September 30-October 2, 2015
San Francisco, CA, USA

I0038029

**Association for
Computing Machinery**

Advancing Computing as a Science & Profession

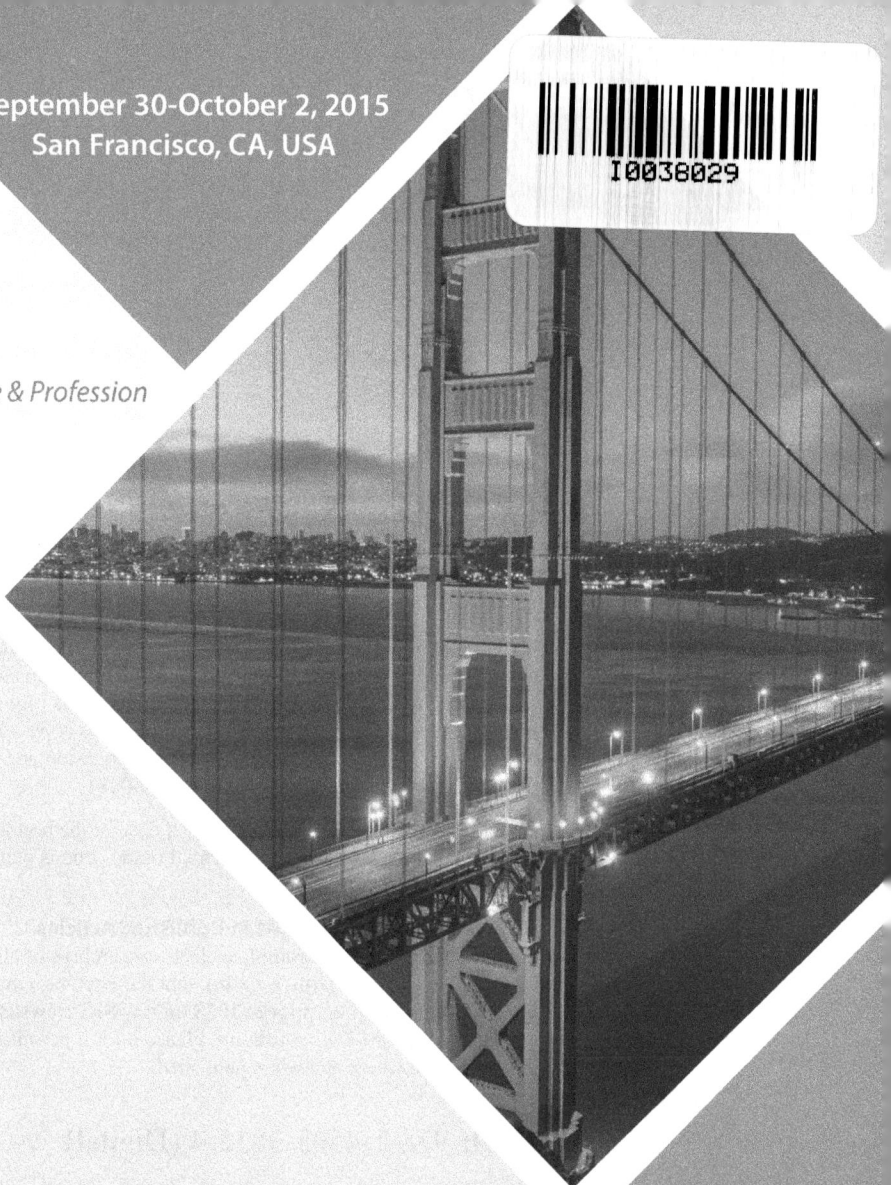

ICN'15

Proceedings of the 2nd International Conference on
Information-Centric Networking

Sponsored by:
ACM SIGCOMM

Supported by:
CISCO, Huawei, PARC, Verisign, & Intel

**Association for
Computing Machinery**

Advancing Computing as a Science & Profession

The Association for Computing Machinery
2 Penn Plaza, Suite 701
New York, New York 10121-0701

Notice to Past Authors of ACM-Published Articles
ACM intends to create a complete electronic archive of all articles and/or other material previously published by ACM. If you have written a work that has been previously published by ACM in any journal or conference proceedings prior to 1978, or any SIG Newsletter at any time, and you do NOT want this work to appear in the ACM Digital Library, please inform permissions@acm.org, stating the title of the work, the author(s), and where and when published.

ISBN: 978-1-4503-3855-4 (Digital)

ISBN: 978-1-4503-4098-4 (Print)

Additional copies may be ordered prepaid from:

ACM Order Department
PO Box 30777
New York, NY 10087-0777, USA

Phone: 1-800-342-6626 (USA and Canada)
+1-212-626-0500 (Global)
Fax: +1-212-944-1318
E-mail: acmhelp@acm.org
Hours of Operation: 8:30 am – 4:30 pm ET

Printed in the USA

Foreword

Welcome to the 2nd ACM conference on Information-Centric Networks. After a very successful conference in 2014 it became clear that ACM ICN would become the heart of the ICN research. With Paris as the backdrop, the first conference drew researchers from around the world. In 2015 we decided to hold the conference in San Francisco to tap into some of the American research interest.

Information-Centric Networks have become over the last few years one of the hot research topics in computer networks. The paradigm shift in how the network is viewed lets us take a different perspective on some of the old problems to look for solutions that were impossible before.

While we have seen many advances in the base architecture, ICN still needs a considerable amount of work to address some of the unknowns. Last year we had a number of research papers focused on routing and caching. This year we'll continue looking at some of these issues but we'll also expand more into the areas of scalability.

This year we received 55 full paper submissions from around the world with a good mix of industrial and academic research. After a tough review process we accepted 19 for an acceptance rate of 35%. To round off the technical program we also accepted 8 posters and 10 demos. As we did in 2014, we plan to have a full day of tutorials. Here you will be able to learn about the latest changes in some of the prevalent ICN architectures and get some hands on experience with their code. Van Jacobson will be giving the keynote speech and we have also prepared an engaging panel for a lively discussion so we hope this year will be as valuable as last year.

Getting everything ready for ACM ICN 2015 took a lot of effort. We appreciate all the authors who submitted papers to create this wonderful program. We would like to thank the program committee for donating their time and expertise to evaluate the submissions and provide their peer review. ACM SIGCOMM made it all possible through their sponsorship. Finally, we would like to thank our industrial supporters, Cisco, Huawei, PARC, Verisign and Intel.

Once again, we welcome you to ACM ICN 2015. We hope you enjoy the program we put together for you; we certainly enjoyed organizing it.

Ignacio Solis
ICN 2015 General Chair
PARC, USA

Technical Program Committee Chairs' Welcome

It is our great pleasure to welcome you to *ICN 2015*, the *2nd ACM Conference on Information-Centric Networking*, held from September 30 to October 2, 2015, in San Francisco, CA, USA! We have worked to put together a strong technical program that would be of interest to researchers, industrial practitioners, and students in the field of Information Centric Networking. The program includes technical research paper presentations, a keynote presentation, as well as two tutorials, technical demonstrations, poster presentations, and a panel discussion.

This year, the technical program of ICN attracted 55 submissions. The Program Committee proceeded with a two phase selection process. In the first phase, three members of the program committee reviewed each one of the 55 submissions. We then selected those papers with at least one positive review or with no decidedly negative reviews for a second phase. The 45 papers that went to the second phase then received one or two additional reviews, and based on all the reviews we then selected 38 papers to discuss in the Program Committee meeting, which was held in Prague, Czech Republic in July. At the end of an all-day meeting, the Technical Program Committee selected 19 for publication and presentation at the conference. A subsequent decision resulted in a final program comprising 18 papers.

The Technical Program Committee comprised 36 members, including the two TPC Co-Chairs. The TPC members were chosen for their expertise in the field and for their excellent track record on making balanced evaluations and providing thorough feedback to the authors. Just as with the submitted papers, the TPC members also were from all over the world, reflecting the significant wide-spread interest in ICN. We sincerely thank the TPC members for their dedication and hard work in reading and providing detailed feedback on the papers, and we hope the authors of all the papers would appreciate the feedback provided in the reviews to help improve their work.

The resulting technical program is arranged over six sessions of paper presentations over the two days of the main conference. It is intended to give authors and attendees a chance to present and discuss new ideas and theoretical as well as experimental results in the general area of Information Centric Networking. The program covers a wide range of research topics, from network architectures, to routing, name resolution, router design and implementation, transport protocols, caching, security, and applications. The technical program is the backbone of the ICN conference.

The keynote speaker is Van Jacobson, who has made long-term and foundational contributions to the Internet, and who is also a very influential proponent and architect of the notion of Information Centric Networking.

In addition to the main technical program, the conference includes two tutorial presentations covering important technical features of the CCN and NDN systems, respectively; an open discussion lead by a panel of experts and practitioners on the future prospects for ICN in research, applications, deployments, and also in its economic aspects; a session dedicated to posters and demos intended as a venue to present and discuss compelling initial ideas and other advances in research and engineering for ICN, including the demonstration of concrete systems, tools, and applications.

In conclusion, we worked to assemble a compelling technical program to advance and consolidate knowledge and technology in the area of Information Centric Networking. We also wanted to create a venue to support, foster, and facilitate the exchange of ideas and to grow and strengthen the ICN research community. We hope we succeeded and we hope you enjoy the conference!

Antonio Carzaniga and K. K. Ramakrishnan
ICN 2015 Program Co-Chairs

Table of Contents

Session: Tutorial 1

Session: Tutorial 2

Keynote Speech

Session 1: Routing

Session 2: Node Architecture

Session 4: In-network Caching

Session 5: Content and Applications

Session 6: Internetworking and Access Control

Session 7: Security

Poster Presentations

Demonstrations

ICN 2015 Conference Organization

General Chair: Ignacio Solis *(PARC, USA)*

Local Chair: Laura Hill *(PARC, USA)*

Program Chairs: Antonio Carzaniga *(USI, Switzerland)*
K.K. Ramakrishnan *(UC Riverside, USA)*

Tutorial & Panel Chair: Christos Papadopoulos *(Colorado State University, USA)*

Demo Chair: Eve M. Schooler *(Intel, USA)*

Poster Chair: Gareth Tyson *(Queen Mary, University of London, UK)*

Finance & Registration Chair: George Xylomenos *(AUEB, Greece)*

Publication Chair: Paulo Mendes *(COPELABS / University Lusofona, Portugal)*

Travel Grant Chair: Lan Wang *(University of Memphis, USA)*

Communication Chair: Matthias Wählisch *(Freie Universität Berlin, Germany)*

Steering Committee Chair: George C. Polyzos *(AUEB, Greece)*

Steering Committee: Giovanna Carofiglio *(Cisco, USA)*
Van Jacobson *(Google, USA)*
Dirk Kutscher *(NEC Laboratories Europe, Germany)*
Giacomo Morabito *(University of Cantania, Italy)*
Luca Muscariello *(Orange Labs, France)*
Börje Ohlman *(Ericsson Research, Sweden)*
Jörg Ott *(Aalto University, Finland)*
Ignacio Solis *(PARC, USA)*
Lixia Zhang *(UCLA, USA)*

Program Committee: Mayutan Arumaithurai *(Universität Göttingen, Germany)*
Giuseppe Bianchi *(University of Rome Tor Vergata, Italy)*
Nicola Blefari-Melazzi *(University of Rome Tor Vergata, Italy)*
Jeff Burke *(UCLA, USA)*
Kenneth Calvert *(University of Kentucky, USA)*
Giovanna Carofiglio *(Cisco, USA)*
Patrick Crowley *(Washington University in St. Louis, USA)*
Christian Esteve Rothenberg *(University of Campinas, Brazil)*
JJ Garcia-Luna-Aceves *(UC Santa Cruz, USA)*
Toru Hasegawa *(Osaka University, Japan)*
Jussi Kangasharju *(Helsinki University, Finland)*

ACM-ICN 2015 Sponsor & Supporters

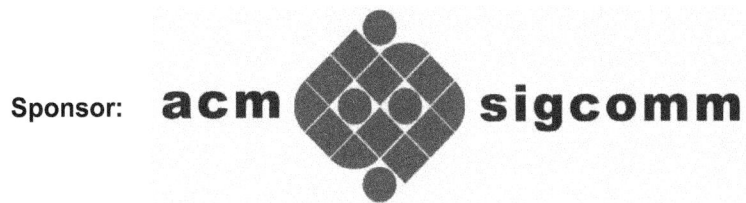

Sponsor: acm sigcomm

Supporters: CISCO

HUAWEI

parc
A Xerox Company

VERISIGN

intel

CCNx 1.0 Tutorial

Theory and Practice

Ignacio Solis
Palo Alto Research Center
Palo Alto, CA, USA
Ignacio.Solis@parc.com

Marc Mosko
Palo Alto Research Center
Palo Alto, CA, USA
Marc.Mosko@parc.com

Glenn Scott
Palo Alto Research Center
Palo Alto, CA, USA
Glenn.Scott@parc.com

Alan Walendowski
Palo Alto Research Center
Palo Alto, CA, USA
Alan.Walendowski@parc.com

ABSTRACT

This is a tutorial of the CCNx 1.0 protocol and the CCNx codebase. It will cover the basic CCNx architecture and provide hands on experience with the code.

Categories and Subject Descriptors

C.2.1 [**Networks**]: Architecture and Design

General Terms

CCN, ICN

1. INTRODUCTION

ICN has been gaining quite a bit of traction in the research community. CCN has been at the core of the surge in interest. The CCN protocol has become the basis of comparison to the various ICN architectures. The original CCNx codebase (0.x) acted as the first playground for developing and evaluating ICN. It became the base of various projects enabling a large number of research projects. With time CCN has grown throughout the past few years. The protocol has changed and the codebase has been rewritten to reflect the new functionality. A binary version of CCNx (compatible with the 1.0 protocol spec) was released at ICN 2014 for early experimentation. A source release of CCNx was made available this year under a technology evaluation program for both academia and universities as well as commercially interested entities. ICN 2015 is the perfect venue to give an overview of the CCN protocol and CCNx code base. The protocol has added a few features (like manifests) and the code has been updated with the new functionality. A CCNx tutorial would cover both the protocol changes as well as the code (in both binary and source form).

ICN'15, Sept. 30–Oct.2, 2015, San Francisco, CA, USA.
ACM 978-1-4503-3855-4/15/09.
DOI: http://dx.doi.org/10.1145/2810156.2815104

2. TUTORIAL DESCRIPTION

2.1 Structure and Length

This tutorial takes up a whole day.

2.1.1 Morning - Theory and Architecture

In the morning the tutorial will focus mostly on the theory and architecture of CCN. This will touch on the 1.0 protocol including:

- Naming, Matching and Forwarding
- Messages and Manifests
- Transport and Routing
- PIT and FIB
- Framing headers and Encoding
- Validation

2.1.2 Afternoon - Code and Practice

The second half of the tutorial will focus on practical experience and working with the code. Specifically, we will cover:

- CCNx Forwarder
- CCNx Transport Stack
- CCNx Assembly Framework
- CCNx Coding conventions
- PARC Memory and PARC Object

Using the knowledge gained in the first part of the second half atendees will then write code in the final part of the tutorial. Help will be available.

2.2 Intended Audience

The first section of the tutorial will require a general understanding of networking. Previous experience with CCN is not required. The second part of the tutorial will require familiarity with CCN. This will be effectively provided by the first half.

2.3 Materials

All the materials to be used for this tutorial will be available through the CCNx website. Please refer to http://www.ccnx.org/ for more information.

Tutorial: Security and Synchronization in Named Data Networking (NDN)

Hila Ben Abraham
Washington University
in St. Louis
hila@wustl.edu

Alex Afanasyev,
Yingdi Yu, Lixia Zhang
UCLA IRL
{afanasyev, yingdi, lixia}
@cs.ucla.edu

Steve DiBenedetto
Colorado State University
dibenede@cs.colostate.
edu

Jeff Thompson
Jeff Burke
UCLA REMAP
{jefft0, jburke}
@remap.ucla.edu

ABSTRACT

This full day tutorial on synchronization and security in Named Data Networking (NDN) will share important architectural concepts we are exploring in these areas, the software we have built to perform these tasks, and remaining open issues. In particular, it will emphasize how the existing open source toolset provides a platform for exploring the open research questions.

1. INTRODUCTION

Named Data Networking (NDN) is one of the most prominent ICN architectures and software platforms available to the research community. The NDN codebase is published under an open source license and widely used in experimentation; a 26 node international testbed is available for research use. In previous years, the NDN project team has presented tutorials to introduce the basics of the architecture and its software platform, both to promote related research and to encourage community contribution to the open source software platform. These earlier tutorials focused primarily on introductory material—in particular, Interest/Data exchange mechanisms and basic content verification. However, many of the field's most interesting research challenges lie in areas that build on these basics. In particular, **mechanisms for access control and trust verification, along with new transport protocols building on Interest/Data exchange**, are important areas of work for the NDN project team.

This tutorial will share important architectural concepts we are exploring in these areas, the software we have built to perform these tasks, and remaining open issues. In particular, it will emphasize how the existing open source toolset provides a platform for exploring the open research questions.

We hope to engage participants both in using deeper and emerging features of the available toolset, and in tackling these critical problem spaces with us. In addition to referencing a variety of existing examples, the tutorial will use the creation of a modern browser-based application to illustrate three such topics where the ideas have progressed such that we can build experimental libraries to work with them: **1) multi-party synchronization, 2) schematized trust, 3) encryption-based access control.**

2. TYPE OF TUTORIAL

Combination of introductory material about the architectural concepts, solution space, and available open source prototype implementations, with motivation/demonstration examples that can be followed in real-time by the tutorial participants. We expect the duration of the tutorial to be a full day, approximately 7.5 hours including a 1-hour working lunch break.

3. CONTENT OUTLINE

3.1 Welcome and introduction, recap of NDN software platform and testbed
(45 minutes)

Objective: Review architecture, platforms and key challenges, motivation of tutorial topics.
a. Recap of NDN libraries, NFD forwarder, and repository implementations, focused on typical configuration concerns and the emphasis of the tutorial.
b. Review of storage options—forwarder content store, repository, application in-memory storage. Discuss the data custodian design pattern used in the rest of the tutorial.
c. Introduction of basic NDN data-centric security and the minimum requirements and recommendations for NDN applications.

3.2 Running application example
(15 minutes)

Objective: Present the running example of the tutorial: *Build a secure, peer-to-peer browser-based messaging system (vis-à-vis Slack[1]), using NDN to provide Firebase[2]-like features with local data custodians instead of cloud infrastructure.*

3.3 Multi-party Synchronization (Part 1)
(45 minutes)

Objective: Introduce the practical role of sync as a communication protocol, and available tools.

a. **Motivation & concept**: Synchronization as a new transport approach, open questions, and envisioned use cases. How we are moving from general sync concept to specific sync designs, role that sync plays in the sample application.
b. **Design patterns:** Introduction and comparison of application design patterns based on current applications, including ChronoShare, NLSR, NDNFit. Achieving related patterns in higher layers of the TCP/IP world (e.g., Firebase).

---

[1] http://slack.com/

[2] http://firebase.com/

c. **Solution space**: Discuss challenges and options in creating sync-based protocols, including ChronoSync, CCNx Sync, ISync, and others. Provide overview of libraries and code available for exploration by others.

3.4 Multi-party Synchronization (Part 2)
(45 minutes)

a. **Application example:** Illustrate sync in action by starting to build our running example - a simple browser-based, peer-to-peer messaging application using sync. Begin by creating a simple library with features similar to *Firebase*. Participants can optionally follow along using NDN-JS in their browser.

b. **Future work**: Brief introduction to research challenges and moving forward with sync-based designs.

3.5 Beyond Static Content Distribution
(60 minutes, during lunch)

a. **Presentation**: *Why caching is not the most exciting part of NDN*. Opportunities to use the open source platform to explore NDN advantages related to the tutorial topics for important applications beyond static content distribution. Topics including: Support for ad hoc connectivity; potential solutions to design and security challenges for IoT and M2M; supporting content distribution on the web.

b. **Discussion**: Review and discuss available, upcoming, and desired open source software tools for NDN research beyond content distribution. Opportunities to become involved in the open source development of NDN.

3.6 Schematized Trust (Part 1)
(45 minutes)

Objective: Introduce schematized trust verification for Data using the current NDN security library, and discuss related developments such as certificate formats and library support.

a. **Motivation & concept**: Introduction to trust schema: Creating powerful, named-based schemes for verification of data authenticity and supporting automated generation of keys. Role that schematized trust plays in the sample application.

b. **Design patterns**: Examples of hierarchical trust schema that the NDN team is exploring in different applications, such as routing security, building automation, and mobile health.

c. **Solution space**: Current and planned NDN Certificate format; library support for trust schema; tools available to create key hierarchies; and a brief introduction on example ways keys can get certified by local trust anchors (e.g., NDN testbed root or other). Pointers to how other types of verification (e.g., "web of trust") can be implemented using the available libraries.

3.7 Schematized Trust (Part 2)
(60 minutes)

Objective: Introduce schematized trust verification for Data using the current NDN security library.

a. **Application example**: Updating the example application to provide hierarchical verification that messages are from the authorized members of the tutorial group.

b. **Future work**: Discussion of how open research questions can be explored by building on the available platforms.

3.8 Encryption-based Access Control, Briefly
(90 minutes)

Objective: Introduce encryption-based access control using NDN and extend the sample application via experimental NDN libraries for group encryption.

a. **Motivation & concept**: Briefly introduce the notion of data-centric security and compare to channel-based security. Concept for access control in the sample application.

b. **Design patterns**: Access control patterns emerging in current applications explored by the NDN team, as well as other related previous work in other fields.

c. **Solution space**: Available open source tools and libraries and upcoming plans for development.

d. **Application example**: Using the NDNFit application as an example, illustrate basic encryption-based access control.

3.9 Conclusion and wrap-up discussion
(30 minutes)

4. Previous Tutorials
The NDN team has provided tutorials, including hands-on workshops, at venues including: GENI Engineering Conference 21, October 20-23, 2014, Indiana University; ACM 1st Information-Centric Networking (ICN) Conference, September 24, 2014, Paris, France; NDN Community Meeting 2014, September 3, UCLA; AsiaFI NDN Hands-on Workshop, March 19-21, 2012, Seoul National University, Korea. These previous tutorials have focused on how to get started using the NDN codebase to build applications using basic Interest/Data exchange. Given that many in the ICN community are now familiar with this topic, we propose in this tutorial to cover the two "intermediate" topics of multi-party synchronization and security (specifically, hierarchical trust verification and encryption-based access control) that we expect will be beneficial to researchers in the community and also bring additional feedback to the NDN team as we develop tools in these important areas.

5. Requirements for the Tutorial Room
The tutorial room must provide: 1) At least one data projector, XGA resolution or better, on which code examples can be clearly viewed by all participants. Preferred are two independently fed data projectors – one for a running code example and one for slides / reference material. 2) Sound reinforcement (microphone) for presenters, at a minimum. 3) Wired internet access, preferably unfiltered with a static IP. Either the conference organizers (preferred) or the NDN project team (if necessary) will provide: 1) A NAT-capable router with a local LAN segment dedicated to the tutorial, connected to the above wired internet service. There should be no restrictions on local traffic. 2) Wireless access points connected to the LAN side of the router sufficient to provide access for all tutorial participants. Finally, the NDN team will include a few tutorial helpers that will walk around to provide hands-on assistance where necessary. The room layout should support this, if possible (i.e., relatively wide aisles between seating rows, etc.).

6. Requirements for the Attendees
Attendees must bring a laptop capable of running the most recent version of Chrome and/or Firefox. All required examples will be in Javascript. Ideally, laptops should also have pre-installed and tested the full Named Data Networking platform, which has been tested most extensively on modern versions of Ubuntu Linux and Mac OS X. Time will not be allocated in the tutorial for

troubleshooting participants' installations. *For those who wish to work with it, the NDN Platform must be installed and tested prior to the tutorial; we will provide limited email support to participants who encounter any trouble in the weeks leading up to the tutorial.*

Attendees should have some reasonable conceptual and practical familiarity with the NDN architecture and the fundamentals of Interest/Data exchange. Ideally, they should be comfortable with Javascript, including the basic debugging tools available in the browser, as well as getting around in the Unix shell.

Prior to the tutorial, we will distribute key references on the architecture to the participants, as well as recommendations for hands-on examples that will build familiarity with basic functions in the NDN Javascript library and serve as a recap of the needed understanding of the language itself. Unlike previous years, this is not a basic introduction to NDN applications. It is an intermediate level tutorial that requires either some basic experience with NDN or similar ICN architectures, *or* a willingness to follow along with topics that build on basics that will only be covered briefly.

7. LIMITATIONS ON PARTICIPATION

As long as all participants can work comfortably on their own laptop, with power and network access, as well as access to local resources on a network that we provide, we do not see that any limitations will be needed.

8. REPRESENTATIVE REFERENCES

[1] claffy, kc, J. Polterock, A. Afanasyev, J. Burke, L. Zhang. "The First Named Data Networking Community Meeting (NDNcomm)", In submission to *ACM SIGCOMM Computer Communication Review (CCR)*, 2015.

[2] Jacobson, Van, et al. "Networking named content." *Proceedings of the 5th international conference on Emerging networking experiments and technologies.* ACM CoNEXT, 2009.

[3] Shang, W., J. Thompson, M. Cherkaoui, J. Burke, L. Zhang. "NDN.JS: A JavaScript Client Library for Named Data Networking." *Proceedings of IEEE INFOCOMM 2013 NOMEN Workshop*, April 2013.

[4] Yu, Y., A. Afanasyev, D. Clark, k. claffy, V. Jacobson, L. Zhang. "Schematizing and Automating Trust in Named Data Networking." *NDN Technical Report NDN-0030*, Revision 2, June 2, 2015.

[5] Zhu, Z., A. Afanasyev. "Let's ChronoSync: Decentralized Dataset State Synchronization in Named Data Networking," *Proceedings of the 21st IEEE Intl. Conf. on Network Protocols (ICNP 2013)*, Goettingen, Germany, October 2013.

Improving the Internet with ICN

Van Jacobson
UCLA

Abstract

Efficient static content distribution is the focus of most ICN efforts. But content distribution is just one of many Internet pain points. An Information Centric approach could potentially spur major advances on most of the Internet's most pressing problems. This talk will discuss where, why, and how ICN could make a difference on a broader scale.

Categories and Subject Descriptors:
H.3.4 [**Information Systems**]: Systems and Software; C.2.1 [**Computer Systems Organization**]: Network Architecture and Design

Keywords
information-centric networking; named-data networking

Short Bio

Van Jacobson's algorithms for the Transmission Control Protocol (TCP) helped solve the problem of congestion and are used in over 90% of Internet hosts today. He is renowned for his pioneering achievements in network performance and scaling. Widely credited with enabling the Internet to expand in size and support increasing speed demands, he helped the Internet survive a major traffic surge (1988-89) without collapsing.

Jacobson has co-written many network diagnostics tools (traceroute, pathchar, and tcpdump) that are widely used by the Internet research and development community. Besides authoring dozens of seminal, Internet-defining documents, he also helped lead the development of the Internet Multicast Backbone (MBone) and the popular Internet audio and video conferencing tools (vic, vat, wb) that laid the groundwork and defined the standards for current Internet VoIP and multimedia applications.

ICN'15, Sept. 30–Oct.2, 2015, San Francisco, CA, USA.
ACM 978-1-4503-3855-4/15/09.
DOI: http://dx.doi.org/10.1145/2810156.2810157

Pro-Diluvian: Understanding Scoped-Flooding for Content Discovery in Information-Centric Networking

Liang Wang
University of Cambridge, UK
lw525@cam.ac.uk

Suzan Bayhan
University of Helsinki, Finland
bayhan@hiit.fi

Jörg Ott
Aalto University, Finland
jo@netlab.tkk.fi

Jussi Kangasharju
University of Helsinki, Finland
jakangas@helsinki.fi

Arjuna Sathiaseelan
University of Cambridge, UK
as2330@cam.ac.uk

Jon Crowcroft
University of Cambridge, UK
jac22@cam.ac.uk

ABSTRACT

Scoped-flooding is a technique for content discovery in a broad networking context. This paper investigates the effects of scoped-flooding on various topologies in information-centric networking. Using the proposed ring model, we show that flooding can be constrained within a very small neighbourhood to achieve most of the gains which come from areas where the growth rate is relatively low, i.e., the network edge. We also study two flooding strategies and compare their behaviours. Given that caching schemes favour more popular items in competition for cache space, popular items are expected to be stored in diverse parts of the network compared to the less popular items. We propose to exploit the resulting divergence in availability along with the routers' topological properties to fine tune the flooding radius. Our results shed light on designing efficient content discovery mechanism for future information-centric networks.

Categories and Subject Descriptors

C.2.1 [**Network Architecture and Design**]: Network communications; C.4 [**Performance of Systems**]: Modeling techniques

General Terms

Theory; Design; Performance

Keywords

Information-Centric Networking; Scoped-flooding; Content Discovery; Optimisation; Graph Theory

1. INTRODUCTION

Content, especially popular content, in an information-centric network (ICN) [1–4] may reside "anywhere", there-

ICN'15, September 30–October 2, 2015, San Francisco, CA, USA.
© 2015 ACM. ISBN 978-1-4503-3855-4/15/09 ...$15.00.
DOI: http://dx.doi.org/10.1145/2810156.2810162.

fore the distribution efficiency heavily relies on the effectiveness of content discovery mechanisms. Considering the gap between large content objects and scarce router resources, designing intelligent content discovery to balance protocol simplicity, computational complexity and traffic overhead is crucial in every ICN architecture.

Content discovery is generally achieved by resolution-based [2–8] or routing-based [1,9,10] solutions. Resolution-based discovery is a deterministic solution which maps requesters with providers at rendezvous points. The rendezvous point can be either statically configured or referred by proper content addressing [3,7,8]. Though resolution-based discovery has relatively small traffic footprint, its performance may degrade quickly in face of large and dynamic content demands. On the other hand, the routing-based discovery usually provides a probabilistic solution. The chances of finding the content can be improved by exploring a larger area of the network, i.e., via collaboration or flooding. In practice, naive network-wide flooding is rarely used due to its significant traffic overhead. A flooding operation is usually constrained within a well-defined neighbourhood (or scope) which is often referred to as *scoped-flooding*. Technically, such constraint on the neighbourhood size is achieved by setting a hop limit for each flooding (e.g., TTL limit).

The use of flooding is based on the following considerations. First, flooding can significantly reduce the protocol complexity and simplify the design, which is very desirable in an unstable environment [11]. Second, in addition to the well-known temporal locality, user requests also possess strong spatial locality [12]. The two localities together indicate that it is highly likely to discover a popular content among nearby neighbours. Third, flooding can reduce the state maintained in the network for a routing-based discovery [13]. Fourth, the communication between close neighbours is relatively cheap (regarding delay, transmission cost and etc.) compared to using backhauls in many cases. Therefore, flooding remains as the default fallback strategy for content discovery if normal forwarding fails in CCNx [14], and also used in various routing and caching designs [10,13,15–17,41].

Despite its wide application (e.g., in ICN [1,41], P2P [18,19], MANET [20,21]), a thorough understanding of how scoped-flooding impacts content discovery is still lacking. More precisely, the following key questions are awaiting answers: (1) what is the optimal radius of scoped-flooding? (2) where do most of the gains come from in a network? (3)

how do topological properties of a network impact scoped-flooding? The answers will shed light on designing more intelligent strategies by *flooding for the proper content at the right place with the optimal radius*.

In this paper, to address the aforementioned problems, we propose a node-centric, ring-based model to analyse scoped-flooding. Based on the ring model, we first investigate neighbourhood growth model on general network topologies. The results show that average growth rate increases at least exponentially and can be well estimated using the information within 2-hop neighbourhood. Along with Bayesian techniques, we solve the optimal radius problem and further compare two flooding strategies (static and dynamic) on specific network models.

Specifically, our contributions are:

1. We perform a theoretical analysis on the effects of scoped-flooding using the proposed node-centric ring-based model.

2. The analytical results along with the evaluations show optimal flooding radius is very small (no more than 3 hops).

3. Most of the gains of scoped-flooding are from very small neighbourhoods located at network edges, indicating flooding is more proper at network edge instead of core.

2. SYSTEM MODEL

We assume an information-centric network whose topology is represented with a graph $G = (V, \rho)$, where V is a set of nodes characterized with degree distribution ρ. ρ_k denotes the probability that a node has exactly degree k. The distribution can be arbitrary. For a node v_i, we organize its neighbourhood into r concentric rings according to the lengths of shortest paths between v_i and its neighbours. We denote n_r as average number of r-hop neighbours on the rth ring. We refer to this model as node-centric ring-based model, or simply a *ring model*. In reality, nodes may break down resulting in lost messages. We model the stability with $\gamma \in (0, 1]$ which denotes the probability that a router is up and working properly, i.e., the reliability rate. Equivalently, $(1 - \gamma)$ denotes the failure rate.

Designing a fully-fledged protocol is out of the scope of this paper. Instead, we briefly describe general flooding behaviours in the following. Nodes in a network receive requests from either directly connected clients or neighbours. We exclude clients from the model and focus only on core network. Whenever a request arrives, a node first looks for a match in its local cache. If the node cannot find the requested content locally, it decides whether to initiate a scoped-flooding before simply forwarding the request to the next hop along the path to original content providers. The flooding is constrained within a r-hop neighbourhood by maintaining a hop counter in packet header. The node terminates the flooding if the hop counter reaches r. If the content is discovered, we assume the content can always return to the initial flooding node in a reverse route similar to CCNx. To prevent loops, nodes do not re-flood the messages they have seen before.

For simplicity, we do not consider the case of partially matched content. A node i either has the exact requested content or not. The value of response R is described as an

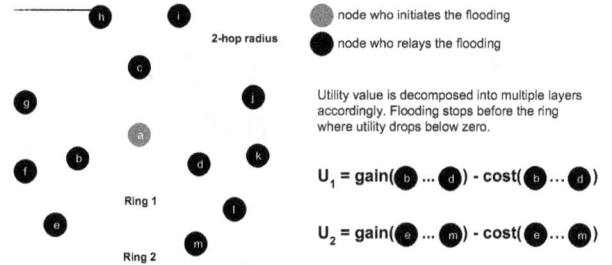

Figure 1: In a ring model, to estimate whether the utility on the $(r + 1)^{th}$ ring drops below zero, a node on the rth ring needs to know three pieces of information (1) which ring it is; (2) how its neighbourhood grows; (3) content availability.

i.i.d random variable which follows a Bernoulli distribution $R \sim \text{Bernoulli}(p)$, with 1 representing a successful discovery and 0 otherwise. p is often referred to as *content availability*. Note that p itself can follow different distributions to model content availability (e.g., Zipf or Weibull). By definition, we let $q \triangleq 1 - p$ denote the probability of failing to find the matched content on a node. Fig. 1 illustrates the ring model under our investigation. Note that there will be less symmetry at network edges but the model remains the same.

There are many resource constraints in a network such as energy, bandwidth and storage. In our model, we use c to represent the cost induced by receiving and processing flooding requests. Besides, consecutive requests may also impact content delivery in terms of added queueing and processing delay which we assume to be roughly proportional to the number of messages. However, the cost can increase faster and requests may be dropped in a busy network. To generalise, the cost is modelled as a linear function of number of nodes involved in a flooding.

3. NEIGHBOURHOOD GROWTH MODEL

The first step to solve optimal radius is to understand how neighbourhood grows as a function of flooding radius. Newman derived this functional relation in [22] using a general graph model $G = (V, \rho)$. We recap briefly the major steps of the derivation in Section 3.1, based on which we investigate two specific types of networks, i.e., random networks and scale-free networks. Then we examine the accuracy of estimates on both synthetic and realistic networks.

3.1 Average Number of r-Hop Neighbours

The effective topology due to a flooding can be viewed as a distribution tree. On non-trivial topologies, such a tree cannot be easily decomposed into multiple linear models (from root to leaves). We apply ring model to organize the neighbourhood of node v into r concentric rings according to the neighbour's distance to v so that we can study the growth ring by ring. Calculating n_1, namely the average number of directly connected neighbours, is trivial. Let $\langle k \rangle$ denote the mean of a given degree variable k. Average number of 1-hop neighbours equals the node's average degree as follows:

$$n_1 = \langle k \rangle = \sum_{k=0}^{\infty} k \rho_k. \tag{1}$$

However, calculating n_r $(r \geq 2)$ is not as straightforward as n_1 since the degree distribution of a node's neighbour is not the same as the general degree distribution of the whole network [24]. Let v_j be one of v_i's next-hop neighbours and τ_k be the probability of v_j having k emerging edges which lead to k new next-hop neighbours. Note that we exclude the edge leading back to v_i from v_j since it does not contribute to new nodes. The results in [25] show τ_k is proportional to both v_i's degree and general degree distribution of the network. The reason is the edges of a high-degree node have a higher chance to connect to any given edge in the network. The probability of v_j having k new next-hop neighbours is:

$$\tau_k = \mathbf{Pr}[deg(v_j) = k|\rho] = \frac{(k+1)\rho_{k+1}}{\sum_m m\rho_m}.$$

Therefore, the average number of new nodes from v_j is:

$$\sum_{k=0}^{\infty} k\tau_k = \frac{\sum_{k=0}^{\infty} k(k+1)\rho_{k+1}}{\sum_m m\rho_m} = \frac{\sum_{k=0}^{\infty} k(k-1)\rho_k}{\sum_m m\rho_m}$$
$$= \frac{\langle k^2 \rangle - \langle k \rangle}{\langle k \rangle}.$$

Because we did not assume v_i is on any specific concentric ring except $r \geq 2$, we can use the same τ_k and the same logic above to calculate arbitrary r-hop neighbours. Namely, n_r equals the average number of nodes on the $(r-1)^{th}$ ring multiplied by their average out-degree to the rth ring.

$$n_r = n_{r-1} \sum_{k=0}^{\infty} k\tau_k = \frac{\langle k^2 \rangle - \langle k \rangle}{\langle k \rangle} n_{r-1}$$
$$= \left[\frac{\langle k^2 \rangle - \langle k \rangle}{\langle k \rangle} \right]^{r-1} \cdot \langle k \rangle \qquad (2)$$

Eq.(2) shows that the number of r-hop neighbours is a function of the degree variable. Using eq. (2), we can calculate $n_2 = \langle k^2 \rangle - \langle k \rangle$. As we know $n_1 = \langle k \rangle$, by applying the replacement recursively, we can rewrite eq. (2) as below, which eventually leads us to the same function found in [22].

$$n_r = \left[\frac{n_2}{n_1} \right]^{r-1} \cdot n_1. \qquad (3)$$

Eq.(3) shows that n_r can also be expressed as a function of the ratio between average number of 2-hop and 1-hop neighbours. The neighbourhood size only converges if there are fewer 2-hop neighbours than 1-hop ones, i.e., $\frac{n_2}{n_1} < 1$, which actually implies the network has multiple components with high probability. We define *neighbourhood growth rate* β as

$$\beta \triangleq \frac{n_2}{n_1} \triangleq \frac{\langle k^2 \rangle - \langle k \rangle}{\langle k \rangle}. \qquad (4)$$

Note that the derivation above applies to any general network of arbitrary degree distributions. The result gives an interesting implication on the topological inference, which says a node can approximate β by utilizing the local knowledge within its 2-hop neighbourhood. In the following, we focus on the growth rate β and study two specific network models: random network and scale-free network. Both are prominent in networking research due to their representativeness of many realistic networks [27–29]. Specifically, empirical evidence shows mobile and opportunistic networks can be either random [29] or scale-free [30], whereas fixed and wired networks are mostly scale-free [27, 28].

3.2 Case 1: Random Networks

Random networks have a binomial degree distribution $B(|V|, \rho)$ which is given by the following formula [23]

$$\rho_k = \binom{|V|-1}{k} \rho^k (1-\rho)^{|V|-k-1}.$$

For very big $|V|$ and small ρ, the binomial distribution above converges to the Poisson distribution in its limit. Then, the degree distribution ρ_k becomes:

$$\lim_{|V| \to \infty} \rho_k = \frac{\langle k \rangle^k e^{-\langle k \rangle}}{k!}.$$

For calculating β in eq.(4), we need to derive the second moment of random variable k, i.e., $\langle k^2 \rangle$. Using Touchard polynomials [1], the rth moment of a variable with Poisson distribution can be calculated as eq. (5) shows. $\left\{ {r \atop k} \right\}$ denotes *Stirling numbers of the second kind* [23] which represents the number of ways to partition a set of r objects into k non-empty subsets, and is known for calculating $\langle k^r \rangle$.

$$\langle k^r \rangle = e^{-\langle k \rangle} \sum_{k=0}^{\infty} \frac{\langle k \rangle^k \cdot k^r}{k!} = \sum_{k=1}^{r} \left\{ {r \atop k} \right\} \langle k \rangle^k \qquad (5)$$

Combining eq. (5) and eq. (2) yields

$$n_2 = \left\{ {2 \atop 2} \right\} \langle k \rangle^2 + \left\{ {2 \atop 1} \right\} \langle k \rangle - \langle k \rangle = \langle k \rangle^2. \qquad (6)$$

Similarly, by applying the replacement recursively, we get

$$n_r = \langle k \rangle^r \implies \beta = \langle k \rangle \qquad (7)$$

Eq. (7) shows that $n_1, n_2, n_3 \ldots$ form a geometric series. The growth rate is $\beta = \langle k \rangle$. It is worth noting that many topological properties (e.g., average degree, density etc.) are homogeneous on random networks. In other words, a randomly chosen sub-network possesses similar characteristics as the whole network which is also known as self-similarity.

3.3 Case 2: Scale-free Networks

Although random networks give a very neat form of growth rate, many realistic networks are scale-free and the node degree follows a power-law distribution, i.e., $\rho \propto k^{-\alpha}$ with $\alpha > 2$ [27, 28, 30]. For a power-law distribution, the rth moment of random variable k equals:

$$\langle k^r \rangle = k_{min}^r \cdot \frac{\alpha - 1}{\alpha - 1 - r} \qquad \forall \alpha > r + 1 \qquad (8)$$

Note that a power-law distribution is extremely right-skewed and has a heavy tail. Only the first $\lfloor \alpha - 1 \rfloor$ moments exist, the other moments are infinite. If we plug eq.(8) into eq.(2) and let $k_{min} = 1$, the growth rate equals:

$$\beta = \frac{1}{\alpha - 3} \qquad \forall \alpha > 3 \qquad (9)$$

Eq. (9) means that though most real-life networks have a well-defined average node degree, their variance is infinite, which further indicates the growth rate β is unbounded.

---

[1]We can also use moment generating functions for a Poisson random variable with parameter λ, i.e., $M_X(t) = e^{\lambda(e^t - 1)}$, and we derive $\langle k^2 \rangle$ by calculating $M_X''(t = 0)$. This gives us: $\langle k^2 \rangle = \langle k \rangle^2 + \langle k \rangle$. $\langle k^r \rangle$ can be calculated using higher order moments similarly.

Table 1: Overestimation of the model at each hop for various network graphs. V: Number of nodes and E: Number of nodes in the generated instance of the graph, l: average path length. Shaded cells represent the cases where the error is below 0.20.

Id	Topology	V	E	$\langle k \rangle$	l	Clustering	Overestimation of the model				
							$r=2$	$r=3$	$r=4$	$r=5$	$r=6$
1	Random	339	338	1.994	23.07	0	0.327	1.046	2.359	4.692	9.092
2	Random	8030	9761	2.431	12.03	0	0.152	0.371	0.642	0.972	1.399
3	Random	9426	15068	3.197	8.30	0.00040	0.060	0.130	0.212	0.332	0.565
4	Random	9811	20073	4.091	6.75	0.00049	0.023	0.053	0.106	0.259	0.873
5	Random	9928	25060	5.048	5.88	0.00048	0.004	0.017	0.079	0.419	2.79
6	Random	9989	35020	7.011	4.95	0.00066	0.003	0.030	0.229	2.139	54.124
7	Scale-free, $\alpha =3.24$	7141	9648	2.70	7.88	0.00057	0.093	0.271	0.529	1.069	2.599
8	Scale-free, $\alpha =3.35$	5869	7347	2.50	8.66	0.00076	-0.115	-0.174	-0.194	-0.16	0.013
9	Scale-free, $\alpha =3.50$	5960	7357	2.47	8.99	0.00013	-0.356	-0.555	-0.68	-0.757	-0.794

For $3 < \alpha < 4$, the growth rate is bounded but the neighbourhood size never converges. It is also interesting to notice when $\alpha > 4$, n_r converges to zero at its limit $r \to \infty$. The reason is the existence of super hubs with extremely high degrees which strengthens the small-world effect and makes the network diameter extremely short. We refer to [23] for more thorough and interesting discussions on graph topological properties. For both random network and scale-free network, we can see neighbourhood growth is at least exponential which sheds light on the flooding strategy design.

3.4 Accuracy on Estimating β

To assess the model accuracy, we generate random and scale-free topologies for which we calculate the actual average neighbourhood at each hop distance, i.e, $\bar{n}_r$. To derive the n_r estimated by the model, we first find the parameter of a corresponding degree distribution, i.e., Poisson for Erdős-Rényi random graph and power-law for scale-free graph, by maximum likelihood estimation.[2] After finding the distribution parameter, we calculate n_r using eq.(7) or eq.(9) and compute the deviation from $\bar{n}_r$ by $(n_r - \bar{n}_r)/\bar{n}_r$. For both topologies, we set the number of nodes to $N = 10000$. If a generated network is not connected, we use the largest component hence V can be smaller than N. The link probability parameter ρ determines the number of edges in an Erdős-Rényi graph, similar to the exponent α in a scale-free network.

Table 1 summarizes the network properties along with the deviation, i.e., overestimation ratio. $r = 1$ is excluded as it converges to 0 for all settings. For almost every setting, the model overestimates the reality only slightly for $r = 2$ and $r = 3$. For $V = 339$, we attribute the deviation to both the finite size effect as well as the absence of random graph property, i.e., the network does not exhibit Poisson degree distribution as the model assumes. Increasing hop count makes the model deviate significantly from the reality, especially when $r \geq l$, which is expected as a result of finite size of the networks. For $r = 4$, the model captures the reality quite well for large V and moderate $\langle k \rangle$ – the region where the random graph property exists but the network is not so densely connected. The deviation is higher for the settings with higher $\langle k \rangle$ due to higher clustering and smaller network diameter.

For scale-free networks, eq.(9) may either underestimate or overestimate depending on the power-law exponent α. For $\alpha \approx 3$, the expected growth rate is very large resulting in overestimation in neighbourhood (e.g., topology-7 in Table 1). For $\alpha > 3$, the estimated growth is more stable which leads to underestimation of the real growth, e.g, topology-8 and topology-9. We attribute this dispersion to the diversity of the degree distribution in a scale-free network and limitations of our model to represent this diversity accurately.

The ISP networks are smaller, ranging from a couple of hundreds to thousands of nodes [27], which results in a slower growth after certain hops. To understand this effect, we derive the growth rate at r^{th} hop as $\beta_r = \frac{n_{r+1}}{n_r}$ and plot them in Fig.2 for eight ISP networks. Recall that in the analysis we have a single β value for the whole networks with $N \to \infty$. As the figure shows, the growth rate decreases with increasing hop due to the finite size of the network. Although the growth rate is a decreasing function of r, we can observe in Fig. 2 that the neighbourhood keeps growing for several hops, e.g., $r \approx 5$. β_r takes values below 1 for r greater than average path length that varies between 3.36 hops to 5.51 hops. In general, the neighbourhood growth model performs very well within a moderate scope on both synthetic and realistic networks.

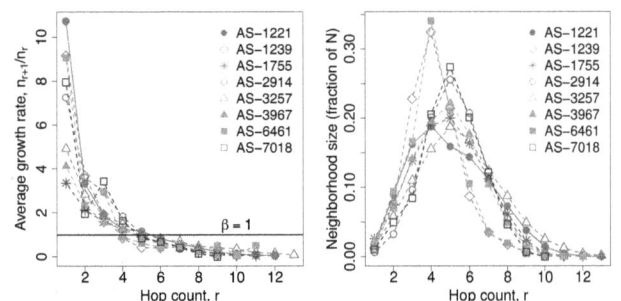

(a) Growth rate at each hop. (b) Neighbourhood size growth.

Figure 2: Change in neighbourhood in real ISP networks. We can see that the neighbourhood growth is constrained by the finite size of real networks. The growth rate slows down when it is beyond 4 hops.

---

[2] For scale-free networks, we use the method described in [31].

4. OPTIMAL FLOODING RADIUS

Based on the previous growth model, we continue our study on calculating the optimal flooding radius in two cases: with and without prior knowledge on content availability.

4.1 Effective Nodes

Since nodes may be up or down, we let γ denote the probability that a node is up, namely a node's reliability rate. We define the *effective nodes* $\hat{n}_r$ as the nodes that are working and also reachable on the rth ring. Since only the effective nodes contribute to flooding messages, i.e., improving content discovery, it is crucial to know the growth of effective nodes for a specific γ in order to derive the optimal radius.

Given a node has n_1 1-hop neighbours, its effective 1-hop neighbours equals $\hat{n}_1 = \gamma n_1$ by assuming a node's state (up or down) is independent of each other. Given growth rate β, the effective 2-hop neighbours equals $\hat{n}_2 = \beta \gamma^2 n_1$. Similarly, we can calculate $\hat{n}_3$ using $\hat{n}_2$. Applying iteratively, we calculate the effective nodes on the rth ring as follows:

$$\hat{n}_r = (\beta \gamma)^{r-1} \gamma n_1 = \gamma^r n_r. \tag{10}$$

It is easy to see the similarity between eq.(3) and eq.(10). In fact, $\hat{n}_1 = \gamma n_1$ is the effective 1-hop neighbours and $\beta \gamma$ can be viewed as effective growth rate given nodes may fail with certain probability $(1 - \gamma)$. For low reliability rates, the gap between the number of effective nodes and the r-hop neighbourhood will quickly increase with an increasing r.

4.2 Content Availability as A Priori

The purpose of flooding is to increase the chance of discovery by visiting enough nodes. Given n visited nodes, the probability of finding the content of availability p equals $(1 - q^n)$ which we use to represent the gain from a flooding. On the other hand, a bigger n also introduces larger cost which limits the utility U as eq.(11) shows:

$$U = (1 - q^n) - n \cdot c. \tag{11}$$

$-U$ in eq.(11) is apparently convex as an exponential function is convex and the linear combination of convex functions preserves convexity. To maximise U, the optimal number of nodes n^* we need to visit can be calculated as below:

$$U'(n) = 0 \implies -q^n \cdot \ln q - c = 0 \implies n^* = \frac{\ln c - \ln \ln q^{-1}}{\ln q}.$$

n^* represents the optimal total number of nodes. Using eq.(10), we can calculate the optimal radius by summing up the effective nodes from ring 1 to r then solving the equation below.

$$\sum_r \hat{n}_r = \sum_r (\beta \gamma)^{r-1} \gamma n_1 = n^*$$

4.3 Inferring the Content Availability

We previously assumed that the content availability p is known *a priori*. Technically, we can set up monitoring nodes to sample request streams. However, monitoring can be expensive and sometimes may not even be feasible. Nevertheless, the probability of finding a specific content in a neighbourhood is a good indicator for its actual availability, since the more popular a content is, the more probable it is to find it among nearby neighbours. We use the Bayesian technique proposed in [32] to estimate content availability.

Eq.(12) is the probability density function of p conditioned on previous i negative (i.e., unsuccessful) queries.

$$f(p|i) = \frac{\mathbf{Pr}(i|p) \cdot f(p)}{\int_0^1 \mathbf{Pr}(i|p) \cdot f(p) dp} \tag{12}$$

Because $\mathbf{Pr}(i|p) = q^i$, if we use the Bernoulli distribution and let $f(p) = 1$, then we have

$$f(p|i) = \frac{q^i}{\int_0^1 q^i dp} = (i+1) q^i.$$

After getting the posterior of p, we can calculate the expected p after i negative queries as below

$$\langle p \rangle = \int_0^1 p(i+1) q^i dp = \int_0^1 (i+1)(1-q) q^i dq = \frac{1}{i+2}. \tag{13}$$

Note that neither p nor q appears in eq.(13). The derivation above gives a very clean estimation of content availability especially when monitoring is not possible or the content has never been observed before.

4.4 Content Availability as Posteriori

Without prior knowledge on content availability, we cannot apply the conventional optimization as that in Section 4.2. Even with the Bayesian inference introduced in Section 4.3, deciding the optimal radius can be difficult, especially when the request comes from directly connected clients or does not carry any information about the number of nodes it has traversed. To get around this challenge, we let a node flood its 1-hop neighbours by default to bootstrap the inference on p. Then we consider the utility of each ring separately and adaptively adjust the estimate of p on every ring. The general mechanism can be summarized as follows:

1. If a request does not contain useful information for estimating the availability (e.g., number of nodes queried), a node initiates a flooding to its directly connected neighbours. A flood message carries 3 pieces of information: the node's local growth rate $\beta = \frac{n_2}{n_1}$; number of 1-hop neighbours n_1; a counter r to record the number of hops it has travelled.[3]

2. When a node receives a flood message, it first estimates the availability p using β, n_1 and r embedded in the message by assuming the requested content cannot be found so far (within r-hop neighbours). More particularly, as follows:

$$\langle p \rangle = \frac{1}{\beta^{r-1} \gamma^r \cdot n_1}$$

Using this estimated p, the node then estimates the potential utility of the next ring. Based on the estimated utility, the node decides whether to continue the flooding or terminate.

More specifically, the overall utility of scoped-flooding is decomposed according to our ring model. Given that R_r and C_r represent the aggregated gain and the aggregated cost on the rth ring respectively, the net utility of a flooding

---

[3]Note that β, n_1, and n_2 here refer to the **local** properties of a specific node instead of the global average. We avoid new notations because the following derivation on optimal radius applies to both local and global cases which is independent on the parameters plugged in. As we will show in Section 5, Dynamic flooding uses local parameters while Static uses global ones.

is as follows:

$$U = \sum_r U_r = \sum_r (R_r - C_r).$$

According to eq.(10), the average cost on the rth ring is:

$$E(C_r) = \hat{n}_r c = \gamma^r n_r c$$

and the average value of gross gain R_r is:

$$E(R_r) = 1 \cdot (1 - q^{\gamma^r n_r}) + 0 \cdot q^{\gamma^r n_r} = 1 - q^{\gamma^r n_r}.$$

The net utility value from the rth ring therefore can be expressed as the difference between $E(R_r)$ and $E(C_r)$, namely

$$U_r = E(R_r) - E(C_r) = (1 - q^{\gamma^r n_r}) - \gamma^r n_r c. \quad (14)$$

An intermediate node forwards the flooding message to its next-hop neighbours only if the next ring can bring positive net utility, which can be easily tested with eq.(14). The flooding radius should stop increasing whenever the expected utility of next ring falls below zero. Technically, this is solved by calculating the root of eq.(14) which is the maximum number of effective nodes on the rth ring. Note that $U_r \geq 0$ indicates $c \leq \frac{1-q^{\gamma^r n_r}}{\gamma^r n_r}$ which provides a clear decision boundary on whether to continue a flooding operation.

Given $\gamma = 1$, which indicates a stable network of no failures, the root of eq.(14) above reduces to:

$$1 - q^{n_r} = n_r c.$$

The mixture of exponential and polynomial functions can be solved with the Lambert W function, which gives:

$$n_r^* = -\frac{1}{\ln q} W_k \left(\frac{\ln q}{c} e^{\frac{\ln q}{c}} \right) + c^{-1}. \quad (15)$$

n_r^* represents the maximum number of nodes that the rth ring can have in order to keep the cost smaller than the gain. By plugging eq.(15) into eq.(2), we can easily derive the optimal flooding radius r^* as a function of cost, content availability and neighbourhood growth rate.

$$n_r = \beta^{r-1} n_1 = n_r^* \implies (r-1)\ln\beta + \ln\langle k \rangle = \ln n_r^* \quad (16)$$

$$\implies r^* = \frac{\ln n_r^* + \ln\beta - \ln\langle k \rangle}{\ln\beta} \quad (17)$$

Given $0 < \gamma < 1$, we have the same derivation except $\hat{n}_r$ replaces n_r in eq.(16). After some manipulations, we have

$$\hat{n}_r = \gamma^r \beta^{r-1} n_1 = n_r^* \implies r^* = \frac{\ln n_r^* + \ln\beta - \ln\langle k \rangle}{\ln\gamma + \ln\beta}. \quad (18)$$

Obviously, $\gamma = 1$ indicates $\ln\gamma = 0$, then eq.(18) reduces to eq.(17) as expected. Since $\ln\gamma$ is a monotonically increasing function and only appears in the denominator of eq.(18), r^* is hence a decreasing function of γ. In practice, eq.(18) means the flooding radius tends to be bigger in an unstable network to achieve the same gain. On the other hand, for a given reliability rate γ, the optimal radius r^* is a decreasing function of the growth rate β.

5. TWO FLOODING STRATEGIES

We first discuss the design rationale behind a scoped-flooding, then introduce two strategies for the later comparison.

5.1 Design Guidelines

A good flooding strategy requires that: (1) a node is aware of its neighbourhood with an accurate topological inference; (2) a node is aware of content availability with an accurate statistical inference on user request streams. These two awareness (solved in Section 3 and 4 respectively) together enable a node to decide its optimal flooding radius based on the estimated utility. In addition, the flooding radius should be adjusted adaptively in different areas according to local topological properties because the network structure may not be homogeneous, i.e., some parts are denser and some parts are sparser (regarding degree distribution). Hence a predetermined radius may lead to suboptimal performance.

5.2 Static Flooding

Static flooding uses a predetermined and fixed flooding radius for all the nodes. The flooding radius is optimized over the whole network topology by e.g., the network operator for each availability value. The average growth rate is calculated using the average number of 1-hop neighbours and 2-hop neighbours of the whole network then plugged into either eq.(17) or eq.(18) to derive the optimal radius. Therefore static flooding ignores the heterogeneity of the topological properties in different areas of the network. Static flooding is simple and popular but it is only suitable for random networks wherein the network structure is homogeneous and nodes have similar growth rates. We include static flooding in our evaluation as a baseline for comparison.

5.3 Dynamic Flooding

Compared to static flooding, dynamic flooding is more attendant to the differences among the nodes and it assigns a specific radius for each node individually. Considering that the degree distribution in a scale-free network is not homogeneous, dynamic flooding lets each node use its own 1-hop and 2-hop neighbours to calculate the local growth rate. Then each node optimises locally within its neighbourhood, hence each has its own optimal flooding radius. Such local optimisation strategy takes a node's position in a network into account. Nodes in denser areas tend to have smaller radius while nodes in sparser areas tend to have bigger radius.

For less available content, a node may prefer routing towards the original content provider rather than initiating flooding. By letting $r = 1$, eq.(14) calculates the availability threshold of whether initiating a flooding as below

$$U_1 > 0 \implies q^{\gamma n_1} < 1 - \gamma n_1 c \implies p > 1 - \sqrt[\gamma n_1]{1 - \gamma n_1 c}.$$

If the availability falls far below the threshold, a node will not flood the request. If content availability is unknown, dynamic strategy floods its 1-hop neighbours by default to bootstrap the inference as described in Section 4.4. As we can expect, without content availability information, dynamic flooding is supposed to introduce more overhead due to its aggressive 1-hop flooding. However, the evaluation in Section 6 shows that such overhead is almost negligible.

6. EVALUATION

We evaluate the two flooding strategies on various topologies to gain a comprehensive understanding of their pros and cons. Our evaluations focus on two network models: random networks and scale-free networks. Both models have a network of 10,000 nodes and 60,000 edges but their degree distributions are different, namely one is Poisson and

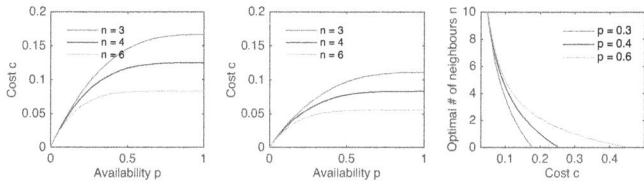

(a) c vs. p, $\gamma = 1$.   (b) c vs. p, $\gamma = 0.5$.   (c) n vs. c, $\gamma = 1$.

Figure 3: Ring model behaviours with different p and c.

the other is power-law. We experimented with a large number of network parameters and various availability and cost values to guarantee the robustness and consistency of our claims.

6.1 Impact of Availability and Cost

Fig. 3 depicts the model behaviours with different cost and availability parameters. In Fig. 3a and 3b, the curves are the decision boundaries below which a node will initiate a flooding for given cost and availability values. The lower cost for higher n_r shows that a node with a large neighbourhood is more parsimonious in flooding compared to a node with a smaller neighbourhood, and only initiates flooding for lower costs. Fig. 3b is a condensed version of Fig. 3a due to setting $\gamma = 0.5$, indicating that an unstable network cannot tolerate high cost values. For both figures, the steep increase in the interval $[0, 0.4]$ indicates the strong preference on high available content in scoped-flooding. Fig. 3c shows when the cost slightly increases from its minimum (i.e., zero), the optimal number of neighbours drops drastically regardless of content availability. After a certain point, e.g., 5 or 6 nodes, the figure shows a slower decrease for content with high availability. Fig. 3c indicates that for higher availability content, it is worth flooding to more neighbours since the content will be discovered with high probability therefore the gain is guaranteed. Whereas for low availability content, even with relatively low cost, the flooding is rather conservative.

6.2 Flooding Radius Distribution

Fig. 4a shows the CDF of nodes' optimal radii using different p on both random (upper figure) and scale-fee (lower figure) networks. By increasing p from 0.1 to 0.9, the CDF curves shift towards right indicating high available content is worth large radius. In random network, the shapes of the curves are mostly identical, whereas in scale-free network, the curves are more stretched for higher p values, which indicates more heterogeneity in scale-free networks. Fig. 4b and 4c specifically plot the radius distributions for $p = 0.8$. The scale-free network has smaller flooding radii than the random network in both dynamic and static flooding. The two red vertical lines in Fig. 4c represent the optimal radii of static flooding, i.e., 2.320 for scale-free and 2.783 for random network. For dynamic flooding, the mean and variance of the radii are 2.447 and 0.094 on the scale-free (red area), and 2.805 and 0.014 on the random (blue area). Static flooding ignores the difference of topological characteristics between two nodes. Fig. 4b shows that over 60% of the nodes in scale-free network have a radius less than 2.5 whereas almost all the nodes' radii in random network are bigger than 2.5. In both Fig. 4b and 4c, the left tail of scale-free network

is heavier than that of random network due to the existence of high-degree nodes. The radius distribution of random network is more condensed in a smaller range (reflected as a small variance 0.014) because of its homogeneous structure.

There is a relatively strong negative correlation between optimal radius and node's degree as well as optimal radius and node's betweenness centrality. We report the results for betweenness centrality in Fig. 4d. Fig. 4d plots the betweenness centrality as a function of radius for the scale-free network. Note the logarithmic scale in the axis. We attribute the negative correlation to the nodes with high betweenness centrality that are located in the the well-connected parts of the network wherein the link density is very high and therefore the radius is small due to the high growth rate.

6.3 Utility and Its Improvement Distribution

Inspired by [42], fig.5a and 5b plot betweenness centrality as a function of a node's utility. Fig.5b is log-log plot. We observe a strong negative correlation between the two variables. The corresponding Pearson correlation can reach -0.93 and -0.80 for random and scale-free network, respectively. The reason for the negative correlation is that, in the dense area where a node has a high betweenness centrality value, its neighbourhood size is usually big. Although the radius is also small, the node may still include more neighbours than necessary (the optimum) which renders a higher cost and drags down the net utility. Sometimes, even 1-hop neighbours include too many nodes. On the other hand, the growth rate in the sparser area is much lower, so nodes have a better control over the neighbourhood size by fine-tuning their radius leading to smaller cost and better net utility.

To compare dynamic flooding against static one, we let U_{dy} denote the optimal utility achieved by dynamic flooding and U_{st} by static flooding. Then, we calculate the utility improvement as: $\frac{U_{dy} - U_{st}}{U_{st}}$. Fig. 5c plots the CDF of the utility improvement. We notice that dynamic flooding is less effective on random networks, only 10% of the nodes actually improve their performance and over half have less than 10% improvement. Such lower effectiveness of dynamic flooding is due to the homogeneous structure of the random network. As we showed in the previous section, the static optimal radius deviates from the dynamic optimal radius only slightly for a random network. Hence, the improvement in utility is marginal. On the other hand, nodes in scale-free network have much more significant utility improvement, namely about 30% of the nodes are improved, among which over 60% have larger than 10% improvement.

Specifically, we take a closer look at those nodes with improved utility, i.e., the 10% in random and 30% in scale-free network. Fig. 5d and 5e plot local growth rate β as a function of improvement. Note the difference in both X-range and Y-range of the two figures. As for X-range, the utility shows a wider range of improvement in scale-free networks due to the diverse growth rate of the nodes shown on the Y-axis. Scale-free network has a larger β due to hub nodes compared to the random network with more homogeneous node characteristics. Fig.5d shows that the correlation between β and the utility improvement on random network is close to zero, more precisely -0.0031, indicating that the significance of improvement is irrelevant of a node's growth rate and its position in the network. Meanwhile, such correlation on scale-free network is much stronger, with Pearson correlation being -0.5273. The results indicate that

15

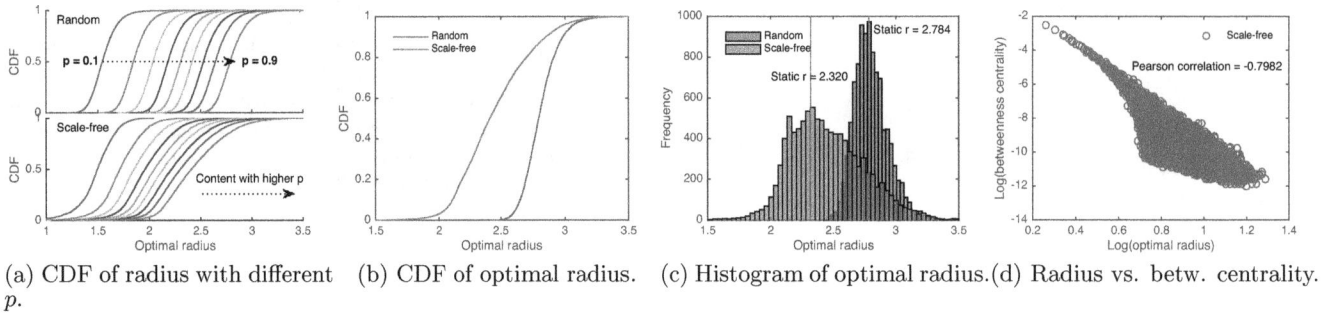

(a) CDF of radius with different (b) CDF of optimal radius. (c) Histogram of optimal radius.(d) Radius vs. betw. centrality.
p.

Figure 4: Optimal radius distribution in dynamic flooding, the radius negatively correlates to nodes' betweenness centrality.

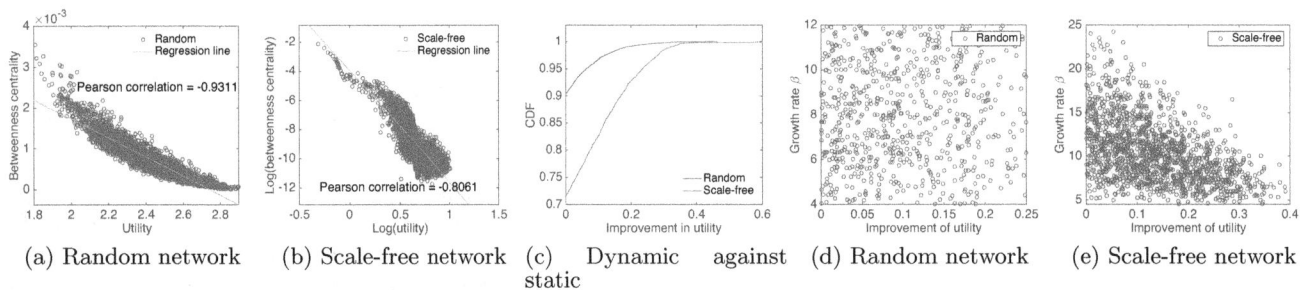

(a) Random network (b) Scale-free network (c) Dynamic against (d) Random network (e) Scale-free network
static

Figure 5: In dynamic flooding, the utility distribution strongly correlates to nodes' positions. However, regarding improvements, the strength of correlation between the significance of improvement and the position depends on the network model.

Table 2: Results for each metric are in the format of *network-wide|static|dynamic* flooding. The cost is measured by the # of flood messages and normalized with the maximum value.

AS	Byte hit rate			Cost			Avg. hops		
	nw	st	dy	nw	st	dy	nw	st	dy
1239	0.44	0.40	0.43	1.0	0.27	0.28	1.90	1.60	1.62
2914	0.49	0.42	0.47	1.0	0.31	0.32	1.75	1.55	1.58
3356	0.42	0.39	0.42	1.0	0.25	0.27	2.02	1.69	1.74
7018	0.47	0.41	0.45	1.0	0.26	0.28	1.87	1.54	1.63
Guifi	0.51	0.44	0.49	1.0	0.22	0.23	1.71	1.32	1.38

nodes with high growth rate β are less likely to have significant improvement by using dynamic flooding. The reason is that the optimal radii of the nodes with high β values in both static and dynamic flooding are small and close to each other. However, dynamic flooding usually significantly increases the radius of the nodes with low β.

6.4 Flooding in the Wild

To confirm our analysis on realistic networks, we choose four realistic ISPs along with one community network (i.e., Guifi Catalunya region) [27, 28] to compare network-wide, static, and dynamic flooding. Note that dynamic flooding is not aware of content availability but use the inference technique in the evaluations. In case there are multiple components in a network, we use the biggest one. The smallest network (AS 3356) has 3,107 nodes and 6,097 edges while the biggest one (AS 7018) has 9,732 nodes and 10,047 edges. Each node is equipped with a 4 GB cache using LRU for cache replacement, and assigned a pair of geographical co-

ordinates according to the topology traces. The content set is based on the Youtube Entertainment Category trace [33] which contains 1,687,506 objects (average size is 8.0 MB and aggregated size is 12.87 TB). The trace contains video id, length, views, rating and etc. All the nodes of degree 1 are considered as content requesters while 10 to 20 content providers (proportional to the network size) are randomly selected among the nodes in the network. A node cannot be a requester and a provider at the same time. To take into account both temporal and spatial locality, we use Hawkes process-based algorithm [34] with different *spatial locality factors* $[0, 1)$ to generate user request streams. Locality factor 0 indicates the request pattern reduces to *Independent Reference Model*, 1 indicates high spatial localisation. The "warm-up" period for pre-filling the caches is excluded from an evaluation and the result is averaged over at least 50 runs.

Table 2 reports the results with spatial locality factor 0.5. Although network-wide flooding always achieves the best byte hit rate, the improvement is rather marginal over dynamic flooding (less than 5%). On the other hand, such a small gain in cache hits is at the price of $2 \sim 3$ times increase in the number of control messages as the second column shows. Intuitively, without prior knowledge on content availability, the performance of dynamic flooding is mostly affected by network topology and should be worse than static flooding which can exploit such knowledge. The results however show that dynamic flooding consistently outperforms static one, which further attests the effectiveness of Bayesian inference and justifies the design of dynamic flooding. Compared to static one, dynamic flooding has slightly higher cost because it tends to explore more nodes (recall the default flooding to 1-hop neighbours in dynamic flooding), which also explains its gain in byte hit rate. The third column shows the average hops between a requester and the first discovered content. Network-wide flooding has the worst values and static flooding is slightly higher than dynamic one. In all cases, most content are discovered within 2 hops.

We investigate the effects of spatial locality by varying the factor between 0 and 1. For network-wide flooding, spatial locality does not appear to have any noticeable impacts on the byte hit rate and the cost except that high factor values lead to shorter average hops. On the other hand, higher spatial locality factor improves byte hit rate and average hop count in both static and dynamic flooding. For dynamic flooding, by increasing the locality factor from 0.1 to 0.9, the byte hit rate improves $9\% \sim 22\%$ and essentially reaches the performance of network-wide flooding. The average hops metric has $7\% \sim 19\%$ improvement. In terms of byte hit rate, the difference of all three strategies becomes smaller as the locality factor increases but dynamic flooding consistently outperforms static one by at least 7.5%. Meanwhile, the cost of all three strategies almost remain unchanged. The reason is that content availability and local topological property are the determinant factors of the cost (due to being a function of p and r) in static and dynamic flooding respectively, neither will be affected by changing the locality factor.

6.5 Summary and Discussion

Our results indicate that dynamic flooding is more effective on the networks of heterogeneous topological structure, and most of the gains come from sparse areas wherein local growth rate is low, namely at network edges. The optimal flooding radius in a dense area is small and nodes suffer from high flooding cost. On realistic networks for which the evaluations further take the spatial locality of content into account, dynamic flooding is consistently superior to static one even without prior knowledge on content availability, and quickly approaches the byte hit rate of network-wide flooding but with much smaller cost in control messages.

7. RELATED WORK

We can categorize the literature into two as *resolution-based discovery* and *routing-based discovery*.

Resolution-based discovery [2–8] provide deterministic solutions, i.e., at least one copy will be found as long as the content is stored within the network. Therefore, such solutions either require complete knowledge on content distribution and network topology [2,4,5] or utilize hash-based content addressing [3,6–8]. Essentially, demands and supplies meet at *rendezvous points* (the actual name differs depending on specific architecture). The rendezvous point either returns a locator or copy of the requested content [2,3], or redirects the request to one content provider [5,7], or constructs a distribution topology [4] depending on an actual design. Resolution-based solutions can reach high success rate but have to maintain the states of content distribution in a network hence are confronted with scalability issue when dealing with large and highly dynamic content demands.

Routing-based discovery [1,9,10,32] usually only provides opportunistic solutions, i.e., content will be found with certain probability. The chances of discovery can be improved by either collaborating with nearby nodes [10,35] or exploring a network via flooding [9, 15, 16, 32, 36]. Both introduce extra traffic overhead. [35] propose using Bloomfil-

ters to exchange information on content availability to improve caching performance. [15, 16, 37] empirically showed that opportunistic flooding can improve content discovery and delivery, also reduce the states maintained in a network. [9, 36, 38, 41] showed that flooding is especially preferred in an unreliable environment to compensate for potential message loss. Empirically or analytically, all [9,16,32,38] attested that naive flooding is hardly viable in practice, the scope needs to be regulated carefully to reduce the cost.

Scoped-flooding also relates to *Gossip Protocol* and *Expanding Ring Search (ERS)*. Gossip protocol has been shown as a simple, robust, and scalable solution on large distributed systems [11]. ERS is supported in reactive routing protocols in MANET such as DSR [39] and AODV [40]. Since nodes cache routes information like content caching in ICN, ERS is rather similar to scoped-flooding. Prior work [19–21] showed that the radius is very small in practice. Regarding the neighbourhood growth model, besides [22, 24, 25], another important line of research is *expander graph* [26]. In general, the advances in graph theory has improved our understanding on network graphs and laid the foundation of this work. Nonetheless, as far as we can tell, none carefully analysed the scoped-flooding for content discovery from network topology perspective, not to mention examining the distribution of gains and improvements within a network.

8. CONCLUSION

This paper aims to comprehend scoped-flooding for content discovery in ICN. Using the proposed ring model, we studied the functional relation between the neighbourhood growth and flooding radius, based on which we derived the optimal search radius. Both our theoretical analysis and empirical evaluations suggest that due to the exponential growth of neighbourhood size, the optimal flooding radius is usually very small (i.e., a couple of hops). Most of the gains of flooding come from the sparse area at the network edge where the neighbourhood growth rate is low. To certain extent, our results justify the rationale of deploying caches at network edge from content discovery perspective. Dynamic flooding is consistently superior to static one, especially on scale-free networks. With strong spatial locality, the performance of dynamic flooding quickly converges to network-wide flooding but with much smaller cost. However, we acknowledge that the following aspects need further investigation in future: (1) current neighbourhood growth model does not take clustering coefficient into account which leads to overestimation in small networks. (2) Our utility model assumes sub-linear gain and linear cost which requires further reality checks. (3) Other in-network caching algorithms can be more effective than simple LRU and a thorough comparison is definitely needed to gain a deeper understanding.

9. ACKNOWLEDGEMENT

The research leading to these results has received funding from the European Union's (EU) Horizon 2020 research and innovation programme under grant agreement No.645124 (Action full title: Universal, mobile-centric and opportunistic communications architecture, Action Acronym: UMO-BILE), and No.644663 (Action full title: architectuRe for an Internet For Everybody, Action Acronym: RIFE) This paper reflects only the authors' views and the Community is not liable for any use that may be made of the information contained therein.

10. REFERENCES

[1] V. Jacobson, et al., "Networking named content," in *Proceedings of the 5th ACM Conext.* ACM, 2009.

[2] C. Dannewitz, et al., "Netinf - an information-centric networking architecture," *Comput. Commun.*, 2013.

[3] M. D'Ambrosio, et al., "MDHT: a hierarchical name resolution service for information-centric networks," in *ACM SIGCOMM workshop on ICN*, ACM, 2011.

[4] D. Trossen, et al., "PURSUIT conceptual architecture: pinciples, patterns and sub-components descriptions," 2011.

[5] T. Koponen, et al., "A data-oriented (and beyond) network architecture," *Comput. Commun. Rev.*, 2007.

[6] D. G. Thaler, et al., "Using name-based mappings to increase hit rates," *Transactions on Networking*, 1998.

[7] L. Wang, et al., "MobiCCN: Mobility support with greedy routing in Content-Centric Networks," in *Globecom*, 2013.

[8] S. Roos, et al., "Enhancing Compact Routing in CCN with Prefix Embedding and Topology-aware Hashing," in *Mobicom workshop on MobiArch'14*, 2014.

[9] M. Varvello, et al., "On the design of content-centric MANETs," in *WONS*, 2011.

[10] W. Wong, et al., "Neighborhood search and admission control in cooperative caching networks," in *Globecom*, IEEE, 2012.

[11] P. Eugster, et al., "Epidemic information dissemination in distributed systems," *Computer*, 2004.

[12] S. Traverso, et al., "Temporal locality in today's content caching: why it matters and how to model it," *Computer Communication Review*, ACM, 2013.

[13] E. Baccelli, et al., "Information centric networking in the IoT: Experiments with NDN in the wild," in *ICN'14*.

[14] PARC, "CCNx 1.0 protocol specifications," 2014.

[15] M. Badov, et al., "Congestion-aware caching and search in information-centric networks," in *ICN'14*.

[16] R. Chiocchetti, et al.,"Exploit the known or explore the unknown? Hamlet-like doubts in ICN," in *ICN'12*.

[17] J. Garcia-Luna-Aceves, "Name-based content routing in information centric networks using distance information," in *ICN'14*, ACM, 2014.

[18] Q. Lv, et al., "Search and replication in unstructured peer-to-peer networks," in *ICS'02*, ACM, 2002.

[19] H. Barjini, et al., "Shortcoming, problems and analytical comparison for flooding-based search techniques in unstructured P2P networks," *P2P Netw. and Appl.*, 2012.

[20] J. Hassan, et al., "Optimising expanding ring search for multi-hop wireless networks," in *GLOBECOM'04*.

[21] J. Deng, et al., "On search sets of expanding ring search in wireless networks," *Ad Hoc Netw.*, 2008.

[22] M. Newman, "Random graphs as models of networks", Wiley, 2003.

[23] S. Bornholdt, et al., "Handbook of graphs and networks", Wiley, 2003.

[24] M. Molloy, et al., "A critical point for random graphs with a given degree sequence," *Random Struct. Algorithms*, 1995.

[25] S. L. Feld, "Why your friends have more friends than you do," *The American Journal of Sociology*, 1991.

[26] S. Hoory, et al., *"Expander graphs and their applications"*, Bulletin of the American Mathematical Society, 2006.

[27] N. Spring, et al., "Measuring ISP topologies with Rocketfuel," in *SIGCOMM*, ACM, 2002.

[28] D. Vega, et al., "Topology patterns of a community network: Guifi.net," in *WiMob*, IEEE, 2012.

[29] R. Hekmat, et al., "Connectivity in wireless ad-hoc networks with a log-normal radio model," *Mob. Netw. Appl.*, 2006.

[30] E. Yoneki, et al., "Distinct types of hubs in human dynamic networks," in *Social Network Systems*, 2008.

[31] A. Clauset, et al., "Power-law distributions in empirical data," *SIAM review*, 2009.

[32] E. Hyytiä, et al., "Searching a needle in (linear) opportunistic networks," in *MSWiM '14*, ACM, 2014.

[33] M. Cha, et al., "I tube, you tube, everybody tubes: analyzing the world's largest user generated content video system," in *IMC'07*, ACM, 2007.

[34] A. Dabirmoghaddam, et al., "Understanding optimal caching and opportunistic caching at "the edge" of information-centric networks," in *ICN'14*, 2014.

[35] M. Lee, et al., "Content discovery for information -centric networking," *Computer Networks*, 2014.

[36] N. Chang, et al., "Controlled flooding search in a large network," *Transactions on Networking*, 2007.

[37] G. Rossini, et al., "Coupling caching and forwarding: Benefits, analysis, and implementation," in *ICN'14*.

[38] C. Liu, et al., "An optimal probabilistic forwarding protocolin delay tolerant networks," in *MobiHoc'09*.

[39] J. Broch, et al., "The dynamic source routing protocol for mobile ad hoc networks," *IETF draft*, 1999.

[40] C. Perkins, et al., "Ad-hoc on-demand distance vector routing," in *WMCSA'99*, 1999.

[41] A. Sathiaseelan, et al., "SCANDEX: Service Centric Networking for Challenged Decentralised Networks," in *Mobisys workshop on DIYNet*, 2015.

[42] L. Wang, et al., "Effects of Cooperation Policy and Network Topology on Performance of In-Network Caching," in *Communications Letters, IEEE*, 2014.

Scalable Name-Based Packet Forwarding: From Millions to Billions

Tian Song
School of Computer Science
and Technology
Beijing Institute of Technology
Beijing, P.R.China 100081
songtian@bit.edu.cn

Haowei Yuan
Dept. of Computer Science
and Engineering
Washington University
St. Louis, MO 63130
hyuan@wustl.edu

Patrick Crowley
Dept. of Computer Science
and Engineering
Washington University
St. Louis, MO 63130
pcrowley@wustl.edu

Beichuan Zhang
Dept. of Computer Science
The University of Arizona
Tucson, Arizona 85721
bzhang@cs.arizona.edu

ABSTRACT

Named-based packet forwarding represents a core characteristic of many information-centric networking architectures. IP-inspired forwarding methods are not suitable because a) name-based forwarding must support variable-length keys of unbounded length, and b) namespaces for data are substantially larger than the global address prefix rulesets used in today's Internet. In this paper, we introduce and evaluate an approach that can realistically scale variable-length name forwarding to billions of prefixes. Our methods are driven by two key insights. First, we show that, represented by binary strings, a name-based forwarding table of several millions of entries can be notably compressed by a Patricia trie to fit in contemporary fast memory of a line card. Second, we show that it is possible to design and optimize the data structure to make its size dependent only upon the number of rules in a ruleset, rather than the length of rules.

We reduce our designs to practice and experimentally evaluate memory requirements and performance. We demonstrate that a ruleset with one million rules based on the Alexa dataset only needs 5.58 MiB memory, which can easily fit in fast memory like SRAM, and with one billion synthetic rules it takes 7.32 GiB memory, which is within the range of DRAM in a line card. These are about an order of magnitude improvement over the state-of-the-art solutions. The above efficient memory size produces high performance. Estimated throughput of the SRAM- and DRAM- based solutions are 284 Gbps and 62 Gbps respectively.

ICN'15, September 30–October 2, 2015, San Francisco, CA, USA.
Copyright is held by the owner/author(s). Publication rights licensed to ACM.
ACM 978-1-4503-3855-4/15/09 ...$15.00.
DOI: http://dx.doi.org/10.1145/2810156.2810166 .

Categories and Subject Descriptors

C.2.1 [**Network Architecture and Design**]: Store and forward networks; C.2 [**COMPUTER-COMMUNICATION NETWORKS**]: Miscellaneous

General Terms

Algorithms

Keywords

Information-Centric Networking, Named Data Networking, Name-based Packet Forwarding, Longest Prefix Matching, Speculative Forwarding

1. INTRODUCTION

Recent information-centric networking (ICN) [1] concepts, such as Named Data Networking (NDN) [4], seek to address weaknesses in today's Internet by shifting the communication abstraction away from machine addresses and toward data names. Rather than forwarding packets based on their destination addresses, ICN forwards packets based on data names, such as URL like name prefixes in NDN. Benefits aside, this shift introduces a new, and some would argue more difficult, problem: forwarding name-based packets with variable-length names based on longest-prefix match against a global data namespace toward high throughput and strict memory requirements.

Longest prefix match (LPM) methods for IP forwarding have been remarkably successful. While innovation continues in this area, the core ideas introduced in the late 1990s, refined with strong ideas [6] [10] [12] based on prefix expansion and bitmap representations, have been sufficient to enable vendors to implement cost-effective LPM solutions across all performance tiers. With fixed-length IPs and fewer than 500 K rules [11], modern LPM implementations enable Internet-scale rulesets to fit comfortably within a few mega-bytes of fast memory, such as TCAM and SRAM, in order to achieve high performance. For IP, most agree that LPM has been a solved problem for some time.

However, those approaches for IP do not work well for name-based forwarding. Traditional LPM methods are optimized for IP prefixes but not designed for general namespaces, such as those used in ICN. Specifically, a scalable and efficient name-based forwarding scheme needs to successfully address the following challenges.

Complex name structure: Names, identifiers to data, have more complex and unrestrained formats than IPs. Different ICNs adopt different naming schemes. NDN uses URL-like hierarchical names [4], while some other ICN architectures [2] [3] use flat self-certifying names. A scalable name-based packet forwarding solution should be agnostic to naming schemes.

Large forwarding table: Compared to the size of forwarding information base (FIB) in core IP routers, the size of FIB for name prefixes can be much larger. Referring to the scale of DNS domain names, So et al. [24] estimated that the name-based FIB is at the scale of $O(10^8)$, two orders of magnitude larger than IP's. As more contents are made available through ICNs over time, the FIB size may eventually reach the level of billions of rules.

High throughput: As 100 Gbps Ethernet is approaching in practice, name-based forwarding needs to be fast enough to keep up with the wire speed. Although ICN's data plane do not forward every request due to in-network caching, a forwarding scheme should be scalable to higher throughput under the worst-case scenario.

Most existing work in name-based forwarding [18] [31] [23] [24] assumes URL-like hierarchical names, i.e., multiple name components delimited by a slash ('/'). The ruleset is often stored in a hash table, and to find the longest prefix match for a key, the key's prefixes of different length are looked up against the hash table. This approach works only for the particular name structure and often results in large hash tables due to the storage of redundant information in the ruleset. Moreover, its efficiency depends on the length of the names, making it difficult to scale to long names.

In this work, we have intentionally avoided making strong assumptions about the precise features of future namespaces. As we will see, flat and heavily hierarchical namespaces each admit opportunities to engineer feasible one-off optimizations of our core ideas. We will discuss these, but our primary aim is to design and evaluate an approach that will work for large future namespace, regardless of their particular characteristics.

In this paper we propose a binary Patricia trie based approach to name-base forwarding. Our methods are driven by two key insights. First, we show that, represented by binary strings, a name-based FIB can be notably compressed by a trie data structure to fit within contemporary fast memory of a line card, even with several million names. Second, we show that it is possible to design and optimize a trie-based data structure whose size is dependent upon the number of rules in a ruleset, rather than the length of the rules.

Our discussion considers several cross-cutting ideas, from algorithm design to namespace characteristic to forwarding methodology. To clarify the overall presentation, the paper is organized to discuss contributions in sequence, as follows.

- We first present the tokenized binary Patricia trie as an efficient data structure to store name-based forwarding tables (Section 3).

- To support FIBs at the scale of billions, we introduce a novel forwarding method, *speculative forwarding*, and its specific data plane (Section 4). Speculative forwarding trades transmission bandwidth for reduced memory size by doing longest prefix classification (LPC) instead of LPM.

- A data structure, *dual binary Patricia*, is described to realize speculative forwarding. Its size is dependent only upon the number of rules rather than the length of the rules. Further analysis and optimizations are also presented in Section 5.

To evaluate our designs, we experimentally validate the memory requirements and performance over namespaces ranging from 1 million to 1 billion rules. The smaller rulesets are real-world ones drawn from today's Internet; the larger ones are synthetically generated with similar characteristics to the real-world datasets.

The results show that only 5.58 MiB[1] memory is needed for a 1 M ruleset, and 7.32 GiB for a one-billion ruleset, about an order of magnitude improvement over the state-of-the-art solutions. Our SRAM- and DRAM-based solutions are estimated to be able to achieve throughput of 284 Gbps and 62 Gbps respectively.

2. DESIGN RATIONALE

Scalable packet forwarding has two fundamental requirements: fast FIB lookup and small memory footprint, and these two requirements are highly related. The main contributor to FIB lookup time is memory access time, which depends on the type of memory used to store the FIB. TCAM has a search time of 2.7 ns [26] for one lookup, while SRAM can achieve each access time of 0.47 ns [27] but one lookup requires multiple memory accesses. These two types of fast memories are commonly used in a line card for FIB lookup, but their sizes are limited. TCAM is available in no more than 10 MiB and SRAM can be available up to 135 MiB. DRAM, on the other hand, has a read latency of 50 ns and access time of 3 ns, but can be available in tens of GiB. It is usually used for packet buffer in line cards.

While IP-based FIBs are stored in data structures that can fit in TCAM or SRAM for fast lookup, it is a challenge to name-based FIB. Existing solutions, such as [23] [24] [31], would cost hundreds of MiB to store even a few million name prefixes. Therefore they use DRAM to store FIB and rely on massive parallel processing to speed up lookup operations.

Our design goal is to have a compact data structure so that FIBs with a few million entries can still fit in SRAM for fast lookup, and when the FIB grows to hundreds of million or even a billion entries in the future, its memory footprint is still scalable in that it only depends on the number of entries rather than the length of names, which would allow effective and efficient parallel lookups to provide high and scalable performance.

To make the FIB data structure compact, we need to avoid storing redundant information. Existing hash-table based work incurs large memory footprint because they store all the rules and there're significant redundant information across different rules. We propose to use **binary Patricia**

---

[1]Mi is *mebi*, multiplied by a power of 1024, while M is *mega* with a power of 1000. We also use k (*kilo*), Ki (*kibi*), G (*giga*), and Gi (*gibi*) in this paper.

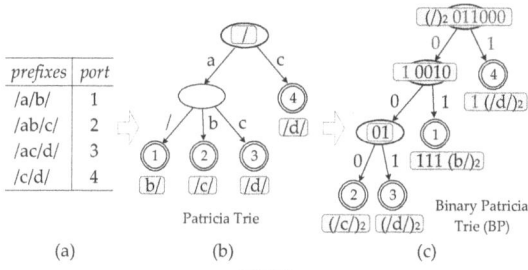

Figure 1: A Patricia and Binary Patricia trie: (a) A small set of prefixes; (b) Patricia representation; (c) binary Patricia representation.

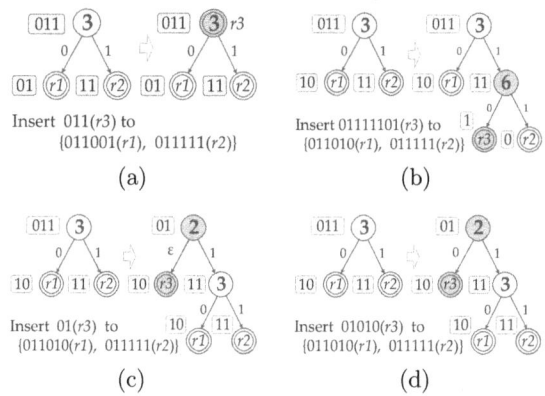

Figure 2: Four possible cases in key insertion.

trie data structure to minimize the redundant information stored. Evaluations showed that this is enough to compress FIBs of a few million entries to fit in tens of MiB of SRAM, the first part of our goal.

To achieve the second part of our goal, which is to scale to billions of FIB entries, we further reduce the data structure to store only the differentiating bits between different rules, not the rules themselves. The result is a minimal data structure that can scale ten times better than existing work, and a corresponding forwarding behavior that we termed "speculative forwarding". While speculative forwarding may cost extra bandwidth when the packet carries a name which doesn't match any prefix in the FIB, we think this is a favorable tradeoff between bandwidth and memory used to support billions of name prefixes.

3. BINARY PATRICIA FOR NAME-BASED LPM

3.1 Binary Patricia for Small Tables

Patricia trie [13], also known as radix tree, is a space-optimized general trie structure. It is generated from a character-based prefix trie by merging every single-child node with its child. The internal nodes in Patricia trie are used to branch by discrimination characters while leaf nodes contain the match information, i.e., the prefix. *Binary Patricia* is a commonly used variant, which treats prefixes as binary strings in building the trie.

In a binary Patricia, a key is represented as $k = b_0, ..., b_{l-1}$ where $k[i] = b_i \in \{0, 1\}, 0 \le i < |k|, |k| = l$ representing the width of k. A key k' is said to be a proper (strict) prefix of key k, denoted by $k' \prec k$, iff $|k'| \prec |k|$ and $k'[i] = k[i], 0 \le i < |k'|$. If two keys are identical, they are considered as one key. A binary Patricia is a full binary tree in which every non-leaf node has exact two children.

Fig.1 illustrates a character-based Patricia and a binary Patricia built from the same FIB. In a character-based Patricia, each internal node may have at most 256 children, branched by octet characters. From the root to a leaf, all tokens stored in the nodes and characters along the arrows together form a complete prefix. The delimiter ('/') is treated as a character as well. To build a binary Patricia, we use the ASCII code to represent prefixes. Other coding schemes can be used too. Each node has at most two children, branched by a bit of 0 and 1. All bits in the nodes and along the arrows from the root to a leaf together form

a complete prefix. This binary Patricia is also called as *tokenized binary Patricia* in this paper, since a prefix is divided to a sequence of tokens. Especially, the branched 0 and 1 in an internal node are part of the sequence.

While the use of binary Patricia in IP lookup dates back to BSD kernel implementation [22], using it for name-based forwarding is novel; most existing work store prefixes in hash tables. We choose binary Patricia for three reasons. First, the binary representation provides the most opportunity to compress shared parts between different prefixes. In the widely used component-based approach, only common components can be compressed; in binary Patricia, arbitrary common bit sequences can be compressed. Second, treating names as bit strings means that we do not assume any property of names, therefore our design can be applied to any name scheme. Third, since names are encoded as binary strings on the wire during transmission, we can directly use the name's wire format in table lookup and forwarding without parsing the name. The component-based approach, however, would need to parse the wire format to figure out the component boundaries before table lookup, which can incur significant processing overhead. Therefore, although component-based approach is more intuitive, binary Patricia is more generic and costs less in memory and processing.

3.2 Binary Patricia Details

A binary Patricia is built by inserting FIB entries one by one into an initial empty tree. Alg.1 details the *key-insertion* algorithm. More specifically, a common prefix is first found by comparing the token which is stored in the root with the key, k. There are three terminated cases: if this common prefix a) equals to both k and the *token* (Fig.2(a)), b) does not equal to either of them (Fig.2(d)), and c) equals to k (Fig.2(c)). If the common prefix equals to the *token* but not k, another iteration is needed to search lower level nodes of the trie with the remaining sequence of k (Fig.2(b)). We omit some details, such as labeling bit positions and creating new nodes, which are described in [13] [15]. The structure of a binary Patricia is independent of key insertion order, i.e., there is a unique trie for any given set of keys.

Removing a key from a binary Patricia requires a key query to locate its leaf node first, then deletes the leaf node and recursively merges all single-child nodes with their children along the path back. Updating a key is the combination of deleting the old key and inserting the new one.

Algorithm 1 Key Insertion Algorithm in BP

Input:
> t: binary Patricia, **static**, initial is $t[0]$
> k: binary digits of a key

Output:
> t: binary Patricia with k

1: cp=find_common($t[0]$.token, k); i=0;
2: **while** TRUE **do**
3:   **if** cp==t[i].token **and** cp==k **then**
4:     mark t[i] with k's next-hop {as Fig.2(a)}
5:   **else if** cp==t[i].token **then**
6:     i=t[i].next[$k[|cp|]$]
7:     cp=find_common(t[i].token,$k[|cp|+1:]$){Fig.2(b)}
8:     **continue**
9:   **else if** cp==k **then**
10:     add two nodes with an ε label {as Fig.2(c)}
11:   **else**
12:     add two nodes {as Fig.2(d)}
13:   **end if**
14:   **break**
15: **end while**

Suppose l_m is the maximum length in a set with n keys, the construction time and space complexity of a binary Patricia is $O(n \times l_m)$ and $O(n)$ respectively. The time complexity of update and search is $O(l_m)$.

4. SPECULATIVE FORWARDING

Although binary Patricia is more compact, its scalability is still similar to other solutions in that its size depends on the length of names. The memory footprint of a binary Patricia consists of two parts: the memory for the trie structure, which is really the differentiating bits between prefixes, and the memory for all the tokens. Note that the binaries of 0 and 1 on the arrows in Fig.1 are counted as part of the trie, not the tokens. Given it is a full trie, a binary Patricia trie has *n-1* internal nodes and *n* leaf nodes for *n* keys. The memory for this structure is independent to the length of the names. The tokens, however, are determined by the length of names. The longer the names, the more memory needed by storing them. A FIB with a few hundreds of thousands of long prefixes may well exceed the capacity of SRAM, let alone FIBs with billions of entries. This is a unique problem arisen in name-based forwarding but not in IP.

The idea to solve this problem, under the context of binary Patricia, is to remove the tokens from the Patricia. This will leave only the differentiating bits in the data structure and make it independent to the length of name prefixes. If this works, it will fundamentally change the scalability property. It will lead to small memory footprint, faster processing, and resilience to attacks that exploit very long names. However, removing the tokens from binary Patricia also changes the lookup behaviour from longest-prefix match (LPM) to longest-prefix classification (LPC). From the perspective of matching, LPM generally consists of two steps: longest-prefix classification and verification. LPC is a step to filter some candidate rules, and an additional verification is required to affirm the right one.

In this section, we will discuss the data-plane forwarding behavior which removes verification from LPM to LPC and the corresponding memory-efficient data structure.

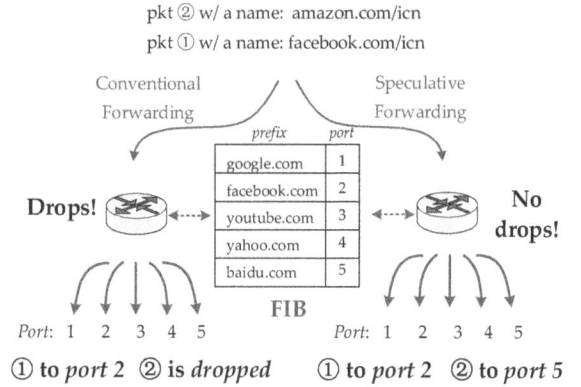

pkt ② w/ a name: amazon.com/icn
pkt ① w/ a name: facebook.com/icn

Figure 3: Speculative forwarding vs. conventional forwarding: an example.

4.1 Speculative Data Plane

We present *speculative forwarding*, which is defined as a forwarding policy that relays packets by LPC instead of LPM. In conventional LPM lookup, if there is a match, the packet will be forwarded to the corresponding nexthop, otherwise it will be dropped. LPC lookup guarantees that if there is a match, the packet will be forwarded to the same nexthop that LPM would use, but if there is no match, the packet is still forwarded.

4.1.1 Forwarding Behaviors

For example, in Fig.3, assume the FIB has already been populated by five prefixes. When the first packet with name *facebook.com/icn* arrives, both conventional forwarding and speculative forwarding will find the same matching prefix in the FIB and forward the packet out via port 2. This is because both data structures contain the same trie structure, therefore the lookup will end up with the same leaf node.

When the second packet with a name *amazon.com/icn* arrives, its name will be used to look up against the trie structure and end up with a leaf node. In conventional forwarding, the leaf node contains the prefix tokens, which will be used to verify whether the FIB entry indeed is a prefix to the packet name, and in this case the verification fails and the packet is dropped. However, in speculative forwarding, since the tokens have been removed from storing, there is no verification step, thus the packet will be forwarded out.

Speculative forwarding can guarantee correct known-prefix lookup and forwarding, but will *wrongly* relay (instead of drop) unknown-prefix packets. In return, it can reduce the memory footprint significantly by not storing rules for verification. Two issues should be further resolved: a) how to design a complete data plane which can work well with speculative forwarding, and b) how to design a data structure to support LPC in all cases for speculative forwarding.

4.1.2 Speculative Data Plane

We propose to use speculative forwarding in default-free zone (DFZ) and conventional forwarding in places with default routes, for the following reasons. DFZ routers are those need to support all global name prefixes and need to forward at high wire speed. Thus they can benefit the most from using speculative forwarding that gives smaller routing table and faster lookup. For routers in edge networks, they need

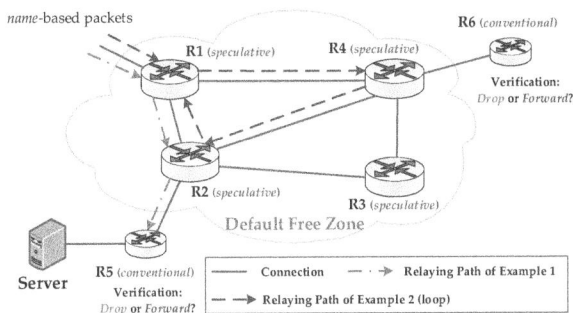

Figure 4: Speculative data plane: an example.

to support much fewer number of prefixes when using the default route. They probably can afford storing all the tokens in the binary Patricia, and they can serve as termination points for those packets wrongly forwarded by speculative forwarding. The combination of edge routers running conventional forwarding and core routers running speculative forwarding forms our global data plane.

We use two examples to explain the forwarding behaviors in this data plane. Fig.4 illustrates a network where there are 6 routers, 4 of which (R1 through R4) are in DFZ running speculative forwarding and 2 (R5, R6) in non-DFZ running conventional forwarding.

4.1.3 Example 1: Packet Forwarding

When a packet from edge networks arrives at R1, R1 performs a FIB lookup by LPC, which will always return nexthop such as R2. R2 does the same thing and forward the packet to R5. Now the packet has left DFZ and arrives at R5, which will perform LPM lookup. There are two possible outcomes. If the packet name matches a known prefix, R5 will forward it and we know that R1 and R2 must also have made the correct forwarding decisions to this packet. Otherwise the packet name doesn't have any match in the FIB, or strictly speaking, it matches R5's default route which is where the packet comes from. R5 will then drop the packet. The packet should have been dropped when it arrives at R1 if R1 runs conventional routing, but now it is dropped some time later at R5 for the purpose of reducing memory footprint at all core routers in DFZ.

4.1.4 Example 2: Loop Handling

Forwarding loops can happen with speculative forwarding. In Fig.4, when an unknown-prefix packet arrives at R1 from edge networks, it could be forwarded to R4, then R2, and R2 send it back to R1, forming a loop. Whether it happens or not depends on the actual content of the FIB, the network topology, and the packet's name. While IP's data plane doesn't handle loops and only relies on TTL exhaustion as the last resort, ICN architectures, especially NDN, employs stateful data plane, which can actually detect and drop looped packets. For example, if this is an NDN network, R1 would store forwarded Interests in the Pending Interest Table (PIT), whose purpose is to guide Data packets back to the data consumer. If the Interest packet somehow loops back to R1, R1 will be able to tell this is a looped packet by looking it up in PIT and as a result drop the packet. The packet doesn't complete the loop again and again until

TTL exhaustion. Therefore the damage of looping packets, if it happens, is much smaller than that in IP networks.

4.1.5 Feedback from the Edge

A feedback mechanism can be applied to a speculative data plane to reduce the overhead of wrongly forwarded packets. In a stateful data plane like NDN's, unknown-prefix Interest packets are stored in PIT, and will be removed after a timeout since it will not bring back any data. Optionally the edge router that dropped the unknown-prefix packet can send back a feedback packet (such as a NACK packet [20]), which will explicitly inform all nodes along the path to delete related pending Interest entries, and may be cached for a while to suppress other interests under the same unknown prefix. This mechanism may immediately reduce the memory overhead of unknown-prefix packets.

4.1.6 Prefixes Over Different Routers

Speculative data plane uses both traditional forwarding and speculative forwarding, and the combination is flexible and configurable. For core routers in DFZ, they may choose to exploit speculative forwarding to reduce its memory footprint of prefixes, or use traditional forwarding when resources are not in count. For other routers, they are configured as traditional forwarding.

For a unknown-prefix named packet whose name contains not any prefix in FIB, it will be forwarded, matched and eliminated by routers in traditional data plane. It may also be relayed and eliminated by routers in speculative data plane. The only difference is that the routers in DFZ can only relay but not drop those packets, because speculative forwarding can only filter but not verify prefixes of names.

4.2 Data Structure: Dual Binary Patricia

In this section, we describe *dual binary Patricia* to support LPC in a speculative data plane. (*dual Patricia* and *DuBP* for short in the rest of text and in the figures)

Generally speaking, a given FIB table (S) can be classified into two subsets. One (F) consists of all flat name prefixes (i.e., no one is a proper prefix of another one), and the other (P) consists of all entries where their names are covered by some entries in the flat subset. Thus, $S=F+P$. As its name implies, dual Patricia is a data structure that consists of two different styles of Patricia: a (tokenized) binary Patricia for subset P and a speculative binary Patricia for subset F.

4.2.1 Speculative Binary Patricia

Speculative binary Patricia (denoted as *sBP*) is a variant binary Patricia which is proposed by our work. It does not store any token in internal or leaf nodes. Instead, every internal node stores a value representing a bit position, namely a *discrimination bit position*. Every lookup in an internal node is branched by identifying the digit of that position in the lookup name

Fig.5(b) shows an example of speculative binary Patricia for FIB in Fig.5(a). The root node is labeled with *p:15*. It means that the root will check the *15th* bit of the lookup name. If that bit is 0 in the name, go to the left child, otherwise go to the right. The whole trie does not store any token to verify correctness of other bit positions except discrimination bits.

Speculative Patricia has a similar building process to the binary Patricia described in Section.3.

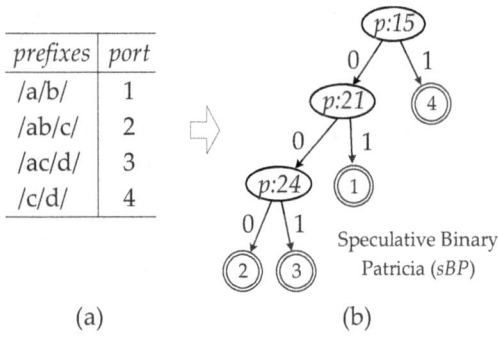

prefixes	port
/a/b/	1
/ab/c/	2
/ac/d/	3
/c/d/	4

(a)

(b)

*: $p{:}\#$ stands for the $\#\,th$ bit position in a queried name or prefix.

Figure 5: Speculative binary Patricia trie: (a) A small set of prefixes; (b) speculative binary Patricia representation.

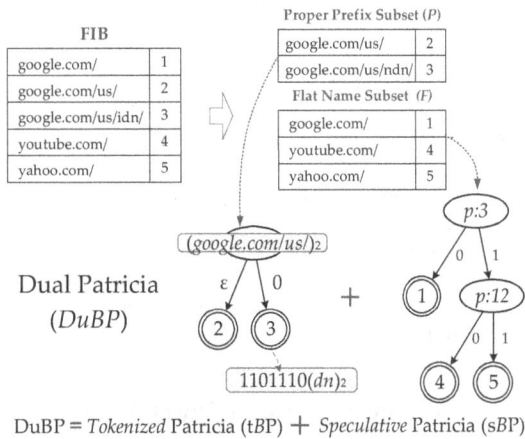

DuBP = *Tokenized* Patricia (tBP) + *Speculative* Patricia (sBP)

Figure 6: Dual Patricia: an example.

4.2.2 Dual Binary Patricia

Fig.6 illustrates a dual Patricia built for a FIB with 5 entries. The prefixes are classified to (only) two subsets. For the subset P with 2 prefixes, we build a tokenized Patricia to perform LPM. For the subset F with 3 flat entries, we build a speculative Patricia to perform LPC.

For an incoming packet, name lookup has two steps. First, the name is given to the tokenized Patricia to preform LPM. If there is no match found, the name is then given to the speculative Patricia to perform LPC among flat names. Since speculative Patricia always returns to a port for a name, the packet will be relayed to that port. Thus dual Patricia overall provides longest prefix classification for speculative forwarding. If a name is related to multiple ports, it is the duty of forwarding strategy to choose one of them.

4.2.3 Discussions about Dual Patricia

The reason that two different Patricia are required is because in the case of a prefix covered by another, such as *google.com/* and *google.com/us/*, a speculative binary Patricia cannot distinguish them apart. Since there are no tokens available in terms of LPC and *google.com/* is along the path to *google.com/us/* in Patricia, a given name cannot be verified whether it matches the internal node which

represents *google.com/* or it should go further to match the leaf node which represents *google.com/us/*. Thus, we distinguish proper prefixes from flat names and build two types of Patricia for them separately.

This design of data structure actually fits well with the design of data plane, where edge routers perform LPM and core routers perform LPC. Edge routers have default route, which covers all other prefixes. Therefore by our trie construction procedure, the entire dual Patricia becomes a binary tokenized Patricia, and the other speculative trie is empty. This naturally leads to LPM for any router that has a default route. Actually, dual Patricia is a general framework to consist of both traditional forwarding with LPM and speculative forwarding with LPC. The configuration is on user's choice.

Binary Patricia, speculative Patricia and dual Patricia (built from the first two) are slightly different variants of Patricia. Since they all have identical trie structure to the traditional Patricia, the analysis and optimization in next Section 5 are applicable to all of them.

5. ANALYSIS AND OPTIMIZATIONS

Two quantities of a Patricia are of special interests: the *depth of a leaf* (search time) and the *length of all tokens* (token memory). This section gives mathematical analysis of the average complexity and optimizations for Patricia. Besides, optimal and practical approaches to place Patricia in memory is also discussed.

5.1 Performance Analysis and Optimization

Different from general key searching in a tree, almost all of the searches in name-based lookup are *successful* search that can lead to leaf nodes. For a Patricia with n keys, the average depth of all leaf nodes, ED_n, is [14]

$$ED_n = \frac{1}{h_1}[lnn + \rho] \qquad (1)$$

where $ln(\cdot)$ denotes the natural logarithm. Here,

$$h_k = (-1)^k \sum_{i=0}^{1} p_i lnp_i \text{ and } \bar{h}_k = (-1)^k \sum_{i=0}^{1} p_i(1 - lnp_i)$$

while p_0, p_1 are the probability of digits 0 and 1 in the set. $\rho \overset{def}{=} \gamma - \bar{h_1} + h_2/(2h_1)$, where $\gamma = 0.5772$[2].

If the probabilities of digits 0 and 1 are equal in keys, the average depth of Patricia is $logn + 0.3327$. Considering the broad range of probabilities and the scale of the key set, the average depths for different cases are shown in Fig.7(a). On average, there are only about **three** additional steps deeper for a key set that is 10x larger. We can conclude that Patricia scales well and maintains a nearly constant search time. The results in practice are similar.

In terms of data structure, reducing the average depth of leaves is always an important step to improve searching performance. It is a classic issue that has already been heavily studied [15]. We utilize a practical scheme, namely load-balancing hash [30], by importing a hash as a load balancer to shorten the depth and therefore improve the search performance in Patricia.

A FIB rulesets can be split into many subsets by hashing, and Patricia can be built individually in each hash bucket. The hybrid scheme of using Patricia and load balancing hash

---

[2]γ is a *Euler* constant

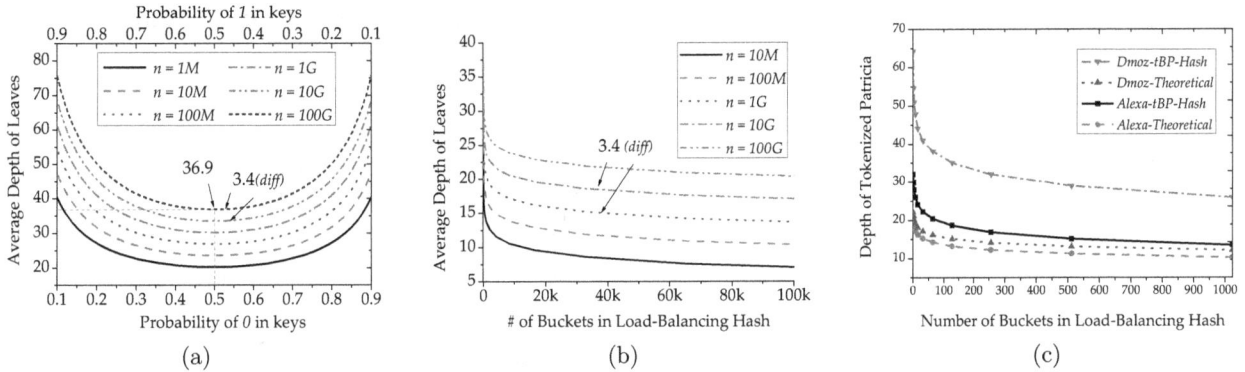

Figure 7: (a) Theoretically average depth of leaves in various possibility of 0 and 1; (b) Theoretical (c) empirical results about average depth using hybrid method with load-balancing hash.

is proven to be efficient to reduce the average depth. Fig.7(b) shows the theoretical average depth of a dual Patricia after importing a load-balancing hash on millions to billions keys. It is important to note that the average depth is a kind of long tail relationship to the number of hash buckets. Smaller hash function is good enough to reduce the depth, even for super-large or super-unbalancing sets.

Besides theoretical analysis, Fig.7(c) presents some empirical results of two real-world data sets with 1 million and 3.7 million rules in Table 1. The one-million set came from Alexa [16], which contains the top 1 M most popular sites. The 3.7 million set was collected from Dmoz [17], which is the largest and most comprehensive directory of the Web. For Alexa set, the depth decreases from 32 to 14; for Dmoz, from 65 to 26 with only hundreds of buckets. We conclude that 1 K buckets in a hash table are good enough to get practical minimum depth.

In practice, the depth is not the only parameter of performance because of memory hierarchical system, especially several levels of cache. Searching a trie could be extremely fast if paths and nodes are already in cache. To provide a nearly constant lookup time, our major design goal is to make the data structure small enough or flexible enough to reside in fast memory (SRAM) or cache in DRAM, then to reduce the depth of leaf nodes.

5.2 Memory Layout and Optimization

The memory layout which places a data structure in memory is as important and critical as the data structure in practice. It compacts memory footprint and impacts the lookup speed. An efficient memory layout should balance the flexibility between random access for high speed and the effectiveness of memory usage.

Basically, binary Patricia is a trie data structure. The memory layout issue is to efficiently *link* all nodes and *store* tokens. Tokenized and speculative Patricia are full binary trie, and every internal node has two children. An obvious memory layout in software implementation is to maintain two pointers from an internal node to its children. For example, suppose we have 1 billion keys, i.e., 1 billion internal nodes, a Patricia should maintain 2 billion pointers. On a 64-bit platform, only maintaining those pointers would consume 16 GiB memory.

Our work introduces a concise memory layout, namely *single-address memory layout*, which can use only one point-

Table 1: The data set configurations

data set	# of keys	% of p.p.	avg.len	alphabet
Alexa	999,973	1.03	15.5 B	readable
Dmoz	3,711,540	3.85	27.3 B	readable
Gen100	100 M	5-50/+5	37.6 B	readable
Gen300	300 M	5-50/+5	37.6 B	random
Gen1000	1 G	5-50/+5	37.6 B	random

er to link an internal nodes with its two children in Patricia. The motivation comes from the fact that Patricia is a full, but not a complete, binary tree. So we have to store pointers (or addresses) from internal nodes to their children, but we may need only one, not two, pointer since there are always two children and they can be put together in memory.

In an internal node, a single address is used to locate the memory of its left child as a base address, and an offset is used to calculate the right child by adding to the base. Tokens can be optionally stored within the trie structures. For 1 billion FIB entries, the single-address layout can easily save about 8 GiB memory size. Similarly, a leaf node stores token related fields and its next-hop information of the corresponding FIB entry. An additional bit is also needed to distinguish leaf nodes and internal nodes for different data structures [15].

Although this single address memory layout may not be the most memory efficient solution for Patricia, it remains a simple way to point to children of nodes and a flexible placement of nodes in memory. Each pair of children can be stored individually, and they are small enough for a cache system to fetch and keep as a fragment of the whole tree. These merits improve the performance by using cache system in software implementation, and enable the hardware implementation to gain high performance by applying on-chip memory.

6. EXPERIMENTAL RESULTS

6.1 Methodology and Setup

To evaluate the above approaches, we collected five data sets, shown in Table 1, from one million to one billion keys to model realistic routing tables in different scales. Two of them are real-world sets, as mentioned in Section 5. We gen-

Table 3: The memory devices in a line card

device	single-chip	#	total size	lookup
TCAM [26]	2.5 MiB	4	10 MiB	2.7 ns
SRAM [27]	33.75 MiB	4	135 MiB	0.47 ns
DRAM	4 GiB	4-8	16-32 GiB	50 ns

erated another three sets. Gen100 set was built on a human readable character set by combining three random English words in the dictionary and one of 271 TLDs from INNA. The other two sets were generated by random bytes and TLDs. To evaluate the cases of highly hierarchical namespace, all generated sets has 5% to 50% of proper prefixes (p.p.) with a step of 5%, where 5% is set as default. We suppose that every router can support the maximum of 256 next hops. If experimental results come from any random related circumstance, they are the average of 10 tries.

6.2 Memory Footprint and Comparison

To normalize results from different scale data sets, we use *memory per million keys* as a unit. In some cases, we also use absolute values directly. For fairness, the single-address memory layout is used as default.

Fig.8(a) presents the memory size of a binary (tokenized) Patricia in conventional forwarding with detailed trie and token memory for five data sets. The memory cost per million keys remains stable in different scales from millions to billions. The slight differences come from the token memory size, which is related to the data sets. For Alexa and Dmoz, both token memory account for about 60% of all memory, which gives us an idea of real-world namespaces.

Fig.8(b) gives the memory cost of a dual Patricia for speculative forwarding. Compared to Fig.8(a), token memory is reduced heavily because no tokens in speculative Patricia is stored for flat names. Because of proper prefixes in the subset P, dual Patricia also consumes some memory for tokens.

All results with detailed values are shown in Table.2. It shows that dual Patricia in speculative forwarding consumes only about 40% of the memory of binary Patricia, achieving 2.5 times memory efficiency. Even for tokenized Patricia, 64.80 MiB for 3.7 million DMOZ set also gains more than 5 times better than other approaches in the literatures, as shown in Table 4. In this table, all memory and performance results of other approaches are extracted from those papers. For memory footprint, the comparison is fair enough, however, for performance, different approaches may build on different platforms, so the results are just for reference.

In the real-world sets in Table 1, there is a very limited proportion of proper prefix keys. To evaluate the cases of highly hierarchical namespace, we extended three generated sets to have from 5% to 50% of proper prefixes, with a step size of 5%. Fig.8(c) gives the memory footprint for dual Patricia. The results indicate a nearly linear scalable trend.

Table 3 lists different configurations of memory devices provided in a line card. Compared to the results in Table.2 (the bottom two lines), it can be calculated that a 135 MiB SRAM-based solution which consists four channels of 33.75 MiB single-chip SRAMs can host 7.71 M FIB entries in conventional forwarding and 16.11 M FIB entries in speculative forwarding. Because 10 M FIB entries are expected as a practical target [23], our approach successful builds the target within fast memory of a contemporary line card.

6.3 Performance and Comparison

6.3.1 Average Depth

We have addressed the average depth of Patricia in Section 5 from theoretical analysis down to optimizations in Fig.7(a), Fig.7(b) and Fig.7(c). It shows that, for names from millions to billions, an average depth is 15 to 20 in both theoretical and practical cases.

Patricia searches a key step by step from the root to leaf, so we assume that there is one memory access for each step deeper. Therefore, we use 15 memory accesses for millions names and 20 for billions to estimate the real performance in the worse scenarios. Actually, cache and other techniques can greatly reduce the requirement of one memory access per step. Although dual Patricia has two separate Patricia, it can be regarded as one Patricia with 15 to 20 steps because the binary Patricia for proper prefixes, tokenized Patricia, hosts very small number of FIB names according to the characteristics of real-world data sets.

6.3.2 Performance Estimation and Comparison

We estimate SRAM-based performance by using parameters in Table 3, in which each memory access to QDR SRAM consumes 0.47 *ns*. For millions of names, a complete key lookup requires 7.05 *ns*, thus 142 million searches per second (MSPS).

For billions of names, DRAM-based solution with massive parallel computing is the only choice. Different from general computer systems, a line card already supports parallel and low-level hardware specific programming for fast speed. Optimizing a tree search in DRAM has been studied before [29], which exploits pipeline and multiple DRAM channels to achieve near one DRAM access performance for a complete key query. We desire that approach and evaluate our performance based on it. According to Table 3, DRAM-based performance may achieve 20 MSPS.

It is complicated to estimate ICN throughput that an approach can support, because only Interest packets are delivered to FIB lookup in NDN architecture and in-network caching can reduce the lookup requirements. We use a similar estimation approach used by So et al. [23] that each lookup handles 256-byte packet in average. Accordingly, our SRAM-based solution can provide a throughput of 284 Gbps, while DRAM-based solution can achieve 62 Gbps. Finally, our results are compared with other approaches in Table 4.

We have memory and performance results in Table 4 for real and generated data sets. Only memory results are evaluated in real systems. The performance values are all estimated, just for reference, according to hardware behaviour and our experiences on them. The future work is to extend our implementation to various hardware systems to further evaluate our approach.

7. CONCLUSIONS

Named-based forwarding poses unique challenges due to complex name structures, unbounded namespace, and high-speed requirement. We propose to use binary Patricia as the basis for compact name-based FIBs, and further improves its scalability by introducing speculative forwarding as a concept to build a novel forwarding plane and dual Patricia as a data structure to carry longest prefix classification rather than longest prefix match. Evaluations have shown more than an order of magnitude reduction in memory footprint

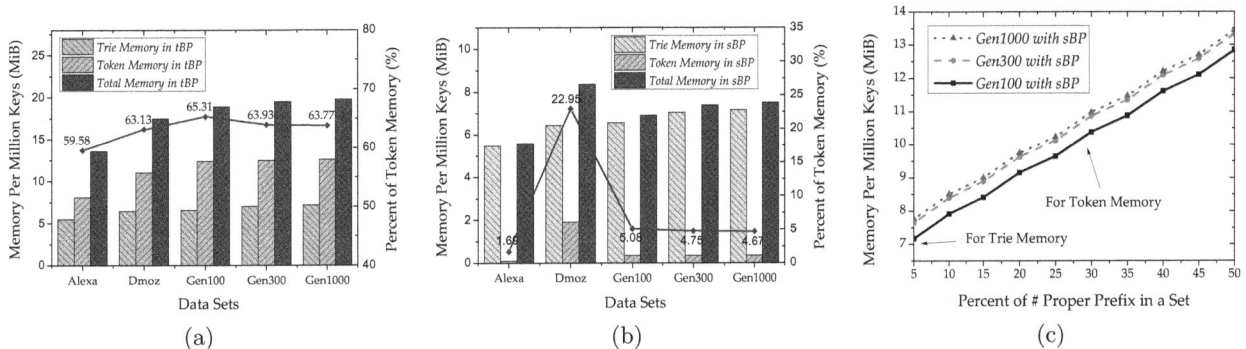

Figure 8: Memory size in a (a) tokenized Patricia, (b) dual Patricia for speculative forwarding,(c) different proper prefix sets.

Table 2: The memory cost of different data structures with one-address memory layout

| Data Set | Tokenized Patricia(tBP) | | | | Dual Patricia($DuBP$) | | | | $DuBP/tBP$ | Memory Efficiency |
	Trie	Token	Total	Devices	Trie	Token	Total	Devices		
Alexa (**MiB**)	5.48	8.08	**13.56**	SRAM	5.48	0.10	**5.58**	SRAM	41.1%	2.43
Dmoz (**MiB**)	23.89	40.91	**64.80**	SRAM	23.89	7.12	**31.01**	SRAM	47.8%	2.09
Gen100 (**GiB**)	0.64	1.21	1.85	DRAM	0.64	0.034	0.67	DRAM	36.2%	2.89
Gen300 (**GiB**)	2.06	3.62	5.68	DRAM	2.06	0.103	2.16	DRAM	38.0%	2.63
Gen1000 (**GiB**)	6.98	12.05	**19.03**	DRAM	6.98	0.342	**7.32**	DRAM	38.5%	2.60
7.71 M Rules	← 135 MiB			SRAM						
16.11 M Rules				SRAM	← 135 MiB					

than state-of-the-art solutions. Thus several million of FIB rules can fit into contemporary SRAM in commercial line cards to achieve the wire speed. Future work includes further investigation on speculative data plane, and extending the binary Patricia to other name-based functionality such as content stores and pending interest tables.

8. ACKNOWLEDGMENTS

This work is supported by the National Natural Science Foundation of China under grant No.61272510, the National Science Foundation under grants CNS-1040643, CNS-1345282, CNS-1455794 and CNS-1513505, and Jiangsu Future Networks Innovation Institute of China under the Prospective Research Project on Future Networks No. BY2013095-1-09. Any opinions, findings, and conclusions or recommendations expressed in this material are those of the authors and do not necessarily reflect those of the funding sources.

9. REFERENCES

[1] Ahlgren, Bengt, Christian Dannewitz, Claudio Imbrenda, Dirk Kutscher, and Börje Ohlman. "A survey of information-centric networking." Communications Magazine, IEEE 50, no. 7 (2012): 26-36.

[2] Ahlgren, B., M. D?ambrosio, C. Dannewitz, A. Eriksson, J. Golic, B. Grönvall, D. Horne et al. "Second netinf architecture description." 4WARD EU FP7 Project, Deliverable D-6.2 v2.0 (2010).

[3] Koponen, Teemu, Mohit Chawla, Byung-Gon Chun, Andrey Ermolinskiy, Kye Hyun Kim, Scott Shenker, and Ion Stoica. "A data-oriented (and beyond) network architecture." In ACM SIGCOMM Computer Communication Review, vol. 37, no. 4, 2007.

[4] Zhang, Lixia, Deborah Estrin, Jeffrey Burke, Van Jacobson, James D. Thornton, Diana K. Smetters, Beichuan Zhang et al. "Named data networking (ndn) project." Technical Report NDN-0001 (2010).

[5] Yuan, Haowei, Tian Song, and Patrick Crowley. "Scalable NDN forwarding: Concepts, issues and principles." In Computer Communications and Networks (ICCCN), 2012 21st International Conference on, pp. 1-9. IEEE, 2012.

[6] Degermark, Mikael, Andrej Brodnik, Svante Carlsson, and Stephen Pink. "Small forwarding tables for fast routing lookups." Vol. 27, no. 4. ACM, 1997.

[7] Eatherton, William N. "Hardware-based internet protocol prefix lookups." Master's thesis, Washington University, 1999.

[8] Jiang, Weirong, and Viktor K. Prasanna. "A memory-balanced linear pipeline architecture for trie-based IP lookup." In High-Performance Interconnects, 2007. HOTI 2007. 15th Annual IEEE Symposium on, pp. 83-90. IEEE, 2007.

[9] Eatherton, Will, George Varghese, and Zubin Dittia. "Tree bitmap: hardware/software IP lookups with incremental updates." ACM SIGCOMM Computer Communication Review 34, no. 2 (2004): 97-122.

[10] Srinivasan, Venkatachary, and George Varghese. "Faster IP lookups using controlled prefix expansion." In ACM SIGMETRICS Performance Evaluation Review, vol. 26, no. 1, pp. 1-10. ACM, 1998.

[11] Smith, P.. "Weekly routing table report." http://thyme.rand.apnic.net.

[12] Doeringer, Willibald, Günter Karjoth, and Mehdi Nassehi. "Routing on longest-matching prefixes."

Table 4: Comparison with other approaches

Method Names	Alexa Mem	Dmoz Mem	Performance	Throughput	Scalability	Comments
Compressed Trie [25]	N/A	400.8 MiB	0.15 MSPS	0.3 Gbps	N/A	
NCE [18]	79.64MiB	272.27 MiB	0.91 MSPS	1.82 Gbps	N/A	3M Dmoz rules
MATA [31](GPU)	N/A	197.6 MiB	63.52 MSPS	127 Gbps	millions	*latency* 100 us
Hash [24](GPU)	153 MiB	587 MiB	8.8 MSPS	17.6 Gbps	millions	massive parallel
Binary Patrica (SRAM)	13.56 MiB	64.80 MiB	142 MSPS	284 Gbps	≤ 7.71 M	3.7M Dmoz rules
Dual Patrica (SRAM)	5.58 MiB	31.01 MiB	**142 MSPS**	**284 Gbps**	≤ **16.1 M**	3.7M Dmoz rules
Dual Patrica (DRAM)	5.58 MiB	31.01 MiB	20 MSPS	62.02 Gbps	billions	w/ pipeline

IEEE/ACM Transactions on Networking (TON) 4, no. 1 (1996): 86-97.

[13] Morrison, Donald R. "PATRICIA?practical algorithm to retrieve information coded in alphanumeric." Journal of the ACM (JACM) 15, no. 4 (1968): 514-534.

[14] Szpankowski, Wojciech. "Patricia tries again revisited." Journal of the ACM (JACM) 37, no. 4 (1990): 691-711.

[15] Knuth, Donald Ervin. "The art of computer programming: sorting and searching." Vol. 3. Pearson Education, 1998.

[16] Alexa: http://www.alexa.com/.

[17] Dmoz: http://www.dmoz.org/.

[18] Wang, Yi, Keqiang He, Huichen Dai, Wei Meng, Junchen Jiang, Bin Liu, and Yan Chen. "Scalable name lookup in NDN using effective name component encoding." In Distributed Computing Systems (ICDCS), 2012 IEEE 32nd International Conference on, pp. 688-697. IEEE, 2012.

[19] Wang, Yi, Yuan Zu, Ting Zhang, Kunyang Peng, Qunfeng Dong, Bin Liu, Wei Meng et al. "Wire Speed Name Lookup: A GPU-based Approach." In NSDI, pp. 199-212. 2013.

[20] Yi, Cheng, Alexander Afanasyev, Lan Wang, Beichuan Zhang, and Lixia Zhang. "Adaptive forwarding in named data networking." ACM SIGCOMM computer communication review 42, no. 3 (2012): 62-67.

[21] Yi, Cheng, Alexander Afanasyev, Ilya Moiseenko, Lan Wang, Beichuan Zhang, and Lixia Zhang. "A case for stateful forwarding plane." Computer Communications 36, no. 7 (2013): 779-791.

[22] Sklower, Keith. "A tree-based packet routing table for Berkeley unix." In USENIX Winter, vol. 1991, pp. 93-99. 1991.

[23] So, Won, Ashok Narayanan, Dave Oran, and Yaogong Wang. "Toward fast NDN software forwarding lookup engine based on hash tables." In Proceedings of the eighth ACM/IEEE symposium on Architectures for networking and communications systems, 2012.

[24] So, Won, Ashok Narayanan, and David Oran. "Named data networking on a router: Fast and DoS-resistant forwarding with hash tables." In Proceedings of the ninth ACM/IEEE symposium on Architectures for networking and communications systems, 2013.

[25] Shue, Craig A., and Minaxi Gupta. "Packet forwarding: Name-based vs. prefix-based." In IEEE Global Internet Symposium, pp. 73-78. 2007.

[26] Renesas TCAM: http://www.am.renesas.com/

[27] Cypress QDR SRAM: http://www.cypress.com/

[28] Sahasra Processor: http://www.broadcom.com

[29] Kumar, Sailesh, Michela Becchi, Patrick Crowley, and Jonathan Turner. "CAMP: fast and efficient IP lookup architecture." In Proceedings of the 2006 ACM/IEEE symposium on Architecture for networking and communications systems, pp. 51-60. ACM, 2006.

[30] Fagin, Ronald, Jurg Nievergelt, Nicholas Pippenger, and H. Raymond Strong. "Extendible hashing?a fast access method for dynamic files." ACM Transactions on Database Systems (TODS) 4, no. 3 (1979): 315-344.

[31] Wang, Yi, Tian Pan, Zhian Mi, Huichen Dai, Xiaoyu Guo, Ting Zhang, Bin Liu, and Qunfeng Dong. "NameFilter: Achieving fast name lookup with low memory cost via applying two-stage bloom filters." In INFOCOM, 2013 Proceedings IEEE, pp. 95-99., 2013.

A New Approach to Name-Based Link-State Routing for Information-Centric Networks

Ehsan Hemmati[1] and J.J. Garcia-Luna-Aceves[1,2]
[1]Department of Computer Engineering, University of California, Santa Cruz, CA 95064
[2]Palo Alto Research Center, Palo Alto, CA 94304
ehsan@soe.ucsc.edu, jj@soe.ucsc.edu

ABSTRACT

The Link State Content Routing (LSCR) protocol is presented, which supports routing over multiple paths to named content using link-state information. LSCR uses two types of link-state advertisements (LSAs): a *Router LSA* that contains information about links connected to each router, and an *Anchor LSA* that carries information regarding a name prefix and the router that advertises being attached to that name prefix, also called an anchor of the prefix. *Anchor LSAs* are propagated selectively based on a diffusing mechanism. In contrast to prior content routing solutions based on link-state information, LSCR allows routers to establish multiple routes to name prefixes, without requiring each router to know about all the instantiations of each prefix. LSCR is shown to avoid permanent routing loops and to have better performance compared to traditional link-state routing protocols when a name prefix is replicated at multiple sites in the network.

Categories and Subject Descriptors

C.2.2 [**Network Protocols**]: Routing protocols;
C.2.6 [**Internetworking**]: Routers

General Terms

Theory, Design, Performance

Keywords

Information-centric networks; name-based content routing; link-state routing

1. INTRODUCTION

The current Internet architecture was designed many years ago to address the communication needs prevailing at that time, and focused on the need to share limited, expensive, and static computer resources. Since then, the Internet usage pattern has shifted from a host-centric model to a flexible content-oriented model in which users and content are distributed and mobile.

ICN'15, September 30–October 2, 2015, San Francisco, CA, USA.
© 2015 ACM. ISBN 978-1-4503-3855-4/15/09 ...$15.00.
DOI: http://dx.doi.org/10.1145/2810156.2810173.

A number of Information-Centric Network (ICN) architectures have been developed to address the increasing demand of user-generated content [9,13,19,27] in the Internet. ICN architectures are based on location-independent content naming rather than location-oriented host addressing. ICN architectures are implemented based on name resolution and name-based content routing to provide cost-efficient, mobile, and scalable content distribution.

The most promising ICN architectures can be characterized as Interest-based. Content Centric Networking (CCN) [1] and Named Data Networking [3] are the most prominent Interest-based ICN architectures today. In such architectures, content providers, i.e., producers, create named data objects (NDOs), and publish name prefixes associated with these content objects. A name prefix (or simply a prefix), is a location-independent routable name that is associated with a set of NDOs and advertised in the network by the publisher. A content consumer asks for an NDO or name prefix by sending a request, called an *Interest*, which is routed along content routers toward a publisher of the requested content. The producers or any caching sites that have a copy of the requested NDOs satisfy the Interests and send back the corresponding *Data* packets.

Each content router in the network forwards Interests according to its *Forwarding Information Base* (FIB), which stores the next hops towards name prefixes. A routing protocol is needed to maintain the routes needed to populate the FIB entries. An important feature of many such architectures is the caching of named data objects that can be done everywhere and for everything in the network. Designing a reliable routing algorithm that cope with adding and deleting prefixes in caches is challenging task.

Section 2 reviews prior work on name-based content routing for ICNs. As this summary reveals, no prior work has been reported based on link-state information that enables routers to know only subsets of the replicas of name prefixes to support name-based content routing to the nearest prefix replicas.

Section 3 presents **LSCR** (*link state content routing*), a name-based content routing protocol that uses link-state information and information regarding the nearest replicas of prefixes. LSCR relies on router names instead of IP addresses. Like other link-state routing protocols for ICNs, LSCR uses a flooding mechanism to propagate link-state information regarding physical link characteristics and build a map of the network topology at each router. However, instead of flooding publisher information, as it is done in NLSR [22] and OSPFN [23], LSCR propagates publisher information by diffusing the information selectively, based on a distributed computation of preferred publishers. LSCR supports both flat and hierarchical naming schemas; therefore, it can be implemented in different ICN architectures with different naming policies.

Section 4 shows that LSCR computes multiple paths to name prefixes and prevents permanent routing-table loops. A routing table lists the shortest distances to the nearest publishers of NDOs or name prefixes through one or multiple neighbors. Section 5 analyzes the communication, storage, and time complexities of LSCR, traditional link-state routing, and loop-free distance-vector routing.

Section 6 presents the results of simulation experiments comparing LSCR with a link-state approach similar to NLSR and OSPFN [22, 23]. LSCR produces less communication and computation overhead when the number of replicas in the network is more than three. This result follows from the fact that LSCR disseminates only partial publisher information.

2. RELATED WORK

Several ICN architectures have been proposed to handle name resolution and routing [7, 31]. In general, these architectures adopt content routing approaches that adapt traditional routing algorithms designed for networks in which a destination has a single instance [15]. This results in the need to disseminate information about all replicas of prefixes, rely on flooding requests to the entire network, build a spanning tree, use source routing, or use directories and DHTs for redirection. The rest of this section summarizes examples of these various approaches.

Directed Diffusion [24] was one of the first proposals for name-based routing of content. Requests for named content (called interests) are flooded throughout a sensor network, and data matching the interests are sent back to the issuers of interests. DIRECT [30] is similar to directed diffusion and provides named-based content routing in MANETs subject to connectivity disruption.

The name-based routing protocol (NBRP) [20] was one of the earliest proposals for name-based routing of content. Name-prefix reachability is advertised among content routers, and path information is used to avoid permanent loops.

CBCB (combined broadcast and content based) routing is another early development on name-based routing of content [12]. CBCB consists of two components. A spanning tree of the network or multiple per-source trees are established, and publish-subscribe requests for content are sent between consumers and producers of content over the tree(s) established in the network.

Data Oriented Network Architecture (DONA) [26] uses name resolution to map the flat names to corresponding IP addresses that can be local or global.

MobilityFirst [4] relies on an external and fast name resolution system called Global Name Resolution Service (GNRS) to map the data object names to network addresses. Name based routing in both DONA and MobilityFirst is accomplished using traditional IP routing and forwarding.

In Publish Subscribe Internet Technology (PURSUIT) [2, 8], each data object has a unique name that is mapped to the publisher. A Topology Manager (TM) in the network, that runs a link state routing protocol to discover the network topology, is responsible to calculate a route between the publisher and the consumer.

NDN [3] has adopted a traditional link-state approach to name-based content routing. NLSR [22] and OSPFN [23] are the two link-state content routing protocols that have been proposed to date. In NLSR, two types of link state advertisements (LSAs), *AdjacencyLSA* and *PrefixLSA*, propagate topology and publisher information in the network. Each router uses topology information and runs an extension of Dijkstra's shortest-path first (SPF) algorithm to calculate the next hops for each router. The router then maps a prefix to the name of its publisher and creates a routing table for each name prefix. NLSR propagates information regarding all replicas of all prefixes in the network and does not provide any mechanism to rank replicas of the same prefix.

A number of content routing approaches have been developed in the context of content delivery networks (CDN) that direct consumers to the nearest CDN sites and support name-based content routing in the CDN using distance information [18, 29]. Other approaches use distributed hash tables (DHT) as the name resolution tool running on top of the existing inter-domain routing infrastructure [5, 6, 25].

CORD [16] combines redirection of content requests with content routing using a publish-subscribe approach based on a virtual DHT of directories listing the location of content.

Recently, DCR [14] was introduced to support name-based content routing using distance information regarding the nearest instances of NDOs or name prefixes. The main difference between DCR and prior approaches to content routing is that routers compute shortest paths to prefixes or NDOs by disseminating distance information only for the nearest instance of a prefix. As the next section describes, LSCR adopts the same general approach using link-state information.

3. LSCR

We make a number of assumption in the description of LSCR. Routers are assumed to operate and store information correctly. Each router receives LSAs from its neighbors correctly and processes them one at a time within a finite time. Link costs can vary in time but cost values are always positive. The link cost assignment and metric determination mechanisms are beyond the scope of this paper.

Each router in the network has a unique name or identifier, which can be flat or hierarchical and a lexicographic value is assigned to the name.

Every piece of content in the network is a named-data object (NDO), and a set of one or multiple NDOs can be represented by name prefix (or simply *prefix*). Prefixes can be simple and human-readable or more complicated and self certifying, or may even be a cryptographic hash of the content.

A router that has local access to all the content associated with a name prefix is called an *anchor* of the prefix. Each anchor of a prefix advertises the prefix as being locally available to the rest of the network. Routers and content can be assigned flat or hierarchical names.

LSCR relies on two basic mechanisms: name resolution and topology-based routing. Like other link-state routing protocols [11], LSCR propagates link state advertisements (LSAs) to create a local copy of the network topology and a mapping schema from name prefixes to router identifiers (ID) at each router. Based on topology and anchor information, LSCR creates a lexicographic ordering among neighbors and calculates multiple routes to the nearest replicas of prefixes, i.e., to the nearest anchors of prefixes.

3.1 Messages and Data Structures

A link between router i and its neighbor n is denoted by (i, n) and its cost is denoted by l_n^i. The set containing router i and its neighbor routers is denoted by N^i. The lexicographic value of the identifier of a neighbor router n is denoted by $|n|$.

LSCR propagate two types of LSAs. A *Router LSA* (RLSA) is used to advertise the presence of a router and the state and cost of its outgoing links. An *Anchor LSA* (ALSA) is used to advertise the existence of name prefixes locally available, which make the advertising router an anchor of the prefixes. A sequence number is associated to each LSA to identify the message and its order.

An RLSA can be initiated by any router that runs LSCR. The ALSA sent by router i is denoted by $RLSA^i$ and consists of the name of the router i, a message sequence number (msn^i), and a list of outgoing links connected to the router i and the cost associated with each link.

ALSAs can be initiated only by anchors of the prefixs and intermediate routers can forward, drop, or hold these LSAs. The ALSA sent by anchor m regarding prefix j is denoted by $ALSA_j^m$, and consists of the name of the anchor (m); and one "*Prefix Update*" (PU^m).

PU^m states the prefix name j, the sequence number that is assigned to the prefix by the anchor (usn_j^m), and the "ValidFlag" or $vFlag$ indicating if name prefix j is attached to anchor m or detached (vf_j^m).

Anchor m sends just one prefix update per ALSA because of two considerations. First, prefixes have different lengths and can be too large for several prefixes to fit in a single message. Second, every intermediate router that runs LSCR processes a received ALSA based on the prefix and decides whether to forward or hold the ALSA. A router may forward one ALSA with a specific prefix and hold another ALSA that advertises a different prefix from the same anchor.

Router i maintains a Link Cost Table (LT^i) storing the cost of the link from router i to each of its adjacent routers. Each LSCR router exchanges periodic *Hello* messages with its neighbors to detect the addition or deletion of links and routers, as well as any changes in the link cost.

A predefined parameter defines the time interval between the transmission of two consecutive Hello messages. The link to a neighbor is considered to be down if a router does not receive a Hello message for a specified amount of time (a time-out) from that neighbor. Afterward, the router sends recovery Hello messages to detect the recovery with time intervals relatively longer than normal Hello message interval. A router cannot differentiate between a link being down or the neighbor behind that link having failed. However, this distinction does not affect the protocol, because in both cases the neighbor behind a perceived link failure should not be used to forward traffic. Each router that runs LSCR sends an RLSA at startup and whenever it detects a change in one of its links.

Each LSCR router maintains a *Forwarding Table* (FT^i), storing the set of valid next hops for each destination. The row for destination p in FT^i specifies: the name of the router (p); the sequence number ($rsn(p)$) reported by router p; the Distance List (RD_p^i) consisting of the set of shortest distances from each neighbor router $n \in N^i$ to destination p

(rd_{pn}^i); the shortest distance to router p (rd_p^i); and the set of neighbors that are valid next hops toward destination p (RS_p^i).

Router i updates FT^i based on RLSAs received from other routers in the network. The RLSA form router k received by router i is denoted by $RLSA_k^i$. The information stored in $RLSA_k^i$ is the router sequence number rsn_j^i, plus the cost of each the links between router j and its neighbors.

Router i stores information about prefixes and their corresponding anchor(s) in its *Prefix Table* (PT^i). The information regarding prefix j is denoted by PT_j^i and consist of the name of the prefix j and the prefix anchor information of prefix j (PAI_j^i).

Each entry of PAI_{jm}^i consists of: the anchor m of the prefix j; a "*valid*" flag; vf_{jm} for anchor m, which indicates whether router m advertises prefix j or not; and the sequence number (sn_{jm}) reported by anchor m for prefix j.

Router i updates PT^i based on ALSAs that are received from anchors. The ALSA form anchor m received by router i regarding prefix j is denoted by $ALSA_{mj}^i$ and consists of: the name of the anchor (m), the prefix name j, the sequence number assigned to the prefix by the anchor (usn_{mj}^i), and the $vFlag$ indicating if name prefix j is attached to anchor m or detached (vf_{mj}^i).

Router i also maintains a *Routing Table* (RT^i) that stores routing information for each known prefix. The information stored in RT^i regarding prefix j is denoted by RT_j^i, and consist of routing information for the nearest anchor of the prefix j. The routing information includes: the name of prefix j, shortest distance d_j^i to nearest anchor of prefix j, the set of neighbors that are valid next hops for prefix j (S_j^i), the king anchor for prefix j (k_j^i), and a neighbor that is the best next hop in the shortest path to anchor k_j^i of j ($s_j^i \in S_j^i$). The king anchor of prefix j is the anchor with the smallest lexicographic name among those anchors that are at the same shortest distance to j

Router i updates PT^i and RT^i based on the other two tables, LT^i and FT^i, and the information available in ALSAs. The ALSA received by router i sent by anchor m regarding prefix j is denoted by $ALSA_{jm}^i$. The information extracted from $ALSA_{jm}^i$ is the sequence number assigned to the prefix by the anchor (usn_{jm}^i) and the vFlag uvf_{jm}^i.

3.2 Routing to Nearest Replicas

A router calculates the best routes to nearest copies of a prefix in two steps. First, the router calculates valid next hops for all the anchors that advertise that prefix. Second, the router selects some of the neighbors from the previous step as valid next hops to the prefix. For every anchor in the network, the result of the first phase is a directed acyclic graph.

3.2.1 Next-Hop Ordering Condition (NOC)

Every router keeps track of the sequence numbers reported by the routers in the network. Whenever a router receives an RLSA from another router, it checks the sequence number. If the message sequence number is greater than the sequence number stored for that router, the router updates the topology information and also forwards it to its neighbors; otherwise, the router drops the message. Using the sequence number and a termination-detection mechanism similar to the one used in OSPF prevents advertisement messages from circulating in the network forever.

Based on the information received from other routers in the network, router i creates the network topology NT^i and calculates the cost of a path to every destination p in the network from each of its neighbors, as well as router i itself. The router executes Dijkstra's SPF algorithm (or any other shortest-path algorithm) on the network topology to construct a source graph, which constitutes shortest-path trees to every destination from every neighbor. The results are stored in the Distance List of the Forwarding Table (RD_p^i). The router also stores the shortest distance d_p^i.

Router i selects a subset of its neighbors as valid next hops to reach destination p based on the following Next-Hop Ordering Condition (NOC), which we will show prevents permanent routing loops from being created.

NOC: Router i can select its neighbor $n \in N^i$ as a valid next hop to reach destination p if:

$$rd_{pn}^i < \infty \wedge (rd_{pn}^i < rd_p^i \vee (rd_{pn}^i = d_p^i \wedge |n| < |i|)) \quad (1)$$

Router i selects router n as next hop to reach destination p if the neighbor n is closer to the destination or neighbor n and router i are at the same distance to p and $|n| < |i|$.

Figure 1 shows an example network topology. The number next to the node representing a router denotes the distance from the router to destination p.

Figures 2 a,b, and c show the valid next hops for each router to reach destinations p, q, and r, respectively. The arrowheads point to valid next hops for each destination. For instance, router u can be selected as next hop in routers s and t to reach destination p, and u itself can select routers l and f to forward messages to p.

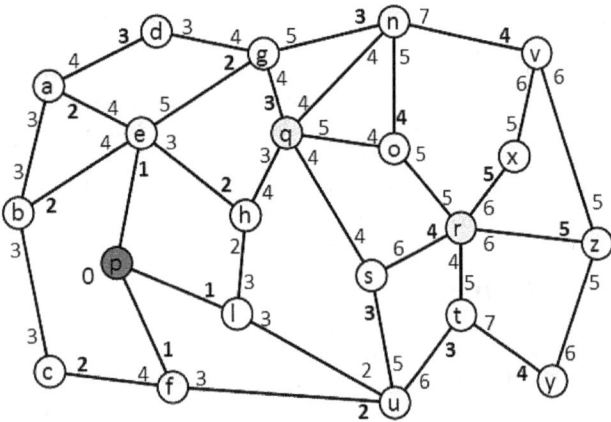

Figure 1: Sample network

Algorithm 1 illustrates how a router updates its forwarding table when it receives an RLSA. We assume that a router waits for a reasonable time after it receives the last RLSA before it executes Algorithm 1, and that the router will not process any other RLSAs while it is executing the algorithm.

3.2.2 King-Anchor Selection Condition (KSO)

Based on the information available in an ALSA received by router i, the router looks up its forwarding table and ranks the next-hops for each prefix based on their costs to reach the anchor(s). Each router selects the *king* anchor of a prefix among all the anchors it knows for the same prefix. If two or more anchors are at the same smallest distance from router i, the router selects the lexicographically smallest anchor as the king anchor. Whenever router receives a new ALSA, i.e., an ALSA with the up-to-date sequence number and valid flag equal to 1, the router updates its Prefix Table and calculates the king anchor.

Algorithm 1 Update FT^i

Input: $RLSA_k^i, LT^i, FT^i$
1: **if** $rsn_k^i > rsn(k)$ **then**
2:     $rsn(k) = rsn_k^i$
3:     Create the Network Topology T^i
4:     Run Dijkstra's algorithm and Update rd_p^i
5:     **for** (every $n \in N^i$) **do**
6:         Run Dijkstra's algorithm on n;
7:         **for** (every router $p \in T^i$) **do**
8:             Update rd_{pn}^i
9:         **end for**
10:    **end for**
11:    **for** every router $p \in T^i$ **do**
12:       $RS_p^i := \varnothing$
13:       **if** $rd_p^i < \infty$ **then**
14:         **for** every $n \in N^i$ **do**
15:             **if** $(rd_{kn}^i < rd_k^i) \vee (d_{kn}^i = d_k^i \wedge |n| < |i|)$
    then $RS_p^i = RS_p^i \cup \{n\}$
16:         **end if**
17:       **end for**
18:       **end if**
19:    **end for**
20: **end if**

Algorithm 2 illustrates how router i updates its Prefix Table PT^i, when it receives a fresh ALSA from anchor m regarding prefix j.

Algorithm 2 Update PT^i

Input: $ALSA_{mj}^i, PT^i$
1: **if** $usn_{mj}^i > sn_{mj}^i$ **then**
2:     $sn_{mj}^i = usn_{mj}^i$
3:     $vf_{mj}^i = uvf_{mj}^i$
4: **end if**

A router forwards an ALSA and sets the forwarded flag if the anchor is the king anchor; otherwise it HOLDs the LSA (i.e., it does not propagate the ALSA). If that anchor becomes the king anchor as a result of topology changes or because the current king anchor stops publishing the prefix, then the router restores the ALSA, sets the forwarded flag in the Prefix Table, and forwards the ALSA. Router keeps track of forwarded LSAs and uses this forwarded flag information to avoid sending duplicate ALSAs. Detach ALSAs (ALSA with $vFlag = 0$) are always forwarded, regardless of whether they come from king anchors or not.

KSO: Router i can select anchor m as the king anchor of prefix j (i.e., k_j^i) if the following statement is true:

$$vf_{mj}^i = 1 \wedge \forall [a, vf_{aj}^i] \in PI_j^i,\ vf_{aj}^i = 1 \wedge$$
$$[rd_m^i < rd_a^i \vee (rd_m^i = rd_a^i \wedge |m| < |a|)] \quad (2)$$

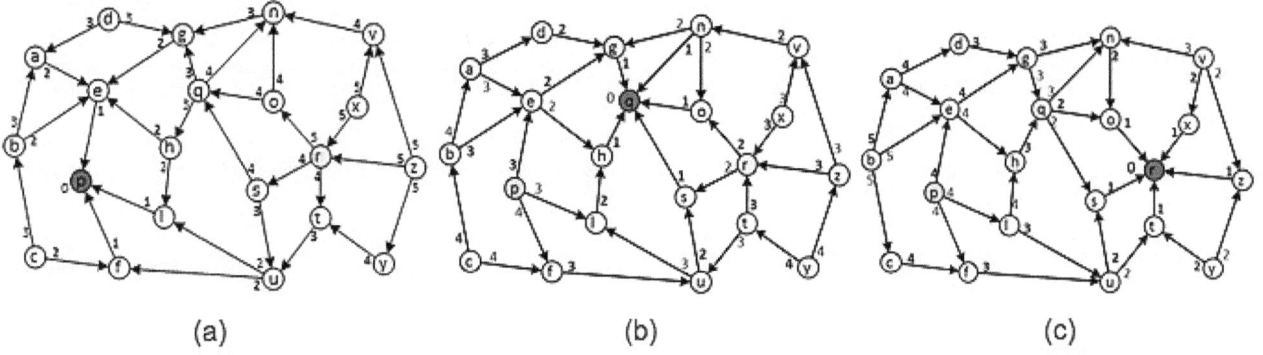

Figure 2: Valid next hops to destinations: (a) destination p, (b) destination q, (c) destination r

The king anchor of a prefix is an active anchor that is the smallest closest anchor among all active anchors of the prefix. The distance to prefix j is the minimum of the distances to anchors advertising j and is equal to the distance to the king anchor of the prefix. Thus,

$$d_j^i = Min\{rd_m^i | m \in PAI_j^i\} = rd_{k_j^i}^i.$$

If no active anchor advertises prefix j or none of the active anchors are reachable, then $PAI_j^i = \varnothing$ and $d_j^i = \infty$ and prefix j is marked as unreachable.

Router i uses Algorithm 3 to select the king anchor of a prefix. After selecting the king anchor, the router selects valid next hops to it. A neighbor can be selected as valid next hop for a prefix if it is valid next hop for the anchor that advertise that prefix and that neighbor is closer to the prefix or it is at the same distance but has lexicographically smaller names.

Algorithm 3 King selection for prefix j

Input: FT^i, PT^i
1: $k_j^i := null; d_j^i := \infty$
2: **for** ecery $m \in PI_j^i$ **do**
3:     **if** $vf_{mj}^i = 1$ **then**
4:         **if** $rd_m^i < d_j^i \vee (rd_m^i = d_j^i \wedge |m| < k_j^i)$ **then**
5:             $d_j^i = rd_m^i$
6:             $k_j^i = m$
7:         **end if**
8:     **end if**
9: **end for**

3.2.3 Successor-Set Ordering Condition (SOC)

The distance from neighbor n to prefix j at router i (d_{jn}^i) is the minimum of the distances to anchors of prefix j through n known by router i:

$$d_{jn}^i = Min\{rd_{mn}^i | m \in PAI_j^i\} \qquad (3)$$

Router i selects router n as a valid next hop to prefix j if the following statement is true:

$$d_{jn}^i < \infty \wedge (d_{jn}^i < d_j^i \vee (d_{jn}^i = d_j^i \wedge |n| < |i|)) \qquad (4)$$

Router i can select its neighbor n as a next hop toward prefix j if the neighbor is closer to the prefix than router i, or routers i and n are at the same distance from the destination,

but neighbor n has a lexicographically smaller name than router i.

Figure 3 shows the final state after executing LSCR assuming routers p, q, and r are all anchors of prefix j. The bold lines in the figure indicate links pointing to the best next hop of each router. For instance, both f and l offer paths of distance two to router u. However, router f is selected as the best next hop at router u toward destination p, because $|f| < |l|$.

Each tuple on a link in Figure 3 represents the closest smallest anchor and distance to that anchor through that link. In this figure, the minimum distance from router d to prefix j is through neighbor g and costs two. Consider router a, router d can reach destination p in three hops via its neighbor a, because a is a valid next hop for that destination and also a is two hops away from prefix j (anchor p) and $|a| < |d|$. These conditions satisfy Eq. 5; therefore, neighbor a is selected as a next hop to reach prefix j.

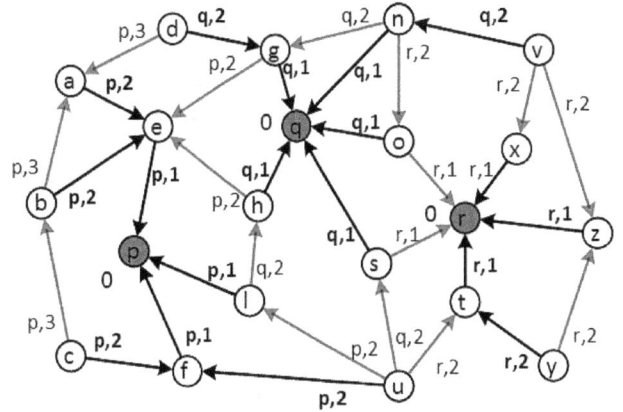

Figure 3: Valid next hops to prefix j

Whenever a router receives an up-to-date LSA indicating a change in the network, it executes Algorithms 1 or 2, depending on whether it receives an RLSA or an ALSA, and then executes Algorithm 4 to update its routing table.

3.3 Naming

The naming schema used in LSCR depends on the ICN architecture in which it is implemented. A hierarchical naming schema such as the one introduced for NLSR can be used for both routers and signaling messages. According this schema, each router is named in the following format: $/ <network> / <site> / <router> /$, where $network$ and $site$ are assigned based on the network and specific site the router belongs to and $router$ is a unique name in that network and site.

LSA messages use the naming schema like: $/<network>/<site>/<router>/LSCR/LSA/TypeID/$ $<sequence\ num>$. The first part is the name of router initiating the LSA, typeID field distinguishes between $Router LSA$ and $ALSA$ and $sequencenum$ is the sequence number assigned by the router for that LSA.

Algorithm 4 Update RT_j^i

Input: LT^i, FT^i, PT^i, prefix j
1: Ecexute Algorithm 3;
2: **if** $d_j^i < \infty$ **then**
3:    **for** (every $n \in N^i$) **do**
4:       $d_{min}^n = \infty$
5:       **for** (every $m \in PAI_j^i$) **do**
6:          **if** $rd_{mn}^i < d_{min}^n$ **then**
7:             $d_{min}^n = rd_{mn}^i$
8:          **end if**
9:       **end for**
10:       **if** $d_{min}^n < \infty$ **then**
11:          **if** $(d_{jn}^i < d_j^i) \vee (d_{jn}^i = d_j^i \wedge |n| < |i|)$ **then**
12:             $S_j^i = S_j^i \cup \{n\}$
13:          **end if**
14:       **end if**
15:    **end for**
16: **end if**

---

4. CORRECTNESS OF LSCR

The following theorems prove that LSCR obtains correct routing entries for routing to the nearest anchor of each prefix, which means that routing tables do not contain any permanent loops. Our proofs rely on known results that sequence numbers can be used to determine that a link-state update is more recent than stored information [11].

We assume that there is a finite number of link-cost and anchor changes up to time t_0, and no more changes occur after that time. We also assume that routers can determine which updates are more recent than others. Also, we assume that every router has correct information about the network topology, which can be be done in many ways for complete or partial topology information [10, 11, 17].

LEMMA 1. *The king anchor is the same for all the routers along the shortest path from each router to the king anchor.*

PROOF. The proof is by contradiction. Assume that the shortest path P_i from router i to its king anchor of prefix j m_j^i consists of h hops and each router selects its next hop according to Equations 3 and 4.

Let $P_i = \{n_1, n_2, S, n_h\}$, where $n_1 = i$, $n_h = m_j^i$, and $n_{k+1} \in RS_m^n$ for $1 \leq k \leq h-1$. We know that $rd_m^i = rd_{n_k}^i + rd_m^{n_k} \forall k, 1 \leq k \leq h-1$. Assume that router n_p selects router $a \neq m$ as the king router for prefix j; therefore, either $rd_a^{n_p} < rd_m^{n_p}$ or $rd_a^{n_p} = rd_m^{n_p} \wedge |a| < |m|$.

If $rd_a^{n_p} < rd_m^{n_p}$ then $rd_{n_p}^i + rd_a^{n_p} < rd_{n_p}^i + rd_m^{n_p}$. Accordingly, $rd_a^i < rd_m^i$. Hence, router a is the king anchor, which contradict our assumption that m is the king anchor.

If $rd_a^{n_p} = rd_m^{n_p} \wedge |a| < |m|$ then $rd_{n_p}^i + rd_a^{n_p} = rd_{n_p}^i + rd_m^{n_p} \wedge |a| < |m|$. Therefore, $rd_a^i = rd_m^i \wedge |a| < |m|$. Again, router a is the king anchor, which contradict our assumption that m is the king anchor. $\square$

LEMMA 2. *Each router that receives an ALSA from the closest anchor of a prefix advertises that prefix.*

PROOF. There are two types of ALSAs based on the $vFlag$ parameter. Detach LSAs (i.e., ALSAs with $vFlag = 0$) are propagated in the network using the intelligent flooding mechanism and termination detection is based on sequence numbering. Therefore, every router receives a Detach LSA from each anchor, including the closest one.

ALSAs with $vflag = 1$ are propagated using a diffusion mechanism. Based on Lemma 1, all the routers along the shortest path from the king anchor to the router has the same king anchor. Based on the LSA forwarding mechanism, each router forwards an ALSA form the king anchor.

Assume that router i did not receive any ALSA from its new king anchor m. Also assume that the shortest path P_i from router i to the king anchor of prefix j, m_j^i, consists of h hops. Assume that $P_i = \{n_1, n_2, S, n_h\}$ is such a path. King anchor k is the king anchor of $n_p, 1 \leq p \leq h-1$. Also assume that a router $n_m \in P_i$ did not forward the ALSA from its king anchor. This is in contradiction to the forwarding mechanism used for ALSAs. Therefore, router i should have received the ALSA form its king anchor. $\square$

THEOREM 3. *All routers in a network running LSCR must converge to the shortest distance to their nearest anchors of each prefix a finite time after t_0.*

PROOF. Note that there is a finite number of prefixes and there is a finite number of anchors for each prefix. Furthermore, each router processes and forwards each unique LSA only once based on sequence numbers.

Without loss of generality, we focus on a specific prefix j. The prefix can be considered as a virtual node connected to its anchor via a virtual link. Prefix detachment and attachment to the anchor can be considered as a link failure and a link recovery, respectively. For each direction of a link, there is one router (the head of the link) that detects and reports the change in the link in one direction. Therefore, for any link l_i, which can be a physical link or virtual link, each router sends at most one LSA for that link after t_0.

Consider an arbitrary router r_0 that never terminates executing LSCR. That router must send an infinite number of LSA messages after time t_0.

Because the network is finite, there is a finite number of links, and r_0 must process an infinite number of LSAs for at least one link l_f. Because no changes occur after time t_0, router r_0 cannot originate an infinite number of LSAs for any adjacent think after t_0. Furthermore, it is not possible for a router to send an infinite number of messages regarding l_f as a result of receiving an infinite number of LSAs regarding link l_h. It follows that router r_0 can forward an infinite number of LSAs regardingl_f only if it receives an infinite number of LSAs regarding l_f from at least one neighbor.

Accordingly, at least one of the neighbors of router r_0, call it r_1, must send an infinite number of LSAs containing updates for link l_f that makes r_0 process and forward an unlimited number of LSAs. By the same token, neighbor r_1 can send an infinite number of LSAs regarding l_f only if at least one of its neighbors, call it r_2, forwards an infinite number of LSAs regarding l_f to router r_1. However, it is impossible to continue the same line of argument indefinitely because the head node of any link can generate at most one update for that link after time t_0 and the network is finite.

Therefore, LSCR can produce only a finite number of LSAs for a finite number of link or prefix changes and must stop within a finite time after t_0. $\square$

THEOREM 4. *If topology information is correct at each router, no routing-table loops can be formed if NOC is used to select the next hops to the anchor of a prefix at each router.*

PROOF. The proof is by contradiction. Assume that a routing loop L_m for anchor m is formed at time $t_1 > t_0$ when routers update their next-hops satisfying NOC. Assume that $L_m = \{r_0, r_1, S, r_{q-1}\}$ consisting of q routers is such a loop.

We can consider L_m as a path $P_m = \{r_0, r_1, S, r_{q-1}, r_q\}$, where $r_0 = r_q$. Note that $rd_{r_q}^{r_0} = rd_{r_0}^{r_0} = 0$ and $rd_m^{r_q} = rd_m^{r_0}$. Router n_i selects its next hop from $RS_m^{n_i}$ for $0 \leq i \leq q-1, r_{i+1} \in RS_m^{n_i}$.

Based on NOC, for every router $n_i \in P_m$, it must be true that $rd_{mn_{i+1}}^{n_i} < rd_m^{n_i}$ or $rd_{mn_{i+1}}^{n_i} = rd_m^{n_i}$ and $|n_{i+1}| < |n_i|$. By definition, $rd_{mn_{i+1}}^{n_i}$ is the distance from $n+1$ to m calculated at router i. Routers i and n have the same topology information by assumption. Accordingly, $rd_{mn_{i+1}}^{n_i} = rd_m^{n_{i+1}}$. This results in the following:

$$(rd_m^{n_{i+1}} < rd_m^{n_i}) \vee (rd_m^{n_{i+1}} = rd_m^{n_i} \wedge |n_{i+1}| < |n_i|) \quad (5)$$

Note that $\forall r_i \in P_m, rd_m^i \neq \infty$. A next hop cannot have an infinite distance to the destination, because that would contradict NOC. Therefore, for any two routers $r_u, r_v \in P_m$ and $0 \leq u < v \leq q$ we have:

$$(rd_m^{r_v} < rd_m^{r_u} \vee (rd_m^{r_v} = rd_m^{r_u} \wedge |r_v| < |r_u|) \quad (6)$$

The equation is valid for any two routers $r_u, r_v \in P_m$ including r_0 and r_q. Hence, it must be true that $rd_m^{r_0} < rd_m^{r_q}$ or $rd_m^{r_0} = rd_m^{r_q} \wedge |r_0| < |r_q|$, which contradict our assumptions. $\square$

LEMMA 5. *For every router i and its neighbor n and for any arbitrary prefix j, it is true that $d_{jn}^i = d_j^n$*

PROOF. The distance of router n from prefix j is the distance of router n from its king anchor: $d_j^n = rd_{k_j^n}^n$. Every router forwards the ALSA from its king anchor; therefore, router i is aware of anchor k_j^n, and so $k_j^n \in PAI_j^i$. From Eq. 3, we have $d_{jn}^i = Min\{rd_{mn}^i | m \in PAI_j^i\} = rd_{k_j^n}^n$. The last equality is derived from Lemma 2, Eq. 2, and the fact that $(k_j^n \in PAI_j^i \wedge k_j^n \in PAI_j^n)$. Therefore, $d_{jn}^i = d_j^n$. $\square$

THEOREM 6. *No routing-table loops can be formed if all routers use LSCR to calculate routes to prefixes and routers have correct topology information.*

PROOF. If the prefix is advertised by just one anchor, based on Theorem 4 no loops can be formed. If more than one anchor advertises a given prefix j, the same conclusion can be derived using Lemma 5 and an argument similar to the proof of Theorem 4. $\square$

5. ROUTING COMPLEXITY

We compute the communication, time, and storage complexities of LSCR and compare it with the complexities of traditional link-state routing and loop-free routing based on distances. The communication complexity of a routing protocol is the number of messages that must be transmitted for the routing protocol to have information required to compute correct routing tables for all the destinations at each router. The storage complexity is the amount of information that must be stored at each router to obtain correct routing tables. The time complexity of a routing protocol is the maximum time needed for all routers to have correct routing information for all destinations.

We use N and E to denote the number of routers and links in the network, respectively. The number of distinct anchors available in the network is denoted by D, the average number of instances of the same destination is denoted by R, the average number of neighbors per router is l, the network diameter is denoted by d, and C denotes the number of distinct prefixes in the network.

Traditional Link-State Routing (LSR):
Both network topology and prefix information are flooded to the entire network when LSR is used. A router that runs LSR sends adjacency LSA and prefix LSAs, one for each local prefix, and each LSA must be sent to all the other routers in the network. Every router stores the complete topology information as well as all instances of all prefixes in the network. Furthermore, the maximum distance between a source and a destination is the network diameter. Accordingly, the time, communication, and storage complexities of LSR are:

$$TC_{LSR} = O(d); \quad CC_{LSR} = O(ERC + lEN); \quad (7)$$
$$SC_{LSR} = O(RC + E)$$

Loop-free Distance-Vector Routing:
Because of the looping problems of traditional distance-vector routing protocols, the traditional distance-vector routing algorithms cannot be used for routing in ICNs with multi-instantiated prefixes [15]. The Distance-based Content Routing (DCR) protocol solves this problem [14], and maintains routes to the nearest replicas of prefixes that are loop-free at every instant. Hence, we use this protocol as the example of distance-vector routing.

For a given prefix, a router disseminates only its distance to the nearest anchor of the prefix, independently of the number of prefix replicas in the network. Hence, the information a router stores and communicates for a given prefix in DCR is only its distance to the nearest anchor of the prefix, plus the anchor name and the latest sequence number created by that anchor.

As the number of replicas increases, the distances from a router to the nearest replica of a prefix decreases, and it is always the case that the number of hops from any router to the nearest replica of a prefix (x) is at most d hops.

DCR does not incur any routing-table loops, which means that any routing information propagates as fast as the shortest path between its origin and the recipient. Furthermore, the number of messages required for all routers to have a correct distance to a given prefix is $O(E)$, regardless of the number of times R the prefix is replicated. Given that there are C prefixes in the network, the time, communication, and storage complexities of DCR are:

$$TC_{DCR} = O(x); \quad CC_{DCR} = O(EC); \quad (8)$$
$$SC_{DCR} = O(C)$$

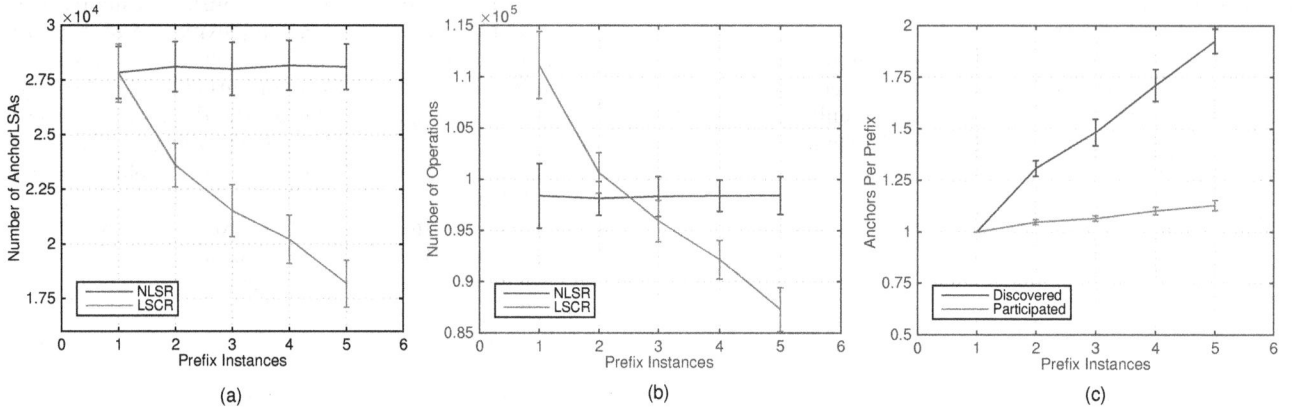

Figure 4: LSCR Performance: (a) average number of LSAs packets sent, (b) average number of operations, (c) average number of discovered anchor and number of anchors selected for routing per prefix per node

Link-State Content Routing (LSCR):

The information required for LSCR to find correct shortest paths to the nearest anchors of prefixes is the complete topology, and the prefix information from the nearest anchor (anchor name and sequence number created by that anchor). Therefore, the storage complexity of LSCR is independent of the number of anchors advertising each prefix.

Given that every router needs the complete topology information, the time required to receive LSAs for all links is the time that a message traverses across the the network diameter d. On the other hand, the distance from any router to the nearest anchor of a prefix can be at most d.

The number of messages exchanged to create the complete topology is $O(lEN)$, just as with traditional link-state routing, given that each of the N routers has l neighbors and LSAs must be flooded. In addition, each router needs to know its nearest anchor to each prefix and also needs to delete anchors and even prefixes due to failures. Based on the diffusion mechanism, LSCR only propagates specific valid ALSAs and the communication complexity incurred for this is just $O(C)$. However, the communication complexity of sending ALSAs for the deletion of a prefix is (CER), where R is number of replicas for a given name prefix.

The storage required by LSCR consists of all the links in the network and all the prefixes in the network. Accordingly, the time, communication, and storage complexities of LSCR are:

$$TC_{LSCR} = O(d); \quad CC_{LSCR} = O(CER + lEN); \quad (9)$$
$$SC_{LSCR} = O(C + E)$$

6. PERFORMANCE COMPARISON

We compared the performance of LSCR with an optimized version of NLSR using the SCoNET-Sim tool, which is an NS-3 based simulator for content centric networks [28].

To eliminate the differences in performance due to sender-initiated or receiver-initiated modalities, we implemented LSCR and NLSR using sender-initiated signaling, in which control messages are simply Interest messages that carry a payload containing control information. As a result, our implementation of NLSR in the simulation uses a single transmission per LSA, rather than sending LSAs as a result of Interests after neighbor routers determine the differences in

their local databases. NLSR propagates LSAs using intelligent flooding.

The scenarios used in our performance comparison assume the The AT&T core network topology, which is a realistic ISP topology [21] consisting of 154 nodes and 184 links. A node has 2.4 neighbors on average, and there are 14 nodes with only one neighbor. Each node has a unique identifier in the simulation model. The existence of a link-level protocol assures that every node detects the loss or recovery of connectivity with its neighbor in a finite time after a router fails to receive the proper control messages a repeated number of times. All messages, link failures, and link recoveries are processed one at time in the order in which they occur and within a finite time. We used a total of 210 content objects and 30 anchors that advertise prefixes in the network. The anchors are selected randomly, and some anchors may have some prefixes in common. On each simulation run, the input event generated was a single link failure or recovery, and a single prefix addition or deletion.

The performance metrics we used to compare NLSR and LSCR were the number of messages, number of events, number of operations, and the average number of replicas per prefix stored in each router. These metrics are measured for five different cases: the initialization process, a link failure, a link recovery, a prefix addition, and a prefix deletion. The number of prefix replicas (prefix instances) is varied from one anchor per prefix to five anchors per prefix.

Figure 4 shows the result of simulations for the number of prefix replicas increasing from one to five. Figure 4-a shows the number of ALSAs sent. As the number of replicas increases, the number of LSAs sent in LSCR decreases, because routers disseminate only LSAs for nearest anchors. The number of operations is the total number of operations performed by each protocol, and is incremented whenever an event occurs or the statements within a for or while loop used in the algorithms that compute shortest paths are executed. Both LSCR and NLSR run Dijkstra's SPF algorithm to find shortest paths to destinations, and in both approaches SPF is run at a node as many times as a node has neighbors.

Figure 4-c illustrates the average number of anchors that LSCR stores for each prefix and the average number of anchors that are participated in routing per prefix per node. As the number of replicas increases the number of replicas

36

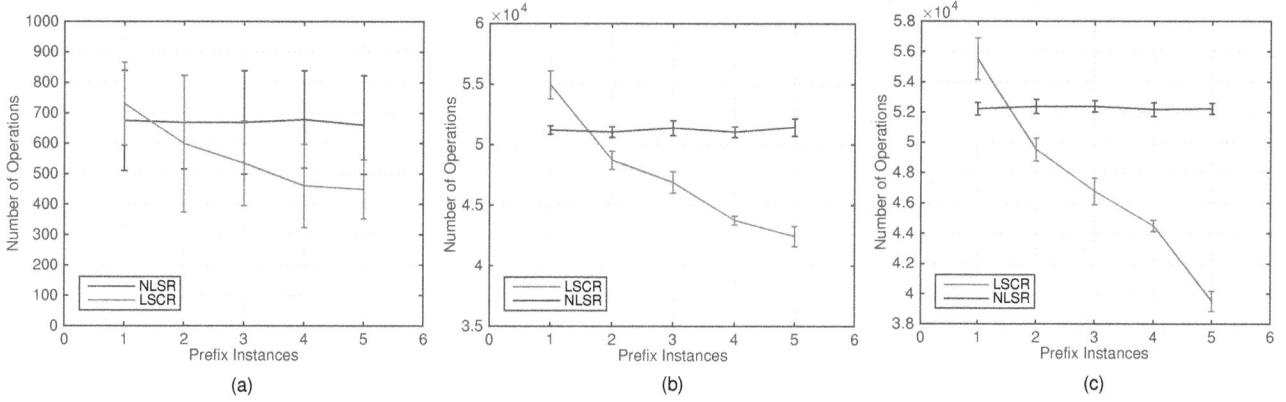

Figure 5: Computational overhead of LSCR: (a) prefix deletion, (b) link failure, (c) link recovery

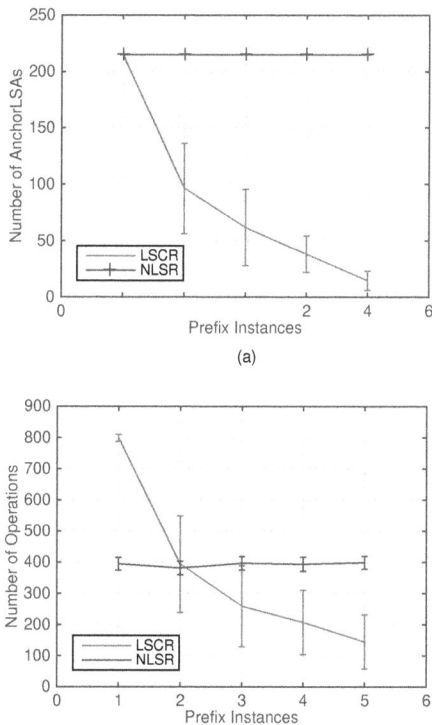

Figure 6: Impact of adding a new prefix: (a) average number of LSAs packets sent, (b) average number of operations

stored in the node also increases but even in a network in which five anchors advertise a prefix, LSCR stores less than two anchors on average, while NLSR stores information for all five anchors.

Figure 5 illustrates the computational overhead of LSCR compared to NLSR for the cases of prefix deletion, link failure and in recovery. A link is selected randomly and deleted from the network. After the deletion, the statistics are measured once the protocols are allowed to converge to the steady state, which means that all messages are processed and no further changes are made to the routing tables.

Then the deleted link were added to network, i.e., the link becomes operational, and the statistics are measured after steady state is reached again. In the case of prefix deletion, an anchor is selected randomly and from that anchor a prefix is deleted. The performance are almost the same in all these cases. However, LSCR has better performance when the number of prefix replicas is larger than three.

Figure 6 shows the number of LSAs propagated and the number of operations executed after an anchor advertises a new prefix. In this case an anchor is selected randomly and then it starts to advertise a prefix that is new for that anchor. As the number of replicas increases, the number of LSAs needed to propagate the new anchor information decreases. The number of propagated LSAs in LSCR is almost half the number of LSAs in NLSR when the number prefix instances is two. The computation overhead also decreases in LSCR as the number of replicas for each prefix increases. For instance, the computation overhead of LSCR is half the computation overhead of NLSR when the number prefix instances is four.

7. CONCLUSION

The Link State Content Routing (LSCR) protocol was introduced for name-based content routing in ICNs. LSCR provides multiple paths to the nearest replicas of NDOs or name prefixes. LSCR relies on full-topology information and information about nearest prefix replicas, rather than all prefix replicas. Therefore, its communication and storage complexities are smaller compared to content routing approaches based on the traditional link state approach exemplified by NLSR and OSPFN.

Routers exchange two types of information: Topology information and anchor information. Each router builds a complete network topology based on topology information. A shortest-path routing algorithm is used to calculate the distance to a given destination through each neighbor of a router. Then neighbors are ranked lexicographically based on their distances.

Routers that run LSCR forward anchor information selectively based on a distributed computation of preferred publishers. We showed that routes to prefixes are loop-free once routers have correct topology information, even when the prefixes have multiple replicas.

Although LSCR is more efficient than the traditional link-state approach to name-based content routing, more work is needed to attain higher efficiency. Possible approaches include: communicating partial topology information [10], reducing the frequency with which LSAs have to be sent [17], and improving the way in which routers update anchor information after resource failures.

8. REFERENCES

[1] Content centric networking project (CCN). http://www.ccnx.org.
[2] Fp7 PURSUIT project. http://www.fp7-pursuit.eu/PursuitWeb/.
[3] Named data network project. http://www.named-data.net/.
[4] Nsf mobility first project. http://mobilityfirst.winlab.rutgers.edu/.
[5] Publish subscribe internet technology (PURSUIT) project. http://www.fp7-pursuit.eu/PursuitWeb/.
[6] Scalable and adaptive internet solutions (SAIL) project. http://www.sail-project.eu/.
[7] B. Ahlgren, C. Dannewitz, C. Imbrenda, D. Kutscher, and B. Ohlman. A survey of information-centric networking. *Communications Magazine, IEEE*, 50(7):26–36, July 2012.
[8] M. Ain, D. Trossen, P. Nikander, S. Tarkoma, K. Visala, K. Rimey, T. Burbridge, J. Rajahalme, J. Tuononen, P. Jokela, J. Kjällman, J. Ylitalo, J. Riihijärvi, B. Gajic, G. Xylomenos, P. Savolainen, and D. Lagutin. D2.3 - architecture definition, component descriptions, and requirements. In *Deliverable, PSIRP 7th FP EU-funded project,*, 2009.
[9] M. Bari, S. Chowdhury, R. Ahmed, R. Boutaba, and B. Mathieu. A survey of naming and routing in information-centric networks. *Communications Magazine, IEEE*, 50(12):44–53, December 2012.
[10] J. Behrens and J.J. Garcia-Luna-Aceves. Hierarchical routing using link vectors. In *INFOCOM '98. Seventeenth Annual Joint Conference of the IEEE Computer and Communications Societies. Proceedings. IEEE*, volume 2, pages 702–710 vol.2, Mar 1998.
[11] D. Bertsekas and R. Gallager. *Data Networks (2Nd Ed.)*. Prentice-Hall, Inc., Upper Saddle River, NJ, USA, 1992.
[12] A. Carzaniga, M. Rutherford, and A. Wolf. A routing scheme for content-based networking. In *INFOCOM 2004. Twenty-third AnnualJoint Conference of the IEEE Computer and Communications Societies*, volume 2, pages 918–928 vol.2, March 2004.
[13] J. Choi, J. Han, E. Cho, T. Kwon, and Y. Choi. A survey on content-oriented networking for efficient content delivery. *Communications Magazine, IEEE*, 49(3):121–127, March 2011.
[14] J.J. Garcia-Luna-Aceves. Name-based content routing in information centric networks using distance information. In *Proceedings of the 1st International Conference on Information-centric Networking*, ICN '14, pages 7–16, New York, NY, USA, 2014. ACM.
[15] J.J. Garcia-Luna-Aceves. Routing to multi-instantiated destinations: Principles and applications. In *Proceedings of the 2014 IEEE 22Nd International Conference on Network Protocols*, ICNP '14, pages 155–166, Washington, DC, USA, 2014. IEEE Computer Society.
[16] J.J. Garcia-Luna-Aceves, Q. Li, and T. Karadeniz. Cord: Content oriented routing with directories. In *Computing, Networking and Communications (ICNC), 2015 International Conference on*, pages 785–790, Feb 2015.
[17] J.J. Garcia-Luna-Aceves and M. Spohn. Scalable link-state internet routing. In *Network Protocols, 1998. Proceedings. Sixth International Conference on*, pages 52–61, Oct 1998.

[18] J.J. Garcie-Luna-Aceves. System and method for discovering information objects and information object repositories in computer networks, Jan. 9 2007. US Patent 7,162,539.
[19] A. Ghodsi, S. Shenker, T. Koponen, A. Singla, B. Raghavan, and J. Wilcox. Information-centric networking: Seeing the forest for the trees. In *Proceedings of the 10th ACM Workshop on Hot Topics in Networks*, HotNets-X, pages 1:1–1:6, New York, NY, USA, 2011. ACM.
[20] M. Gritter and D. R. Cheriton. An architecture for content routing support in the internet. In *Proceedings of the 3rd Conference on USENIX Symposium on Internet Technologies and Systems - Volume 3*, USITS'01, pages 4–4, Berkeley, CA, USA, 2001. USENIX Association.
[21] O. Heckmann, M. Piringer, J. Schmitt, and R. Steinmetz. On realistic network topologies for simulation. In *Proceedings of the ACM SIGCOMM Workshop on Models, Methods and Tools for Reproducible Network Research*, MoMeTools '03, pages 28–32, New York, NY, USA, 2003. ACM.
[22] A. K. M. M. Hoque, S. O. Amin, A. Alyyan, B. Zhang, L. Zhang, and L. Wang. Nlsr: Named-data link state routing protocol. In *Proceedings of the 3rd ACM SIGCOMM Workshop on Information-centric Networking*, ICN '13, pages 15–20, New York, NY, USA, 2013. ACM.
[23] M. Hoque, C. Yi, A. Alyyan, , and B. Zhang. Ospfn: An ospf based routing protocol for named data networking. Technical report, NDN Technical Report NDN, July 2012.
[24] C. Intanagonwiwat, R. Govindan, and D. Estrin. Directed diffusion: A scalable and robust communication paradigm for sensor networks. In *Proceedings of the 6th Annual International Conference on Mobile Computing and Networking*, MobiCom '00, pages 56–67, New York, NY, USA, 2000. ACM.
[25] K. V. Katsaros, N. Fotiou, X. Vasilakos, C. N. Ververidis, C. Tsilopoulos, G. Xylomenos, and G. C. Polyzos. On inter-domain name resolution for information-centric networks. In *Proceedings of the 11th International IFIP TC 6 Conference on Networking - Volume Part I*, IFIP'12, pages 13–26, Berlin, Heidelberg, 2012. Springer-Verlag.
[26] T. Koponen, M. Chawla, B.-G. Chun, A. Ermolinskiy, K. H. Kim, S. Shenker, and I. Stoica. A data-oriented (and beyond) network architecture. In *Proceedings of the 2007 Conference on Applications, Technologies, Architectures, and Protocols for Computer Communications*, SIGCOMM '07, pages 181–192, New York, NY, USA, 2007. ACM.
[27] J. Kurose. Information-centric networking: The evolution from circuits to packets to content. *Computer Networks*, 66:112 – 120, 2014. Leonard Kleinrock Tribute Issue: A Collection of Papers by his Students.
[28] J. Mathewson, M. Barijough, E. Hemmati, J.J. Garcia-Luna-Aceves, and M. Mosko. Sconet : Simulator content networking. In *CCNxCon*, 2015.
[29] J. Raju, J.J. Garcia-Luna-Aceves, and B. Smith. System and method for information object routing in computer networks, June 23 2009. US Patent 7,552,233.
[30] I. Solis and J.J. Garcia-Luna-Aceves. Robust content dissemination in disrupted environments. In *Proceedings of the Third ACM Workshop on Challenged Networks*, CHANTS '08, pages 3–10, New York, NY, USA, 2008. ACM.
[31] G. Xylomenos, C. Ververidis, V. Siris, N. Fotiou, C. Tsilopoulos, X. Vasilakos, K. Katsaros, and G. Polyzos. A survey of information-centric networking research. *Communications Surveys Tutorials, IEEE*, 16(2):1024–1049, Second 2014.

Bloom Filter based Inter-domain Name Resolution: A Feasibility Study

Konstantinos V. Katsaros, Wei Koong Chai, George Pavlou
Dept. of Electrical & Electronic Engineering, University College London
WC1E 7JE, Torrington Place, London, UK
{k.katsaros, w.chai, g.pavlou}@ucl.ac.uk

ABSTRACT

The enormous size of the information space raises significant concerns regarding the scalability of name resolution in Information-Centric Networks, especially at a global scale. Recently, the use of Bloom filters has been proposed as a means to achieve a more compact representation of name resolution state. However, little attention has been paid to the expected performance or even the feasibility of such an approach. In this paper, we aim to fill this gap, presenting a feasibility study and performance analysis of Bloom filter based *route-by-name* inter-domain name resolution schemes. We propose a methodology for assessing the memory and processing resource requirements of the considered schemes and apply it on top of the inter-domain topology. Our investigation reveals that the skewed distribution of state across the inter-network results in a hard to balance trade-off between memory and processing resource requirements. We show that hardly any Bloom filter configuration i.e., size and bits-per-element, is able to reduce both types of resource requirements for all Autonomous Systems (ASes) in the network, while lowering resource requirements at one area of the inter-domain topology inflates resource requirements at another. Detailed simulations further show that the direct connection of multiple stub networks to tier-1 ASes, results in a dramatic increase of false positives, questioning the reliability of a BF-based inter-domain name resolution scheme.

Categories and Subject Descriptors

C.2.1 [**Computer-Communication Networks**]: Network Architecture and Design—*Distributed networks*

Keywords

ICN; scalability; false positive; DONA; CURLING.

1. INTRODUCTION

The Information-Centric Networking (ICN) paradigm focuses on the dissemination and retrieval of information rather that the pairwise communication between end hosts. In ICN, information is organized into named Information Objects (IOs) and a name resolution process is responsible for guiding forwarding decisions based on the names of the requested IOs. This mode of operation enables a series of desirable features such as in-network caching, multicast and mobility support, that have motivated substantial research efforts for the adoption of ICN in the context of the Internet (e.g., see [25] and references therein).

The applicability of the ICN paradigm at the Internet-scale heavily depends on the scalability of the name resolution system (NRS). At this scale, the NRS is required to support routing and forwarding for the entire IO population in the Internet, whose sheer size raises significant feasibility concerns. The size of the indexable Web has been estimated in the order of 10^{12} web pages [12], while the advent of the Internet of Things / Internet of Everything, yields an expectation for even up to 50 billion interconnected devices [8]. These estimations have led to different projections for the size of the IO namespace, ranging from 10^{13} [18] to 10^{17} [6]. Obviously the actual impact on the NRS heavily depends on the granularity of the selected naming scheme, which is yet to reach consensus in the ICN research community[1].

Currently on-going research efforts aim to address this scalability concern with the use of Bloom filters (BFs) [3], under the premise that with a *small* cost of possible but rare incorrect content request resolution, the entire system gains *much* in terms of scalability and performance. In such schemes, IO names are inserted into fixed size BFs which are maintained throughout the inter-domain topology so as to denote the availability of the corresponding content in neighboring Autonomous Systems (ASes). Using BFs results in the compact representation of content availability. It is also expected to lower network traffic and lookup overheads i.e., only a single operation is required to check IO availability in a BF, as opposed to a search procedure through the entire corresponding set of IO names. The cost of these benefits is the possibility of having false positives, in which BF membership queries erroneously report content availability leading to a failing name resolution process.

So far, the use of BFs for the support of inter-domain name resolution schemes in ICN has only been investigated at a coarse level, largely neglecting the details of the BF configuration, namely, the size and *bits-per-element* ratio of BFs, as well as their impact on both the performance and the resource requirements of the resulting NRS. In this

ICN'15, September 30–October 2, 2015, San Francisco, CA, USA.
© 2015 ACM. ISBN 978-1-4503-3855-4/15/09 ...$15.00.
DOI: http://dx.doi.org/10.1145/2810156.2810175.

---

[1]In this paper, we take a conservative approach, assuming a total population of $S = 10^{13}$ IO names.

paper, we aim at filling this gap by delving into the details of the complex inter-dependent impact factors contributing to the tradeoffs of the resolution system utilizing BFs. Our study seeks to verify if the exploitation of BFs can actually fulfill its promise on solving the scalability issue of NRS in ICN. We provide quantitative and illustrative answers to questions on how *small* exactly is the price we need to pay and how *much* it is the individual ASes and the system as a whole stand to gain.

Specifically, we first provide a model enabling the assessment of the suitability of a BF configuration in terms of resource requirements, paying particular attention to the role of the distribution of name resolution states across the inter-domain topology. Focusing on the case of a *route-by-name* name resolution model, e.g., [19, 5], we study this interplay, based on the AS-level Internet graph inferred by the CAIDA BGP traces [1]. Our study reveals that the need for a fixed Internet-wide BF configuration results in considerably diverse resource requirements throughout the inter-domain topology. Namely, large BFs result in large volumes of underutilized computational resources for stub ASes, which constitute the vast majority of ASes in the Internet, since in these domains, BFs tend to be sparse due to the low number of the registered IOs. On the other hand, smaller BF sizes substantially increase resource requirements at the higher tiers of the inter-domain hierarchy for two reasons: (i) smaller BF sizes result in a larger number of BFs to be looked-up for each name resolution request, (ii) for a larger number of BFs, a higher number of BF bits-per-element is required to avoid inflating the system-wide false positive ratio. Building on the introduced model and the CAIDA trace set, we conduct a realistic empirical study on the selection of an appropriate BF configuration and discuss the respective costs, gains and tradeoff space.

Furthermore, we complement our investigation with detailed packet-level simulations to shed light on a set of important, but rather complex to model, aspects of the envisioned BF-based NRSes. Namely, we assess the impact of false positives on the overall NRS performance, across the Internet. Moreover, we assess the effectiveness of applying a *bin-packing* algorithm for the consolidation (i.e., merging) of BFs during state propagation. Finally, we assess the processing overheads associated with the volume of name resolution requests across then network.

The findings of this paper are summarized as follows:

- There is no BF configuration that can lower both memory and processing resource requirements for *all* AS in the inter-domain topology, compared to a BF-agnostic scheme.

- There is no BF configuration that can lower the volume of one type of resources (i.e., memory or processing) without inflating the requirements on the other, either locally or in some other area of the inter-domain topology.

- The direct connection of multiple stub networks to tier-1 ASes inflates the number of BFs maintained by the latter, dramatically increasing the rate of false positives.

The remainder of this paper is organised as follows. In Section 2 we provide a detailed description of the current state-of-the-art in inter-domain name resolution in the context of ICN, motivating the need for the feasibility study presented in this work. Next, in Section 3 we present the Bloom filter configuration parameters and their impact on the resulting resource requirements, revealing important configuration trade-offs. In Section 4 we investigate the interplay between the state distribution across the inter-domain hierarchy and the configuration of BFs, quantifying its impact on the resulting memory and processing resource requirements across the topology. In Section 5, we further employ simulations to shed some light on more complicated aspects of the considered NRSes.

2. BACKGROUND

Research efforts on the support of inter-domain name resolution, largely fall into two basic categories. *Lookup-by-name* approaches decouple name resolution from data forwarding by realizing name resolution as a directory service [6, 17, 15]. In most cases, such solutions rely on Distributed Hash Tables (DHTs) in order to perfectly load balance the overheads imposed from the enormous size of the IO namespace, i.e., memory requirements for name resolution state, processing overheads for lookup operations. However, it has been shown that such approaches present inefficient routing due to stretched name resolution paths and inter-domain routing policy violations [11, 17].

Route-by-name approaches, on the other hand, offer shortest path, BGP-compliant routing. In the classic route-by-name approach, DONA [19], each IO is associated with a *principal* that can be considered as its owner. The DONA design involves an overlay of *Resolution Handlers* (RHs) with at least one logical RH placed at each AS. The role of RHs is to register and maintain name resolution state, as well as to guide the propagation of name resolution requests until they are resolved. To this end, RHs interconnect following the hierarchical business relationship interconnection of their ASes, forming a corresponding RH hierarchy. The RH hierarchy is further enhanced with peering links, i.e., RHs of peering domains are also linked in the RH overlay[2].

Principals issue REGISTER messages towards their local RH(s) to advertise their IO's to the network. A local RH propagates a REGISTER message upwards to its providers in the inter-AS hierarchy and to RHs at peering ASes, thus setting up the name resolution state throughout the network. The propagation of REGISTER messages terminates at the top-most AS level, i.e., at tier-1 RHs (see Section 4). ASes not willing to transit name resolution requests and/or data do not propagate REGISTER messages received over peering links. Since tier-1 ASes all peer with each other, each tier-1 AS will be aware of all IOs in the network. The resolution state at each RH is in the form of <IO name, next hop RH> pairs, i.e., mappings between advertised IO names and a pointer to the previous RH in the corresponding REGISTER propagation path.

Clients (i.e., end hosts) issue name resolution requests in the form of FIND messages submitted to their local RH(s). FIND messages are also propagated upwards via provider-customer links in the domain hierarchy according to the inter-domain routing policies, but not over peering links. In the worst case, a FIND message has to reach a tier-1 AS

---

[2]Since peering links introduce cycles in the inter-domain network graph, the topology is not strictly hierarchical.

in order to locate an IO, or determine that no such IO exists. Upon a name match with an RH entry, FIND messages follow the reverse registration path to reach the local RH of the appropriate principal, which triggers the data transfer.

CURLING [5] follows a similar approach, also adapting to the inter-domain topology structure for name registration and resolution. However, in CURLING, *Content Resolution Servers* (CRS)[3] propagate registration and resolution requests only to their provider ASes. In effect, both REGISTER and FIND messages follow a subset of the underlying routing relationships, as they do not cross peering links. As a result, when a FIND request reaches a tier-1 AS, it will have to be broadcasted to all other tier-1 ASes to guarantee resolution. CURLING however allows optimizing the data paths to allow the utilization of peering links in the delivery of the content itself.

The compliance of name resolution paths to valid BGP shortest path, in DONA and CURLING, comes at the cost of non-negligible replication of name resolution states across the Internet. This results in extensive resource requirements to be satisfied by the participating ASes. As shown in our previous work [18], for a population of $S = 10^{13}$ IOs, the memory footprint of name resolution state reaches 420 TB. This corresponds to the capacity of an entire small to medium scale data center, if state is to be maintained in RAM, e.g., the DONA scheme would require more than 26,000 16GB RAM servers for tier-1 ASes, on average.

These enormous resource requirements have triggered alternative approaches, focusing on a more space-efficient representation of name resolution state. To this end, the use of Bloom filters [3] has been proposed in [21, 14]. Liu *et al.* proposed the use of Bloom filters for the representation of name resolution state [21]. Though promising a significant reduction of the name resolution state size, the presented scheme employs DHTs in the name resolution process, raising the aforementioned concerns on routing quality. Hong *et al.* present an alternative approach, in which name resolution state is disseminated following the inter-domain hierarchy, similarly to DONA and CURLING, thus promising efficient name resolution paths. All NRS nodes in the inter-domain topology use the same set of hash functions to add the names of IOs of local content providers into globally fixed size BFs. Each NRS node maintains a name lookup table that contains the mappings between the IO identifiers registered by CPs in the local domain and the corresponding network locators, i.e., the information required to reach the content. Additionally, an NRS node maintains a set of Bloom filters describing the availability of IOs in customer and (possibly) peering domains[4]. Each NRS node further creates a BF for the locally registered state and forwards it to each provider and (possibly) peering domain along with the BFs received from customer domains. The propagated BF(s) constitute(s) the union[5] of all BFs received from customer domains (along with the entries for locally registered content). Following [14], we assume BFs being periodically propagated by participating nodes, so that the overhead of updating the corresponding name resolution state is controlled. The propagation of BFs and name resolution requests follows the underlying topology, in a fashion similar to DONA and/or CURLING. We thus term the corresponding BF-enabled schemes as DONA-BF and CURLING-BF, depending on whether BFs are propagated over peering links.

Though BFs appear as a promising solution towards the alleviation of the discussed state size related overheads, we still lack a good understanding of the behaviour of a BF-based NRS. The existence of BF false positives calls for a detailed investigation of the configuration of the BFs, i.e., the size and *bits-per-element*, so as to gain insights into the overall performance of a BF-enabled NRS. This includes both the failure of the system to resolve names and the resulting resource requirements, which are affected by the distribution of IOs across the Internet i.e., the volume of name resolution state to be represented. In the following section, we provided a detailed description of a proposed framework for the evaluation of the considered NRSs.

3. IMPACT OF BF CONFIGURATION

In this section, we discuss the parameters that are available to configure BFs with, which we can use as "tuning knobs", and their related impacts and tradeoffs to the system performance and resource requirements.

3.1 Bloom Filter Preliminaries

Bloom filters (BFs) are probabilistic representations of sets [3]. A BF is represented as an array of m bits initially set to 0. An element is inserted into a BF with the help of k hash functions, i.e., each function maps the hash of the inserted element to a position in the bit array which is set to 1. To check whether an element belongs to a set, the k bit array positions indicated by the hash functions are checked. If an element belongs to a BF, then all k positions are set to one and the item is found with probability 1. BFs present a non-zero *false positive ratio* (R), i.e., a BF may falsely report the presence of an element. Given the length of the BF (m), the number of inserted elements (n), and the number of hash functions (k), R can be calculated as follows:

$$R \approx (1 - e^{-kn/m})^k \qquad (1)$$

Using the optimal number of hash functions $k = \frac{m}{n} ln2$, we can calculate the bits-per-element ratio for a certain upper limit of R (defined as R_{max}), i.e.,

$$\frac{m}{n} = -\frac{ln R_{max}}{(ln2)^2} \qquad (2)$$

Based on Equation 2, we can calculate the maximum number of items that can be inserted in a BF without exceeding R_{max}, for a given value of m, namely the *capacity* (C_{BF}) of the BF. Table 1 summarizes the notation used in this paper.

3.2 Configuring BFs

The non-zero false positive ratio of BFs has obviously an impact on the expected correctness of the name resolution process, i.e., false positives would lead to name resolution requests forwarded towards areas of the network where the corresponding content does not exist. Consequently, the design of a global scale NRS should aim at imposing an upper

---

[3]For simplicity, we will use the term RH for both DONA and CURLING, as RHs and CRSs offer similar functionality with respect to the aspects investigated.

[4]Though not explicitly described in [14], it is assumed that BFs are maintained per corresponding neighbor, so that a positive membership query can yield the appropriate forwarding information.

[5]Achieved by simply applying the bit-wise OR operation.

Table 1: Notation

Symbol	Definition
m	Size of BF (bits)
k	Number of hash functions
n	Number of elements inserted in a BF
R	False positive ratio
R_{max}	Maximum allowed R per BF
R_{max}^{Node}	Maximum allowed R per node
C_{BF}	BF capacity (under R_{max})
S	Number of unique IOs in the network
s	Number of IO registrations at a node
s_l	Number of IO registrations in s originating from local content providers
F	Number of BFs maintained by a node
M	State size maintained at a node (bytes)
LO	Number of BF lookups performed at a node, per single resolution request
RL	Number of resolution requests received by a node
b_{NonBF}	Byte overhead per plain registration
b_{BF}	Byte overhead per BF
p	Probability an IO is registered at a node
P_{TP}	Probability a registered IO is found in the locally maintained BFs
P_P	Probability of a positive (multi-)BF lookup
P_N	Probability of a negative (multi-)BF lookup
N	Number of name resolution nodes
w	Resource wastage per node
W	Resource wastage across all N nodes

limit for this impact so as to guarantee a minimum control on the reliability of the NRS. To this end, in this paper, we consider such a limit on an NRS node level, i.e., we define a global upper limit for the false positive ratio experienced at any NRS node (denoted as R_{max}^{Node})[6].

The experienced R_{max}^{Node} depends on the number of BFs used to represent the overall state. The representation of s items, requires F BFs of capacity C_{BF},

$$F = \left\lceil \frac{s}{C_{BF}} \right\rceil \qquad (3)$$

Equation 3 expresses the optimal case of a perfect assignment of IO names to BFs. In practice, the total number of BFs maintained by a NRS node depends on the union (or *merging*) operation applied by each node (see Section 2). In this work we consider this merging process to be enabled by a bin-packing algorithm in which BFs represent the bins to be filled with items in BFs received from customer ASes. All bins have capacity C_{BF}. Obviously, items in a received BF can only be merged into a new BF as a whole i.e., either all items in a received BF or none. Hence, the size of each item in the bin packing algorithm corresponds to the total number of items included in the received BF, which can be estimated or explicitly denoted by an item counter. As the merging process proceeds throughout the inter-domain hierarchy, received BFs are merged into new ones with increasingly more items. In effect the distribution of item sizes throughout the

hierarchy varies. To the best of our knowledge, modelling the expected performance of bin-packing algorithms with a variable distribution of item sizes constitutes a research challenge on its own, and it is beyond the scope of this paper. We revisit the impact of this simplification in our model in Section 5.

Under these assumptions, R_{max}^{Node} is given by Equation 4,

$$R_{max}^{Node} = 1 - (1 - R_{max})^F \qquad (4)$$

It follows then that in order to guarantee R_{max}^{Node}, we need to select the C_{BF} and m values as shown in Equation 5. In the following, we term these two parameters as the *BF configuration*. In practice, and based on Equation 5, we can define different BF configurations by simply selecting different C_{BF} capacity values for a fixed R_{max}^{Node} constraint.

$$m = -C_{BF} \frac{ln(1 - (1 - R_{max}^{Node})^{\left\lceil \frac{1}{C_{BF}} \right\rceil})}{(ln2)^2} \qquad (5)$$

Since a globally fixed BF configuration is required to guarantee inter-domain compatibility and the R_{max}^{Node} constraint applies to all nodes, the selected BF configuration should satisfy Equation 5 for all s values encountered across the Internet, even when the maximum possible number of elements is inserted in a BF. In our context, this is the case of tier-1 ASes, which need to maintain name resolution state even for the entire set of IOs in the Internet (S), in the case of DONA (see Section 2). Therefore, we consider the selection of a BF configuration among the ones satisfying Equation 5 for $s = S$.

3.3 BF Configuration Tradeoff

There are multiple candidate configurations satisfying the R_{max}^{Node} constraint and the exact selection requires the definition of the appropriate evaluation metrics. In the following section, we first define the main two evaluation metrics considered in this work, namely the memory and processing requirements and then discuss how the BF configuration impacts the system, whereby finding a Internet-wide optimal balance is not a trivial issue.

3.3.1 Memory requirements

As discussed in Section 1, the use of BFs is originally motivated by the need to constrain the overall state size to a scalable level (i.e., to reduce the requirements in memory resources to a level supportable by the current technologies). Here, we consider the case where all name resolution states are maintained in the main memory (i.e., RAM) so as to enable fast name resolution. In the context of our generic DONA-/CURLING-BF NRSs, the total memory requirements at a node hosting s registrations (out of a total population of S IOs), is given as follows:

$$M^x = b_{NonBF} \cdot s_l + b_{BF} \cdot F \qquad (6)$$

where M^x is the total state size expressed in bytes, $x \in \{CURLING\text{-}BF, DONA\text{-}BF\}$, s_l is the number locally registered IO names i.e., $s_l < s$, $b_{NonBF} = 42$, is the byte overhead per local state entry[7] and $b_{BF} = (m + log_2 C_{BF})/8$ is

---

[6]Note that R_{max}^{Node} does not represent the overall probability of a name resolution request failing due to a false positive. We revisit this issue in Section 5 where we assess this probability with simulations.

[7]b_{NonBF} corresponds to a 40 byte object identifier and a 2 byte pointer to the next RH i.e., a bitmap for the node's interfaces to the neighboring node[19].

the byte overhead of each BF, considering the size of the BF and the overhead of an item counter required to facilitate BF merging (see Section 3.2)[8]. Obviously for $x \in \{CURLING, DONA\}$, we have:

$$M^x = b_{NonBF} \cdot s \qquad (7)$$

3.3.2 Processing overheads

Name resolution also incurs processing overheads related to the search of a IO name in the maintained name resolution state. The overall overhead depends on the number of BF lookup operations per received request, denoted here as the *lookup overhead* (LO). We approximate this (LO^x), for $x \in \{CURLING, DONA\}$, as follows:

$$LO^x = \alpha \cdot log(s) + c \qquad (8)$$

where α denotes a positive real number[9]. When BFs are employed, the look-up overhead is affected by the total number of entries maintained by the nodes, which determines both the probability that an item is registered locally (i.e., $p = \frac{s}{S}$), and the number of BFs maintained, for a certain BF configuration. When $F > 1$ we assume that the maintained BFs are looked-up sequentially. In effect, the number of look-up operations is further affected by the false positive ratio i.e., a false positive results in no subsequent BF lookups. Hence, we estimate the expected look-up overhead as follows:

$$LO^x = F \cdot P_N^F + \frac{P_P}{P_N} \cdot \sum_{i=0}^{F} i P_N^i \qquad (9)$$

for $x \in \{CURLING\text{-}BF, DONA\text{-}BF\}$, with P_P denoting the probability of a positive BF look-up response:

$$P_P = (1 - P_{TP}) R_{max}^{FP} + P_{TP} \qquad (10)$$

where $P_{TP} = \frac{p}{F}$, is the probability that an existing entry is located in one of the maintained BFs and $P_N = 1 - P_P$.

The overall processing overhead at an NRS node also depends on the total number of name resolution requests received by the node, denoted here as the *resolution load* (RL). This overhead heavily depends on the structure of the inter-domain topology, as well as the effect of false positives. Given the complexity of the inter-domain topology we assess this aspect of processing overheads through simulations in Section 5.

3.3.3 Tuning BF Configuration

Inspecting Equations 6 and 9 shows that the overall resource requirements at each node of the considered BF-based NRS depend on the number of BFs maintained F, which in turn depends on the relation between the C_{BF} and the number of IO names, s. It follows that for a given value of s, the amount of memory and processing resources depends on the selected BF configuration.

---

[8]To simplify our analysis we neglect data structure overheads. We also do not consider interface pointer overheads, since BFs are maintained in a distinct set per neighbor.

[9]We base this approximation on the $O(logn)$ scalability properties of search algorithms, assuming that the size of the IO name space is sufficiently large to roughly approximate an asymptotic behaviour.

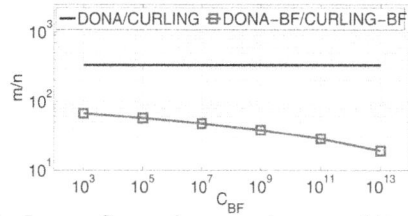

Figure 1: Lower C_{BF} values require more bits-per-element to satisfy the R_{max}^{Node} constraint. Both axes are in logarithmic scale.

On the one hand, selecting $C_{BF} >> s$ results in considerably sparse BFs. In such cases, the corresponding NRS nodes under-utilize the memory resources allocated for the maintenance of the resulting BF. Similarly, the propagation of such sparse BFs across the inter-domain hierarchy results in the waste of the corresponding bandwidth. As shown in [22], a reduction of network traffic in the order of 30% could be theoretically achieved by compression techniques, while not inflating the false positive ratio. However, this neglects the issue of the excessive demand for memory resources.

These concerns cannot be addressed by merely selecting low capacity BFs. Selecting $C_{BF} << s$ increases the number of BFs maintained by the node, correspondingly leading to increased look-up processing overheads (see Equation 9). Moreover, lower C_{BF} quire a higher number of bits-per-element to support the R_{max}^{Node} constraint. Figure 1 shows the bits-per-element required for various example C_{BF} values, according to Equation 5. At the same time, the increase of the bits-per-element ratio, further increases the processing overheads as it corresponds to a higher number of hash functions to be applied to the IO name included in an incoming name resolution request.

In all, it becomes apparent that for a certain number of IO names, s, the selection of a BF configuration should strike a balance between the resulting memory and processing resource requirements. At first glance, selecting $C_{BF} = s$ offers the best compromise between memory and processing overheads. However, as we show in the following, the need for a single, globally fixed BF configuration, along with the highly skewed distribution of state across the inter-domain topology, render the selection of a BF configuration particularly hard.

4. INTERNET-WIDE BF-BASED NRS

In this section, we empirically explore the range of gains that can be obtained through different BF configurations, for different types of ASes. We engage in a detailed, quantitative study of the distribution of name resolution state in the inter-domain topology. Our target is to investigate the identified interplay between the state distribution and the BF configuration, quantifying its impact on the resulting memory and processing resource requirements.

4.1 Methodology

Our study is based on the AS-level Internet graph inferred by the CAIDA BGP traces[10] [1]. We classify the ASes appearing in the CAIDA trace set into four tiers based on the

---

[10]The traces are created by first collecting traceroute-like IP-level topology data from several vantage points in the Inter-

size of their customer *cone*, i.e., the total number of their downstream customers [23]. The four tiers are:

1. *Stub* networks, i.e., domains with no more than 4 customer networks, which includes all access networks. As shown in Table 2, these networks constitute the large majority (93.38%) of ASes in the Internet,

2. *Small ISPs*, i.e., small Internet Service Provider ASes that have a cone size between 5 and 50,

3. *Tier-1* ASes, i.e., ASes at the highest level of the hierarchy that do not act as customers for another AS,

4. *Large ISPs*, a category which includes the remaining ASes that have a larger cone than small ISPs but are not tier-1 members.

We parse this graph with a custom, Java-based DONA / CURLING simulator which simulates the registration of IOs across the domains by traversing the appropriate parts of the graph. We first assume that content is uniformly distributed across content providers, which uniformly reside at the leafs of the inter-domain hierarchy. Table 2 provides the average and median percentage of total IO entries held by each AS across all tiers and per tier [18]. We notice a heavily skewed distribution of state across the topology tiers. For instance, more than 93% of the ASes are expected to maintain only up to 0.003% of the total IO entries, in CURLING, while only a small set of tier-1 ASes are burdened with the entire name resolution state in the Internet, in the case of DONA. Moreover, by not exchanging state across peering links, CURLING results in a considerably lower state overhead, especially at the lower tiers. We next utilize the derived results to assess the impact of different BF configurations on the resulting resource requirements.

4.2 Empirical observations

4.2.1 Gains

The heavily skewed distribution of IO entries across the inter-domain topology, results in a correspondingly skewed distribution of resource requirements. Figures 2 and 3 show the memory (M) and processing (LO) resource requirements of DONA-BF and CURLING-BF schemes, for various BF configurations, reaching a maximum $C_{BF} = S$. The figures further illustrate the corresponding requirements of DONA and CURLING.

As expected, memory requirements are in all cases of C_{BF} lower for tier-1 ASes, for both DONA-BF and CURLING-BF, against their non-BF counterparts, since $C_{BF} < s \leq S$. In the extreme case of $C_{BF} = S$, a single 23.96 TB BF would be required to represent all states at all tiers of the topology, for $R_{max}^{Node} = 10^{-4}$. This corresponds to approximately 94,29% decrease in the size of the maintained state at tier-1 ASes, compared to DONA (90,25% in CURLING). Though this reduction confirms the initial motivation for employing BFs, it also questions the practical feasibility of such BF configurations. Supporting efficient lookup operations for name resolution requests requires the queried BF(s) to reside in main memory (instead of storage), leading to limitations by current hardware capabilities. Typical data center servers

are configured with only some tens on GB of RAM, constituting a cloud based approach infeasible. Current high end servers, on the other hand, have only just started reaching such capacities[11].

At the same time, selecting such large sized BFs raises concerns about the memory requirements at lower tier ASes which present substantially lower volumes of IO name registrations (i.e., $C_{BF} >> s$). We see that in both cases of DONA-BF and CURLING-BF, large C_{BF} values result in memory resource requirements that exceed those of plain DONA and CURLING, thus providing no incentives for the vast majority of ASes to adopt a BF-based approach. A closer inspection shows that preserving these incentives across the inter-domain topology, in terms of memory requirements, calls for BFs smaller than $C_{BF} = 2^{31}$, $m = 9.86$ GB (we denote this upper limit as C_{BF}^{max}). For instance, the use of 718.88 KB BFs (i.e., $C_{BF} = 10^5$) would result in only an average of approximately 1.95 GB of total memory space for the BF-based representation of state at stub domains, in CURLING-BF, against 359.43 GB, for $C_{BF} = 10^{11}$, and 11.37 GB when not using BFs.

On the other hand, as demonstrated in Figures 2 and 3, using multiple, lower size BFs so as to limit the memory requirements of lower tier ASes, increases the number of lookup operations per name resolution request. For instance, each resolution request reaching a tier-1 AS in DONA-BF, using $C_{BF} = 10^5$ and $m = 718.88$ KB, would require an average of 8.39×10^8 BF lookup operations, against a load in the order of several tens of operations for DONA. This observation becomes especially important when considering that a major fraction of name resolution requests are actually served by tier-1 ASes [18]. On a closer inspection, preserving these incentives across the inter-domain topology, in terms of processing requirements, calls for BF larger than $C_{BF} = 2^{37}$, $m = 482.75$ GB (we denote this lower limit as C_{BF}^{min}).

It follows that a BF configuration lowering both the memory and processing requirements should fall into the $[C_{BF}^{min} .. C_{BF}^{max}]$ range. However, we observe that $C_{BF}^{min} > C_{BF}^{max}$, which means there is no single BF configuration that can yield both lower memory and processing resource requirements for all ASes in the inter-domain topology, compared to a BF-agnostic scheme.

4.2.2 Costs

Since all BF configurations result in the wastage of resources at some areas of the inter-domain topology, we are next interested in identifying the extend of the wastage as well as the areas of the inter-domain topology it affects most. Our target is to get a better understanding on how much the various BF configurations affect the incentives of stakeholders to invest on a BF-based NRS, considering both types of memory and processing resources simultaneously. Towards this end, we first express the wastage (w) brought to an AS by a BF configuration for each type of resource compared to plain DONA or CURLING, as follows:

$$w_{i,x-BF}^y = max\{0, 1 - \frac{y_i^x}{y_i^{x-BF}}\} \tag{11}$$

---

net and subsequently identifying the involved ASes from the traced IP addresses.

[11]See for instance: https://www.oracle.com/servers/sparc/m6-32/index.html

Type	(%)	DONA		CURLING		
		Average	**Median**	**Average**	**Median**	**Avg. gain**
All Tiers	100.00%	3.778%	0.003%	0.060%	0.003%	62.97%
Tier-1	0.03%	100.00%	100.00%	59.895%	61.769%	1.67%
Large ISP	1.35%	36.701%	42.687%	2.758%	0.298%	13.31%
Small ISP	5.23%	15.599%	0.097%	0.029%	0.018%	537.90%
Stub	93.38%	2.039%	0.003%	0.003%	0.003%	679.67%

Table 2: State size per AS expressed as a percentage of the total state size throughout the inter-network (%).

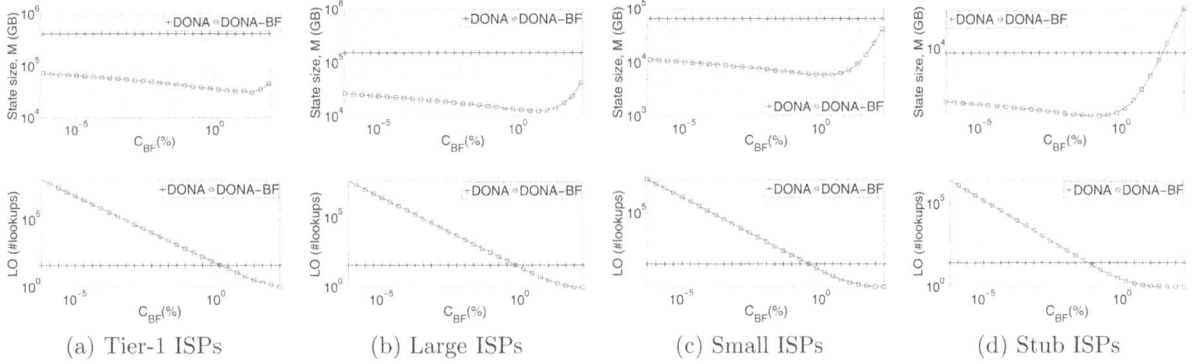

(a) Tier-1 ISPs   (b) Large ISPs   (c) Small ISPs   (d) Stub ISPs

Figure 2: Comparison of memory and processing overheads between DONA and DONA-BF for different BF configurations ($R_{max}^{Node} = 10^{-4}$, $S = 10^{13}$). Here C_{BF} is expressed as a percentage of the total number of IOs in the inter-network. Note that both axes are in log-scale.

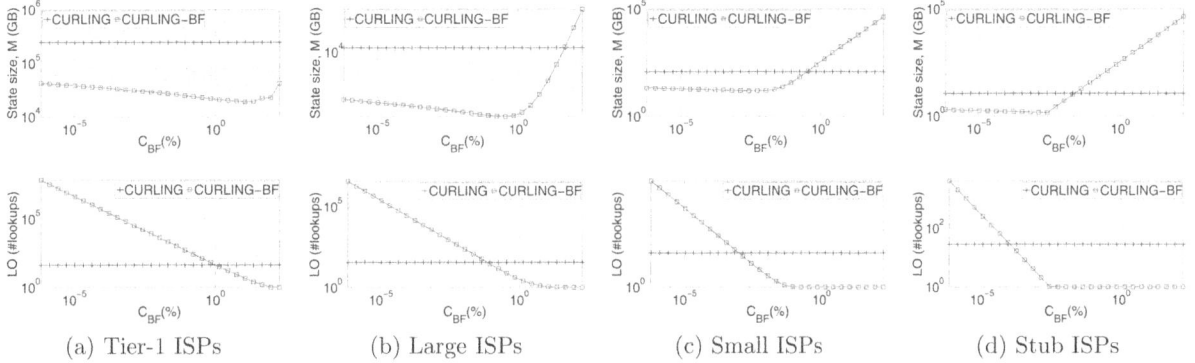

(a) Tier-1 ISPs   (b) Large ISPs   (c) Small ISPs   (d) Stub ISPs

Figure 3: Comparison of memory and processing overheads between CURLING and CURLING-BF for different BF configurations ($R_{max}^{Node} = 10^{-4}$, $S = 10^{13}$). Here C_{BF} is expressed as a percentage of the total number of IOs in the inter-network. Note that both axes are in log-scale.

where $y \in \{M, LO\}$, $x \in \{DONA, CURLING\}$, i is the index of an AS, with $i \in [1, .., N]$, and N denotes the total size of the AS population. Equation 12 expresses the normalised total waste of a BF configuration.

$$W^y = \frac{\sum_{i=1}^{N} w_{i,x-BF}^y}{N} \qquad (12)$$

Figure 4 depicts the total wastage W at the various tiers of the inter-domain topology in the case of DONA-BF and CURLING-BF. We first see that, for both DONA-BF and CURLING-BF, resource wastage at Stub networks is reduced across both types of resources, for C_{BF} values in the range of 10^{-4} to $10^{-2}\%$ of the total IO catalogue size (S), e.g., from $C_{BF} = 2^{23}$, $m = 50.63$ MB to $C_{BF} = 2^{32}$, $m = 19$ GB for $S = 10^{13}$. This constitutes the vast majority of the ASes in the Internet, thus motivating the selection of a BF configuration in this range. Nevertheless, at this range,

we notice a substantial wastage of processing resources for tier-1 ASes, with Large and Small ISPs also being substantially affected in the case of DONA-BF. In all, it becomes evident that even if a subset of the ASes in the Internet is willing to tolerate the wastage of some type of resource, over the other (e.g., Stub networks tolerate some increased processing resource requirements in order to reduce their memory costs in the aforementioned range), still, this would have a substantial impact in other areas of the network, particularly dis-incentivising the corresponding ASes (e.g., tier-1 ASes). Evidently, this observation renders the selection of a globally fixed BF configuration infeasible.

5. SIMULATION EVALUATIONS

Though enabling the identification and assessment of the tradeoffs emerging in the design and configuration of the considered BF-based NRS approaches, the methodology employed in the previous section presents some limitations.

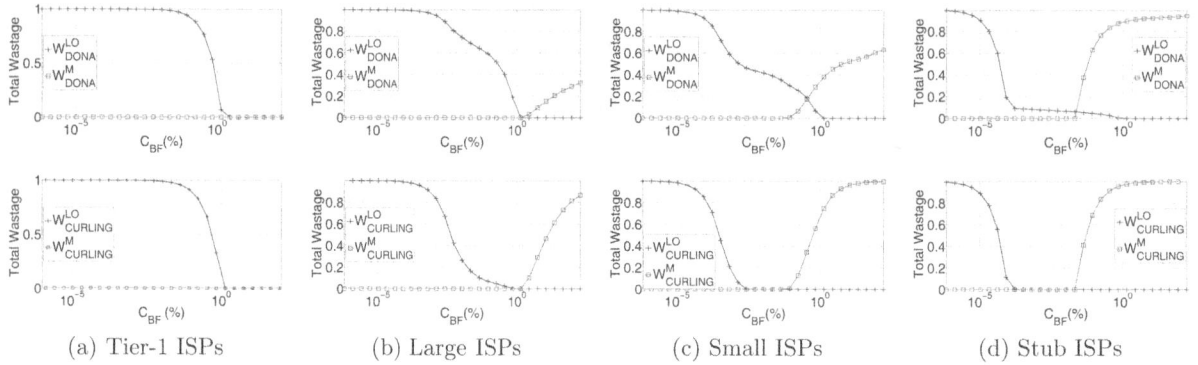

| (a) Tier-1 ISPs | (b) Large ISPs | (c) Small ISPs | (d) Stub ISPs |

Figure 4: Total wastage observed across the inter-domain topology tiers, for DONA-BF and CURLING-BF.

First, our analysis is based on the simplifying assumption of a perfect allocation of IO name registrations into BF containers, while the actual number of BFs depends on the merging process throughout the hierarchy (see Section 3). Second, the assessment of the processing overheads calls for a closer look at the actual number of name resolution requests reaching each node. Third, our analysis does not provide insights on the overall impact of false positives on the entire inter-domain topology, as it focuses on a per node upper limit, i.e., R_{max}^{Node}.

In this section, we address these limitations by resorting to packet level simulations, which enable the investigation of the dynamics of the name resolution system and the actual impact of the complex inter-domain topology structure on the identified performance metrics.

5.1 Simulation environment

As the size of inter-domain topology graph presents significant scalability challenges for our simulation environment (i.e., more than 45K ASes and approximately 200,000 annotated links [1]), we employ scaled-down inter-domain topologies generated by the algorithm proposed by Dimitropoulos et al. [7], which present a manageable size for our evaluation purposes while maintaining the same properties of the original CAIDA graph. Specifically, we employ a topology of 400 ASes inter-connected with multi-homing and peering links. On top of this topology, we deploy one RH node per AS. We neglect intra-domain communication overheads and focus our study on the effects of the inter-domain topology structure on the performance of the considered NRSes. In these scaled-down topologies, we classify the ASes according to their minimum hop-count distance to the top level of the hierarchy. Finally, we use a synthetic workload which considers a detailed mixture of various traffic types (e.g., Web, Video, P2P). For this purpose, we employed the GlobeTraff traffic generator tool [16], to generate workload instances with an average IO catalogue size of 79,821 items and 190,065 resolution requests. Each simulated scenario consists of two phases. In the first phase, the entire catalogue of IOs is registered to the NRS. Then, the entire set of resolution requests is injected into the network from randomly selected leaf ASes (i.e., ASes with an empty cone). We consider various values of C_{BF} ranging from $C_{BF} = 10$ to $C_{BF} = 10^5$, and set $R_{max}^{Node} = 10^{-4}$.

5.2 Results

Based on the described simulation environment, we first validate the methodology and findings presented in the pre-

vious sections. To this end, we assess the distribution of the states across the inter-domain topology, along with processing overheads as defined in Section 3.3.3.

State size. Figure 5 shows the average state size for all considered schemes and various BF configurations. We see that the state size varies in a similar pattern to our analytical model, with large C_{BF} values eventually leading to state sizes that exceed those observed for plain DONA and CURLING.

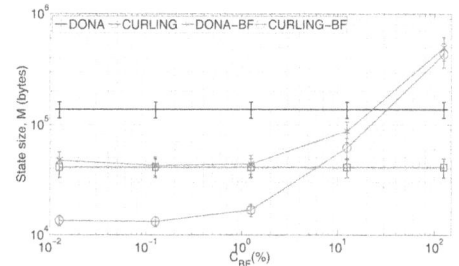

Figure 5: Average state size (M) per AS across the inter-domain topology.

Processing overheads. Figure 6(a) shows the average number of lookup operations (LO) per received name resolution request, across all ASes. As previously described, this metric expresses the processing overheads associated with each request. As we see, these overheads are directly related to the BF configuration, presenting a trend corroborating our analytical model.

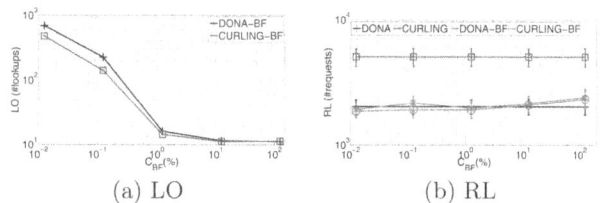

| (a) LO | (b) RL |

Figure 6: Processing overheads for various C_{BF} values. In 6(a): average LO per AS across the inter-domain topology. In 6(b): average RL per AS across the inter-domain topology.

In Figure 6(b), we further show the average total number of name resolution requests received at each AS in the topology (i.e., RL, see Section 3). We notice that CURLING presents the highest load among the considered schemes. As shown in [18], this is because no state is exchanged over peering links in CURLING, resulting in name resolution requests being propagated further up in the hierarchy. Both BF-based schemes present a performance similar to DONA, with slightly higher overheads in the case of the largest C_{BF} values. At such values, BFs are sparser and thus present a lower false positive ratio, thus allowing requests to further propagate in the inter-domain topology (see also Figure 8). In all, Figure 6(b) suggests that the BF configuration has a minor impact on the total number of resolution requests received by each AS.

BF merging efficiency. As mentioned above, our assumption on perfect assignment of IO registrations to BFs only supports a baseline understanding of the identified trade-offs. In order to assess the efficiency of a realistic merging process we resort to simulations. In our model we employ the *Best First Decreasing* bin-packing algorithm. We consider an offline algorithm since we assume a periodic state update mechanism (see Section 2).

We measure the efficiency of the bin-packing algorithm with the help of the *merging overhead* metric, which corresponds to the ratio of the actual number of BFs over the theoretically optimal F. Figures 7(a) and 7(b) present this overhead for each inter-domain topology level, for DONA-BF and CURLING-BF respectively. In both cases, large C_{BF} values result in considerable overheads at all layers with the highest impact on Level 1 ASes, i.e., tier-1. A close inspection of the inter-domain topology structure reveals that this is the direct consequence of a large number of ASes being directly connected to tier-1 ASes. Specifically, we observe that approximately 48% of the leaf nodes in the entire topology are directly connected to some tier-1 AS, corresponding to ASes that aim to minimize transit overheads [20]. This has the effect of multiple BFs arriving directly to tier-1 ASes without having been previously merged with each other at some intermediate AS. It is noted that tier-1 ASes do not merge incoming BFs from multiple customer ASes as this would not allow them to preserve forwarding information.

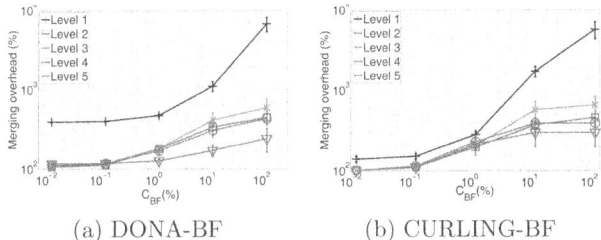

Figure 8: Average false positive ratio (R) across the inter-domain topology.

same node will deterministically lead to false positives.[12] To further assess the impact of IO popularity on the perceived false positive ratio, Figure 8 further depicts the observed values for an alternative workload with a unique request per IO in the network (denoted as DONA-/CURLING-BF (Unique)). This removes the effect of repeated false positive events for the same resolution requests (i.e., the overall rate of false positive events) and reflects the false positive probability. We notice a substantial reduction to values in the order of 40%, which are still considered impractical.

To further shed some light on this finding, we inspect the distribution of the observed false positive events across the levels of the inter-domain topology. Figures 9(a) and 9(b) show that in both cases of DONA-BF and CURLING-BF, the vast majority of false positives takes place at tier-1 ASes. This is a direct outcome of the observed concentration of large numbers of BFs at tier-1 ASes from directly attached leaf ASes. Though the R_{max}^{Node} constraint is enforced through the configuration of BFs, the structure of the inter-domain topology results in a volume of BFs that increases the overall probability of suffering a false positive (see Appendix). Moreover, it must be noted that the overall false probability ratio is further increased by the multi-hop resolution process i.e., the false positive ratio at each node has a cumulative effect.

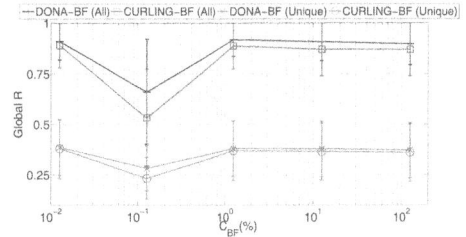

(a) DONA-BF   (b) CURLING-BF

Figure 7: Average merging overhead across the inter-domain topology levels for various C_{BF} values.

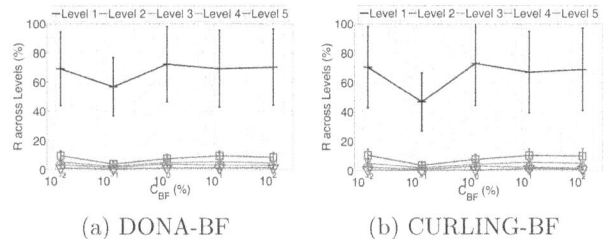

(a) DONA-BF   (b) CURLING-BF

Figure 9: Distribution of average False Positive ratio across the levels of the inter-domain topology.

Overall False Positive Ratio. Figure 8 shows the overall false positive ratio observed across the hierarchy, i.e., the ratio of the total number of name resolution requests that suffered a false positive response, over the entire population of name resolution requests in our workload (denoted as DONA-/CURLING-BF (All)). Interestingly, we see a considerably high false positive ratio in the order of 90%. To get a better understanding of this result, we first note that, following widely studied popularity models, our workload included multiple requests for the most popular IOs [16]. This means that if a request leads to a false positive at a certain node, then all subsequent requests for the same IO at the

6. CONCLUSIONS AND FUTURE WORK

Promising a compact representation of name resolution state, BFs have been considered as a potential solution towards the scalability concerns stemming from the enormous size of the information namespace. In this paper, we have attempted to shed some light on the properties of BF-based inter-domain name resolution schemes, focusing on the resulting resource requirements and the interplay between the

---

[12]This assumes that between consecutive name resolution requests, the queried BFs along the name resolution path remain unchanged. We leave this issue for future investigation.

BF configuration and the distribution of state across the inter-domain Internet topology. Our findings show that the skewed distribution of name resolution state renders the selection of a BF configuration particularly problematic. According to our findings: (i) it is not possible to select a BF configuration such that both the memory and processing resource requirements are reduced for all ASes, compared to BF-agnostic NRSes, (ii) reducing memory resource requirements for the majority of ASes in the Internet, inevitably inflates processing resource requirements at tier-1 ASes, (iii) the multiplicity of customer-provider routing relationships between tier-1 and stub networks inflates the number of BFs maintained by the former, dramatically increasing false positives, and thus deteriorating the reliability of the NRS.

These results directly question the feasibility of BF-based inter-domain NRSes. The resulting resource requirements lead to a conflict of interests in the inter-domain topology with ASes at different tiers presenting contradictory requirements. Even worse, the structure of the inter-domain topology results in inflated false positive ratios that question the reliability of the name resolution process.

In view of these conclusions, the investigation of alternative probabilistic data structures appears as the next step. To this end, a series of BF enhancements and alternative structures has been proposed, offering some appealing properties [24]. Scalable BFs [2] and Dynamic BFs [13] target at dynamically adapting to varying and/or potentially large set sizes. Counting BFs (CBFs) [10] and d-left CBFs [4] further enable the deletion of registered items, thus avoiding the periodic update of the entire name resolution state. Finally, the Cuckoo [9] filter was recently proposed as a BF alternative presenting lower memory and processing requirements, while reducing false positive rates.

Acknowledgments

The research leading to these results has received funding from the European Community's Seventh Framework Programme FP7-ICT-2011-8 under grant agreement no. 318708 (C-DAX) and the CHIST-ERA / EPSRC UK project CONCERT (grant no. EP/L018535/1). The authors alone are responsible for the content of this paper.

7. REFERENCES

[1] Caida dataset. http://www.caida.org/research/topology/#Datasets, 2008. [Online; accessed 19-July-2008].

[2] P. S. Almeida et al. Scalable bloom filters. *Information Processing Letters*, 101(6):255 – 261, 2007.

[3] B. H. Bloom. Space/Time Trade-offs in Hash Coding with Allowable Errors. *Commun. ACM*, 13(7):422–426, July 1970.

[4] F. Bonomi et al. An improved construction for counting bloom filters. In Y. Azar and T. Erlebach, editors, *Algorithms âĂŞ ESA 2006*, volume 4168 of *Lecture Notes in Computer Science*, pages 684–695. Springer Berlin Heidelberg, 2006.

[5] W. K. Chai et al. Curling: Content-ubiquitous resolution and delivery infrastructure for next-generation services. *IEEE Communications Magazine*, 49(3):112 –120, 2011.

[6] C. Dannewitz et al. Hierarchical DHT-based name resolution for information-centric networks. *Computer Communications*, 36(7):736–749, Apr. 2013.

[7] X. Dimitropoulos et al. Graph annotations in modeling complex network topologies. *ACM Transactions on Modeling and Computer Simulation*, 19:17:1–17:29, November 2009.

[8] D. Evans. The Internet of Everything: How More Relevant and Valuable Connections Will Change the World. White Paper, February 2012.

[9] B. Fan et al. Cuckoo filter: Practically better than bloom. In *Proceedings of the 10th ACM International on Conference on Emerging Networking Experiments and Technologies*, CoNEXT '14, pages 75–88, New York, NY, USA, 2014. ACM.

[10] L. Fan et al. Summary Cache: a scalable wide-area web cache sharing protocol. *IEEE/ACM Transactions on Networking*, 8(3):281–293, 2000.

[11] N. Fotiou et al. H-Pastry: An inter-domain topology aware overlay for the support of name-resolution services in the future Internet. *Computer Communications*, 62:13 – 22, 2015.

[12] Google. *We knew the web was big, July 2008*.

[13] D. Guo et al. The dynamic bloom filters. *Knowledge and Data Engineering, IEEE Transactions on*, 22(1):120–133, Jan 2010.

[14] J. Hong et al. Bloom Filter-based Flat Name Resolution System for ICN. Internet-Draft draft-hong-icnrg-bloomfilterbased-name-resolution-03.txt, IETF Secretariat, Mar. 2015.

[15] R. Jarno et al. On name-based inter-domain routing. *Computer Networks, Elsevier*, 55:975–986, March 2011.

[16] K. Katsaros et al. GlobeTraff: A Traffic Workload Generator for the Performance Evaluation of Future Internet Architectures. In *New Technologies, Mobility and Security (NTMS), 2012 5th International Conference on*, pages 1–5, May 2012.

[17] K. V. Katsaros et al. On inter-domain name resolution for information-centric networks. In *Proc. of the IFIP TC 6 Conference on Networking*, pages 13–26, 2012.

[18] K. V. Katsaros et al. On the Inter-domain Scalability of Route-by-Name Information-Centric Network Architectures. In *Proc. of the IFIP TC 6 Conference on Networking*, pages –, 2015.

[19] T. Koponen et al. A data-oriented (and beyond) network architecture. In *Proc. of the ACM SIGCOMM*, pages 181–192, 2007.

[20] C. Labovitz et al. Internet inter-domain traffic. In *Proc. of the 2010 ACM SIGCOMM*, pages 75–86, New York, NY, USA, 2010. ACM.

[21] H. Liu et al. A multi-level DHT routing framework with aggregation. In *Proc. of the 2012 ACM SIGCOMM Workshop on Information-centric networking (ICN'12)*, pages 43–48. ACM, 2012.

[22] M. Mitzenmacher. Compressed Bloom Filters. *IEEE/ACM Trans. Netw.*, 10(5):604–612, Oct. 2002.

[23] R. Oliveira et al. The (in)completeness of the observed internet AS-level structure. *IEEE/ACM Transactions on Networking*, 18:109–122, February 2010.

[24] S. Tarkoma et al. Theory and practice of bloom filters for distributed systems. *Communications Surveys Tutorials, IEEE*, 14(1):131–155, First 2012.

[25] G. Xylomenos et al. A Survey of Information-Centric Networking Research. *IEEE Communications Surveys and Tutorials*, 16(2):1024–1049, 2014.

APPENDIX

As discussed in Section 5, the direct connection of multiple leaf ASes to Tier-1 ASes results in the latter maintaining a large number of BFs, considerably sparse in the case of large C_{BF} values. In turn the false positive rate at Tier-1 ASes is inflated. This is because for a certain BF configuration and a certain number of IOs s, the use of multiple sparse BFs increases the effective false positive ratio compared to fewer but denser BFs. Considering a positive integer $\beta \in \mathbb{Z}$:

$$s < \beta s \Leftrightarrow$$
$$R(s) < R(\beta s) \Leftrightarrow$$
$$(1 - R(s))^{\beta} < (1 - R(\beta s))^{\beta} \Leftrightarrow$$
$$1 - (1 - R(s))^{\beta} > 1 - (1 - R(\beta s))^{\beta} > 1 - (1 - R(\beta s)) \Leftrightarrow$$
$$R^{Node}(s, \beta) > R(\beta s)$$

where $R(s)$ is the false positive ratio of a BF with s elements inserted and $R^{Node}(s, \beta)$ is the false positive probability at a node maintaining β BFs of s elements each.

Pending Interest Table Sizing in Named Data Networking

Giovanna Carofiglio
Cisco Systems
gcarofig@cisco.com

Massimo Gallo
Bell Labs, Alcatel-Lucent
massimo.gallo@alcatel-lucent.com

Luca Muscariello
Orange Labs Networks
luca.muscariello@orange.com

Diego Perino
Bell Labs, Alcatel-Lucent
diego.perino@alcatel-lucent.com

ABSTRACT

Named Data Networking (NDN) has emerged as a promising candidate for shifting Internet communication model from host-centric to content-centric. A core component of NDN is its stateful forwarding plane: Content Routers keep track of pending requests (Interests) storing them in dedicated tables at routers (Pending Interest Tables). A thorough analysis of PIT scalability is fundamental for deploying NDN as a whole and questions naturally arise about memory requirements and feasibility at wire-speed. While previous works focus on data structures design under the threat of PIT state explosion, we develop for the first time an analytical model of PIT dynamics as a function of relevant system parameters. We provide a closed form characterization of average and maximum PIT size value at steady state. We build an experimental platform with high speed content router implementation to investigate PIT dynamics and to confirm the accuracy of our analytical findings. Finally, we provide guidelines on optimal PIT dimensioning and analyze the case of an ISP aggregation network with a trace-driven packet delay distribution. We conclude that, even in absence of caching and under optimal network bandwidth usage, PIT size results to be small in typical network settings.

Categories and Subject Descriptors

C.2.1 [**Computer-Communication Networks**]: Network Architecture and Design—*Network communications*

Keywords

Information-Centric Networking; Performance; Scalability.

1. INTRODUCTION

Internet architecture has been undergoing a tremendous transformation from a network of computers into an ubiquitous interconnection of data, things and ultimately people. Under the stress of a richer, mobile and dynamic user demand, Internet communication principles show their limita-

ICN'15, September 30–October 2, 2015, San Francisco, CA, USA.
© 2015 ACM. ISBN 978-1-4503-3855-4/15/09 ...$15.00.
DOI: http://dx.doi.org/10.1145/2810156.2810167.

tions and are today at the center of research investigations. Various future Internet proposals have emerged in the research arena, innovating the network architecture and its communication primitives around a content (or information) centric communication.

The most popular, [9, 18] CCN/NDN advocates a name-based communication, controlled by the end-user and realized via name-based routing and forwarding. Such connectionless communication model naturally takes advantage of multipath/multicast network capabilities and in-network caching. To this goal, NDN requires a stateful data plane. End -user name-based requests (Interests) are interpreted by NDN nodes and, when not satisfied by a local cache (Content Store, CS), forwarded according to the name-based FIB. NDN nodes keep track of the state of all pending Interests in dedicated data structures called PIT (Pending Interest Tables). The PIT is an essential element of NDN forwarding plane and is used to: (i) guarantee Data delivery to the requesting user(s) on Interests' reverse path, (ii) realize Interest aggregation, enabling native support for multicast and (iii) enable advanced forwarding features as hop-by-hop forwarding, loop detection, etc. The design of a router implementing the NDN data-plane (Content Router) is a challenging task. Name based FIB and CS are similar to today's router data structures (IP FIB and packet buffer), and their design and implementation is already a challenging research problem.

The PIT is a novel data structure and two main aspects require thorough investigation: (i) the feasibility of wire speed PIT implementation; (ii) the analysis of the PIT size evolution. Most of the previous works address ed feasibility issues [7, 16, 11, 17, 13], while PIT size analysis received little attention so far [7, 14]. However, none of the previous works analyze PIT dynamics as a function of content request workload and network conditions.

In this paper, we develop for the first time an analytical model of PIT dynamics under the assumption of a single PIT per node, and no a priori size or request lifetime limitations. Our traffic model assumes elastic flows only. Indeed, inelastic flows do not impact PIT dynamics when their rate is smaller than the bottleneck's fair rate, and are most likely stopped by the users otherwise. More in detail:

- We develop a fluid model of instantaneous rate, queue length and PIT size over time and derive a closed form characterization of average and maximum PIT size at steady state in a single bottleneck scenario.

- We extend our model to general network topologies and multi-bottlenecks scenarios.

- We build an experimental testbed including high-speed content router and custom application layer NDN client, repository to analyze PIT dynamics and to assess model accuracy.

- We provide guidelines on optimal PIT dimensioning and analyze the case of an ISP aggregation network in presence of a realistic trace-driven packet delay distribution.

The conclusion of our study is that, even in absence of in-network caching and under optimal use of network bandwidth, PIT size results to be small in typical network settings. The remainder of the paper is organized as follow. Sec. 2 presents the related work. In Sec.3 we describe the NDN communication principles, and introduce our modeling framework. Analytical results are gathered in Sec.4. We carry out an experimental evaluation in Sec.5, with the twofold objective of analyzing PIT dynamics in realistic settings and assessing model accuracy. Sec.6 provides guidelines on PIT dimensioning based on our analytical tool. Finally, Sec.7 concludes the paper.

2. RELATED WORK

PIT feasibility has been studied for the first time in [7]. By analyzing an IP trace, authors provide an approximate quantification of PIT size, and propose Name Component Encoding as well as PIT placement on outgoing router line-cards in order to reduce PIT size and accelerate management operations. Other PIT compression methods exploiting Bloom filters have been also proposed in [16, 11]. Authors of [17] provide design guidelines for high-speed PIT implementation: in order to limit memory requirements and access frequency content names are replaced with fingerprints. A performance comparison of encoding methods and hash-based methods can be found in [13]. Authors evaluate content router requirements under the assumptions of limited request lifetime and homogeneous network links with an average global RTT of 80 ms.

Motivated by the threat of PIT size explosion, authors of [12] propose a semi-stateless forwarding scheme for NDN. Their design propose to keep track of forwarded requests every d hops instead of every hop as in the original CCN/NDN proposal. PIT security analysis also received particular attention in some related works. In [15], authors derive an analytical model for denial of service attack detection. Threats to the PIT stability and security are also analyzed in [14] through analytical modeling and experimental evaluation. None of the previous work has focused on the analysis of PIT dynamics as a function of relevant system parameters. To the best of our knowledge, this is the first paper to characterize PIT dynamics and to investigate them means of experiments with a realistic platform and trace-driven packet delay distribution.

Other bodies of work in the literature are significant to this paper: buffer sizing in Internet routers and scalability of stateful schedulers. In particular dimensioning is made in [2] by using the Gaussian quantile of a core router queue occupancy created by a large number of bottlenecked flows. Flow table in [10] is sized by computing the distribution of the number of active flows in a per-flow scheduler, under dynamic workload. Our approach is similar to these works but we focus on PIT sizing instead of buffer or flow table dimensioning. We require a finer characterization of the queue

evolution and its relation with the flow controller characteristics under dynamic setting which constitutes in itself a novel contribution.

3. PROBLEM DESCRIPTION

Our work builds on Named Data Networking assumptions [9, 18]. In the following we briefly revise NDN communication principles.

3.1 System description

NDN uses hierarchical names similar to URIs to address content. Content items are split into a sequence of chunks (or Data packets) uniquely identified by the content name plus the chunk identifier. Clients express per chunk requests (or Interests) to retrieve the complete content item and regulate the request rate via a window-based multipath congestion control algorithm. NDN nodes process incoming packets using the name carried in the packet header. Upon Interest packet reception, an NDN node first checks if the requested Data packet is stored in the local cache (Content Store in the NDN terminology). In this case, it sends the Data back through the requesting interface(s), satisfying the Interest. Otherwise, it checks if the PIT stores requests for the same ongoing Data request. If it is the case, it adds the requesting interface to the list of interfaces waiting for the Data packet and discards the Interest packet. Finally, if both CS and PIT lookups give negative response, the NDN node forwards the Interest to the next hop according to the name-based longest prefix match on the FIB and creates a corresponding PIT entry. If there is no match in the FIB, the Interest is discarded. When a Data packet arrives, the NDN node checks the PIT to retrieve the list of requesting interfaces and forwards the Data back to such interfaces. Also, the NDN node potentially stores the packet in the local CS for future reuse. The Data packet is discarded if there are no matching entries in the PIT.

3.2 Modeling framework

We model system dynamics at the timescale of content retrievals through a deterministic fluid model, where the discrete packet representation is replaced by a continuous one, either in space and in time. Similar fluid models have been adopted to analyze TCP/UDP dynamics (e.g.,[8]). Like in the TCP/UDP case, the continuous space representation captures the aggregate flow behavior neglecting microscopic packet-level dynamics. Thus, the smaller the packet size and the larger the number of multiplexed flows/packets, the more accurate is the fluid approximation of system dynamics. However, previous work neglect the fine-grained analysis of queue dynamics and its oscillations, which we provide in this paper. An accurate characterization of queue and PIT size variations is important for PIT size prediction and dimensioning. Let us summarize the main assumptions and provide the notation (Tab.1).

3.2.1 Network model

- The network is modeled as a directed graph $\mathcal{G} = (\mathcal{V}, \mathcal{L})$ with bi-directional arcs.

- Links have finite capacities $C_{ij} > 0$, $\forall (i,j) \in \mathcal{L}$. For a line topology (Fig.1) we simplify the notation, $C_i \equiv C_{i-1,i}$ (same notation for other link variables). We consider downlink bandwidth limitations only.

- A content retrieval (flow) $n \in \mathcal{N}$ is univocally associated to a user node and to a set of available sources.

- According to NDN symmetric routing principle, if Interests of flow n traverse link (i, j), corresponding Data packets are pulled down over link (j, i).

- We study PIT dynamics with no caching, no Interest aggregation nor PIT timeouts as a worst case for PIT dimensioning. Note that caching before the bottleneck will have a mitigating effect on PIT size.

- We consider infinite output buffers at downlink: Data packet losses are anticipated by request rate decrease.

3.2.2 Source model

- The variables X^n, $\tilde{X}^n$, respectively denote Data, Interest rate of flow n and can be specified at the receiver (index 0) or over a link. In a line network as in Fig.1, $X_i^n(t)$ denotes the downlink Data rate of flow n, at time t and at the ith link, in packet/second.

- The round trip delay of flow n at time t, $R_n(t)$, is assumed to be the sum of a constant round trip propagation delay, R_{min}^n and of a variable queuing delay considering all traversed queues. In a line network with L links as in Fig.1 and for homogeneous flows, $R(t) \equiv R(t) = R_{min} + \sum_{i=1}^{L} Q_i(t)/C_i$, where $Q_i(t)$ denotes the instantaneous downlink queue length at link i at time t.

- Interests of flow n are issued by the user at a rate modulated by a Remote Adaptive Active Queue Management (RAAQM) controller, such as the one presented in ([6],[5]), where initial slow start phase and fast recovery are neglected. As described in [6], the Interest window $W(t)$ at the receiver (we omit the index 0 identifying the receiver), increases by a factor η every window of Data packets received in a round trip delay $R(t)$, and decreases by a multiplicative factor β proportionally to the Data packet rate and to a decrease probability $p(t)$. Since $\tilde{X}(t) = W(t)/R(t)$ by Little's law, the rate evolution over time at the receiver follows the DDE (Delay Differential Equation):

$$\frac{d\tilde{X}(t)}{dt} = \frac{\eta}{R(t)^2} - \beta \tilde{X}(t) X(t) p(t - R(t)) \quad (1)$$

$$p(t) = p_{min} + \Delta p \min\left(\frac{R(t) - R_{min}}{\Delta R}, 1\right) \quad (2)$$

where $\Delta p \equiv p_{max} - p_{min}$, $\Delta R \equiv R_{max} - R_{min}$ and $X(t)$ reflects the Interest rate $\tilde{X}(t - R(t))$ associated to the round trip delay before.

The decrease probability $p(t)$ is a RAAQM parameter: p_{min}, p_{max} are two AQM thresholds, assumed to be fixed in our analysis, while in the experiments they are adapted over time by the transport protocol according to round trip time measurements at the receiver (cfr.[6]). If not otherwise specified, $p_{min} = 0$.

$p(t)$ mirrors the delay variation due to queuing delay along the path. Note that $p(t)$ is computed over the round trip delay measurements carried by received Data packets, thus referred to the previous round trip delay. This introduces a delayed component in system DDEs which we will account for in our analysis.

OBSERVATION 3.1. *It is worth noticing that, in this work, we consider the RAAQM controller as it is, to the best of our knowledge, the unique ICN receiver-driven controller proved to be throughput optimal (cfr.[6]). However, the analysis can be easily generalized to any throughput optimal receiver-based rate controller yielding to the same optimal rate allocation.*

4. ANALYSIS OF PIT DYNAMICS

In this section we first model the PIT dynamics in presence of N homogeneous flows and over a single path composed by L cascaded links as in Fig.1 (Node 0 identifies a user node sending requests to node L, associated to the Data repository), hence considering a single bottleneck scenario. In Sec.4.2 we then extend the model to the case of variable number of flows, multi-bottlenecks, and general network topology.

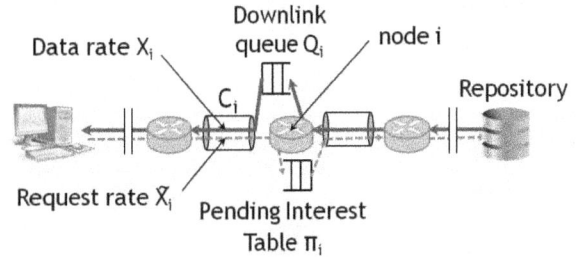

Figure 1: Line network topology.

Every node hosts a PIT keeping track of ongoing requests in uplink. Its length is denoted by $\pi_i(t)$. A downlink transmission queue serving Data packets, $Q_i(t)$, is associated to link i. Since we assume no bandwidth limitations in uplink, $\tilde{X}_i^n(t) = \tilde{X}^n(t)$, $\forall i$. The *system state* is described by $\{\tilde{X}^n(t), X_i^n(t), Q_i(t), \pi_i(t)\}$, $i = 0, \ldots, L$, respectively Interest/Data rates, downlink queue and PIT size at each link. The evolution of system dynamics is described by the following nonlinear DDEs:

$$\frac{d\tilde{X}^n(t)}{dt} = \frac{\eta}{R(t)^2} - \beta \tilde{X}^n(t) X^n(t) p(t - R(t)), \quad (3)$$

$$p(t) = p_{min} + \Delta p \min\left(\frac{R(t) - R_{min}}{\Delta R}, 1\right), \quad (4)$$

$$X_{i-1}^n(t) = X_i^n(t) \mathbb{1}_{\{Q_i(t)=0\}} + \left(C_i - \sum_{k \neq n} X_i^k(t)\right) \mathbb{1}_{\{Q_i(t)>0\}}$$

$$\text{with } i = 1, \ldots, L \text{ and } X_L^n(t) = \tilde{X}^n(t) \quad (5)$$

$$\frac{dQ_i(t)}{dt} = \sum_n X_i^n(t) - C_i \mathbb{1}_{\{Q_i(t)>0\}}, \quad (6)$$

$$\frac{d\pi_i(t)}{dt} = \sum_n \left(\tilde{X}^n(t) - X_{i+1}^n(t) \mathbb{1}_{\{\pi_i(t)>0\}}\right), \quad \forall i. \quad (7)$$

Eqq.(3)-(4) describe the RAAQM receiver-driven rate control applied to every flow n. To the ease of notation, we denote $X^n(t)$, the Data rate at the user. Queue length time evolution is described by the fluid queue equation in Eq.(6) where the input rate is the total Data rate at node i, and the output rate is the ith link capacity, C_i. Finally, the PIT size follows a similar fluid queue equation with input rate, the sum of Interest rates of all flows at node i, and output rate,

$N = \|\mathcal{N}\|$	Number of flows
L	Number of links in the line topology
$\tilde{X}_{i,j}(t)$	Interest rate at link ij,
$X_{i,j}(t)$	Data rate at link ij,
$\tilde{X}_i, X_i$	Interest/Data for a line
$Q_{i,j}(t)$	Downlink Queue size at link ij, Q_i for a line
$\pi_i(t)$	PIT size at node i and time t
$C_{i,j}$	Capacity of link ij, C_i for a line
$R(t), \Delta R$	Round trip delay and variation
$p(t), \Delta p$	Packet loss probability and variation
η, β	Rate increase, decrease factor
σ_n	Mean flow size (in # of packets) of flow n.

Table 1: Notation

the total Data rate of such flows at time t. Indeed, ongoing requests of flow n are recorded in the PIT until reception of the corresponding Data packets, when they are eventually removed from the table.

4.1 Main results

We consider the case of a fixed number N of homogeneous flows traversing the series of L cascaded links in Fig.1. Each flow is controlled by the optimal RAAQM controller defined by Eqq.(1)-(2).With no loss of generality, we assume that the system starts empty, i.e. $\tilde{X}^n(0) = Q_i(0) = 0$, $\forall n = 1, \ldots, N, i = 1, \ldots, L$. Since flows are assumed to be homogeneous, $\tilde{X}^n(t) \equiv \tilde{X}(t)$, $X_i^n(t) \equiv X_i(t)$.

4.1.1 Scaling with the number of flows

Let us study how the system scales with the number of flows, N.

PROPOSITION 4.1. *System dynamics in presence of N flows as described by DDEs (3)-(7) are equivalent to those of a single flow, under the following linear scaling of parameters:* $N\eta \leftarrow \eta$, $N\Delta R \leftarrow \Delta R$.

PROOF. The evolution over time of the total flow rate at the receiver, $\tilde{X}^{tot}(t) \equiv N\tilde{X}(t)$, is given by

$$\frac{d\tilde{X}^{tot}(t)}{dt} = \frac{N\eta}{R(t)^2} - \beta\tilde{X}^{tot}(t)X^{tot}(t)p_N(t - R(t)), \quad (8)$$

where $p_N(t) = \frac{\Delta p}{N\Delta R}p(t)$. Queue dynamics become

$$\frac{dQ_i(t)}{dt} = X_i^{tot}(t) - C_i \mathbb{1}_{\{Q_i(t)>0\}}, \qquad \forall i \quad (9)$$

where the instantaneous Data rate at link i is given by Eq.(5), replacing the flow rate with X^{tot}. Similarly, the evolution of PIT size at different nodes still follows Eq.(7), replacing the flow rate with X^{tot}.

It follows that system dynamics in presence of N flows can be derived from those of a single flow by applying the linear scaling of parameters: $N\eta \leftarrow \eta$, $N\Delta R \leftarrow \Delta R$. $\square$

To the ease of notation, results below are proved for $N = 1$.

4.1.2 Transient analysis

Starting from an empty system, the Interest flow rate initially grows linearly in time according to the additive increase term η/R_{min}^2, until it reaches the smallest link capacity, C_{i^*}, where $i^* = \arg\min_i C_i$. At this point in time, that we refer to as t^*, the downlink queue of the slowest link, Q_{i^*} starts filling in and the output rate is throttled to C_{i^*}. Thus, we can prove what follows.

PROPOSITION 4.2. *It exists a time instant $t^* > 0$, such that for $t > t^*$ the output rate of the bottleneck queue Q_{i^*} is equal to the bottleneck link capacity, $X_{i^*}(t) = C_{i^*}$, and downlink queues below the bottleneck remain empty, $Q_j(t) = 0$, for $j < i^*$.*

PROOF. Let us use the above definition for t^*. Proving that the output Data rate at the bottleneck remains equal to C_{i^*}, it is equivalent to show that the bottleneck queue does not remain empty for a positive interval of time. To see this, it suffices to observe that if the bottleneck queue instantaneously empties, the rate decrease term in Eq.(3) becomes zero, as well as the queue decrease term in Eq.(6). Thus, the Interest rate instantaneously increases, hence the queue derivative (Eq.(6)) and consequently the queue itself. Also, by definition of smallest link capacity, we have that $Q_j(t) = 0$, for $j < i$, $\forall t > t^*$, as the input rate C_{i^*} never exceeds C_j. $\square$

OBSERVATION 4.3. *Round trip and bottleneck queuing delay* We have observed that queues below the bottleneck remain empty after a transient phase. Above the bottleneck, queue occupancy depends on instantaneous flow rate values. In the following results, we will consider queues above the bottleneck to be empty as well, so neglecting their contribution to the round trip delay, $R(t)$. Clearly, such condition is always verified when the maximum flow rate value $\tilde{X}_{max}(t) < C_{i^{**}}$, with i^{**} identifying the second smallest capacity link after i^*, i.e. $i^{**} = \arg\min_{i \neq i^*} C_i$. The characterization of X_{max} in steady state can be derived from that of the maximum bottleneck queue/PIT value in Sec.4.1.4. One can then identify the parameters' region where the round trip delay happens to be affected mostly by the bottleneck delay. Our experiments in Sec.5 also confirm that such simplifying assumption holds in typical network settings.

4.1.3 Bottleneck queue and PIT size equivalence

The following result allows us to derive PIT size from bottleneck queue occupancy.

PROPOSITION 4.4. *It exists a time instant $t^* > 0$, such that, for $t > t^*$, PIT sizes, $\pi_i(t)$, are empty above the bottleneck ($i \geq i^*$) and equal to the bottleneck queue length, $Q_{i^*}(t)$ below the bottleneck ($i < i^*$), that is:*

$$\pi_i(t) = \begin{cases} Q_{i^*}(t), & \forall i < i^*, \\ 0, & \forall i \geq i^*, \end{cases} \quad (10)$$

where $i^* = \arg\min_{i=1,\ldots,L} C_i$, identifies the bottleneck link.

PROOF. Let us use the above definition for t^*. For $t > t^*$ and $\forall i > i^*$, we have that $Q_i(t) = 0$, hence $X_i(t) = \tilde{X}(t)$. By invoking Eq.(7), we derive that $\pi_i(t) = 0 \ \forall i \geq i^*$. Instead, for $t > t^*$ and $\forall i < i^*$, $X_i(t) = C_{i^*}$, hence Eq.(6) and Eq.(7) coincide and $\pi_i(t) \equiv Q_{i^*}(t)$. $\square$

4.1.4 Steady state equilibrium

Given previous results in Propp.4.1, 4.2, 4.4, we can focus on the following system of DDEs:

$$\frac{d\tilde{X}(t)}{dt} = \frac{\eta}{R(t)^2} - \beta\tilde{X}(t)C_{i^*}p(t - R(t)),$$

$$p(t) = p_{min} + \Delta p_{\min}\left(\frac{R(t) - R_{min}}{\Delta R}, 1\right),$$

$$\frac{d\pi_i(t)}{dt} \equiv \frac{dQ_{i^*}(t)}{dt} = \tilde{X}(t) - C_{i^*}, \forall i < i^* \quad (11)$$

and study its steady state solution. Recall that $Q_i(t) = 0$, $\forall i \neq i^*$, and $\pi_i(t) = 0$, $i \geq i^*$.

PROPOSITION 4.5. *The system of DDEs in Eqq.(11) admits a steady state solution characterized by*

$$\bar{\bar{X}} = \bar{X} = C_{i^*}, \bar{\pi}_i = \bar{Q}_{i^*} = \left(\frac{\eta C \Delta R}{\beta \Delta p}\right)^{1/3}, \quad i < i^*. \quad (12)$$

which generalizes to

$$\bar{\bar{X}}^n = \bar{X}^n = C_{i^*}/N, \bar{\pi}_i = \bar{Q}_{i^*} = \left(\frac{N^2 \eta C \Delta R}{\beta \Delta p}\right)^{1/3}, i < i^*. \quad (13)$$

in case of N homogeneous flows.

PROOF. By considering only the bottleneck link i^*, which is the unique non empty queue according to Prop.4.2, we compute the steady state regime by setting the derivatives to zero. We omit the link identifiers to simplify the notation. Notice that, by assuming the bottleneck queue not empty (Prop.4.2), $\bar{X} = C$. Also, $\frac{\eta C^2}{\bar{Q}^2} - \beta C \bar{\bar{X}} \frac{\bar{Q}\Delta p}{C \Delta R} = 0$, where we considered $R_{min} << \bar{Q}/C$ to the ease of computation. From which we obtain a unique stationary point (which can be computed also in presence of R_{min}). The generalization to the case of N flows derives from Prop.4.1. $\square$

4.1.5 Maximum PIT size in steady state

Beside the average PIT size value, it is interesting for analysis and dimensioning purposes, to compute the maximum value attained by $Q_{i^*}(t)$, thus by the PIT size. To this aim, we linearize the DDEs in Eqq.11 around the stationary point computed above and compute the maximum through the equivalence with the maximum value of the Laplace transform. We provide the two following auxiliary results.

PROPOSITION 4.6. *The Laplace transform of the queue $Q(t)$ is given by*

$$Q(s) = \frac{\bar{Q}(\kappa_2 + \kappa_3) - sC}{s^2 + \kappa_1 s + \kappa_2 + \kappa_3 e^{-sR}}$$

with $\kappa_1 = \beta \frac{\bar{Q}}{N} \frac{\Delta p}{\Delta R}$, $\kappa_2 = \frac{2\eta N C^2}{\bar{Q}^3} = 2\kappa_3$, $\kappa_3 = \beta \frac{C}{N} \frac{\Delta p}{\Delta R}$

PROOF. The following DDEs can be linearized around the stationary point by assuming that the queue never empties (Prop.4.2),

$$\frac{d\tilde{X}_t}{dt} = f(X_t, Q_t, Q_{t-R}) \qquad \frac{dQ_t}{dt} = \tilde{X}(t) - C,$$

The linearized system gives the following DDEs.

$$\frac{d\tilde{X}_t}{dt} = -\kappa_1(\tilde{X}_t - C) - \kappa_2(Q_t - \bar{Q}) - \kappa_3(Q_{t-R} - \bar{Q})$$

$\kappa_1 = -\frac{\partial f}{\partial \tilde{X}_t}$, $\kappa_2 = -\frac{\partial f}{\partial Q_t}$, $\kappa_3 = -\frac{\partial f}{\partial Q_{t-R}}$. By transforming using the Laplace operator

$$sX(s) = -\kappa_1(X(s) - C) - \kappa_2(Q(s) - \bar{Q}) + \\ - \kappa_3(Q(s)e^{-sR} - \bar{Q})$$

$$s(sQ(s) + C) = -s\kappa_1 Q(s) - Q(s)(\kappa_2 + \kappa_3 e^{-sR}) \\ + \bar{Q}(\kappa_2 + \kappa_3)$$

we obtain the Laplace transform of the linearized equation. $\square$

Note that $R \to 0$ the Laplace transform can be easily inverted by analyzing the poles of $Q(s)$, $s_{1,2} = -\frac{1}{2}\kappa_1 \pm j\omega_0$ with $\omega_0^2 = 3\kappa_3 - \kappa_1^2/4$.

PROPOSITION 4.7. *If $R = 0$ then*

$$\max_{t>0} Q(t) \leq \bar{Q}\left(1 + 3\beta \left(\frac{T}{2\pi}\right)^2 \frac{C}{N} \frac{\Delta p}{\Delta R}\right)$$

PROOF. When $R = 0$ the Laplace transform of the queue admits poles with negative real part if

$$\beta \frac{\Delta p_{\max}}{\Delta R} < \frac{C/N}{2(\bar{Q}/N)^2}\left(1 + \sqrt{1 + \frac{2\eta}{\bar{Q}/N}}\right) \approx \frac{C/N}{(\bar{Q}/N)^2}$$

. The Laplace transform $Q(s)$ can be easily inverted to obtain the solution

$$Q(t) = Ae^{-\kappa_1 t/2}\sin(2\pi t/T + \phi)$$

$T = 2\pi/\omega_0$ and

$$A = \frac{CT}{2\pi}\sqrt{1 + \left(\frac{T\bar{Q}(\kappa_2 + \kappa_3)}{2\pi C}\right)^2} \approx \bar{Q}\left(\frac{T}{2\pi}\right)^2 (\kappa_2 + \kappa_3)$$

$$(14)$$

$$= 3\beta\left(\frac{T}{2\pi}\right)^2 \bar{Q} \frac{C}{N} \frac{\Delta p}{\Delta R} \quad (15)$$

This is illustrated in Fig.2. Observing that $\max_{t>0} Q(t) \leq A$ we conclude the proof. $\square$

Let us now state the main result about bottleneck queue, hence PIT size maximum value.

PROPOSITION 4.8.

$$\max_{t>0} Q(t) = \max_{t>0} \pi_i(t) \leq \bar{Q} + \frac{CR}{2\sqrt{3}} = \bar{Q}\frac{1 + 2\sqrt{3}}{2\sqrt{3}}, i < i^*$$

where $Q(t) \equiv Q_{i^*}(t)$, $C \equiv C_{i^*}$.

PROOF. The proof is based on the analysis of the modulus of the Laplace transform $|Q(s)|$. $\max_{s \in \mathbb{C}} Q(s)$ gives the value of the maximum fluctuation of $Q(t)$ from the stationary point $\bar{Q}$. In the complex plain the analysis can be easily made by focusing only on the dominant poles that can be computed by using a second order Padé approximation of the delay term

$$e^{-sR} = \frac{1 - sR/2 + s^2 R^2/12}{1 + sR/2 + s^2 R^2/12}$$

We have two additional dominant complex conjugate poles, $s_{1,2} = \frac{-3 \pm \sqrt{3}}{R}$ for the Laplace transform $Q(s)$, when compared to the case $R = 0$. The frequency $\frac{\sqrt{3}}{R}$ gives the fundamental frequency at which the system oscillates around its stationary value $\frac{2\pi}{\sqrt{3}}R \approx 3R$. Such frequency dominates over the other frequencies when $3/R < \kappa_1/2 = \frac{\beta}{2}\frac{\bar{Q}}{N}\frac{\Delta p}{\Delta R}$, i.e. $R > 6\frac{N}{\bar{Q}}\frac{\Delta R}{\beta\Delta p}$. In this case the maximum can be obtained by derivation of $|Q(j\omega)|$ which gives that $\max_{s \in \mathbb{C}} Q(s) = \frac{CR}{2\sqrt{3}}$ is the maximum oscillation around the stationary point. The maximum value of the queue is then obtained as

$$\bar{Q} + \frac{CR}{2\sqrt{3}} = \bar{Q}\left(\frac{1 + 2\sqrt{3}}{2\sqrt{3}}\right)$$

$\square$

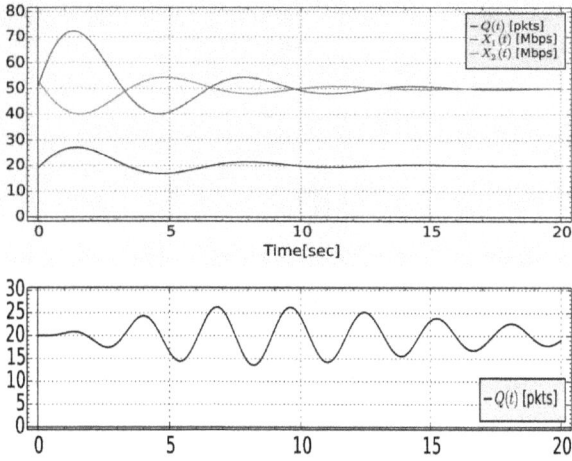

Figure 2: Flow rates and bottleneck queue time evolution, with $R = 0$ (top) and queue evolution when $R > 0$ (bottom).

4.2 Model extensions

In this section we generalize our PIT dynamics analysis to the case of variable number of flows, multiple bottlenecks and general network topology. Eqq.(3-7) hold pathwise, where downlink queues and PITs occupancy results of the contribution of all traversing classes of flows. To compute the average PIT size in general network setting, let us recall that the network topology is represented by a directed graph $\mathcal{G} = (\mathcal{V}, \mathcal{L})$ composed of a set of nodes $\mathcal{V}$ and links $\mathcal{L}$. We group flows according to classes of equal routing, referred to by the index r. Flows belonging to a given class r, share the same sequence of directed links from a user node to a repository node and, hence, the same bottleneck link ij_r^*. We introduce the additional notation $\mathcal{R}_{ij}$ for the set of routes crossing link ij and $\mathcal{L}_v$ for the set of links having node v as egress node. We further distinguish routes bottleneck upstream and downstream within $\mathcal{R}_{ij}$, respectively $\mathcal{R}_{ij}^u$ and $\mathcal{R}_{ij}^d$. Clearly, according to the definition $\mathcal{R}_{ij}^u \cup \mathcal{R}_{ij}^d = \mathcal{R}_{ij}$, $\mathcal{R}_{ij}^u \cap \mathcal{R}_{ij}^d = \emptyset$.

The number of ongoing flows associated to route r, is N_r. We assume flows arrival rate λ_r and average file size of σ_r packets. Let $\rho_{ij} = \sum_{r \in \mathcal{R}_{ij}} \lambda_r \sigma_r / C_{ij}$ denote the load offered to link ij. In case of congestion, link capacity is shared according to max-min fairness and each flow in class r gets the fair share X_r, i.e. $\sum_{r \in \mathcal{R}_{ij}} X_r N_r \le C_{ij}, \forall ij$ (See [3] for an example of max-min fairness applied to ICN). Thus, $\forall r$ there exists at least one bottleneck link such that

$$\sum_{r \in \mathcal{R}_{ij}} X_r N_r = C_{ij} \text{ and } X_r = \max_{r' \in \mathcal{R}_{ij}} X_{r'}.$$

Such conditions uniquely define the max-min shares X_r across route r. N_r is a Markov process positive recurrent under the stability condition $\rho_{ij} < 1$ for each link on route r.

According to the model presented in Sec.4.1 the queue occupancy at every bottleneck link ij, Q_{ij} is caused only by

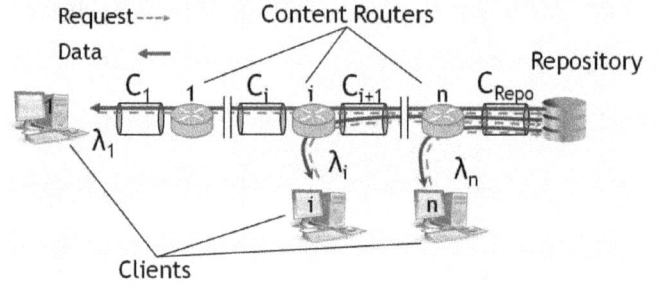

Figure 3: Test topology.

the flows in progress bottlenecked at link ij. Also

$$Q_{ij}\left(\sum_{r \in \mathcal{R}_{ij}} N_r\right) = Q_{ij}(1) \sum_{r \in \mathcal{R}_{ij}} N_r \qquad (16)$$

We compute the average PIT size in steady state at node v as:

$$\mathbb{E}[\pi_v] = \mathbb{E}\left[\sum_{ij \in \mathcal{L}_v} \sum_{r \in \mathcal{R}_{ij}} Q_r\right] = \sum_{ij \in \mathcal{L}_v} \sum_{r \in \mathcal{R}_{ij}} \mathbb{E}[Q_r] \qquad (17)$$

$$= \sum_{ij \in \mathcal{L}_v}\left(\sum_{r \in \mathcal{R}_{ij}^u} \mathbb{E}[N_r]\mathbb{E}[Q_r|N_r=1] + \sum_{r \in \mathcal{R}_{ij}^d} \mathbb{E}[N_r]\mathbb{E}[Q_r|N_r=1]\right)$$

$$= \sum_{ij \in \mathcal{L}_v} \sum_{r \in \mathcal{R}_{ij}^u} \mathbb{E}[N_r]\mathbb{E}[Q_r|N_r=1]$$

$$= \sum_{ij \in \mathcal{L}_v} Q_{ij}(1) \sum_{r \in \mathcal{R}_{ij}^u} \mathbb{E}[N_r] \le \sum_{ij \in \mathcal{L}_v} Q_{ij}(1) \sum_{r \in \mathcal{R}_{ij}^u} \frac{\rho_r}{1 - \rho_r}.$$

The PIT occupancy at node v is decomposed into the sum of the contributions associated to each incoming link $ij \in \mathcal{L}_v$ and for each of them into the contribution of each class of flows $r \in \mathcal{R}_{ij}$. Proposition 4.2 allows us to exclude the flows bottlenecked downstream as they do not contribute to the PIT. The linear dependence of the bottleneck queue, hence of PIT contributions, from the number of active flows allows to isolate in the computation the expected number of flows, $\mathbb{E}[N_r]$. According to the max min fairness model, $\mathbb{E}[N_r]$ can be upper bounded by the average number of packets in a M/M/1 queue, $\mathbb{E}[N_r] \le \frac{\rho_r}{1-\rho_r}$, as in [4].

5. EXPERIMENTAL EVALUATION

In this section we experimentally evaluate PIT dynamics and assess our analytical model accuracy. We consider different scenarios on a parking lot topology with fix/variable number of parallel downloads (e.g., flows) and single/multiple bandwidth bottlenecks. Finally, we analyze the realistic case of an ISP aggregation network.

5.1 Testbed

Our experimental platform is composed of: i) a content router testbed, with a set of hardware nodes running the NDN data plane described in Sec. 3.1; ii) a set of general purpose servers running a custom application layer NDN client/repository implementation. Servers are connected to the content router testbed via optical fibers; iii) a controller, running on a general purpose server to orchestrate the experimental platform and collect statistics.

Content Router – The content router consists of a micro telecommunications computing architecture (μTCA) chassis for advanced mezzanine cards (AMCs). Four slots are occupied by AMC boards equipped with a network processor unit (NPU), 4GB off-chip DRAM, a set of 10GbE interfaces. Each NPU has a 12 cores 800 MHz 64-bits MIPS processor with 16-KB L1 cache per core, and 2MB L2 shared cache. An Ethernet switch enables communications between the different slots of the chassis. In the testbed, every board represents a single content router implementing NDN data plane and network topologies are configured by means of hardware traffic shapers and L2 tunnels among boards. The PIT is implemented using an optimized open-addressed hash table and hardware timers for managing PIT timeouts as in [13]. A detailed description of all data structures (including FIB and CS) is omitted for lack of space. Finally, content router software is instrumented to sample PIT and Queue size values. Samples are collected by an platform controller that computes average and maximum values. We do not process samples inside the board in order to minimize the impact of measurements on processing performance.

Client/repository application – Client/repository applications are written in C and run on general purpose Linux servers. The repository consists of one or multiple UDP/IP socket(s) listening for incoming requests (Interests). Whenever the repository receives an Interest packet, it replies with a fixed size Data packet with the requested chunk name in the header and a dummy payload. The client consists in a local UDP/IP socket sending Interests in order to retrieve a named file. The Interest rate is controlled by the RAAQM mechanism described in Sec. 3.2. Unless otherwise specified we set the controller parameters to $\eta = 1$, $\beta = 0.4$, $\Delta p = 0.02$. The client application is instrumented to report measured round trip delay for each chunk (i.e. the time between a chunk request and the reception of the corresponding data). We use such measures to compute ΔR value used by our model to estimate queue an PIT size (See Prop. 4.5, 4.8.)

Repository and client applications use UDP/IP stack to directly send/receive packets to/from the first directly connected content router. Indeed, the NDN header carries the name of the requested chunk encapsulated in a UDP/IP packet. Content items (each one composed of σ chunks), are requested by clients according to a specific workload (*i.e.*, Poisson arrival). Data and Interest packets are 1,422 Bytes and 92 Bytes respectively including Ethernet, IP, UDP and NDN.

Platform controller – The experimental platform is controlled by a centralized application running on a general purpose server. The controller is in charge of configuring the content router testbed, run client/server application and collect statistics. It is also in charge of the post-processing of the collected data to gather the desired statistics.

5.2 Static case

We consider a static scenario with N parallel flows (*i.e.*, file downloads) and single bottleneck link. We use the network topology in Fig. 3 with $L = 4$, $C_3 = 100$ Mbps, $C_1, C_2, C_{Repo} = 5$ Gbps, we disable caching, and set the maximum queue size of every link to 1,000 packets. Clients run on server 1 connected to CR_1, and retrieve N content items from the repository using route 1 (*i.e.*, the one between server 1 and the repository). Every item is composed

of $\sigma = 1$ million Data packets emulating long lived data transfers.

Fig. 4(a) reports the average/maximum PIT and downlink queue sizes at Content Router j (π_j and Q_j respectively) measured from the test and estimated analytically (computed according to Prop. 4.5, 4.8 respectively), as a function of $N = [1 : 30]$. ΔR is set according to the monitored round trip delay variability at the receiver. Note that for each of the following experiments the congestion controller is observed to achieve a fully efficient and fair rate equilibrium as expected (cfr. [6]). Also note that there are not timer expiration: data packet losses are anticipated by a request rate decrease of the controller before the queue of any link gets full.

Fig. 4(a) shows four main results. (i) The queue size of the bottlenecked link (e.g., link 3 in our experiment) is equivalent to the PIT size in the content routers below the bottleneck (e.g., CR 1,2 in our experiment). (ii) The downlink queue and PIT sizes on the nodes that are above the bottlenecked (e.g., CR 3 in our experiment) link are approximately zero. (iii) The PIT size linearly increases with the number of parallel flows N. (iv) Results confirm the trends predicted by the analytical model and the average/maximum PIT size prediction derived in Prop. 4.5, 4.8 appear to be very accurate.

In Fig. 4(b) we plot the average experimental and analytical PIT size at Content Router 2 as a function of the bottleneck capacity, $C_3 = [100 : 1000]$ Mbps, with $N = [10, 20, 30]$ parallel flows. The most striking result is that the PIT size does not depend on the the bottleneck capacity but only on the number of parallel flows N. While Prop. 4.5 highlights the PIT size is related to the ratio $C/\Delta R$, we observe ΔR decreases proportionally with C: it follows the ratio $C/\Delta R$ remains constant for all values of C and the PIT size only depends on N. Also, the figure shows the PIT size prediction of Prop. 4.5 remains very accurate for all bottleneck capacities.

Finally, Fig.4(c) reports the PIT size at Content Router 2 with different congestion control algorithm parameters (namely Δp and β) with $N = 10$ and $C_3 = 100$ Mbps. Two main observations can be made. First, a proper setting of the congestion control parameters can reduce the PIT size while fully utilizing the available capacity. Second, the analytical model is able to correctly predict the PIT size independently from the parameters used by the congestion control algorithm.

5.3 Dynamic case

In this section we consider dynamic scenarios where the number of parallel flows (*i.e.*, file downloads) varies during the experiment. Content requests are generated at servers according to a Poisson process of rate λ and retrieve items from the content repository. Three routes are available to retrieve items from servers 1,2,3 to the repository and are identified as route 1,2,3 respectively. Requested content items belong to a fixed size catalog of 10000 items, divided in $\sigma = 15000$ Data packets each, while content popularity is Zipf distributed with shape parameter $\alpha = 0.8$. It is worth observing that as cache size is set to zero, file popularity does not influence PIT size evolution. We also disable the PIT request aggregation mechanism.

We start the analysis of the dynamic case with a single bottleneck scenario in which content requests are generated

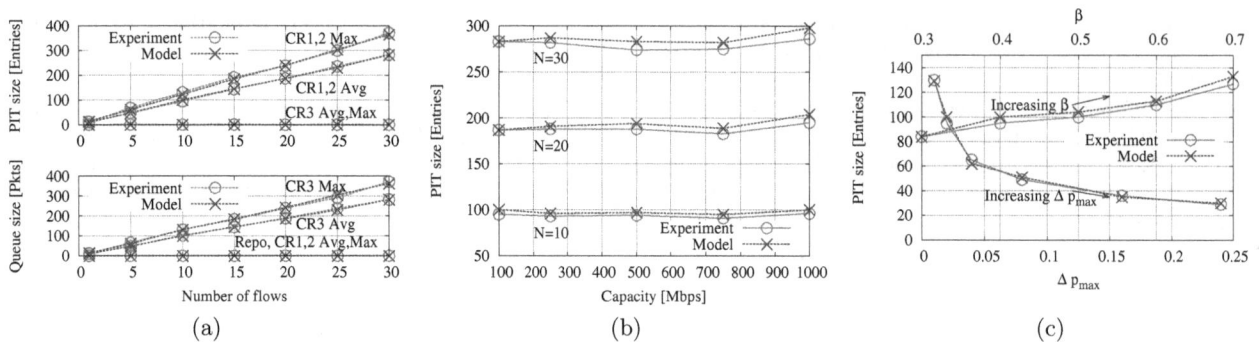

Figure 4: Static scenarios.(a) Average PIT and queue size as function of the Number of flows $N \in [1:30]$, (b) Average PIT size as function of Link capacity $C_3 \in [100:1000]$ Mbps, (c) Average PIT size as function of $p_{max} \in [0.01, 0.24]$ and $\beta \in [0.3, 0.7]$.

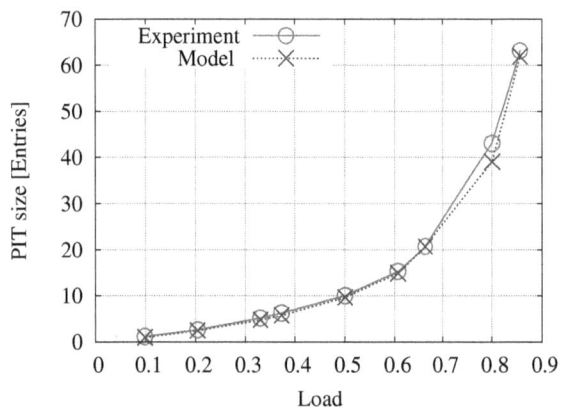

Figure 5: Dynamic scenario, single bottlenecked link: average PIT size as function of the link load $\rho \in [0.1:0.9]$.

Scenario	PIT size [Entries] / Queue size [Pkt]		
bottlenecks	π_1/Q_2	π_2/Q_3	π_3/Q_{repo}
(Link 3)	32.48/0	63.92/0	93.14/91.2
(Links 1,3)	15.69/12.1	42.61/0	78.7/75.6

Table 2: Dynamic scenario, single and multiple bottleneck links. Experimental average PIT size/queue size.

at server 1 only. We set $C_2 = 100$ Mbps, $C_1, C_3, C_{Repo} = 5$ Gbps, i.e., link 2 is the bottleneck, and we vary λ_1 in the range [0.058:0.52] downloads/second in order to vary the link load ρ_2. Fig.5 shows PIT size at Content Router 1 as a function of link load ρ_2; the analytical value is computed with Eq.17. We observe the PIT size increases with the load and the model is very accurate in predicting the measured value.

We now consider a second dynamic scenario with a single bottleneck link and multiple sets of content requests Poisson-generated by all servers according to the rate $\lambda_1 = \lambda_2 = \lambda_3 = 1.75$ requests/second. Link capacities are set to $C_1, C_2, C_3, C_{Repo} = 5$ Gbps, with link towards the Repo representing the bottleneck for all routes. Tab.2 (top row) reports the experimental average PIT size at content routers $j = 1, 2, 3$, and the average downlink queue size at content router $j = 2, 3$ and at the repository. As predicted by our

analytical model, the PIT size after the bottlenecked link π_3 is equal to the sum of the PIT entries generated by route 1,2,3 that are bottlenecked on link 3. We also observe that all packets are queued at the node before the bottleneck (i.e., at the repository), and the other queues are empty (as expected from Prop.4.2).

Finally, we consider a third scenario with two bottleneck links and requests Poisson-generated by all servers according the rates $\lambda_1 = 0.35$, $\lambda_2 = 2.63$, $\lambda_3 = 2.63$ requests/second. Link capacities are set to $C_2 = 100$ Mbps, $C_1, C_3, C_{Repo} = 5$ Gbps, with link 1 and 3 representing the bottlenecks for route 1 and route 2,3 respectively. Tab.2 (bottom row) reports the results for this scenario. Unlike the previous scenario, route 1 is bottleneck on link 1 and π_1 does not contribute to π_3. We also observe that packets following route 1 are mostly queued before its bottleneck (i.e., at CR_2), while packets following route 2,3 are queued at the repository.

5.4 ISP network case

In this section we consider a realistic scenario to show how our analytical model can be used as a tool providing useful estimations of the PIT size for different network equipments. We focus on three types of equipments: an OLT (optical line terminator) in the access network, an IP edge router in the backhaul and a backbone router interconnecting the backhaul to the transit network. These three equipments have very different user fan out, starting from a typical 1024 for an OLT for 1Gbps GPON (Gigabit Passive Optical Network) to about 50 000 for IP edge routers in backhaul ring deployments. A router interconnecting the backhaul to the transit network may achieve a user fan out around 5 millions users. The network scenario is depicted in Fig.6(a).

Using our experimental platform we reproduce the upstream link of these network elements serving two classes of users: flows belonging to the first group are bottlenecked at user access gateways, while flows belonging to the second group are bottlenecked outside the aggregation network, i.e., after the backbone router. We assume the load between the OLT and the backhaul network to be equal to $\rho = 0.65$ which is a typical maximum load in operations. The fraction of users belonging to each class is varied from 0% to 100%. The experiments are run using packet delays derived from real traces collected at an OLT of a major European ISP.

Fig.6(b) shows the model prediction and the experimental measurements of the PIT size at the three considered network elements. We observe that the size of the OLT PIT depends on the percentage of flows bottlenecked up-

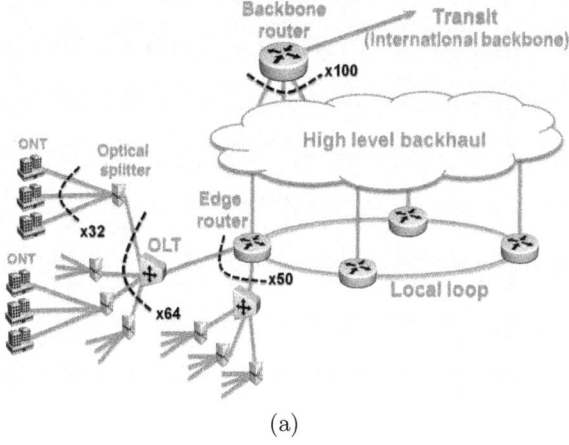

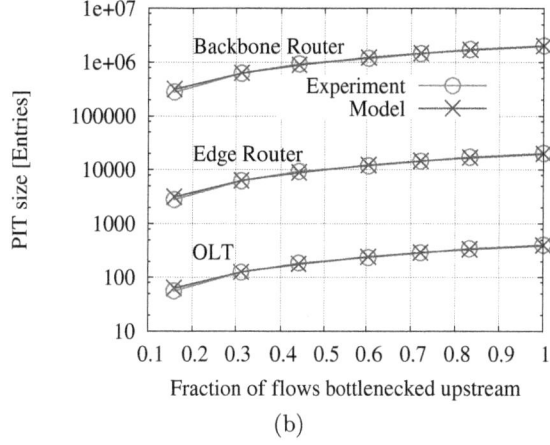

Figure 6: (a) Realistic case topology, (b) Realistic case: PIT size as a function of the percentage of upstream bottlenecked flows.

stream (e.g., peering link between a small ISP and a content provider) and remains very small (about 200 entries) when the percentage of the flows bottlenecked upstream is less than 30%. Even when all flows are bottlenecked upstream the OLT the PIT size does not exceed the 1,000 entries.

The PIT size at backbone routers does not exceed 2 millions entries even in the worst case when all traffic is bottlenecked outside the ISP network. Assuming content names of 40B on average, the memory required to store that many entries is about 400MB in our implementation: this amount of memory is available in today's platforms and allows to perform PIT operations at wire speed up to 40Gbps with current technology.

In addition, we observe that the PIT size is dramatically reduced when part of the traffic is bottlenecked within the backhaul, the access or in the home network. This is typically the case today because content servers are rarely bottlenecks, due to the massive usage of CDNs for popular web applications. On the one hand, a small portion of today's customers have access to very high speed rate fiber at 500 Mbps, capable to create congestion in the backhaul network. On the other hand, we expect user available rates to significantly increase in the following five years: (i) in wireless network thanks to the massive deployment of 4G that will replace all previous data mobile technologies;(ii) in wired access due to the growth of fiber-to-the-home especially in Europe. Finally, we observe that the PIT size at an edge router never rises feasibility issues.

6. PIT SIZING

In this section we present a simple dimensioning tool based on the 95% quantile estimation of the PIT size derived from the analysis in Sec.4. We recall that the number of entries in the PIT at node v is the aggregate sum of the number of packets in routes bottlenecked upstream node v. The number of packets queued at the bottleneck has been computed in Sec.4 and has average $\bar{Q}^3 = N\frac{\eta C \Delta R}{\beta \Delta p}$. If the parameter ΔR of the flow controller is optimally set, i.e $\Delta R = NQ_{max}/C = N\bar{Q}(1 + 1/2\sqrt{3})/C$. Hence $\bar{Q}^3 = N^2\frac{\eta C Q_{max}}{C\beta \Delta p} = N^2\frac{\eta \bar{Q}(1+1/2\sqrt{3})}{\beta \Delta p}$, where we set ΔR equal to N times the value for $N = 1$ (see Prop.4.1). By replacing ΔR

with Q_{max}/C (neglecting R_{min}) and using Prop.4.7, we get $\bar{Q}_N = N\sqrt{\frac{\eta}{\beta \Delta p}(1 + 2\sqrt{3})}$. By taking the expectation of N (Sec.5.3) we obtain an average PIT size

$$\mu = \mathbb{E}[N]\bar{Q}_1 = \mathbb{E}\left[\sum_{r=1}^{M} N_r\right]\bar{Q}_1 = \sum_{r=1}^{M} \frac{\rho_r}{1 - \rho_r}\bar{Q}_1$$

The standard deviation σ can be computed approximating the queue size distribution with a uniform random variable with range $[0, Q_{max}]$. The variance is then $\frac{Q_{max}^2}{12}$, hence

$$\sigma^2 = \mathbb{E}[N^2]\frac{Q_{max}^2}{12} = \sum_{r=1}^{M} \frac{\rho_r(1 + \rho_r)}{(1 - \rho_r)^2}\frac{\eta(1+2\sqrt{3})^3}{12^2\beta \Delta p}$$

Once mean and variance known as a function of the loads, we can use the central limit theorem to estimate the 95% percentile of the Gaussian distribution, with mean μ and variance σ^2 and set the PIT size to $\mu + \sigma z_\alpha$, with $\alpha = 0.05$ being z_α the $1 - \alpha$ quantile of the standard Gaussian distribution. Let us consider a simple case when all M routes traversing node v have the same load $\rho_r = \rho$ then

$$\mu = M\frac{\rho}{1 - \rho}\sqrt{\frac{\eta}{\beta \Delta p}(1 + 2\sqrt{3})}$$

and

$$\sigma = \mu(1 + 1/2\sqrt{3})\sqrt{1 + 1/\rho}/\sqrt{M}$$

The PIT size can be set to

$$\mu(1 + z_\alpha c_v)$$

being $c_v = (1+1/2\sqrt{3})\sqrt{1 + 1/\rho}/\sqrt{M}$ the coefficient of variation.

The estimation of the PIT size is reported in Fig.6 as a function of the load of M different routes bottlenecked upstream the node under consideration. We note that in practice it is unlikely to observe many routes bottlenecked upstream, on a backbone router for instance, because networks are operated to have bottlenecks in the user's access. A backbone router also is usually not operated above 60% load so that the PIT size would be counted in hundreds of entries or a few thousands at normal loads.

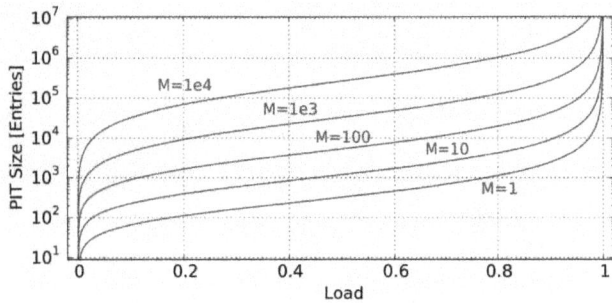

Figure 7: PIT sizing at different loads for a variable number of routes M bottlenecked upstream with respect to the considered router ($\beta = 0.4$, $\Delta p = 0.02$, $\eta = 1$).

7. CONCLUSIONS

The PIT is a key element of NDN design and its sizing is a critical factor for the feasibility of NDN deployment as a whole. In this paper we carry out, to the best of our knowledge, the first analytical investigation on PIT dynamics, deriving average and maximum stationary values. The closed-form characterization of stationary PIT size allows us to provide guidelines on optimal PIT dimensioning. We also build an experimental high speed platform allowing us to assess the accuracy of our model in presence of synthetic traffic workload and trace-driven packet delay distribution. Concerns about PIT state explosion expressed by previous works on the basis of approximate estimations are disproved by our study. We show PIT size is small in typical network settings even without in-network caching and under efficient use of network bandwidth.

In this work we have assumed clients express requests that are flow controlled by a throughput optimal congestion controller that we take from [6]. By considering controlled requesters we neglect congestion collapse scenarios or denial of service attacks that might happen in practice and should be faced by using active PIT management mechanisms (e.g. [1]). In such cases, PIT size minimization can be performed by explicit flow management at a finer-grained scale. Flow drops can be orchestrated via PIT entry removal on a per application basis and for different purposes,e.g.,admission control or overload control in a hop-by-hop fashion. Such decisions, leveraging PIT state over time may enable adaptive re-routing of flows or fast reaction to congestion phenomena by in-network congestion control. Further research is required to design and analyze such PIT management schemes.

Acknowledgments

This research work has been partially funded by the Technological Research Institute SystemX, within the project "Network Architectures" hosted at LINCS.

8. REFERENCES

[1] A. Afanasyev, P. Mahadevan, I. Moiseenko, E. Uzun, and L. Zhang. Interest flooding attack and countermeasures in named data networking. In *IFIP Networking Conference, 2013*, pages 1–9, May 2013.

[2] G. Appenzeller, I. Keslassy, and N. McKeown. Sizing Router Buffers. In *Proc. of ACM SIGCOMM*, 2004.

[3] G. Carofiglio, M. Gallo, and L. Muscariello. Joint hop-by-hop and receiver-driven interest control protocol for content-centric networks. In *proc. of ACM Sigcomm ICN workshop*.

[4] G. Carofiglio, M. Gallo, and L. Muscariello. Bandwidth and Storage Sharing Performance in Information Centric Networking. *Elsevier Science, Computer Networks Journal, Vol.57, Issue 17*, 2013.

[5] G. Carofiglio, M. Gallo, L. Muscariello, and L. Papalini. Multipath congestion control in content-centric networks. In *Proc. of IEEE INFOCOM NOMEN*, 2013.

[6] G. Carofiglio, M. Gallo, L. Muscariello, M. Papalini, and S. Wang. Optimal Multipath Congestion Control and Request Forwarding in Information-Centric Networks. In *Proc. of IEEE ICNP*, 2013.

[7] H. Dai, B. Liu, Y. Chen, and Y. Wang. On Pending Interest Table in Named Data Networking. In *Proc. of ACM ANCS 2012*.

[8] C. Hollot, V. Misra, D. Towsley, and W. Gong. Analysis and design of controllers for AQM routers supporting TCP flows. *IEEE Transactions on Automatic Control*, 47(6):945 –959, 2002.

[9] V. Jacobson, D. Smetters, J. Thornton, and al. Networking named content. In *Proc. of ACM CoNEXT*, 2009.

[10] A. Kortebi, L. Muscariello, S. Oueslati, and J. Roberts. Evaluating the Number of Active Flows in a Scheduler Realizing Fair Statistical Bandwidth Sharing. In *Proc. of ACM SIGMETRICS*, 2005.

[11] Z. Li, J. Bi, S. Wang, and X. Jiang. Compression of Pending Interest Table with Bloom Filter in Content Centric Network. In *Proc. of ACM CFI 2012*, Seoul, Korea.

[12] C. Tsilopoulos, G. Xylomenos, and Y. Thomas. Reducing Forwarding State in Content-Centric Networks with Semi-Stateless Forwarding. In *Proc. of IEEE INFOCOM*, 2014.

[13] M. Varvello, D. Perino, and L. Linguaglossa. On the Design and Implementation of a wire-speed Pending Interest Table. In *Proc. of IEEE INFOCOM NOMEN workshop*, 2013.

[14] M. Wählisch, T. C. Schmidt, and M. Vahlenkamp. Backscatter from the Data Plane – Threats to Stability and Security in Information-Centric Network Infrastructure. *Computer Networks Journal*, Nov. 2013.

[15] K. Wang, J. Chen, H. Zhou, Y. Qin, and H. Zhang. Modeling denial-of-service against pending interest table in named data networking. *International Journal of Communication Systems*, 2013.

[16] W. You, B. Mathieu, P. Truong, J. Peltier, and G. Simon. DiPIT: A Distributed Bloom-Filter Based PIT Table for CCN Nodes. In *Proc. of IEEE ICCCN*, 2012.

[17] H. Yuan and P. Crowley. Scalable Pending Interest Table Design: From Principles to Practice. In *Proc. of IEEE INFOCOM*, 2014.

[18] L. Zhang and al. Named Data Networking (NDN) Project, 2010. http://named-data.net/ndn-proj.pdf.

Hierarchical Content Stores in High-speed ICN Routers: Emulation and Prototype Implementation

Rodrigo B. Mansilha
INF/UFRGS &
Telecom ParisTech
Porto Alegre, Brazil
rbmansilha@inf.ufrgs.br

Lorenzo Saino
University College London
London, UK
l.saino@ucl.ac.uk

Marinho P. Barcellos
INF/UFRGS
Porto Alegre, Brazil
marinho@inf.ufrgs.br

Massimo Gallo
Bell Labs, Alcatel-Lucent
Nozay, France
massimo.gallo@alcatel-
lucent.com

Emilio Leonardi
Politecnico di Torino
Torino, Italy
emilio.leonardi@tlc.polito.it

Diego Perino
Bell Labs, Alcatel-Lucent
Nozay, France
diego.perino@alcatel-
lucent.com

Dario Rossi
Telecom ParisTech
Paris, France
dario.rossi@telecom-
paristech.fr

ABSTRACT

Recent work motivates the design of Information-centric routers that make use of hierarchies of memory to jointly scale in the size and speed of content stores. The present paper advances this understanding by (i) instantiating a general purpose two-layer packet-level caching system, (ii) investigating the solution design space via emulation, and (iii) introducing a proof-of-concept prototype. The emulation-based study reveals insights about the broad design space, the expected impact of workload, and gains due to multi-threaded execution. The full-blown system prototype experimentally confirms that, by exploiting both DRAM and SSD memory technologies, ICN routers can sustain cache operations in excess of 10Gbps running on off-the-shelf hardware.

Categories and Subject Descriptors

C.2.1 [**Network Architecture and Design**]: Network communications, Packet-switching networks

General Terms

System Design; Emulation; Prototype

Keywords

Information centric router; Hierarchical content store

1. INTRODUCTION

The success of the ICN paradigm heavily depends on the ability of equipping routers with large caches [8] able to operate at line speed [3]. However, given the technological limits of current off-the-shelf memory technologies, it is difficult to satisfy both requirements together. On one hand, memory technologies that are suitable to meet line-speed constraints of ICN routers are relatively costly and have limited size; for example, DRAM technologies achieve access latencies of $O(10ns)$ with $O(10GB)$ per bank and $O(10\,USD/GB)$ price. On the other, technologies that are appealing due to their large size and low price cannot achieve the speeds required for line-rate operation; this is the case of SSD technologies, with $O(1TB)$ size and $O(1USD/GB)$ price, but unfortunately access latency of $O(10\mu s)$. As a result, the maximum memory size that can sustain a data rate of 10 Gbps is estimated to be around 10 GB [3, 15].

Yet, our previous work [18] proposes a novel scheme for the management of a Hierarchical Content Store (HCS) that bypasses the above limit by exploiting a peculiarity of the request arrival pattern in ICN. Specifically, there is an intrinsic correlation among requests for chunks of the same content, as the arrival of a request for a given chunk can be used as a predictor of future requests for subsequent chunks of the same content. In turn, this correlation can be exploited by proactively moving *batches of chunks* (to be requested) from a large but slow cache such as SSD to a fast but small memory swap area such as DRAM. Batching memory transfer operations is crucial to move the HCS system from an operational point whose the bottleneck is the SSD *memory access time* (as it would be accessing individual chunks) to an operational point whose bottleneck is the SSD *external data rate* – gaining over an order of magnitude in terms of data-rate scalability [18].

In this paper we make a significant step forward with respect to [18], providing an emulation-based study to assess the practical feasibility of an HCS system and to guide its design, as well as a prototype implementation and benchmarking, both using off-the-shelf hardware. To summarize our main contributions: (i) we perform an independent assessment of the NDN Forwarding Daemon (NFD) performance, paying special attention to its content store and forwarder modules, and modify NFD to support hierarchical operations (NFD-HCS); (ii) limitedly considering the content store operations, we use NFD-HCS to conduct a broad investigation of the design space (including parallel vs serial modes of operation, hyper-threading vs OS scheduler in

ICN'15, September 30–October 2, 2015, San Francisco, CA, USA.
© 2015 ACM. ISBN 978-1-4503-3855-4/15/09 ...$15.00.
DOI: http://dx.doi.org/10.1145/2810156.2810159.

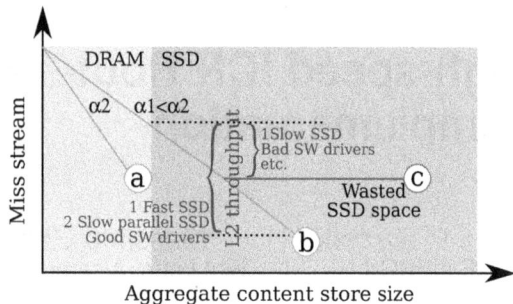

Figure 1: Expected performance of the multi-threaded HCS

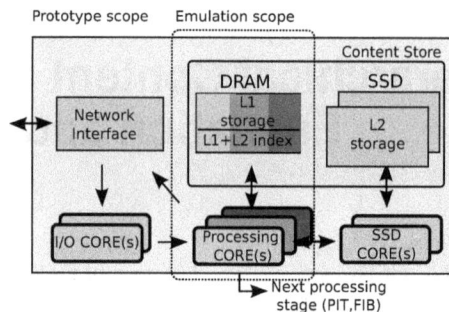

Figure 2: Synoptic of HCS system design

multi-threading, etc.) and a sensitivity analysis of our results along multiple axes (including L1 size, L2 data rate speed, input workload type, hardware setup, etc.) by emulating NIC and SSD technologies; (iii) we implement a high-speed prototype (DPDK-HCS) considering all necessary aspects that were in part abstracted in the emulation-based study (i.e., packet processing in DPDK, software load balancing across cores, SSD management with specialized drivers, and memory management for efficient lookups); (iv) we benchmark the DPDK-HCS prototype, equipped with O(10GB) DRAM and O(100GB) SSD, against a realistic traffic pattern, achieving in excess of 10 Gbps throughput.

In the remainder of this paper, we first clarify our overall goals and position our investigation in the context of related work (Sec. 2). Next, we describe the emulation setup (Sec. 3) and the results it provided (Sec. 4), followed by a description of the prototype design (Sec. 5) and its benchmarking (Sec. 6). We conclude with a summary of key findings and perspectives for future work (Sec. 7).

2. HCS OVERVIEW

In order to enable hierarchical caching in high-speed ICN routers, we first introduce our main performance goals (Sec. 2.1), then overview our design (Sec. 2.2) and contrast it to related effort (Sec. 2.3).

2.1 Performance goal

According to the analysis in [18], expected system performance can be sketched as in Fig. 1. Assuming the router receives requests at full line rate, the picture shows the miss stream (y-axis) as a function of the overall cache memory size (x-axis). Clearly, the larger the portion of catalog that fits the router memory, the lower the request miss stream exiting the router. Fig. 1 highlights regions corresponding to different memory technologies (i.e., DRAM, SSD), and the slope of the curve depends on the workload (i.e., the catalog size $|C|$ and Zipf skew α). L1 misses causes a stream of request to L2 and, for any given aggregate memory size (i.e., DRAM + SSD), the system works at the expected operational point (i.e., follows the slope) until the miss stream from L1 to L2 exceeds the aggregated data rate of the physical L2 units. Read throughput from L2 depends linearly on the hit probability at L2, so increasing the storage space in L2 also increases the throughput demand from L2: this holds up to a point at which the system is bottlenecked by L2 throughput, and where increasing further the SSD size brings no benefits, as it is not possible to read content at the requested speed. Thus, operating at points such as ⓐ or ⓑ

is desirable, while situations such as ⓒ are to be avoided. Yet, the transfer rate between L2 and L1 does not only depend on the physical properties (e.g., L2 external data rate, PCIx bus speed, use of multiple physical SSDs in parallel), but also to software aspects (e.g., SSD driver and memory management) for which is not straightforward to design an HCS system that avoid operating at ⓒ.

2.2 System Design

A high level view of the system we propose is provided in Fig. 2. When a packet arrives to the router, it is handled by a pipeline of cores (or threads) performing respectively packet I/O, packet processing and SSD I/O. For the sake of simplicity, we neglect the NDN packet forwarding stage (e.g., PIT and FIB lookup operations) and focus on hierarchical content store only.

Packet batches are dispatched from NICs to I/O cores, whose main task is to distribute batches to processing cores according to the hash value of a *batch identifier* – ensuring that chunks of a specific batch are always handled by the same processing core, and enabling therefore lock-free multi-thread operations.

Afterwards, batches are handled by the corresponding processing core that returns a data packet if it is stored in the L1 content store. Otherwise, if the requested data is cached in L2, the request is handed over to an SSD I/O core. The rationale for the separation between DRAM (processing) and SSD cores is to deal with different memory access latencies and avoid starvation. Multiple SSD drives can be used to perform parallel data read/write operations to improve SSD throughput. Finally, if the data is not cached locally, the request is further processed by the router (i.e., PIT and FIB lookup) and forwarded to the next hop.

HCS performance is affected by many factors, including physical hardware components or software bottlenecks, that we investigate in two ways. First, we use emulation to broadly explore the software design space of the processing operations without being restricted by a specific hardware choice. Then, we nail down all details including NIC and SSD management, to a specific software prototype, running on a specific off-the-shelf hardware setup.

2.3 State of the art

A number of custom NIC drivers have been recently proposed to bypass standard OS bottlenecks and support 10Gbps operations. Examples include PF_RING with Threaded NAPI [7], Netmap [17], PacketShader [9], and DPDK [1]. Keys to achieve such performance include limiting IRQs overhead by avoiding per-packet operations (e.g.

interrupt coalescence), exposing memory of packet buffers to user-space for DMA access with zero-copy, load balancing flows among threads using different Receive Side Scaling (RSS) queues and exploiting Non-Uniform Memory Access (NUMA).

The kind of applications enabled by such drivers is rather diverse and include IPv4 forwarding [9], on-the-fly traffic classification [19], intrusion detection [11] and traffic monitoring [13]. With respect to the narrower domain of ICN, so far only *high-speed forwarding* has been investigated, with valuable work focusing on their design [3, 15] or prototype implementation [21, 16, 10].

To the best of our knowledge, *high-speed content store* implementations are yet to appear. The closest work to ours includes our own previous design, analysis and simulation of a hierarchical content store [18], and the micro-benchmarking of SSD technologies to assess their suitability for the purpose [20]. The present paper goes beyond both [18, 20] by (i) employing complementary methodologies to [18], namely emulation and prototypes; (ii) carrying out an extensive emulation of the design space using open-source software; (iii) presenting a complete system implementation over DPDK, as opposite to a benchmark of a specific component as in [20].

3. EMULATION DESIGN

This section presents the emulation-based methodology, starting with an overview of the emulation design principles (Sec. 3.1), followed by details of the scenario and workload (Sec. 3.2).

3.1 NFD-HCS Design principles

Our emulation study is based on off-the-shelf hardware and open-source software, namely NDN Forwarding Daemon (NFD) [2], that we modify to support HCS operation. For the sake of simplicity, NFD-HCS performs only the main operations on L1 and L2 similarly to what described in [18]. To begin with, we avoid optimizations such as prefetching immediately before a batch eviction, or keeping in L1 the first chunk of all contents in L2 to avoid the first miss. Second, the reading method of NFD-HCS is serial: it first attempts to read a chunk from L1. On a hit, the corresponding data is returned; otherwise, a batch is read from L2 and each chunk of the batch is written on L1. After the L2→L1 transfer, the data corresponding to the immediate request is returned (while a serial design may seem naïve at first, we discuss parallel design in Sec. 4.3).

NFD-HCS implements the two memory layers and their operations (i.e., $L1.lookup$, $L1.insert$, $L2.read$). The L1 of HCS is instantiated as an NFD Content Store (CS) and employs a FIFO chunk eviction policy[1]. From the literature, similarities of LRU vs random [6] and equivalence of FIFO vs random [14] replacement are known: thus, we do not expect this detail to have a dramatic importance and leave implementation of other replacement policies for future.

Whereas all the required *software* operations are performed as in a real hierarchical system, to avoid gathering results that are representative of very specific NIC and memory technologies we emulate the NIC as well as L2 *hardware and drivers*. As several NIC drivers [17, 9, 1] offer line-speed operation in user space, we assume the delay due to packet

---

[1]More precisely, CS employs a prioritized FIFO, composed of multiple eviction queues; however, in this study we force all chunks go through the same FIFO queue.

Table 1: Emulation settings

	Meaning	Param	Range
Software	Batch Size	B	10 chunks
	L1 Size	$|L1|$	[100MB-10GB]
	L2 Size	$|L2|$	10 GB
	L2 Throughput	τ_{L2}	[1,32] Gbps
	Chunk size	$|c|$	8KB

	Label	Param	Value
Hardware	Local	CPU	1.90 GHz Intel E52420
		NUMA	1 node, 6 cores
		RAM	32GB - 1333 MHz (0.8 ns)
		Opts.	CPU Gov., Hyper-threading
	Cloud	CPU	2.00 GHz Intel E52698B
	(Microsoft	NUMA	1 node, 8 cores
	Azure G3)	RAM	112GB (speed unknown)
		Opts.	None

	Meaning	Param	Value
Real workload	Catalog size	$|C|$	(up to) 10^3 objects
	Request arrival rate	λ	1 Hz
	Zipf skew	α	1
	Streaming rate		512 Kbps (8 chunks/s)
	Streaming duration		160 seconds
	Stream size		10.25 MB (1,280 chunks)

processing in the NIC to be negligible. We also assume the NIC is capable of performing hash operations on non-IP header fields, so that batches are consistently mapped to cores to preserve catalog locality and enable lock-free multi-threading.

L2 instead emulates a slower memory technology (e.g. SSD) by waiting some time before returning the data. This is performed through *busy waiting*[2], which consumes CPU cycles useful for other HCS operations but enables more precise emulation. We point out that, aside the waiting detail, L2 in NFD-HCS is fully functional so that NFD-HCS could be used for experiments and not only for emulation. This implies that both L1 and L2 store actual data on the main DRAM memory, which limits the size of L2 we can benchmark (implications and alternatives design will be discussed later in Sec. 4 and Sec. 7 respectively).

3.2 Emulation scenario

We now describe the most relevant details of our software, hardware and workload setup. For the sake of readability, we summarize these settings in Tab. 1.

3.2.1 Software settings

NFD-HCS has four parameters: batch size, L1 and L2 size and L2 throughput. Batch size[3] B defines the amount of data transferred from L2 to L1 per $L2.read$ operation, whereas $|L1|$ and $|L2|$ refer to the memory space available at layers 1 and 2, respectively. The L2 throughput τ_{L2} is our L2 control knob, lumping together the speed of individual disks, the number of multiple disks in parallel, the SSD drivers, static delay components, etc. from which we gather the duration of the active sleep $d_{L2.read}$ for a batch of B chunks having fixed size $|c|$ as $d_{L2.read} = Bc/\tau_{L2}$.

In this work, we explore aggregated rates in the range $\tau_{L2} \in [1,32]$ Gbps, modeling respectively a single slow SDD to several faster SDDs in parallel[4] and by default use $\tau_{L2} =$

---

[2]i.e., running an idle loop of a given size, which we have carefully dimensioned.

[3]We interchangeably express size in terms of chunks, bytes, or bits depending on the context.

[4]It can be expected that a linear scaling will hold up to a point after which an expected (e.g., PCIx bus capacity, disk

4 Gbps, close to the nominal one of the SSDs used in proto-type. Notice that our L2 emulation model fails to capture the impact of the batch size in the emulation, so that we do not consider it as a free variable and perform a micro-benchmark of its effect with the prototype (Sec. 6).

3.2.2 Hardware settings

We use two different hardware platforms in the emulation study, as follows. One is a local host, which offers a fully controlled environment and has the advantage of allowing options and parameters such as hyper-threading to be adjusted and evaluated. On the other hand, its computing power and memory are somewhat limited. The second platform is a VM hosted at a powerful public cloud server. Because it is a public cloud, experiments run on shared resources and are subject to interference. However, statistically valid results can be extracted from multiple runs and reproduced by other researchers with access to the same cloud. We use the same software set in both machines: namely, Linux Ubuntu 12.04 LTS, NFD package v0.3.1, ndn-cxx library v0.3.1, and Boost Libraries v1.54.

3.2.3 Workload settings

We consider sequential (*seq*), random uniform (*unif*), and realistic (*real*) workloads. The *seq* and *unif* workloads are included as best-case and worst-case references: in the former, each chunk of each content is requested sequentially whereas in the latter, chunks are randomly chosen with a uniform probability. In the *real* workload, which is instead included to yield expected performance in the typical usage, requests for the first chunk of a new object with Zipf popularity of shape α arrive according to a Poisson process of rate λ, after which requests for subsequent chunks are subject to the streaming rate constraint and are periodically spaced (i.e., no interest shaping nor congestion control). The length of the generated sequence includes a warm-up period to pre-fill the content store (hot start), and the catalog size $|C|$ varies across scenarios: purposely, to gather NFD performance that only depends on content store data structures, but not on other structures such as PIT and FIB (due to miss-stream lookups), we cap the catalog size to L2 size, to avoid raising miss events.

4. EMULATION RESULTS

This section is organized as follows. We start by presenting a baseline evaluation of NFD (Sec. 4.1). We then compare a single-core NFD-HCS emulation results with the expected performance of simple analytical models to validate our methodology and assess the performance of multi-core NFD-HCS (Sec. 4.2). We finally present a sensitivity analysis of our results with respect to software design choices and hardware characteristics (Sec. 4.3). All experimental results are collected from five runs with different random seeds and are shown with 95% confidence interval (Students t-distribution with 4 degrees of freedom).

4.1 Baseline NFD performance

We gather baseline single-threaded NFD performance for both (i) the forwarding engine (FWD) and (ii) the single-layer content store (CS). Aiming at getting an upper-bound of NFD performance, we engineer the scenarios such that

controller) or unexpected bottleneck (e.g., software CPU, OS scheduler) will kick in yielding to sublinear gains.

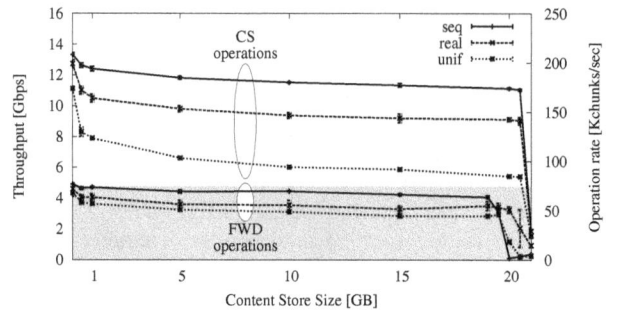

Figure 3: NFD Microbenchmark: Forwarding and Content store Throughput

contents always fit entirely in the router memory. We evaluate different catalog sizes 10MB (that in principle fits the CPU cache), 100MB (that no longer fits the CPU cache), and 1GB, 2GB, 3GB...32GB (all within DRAM memory capacity). By capping the catalog size, we can focus on performance of core NFD operations involving CS (such as name lookup, CS access for data, etc.) avoiding to emulate other operations that CS misses would forcibly imply (such as generating interests packets, PIT management, FIB lookup, etc.).

To separate FWD from CS operations, we develop microbenchmark NFD modules that include only the relevant functionalities. The throughput of these modules, expressed in terms of Gbps as well as the number of chunks operations per second, is reported in Fig. 3. Two families of curves are shown: the bottom ones correspond to FWD operations, whereas the upper ones, to CS operations. Comparison between the families shows FWD operations to be the fundamental bottleneck in these scenarios: hence, as long as any re-engineering of NFD does not slow down CS operations below the FWD bottleneck (shaded region), then we can expect these changes to be transparent to the current NFD implementation.

Next, notice that for all curves performance is tri-modal (particularly visible in the CS family): (i) when the catalog fits the cache, CS throughput is especially high, then (ii) throughput exhibits a large plateau in the range 1-20GB, stabilizing to values that depend on the workload, after which (iii) throughput drops, as a consequence of memory management from the OS (part of the CS is then stored on disks, increasing the number of page faults and decreasing the CPU usage).

The throughput plateau demonstrates that single level memory can scale well up to the intrinsic DRAM limit. At the same time, it also shows that native OS memory management can move the bottleneck from CPU to IO even for relatively small CS sizes, making the system potentially unstable and showing the interest of a hierarchical solution as the one investigated here.

Finally, another important observation is that statistical properties of request process have a significant impact on throughput. The consistent difference between the three curves in each family confirms our choice of sequential and uniform access patterns as the best and the worst cases, respectively. Due to space constraints, and as we expect average system performance to be more important, we avoid reporting a detailed explanation (tied, e.g., to the lookahead policy of DRAM memories).

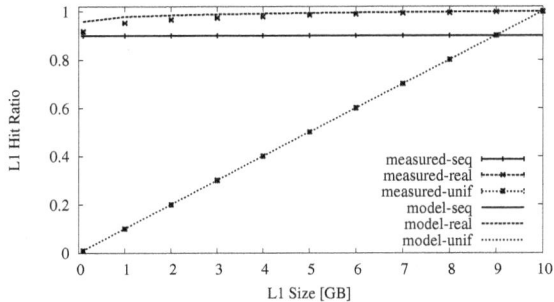

Figure 4: HCS hit ratio: comparison of analytic and HCS-NFD emulation results at L1

4.2 NFD-HCS Performance

Turning our attention to the two-layer CS architecture, we begin by contrasting NFD-HCS results with the expectation of simple analytical models: the purpose is to proceed in steps, validating our emulation methodology before assessing the performance of a more complex multi-threaded system, were we will no longer be able to model software and hardware dependencies.

4.2.1 Validating Emulation via Analytical Modeling

Intuitively, the hit ratio on L1 has a fundamental impact on the hierarchical memory performance, as the L2 request rate depends on the miss stream at L1. Hence, we start our analysis by modeling the L1 hit probability for the different workloads. For the uniform request model, the hit probability necessarily equals the fraction of the catalog that is stored in the L1 cache, independently from the identity of contents which are stored in the cache:

$$\mathbb{E}[P_{\text{uni}}] = |\text{L1}|/|C| \qquad (1)$$

where $|\text{L1}|$ and $|C|$ are the size of the L1 cache and catalog, respectively. Under the sequential request model, the request associated to the first chunk within every batch yields a cache miss while, due to prefetching, the remaining chunks of the batch yield a hit. Denoting by B the batch-size we have:

$$\mathbb{E}[P_{\text{seq}}] = 1 - 1/B \qquad (2)$$

Under a realistic request process with Poisson arrivals of Zipf-popular content, the first chunk of batch i is found in L1 from the arriving request with a probability $P_{\text{real},i}^{1st}$ while all the other chunks within the batch are found in L1 w.h.p as for the previous case, thus:

$$\mathbb{E}[P_{\text{real},i}] = \frac{P_{\text{real},i}^{1st}}{B} + \left(1 - \frac{1}{B}\right) \qquad (3)$$

The value of $P_{\text{real},i}^{1st}$ can be estimated numerically using a recently proposed extension of Che's approximation for FIFO caches [4, 14],

$$P_{\text{real}}^{1st} = \sum_k \frac{\lambda_k^2 t_c}{1 + \lambda_k t_c} \qquad (4)$$

with t_c the only solution of

$$\sum_k \frac{\lambda_k t_c}{1 + \lambda_k t_c} = |\text{L1}| \qquad (5)$$

where $|\text{L1}|$ is the cache size expressed in chunks.

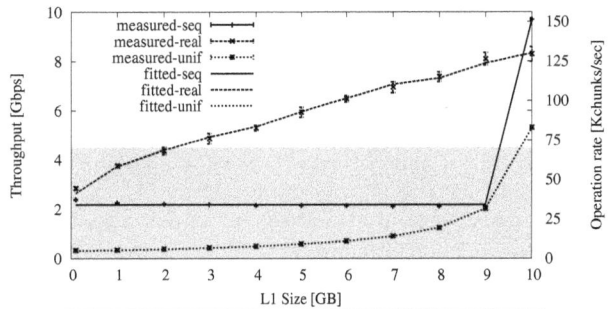

Fitting	*real* sequence	Asymptotic error
$d_{\text{L1.lookup}}$	$7.4 \pm 0.06\ \mu s$	0.9%
$d_{\text{L1.insert}}$	$42.1 \pm 5.31\ \mu s$	12.6%

Figure 5: HCS throughput: emulation results and fitted model

In the experiments, we configure the system with a fixed batch size B=10 chunks, fix the L2 size to 10GB and L2 throughput to 4Gbps, vary L1 size in the 100MB-10GB range, and generating requests for $O(10^7)$ chunks (including warmup). It is worth stressing that, for the sake of simplicity, we consider that the whole catalog can fit the L2 size, so that in the best case, all content can fit in the NFD-HCS router memory. While clearly this would not make sense so as to gather performance in a realistic scenario, it nevertheless allows us to validate the soundness of our experimental methodology against expected results from well understood and accurate models [6]. Specifically, in Fig. 4 the superposition between each of the three measurement-based curves and their corresponding model-based ones indicates clearly the accuracy of the prediction for L1 hit ratio.

4.2.2 Inferring software bottlenecks

While L2 delays are known (as we emulate them with active sleep) and information concerning L1 memory read/write times is available from data sheets, the software overhead of managing L1 CS in NFD (i.e., the times $d_{\text{L1.lookup}}$, $d_{\text{L1.insert}}$ needed to perform lookup and insert operations in the SkipList data structure) is harder to determine. Unfortunately, instrumenting the NFD code to measure these delays would provide biased results, since clock precisions do not allow accurate timestamping of an individual operation and would likely alter performance. A more promising direction is to infer this temporal variables from a model of HCS system performance:

$$\mathbb{E}[Throughput] = |c|/\mathbb{E}[d] \qquad (6)$$

where $|c|$ is the chunk size and $\mathbb{E}[d]$ the average chunk service time, that can be expressed as:

$$\mathbb{E}[d] = P_{\text{hit}} d_{\text{hit}} + (1 - P_{\text{hit}}) d_{\text{miss}} \qquad (7)$$

where P_{hit} is computed as either (1), (2), or (3), whereas the hit/miss delays account for the different CS operations performed by NFD-HCS. Specifically, for a L1 hit, the service time equals the time needed to access a chunk in L1 (i.e., find a pointer to the content in L1 and access the memory location):

$$d_{\text{hit}} = d_{\text{L1.lookup}} + d_{\text{L1.read}} \approx d_{\text{L1.lookup}} \qquad (8)$$

Upon a L1 miss, the delay in accessing a chunk stored in L2 is given in our implementation by the sum of three terms: a first term $d_{\text{L1.lookup}}$ modeling the time needed to recognize that the content is not in L1, a second term $d_{L2.read}$ to read the content from L2, and a last component $d_{L1.insert}$ to insert the whole batch in L1:

$$d_{miss} = d_{L1.lookup} + d_{L2.read} + d_{L1.insert} \quad (9)$$

By fitting our experimental results (i.e., hit probabilities and throughput) we can infer estimates of $d_{L1.lookup}$ and $d_{L1.insert}$. Fitting results are shown in Fig. 5 and additionally tabulated for the *real* sequence, from which we gather small asymptotic errors (especially for $d_{L1.lookup}$). Several remarks are worth stressing. First, the L1 size slightly above 2GB does not constitute a bottleneck for NFD operations, as the throughput is higher than that of the forwarding module (shaded region reported as a reference). Second, SkipList per-chunk insert and lookup operation have both logarithmic cost: yet, the fitting suggests that inserting *consecutives* chunks of a batch may bring some gain in terms of memory management (as the memory lines prefetched for the insertion of the first chunk are useful for subsequent chunks of the batch). Finally, notice that the lookup duration L1.lookup is $O(10\mu s)$ and would not allow to sustain $O(10Gbps)$ operation: i.e., L1 memory management overhead is about 3 orders of magnitude larger than the DRAM access time of $O(10ns)$. This confirms that CS indexing on an off-the-shelf architecture can become a software bottleneck as well [15]: yet this is not a problem since, while a single-threaded engine would not be able to sustain a 10Gbps throughput, our system design (both emulation and prototype) involves a multi-threading paradigm to avoid software performance bottleneck, which we examine next.

4.2.3 Multi-threaded HCS Performance

We now carry on an emulation based study of multi-threaded HCS throughput. In a nutshell, lock-free operations are achieved by partitioning the contents requests among different threads each of which manages an isolated CS: as CS are isolated, they can run in parallel without requiring synchronized access. In the emulation study, for the sake of simplicity we employ a modulo operation on the *content name* (sub-optimal as all chunks of the same content are directed to the same core, which yields to load imbalance for the core handling the most popular requests; we instead avoid such imbalance in the prototype by considering the *batch name*).

We investigate if this simple strategy can scale up the HCS performance: to this end, we setup the system with $|L1|$=1GB, $|L2|$=10GB, τ_{L2}={4, 32}Gbps and observe the system throughput for the realistic workload for a different degree of parallelism. As we cannot emulate shared access to a single L2 device in a non-blocking multi-threaded fashion, notice that we are implicitly assuming here that (i) each thread accesses a physically separate L2, (ii) the aggregate throughput toward all L2 memories is lower than the PCIx-3 bus capacity of 64Gbps. We also vary the hyper-threading (HT) option: basically, when HT is enabled the Operating System (OS) is offered a number of logical cores which is exactly the double of the number of physically available CPU cores, each of which is running at half the frequency. Grossly, we may say that HT lets either the CPU or the OS manage the scheduling among threads.

Several interesting remarks can be gathered from Fig. 6. First, multi-threading exhibits gains regardless of the physical properties of the system (i.e., L2 throughput), although the effect of increasing the number of threads is more bene-

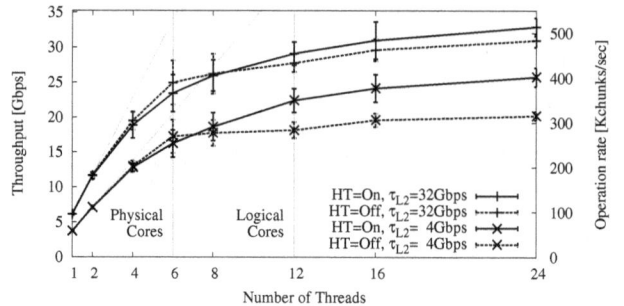

Figure 6: Performance of a multi-threaded HCS for varying number of threads, L2 throughput, and Hyper-threading settings

ficial for systems with large L2 throughput. Second, hyper-threading exhibits larger gains with respect to OS scheduling, and should therefore be enabled by default. Finally, note that multi-threading quickly exhibits diminishing returns, with a logarithmic scaling in the number of threads (the picture is also annotated with linear slopes, interpolating the point with 1 and 2 threads for reference). Further, there is a knee in the curve, where the number of threads exceeds the number of cores, which is especially visible in the most constrained system with HT=Off, and τ_{L2}=4Gbps.

Yet, it is interesting that the gains shown in Fig. 6 do not completely flatten out even when the number of threads significantly exceeds the number of logical cores. This can be explained as follows: (i) increasing the number of threads not only reduces the per-thread CPU operation workload, but also increases the aggregated L2 bandwidth, removing hardware bottlenecks; (ii) by splitting workload into smaller tasks, the difference between the most and the least loaded threads becomes smaller, reducing software bottlenecks. Additionally notice that, while the aggregated system throughput does not exceed PCIx-3 bus speed (so that our former assumption holds), the performance of the actual system may exhibit additional correlation (e.g., among multiple SSD disks). This can lead to sub-linear performance, below the expectation for the actual system.

Nevertheless, the emulation provides optimistic upper bounds of the system performance, as follows. We ignore the overhead associated to some operations, such as fetching incoming packets from the NIC, and forwarding outgoing packets to the NIC. Further, we do not consider the limits of L2 technologies, e.g. efficient driver access to SSD or dependency among reads from parallel SSDs. Yet these correlations are hard to model, so that they fall beyond the scope of the emulation methodology and enter the prototype realm, which we describe and benchmark in later sections (Sec. 5-6).

4.3 Sensitivity analysis

Before turning our attention to the prototype, we finally verify the results outlined in the previous sections to be robust against (i) software design choices (e.g., parallel vs serial execution), as well as (ii) hardware properties (e.g., L2 throughput and PC hardware).

4.3.1 Software: Design space

We first consider a single thread case and assess whether alternative designs to the serial algorithm are worth. All

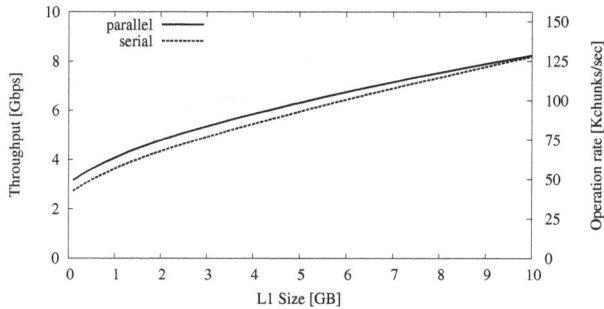

Figure 7: Analytical comparision between fully-serial vs fully-parallel design (realistic workload)

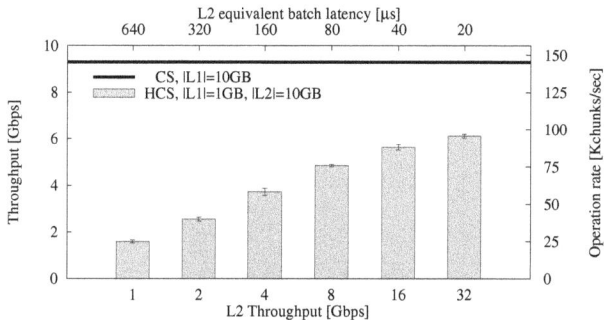

Figure 8: Impact of L2 throughput on the HCS throughput (single-threaded system)

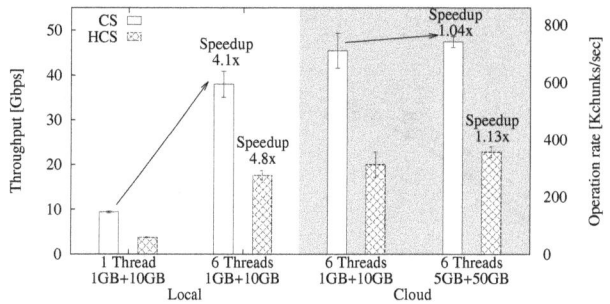

Figure 9: CS and HCS throughput measured on two different off-the-shelf servers: Thread and Memory scalability

possible combination of implementations are comprised between a fully serial and a fully parallel implementation of the key operations ($L1.lookup$, $L1.insert$, $L2.read$). In case of L1 hit, the delay d_{hit} is the same for the both serial and parallel implementation. In case of L1 miss, the delay depends on the design choices: in the fully sequential case, the delay d_{miss}^{ser} is given by (9), wheres in a fully parallel design, the delay is the maximum among:

$$d_{miss}^{par} = Max(d_{L1.lookup}, d_{L1.insert}, d_{L2.read}) \quad (10)$$

Whereas the fully parallel design is likely not feasible in practice, it represents an upper-bound of the gains that can be achieved by ameliorating our simple NFD-HCS implementation. Fig. 7 contrasts modeling results for the sequential vs parallel designs: from the plot, it emerges that, given technological limits for which a single component dominates the others, namely $d_{miss}^{par} \approx d_{miss}^{ser} \approx d_{L2.read}$, the actual gain of a parallel implementation is marginal (the maximum theoretic gain of 2/3 could be achieved when the three components are equal, so that technology evolution may force to re-evaluate this issue at a finer grain).

4.3.2 Hardware: L2 Throughput

We now discuss the impact of hardware limits, such as L2 throughput, on the HCS performance. For the sake of the example, we consider a single-threaded system and fix $|L1|$=1GB, $|L2|$=10GB, B=10 chunks, and depict results in Fig. 8, that reports the throughput of a single-layer CS with $|L1|$=10GB for reference purposes. Two observations are in order. First, given the x-axis logscale, a linear slope testifies a logarithmic return for the system throughput as a function of L2 throughput. Second, HCS approaches, without how-

ever reaching, performance of a single-layer CS of equal size. These trends are likely due to software bottlenecks tied to the additional overhead of handling a second memory layer.

4.3.3 Hardware: Off-the-shelf PCs

We finally check scalability and consistency of our results over different off-the-shelf PCs (recalling Tab. 1, both machines have close specs), considering both CS and NFD-HCS performance. We consider a multi-threaded system with 6 threads and run the realistic workload over six threads in parallel for both CS ($|L1|$=1GB) and HCS ($|L1|+|L2|$ =1GB+10GB, τ_{L2}=4Gbps and B=10 chunks) and since we not fully control the cloud machine, we disable Hyper-threading in this experiment. In the local PC, we assess multi-threading speed-up comparing with a single threaded system. In the cloud server, we additionally test memory scalability with $|L1|+|L2|$=5GB+50GB) where we expect only a slight speedup due to larger L1 but no penalty due to larger L2. Performance is reported in Fig. 9: notice that both multi-threaded systems yield remarkably close performance, thus highlighting (i) emulation results are not biased and (ii) confirming memory and threading scalability of HCS.

5. PROTOTYPE IMPLEMENTATION

The emulation study presented above provides insights for HCS design, but neglects some critical implementation aspects related to fast packet I/O, memory management and constraints of Flash technology. This section illustrates such challenges, discussing the design principles that our DPDK-HCS prototype implementation follows to effectively address them.

NIC. First, it is widely recognized that Linux kernel's packet processing is not efficient and cannot achieve wire-speed [5, 9, 17]. To overcome this issue, we build our prototype leveraging the Intel DPDK packet processing framework [1]. DPDK enables zero-copy packet processing directly at the userspace by efficiently transferring data from/to the NICs bypassing the kernel and using Direct Memory Access (DMA) to reduce CPU utilization.

Multi-threading. Under a traffic load of O(10Gbps), effective multi-thread (or multi-process) application design is crucial to avoid software bottlenecks [19]. While the emulation study considers lock-free multi-threaded design, it however neglects Non Uniform Memory Access (NUMA) ca-

65

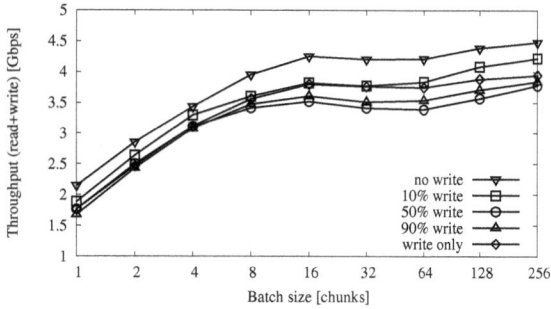

(a) Throghput vs read/write mix

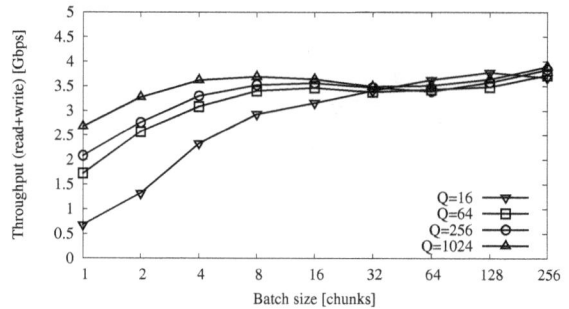

(b) Throughput vs queue depth

Figure 10: Prototype benchmarking: SSD baseline performance

pabilities, that can have an important impact on system performance, and that, as such, our prototype instead exploits.

Load balancing. In order to avoid lock contention, we partition the memory space of both DRAM (L1) and SSD (L2) in as many regions as the number of cores and assign each region to a specific core. Emulation assumes these capabilities are available in hardware and are exported by the NIC drivers, which is not the case: as such, we perform this task in software. The hash function is based on batch identifiers (by using a concatenation of object name and integer part of $chunk\_id/batch\_size$). As a result, read and write operations involving a particular chunk are always performed by the same core, therefore eliminating the need for locks on most operations. In turn, such memory partitioning technique also enables NUMA-aware memory allocation, reducing DRAM access latency.

Batching. Performing per-chunk I/O operations, as normally done by Linux kernel, is expensive and inefficient. In fact, both NIC-CPU and SSD-CPU communication pipelines cannot be effectively saturated by transferring one packet at a time, resulting in limited throughput. To overcome this limitation, our prototype performs all I/O operations (towards NICs or SSDs) over batches instead of single chunks. A side effect of batched operations is the latency increase, especially at low load: to alleviate this problem we use a timeout to cap the maximum waiting time.

SSD I/O. SSD access mechanisms must be carefully designed to achieve a suitable trade-off between latency and throughput. This can be obtained by carefully tuning a number of SSD I/O parameters such as, for example, queue depth (i.e., the number of outstanding access operations executed in parallel by the SSD controller). To access the SSD drives, we use a combination of Direct I/O, Vectored I/O and Asynchronous I/O, which are all standard Linux I/O techniques enabling zero-copy batched transfers between DRAM and SSD. Our SSD interfacing mechanism is similar in principle to the one proposed in [20], that is however just a building block of our complete end-to-end system, unlike in [20].

Lookup. The emulation is based on NFD that, as explained earlier, is designed for completeness rather than performance. As such, a number of software bottlenecks arise in both NFD and NFD-HCS concerning memory manage-

Table 2: Experimental settings

Label	Param	Value
Hardware	CPU	(2 ×) Intel Xeon E5540, 2.53 GHz
	NUMA	2 nodes, 4 cores/node
	RAM	32GB - 1.3GHz (0.8 ns)
	SSD	(2 ×) 200 GB HP enterprise SAS
	NIC	Dual-port 10GbE Intel 82599EB
Software	OS	Ubuntu 12.04 LTS
Workload	Catalog size	1.3M items
	Item size	10 MB
	Chunk size	8 KB
	Zipf skew	1

ment, that are tied to the data structures in use. Specifically, DPDK-HCS memory lookups are managed by a single hash table kept in the main memory for indexing all the chunks currently cached in both L1-DRAM as well as in L2-SSD: every hash table entry indicates whether the chunk is stored in L1 or L2 and the corresponding memory location, reducing the number of lookup operations to be performed. Also, unlike in NFD-HCS, both layers are managed according to the LRU replacement policy and chunks are demoted to L2 upon eviction from L1. As in [16], we manage collisions using open addressing and optimize the memory layout to retrieve a hash table entry within a single memory access. To do so, we store different hash entries in a single cacheline-sized bucket (64B in our architecture), which effectively addresses collisions without the need for chaining in most of the cases.

6. PROTOTYPE BENCHMARKING

We benchmark DPDK-HCS using two general purpose servers (one server running a custom NDN traffic generator), whose characteristics are reported in Tab. 2. We first evaluate and fine-tune SSD performance in isolation (Sec. 6.1) and then measure the overall two-layer cache throughput under realistic workload conditions (Sec. 6.2). Notice that as our focus is on HCS performance, we therefore do not analyze PIT and FIB lookup operations (which our prototype is capable of) that are performed after a content store miss.

6.1 Baseline SSD performance

We investigate SSD throughput as a function of batch size, SSD queue size and read/write mix, fixing as before chunk size $|c|$=8KB. Fig.10(a) reports the cumulative SSD throughput (read + write) as a function of batch size for different read/write mixes (i.e., percentage of SSD read/write

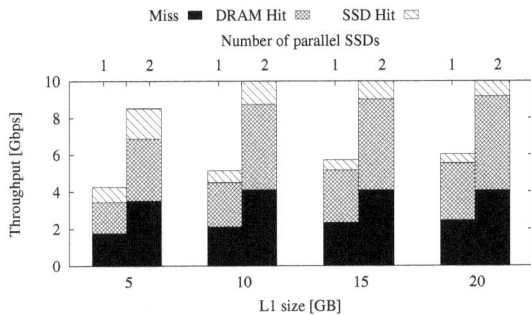

Figure 11: Prototype benchmarking: DPDK-HCS throughput

operations for a random batch) setting SSD queue size to 64 batches. We remark that a batch of $B=16$ chunks (128KB) is sufficient to reach a near-maximum SSD throughput for all read/write mixes. Additionally, $B>16$ does not provide any throughput benefit but yields a latency penalty (from 2.8ms for $B=16$ to 38ms for $B=256$ at 50% write). In addition, notice that while for 100% reads or 100% writes (which are however not realistic for HCS), the measured throughput approaches the external data rate declared by the manufacturer (4.8 Gbps, as per SSD datasheet), with more realistic read-write mixes (e.g., 10-50% writes), the SSD throughput decreases to about 3.5 Gbps.

Fig.10(b) reports the overall SSD throughput as a function of the batch size at 50% write for different SSD queue sizes Q. For small batches, a large SSD queue is beneficial as it improves throughput by increasing the number of outstanding (i.e., parallel) SSD operations. Again, if the batch size is large enough ($B=16$), increasing the queue size beyond 16 batches does not provide significant throughput benefits but only latency penalties (e.g., from 2.8ms for $Q=16$, to 146ms for $Q=1024$).

6.2 DPDK-HCS Performance

Finally, we evaluate the overall DPDK-HCS throughput, using a traffic trace representing a sample of the HTTP requests received by the Wikipedia website, available at [22], whose characteristics are reported in Tab. 2. As in the emulation, interest packets for a content are issued at constant bit rate (i.e., no congestion control). Results of DPDK-HCS for $|L1| \in [5,20]$GB and $|L2|=100$GB (with 1 or 2 SSDs) using $B=16$ and $Q=16$ are reported in Fig.11, with the throughput breakdown indicating the miss rate (requests served by a remote server), DRAM-L1, and SSD-L2 hit rates (notice that hit rates as only apparently low, as due to prefetching L2 increases L1 hits). The most important takeaway lesson is that our system sustains a line rate of 10 Gbps with 96 μs average latency when the L2 cache is spread over two SSD drives, which validates the soundness of our design. Differently, a single SSD cannot achieve a sufficient read throughput to support line speed operations, as sketched in Fig. 1.

7. CONCLUSIONS

This work shows, via emulation and experiments, that line-rate O(10 Gbps) operation of hierarchical content equipped with O(10GB) DRAM-L1 and O(100GB) L2-SSD memory technologies can be achieved in practice. There are a number of interesting points that remain open, though, for both methodologies.

Concerning the emulation part, one possibility would be to decouple L2 size from L1 size (by avoid storing L2 contents and returning dummy data), and to further decouple the catalog size from L2 size (by emulating misses as a network delay). Yet this would make NFD-HCS unusable beyond performance evaluation studies, which question the very same relevance of the effort.

Hence, we believe open points concerning the prototype to be more relevant. With this regard, we have identified a number of directions that can further enhance system performance, and especially SSD management, which is where the performance bottleneck currently is. First, an interesting option to reduce stress on SSD is to require multiple *name* hits [12] before writing to SSD, which would spare SSD throughput avoiding writes for unpopular content. Second, it should be relatively easy to assess up to which level of SSD parallelism returns a linear performance speedup, as well as the number cores needed to manage parallel SSD operations. Third, the `SCHED_DEADLINE` policy, recently introduced in Linux kernel 3.14, could avoid polling mode of NIC cores, freeing CPU cycles for SSD cores. Similarly, moving load balancing operations to the NIC HW would further relieve the software load.

Acknowledgements

This work has been partially funded by the Technological Research Institute SystemX, within the project "Network Architectures", and by the European open innovation organisation EIT Digital under the project n. 15212 ("Information aware data plane for programmable networks"). Rodrigo B. Mansilha was supported by CAPES Foundation (Proc. BEX 3925/14-5). The work has been partially carried out at LINCS – Laboratory of Information, Networking, and Computer Science (`www.lincs.fr`).

8. REFERENCES

[1] Intel DPDK framework. `http://dpdk.org`.

[2] Alexander Afanasyev et al. NFD Developer's Guide. `http://named-data.net/publications/techreports/nfd-developer-guide/`, 2014.

[3] S. Arianfar and P. Nikander. Packet-level Caching for Information-centric Networking. In *ACM SIGCOMM, ReArch Workshop*, 2010.

[4] H. Che, Y. Tung, and Z. Wang. Hierarchical Web caching systems: modeling, design and experimental results. *IEEE JSAC*, 2002.

[5] M. Dobrescu, N. Egi, K. Argyraki, B.-G. Chun, K. Fall, G. Iannaccone, A. Knies, M. Manesh, and S. Ratnasamy. Routebricks: Exploiting parallelism to scale software routers. In *ACM SIGOPS*, 2009.

[6] C. Fricker, P. Robert, and J. Roberts. A versatile and accurate approximation for lru cache performance. In *ITC*, 2012.

[7] F. Fusco and L. Deri. High speed network traffic analysis with commodity multi-core systems. In *ACM IMC 2010*.

[8] A. Ghodsi, S. Shenker, T. Koponen, A. Singla, B. Raghavan, and J. Wilcox. Information-centric networking: seeing the forest for the trees. In *ACM HotNets-X*, 2011.

[9] S. Han, K. Jang, K. Park, and S. Moon. Packetshader: A gpu-accelerated software router. In *ACM SIGCOMM*, 2010.

[10] T. Hasegawa, Y. Nakai, K. Ohsugi, J. Takemasa, Y. Koizumi, and I. Psaras. Empirically modeling how a multicore software icn router and an icn network consume power. In *ACM ICN*, 2014.

[11] M. Jamshed, J. Lee, S. Moon, I. Yun, D. Kim, S. Lee, Y. Yi, and K. Park. Kargus: a highly-scalable software-based intrusion detection system. In *ACM CSS*, 2012.

[12] T. Johnson, D. Shasha, et al. 2Q: A low overhead high performance buffer management replacement algorithm. In *ACM VLDB*, 1994.

[13] N. Kim, G. Choi, and J. Choi. A scalable carrier-grade dpi system architecture using synchronization of flow information. *IEEE JSAC*, 2014.

[14] V. Martina, M. Garetto, and E. Leonardi. A Unified Approach to the pertformance analysis of Caching systems. In *IEEE INFOCOM*, 2014.

[15] D. Perino and M. Varvello. A reality check for content centric networking. In *ACM SIGCOMM, ICN Workshop*, 2011.

[16] D. Perino, M. Varvello, L. Linguaglossa, R. Laufer, and R. Boislaigue. Caesar: A Content Router for High-speed Forwarding on Content Names. In *ACM/IEEE ANCS*, 2014.

[17] L. Rizzo. netmap: A Novel Framework for Fast Packet I/O. In *USENIX ATC*, 2013.

[18] G. Rossini, D. Rossi, M. Garetto, and E. Leonardi. Multi-Terabyte and multi-Gbps information centric routers. In *IEEE INFOCOM*, 2014.

[19] P. M. Santiago del Rio, D. Rossi, F. Gringoli, L. Nava, L. Salgarelli, and J. Aracil. Wire-speed statistical classification of network traffic on commodity hardware. In *ACM IMC 2012*.

[20] W. So, T. Chung, H. Yuan, D. Oran, and M. Stapp. Toward terabyte-scale caching with ssd in a named data networking router. In *ACM/IEEE ANCS, Poster session*, 2014.

[21] W. So, A. Narayanan, and D. Oran. Named data networking on a router: Fast and dos-resistant forwarding with hash tables. In *ACM/IEEE ANCS*, 2013.

[22] G. Urdaneta, G. Pierre, and M. van Steen. Wikipedia workload analysis for decentralized hosting. *Elsevier Computer Networks*, July 2009.

On the Analysis of Caches with Pending Interest Tables

Mostafa Dehghan[1], Bo Jiang[1], Ali Dabirmoghaddam[2], and Don Towsley[1]

[1]College of Information and Computer Sciences, University of Massachusetts, Amherst, MA

[2]Computer Engineering Department, University of California, Santa Cruz, CA

{mdehghan, bjiang, towsley}@cs.umass.edu, alid@soe.ucsc.edu

ABSTRACT

Collapsed forwarding has been used in cache systems to reduce the load on servers by aggregating requests for the same content. This technique has made its way into design proposals for the future Internet architecture through a data structure called Pending Interest Table (PIT). A PIT keeps track of *interest* packets that are received at a cache-router until they are responded to. PITs are considered useful for a variety of reasons *e.g.*, communicating without the knowledge of source and destination, reducing bandwidth usage, better security, etc. Due to the high access frequency to the PIT, it is essential to understand its behavior, and the effect it has on cache performance. In this paper, we consider a TTL-based cache with a Pending Interest Table, and analyze the cache hit probability, mean response time perceived by the users, and size of the PIT, among other metrics of interest. In our analysis, we account for the time it takes for the cache to download a file from the server defined as a random variable. We apply our model to analyze traditional caching policies LRU, FIFO, and RANDOM, and verify the accuracy of our model through numerical simulations.

1. INTRODCUTION

With the accelerating growth in data traffic, caching has been widely acknowledged as one of the most effective means to improve the performance of web applications (*e.g.*, streaming video on-demand). Storing copies of popular content at several locations in the network can greatly reduce network bandwidth usage, load on servers, and more importantly the service delay perceived by the end-users [5]. To further reduce the load on the servers, cache systems (*e.g.*, Squid [1]) usually employ techniques such as *collapsed forwarding*, where multiple user requests for the same content are aggregated and one request is sent out to the back-end server. This technique has been in use in commercial caches built at Akamai since the very early days (circa 1999) [18].

Over the past few years, the research community has been advocating for content-centric networking (CCN), an archi-tecture that emphasizes directly accessible and routable content, arguing that today's Internet is more concerned with *what* a user wants rather than *where* it is located [15]. One important feature of the CCN architecture is the integration of caching in network routers. Named Data Networking (NDN) [12, 24] is one of the most popular designs following the CCN approach. In NDN, a user puts the name of the desired content in an *Interest* packet and sends it to the network. Once the Interest packet reaches a network node that has the content, a *Data* packet is returned to the user by traversing the reverse path taken by the Interest packet.

One of the core components of the NDN architecture is the Pending Interest Table (PIT) which performs collapsed forwarding by keeping track of currently unsatisfied Interest packets. An incoming request, at an NDN router, is forwarded to the next hop only if the PIT finds no pending Interest for the same content name. Once the content is received at the router the entry for the corresponding name is deleted from the PIT. To ensure efficient I/O operations at line speed, a fast and scalable data structure is required for the Pending Interest Table, and an accurate assessment of the PIT size is key to achieving this. Despite many experimental and numerical evaluations [10, 19, 21, 23], there has been no analytic work in modeling Pending Interest Tables. This motivates the current work.

In this paper, we analyze a cache with a Pending Interest Table, to compute the cache hit probability, response time perceived by the users, and the size of the Pending Interest Table. Unlike previous works that assume a file is instantaneously downloaded to the cache in case of a cache miss, we assume a non-zero download delay modeled as a random variable. In our analysis, we consider Time-To-Live (TTL) caches since they provide a unified framework for the analysis of single and networked caches [4, 7]. TTL caches decouple the eviction mechanisms of different files by associating each content with a timer. When a timer expires the corresponding content is evicted from the cache. TTL caches have also proven useful in accurately modeling the behavior of replacement-based caching policies such as LRU, FIFO, and RANDOM among others [8, 11, 13].

Our contributions in this paper can be summarized as follows:

- We model TTL caches with Pending Interest Tables. Our analysis is generic in the sense that it can be used to model single or networked caches assuming the request arrivals can be described as renewal processes. In our analysis, we compute the cache hit probability, mean response time,

ICN'15, September 30–October 2, 2015, San Francisco, CA, USA.
© 2015 ACM. ISBN 978-1-4503-3855-4/15/09 ...$15.00.
DOI: http://dx.doi.org/10.1145/2810156.2810161.

and the distribution of the size of the Pending Interest Table.

- We use our model to analyze popular caching policies LRU, FIFO and RANDOM with Poisson request arrivals, and derive expressions for the cache hit probability, probability of having an entry for a content in the PIT, and the average response time. We also compute the rate at which the cache forwards requests towards the content custodian.

- We perform extensive simulations that demonstrate the accuracy of our models in predicting our metrics of interest.

The remainder of this paper is organized as follows: In the next section, we review the related work. In Section 3, we describe the system model and explain the assumptions. In Sections 4 and 5, we analyze two types of TTL caches, non-reset TTL, and reset TTL, respectively. We use the models developed in these two sections to analyze FIFO and LRU cache in Sections 6 and 7. In Section 8, we evaluate the accuracy of our model through numerical simulations. Finally, we conclude the paper in Section 9.

2. RELATED WORK

2.1 Pending Interest Table

The Pending Interest Table is one of the three fundamental data structures maintained at each router in the NDN architecture. The PIT keeps track of all the Interests that a router has forwarded but are not yet satisfied [24]. Each PIT entry stores the content name, together with the incoming and outgoing interfaces. The names are similar to URLs and are typically tens of bytes long. The URLs for pictures and videos on social networking websites, for example, require more than 80 bytes of storage [23]. A PIT is expected to store on the order of 10^7 entries on average, which makes performing operations at line speed a daunting task [22]. Over the past few years, researchers have made a great effort in design and implementation of fast and scalable Pending Interest Tables [10, 17, 19, 21, 23]. However, despite all the experimental efforts in understanding the dynamics of the PIT size [2, 20], we are unaware of any analytic work in modeling PITs. That is the problem we tackle in this paper.

2.2 Time-To-Live Caches

TTL caches, in which content eviction occurs upon the expiration of a timer, have been employed since the early days of the Internet with the Domain Name System (DNS) being an important application [13]. More recently, TTL caches have regained popularity, mostly due to admitting a general approach in the analysis of caches that can also be used to model replacement-based caching policies such as LRU. The connection between TTL caches and replacement-based (capacity-driven) policies was first established for the LRU policy by Che *et al.* [6] through the notion of cache *characteristic time*, described in Section 3.3. The characteristic time was theoretically justified and extended to other caching policies such as FIFO and RANDOM [11]. This connection was further confirmed to hold for more general arrival models than Poisson processes [16]. Over the past years, several exact and approximate analyses have been proposed

for modeling single caches in isolation as well as cache networks using the TTL framework [4, 7–9]. However, there is little work that accounts for the delay in downloading files to the cache from content servers [3].

In this paper, we focus on analytic models for a single cache with a Pending Interest Table where content is fetched from the back-end server incurring some download delay. However, our model can be applied to a network of caches when request arrivals at all caches can be modeled as renewal processes.

3. MODEL DESCRIPTION

In this section, we introduce our model for a cache with requests arriving for a set of K unique files $F = \{f_1, f_2, \ldots, f_K\}$ of unit size. Throughout this paper, we will use the terms content and file interchangeably. We assume that each file resides permanently at a content custodian.

Once a request arrives for a file that is in the cache, the request is served instantly. However, if the content is not found in the cache, the request will be forwarded to the content custodian. Unlike previous work that assume zero download delay, we consider the case where downloading content $f \in F$ from the custodian incurs a non-zero delay denoted by the random variable D_f. With a misuse of notation, we will use $D_f(\cdot)$ to denote the CDF of D_f. Note that since we can analyze different files individually, we can have different download delay distributions for different files.

It is assumed that the cache employs a Pending Interest Table (PIT) to aggregate requests arriving while the content is being downloaded to the cache. With the arrival of the first request to a file that is not in cache, an entry is created in the PIT. All successive requests during time D_f are aggregated at the PIT and not forwarded to the custodian. Once the content is downloaded, the PIT entry is deleted.

We consider a Time-To-Live (TTL) cache where the cache maintains a timer for each item which indicates the duration of validity for that content. The timer values could be decided by the cache or be imposed by external factors (*e.g.*, content owners). With TTL caches, the caching behaviors of different files are decoupled and thus we can consider files independently. We define T_f to denote the random variable for the TTL of content f and assume the sequence of timers are independent and identically distributed with CDF $T_f(\cdot)$.

TTL-based caching policies generally divide into two classes depending on the behavior of the TTL resets:

- *Non-reset TTL:* The timer is set once the content is downloaded to the cache, and the content leaves the cache after the timer expires.

- *Reset TTL:* The timer is set when the content is downloaded to the cache, and is reset each time a request arrives while the content is still in the cache.

Both of these policies have been properly formalized in the literature [8, 11].

3.1 Metrics of Interest

In our analysis, we are interested in computing the cache hit probability and the response time for individual files as well as the overall expected value. We will also compute the rate at which the cache forwards requests to the content custodians. Since estimating the size of the Pending Interest Table is important in the design of an appropriate data structure, we will capture the distribution of the PIT size. With TTL caches, it is also important to estimate the number of files in the cache. In order to compute the statistics of the cache and PIT size, we first compute the occupancy probability of file f in the cache and in the PIT denoted by o_f and p_f, respectively. We then define Bernoulli random variables O_f and P_f to indicate whether file f resides in cache or PIT. The random variables O_f and P_f take value one with probability o_f and p_f, and zero with probability $1 - o_f$ and $1 - p_f$, respectively. We then define $C = \sum_f O_f$ and $S = \sum_f P_f$ to denote the number of files in the cache and PIT respectively; they follow Poisson Binomial distributions with means $\mu_C = \sum_f o_f$ and $\mu_S = \sum_f p_f$, and variances $\sigma_C^2 = \sum_f o_f(1 - o_f)$ and $\sigma_S^2 = \sum_f p_f(1 - p_f)$, respectively. Assuming a reasonably large number of files, we can approximate the cache and PIT sizes with the Gaussian distribution with means μ_C and μ_S, and variances σ_C^2 and σ_S^2, respectively.

3.2 Renewal Arrivals

Let X_i be the time interval between the $(i-1)$st and the i-th requests for a given file. Inter-request times are assumed to be i.i.d and have distribution function $F(x) = \mathbb{P}(X_i \leq x)$. Let $\lambda = 1/\mathbb{E}[X_i]$ denote the arrival rate for the given file. Without loss of generality, we assume that a request for a file that is not in the cache occurs at $t = 0$, i.e., $X_0 = 0$. Let M_t denote the number of requests for the given file in the interval $(0, t]$. M_t is called the *renewal (counting) process*. Note that the request at $t = 0$ is excluded, i.e., $M_0 = 0$. Also, let

$$\tau_n = X_1 + X_2 + \ldots + X_n, \quad n \geq 1 \quad (\tau_0 = 0),$$

denote the time until the arrival of the nth request. We have

$$\mathbb{P}(\tau_n \leq t) = \mathbb{P}(X_1 + X_2 + \ldots + X_n \leq t) = F^{(n)}(t),$$

where $F^{(n)}(t)$ denotes the n-fold convolution of the distribution function $F(x)$ with itself.

The expected number of renewals for the time duration $(0, t]$ is the *renewal function* $m(t) = \mathbb{E}[M_t]$, and can be expressed as

$$m(t) = \sum_{n=1}^{\infty} F^{(n)}(t), \quad t \geq 0.$$

Poisson Arrivals

A Poisson process is a renewal process with parameter λ whose inter-arrival times have the exponential distribution $F(x) = 1 - e^{-\lambda x}$. For a Poisson process, the renewal function simplifies to $m(t) = \lambda t$. We will use Poisson arrivals in analyzing LRU, FIFO and RANDOM caches in later sections.

3.3 Cache Characteristic Time

Che *et al.* [6] introduced the notion of *cache characteristic time*, and used it to evaluate the hit probability of a cache under the LRU policy with Poisson arrivals. Based on their work, the probability that a request for file f results in a hit can be approximated by

$$h_f = 1 - e^{-\lambda_f T},$$

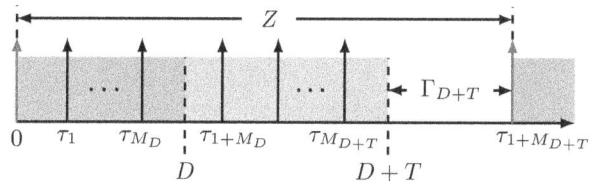

Figure 1: An entry is created in PIT for the file at time $t = 0$. Content enters the cache at time $t = D$, and PIT entry is deleted. Content stays in cache until time $t = D + T$. Only requests marked as red are forwarded to the content custodian.

where λ_f is the request rate for file f, and T is a constant denoting the characteristic time of the cache and is computed as the unique solution to the equation

$$\sum_{f=1}^{K} (1 - e^{-\lambda_f T}) = C,$$

where C is the capacity of the LRU cache. The notion of cache characteristic time has been theoretically justified and generalized to a wider range of caching policies and more general arrival processes [16]. The idea is to compute the probability that file f occupies the cache as a function of the characteristic time $o_f(T)$, and solve for T in the fixed-point equation

$$\sum_f o_f(T) = C.$$

Cache characteristic time maps replacement-based caching policies to TTL-based caching policies. By using this notion, we will apply the analysis we develop in this paper for TTL caches to model LRU, FIFO and RANDOM caches.

4. NON-RESET TTL CACHES

In this section, we model a non-reset TTL cache with a Pending Interest Table with requests arriving according to a renewal process. In this section and the next, we model the dynamics of a single file only, as we are considering a TTL cache with no capacity constraints. We can have different distributions for download delays and TTL timers for different files, but we will use D and T without subscripts here since we are considering a specific file. In Sections 6 and 7, however, we will use subscripts to refer to the metrics of individual files, and explain how they are computed for different replacement policies subject to the cache capacity constraint.

Figure 1 shows the cache dynamics for a given file. It is assumed that initially the requested content is neither in the cache nor the PIT. The first request for the file creates an entry in PIT. It takes some time D for the file to be downloaded to the cache from a content custodian. Requests arriving for the file during D will be aggregated at the PIT, and only the first request is forwarded to the content custodian. Once the file is downloaded to the cache, the PIT entry is deleted and the TTL set to T. The content stays in the cache for T units of time until the TTL expires and the content is evicted from the cache at time $t = D + T$. This process repeats with the arrival of the next request for the file. Here, we are using generic terms D and T without subscripts for a given file, bearing in mind that different files can have different distributions for the download delay, and different values for TTL timers.

The process explained above can be divided into cycles $Z_1, Z_2, \ldots$ separated by consecutive requests sent from the cache to the custodian. These requests are marked red in Figure 1. Note that these cycles are statistically the same. Without loss of generality, consider the cycle starting at $t = 0$. The expected number of requests within this cycle equals $1 + \mathbb{E}[m(D+T)]$, where the expectation is computed with respect to the distribution of download delay D and time T. From these requests, $1 + \mathbb{E}[m(D)]$ on average result in cache misses, and will have to wait for the content to be downloaded to the cache.

Based on the above discussion, the cache hit probability of the file is

$$h = \frac{\mathbb{E}[m(D+T)] - \mathbb{E}[m(D)]}{1 + \mathbb{E}[m(D+T)]}. \tag{1}$$

Moreover, the cache and PIT occupancy probabilities for the given content can be expressed as

$$o = \frac{\mathbb{E}[T]}{\mathbb{E}[Z]} \quad \text{and} \quad p = \frac{\mathbb{E}[D]}{\mathbb{E}[Z]},$$

where $\mathbb{E}[Z]$ denotes the average cycle length. Note that o and p (defined in Section 3.1) can be used to obtain the size of the cache and PIT. To compute $\mathbb{E}[Z]$, we define Γ_t as

$$\Gamma_t := \tau_{1+M_t} - t, \tag{2}$$

to denote the time between t and the arrival of the next request. Γ_t is known as the *excess life* of the renewal process at time t, for which the complementary distribution function is expressed as (see Eq. (6.1) of Chapter 5 in [14])

$$A_\gamma(t) = \mathbb{P}(\Gamma_t > \gamma) \tag{3}$$

$$= 1 - F(t + \gamma) + \int_0^t \Big(1 - F(t + \gamma - x)\Big) dm(x).$$

We can now write the length of a cycle as

$$Z = D + T + \Gamma_{D+T},$$

and hence

$$\mathbb{E}[Z] = \mathbb{E}[D] + \mathbb{E}[T] + \mathbb{E}[\Gamma_{D+T}] \tag{4}$$

$$= \mathbb{E}[D] + \mathbb{E}[T] + \int_0^\infty \int_0^\infty \int_0^\infty A_x(d+t) dx dD(d) dT(t).$$

We can also compute the distribution of the cycle length as in (5). Note that $\mathbb{P}(Z \leq z)$ also defines the distribution of the inter-arrival times of the requests forwarded to the content custodian, referred to as the *miss stream*. The rate of the miss stream for the file then equals $\zeta = 1/\mathbb{E}[Z]$.

As mentioned earlier, requests arriving before time D cannot be immediately served, and will experience a delayed service since the content has to be downloaded to the cache first. Let $w(t)$ denote the expected total waiting time of the requests up to time t. It is characterized by the following recursive equation

$$w(t) = t + \int_0^t w(t-x) dF(x)$$

$$= t + \int_0^t (t-x) dm(x), \tag{6}$$

where the last equality follows from Theorem 4.1 of Chapter 5 in [14]. Dividing the expected total waiting time until time D, i.e., $\mathbb{E}[w(D)]$, by the expected number of the requests in the cycle yields the following expression for the expected response time of the file

$$r = \frac{\mathbb{E}[w(D)]}{1 + \mathbb{E}[m(D+T)]}.$$

5. RESET TTL CACHES

In this section, we analyze a TTL cache where the TTL is reset every time a request arrives for a file that is in the cache. Figure 2 illustrates the cache dynamics with requests arriving for a given content.

With the arrival of the first missed request an entry is created for the file in PIT, and consecutive requests for the file are aggregated until content is downloaded to the cache at time D. When the content enters the cache, the TTL is set to T_0. If the next request arrives after the TTL expires, i.e., $\Gamma_D > T_0$, the content will be evicted from cache at time $t = D + T_0$, similar to the non-reset TTL case. However, if a request arrives before the TTL expires, the TTL will be reset to time T_1. For notational simplicity, we define Y_n to denote the inter-arrival time for the request after the nth hit. Note that Y_n follows the same distribution as X_i and has CDF $F(\cdot)$. The file will remain in the cache as long as successive requests arrive no later than the TTL expires, i.e., $Y_n \leq T_n$. We assume that the sequence of the TTL timers $T_0, T_1, \ldots$ are independent and identically distributed according to $T(\cdot)$, and independent of the request inter-arrival times, Y_n.

For Γ_D we can use (3) to get

$$\mathbb{P}(\Gamma_D \leq \gamma \mid D = d) = 1 - A_\gamma(d) \tag{7}$$

$$= F(d + \gamma) - \int_0^d \Big(1 - F(d + \gamma - x)\Big) dm(x).$$

Note that if $\Gamma_D > T_0$, the cycle Z ends at τ_{1+M_D} with no cache hits. With $\Gamma_D \leq T_0$ we observe the first cache hit. The second hit occurs if $Y_1 \leq T_1$. Assuming that exactly N requests result in cache hits, we must have $Y_n \leq T_n$, $n = 1, 2, \ldots, N-1$, and $Y_N > T_N$. The distribution of the number of cache hits, hence, resembles a geometric distribution. We have

$$\mathbb{P}(N = n \mid D = d) = \begin{cases} q_\Gamma & n = 0, \\ (1 - q_\Gamma)(1 - q_T)^{n-1} q_T & n \geq 1, \end{cases}$$

where

$$q_\Gamma = 1 - \int_0^\infty \mathbb{P}(\Gamma_d \leq t) dT(t),$$

denotes the probability of no cache hits, and

$$q_T = 1 - \int_0^\infty F(t) dT(t),$$

is the probability $\mathbb{P}(Y_i > T_i), i = 1, 2, \ldots, n-1$. This yields

$$\mathbb{E}[N \mid D = d] = (1 - q_\Gamma)/q_T.$$

The expected number of cache hits then equals

$$\mathbb{E}[N] = \frac{\int_0^\infty \int_0^\infty \mathbb{P}(\Gamma_d \leq t) dT(t) dD(d)}{1 - \int_0^\infty F(t) dT(t)}. \tag{8}$$

We can now write the cache hit probability for the given content as the expected number of hit requests divided by the expected total number of requests,

$$h = \frac{\mathbb{E}[N]}{1 + \mathbb{E}[m(D)] + \mathbb{E}[N]}. \qquad (9)$$

Also, assuming N cache hits occur in a cycle, the cycle duration Z can be expressed as

$$Z = \sum_{i=1}^{1+M_D} X_i + \sum_{n=1}^{N} Y_n.$$

Note that N is a stopping time with respect to the sequence $\{T_n - Y_n\}$, corresponding to the rule "stop as soon as $T_n - Y_n \leq 0$." By applying Wald's equation we get

$$\mathbb{E}\left[\sum_{n=1}^{N} Y_n\right] = \mathbb{E}[Y_1]\mathbb{E}[N] = \mathbb{E}[X]\mathbb{E}[N] = \mathbb{E}[N]/\lambda,$$

and therefore

$$\mathbb{E}[Z] = \Big(1 + \mathbb{E}[m(D)] + \mathbb{E}[N]\Big)/\lambda. \qquad (10)$$

The rate of the miss stream then is

$$\zeta = \frac{1}{\mathbb{E}[Z]} = \frac{\lambda}{1 + \mathbb{E}[m(D)] + \mathbb{E}[N]}.$$

We can also write the cache occupancy probability for the content as the expected time spent in cache, colored green in Figure 2, divided by the expected cycle length as

$$o = \frac{\mathbb{E}[\Gamma_D] + \mathbb{E}[N]/\lambda - \mathbb{E}[\Gamma_{t_E}]}{\mathbb{E}[Z]},$$

where t_E denotes the eviction time of the content. It is easy to see, by comparing the above equation with (9), that $h = o$ if the request arrival process is Poisson, since with exponential inter-arrival times we have $\mathbb{E}[\Gamma_D] = \mathbb{E}[\Gamma_{t_E}] = \mathbb{E}[\Gamma_t], \forall t$.

We can also write the probability of having an entry in the PIT for the file as

$$p = \frac{\mathbb{E}[D]}{\mathbb{E}[Z]} = \frac{\lambda\mathbb{E}[D]}{1 + \mathbb{E}[m(D)] + \mathbb{E}[N]}. \qquad (11)$$

As explained in Section 3.1, we can use o and p to compute statistics regarding the number of items in the cache and PIT.

Computing the distribution of the cycle length requires some care. Note that making an assumption on the number of hits affects the distribution of Γ_D. Specifically, let $H_0^d(\cdot)$ denote the distribution of Γ_d (assuming $D = d$) when we do not get any hits in a cycle. We have

$$H_0^d(\gamma) = \int_0^{\infty} \mathbb{P}(\Gamma_d \leq \gamma \mid \Gamma_d > T_0, T_0 = t)\mathrm{d}T(t)$$
$$= \Big(1 - A_\gamma(d)\Big) \int_0^{\gamma} \frac{\mathrm{d}T(t)}{A_t(d)}.$$

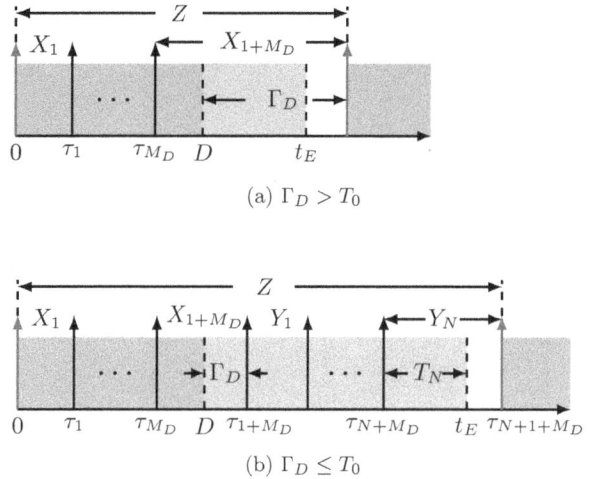

(a) $\Gamma_D > T_0$

(b) $\Gamma_D \leq T_0$

Figure 2: An entry is created in PIT for the file at time $t = 0$. Content enters the cache at time $t = D$, and PIT entry is deleted. (a) The content will be evicted from cache at time $t_E = D + T_0$ if $\Gamma_D > T_0$. (b) The TTL will be reset if $\Gamma_D \leq T_0$, and the content will continue to stay in the cache as long as $Y_n \leq T_n$. Here, $t_E = \tau_{N+M_D} + T_N$ denotes the time that the content is evicted from cache.

Similarly, let $H_1^d(\cdot)$ denote the distribution of Γ_d when there is at least one hit in a cycle. We have

$$H_1^d(\gamma) = \int_0^{\infty} \mathbb{P}(\Gamma_d \leq \gamma \mid \Gamma_d \leq T_0, T_0 = t)\mathrm{d}T(t)$$
$$= \Big(1 - A_\gamma(d)\Big) \int_\gamma^{\infty} \frac{\mathrm{d}T(t)}{1 - A_t(d)}.$$

Moreover, assuming we get N hits in a cycle translates into $Y_1, Y_2, \ldots, Y_{N-1}$ having the distribution

$$L_1(y) = \int_0^{\infty} \mathbb{P}(Y_n \leq y \mid Y_n \leq T_n, T_n = t)\mathrm{d}T(t)$$
$$= F(y) \int_y^{\infty} \frac{\mathrm{d}T(t)}{F(t)},$$

and for Y_N we have

$$L_2(y) = \int_0^{\infty} \mathbb{P}(Y_N \leq y \mid Y_N > T_N, T_N = t)\mathrm{d}T(t)$$
$$= F(y) \int_0^y \frac{\mathrm{d}T(t)}{1 - F(t)}.$$

The cycle length can be expressed as

$$Z = D + \Gamma_D + \sum_{n=1}^{N} Y_n,$$

and since Γ_D and $Y_n, n = 1, \ldots, N$ are conditionally independent given N and D, we can write the distribution

$$\mathbb{P}(Z \leq z) = \int_0^z \int_0^{z-t} \mathbb{P}(D + T + \Gamma_{D+T} \leq z \mid D = d, T = t)\mathrm{d}D(d)\mathrm{d}T(t)$$
$$= \int_0^z \int_0^{z-t} \Big(1 - A_{z-d-t}(d+t)\Big)\mathrm{d}D(d)\mathrm{d}T(t). \qquad (5)$$

function of Z as

$$\mathbb{P}(Z \leq z) = \int_0^z \Big[H_0^d(z)\mathbb{P}(N = 0 \mid D = d) \quad (12)$$

$$+ \sum_{n=1}^{\infty} \Big(H_1^d * L_2 * L_1^{(n-1)} \Big)(z)\mathbb{P}(N = n \mid D = d) \Big]\mathrm{d}D(d),$$

where $(f * g)(\cdot)$ denotes the convolution of f and g, and $L_1^{(n)}$ denotes the n-fold convolution of L_1 with itself.

The service delay experienced by requests arriving before time D will be the same as the non-reset TTL case, and we have

$$w(t) = t + \int_0^t (t - x)\mathrm{d}m(x).$$

The expected response time of the file then equals

$$r = \frac{\mathbb{E}[w(D)]}{1 + \mathbb{E}[m(D)] + \mathbb{E}[N]}. \quad (13)$$

6. FIFO WITH POISSON ARRIVALS

In this section, we consider a FIFO cache of size C with requests arriving to the cache according to a Poisson process. We assume that requests for file f arrive with rate λ_f. It was shown in [7] that a FIFO cache can be modeled as a TTL cache with constant non-reset timers $T_f = T, \forall f$. The constant T is the characteristic time of the FIFO cache; we will explain how to compute T in the remainder of the section.

6.1 Cache Hit Probability

With a Poisson process, the renewal function for file f is $m_f(t) = \lambda_f t$, and hence using (1) we can write the cache hit probability as

$$h_f = \frac{\mathbb{E}[\lambda_f(D_f + T)] - \mathbb{E}[\lambda_f D_f]}{1 + \mathbb{E}[\lambda_f(D_f + T)]}$$

$$= \frac{\lambda_f T}{1 + \lambda_f(\mathbb{E}[D_f] + T)}. \quad (14)$$

Note that when $\mathbb{E}[D_f] = 0$, we obtain

$$h_f = \lambda_f T/(1 + \lambda_f T),$$

which is the expression obtained in [7] for the hit probability of a FIFO cache under the zero download delay assumption. With Poisson arrivals, the cache occupancy probability equals the cache hit probability, i.e., $o_f = h_f$, and hence as explained in Section 3.3, the value of T can be computed by solving the fixed-point equation

$$\sum_{f=1}^{K} \frac{\lambda_f T}{1 + \lambda_f(\mathbb{E}[D_f] + T)} = C.$$

6.2 Size of Pending Interest Table

The expected cycle length can be computed from (4), and for Poisson processes is

$$\mathbb{E}[Z_f] = \mathbb{E}[D_f] + T + 1/\lambda_f.$$

The probability of having an entry for file f in the PIT then is

$$p_f = \frac{\lambda_f \mathbb{E}[D_f]}{1 + \lambda_f(\mathbb{E}[D_f] + T)}. \quad (15)$$

As explained in Section 3.1, the size of the Pending Interest Table, S, can be approximated as a Gaussian random variable with mean $\mu_S = \sum_f p_f$ and variance $\sigma_S^2 = \sum_f p_f(1 - p_f)$.

6.3 Cache Response Time

Using $m_f(t) = \lambda_f t$ for Poisson processes in (6), the total waiting time of requests until time t can be written as $w_f(t) = t + 0.5\lambda_f t^2$. Therefore, the expected response time for file f equals

$$r_f = \frac{\mathbb{E}[D_f + 0.5\lambda_f D_f^2]}{1 + \lambda_f(\mathbb{E}[D_f] + T)}.$$

For the cases of deterministic and exponentially distributed download delays, we can simplify the response time as follows:

- If the delay to download a content to the cache is deterministic, the average response time equals

$$r_f = \frac{D_f + 0.5\lambda_f D_f^2}{1 + \lambda_f(D_f + T)}.$$

- If the download delay follows an exponential distribution, for the expected response time of file f we obtain

$$r_f = \frac{\mathbb{E}[D_f] + \lambda_f \mathbb{E}^2[D_f]}{1 + \lambda_f(\mathbb{E}[D_f] + T)}.$$

6.4 Miss Process

The expected cycle length can be computed from (4) and equals

$$\mathbb{E}[Z_f] = \Big(1 + \lambda_f(\mathbb{E}[D_f] + T)\Big)/\lambda_f.$$

The rate at which the cache forwards requests for file f to the custodian then is

$$\zeta_f = 1/\mathbb{E}[Z_f] = \lambda_f/\Big(1 + \lambda_f(\mathbb{E}[D_f] + T)\Big).$$

We can also compute the distribution of the cycle lengths. First note that for Poisson processes we have

$$A_\gamma(t) = e^{-\lambda_f \gamma}.$$

Therefore, from (5) we obtain

$$\mathbb{P}(Z_f \leq z) = \int_0^{z-T} \Big(1 - e^{-\lambda_f(z-d-T)}\Big)\mathrm{d}D_f(d),$$

which for deterministic and exponentially distributed download delays can be simplified as follows:

- For deterministic download delays

$$\mathbb{P}(Z_f \leq z) = \begin{cases} 0, & z < D_f + T, \\ 1 - e^{-\lambda_f(z-D_f-T)}, & z \geq D_f + T. \end{cases}$$

- For exponentially distributed download delays

$$\mathbb{P}(Z_f \leq z) = \begin{cases} 0, & z < T, \\ 1 - e^{-(z-T)/\mathbb{E}[D_f]} \\ \quad - \dfrac{e^{-(z-T)/\mathbb{E}[D_f]} - e^{-\lambda_f(z-T)}}{\lambda_f \mathbb{E}[D_f] - 1}, & z \geq T. \end{cases}$$

6.5 RANDOM with Poisson Arrivals

It was shown in [7] that a RANDOM cache can be modeled as a TTL cache with exponentially distributed non-reset timers. Repeating the analysis we did in this section for exponentially distributed T with mean $\mathbb{E}[T]$ reveals that all the expressions derived for a FIFO cache can be used for a RANDOM cache by replacing T with $\mathbb{E}[T]$. The only expression that is different is the distribution function for the cycle length $\mathbb{P}(Z_f \leq z)$. For deterministic and exponentially distributed download delays we have

- For deterministic download delays

$$
\mathbb{P}(Z_f \leq z) = \begin{cases} 0, & z < D_f, \\ 1 - e^{-(z-D_f)/\mathbb{E}[T]} \\ \quad - \dfrac{e^{-(z-D_f)/\mathbb{E}[T]} - e^{-\lambda_f(z-D_f)}}{\lambda_f \mathbb{E}[T] - 1}, & z \geq D_f. \end{cases}
$$

- For exponentially distributed download delays, note that D_f, T and Γ_{D_f+T} follow independent exponential distributions. Note that with Poisson arrivals, Γ_{D_f+T} has the same distribution as the inter-arrival times for file f, and hence has CDF $F_f(\cdot)$. Therefore, the distribution of the cycle length follows as

$$
\mathbb{P}(Z_f \leq z) = (D_f * T * F_f)(z), \ z \geq 0.
$$

7. LRU WITH POISSON ARRIVALS

In this section, we model an LRU cache of capacity C with requests arriving to the cache according to a Poisson process. We assume that requests for file f arrive with rate λ_f. It was shown in [7] that an LRU cache can be modeled as a TTL reset cache with constant timers $T_f = T, \forall f$.

7.1 Cache Hit Probability

First, we note that with Poisson arrivals we have

$$
\mathbb{P}(\Gamma_d \leq \gamma) = 1 - e^{-\lambda_f \gamma},
$$

which is independent of d. The above equation suggests that the expected number of cache hits in a cycle is independent of the distribution of the download delay. Using (8), we obtain

$$
\mathbb{E}[N_f] = \frac{1 - e^{-\lambda_f T}}{e^{-\lambda_f T}} = e^{\lambda_f T} - 1.
$$

Based on (9), the hit probability of content f can then be written as

$$
h_f = \frac{e^{\lambda_f T} - 1}{\lambda_f \mathbb{E}[D] + e^{\lambda_f T}}.
$$

Note that $\mathbb{E}[D_f] = 0$ yields $h_f = 1 - e^{-\lambda_f T}$ which is the expression obtained by Che $et\ al.$ [6] for the hit probability of an LRU cache under the assumption of zero download delay.

For Poisson arrivals the cache occupancy probability equals the cache hit probability, $i.e.$, $o_f = h_f$, and hence the value of T is obtained by solving the fixed-point equation

$$
\sum_{f=1}^{K} \frac{e^{\lambda_f T} - 1}{\lambda_f \mathbb{E}[D_f] + e^{\lambda_f T}} = C.
$$

7.2 Size of Pending Interest Table

Based on (10), the expected cycle length equals

$$
\mathbb{E}[Z_f] = \mathbb{E}[D_f] + e^{\lambda_f T}/\lambda_f,
$$

and hence using (11), the probability of having an entry for file f in the PIT is given by

$$
p_f = \frac{\lambda_f \mathbb{E}[D_f]}{\lambda_f \mathbb{E}[D_f] + e^{\lambda_f T}}.
$$

As explained in Section 3.1, the size of the Pending Interest Table, S, can be approximated as a Gaussian with mean $\mu_S = \sum_f p_f$ and variance $\sigma_S^2 = \sum_f p_f(1 - p_f)$.

7.3 Cache Response Time

Considering Poisson processes, the total waiting time of requests until time t (for $t \leq D_f$) is $w_f(t) = t + 0.5\lambda_f t^2$, and using (13) the average response time for file f is

$$
r_f = \frac{\mathbb{E}[D_f + 0.5\lambda_f D_f^2]}{\lambda_f \mathbb{E}[D_f] + e^{\lambda_f T}}.
$$

For deterministic and exponentially distributed download delays, we can simplify the response time as follows:

- For deterministic download delays, we can simply write the expected response time for file f as

$$
r_f = \frac{D_f + 0.5\lambda_f D_f^2}{\lambda_f D_f + e^{\lambda_f T}}.
$$

- If the download delay is exponentially distributed, the expected delay simplifies to

$$
r_f = \frac{\mathbb{E}[D_f] + \lambda_f \mathbb{E}^2[D_f]}{\lambda_f \mathbb{E}[D_f] + e^{\lambda_f T}}.
$$

7.4 Miss Process

The rate at which requests get forwarded to the custodian equals

$$
\zeta_f = \frac{1}{\mathbb{E}[Z_f]} = \frac{\lambda_f}{\lambda_f \mathbb{E}[D_f] + e^{\lambda_f T}}.
$$

8. PERFORMANCE EVALUATION

In this section, we evaluate the accuracy of our models by comparing against numerical simulations. We simulate LRU and FIFO caches of size $C = 1000$, where requests arrive for $N = 10,000$ files. File popularities follow a Zipf distribution with parameter $\alpha = 0.8$, $i.e.$, $\lambda_f \propto 1/f^\alpha$, and the aggregate request rate is assumed to be $\lambda = 10^5$ requests per second. In evaluating the accuracy of the models for individual files, the download delay is set to 100ms. We also compute the average values for different metrics by varying the download delay from zero to 250ms.

8.1 Cache Hit Probability

Figure 3 shows the hit probability of the individual files for LRU and FIFO caches. The hit probability computed by the original characteristic time approximation assuming zero download delay (ZDD) [6] is also shown for comparison. While our models accurately estimate the hit probabilities of the individual files for the LRU and FIFO caches, it is clear that with ZDD assumption the behavior of the system cannot be captured.

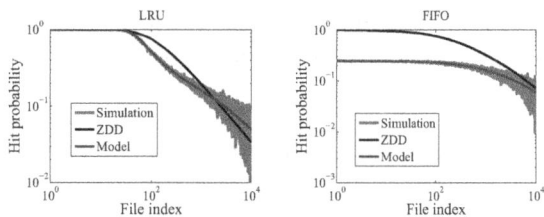

Figure 3: Cache hit probability for individual files.

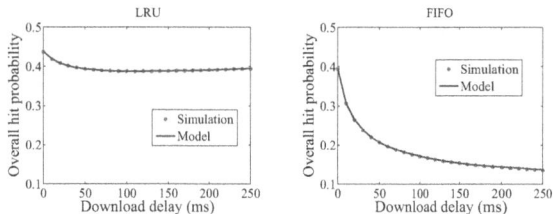

Figure 4: Overall cache hit probability.

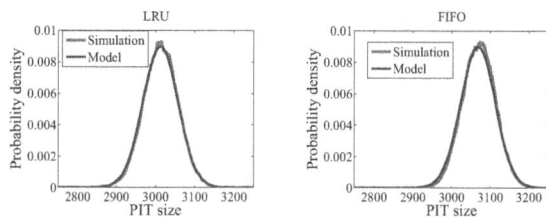

Figure 6: PIT size distribution.

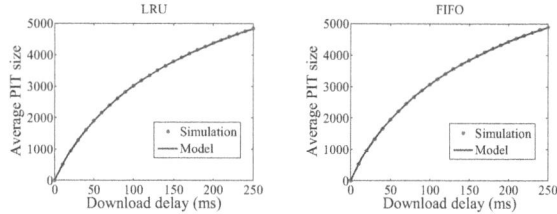

Figure 7: Average PIT size.

Figure 4 shows the overall cache hit probability computed, from simulations and our models, for different values of the download delay. This figure suggests that increasing the download delay drastically affects the hit probability of the FIFO cache, while it has minor impact on the hit probability of the LRU cache.

8.2 Size of Pending Interest Table

Figure 5 shows the probability of having an entry for each file in the Pending Interest Table. Note that for Poisson arrivals this also equals the probability that a request will be aggregated in the PIT and not forwarded to the server.

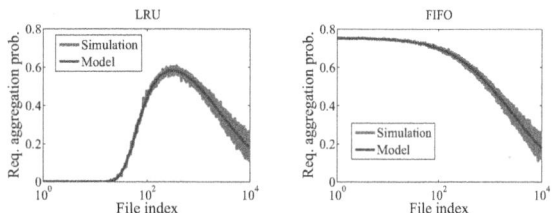

Figure 5: Request aggregation probability in PIT.

In Section 3.1, we advocated the use of the Gaussian distribution to approximate the size of the Pending Interest Table. Figure 6 shows the distribution of the PIT size computed from simulations, as well as a Gaussian distributions with moments computed based on the discussion in Section 3.1. It is clear that the Gaussian distribution accurately represents the distribution of the PIT size for both LRU and FIFO caches. Figure 6 also suggests that a FIFO cache yields a larger Pending Interest Table compared to an LRU cache of the same size.

Figure 7 shows the average PIT size for different values of the cache download delay. As one might expect, as download delay increases, the size of the Pending Interest Table increases, and our model accurately predicts the expected PIT size.

8.3 Cache Response Time

Figure 8 shows the average response time for individual files when the cache download delay is $D = 100$ms. With

the LRU policy, the average response times for the most popular files are zero, which suggests that these files are almost always in the cache. With the FIFO cache, however, even the most popular file has a non-zero average response time. This is due to the non-reset TTL nature of the FIFO policy, i.e., even the most popular file gets evicted from cache T_{FIFO} time after the insertion into the cache, where T_{FIFO} denotes the characteristic time of the FIFO cache.

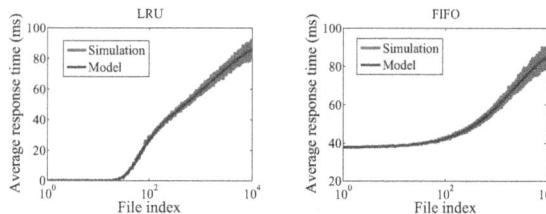

Figure 8: Response time per file.

Figure 9 shows how average response time depends on download delay. Comparing the two plots in Figure 9 we conclude that the LRU cache yields lower average response times compared to the FIFO cache. In fact, for large download delay, LRU achieves a 30% lower average response time.

8.4 Miss Request Forwarding

Figure 10 shows the probability of forwarding a request to other network nodes for each file, and Figure 11 shows the rate at which requests are forwarded. While with an LRU cache, requests for the most popular file are almost never forwarded, with a FIFO cache, the most popular file has the highest request forwarding rate. Figure 11 looks like Figure 5 because the expressions for PIT hit probability and request forwarding rate are related through $p_f = \zeta_f \mathbb{E}[D_f]$.

Figure 12 shows the overall request forwarding rate as a function of download delay. As download delay increases, more requests are aggregated at the PIT and hence fewer requests are forwarded.

8.5 A Larger System

Convinced of the accuracy of our models, we use them to analyze properties of a larger system. We consider a system with $N = 10^7$ files, where file popularities follow

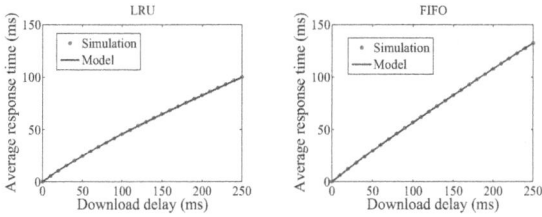

Figure 9: Average response time.

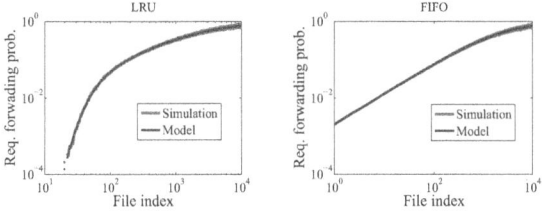

Figure 10: Request forwarding probability for individual files.

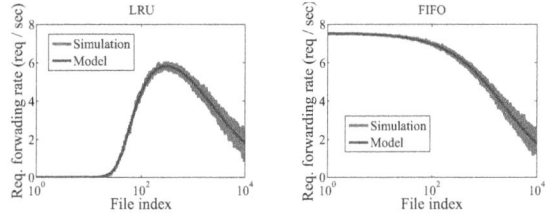

Figure 11: Request forwarding rate for individual files.

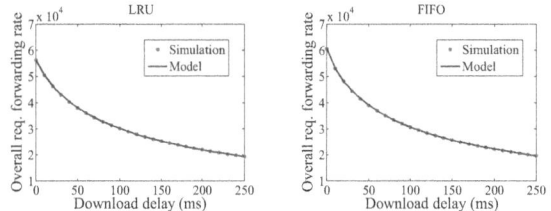

Figure 12: Overall request forwarding rate.

a Zipf distribution with parameter $\alpha = 0.8$. The aggregate request rate at the cache is $\lambda = 10^5$ requests per second. We compute the average cache hit probability, average response time, average PIT size, and the average request forwarding rate for various cache sizes and download delays. When studying the effect of the cache size we set the download delay to $D = 100$ms, and when exploring the effect of the download delay we set the cache size equal to $C = 10^4$. Here, we only present results from the models as it takes a significantly long time to simulate the system explained above.

Figure 13 shows the average hit probability for the LRU and FIFO caches for various values of cache size and download delay. Although the plots seem to be very close for LRU and FIFO caches, the LRU cache achieves up to 60% higher hit probability for some cache sizes. Moreover, this difference increases as download delay increases.

Figure 14 demonstrates the effect of the cache size and download delay on the average response time of the LRU and FIFO caches. For small and very large cache sizes LRU and FIFO caches exhibit similar performance. However, for mid-sized caches, LRU yields up to 20% lower response time. For a given cache size, the response times of the LRU and FIFO caches show linear increase as download delay increases, and the two caches exhibit similar performance.

Figure 15 shows how the average PIT size changes with cache size and download delay. For small and very large cache sizes, the average PIT size is almost the same for LRU and FIFO caches, while for mid-sized caches, the LRU cache saves up to 20% on the PIT size. With a given cache size, the PIT size shows a linear increase with the download delay, and the difference in the PIT sizes of the LRU and FIFO caches is less than 1% for the values of the download delays explored here.

Figure 16 shows the effect of cache size and download delay on the overall request forwarding rate. The average request forwarding rate behaves very similar to response time with respect to the cache size. For small and very large cache sizes the LRU and FIFO policies yield almost the same forwarding rates but for some mid-sized caches up to 18% reduction in forwarding rate can be achieved by using an LRU cache. As one might expect, the request forwarding rate decreases, as the download delay is increased.

9. CONCLUSION

In this paper, we consider the problem of modeling a cache with a Pending Interest Table. It is assumed that in case of a cache miss, it would take some time to download the content to the cache, where the download delay is modeled as a random variable. While the content is being downloaded to the cache, requests arriving for the content are aggregate at the Pending Interest Table, and not forwarded to the content custodian in order to reduce the load on the server. We derive expressions for the cache hit probability, response time perceived by the users, and the size of the Pending Interest Table. We analyze two classes of TTL-based caching policies, where the timer could be set only once, or be reset with every request for the content. Our analysis enables us to model the traditional replacement-based caching policies LRU, FIFO and RANDOM. We perform numerical simulations that demonstrate the accuracy of our approach in modeling caches with Pending Interest Tables.

Acknowledgements

This work was conducted under an NSF grant CNS-1413998 and a MURI ARO grant W911NF-12-10385. Ali Dabirmoghaddam was supported by a UCSC Chancellor's Dissertation-Year Fellowship.

10. REFERENCES

[1] Squid. `squid-cache.org`.
[2] ABU, A. J., BENSAOU, B., AND WANG, J. M. Interest packets retransmission in lossy ccn networks and its impact on network performance. In *ICN* (2014), pp. 167–176.
[3] BAHAT, O., AND MAKOWSKI, A. M. Measuring consistency in ttl-based caches. *Performance Evaluation 62* (2005), 439–455.
[4] BERGER, D. S., GLAND, P., SINGLA, S., AND CIUCU, F. Exact analysis of ttl cache networks. *Performance Evaluation 79* (2014), 2–23.
[5] BORST, S., GUPTA, V., AND WALID, A. Distributed caching algorithms for content distribution networks. In *INFOCOM* (March 2010), pp. 1–9.

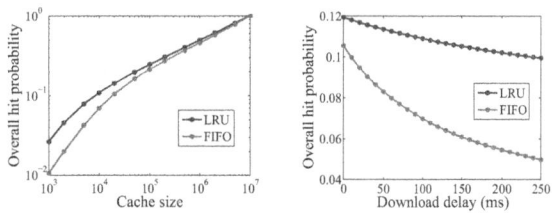

Figure 13: Overall hit probability.

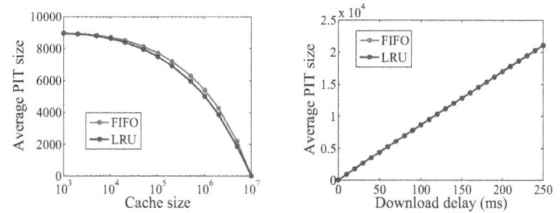

Figure 15: Average PIT size.

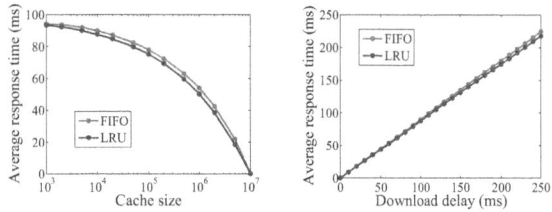

Figure 14: Average response time.

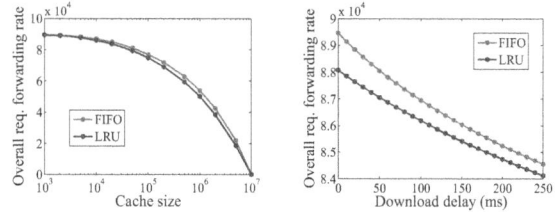

Figure 16: Overall request forwarding rate.

[6] CHE, H., WANG, Z., AND TUNG, Y. Analysis and design of hierarchical web caching systems. In *INFOCOM* (2001), pp. 1416–1424.

[7] CHOUNGMO-FOFACK, N., DEHGHAN, M., TOWSLEY, D., BADOV, M., AND GOECKEL, D. L. On the performance of general cache networks. In *ValueTools* (December 2014).

[8] CHOUNGMO-FOFACK, N., NAIN, P., NEGLIA, G., AND TOWSLEY, D. Analysis of ttl-based cache networks. In *ValueTools* (October 2012), pp. 1–10.

[9] CHOUNGMO-FOFACK, N., NAIN, P., NEGLIA, G., AND TOWSLEY, D. Performance evaluation of hierarchical ttl-based cache networks. *Computer Networks 65* (2014), 212–231.

[10] DAI, H., LIU, B., CHEN, Y., AND WANG, Y. On pending interest table in named data networking. In *ANCS* (2012), pp. 211–222.

[11] FRICKER, C., ROBERT, P., AND ROBERTS, J. A versatile and accurate approximation for lru cache performance. In *ITC* (2012).

[12] JACOBSON, V., SMETTERS, D. K., THORNTON, J. D., PLASS, M. F., BRIGGS, N. H., AND BRAYNARD, R. L. Networking named content. In *CoNEXT* (2009), pp. 1–12.

[13] JAEYEON, J., BERGER, A. W., AND BALAKRISHNAN, H. Modeling ttl-based internet caches. In *INFOCOM* (March 2003), pp. 417–426.

[14] KARLIN, AND SAMUEL. *A first course in stochastic processes*, 2 ed. Academic press, 1975.

[15] KUROSE, J. Information-centric networking: The evolution from circuits to packets to content. *Computer Networks 66* (2014), 112–120.

[16] MARTINA, V., GARETTO, M., AND LEONARDI, E. A unified approach to the performance analysis of caching systems. In *INFOCOM* (April 2014), pp. 2040–2048.

[17] PERINO, D., AND VARVELLO, M. A reality check for content centric networking. In *SIGCOMM Workshop on Information-centric Networking* (2011), pp. 44–49.

[18] SITARAMAN, R. personal communication, April, 2015.

[19] VARVELLO, M., PERINO, D., AND LINGUAGLOSSA, L. On the design and implementation of a wire-speed pending interest table. In *INFOCOM workshops* (April 2013), pp. 369–374.

[20] VIRGILIO, M., MARCHETTO, G., AND SISTO, R. Pit overload analysis in content centric networks. In *SIGCOMM Workshop on Information-centric Networking* (2013), pp. 67–72.

[21] WANG, Y., HE, K., DAI, H., MENG, W., JIANG, J., LIU, B., AND CHEN, Y. Scalable name lookup in ndn using effective name component encoding. In *ICDCS* (2012), pp. 688–697.

[22] YOU, W., MATHIEU, B., TRUONG, P., PELTIER, J., AND SIMON, G. Dipit: A distributed bloom-filter based pit table for ccn nodes. In *ICCCN* (July 2012), pp. 1–7.

[23] YUAN, H., AND CROWLEY, P. Scalable pending interest table design: From principles to practice. In *INFOCOM* (April 2014), pp. 2049–2057.

[24] ZHANG, L., AFANASYEV, A., BURKE, J., JACOBSON, V., CLAFFY, K., CROWLEY, P., PAPADOPOULOS, C., WANG, L., AND ZHANG, B. Named data networking. *ACM SIGCOMM Computer Communication Review 44* (July 2014), 66–73.

Performance and Cost Effectiveness of Caching in Mobile Access Networks

Salah Eddine Elayoubi[*]
Orange Labs, Issy-Les-Moulineaux, France
salaheddine.elayoubi@orange.com

James Roberts
IRT-SystemX, Paris-Saclay, France
james.roberts@irt-systemx.fr

ABSTRACT

The paper considers the use of caching in mobile access networks and seeks to evaluate the optimal memory for bandwidth tradeoff at base station (BS), packet gateway (PGW) and a possible intermediate mobile cloud node (MCN). Formulas are derived for the hit rate under time varying popularity and for a novel cache insertion policy incorporating a pre-filter. The analytical model is applied first to demonstrate that reactive caching is not efficient for nodes with low demand due to the negative impact of content churn. This means BS or MCN caches must be managed proactively with popular content items pre-fetched under some centralized control. Quantifying the tradeoff at each level leads us to conclude that limited caching at BS and MCN levels brings significant savings while to store the vast majority of the content catalogue at the Internet edge at the PGW is clearly cost effective.

Categories and Subject Descriptors

C.2.1 [**Computer communication networks**]: Network Architecture and Design—*packet-switching networks*; C.4 [**Performance of systems**]: [modeling techniques, performance attributes]

General Terms

Algorithms, Performance

Keywords

Cache hit rate; memory-bandwidth tradeoff; mobile access network; time varying popularity

1. INTRODUCTION

Lively debate on the optimal use of caching in information centric networks is still ongoing. A major outstanding issue

---

[*]Both authors are members of the LINCS, Paris, France. See www.lincs.fr.

ICN'15, September 30–October 2, 2015, San Francisco, CA, USA.
© 2015 ACM. ISBN 978-1-4503-3855-4/15/09 ...$15.00.
DOI: http://dx.doi.org/10.1145/2810156.2810168.

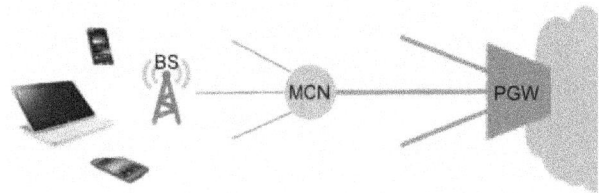

Figure 1: Mobile access network: connects base stations (BS) to Internet via packet gateway (PGW) and optional mobile cloud node (MCN).

is whether caching should be limited to the edge of the Internet or whether the network should be designed to make optimal use of content stores incorporated in routers distributed throughout the core. Based on our own prior work, as well as arguments published in the literature, we tend to believe edge caching is more cost effective and has potential to significantly simplify the network architecture. If this belief is correct, it still remains to more precisely understand where and how caching should be performed within the access infrastructure beyond the edge. Our objective in this paper is to evaluate the performance and cost effectiveness of caching solutions in a mobile access network.

We consider the network depicted in Figure 1 where base stations (BS) are connected to a packet gateway (PGW) at the Internet edge via a so-called mobile cloud node (MCN) and all three levels might host a cache. In current 4G networks the MCN is absent and BSs are connected directly to the PGW via IP tunnels. The MCN is envisaged for 5G mobile access and is intended to fulfill diverse functions including radio link control and offloading of mobile device applications. We suppose the MCN would also perform caching for and in place of its connected BSs. The number of BSs connected to a PGW is around 1000 while the MCN would serve up to 100 BSs.

We consider the placement of caches from the point of view of a network operator seeking to minimize investment by realizing an optimal tradeoff of cache memory for network bandwidth. We assume ongoing tussles between operators and content providers have been resolved so that all stored content can indeed be cached. This implies the network offers content providers the necessary control over content delivery, for billing, accounting or ad placement, say, so that there is no impediment to delivering a content item from a remote cache if available.

Cache placement has previously been considered as an optimization problem where a fixed volume of memory, or "cache budget", must be distributed over a given network topology, typically in order to minimize the average download path length. Fayazbakhsh *et al.* [5] concluded in this way that edge caching was preferable while Rossi and Rossini [12] later showed that the conclusions of [5] would have changed had the authors considered more efficient cache insertion and request forwarding policies. Dabirmoghaddam *et al.* [3] showed that the notion of cache budget is in fact flawed since, obviously, edge caching becomes progressively more attractive as the budget increases while there is no obvious way to determine what the budget should be. In evaluating the memory for bandwidth tradeoff, we do not have to postulate a cache budget but rather to directly weigh the costs of caching against the resulting savings in network transport infrastructure.

At any given network node, the optimal cache size will be that which minimizes, $\text{cost}_b(D) + \text{cost}_m(C)$, where D is busy period demand upstream of the cache in bit/s, C is cache size and cost_b and cost_m are cost functions for bandwidth and caching, respectively. Demand D determines required infrastructure investment. It is proportional to the cache miss rate so that the tradeoff evaluation critically depends on this or, equivalently, on the hit rate $h(C)$. Much recent research has clarified cache hit rate performance under stationary demand, i.e., when the catalogue of content items is fixed and their individual popularities do not change. However, at points low in the access network, like the BS or MCN, where demand is relatively light, it is essential to account for time varying popularity as content churn then becomes the major source of cache misses.

We evaluate tradeoffs assuming cache performance is *ideal* in the sense that it stores the currently most popular items that fit into the cache. It is known that this ideal can be attained under stationary demand by applying a highly selective insertion policy where items are only added to the cache if they have been determined, by a history of previous requests, to have high popularity. The response to changing popularities of such policies is slow, however, and tends to further degrade cache performance in nodes with low demand. When reactive caching fails, it is necessary to envisage proactive caching. This means some external entity determines popularities in real time and ensures remote caches contain the most popular items by pre-fetching. Prefetching requires an appropriate architectural solution allowing the entity in question to infer popularities, typically by monitoring demand from a large user base.

Our first contribution in Section 2 is to derive accurate analytical hit rate approximations for an LRU cache applying a novel selective insertion policy. Hit rates can be evaluated under stationary or time varying popularity for any cache size. These formulas are then used in Section 3 to determine whether reactive or proactive caching should be employed at each of the considered network levels. We discuss the architectural implications of the need to perform pre-fetching when reactive caching is not viable. Lastly, in Section 4, we evaluate the cost tradeoff. We assume the BS would have a fixed-size cache of limited complexity while the PGW and MCN have a modular design, like a data center, allowing a wide range of cache sizes.

N	catalogue size
q_i	popularity of item i, $\sum_{1 \leq i \leq N} q_i = 1$
α	Zipf law exponent
C	cache size
$c = C/N$	normalized cache size
K	pre-filter size
t_C	cache characteristic time
h	overall hit rate
h_i	hit rate for item i
$h_i^{(n)}$	hit rate of nth requests for item i
τ_i	mean lifetime of item i
p_{in}	proba. n requests in item i lifetime
η_i	proba. current request for item i is not last
l_k	mean lifetime of items in class k
f_k	fraction of items in class k
σ	mean requests per item per day
k_b	monthly per Mb/s bandwidth cost
k_m	monthly per GB memory cost
Δ	overall cost
$\delta(c)$	normalized cost
Γ	ratio of zero cache cost to full cache cost

Table 1: Summary of notation..

2. CACHE HIT RATES

We first consider cache performance under stationary demand, applying the independent reference model, before evaluating the impact of changes in popularity over time. Notation used in the following is summarized in Table 1.

2.1 Stationary demand

Assume the content catalogue contains N items of equal size and that demand for item i is proportional to q_i independently of time. This stationarity assumption is reasonable if the q_i are popularities in a relatively short period like 1 day. We normalize the q_i such that $\sum_1^N q_i = 1$. The "items" might typically be chunks of videos or other data objects and are assumed to have the same size.

An ideal cache.

An ideal cache of size C would store just the C most popular items. The hit rate $h(C)$ is then simply the ratio $\sum_1^C q_i / \sum_1^N q_i$. For Zipf($\alpha$) popularity, $q_i \propto 1/i^\alpha$, with $\alpha < 1$ and N large, we have $h(C) \approx (C/N)^{1-\alpha}$.

Ideal cache performance can be realized if item popularities are accurately determined (e.g., by a server aware of demand from a large population of users and able to anticipate changes in popularity) and the cache content is proactively updated by pre-fetching. An alternative is to augment a reactive caching policy like LRU with a pre-filter, as discussed below.

LRU cache.

The hit rate of an LRU cache can be accurately evaluated by the Che approximation [6]. We have $h(C) = \sum_1^N q_i(1 - e^{-q_i t_C})$ where the *characteristic time* t_C satisfies $C = \sum_i (1 - e^{-q_i t_C})$. The characteristic time is the time to receive requests for C distinct items. Figure 2 shows that the performance of LRU can be far from ideal, especially for a cache that has capacity for only a small fraction of the catalogue.

Cache with pre-filter.

Several authors have observed that the performance of an LRU cache can be improved by equipping it with what we term a pre-filter. We illustrate this through the following particular filter design. The identities of the last K items to be requested are recorded in a filter list. If a request is a hit (the item is present in the LRU cache), it is moved to the front of the LRU as usual. If the item is not in the LRU but is in the filter list, it is fetched and placed at the front of the LRU displacing the item at the end. If the item is not in either the LRU or the filter list, it is fetched but not cached.

To evaluate the hit rate, we adapt an approximation proposed by Martina et al. [9] for another type of pre-filter. We assume the states of the pre-filter and the LRU are statistically independent and consider $h_i^{(n)}$, the probability the nth request for item i is a hit. Conditioning on the fate of the nth request, we can write,

$$h_i^{(n+1)} = \left(1 - e^{-q_i t_C}\right)\left(h_i^{(n)} + (1 - h_i^{(n)})(1 - (1 - q_i)^K)\right), \quad (1)$$

where t_C is a characteristic time, to be determined. The first term, $(1 - e^{-q_i t_C})$, is the probability the $(n+1)^{th}$ request arrives within t_C of the nth while the second term is the probability i was already in the LRU following the nth request. Under the present stationarity assumption, we have $h_i^{(n+1)} = h_i^{(n)} = h_i$ and, from (1),

$$h_i = \frac{(1 - e^{-q_i t_C})(1 - (1 - q_i)^K)}{1 - (1 - e^{-q_i t_C})(1 - q_i)^K}.$$

Equating $\sum_1^N h_i$ to C, as in the Che approximation for LRU, gives the equation for t_C and consequently all the individual hit rates. The overall hit rate is $h(C) = \sum_1^N q_i h_i$.

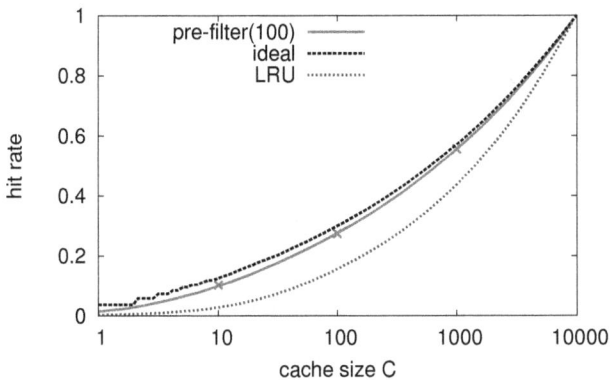

Figure 2: Hit rates with pre-filter of 100 places against cache size: $N = 10^4$ items with Zipf(.8) popularity; crosses are simulation results.

Figure 2 shows the hit rate obtained with a pre-filter of 100 places in comparison to ideal and LRU caching. Crosses are hit rates derived by simulation and illustrate the high accuracy of the approximation based on the independence assumption. The act of filtering preferentially selects the most popular items for insertion so that the cache has close to ideal performance. Performance could be further improved by reducing the size of the filter but this also reduces the reactivity of the cache to changing popularities, as discussed next.

2.2 Time varying popularities

We propose a simple model, following Wolman et al. [15], to account for the fact that content items have finite lifetimes. We suppose that the catalogue remains fixed at N and that at any instant there is an item i with popularity q_i for $1 \leq i \leq N$. However, the item labelled i can change between requests as the current item ends its lifetime and a new one begins. This modelling device allows us to retain the notion of popularity law while accounting for the fact that content churn can significantly reduce the hit rate.

LRU cache.

Let the mean lifetime of items labelled i be τ_i. The rate of misses for such items in an unlimited capacity cache is then $1/(1 + q_i \tau_i)$ (i.e., 1 in an average number of requests of $1 + q_i \tau_i$). For a cache of capacity $C < N$, the first request for a new item i is necessarily a miss and the LRU miss probability for any request after the first is $e^{-q_i t_C}$, as for the IRM, where t_C is the Che characteristic time. The overall hit rate is thus

$$h_i = \left(1 - \frac{1}{1 + q_i \tau_i}\right)\left(1 - e^{-q_i t_C}\right). \quad (2)$$

To compute t_C, note that the cache may contain more than one version of item i. To simplify we exclude this possibility by assuming the old version is overwritten by the new. We then still have the identity $C = \sum h_i$ to compute t_C. However, simulations used to validate the approximation do maintain copies of old versions until they are ejected by the LRU policy.

Note that, in the present case, the Che equation does not necessarily have a solution when the τ_i are small. This is because content churn is too rapid for their ever to be a finite interval in which there are requests for C or more distinct items. In this case we must set t_C to ∞ in (2).

Cache with pre-filter.

Formula (1) constitutes a recursion for calculating the hit rate of the nth request for item i after a renewal, for $n \geq 3$ with $h_i^{(1)} = h_i^{(2)} = 0$. The mean hit rate is

$$h_i = \frac{h_i^{(1)} + h_i^{(2)}(1 - p_{i1)} + h_i^{(3)}(1 - p_{i1} - p_{i2}) + \ldots}{1 + (1 - p_{i1}) + (1 - p_{i1} - p_{i2}) + \ldots}$$

where p_{in} is the probability the number of requests between renewals is n, for $n \geq 1$.

To proceed, we assume the number of requests has a geometric distribution, $p_{in} = (1 - \eta_i)\eta_i^{n-1}$ with $\eta_i = q_i \tau_i/(1 + q_i \tau_i)$. The expression for h_i then simplifies to $h_i = (1 - \eta_i)\sum_n \eta_i^{n-1} h_i^{(n)}$. Multiplying both sides of (1) by η_i^n and summing leads eventually to an equation for h_i with solution,

$$h_i = \frac{\eta_i^2 \left(1 - e^{-q_i t_C}\right)\left(1 - (1 - q_i)^K\right)}{1 - \eta_i\left(1 - e^{-q_i t_C}\right)(1 - q_i)^K}.$$

As for the LRU cache, we determine t_C from the equation $\sum_1^N h_i = C$, letting $t_C \to \infty$ when there is no solution.

Lifetimes.

Traverso et al. have derived some lifetime statistics from trace data [14, Table 2]. The authors give the fractions of items having a lifetime in five intervals: 0 to 2 days, 2 to 5, 5 to 8, 8 to 13, more than 13. They also observe that

class k	interval	l_k	f_k
1	0-2	1.1	.005
2	2-5	3.3	.008
3	5-8	6.4	.005
4	8-13	10.6	.008
5	> 13	365	.974

Table 2: Lifetime in days of most popular items, deduced from Traverso et al. : l_k is the class mean lifetime and f_k the fraction of items in the class.

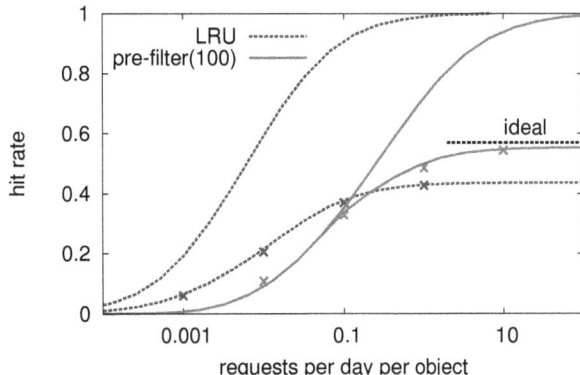

Figure 3: Hit rate against normalized demand σ: analytical results for a cache of size 1000 and an unlimited cache for LRU and LRU+pre-filter of 100; simulation results are shown as crosses for $C = 1000$; $N = 10^4$ items with Zipf(.8) popularity.

lifetimes cannot be measured for the 85% most unpopular items with fewer than 10 requests in the entire trace. Table 2 consolidates the results from [14], grouping in class 5 all items with lifetime > 13 days or less than 10 requests in the entire trace. Somewhat arbitrarily in the absence of data, we suppose the mean lifetime of these items is one year. We discuss the impact of divergence from this assumed lifetime distribution below.

The average item popularity in the classes decreases with increasing mean lifetime. In our evaluations we assume the items in class j are in fact all more popular than the items in class k when $j < k$. While these data are clearly very rough, they do allow us to appreciate the significant impact of time locality on cache performance.

Numerical results.

In the formulas, lifetimes τ_i are normalized with respect to the overall request arrival rate since we have $\sum q_i = 1$. In Figure 3 we plot the overall hit rate against overall demand σ expressed as the mean number of requests per item per day. The corresponding mean lifetimes are then $\tau_i = \sigma N l_k$, for $\sum_{j<k} f_j N < i \le \sum_{j \le k} f_j N$ and $k \le 5$. We choose to normalize with respect to the catalogue size since, for Zipf(α) popularity with $\alpha < 1$, hit rates $h(\sigma, N)$ tend to a limit as $N \to \infty$ (with filter size K increasing proportionally).

Figure 3 plots hit rates against σ for an LRU cache and for a cache equipped with a pre-filter of size 100. The catalogue size is 10^4 and popularity is Zipf(.8). Simulation results for $C = 1000$, derived *without* the assumption that

an old version of item i is removed when a new version is inserted, are shown as crosses and confirm the accuracy of the formulas. Lifetimes in the simulations have geometric distributions with means given in Table 2.

The depicted results demonstrate that, though the pre-filter brings close to ideal performance for stationary demand (i.e., for large σ), performance at moderate demand is worse than LRU. Neither caching strategy is effective when demand is low. The difference between the two policies for an unlimited cache is due to the fact that the pre-filter imposes a miss for the first two requests for a new item whereas LRU imposes only one miss.

The lifetime data constitute the best guess we have but are clearly imprecise. We have therefore examined the impact of deviations from our assumptions. As previously noted, as N increases, the hit rates as a function of σ tend to a limit. The curves in this limit are slightly above those depicted in the figure. Increasing all lifetimes by a common factor gives the same curves translated horizontally by the same factor. Changing the lifetime of class 5 from 1 year to 6 months or 2 years, say, shifts the lower part of the curves by a factor of 2 to the right or the left, respectively without modifying the top that is mainly determined by classes 1 to 4. Slightly modifying the lifetimes of the latter (e.g., lifetimes $l = \{10.6, 6.4, 3.3, 1.1\}$ instead of $\{1.1, 3.3, 6.4, 10.4\}$) has only a small impact on computed hit rates.

3. DEMAND AND CACHING POLICIES

Depending on the volume and characteristics of demand it may or may not make sense to apply a reactive caching policy like LRU or LRU with pre-filter (cf Sec. 2). If demand is too low, we need to envisage a proactive pre-fetching policy where the most popular items are determined externally. Note that cache performance has been shown to be largely independent of chunk size and we therefore choose to express catalogue size as a volume in bytes.

3.1 Traffic mix

For illustration purposes, we consider two types of content with very different catalogue sizes, 1 TB and 1 PB, respectively. The first might represent VoD where the number of titles available in the US is currently around 10^4 and mobile compatible rates limit the mean byte volume per object to around 100 MB. The second 1 PB catalogue corresponds to all other content. This is a rough order of magnitude estimate accounting for the data volume represented by applications like user-generated video content, social networking, file sharing and the web.

In traffic statistics published by Sandvine [13], 95% of mobile access downstream traffic in North America is content retrieval with VoD applications counting for some 20% of this. The VoD proportion has an increasing trend. In fixed networks the VoD proportion already attains 60%.

3.2 Popularity laws

For the sake of simplicity and reproducibility we choose to model popularity for both catalogues using a Zipf law with exponent 0.8. This value is typical of what has been observed for the main part of the popularity law (e.g., [7, 11]). The Zipf law does not accurately model the tail of the law, however, and care must be taken in interpreting the assumed catalogue sizes.

The BitTorrent popularity data described in [11] reveal a significant tail where popularity decreases much faster than Zipf(.8). The observed torrent catalogue was of 1.6 PB with 1.5 PB in the tail counting for 31% of requests. To model this law by a Zipf(.8) having the same weight of requests in the tail, and therefore the same ideal cache hit rates for capacities up to the start of the tail, the catalogue size should be limited to only 500 TB.

The above discussion highlights a deficit in our understanding of popularity, despite numerous published measurements. The common approach of trace analysis appears unable to correctly determine the behaviour of the tail of the law: the trace must typically be very long to observe any requests for the least popular items; on the other hand, we know that popularities can change quite rapidly and can only be measured reliably over a relatively short period.

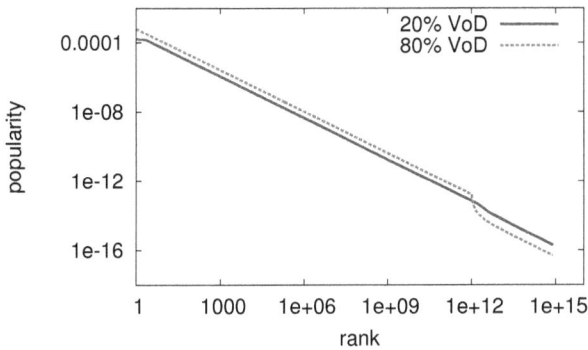

Figure 4: Popularity laws for a composition of 1 TB catalogue, representing VoD, and 1 PB catalogue, representing all other content; both catalogues have Zipf(.8) popularity and the relative traffic volumes are 20:80 and 80:20, respectively.

We consider the 1 TB and 1 PB catalogues individually to evaluate the impact on performance and cost effectiveness of what might be considered two extremes. We also combine the catalogues with traffic proportions 20:80 and 80:20, respectively. The resulting popularity laws are depicted in Figure 4. From traffic data reported in Section 3.1, the 20:80 combination is most plausible.

Time varying popularities.
Figure 3 shows the impact on hit rates of time varying popularities for individual Zipf(.8) catalogues. Figure 5 shows hit rates for an unlimited cache without pre-filter as a function of normalized demand for 100%, 80%, 20% and 0% VoD. The lifetime distribution of Table 2 is applied to each catalogue separately.

Demand σ is normalized with respect to the overall catalogue of 1.001 PB, even when we assume the VoD proportion is 100%. The difference between hit rate plots for 0% and 100% VoD corresponds therefore to a translation by a factor of 1000. These two plots constitute a reference to understand the impact of the mix. When VoD counts for only 20% of demand, the performance of reactive caching is close to that of a single 1 PB catalogue. When VoD represents 80% of demand, the hit rate first behaves like the 100% VoD

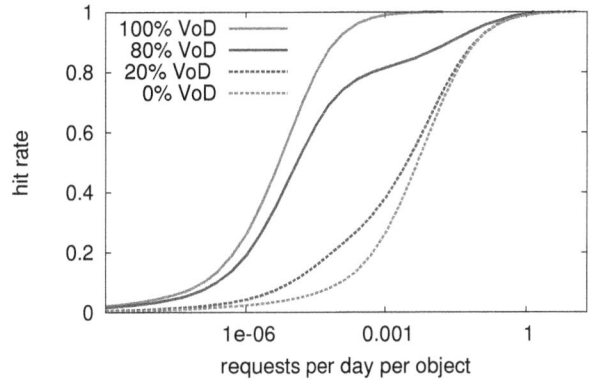

Figure 5: Hit rate against normalized demand σ when content is from two catalogues, a 1 TB catalogue representing VoD and a 1 PB catalogue representing all other content. The proportion of VoD demand varies from 0 to 100%.

plot but differs for the largest hit rates when the tail of the 1 PB catalogue popularity law predominates.

3.3 Traffic volumes

Based on traffic records from a mobile operator, we consider two base station demand scenarios:

- "current demand" with 40 Mb/s busy hour content traffic and 144 GB daily download (8 times the busy hour volume),

- "future demand" with 240 Mb/s busy hour and 864 TB per day, accounting for a possible future sixfold capacity extension.

PGW and MCN concentrate the traffic of 1000 and 100 BS, respectively, and are supposed to have proportional demand with the same popularity laws.

3.4 Caching policies

We suppose the objective is to realize ideal cache performance, either by using a pre-filter cache policy or by proactively filling caches with the most popular items as determined by some external analysis. We discuss which of these policies is viable at each of the considered cache locations.

Base stations.
Even for the most optimistic scenario of 240 Mb/s demand for 1 TB of content (i.e., 100% VoD), the number of requests per day per item (σ = 864 GB / 1 TB) is less than 1 and, according to the lifetimes assumed for Figure 3, the considered reactive caching policies (either LRU or LRU with pre-filter) are not completely efficient. They are even less so for smaller demand (e.g., 40 Mb/s) or a bigger catalogue (e.g., 1 PB). It would be far preferable therefore to perform pre-fetching to populate the cache.

Pre-fetching would need to be orchestrated by a server that is aware of current demand from a much larger population of users than that of a single BS. This server would need to be made aware of all user requests, even those that result in a hit at the BS. It might be located at the PGW or at an upstream node concentrating demand from multiple access networks. Note that to inform such a centralized entity of user requests would also facilitate necessary content provider control over delivery of its particular content items (for billing, accounting, ad placement, etc.), as in current CDN solutions

This server would perform, so far unspecified, data analytics to determine the most popular items for each BS accounting for the nature of its particular population of users. Popularity might for instance be determined using the pre-filter, as long as demand σ is high enough, with changes to local BS content performed incrementally as necessary.

Packet gateway.

The PGW may or may not concentrate sufficient traffic to make reactive caching efficient. We find $\sigma = 144$ with the current demand scenario and a catalogue of 1 TB (meaning the pre-filter gives close to ideal hit rates) but $\sigma = .144$ only, if the catalogue size is 1 PB.

If the latter case applies one would need proactive pre-fetching of the most popular items, even at this highest level of concentration. This is clearly problematic for a mobile provider whose knowledge of demand is limited to that of its own limited population of users. The provider would typically need to be informed of demand from a much larger population of users than its own.

Rather than creating a cache in the PGW, one can thus envisage the creation of a large-scale content store shared by multiple mobile and fixed operators and physically located at the same point of presence at the edge of the Internet. This content store would take the form of a data center with the data analytics capacity needed both to perform content provider functions and to determine the items that need to be pre-fetched to BS caches.

It is significant that this calls for a separation of functions between the mobile access transport infrastructure provider on one hand and a large-scale content store provider on the other. The former would share the cost of the latter, typically by some usage-based pricing scheme.

Mobile cloud node.

The envisaged mobile cloud node plays the role of a BS with 100 times more demand. This would make reactive caching viable for the current and future demand scenario and a catalogue of 1 TB when $\sigma = 14.4$ and 86.4, respectively. Pre-fetching would still be necessary, however, for the larger catalogue of 1 PB since σ is then 1000 times smaller.

3.5 Discussion

The above results and observations may have significant impact on the ICN architecture and business model.

Our conclusion that pre-fetching is necessary to ensure efficient BS caching implies a central server (at the PGW or higher) would need to be made aware of all requests, including BS hits, to be able to track dynamic popularity. This is likely necessary in any case to provide content providers adequate control over delivery of their content. An MCN would improve caching efficiency but still require pre-fetching if our assumption that the catalogue attains 1 PB and not 1 TB is correct.

For the PGW, reactive caching is still only just effective for the larger catalogue. It may be preferable in this case to create a content store that federates the content demand from multiple access network providers. This would lead to

rate (Mb/s)	charge ($)	rate (Mb/s)	charge ($)
10	500	100	850
20	575	200	1025
50	750	300	1220

Table 3: Monthly backhaul connection charges

a separation of functions between the content store operator and the access network operators. The former would likely host content as well as provider control logic (for accounting, ad placement, etc.).

4. MEMORY BANDWIDTH TRADEOFFS

Whether it is profitable to install a cache and what size it should have depends on the realized memory for bandwidth tradeoff. In this section we seek to evaluate this tradeoff at the BS, PGW and MCN locations assuming that caching is ideal thanks either to an efficient reactive cache policy or to pre-fetching.

4.1 Base stations

We propose rough cost estimates and evaluate the tradeoff realized under current and future BS demand scenarios.

Cost of storage.

We suppose base stations would either be equipped with a dedicated cache of some given capacity or have no cache. BS cache capacity is limited for cost and complexity reasons and, for the present evaluation, we suppose this capacity is 1 TB. Such a cache could be realized using a solid state disk with 1 TB hard drives currently priced at around $400. A DRAM cache would cost roughly 20 times more.

To the cost of the hard drive must be added that of its server logic yielding a total caching cost of perhaps $1000. Note that cost trends tracked over many years show the price of memory is decreasing by around 40% each year[1].

Cost of bandwidth.

We assume the backhaul is sized to realize a busy hour utilization of 80%, i.e., required connection bandwidths are 50 and 300 Mb/s for the current and future demand scenarios, respectively. The mobile operator typically pays a fixed network operator for backhaul capacity. We suppose a monthly charge per Mb/s that depends on demand, as given in Table 3. The table is based on current tariffs for optical backhaul in France. These tariffs have been fairly stable over the past 3 years. The charge determines the bandwidth cost of the mobile operator irrespective of the distance from the PGW.

Tradeoff.

An assumed cache cost of $1000 amortized over a 3 to 4 year lifetime corresponds to a monthly charge of barely $25 to be compared to the monthly cost of the connection. According to the tariffs of Table 3, the 1 TB cache would economize $250 ($750−$500) per month for current demand and $470 ($1220 − $750) for future demand if the catalogue were only 1 TB (100% hit rate). On the other hand, bandwidth savings would hardly be worthwhile if the catalogue

[1]J. C. McCallum: http://www.jcmit.com/mem2014.htm

were 1 PB since the hit rate is then less than 10%, even for ideal caching.

For a catalogue composed of 1 TB of VoD and 1 PB of other content in proportions 20:80, an ideal cache of 1 TB would give a hit rate of around 30%. This is significantly more than the 20% obtained by caching exclusively the VoD content. This is because it is more effective to cache the most popular other content items than the least popular VoD items. The average saving would then be around $80 per month per BS in both demand scenarios. Assuming the more favourable proportions of 80% VoD and 20% other content yields an ideal cache hit rate of nearly 85% and savings only slightly less than those given above for an individual 1 TB catalogue.

4.2 Packet gateway

The packet gateway is assumed to concentrate the traffic of 1000 BSs with, therefore, a busy hour downstream demand of 40 Gb/s and 240 Gb/s for the current and future scenarios, respectively. The PGW might have its own dedicated cache or share a co-located cache with other fixed and mobile operators. In the latter case, the tradeoff must be considered as a whole with the assumption that a given operator shares the cost of caching in proportion to its demand.

For the considered large scale cache at this location, we assume linear cost functions and seek therefore to minimize

$$\Delta = k_b T(1 - h(C)) + k_m C, \qquad (3)$$

for particular values of cost coefficients k_b and k_m. Now, for Zipf(α) popularity with $\alpha < 1$ and a large catalogue N, it is known that the hit rate $h(C, N)$ is in fact a function of the ratio $c = C/N$. This is true also for the considered combinations of Zipf catalogues. It is convenient therefore to re-write (3) in a normalized form as follows:

$$\delta(c) = \Gamma(1 - h(c)) + c, \qquad (4)$$

where $\Gamma = k_b T / k_m N$. Γ is the ratio of the cost of no cache to the cost of a full capacity cache and summarizes the combined impact of the demand and cost parameters.

Cost of storage.

We base storage costs on the charges levied for data storage by Cloud providers. This is currently around $.03 per GB per month. The traffic related cost of retrieving data from the cache is small compared to the cost of network bandwidth and is therefore neglected in our tradeoff evaluation.

Cost of bandwidth.

From Table 3, the cost of backhaul bandwidth is a decreasing function of demand and the lowest incremental charge for connections of rate greater than 200 Mb/s is $2 per Mb/s. In the absence of more precise data, we take this as the value of k_b. This would be a charge paid by the mobile operator for traffic retrieved from the Internet. The actual tariffs are certainly more complex than this but they are not public and the linear cost model allows for simpler comparisons.

Tradeoff.

Figure 6 plots normalized cost δ against normalized cache size c for Zipf(.8) popularity assuming ideal caching. The blue lines correspond to different values of Γ between 0.01

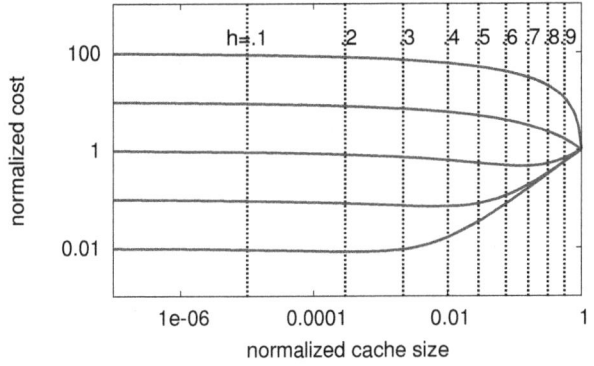

Figure 6: Normalized cost against normalized cache size for Zipf(.8) popularity and ideal caching. The horizontal lines correspond to values of Γ of .01, .1, 1, 10, 100 from bottom to top.

and 100, as determined by their intercept on the y-axis. Vertical lines give the hit rate realized by the given cache size.

From the figure, for most values of Γ, the optimal choice is either no cache ($c = 0$) or a full capacity cache ($c = 1$). As can readily be verified, the cost δ is minimized for some $c \in (0, 1)$ if $\Gamma < 5$. The gain is very limited when Γ is small, however. Maximum gain relative to $c = 0$ or $c = 1$ occurs for $\Gamma = 1$ and $c = .13$ when $\delta = 0.47$.

Using the above cost estimates, $k_b = \$2$ per Mb/s, $k_m = \$.03$ per GB, we have $\Gamma = 2000$ for current demand and a 1 TB catalogue. It is clearly optimal in this case (and *a fortiori* with the future demand scenario) to equip the PGW with a full capacity cache. The choice is less obvious for a catalogue of 1 PB where Γ is only 2 for current demand. Rather than optimizing the cache size (at around 10% of the catalogue), it would make more sense in this case to share a common cache with multiple mobile and fixed operators having co-located facilities at the edge of the Internet, as discussed above in Section 3.

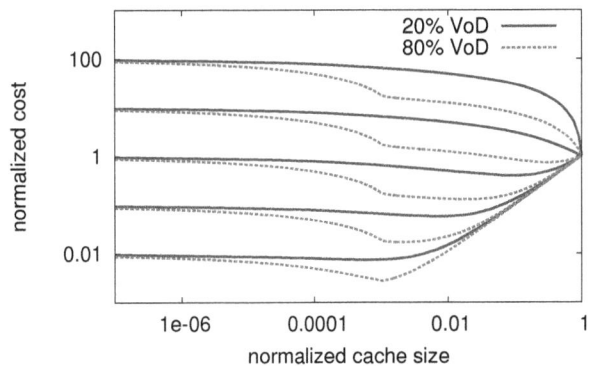

Figure 7: Normalized cost against normalized cache size for mix of popularity laws and ideal caching: VoD and other. The horizontal lines correspond to values of Γ of .01, .1, 1, 10, 100 from bottom to top.

Figure 7 plots the cost δ for the two catalogue mixes with 20% VoD and 80% VoD, respectively. Conclusions for the more plausible 20% VoD mix are broadly the same as for homogeneous Zipf(.8) popularity. When VoD counts for 80% of demand, on the other hand, there is scope for optimizing cache size. For example, for $\Gamma = 2$ (i.e., for the current demand scenario) it would be optimal to equip the cache with a capacity of 40 TB. This would yield a hit rate of 90% with cost reduced by a factor of 4 compared to the cache all solution.

4.3 Mobile cloud node

The MCN node is supposed to be equipped as a small data center performing various network functions and application offloads so that marginal storage charges are appropriate. We suppose these are the same as for a PGW cache. Since demand is greater than 200 Mb/s, we also assume the marginal bandwidth charge of $2 per Mb/s applies to the considered content traffic.

The tradeoff can be derived from Figures 6 and 7 on calculating the appropriate values of Γ. For instance, for current demand bandwidth requirement $T = 5$ Gb/s and catalogue size $N = 1$ TB, we have $\Gamma = 333$ and to cache all content at the MCN would be cost effective. On the other hand, if $N = 1$ PB we have $\Gamma = .33$ and caching brings only marginal gains.

Note that caching at the MCN is an alternative to caching at the BS. Its greater effectiveness constitutes an additional argument for actually creating such a node in future mobile access networks.

4.4 Discussion

At the BS, a 1 TB cache costing $1000 would be beneficial if pre-fetching were used to realize ideal caching (cf. Sec. 3). Cost trends suggest this tradeoff will become more favorable over time as the cost of memory is decreasing faster than the cost of bandwidth.

The charts in Figures 6 and 7 show that it is rarely worthwhile to optimize the size of the cache at the PGW where simply caching the entire catalogue is the most cost effective solution. This is not true for the 80% VoD scenario but this not realistic according to current usage statistics. It must be remembered that this conclusion applies under the simplifying assumption that catalogue popularity is Zipf. If the tail of the popularity law were more accurately represented, with a significant volume of very unpopular items, it would likely make sense to store only a fraction of the catalogue leading to a hit rate of 99%, say.

5. RELATED WORK

The models for cache performance in Section 2 are developments on the approximation originally proposed by Che *et al.* [1] and extended since, notably by Fricker *et al.* [6] and Martina *et al.* [9]. We further extend the approach here to account for time varying popularities for both an LRU cache and our particular design of an LRU cache with pre-filter. The corroborating simulation results presented here confirm the versatility and high accuracy of the Che approach.

The pre-filter cache policy we describe is an adaptation of the discrete persistent access cache proposed by Jelenkovic *et al.* [8]. It is simpler than insertion policies like k-LRU, where the filter is one or more successive virtual LRU caches, and more reactive to changing popularity than probabilistic q-LRU caching, where items are inserted with probability q.

These names were given by Martina *et al.* [9] whose models directly inspired those developed here.

The need to take proper account of time varying popularities has been underscored by recent analyses of trace statistics, notably by Traverso *et al.* [14], Olmos *et al.* [10] and Imbrenda *et al.* [7]. The authors of both [14] and [10] propose a so-called shot noise model where items are born at some instant in time, receive requests at possibly varying rate for a certain lifetime and then die. The overall request process is a superposition of such shots. In our approach, items that die are immediately replaced by a new item with identical popularity, simplifying demand characterization and allowing a straightforward application of the Che approach. This model or content churn was first used by Wolman *et al.* [15] in a study of hit rates in an unlimited capacity web cache. We generalize the model of [15] by considering finite capacity caches with LRU or pre-filter caching policies.

The direct evaluation of the memory for bandwidth tradeoff has received little direct attention in the literature. Cidon *et al.* [2] consider the problem of minimizing the joint cost of bandwidth and storage cost in a tree network but provide no numerical evaluations. Erman *et al.* [4] apply a similar approach to ours for a 3G access network assuming unlimited cache capacity and applying trace data. Our formulation of this issue is derived from prior work on the effectiveness of edge caching [11]. The present work provides a quantified evaluation of the tradeoffs in a mobile access network using our best guess demand and cost data.

6. CONCLUSIONS

To evaluate the effectiveness of caching in the mobile access network we have developed original mathematical models to determine the hit rate as a function of content popularity statistics. We have notably proposed a model to account for time varying content popularities. The results show that using a pre-filter makes an LRU cache have close to ideal performance under stationary popularity but can be counterproductive due to the impact of content popularity churn when the request rate is low.

The analytical models have been applied to determine the effectiveness of reactive caching, using LRU or LRU with a pre-filter and relying, therefore, only on locally gained knowledge of content popularity. Results for the most plausible demand scenarios suggest reactive caching at the BS or MCN levels would not be efficient and that a proactive policy of prefetching would therefore be necessary. This implies some upstream entity must be made aware of requests from a population of users that is large enough that request rates are typically much greater than the rate of churn. Even the PGW may not have sufficient demand to enable efficient reactive caching in the more pessimistic scenarios implying that the upstream entity in question might be located in a common cache at the Internet edge shared by multiple access networks.

The memory for bandwidth tradeoff is favourable at all levels of the considered access network. In the scenario considered most plausible where 20% of demand is for VoD, a relatively small 1 TB cache at the BS would be cost effective in reducing upstream traffic by 30%. The addition of the MCN level would be beneficial by enabling a single cache to be shared by up to 100 BS and, under our assumptions, enabling more flexible cache sizing. A cache at the PGW would generally be cost effective when sized to capture up to 99% of all requests. It may, however, make more economic sense to share a dedicated content store located in proximity to the PGW at the Internet edge between multiple access network providers.

It is clear that the above conclusions rely on input data on demand, popularity and costs that are necessarily questionable. However, we have considered a range of scenarios and illustrated the impact of possible deviations from our best guess data and believe the above conclusions to be robust. The methodology and formulas can of course be applied with alternative, more precise data when these are available. Evaluating the realized memory for bandwidth tradeoff, even imprecisely as here, more directly informs the debate on ICN caching architecture than any consideration of the optimal placement of a hypothetical "cache budget".

Acknowledgment

This research work has been partially funded by the SystemX Technological Research Institute within the "Network Architecture" project hosted at LINCS.

7. REFERENCES

[1] H. Che, Y. Tung, and Z. Wang. Hierarchical web caching systems: modeling, design and experimental results. *IEEE JSAC*, 20(7):1305–1314, 2002.

[2] I. Cidon, S. Kutten, and R. Soffer. Optimal allocation of electronic content. *Computer Networks*, 40(2):205 – 218, 2002.

[3] A. Dabirmoghaddam, M. M. Barijough, and J. Garcia-Luna-Aceves. Understanding optimal caching and opportunistic caching at "the edge" of information-centric networks. In *Proceedings of the 1st International Conference on Information-centric Networking*, INC '14, pages 47–56, New York, NY, USA, 2014. ACM.

[4] J. Erman, A. Gerber, M. Hajiaghayi, D. Pei, S. Sen, and O. Spatscheck. To cache or not to cache: The 3g case. *Internet Computing, IEEE*, 15(2):27–34, March 2011.

[5] S. K. Fayazbakhsh, Y. Lin, A. Tootoonchian, A. Ghodsi, T. Koponen, B. Maggs, K. Ng, V. Sekar, and S. Shenker. Less pain, most of the gain: Incrementally deployable icn. *SIGCOMM Comput. Commun. Rev.*, 43(4):147–158, Aug. 2013.

[6] C. Fricker, P. Robert, and J. Roberts. A versatile and accurate approximation for LRU cache performance. In *Proceedings of ITC 24*, 2012.

[7] C. Imbrenda, L. Muscariello, and D. Rossi. Analyzing cacheability in the access network with hacksaw. In *Proceedings of the 1st International Conference on Information-centric Networking*, INC '14, pages 201–202, New York, NY, USA, 2014. ACM.

[8] P. Jelenkovic, X. Kang, and A. Radovanovic. Near optimality of the discrete persistent access caching algorithm. In *International Conference on Analysis of Algorithms,*, 2005.

[9] V. Martina, M. Garetto, and E. Leonardi. A unified approach to the performance analysis of caching systems. In *INFOCOM, 2014 Proceedings IEEE*, pages 2040–2048, April 2014.

[10] F. Olmos, B. Kauffmann, A. Simonian, and Y. Carlinet. Catalog dynamics: Impact of content publishing and perishing on the performance of a lru cache. In *Teletraffic Congress (ITC), 2014 26th International*, pages 1–9, Sept 2014.

[11] J. Roberts and N. Sbihi. Exploring the memory-bandwidth tradeoff in an information-centric network. In *Teletraffic Congress (ITC), 2013 25th International*, pages 1–9, Sept 2013.

[12] G. Rossini and D. Rossi. Coupling caching and forwarding: Benefits, analysis, and implementation. In *Proceedings of the 1st International Conference on Information-centric Networking*, INC '14, pages 127–136, New York, NY, USA, 2014. ACM.

[13] Sandvine. Global internet phenomena report - 2h 2014. White paper, 2014.

[14] S. Traverso, M. Ahmed, M. Garetto, P. Giaccone, E. Leonardi, and S. Niccolini. Temporal locality in today's content caching: Why it matters and how to model it. *SIGCOMM Comput. Commun. Rev.*, 43(5):5–12, Nov. 2013.

[15] A. Wolman, M. Voelker, N. Sharma, N. Cardwell, A. Karlin, and H. M. Levy. On the scale and performance of cooperative web proxy caching. *SIGOPS Oper. Syst. Rev.*, 33(5):16–31, Dec. 1999.

Object-oriented Packet Caching for ICN

Yannis Thomas
thomasi@aueb.gr

George Xylomenos
xgeorge@aueb.gr

Christos Tsilopoulos
tsilochr@aueb.gr

George C. Polyzos
polyzos@aueb.gr

Mobile Multimedia Laboratory
Department of Informatics
School of Information Sciences and Technology
Athens University of Economics and Business

ABSTRACT

One of the most discussed features offered by Information-centric Networking (ICN) architectures is the ability to support packet-level caching at every node in the network. By individually naming each packet, ICN allows routers to turn their queueing buffers into packet caches, thus exploiting the network's existing storage resources. However, the performance of packet caching at commodity routers is restricted by the small capacity of their SRAM, which holds the index for the packets stored at the, slower, DRAM. We therefore propose Object-oriented Packet Caching (OPC), a novel caching scheme that overcomes the SRAM bottleneck, by combining object-level indexing in the SRAM with packet-level storage in the DRAM. We implemented OPC and experimentally evaluated it over various cache placement policies, showing that it can enhance the impact of ICN packet-level caching, reducing both network and server load.

Categories and Subject Descriptors

C.2.1 [**Computer-Communication Networks**]: [Network Architecture and Design]

Keywords

Information-centric networking; ICN; Caching

1. INTRODUCTION

Reducing the redundancy in Web traffic by exploiting caches to satisfy repeated requests for popular content has long been an active research topic. Analysis from Cisco argues that global IP traffic will increase threefold over the next five years, reaching eventually 1.6 zettabytes per year by 2018 [1]. As a result, considerable investment in network infrastructure will be needed in order to meet these traffic demands, unless caching rises up to the challenge. Numer-ous research studies examining the character of modern Internet traffic have indicated that caching has the potential to greatly reduce network load for a given traffic demand [2, 3, 4]. Indeed, Web caches are vital network elements, bringing popular content closer to the users, contributing to faster data delivery, and reducing network and server load within ISPs and at large stub networks.

However, some studies question the effectiveness of Web caches [5, 6], arguing that redundancy should be detected at a finer granularity, such as packets, instead of objects. These designs, also known as *packet-level caches*, can be significantly more efficient in eliminating repeated content transfers. Nevertheless, they present significant scalability and flexibility issues, such as managing large lookup indexes, performing per packet lookups at wire-speed, operating in more than one link and synchronizing lookup indexes.

Most such weaknesses can potentially be addressed by *Information-Centric Networking* (ICN) [7]. ICN proposes a clean slate network architecture where all network operations concern information itself, in contrast to IP-based networking, where communication is endpoint-oriented. Most ICN initiatives adopt a model of receiver-driven content delivery of self-identified packets that can be temporarily cached by routers, allowing routers to satisfy future requests for the same content. Nevertheless, ICN caching has not yet met these expectations, receiving criticism for its efficiency [8, 9], based on the debatable performance superiority of distributed in-network caching over independent caches at the network edge, as well as on the questionable support for packet-level caching by today's hardware.

In this paper we introduce *Object-oriented Packet Caching* (OPC), a novel packet-level caching scheme for ICN architectures. OPC is designed to improve the performance of ICN packet caches by increasing the usable caching capacity of commodity routers, without requiring additional storage resources. Furthermore, OPC addresses the *looped replacement* and *large object poisoning* effects, two common issues with packet caches that can highly penalize the performance of ICN in-network caching.

The remainder of this paper is organized as follows. In Section 2 we review work in packet-level caching and the issues raised by it in an ICN context. In Section 3 we explain how OPC works and how it addresses these challenges. In Section 4 we present an evaluation study of OPC, showing the gains achieved. We conclude and discuss future work in Section 5.

ICN'15, September 30–October 2, 2015, San Francisco, CA, USA.
© 2015 ACM. ISBN 978-1-4503-3855-4/15/09 ...$15.00.
DOI: http://dx.doi.org/10.1145/2810156.2810172.

2. RELATED WORK

2.1 Packet caches in IP

Packet-level caching in IP networks requires detecting redundancy in arbitrary packets at wire-speeds. The computational cost for avoiding replication via, say, suppressing replicated data [10], deep packet inspection [11] and/or delta coding [12], has prevented Web caches from moving in this direction. Interest in packet-level caching was rejuvenated by a computationally efficient technique for finding redundancy in Web traffic [5], where Rabin fingerprints are used to detect similar, but not necessarily identical, information transfers in real time. As this method is protocol independent, it may even eliminate redundancy among different services, thus greatly widening the scope of application caches.

Unfortunately, this scheme has a limited scope of applicability: it requires placing pairs of caching points at opposite ends of a physical link, replacing redundant data with a special identifier as packets enter and leave that link. The two caching points must also keep their lookup indexes synchronized. A few years later, the application of this technique was explored in an inter-domain scenario [6]. Even though the scheme performed far better than an ordinary object cache, it was once more concluded that this solution can only be applied to limited-scale deployments across specific network links. The authors argued that the usefulness of this technique could be enhanced by new network protocols that would leverage link-level redundancy elimination [6].

2.2 Packet caches in ICN

The distinguishing feature of ICN is the placement of information in the center of network operations, in contrast to endpoint-oriented IP networks [7]. In ICN the functions of requesting, locating and delivering information are directly based on the information itself, rather than on the hosts providing the content. In most ICN proposals, information travels through the network as a set of self-verified data chunks that carry a *statistically unique* identifier. This identifier, which is usually a concatenation of the content's name and the packet's rank/order in the content, is placed in the packet header, relieving ICN nodes from the computational costs of detecting identical packets; if two packets have the same identifier, then they must (statistically) carry the same content. In the vast majority of ICN studies, a chunk refers to the *Maximum Transfer Unit* (MTU) of the network, that is, the maximum packet allowed, hence, we will use below the terms packet and chunk as synonyms.

ICN transport protocols are mostly receiver-driven [13, 14], completing a transmission via numerous independent transfers of self-verified chunks. Each transfer is triggered by a specific *request* packet and is fulfilled by the transmission of the corresponding *data* packet. The pull model allows exploiting on-path caches: ICN routers that use their queueing buffers as temporal repositories for packets can directly respond to later requests for these packets.

ICN has great potential for exploiting packet-level caches, therefore many researchers have investigated the gains of ubiquitous caching [15, 16, 17, 18]. The authors of these papers try to aggregate the caching potential of all on-path routers into a distributed caching system, focusing on achieving the most profitable distribution of content across these routers. However, experience with distributed caching systems suggests that dedicated caching super-nodes at the edges of the network can have the same impact as caching at every in-network node [8]. In addition, some authors advocate caching content only at a subset of network nodes that satisfy certain centrality requirements [19], while others argue that an "edge" caching deployment provides roughly the same gains with a universal caching architecture [20].

To the best of our knowledge, there is only one study in the literature dealing with the internal details of ICN packet caches [21]. This study proposes a two-layer cache model with the goal of improving response time. Specifically, it suggests that groups of chunks should be pre-fetched from the slow memory (SSD) to the fast one (DRAM) in order to respond faster to consequent chunk requests. However, the authors propose this design only for edge routers, due to its storage requirements and static content catalogue. For in-network routers they argue that both SRAM and DRAM should be utilized for wire-speed operation. Most other research simply assumes a *Least Recently Used* (LRU) replacement policy [16, 17, 20, 19, 20, 22] or novel policies for the proper distribution of the cached content along the path [15, 18, 23], without evaluating whether router-cache performance is limited by the size of its fast memory.

3. OBJECT-ORIENTED PACKET CACHING

3.1 Design issues

Based on the previous discussion, we identified three aspects of ICN packet-caching that can be improved:

Limited storage resources: A reasonable requirement for packet-level caching is wire-speed operation. Usually, the cache module is implemented based on a hash-table structure, spread across the fast and slow memory of the system. The hash-table proper is kept on the fast, and expensive, memory of the system, mapping a hashed packet identifier to a pointer to the packet data on the slow, but cheap, memory [18, 24]. Since the vast majority of proposed cache designs assumes 1500 byte chunks and at least 32 byte LRU entries [24], a one-to-one correlation of fast-to-slow memory entries, implies a ratio of fast to slow memory size of approximately 1:46. The largest amount of SRAM memory found in current network routers is 210 Mbits [9], thus being able to index almost 1.2 GBytes of 1500 byte chunks. However, the maximum DRAM memory of a network router is 10 GBytes, thus roughly 88% of the available network storage cannot be indexed at the packet-level. One solution to this problem would be to increase chunk size, so that the hardware specifications would not affect caching performance, but this would penalize the granularity of caching [5, 6] and it would also require changing the network's MTU to preserve the self-identification of network units. Another solution could be to use DRAM for indexing the stored packets. However, this design requires one read to the slow memory for each incoming request, even with zero cache hits, thus making wire-speed operation questionable.

Looped replacement: In contrast to object caches, packet caches may contain only part of an object, depending on the replacement policy and the access pattern. This can be both a benefit and a curse. In most applications, the packets of an object are requested in a sequential ascending order, which means that in an LRU-based cache, the first packets of the object are evicted before the last ones, as they have resided longer in the cache. Consider for example an object consisting of n packets and a cache that can hold m packets, where $n > m$. An object cache would not cache the object at all, but a packet cache could cache some of its packets. However, if the object is accessed sequentially, then after the first m packets are fetched and the cache fills, the $m + 1$-th packet will displace the first packet, and so on until the object completes transmission (Fig.1(a)). When the object is later requested again, the first packet will not be found, so it will be fetched from the source, replacing the earliest packet of the object; this will be repeated until the entire object is fetched again, without even a single cache hit (Fig.1(b) and (c)). We call this the *looped replacement* effect. It can arise with any cache size, as long as we are using the LRU replacement policy, provided that the object is always accessed sequentially and requests for the same object are not too frequent. This effect is also identified by authors in [22], who however do not propose a specific solution.

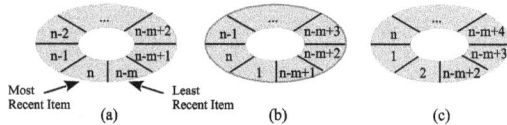

Figure 1: An LRU cache holding m packets, presented as a circular buffer. In (a) an object consisting of n packets ($n > m$) was just downloaded, in (b) and (c) the first and second packet of the same content, respectively, are fetched again.

Large object poisoning: A serious challenge for small in-network caches is handling large but unpopular objects. A cache-anything LRU module stores all the chunks of every incoming object, regardless of its popularity; popularity only influences evictions. This can severely penalize the performance of the cache, especially in cases of large objects that occupy a significant amount of memory space, which cause the cache to waste its resources by storing contents that do not offer any profit.

3.2 Design overview

To address the limitations of packet-based caching schemes in the ICN context, we designed *Object-oriented Packet Caching* (OPC) [25], a scheme which combines the effectiveness of packet-level caching with the resource efficiency of object-level caching. The design of OPC directly attacks the weak aspects of ICN packet-caches: it increases memory utilization, avoids looped replacement, and prevents large object poisoning. OPC achieves these goals without requiring more computational and memory resources than an ordinary LRU packet-cache.

The main concept of OPC is to combine object-oriented cache lookups with packet-oriented cache replacement. Based on the observation that most applications request the packets of an object in a sequential manner, in OPC *the initial part of an object is always cached, from the first to the n-th packet, with no gaps*. Therefore, any partially cached objects are always represented by their first n packets.

The lookup index in OPC holds the object's name and a counter for each (partially) stored object. This counter, also called *last_chunk_id*, indicates the number of cached chunks for that object. For instance, the entry `file/a, 45` means that the cache holds the first 45 chunks of the object `file/a` without gaps. If a request for that object arrives with a rank/order less or equal to the *last_chunk_id*, the cache

can directly respond to the request. When a request with a higher chunk rank/order arrives, then the cache simply forwards the request to its destination. This reduces the indexing costs to one entry per (partially) stored object, or roughly *average_objectsize* times less than an ordinary LRU packet cache.

To ensure that OPC always holds the initial part of an object, we also introduce a novel packet replacement algorithm. OPC inserts a chunk with rank/order i if it is either the object's first chunk, in which case we also create a new index entry for that content, or if we already have stored the $i - 1$ chunk for that object, that is, if *last_chunk_id* for that object is equal to $i - 1$. This guarantees that at any time the cache always holds the first part of each object, without any gaps. If there is no space in slow memory to hold a new chunk, then we use an object-level LRU list and remove the *last* cached chunk of the object at the tail, so as to still hold the first chunks of the object with no gaps. On the other hand, if there is no space in fast memory for a new object, then the index entry for the object at the tail of the object-level LRU is removed, along with the corresponding chunks in the slow memory.[1]

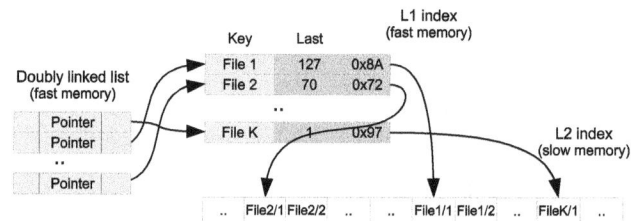

Figure 2: Data structures used by OPC.

3.3 Data structures

An OPC node maintains two data structures for chunk insertions and lookups, and one data structure for chunk evictions. The first two structures, called Layer 1 ($L1$) and Layer 2 ($L2$) indexes, organize data at the object-level and the chunk-level, respectively. The $L1$ index is stored in fast memory (e.g., SRAM) and is implemented as a fixed-sized hash-table with one entry per cached object. Each entry in $L1$ maps a content identifier to a pair of values: the rank/order of the last stored chunk (*last_chunk_id*) of that object and a pointer to the *final* chunk of the object in the $L2$ index (Ptr_{mem}). The $L2$ index on the other hand is basically an array in slow memory (e.g. DRAM) containing the cached chunks of each object in sequential order; we explain how slow memory is managed in Section 3.5.

Upon the receipt of a chunk request, OPC uses the identifier in the request's header to check via the $L1$ index if there are any cached chunks of that item. If so, and the search returns a *last_chunk_id* greater or equal to the rank/order of the requested chunk, then that chunk can be retrieved from address $Ptr_{mem} - (chunk\_id - id) * MSS$, where id is the rank/order of the requested chunk and MSS is the maximum segment size of a data chunk. Note that in order to speed up lookups, the memory array employs MSS bytes per chunk, regardless of the chunk's size. Otherwise, the request is forwarded towards its destination.

---

[1]The hash table can use linear probing, double hashing, or any other technique that does not require additional memory, to handle collisions.

2. RELATED WORK

2.1 Packet caches in IP

Packet-level caching in IP networks requires detecting redundancy in arbitrary packets at wire-speeds. The computational cost for avoiding replication via, say, suppressing replicated data [10], deep packet inspection [11] and/or delta coding [12], has prevented Web caches from moving in this direction. Interest in packet-level caching was rejuvenated by a computationally efficient technique for finding redundancy in Web traffic [5], where Rabin fingerprints are used to detect similar, but not necessarily identical, information transfers in real time. As this method is protocol independent, it may even eliminate redundancy among different services, thus greatly widening the scope of application caches.

Unfortunately, this scheme has a limited scope of applicability: it requires placing pairs of caching points at opposite ends of a physical link, replacing redundant data with a special identifier as packets enter and leave that link. The two caching points must also keep their lookup indexes synchronized. A few years later, the application of this technique was explored in an inter-domain scenario [6]. Even though the scheme performed far better than an ordinary object cache, it was once more concluded that this solution can only be applied to limited-scale deployments across specific network links. The authors argued that the usefulness of this technique could be enhanced by new network protocols that would leverage link-level redundancy elimination [6].

2.2 Packet caches in ICN

The distinguishing feature of ICN is the placement of information in the center of network operations, in contrast to endpoint-oriented IP networks [7]. In ICN the functions of requesting, locating and delivering information are directly based on the information itself, rather than on the hosts providing the content. In most ICN proposals, information travels through the network as a set of self-verified data chunks that carry a *statistically unique* identifier. This identifier, which is usually a concatenation of the content's name and the packet's rank/order in the content, is placed in the packet header, relieving ICN nodes from the computational costs of detecting identical packets; if two packets have the same identifier, then they must (statistically) carry the same content. In the vast majority of ICN studies, a chunk refers to the *Maximum Transfer Unit* (MTU) of the network, that is, the maximum packet allowed, hence, we will use below the terms packet and chunk as synonyms.

ICN transport protocols are mostly receiver-driven [13, 14], completing a transmission via numerous independent transfers of self-verified chunks. Each transfer is triggered by a specific *request* packet and is fulfilled by the transmission of the corresponding *data* packet. The pull model allows exploiting on-path caches: ICN routers that use their queueing buffers as temporal repositories for packets can directly respond to later requests for these packets.

ICN has great potential for exploiting packet-level caches, therefore many researchers have investigated the gains of ubiquitous caching [15, 16, 17, 18]. The authors of these papers try to aggregate the caching potential of all on-path routers into a distributed caching system, focusing on achieving the most profitable distribution of content across these routers. However, experience with distributed caching systems suggests that dedicated caching super-nodes at the edges of the network can have the same impact as caching at every in-network node [8]. In addition, some authors advocate caching content only at a subset of network nodes that satisfy certain centrality requirements [19], while others argue that an "edge" caching deployment provides roughly the same gains with a universal caching architecture [20].

To the best of our knowledge, there is only one study in the literature dealing with the internal details of ICN packet caches [21]. This study proposes a two-layer cache model with the goal of improving response time. Specifically, it suggests that groups of chunks should be pre-fetched from the slow memory (SSD) to the fast one (DRAM) in order to respond faster to consequent chunk requests. However, the authors propose this design only for edge routers, due to its storage requirements and static content catalogue. For in-network routers they argue that both SRAM and DRAM should be utilized for wire-speed operation. Most other research simply assumes a *Least Recently Used* (LRU) replacement policy [16, 17, 20, 19, 20, 22] or novel policies for the proper distribution of the cached content along the path [15, 18, 23], without evaluating whether router-cache performance is limited by the size of its fast memory.

3. OBJECT-ORIENTED PACKET CACHING

3.1 Design issues

Based on the previous discussion, we identified three aspects of ICN packet-caching that can be improved:

Limited storage resources: A reasonable requirement for packet-level caching is wire-speed operation. Usually, the cache module is implemented based on a hash-table structure, spread across the fast and slow memory of the system. The hash-table proper is kept on the fast, and expensive, memory of the system, mapping a hashed packet identifier to a pointer to the packet data on the slow, but cheap, memory [18, 24]. Since the vast majority of proposed cache designs assumes 1500 byte chunks and at least 32 byte LRU entries [24], a one-to-one correlation of fast-to-slow memory entries, implies a ratio of fast to slow memory size of approximately 1:46. The largest amount of SRAM memory found in current network routers is 210 Mbits [9], thus being able to index almost 1.2 GBytes of 1500 byte chunks. However, the maximum DRAM memory of a network router is 10 GBytes, thus roughly 88% of the available network storage cannot be indexed at the packet-level. One solution to this problem would be to increase chunk size, so that the hardware specifications would not affect caching performance, but this would penalize the granularity of caching [5, 6] and it would also require changing the network's MTU to preserve the self-identification of network units. Another solution could be to use DRAM for indexing the stored packets. However, this design requires one read to the slow memory for each incoming request, even with zero cache hits, thus making wire-speed operation questionable.

Looped replacement: In contrast to object caches, packet caches may contain only part of an object, depending on the replacement policy and the access pattern. This can be both a benefit and a curse. In most applications, the packets of an object are requested in a sequential ascending order, which means that in an LRU-based cache, the first packets of the object are evicted before the last ones, as they have resided longer in the cache. Consider for example an object consisting of n packets and a cache that can hold m packets, where $n > m$. An object cache would not cache the object at all, but a packet cache could cache some of its packets. However, if the object is accessed sequentially, then after the first m packets are fetched and the cache fills, the $m + 1$-th packet will displace the first packet, and so on until the object completes transmission (Fig.1(a)). When the object is later requested again, the first packet will not be found, so it will be fetched from the source, replacing the earliest packet of the object; this will be repeated until the entire object is fetched again, without even a single cache hit (Fig.1(b) and (c)). We call this the *looped replacement* effect. It can arise with any cache size, as long as we are using the LRU replacement policy, provided that the object is always accessed sequentially and requests for the same object are not too frequent. This effect is also identified by authors in [22], who however do not propose a specific solution.

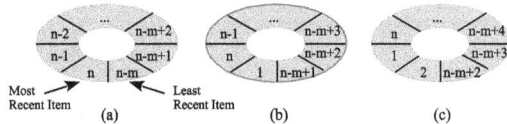

Figure 1: An LRU cache holding m packets, presented as a circular buffer. In (a) an object consisting of n packets ($n > m$) was just downloaded, in (b) and (c) the first and second packet of the same content, respectively, are fetched again.

Large object poisoning: A serious challenge for small in-network caches is handling large but unpopular objects. A cache-anything LRU module stores all the chunks of every incoming object, regardless of its popularity; popularity only influences evictions. This can severely penalize the performance of the cache, especially in cases of large objects that occupy a significant amount of memory space, which cause the cache to waste its resources by storing contents that do not offer any profit.

3.2 Design overview

To address the limitations of packet-based caching schemes in the ICN context, we designed *Object-oriented Packet Caching* (OPC) [25], a scheme which combines the effectiveness of packet-level caching with the resource efficiency of object-level caching. The design of OPC directly attacks the weak aspects of ICN packet-caches: it increases memory utilization, avoids looped replacement, and prevents large object poisoning. OPC achieves these goals without requiring more computational and memory resources than an ordinary LRU packet-cache.

The main concept of OPC is to combine object-oriented cache lookups with packet-oriented cache replacement. Based on the observation that most applications request the packets of an object in a sequential manner, in OPC *the initial part of an object is always cached, from the first to the n-th packet, with no gaps*. Therefore, any partially cached objects are always represented by their first n packets.

The lookup index in OPC holds the object's name and a counter for each (partially) stored object. This counter, also called *last_chunk_id*, indicates the number of cached chunks for that object. For instance, the entry `file/a, 45` means that the cache holds the first `45` chunks of the object `file/a` without gaps. If a request for that object arrives with a rank/order less or equal to the *last_chunk_id*, the cache

can directly respond to the request. When a request with a higher chunk rank/order arrives, then the cache simply forwards the request to its destination. This reduces the indexing costs to one entry per (partially) stored object, or roughly *average_objectsize* times less than an ordinary LRU packet cache.

To ensure that OPC always holds the initial part of an object, we also introduce a novel packet replacement algorithm. OPC inserts a chunk with rank/order i if it is either the object's first chunk, in which case we also create a new index entry for that content, or if we already have stored the $i - 1$ chunk for that object, that is, if *last_chunk_id* for that object is equal to $i - 1$. This guarantees that at any time the cache always holds the first part of each object, without any gaps. If there is no space in slow memory to hold a new chunk, then we use an object-level LRU list and remove the *last* cached chunk of the object at the tail, so as to still hold the first chunks of the object with no gaps. On the other hand, if there is no space in fast memory for a new object, then the index entry for the object at the tail of the object-level LRU is removed, along with the corresponding chunks in the slow memory.[1]

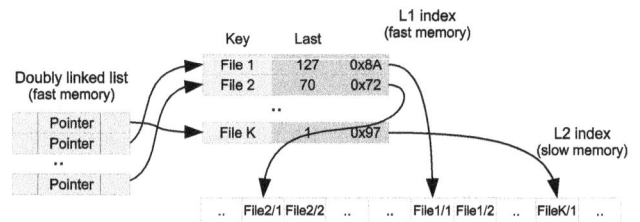

Figure 2: Data structures used by OPC.

3.3 Data structures

An OPC node maintains two data structures for chunk insertions and lookups, and one data structure for chunk evictions. The first two structures, called Layer 1 ($L1$) and Layer 2 ($L2$) indexes, organize data at the object-level and the chunk-level, respectively. The $L1$ index is stored in fast memory (e.g., SRAM) and is implemented as a fixed-sized hash-table with one entry per cached object. Each entry in $L1$ maps a content identifier to a pair of values: the rank/order of the last stored chunk (*last_chunk_id*) of that object and a pointer to the *final* chunk of the object in the $L2$ index (Ptr_{mem}). The $L2$ index on the other hand is basically an array in slow memory (e.g. DRAM) containing the cached chunks of each object in sequential order; we explain how slow memory is managed in Section 3.5.

Upon the receipt of a chunk request, OPC uses the identifier in the request's header to check via the $L1$ index if there are any cached chunks of that item. If so, and the search returns a *last_chunk_id* greater or equal to the rank/order of the requested chunk, then that chunk can be retrieved from address $Ptr_{mem} - (chunk\_id - id) * MSS$, where id is the rank/order of the requested chunk and MSS is the maximum segment size of a data chunk. Note that in order to speed up lookups, the memory array employs MSS bytes per chunk, regardless of the chunk's size. Otherwise, the request is forwarded towards its destination.

[1]The hash table can use linear probing, double hashing, or any other technique that does not require additional memory, to handle collisions.

When a new data chunk arrives, we also consult the $L1$ index: if the object is stored and this is the next chunk in sequence, we store it in the $L2$ index, increment Ptr_{mem} by MSS and increase $last\_chunk\_id$; if the object is not stored and the chunk is the first for that object, we store the chunk in the $L2$ index and create a new entry in the $L1$ index with $last\_chunk\_id$ equal to 1 and Ptr_{mem} pointing at the chunk in the $L2$ index. Otherwise, we ignore the chunk.

The third data structure in OPC is a doubly-linked list used to rank the objects for replacement purposes. This list, also kept in fast memory, shows the least "important" object in the OPC cache; this object will be evicted when additional space is needed. In our implementation, objects are ranked based on their recent usage, i.e. in LRU fashion. However, the way the least important content is defined is not crucial for our design, so cached contents may be organized in an LRU, LFU or FIFO structure. If the eviction is due to lack of $L1$ space, then the $L1$ index entry and all the $L2$ chunks that the selected entry points at are reclaimed. If the eviction is due to lack of $L2$ space though, only the last chunk of the selected entry is reclaimed and the $L1$ entry is updated by decrementing Ptr_{mem} by MSS and $last\_chunk\_id$ by 1. A snapshot of OPC's data structures is illustrated in Fig. 2.

3.4 Caching behavior

We can now explain how the OPC design addresses the limitations of chunk-level caching in the ICN context described in Section 2. First, the *two-level indexing structure* of OPC optimizes the use of both fast and slow memory: the $L1$ index in fast memory uses one entry per object, rather than one entry per chunk. The small size of the $L1$ index allows storing it in fast memory, to speed up lookups, but also substantially augments the volume of data that can be indexed in $L2$ memory, compared to simpler solutions such as LRU and FIFO, thus addressing the *limited storage resources* problem.

Second, to avoid the *looped replacement* issue, OPC always holds the initial chunks of an object, by only inserting chunks sequentially and evicting them in the reverse order. Assuming that chunks are requested in ascending order (as is also the case in [21]), our method extends the time that a cached object can be exploited, thus increasing the cache hit rate. To better illustrate this, consider Fig. 3, which presents the *potential* cache hits of two requests for the same object (y-axis) in an LRU and an OPC cache, depending on the interarrival time of these requests (x-axis). In general, as the chunks of an object are requested sequentially, the number of cached chunks increases, hence the potential for cache hits also grows. In subfigures (a) and (c), the cache size is smaller than the object size, therefore when the cache gets full, the potential for cache hits cannot increase any more. With an LRU cache (subfigure (a)) the *looped replacement* effect causes the next chunks (even of the same object) to displace the *first* chunks of the object, therefore a new sequential request for the object will lead to zero cache hits. In contrast, with OPC (subfigure (c)) chunks are only dropped from the *end* of the object, therefore the potential for cache hits decreases gradually, until all chunks are displaced. Similarly, in subfigures (b) and (d) where the cache size is larger than the object size, after the entire object is cached the potential for cache hits remains constant. When the chunks start getting evicted at a later time, with an LRU cache (subfigure (b)) the potential drops to zero, since the

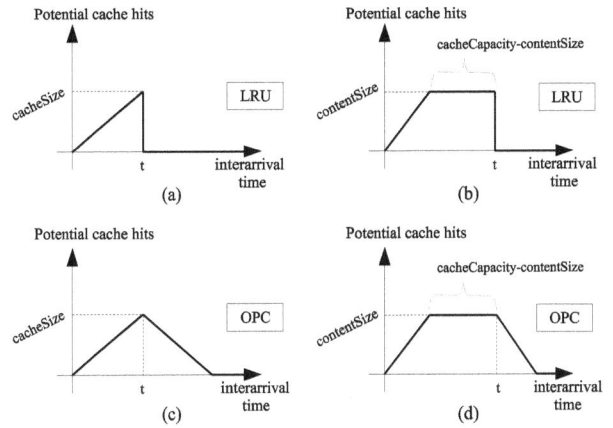

Figure 3: Potential cache-hits of two requests for the same object in an LRU and an OPC cache. In (a) and (c) content size exceeds cache size, whereas in (b) and (d) cache size exceeds content size.

first chunks are evicted, while with OPC (subfigure (d)) it only decreases gradually.

Finally, OPC addresses the *large object poisoning* issue, by applying *object-level filtering* on popularity statistics. Specifically, an $L1$ object-level index following the LRU policy, pushes an object at the head of the LRU list only on cache hits; newly inserted chunks inherit the LRU position of the object, which is commonly not the head. In contrast, with chunk-level LRU, each inserted chunk is placed at the head of the LRU list by default, thus having to traverse the entire LRU list before it is evicted. Consequently, in OPC the eviction of an object depends on the popularity of that object as a whole, while in a cache-anything chunk-based LRU the many individual chunks of the object fill up the LRU list, making it harder to keep popular objects in the cache. As shown in the evaluation section, OPC effectively enhances caching efficiency, by storing chunks with greater popularity, which are expected to produce more cache-hits.

3.5 Space allocation in slow memory

The OPC scheme assumes that slow memory is a large array with fixed size slots of MSS bytes, where adjacent chunks of the same object are placed in contiguous physical memory locations. This allows one-access insertions, evictions and reads from slow memory, since we simply index slow memory based on a pointer in fast memory. However, the number of chunks that must be stored per object is not known a priori, therefore allocating $L2$ memory for a new $L1$ entry is not trivial.

The simplest policy is to provide a fixed-size area per object, based on the $L2\_slots/L1\_slots$ ratio, thus equally distributing slow memory among all cached objects, ignoring the size and caching needs of each object. The efficiency of this approach clearly depends on the nature of network traffic; if most object sizes are close to $L2\_slots/L1\_slots$, then cache performance is not affected, but if objects are much smaller than the fixed-size allocation, then slow memory is underutilized; if they are larger, we can only store their first part, thus potentially reducing cache hits.

To avoid these problems, we have designed a method for dynamic memory allocation that adapts to different types of traffic, retaining one-access chunk insertions and evictions

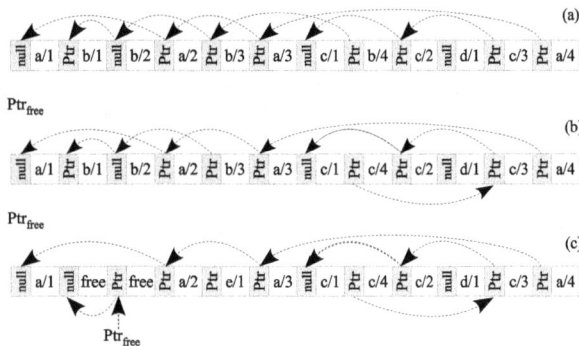

Figure 4: Evolution of slow memory: (a) initially, (b) after object c steals a chunk from object b, (c) after object b is evicted to make space for object e.

from slow memory, at the cost of increasing the accesses for lookups and entire object evictions. In our scheme, chunks of the same object are not stored in contiguous memory space, forming instead a linked-list starting from the last chunk of the object. Therefore, each chunk slot in $L2$ consists of a data chunk and a pointer Ptr_{prev} to the previous chunk of the same object. The combination of Ptr_{mem} ($L1$) and Ptr_{prev} ($L2$) forms a linked-list per object, where the last chunk of the object is the head of the list. In addition, one global pointer, Ptr_{free} points at a list of available chunks, which are also linked via their Ptr_{prev} pointers.

Whenever a new chunk needs to be inserted to the cache, if the list of available chunks is not empty, the entry pointed at by Ptr_{free} is used, and Ptr_{free} is modified to point to the next free chunk. The new chunk is linked to the list of the appropriate object by modifying its $Prev_{ptr}$ to the previous head of that object's list, and making the Ptr_{mem} of that object point at the new chunk. If there are no available chunks (Ptr_{free} is null), then we use the LRU object list to determine which object will lose a chunk, and move the chunk at the head of that object's list to the head of the new object's list, by simply modifying the Ptr_{mem} pointers of the two objects and the Ptr_{mem} pointer of the chunk. These operations require only a single slow memory access to modify the Ptr_{prev} pointer of the selected chunk.

When an entire object is to be evicted, all of its chunks in $L2$ become part of the free list. We first make the Ptr_{free} pointer point at the head of the evicted object's list, then we traverse the list following its Ptr_{prev} pointers and, finally, we modify its last pointer to point at the previous head of the free list. This requires traversing the list of the object that is evicted, thus object eviction is a costlier procedure.

The main overhead of our method is that it does not support one-access cache hits. In order to fetch a cached chunk, OPC must follow the object's linked-list from the last stored chunk until the right chunk is found. Given that chunks are requested in sequential order and that OPC holds the initial part of an object without any gaps, if the first chunk is hit then the rest will follow. Therefore, we expect an average of $n/2$ memory accesses per hit when all chunks of an n-chunk object are hit. Nevertheless, our experiments validate that this overhead is not critical, since it arises only during actual cache hits. Furthermore, an additional latency in the order of nanoseconds is an insignificant expense for a cache-hit that saves several milliseconds of delay.

		Web	P2P	Video	Other
#objects		195386	1	176	10485
#chunks	median	6	687168	8133	4
	max	19929	687167	16977	5120
	std. dev	56.6	0	5261.2	0
#requests	mean	658686	2	326	22352
	max	10984	2	17	1106
	std. dev	53.8	0	2.33	15.3

Table 1: Workload characteristics.

An example of $L2$ management is presented in Figure 4, where $L2$ state is shown at three consecutive snapshots. In Fig.4.(a), the slow memory holds chunks of four objects (a, b, c and d), which are not stored contiguously. In Fig.4.(b), another chunk of object c is inserted, but since there are no free slots, it "steals" the last chunk of object b. In Fig.4.(c), object b is evicted to make space for object e, by first moving all chunks of b to the free list and then using the first free chunk for the first chunk of object e. If at this point we get a cache hit for the first chunk of object c, we need 4 slow memory accesses to traverse the corresponding list.

4. EXPERIMENTAL EVALUATION

4.1 Experiment set-up

We implemented the CCN/NDN forwarding functionality along with various policies for chunk-level cache management[2] over the NS-3 network simulator.[3] We examined 10 scale-free topologies of 50 nodes, created via the Barabási-Albert algorithm [26], as in the experiments in [19]. We assumed a stop-and-wait unicast transport protocol for all applications, as the simpler transport provides a clearer view of system performance. In order to get a realistic traffic mix with variable object sizes and popularities, we employed the GlobeTraff traffic trace generator [27]; the characteristics of the resulting workload are summarized in Table 1. At every access node we placed a fixed-size group of 25 receivers, reserving one access node to host the origin server for all content. The workload was randomly distributed among the receivers, which all started requesting content simultaneously. The experiment ended when all receivers finished pulling their scheduled items.

We investigated the performance of OPC against LRU under three different cache placement policies: universal caching, edge caching and caching based on betweenness centrality. In universal caching, all network nodes operate a caching module, whereas in edge caching, caches are placed only at the access nodes of the network. In betweenness centrality caching, all network nodes deploy a caching module, but data chunks are stored at the on-path node(s) with the highest betweenness centrality degree [19]. Based on the hardware specifications presented in [9], we assume that the most capable caching router is equipped with 210 Mbits of SRAM and 10 GBytes of DRAM. Furthermore, we assume 40 byte LRU entries and 1500 byte chunks, similarly to most previous work [9, 19, 20]. Compared to LRU, the OPC fast memory entry requires two additional bytes for storing the number of cached chunks per object (up to 2^{16} chunks per object). This means that LRU can index up to

---

[2]Implementations available at http://www.mm.aueb.gr/
[3]Available at http://www.nsnam.org/

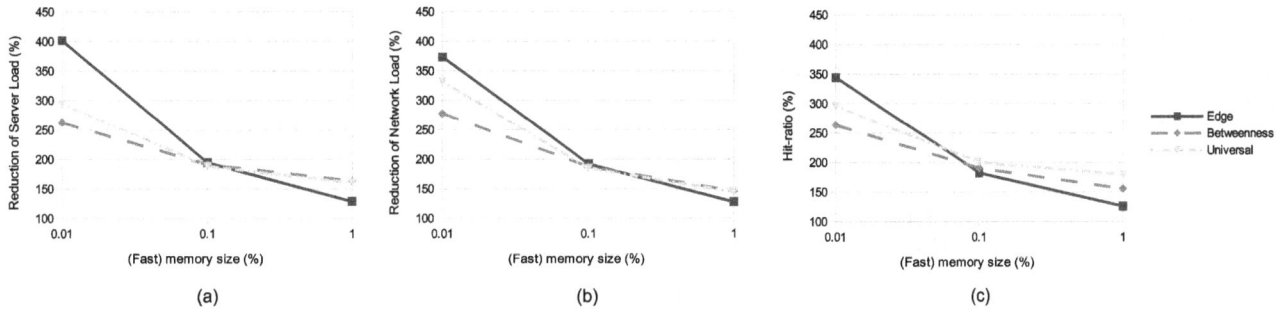

Figure 5: OPC gains normalized to LRU depending on 'fast memory size:catalog size' ratio.

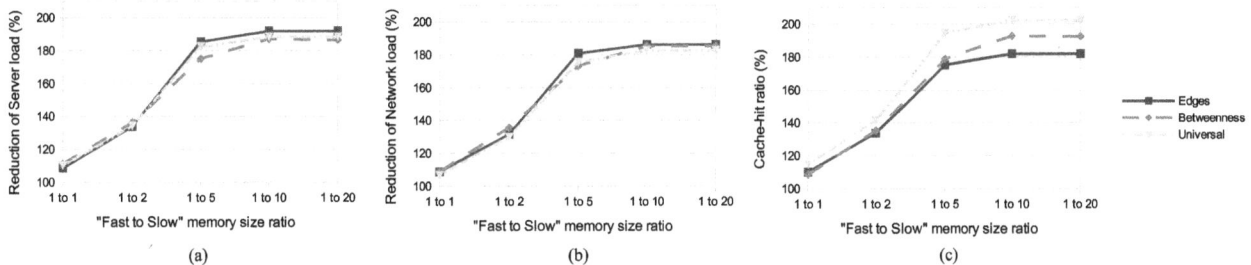

Figure 6: OPC gains normalized to LRU depending on 'fast:slow memory size' ratio.

688,128 items in fast memory, while OPC can only index up to 655,360 items. However, since LRU requires one index entry per packet, the ratio of fast to slow memory items must be 1:1, while with OPC each index entry can point at many packets; with these memory sizes, the fast to slow memory item ratio is around 1:11, i.e., one index entry per 11 chunks.

4.2 Network Performance assessment

We first investigate the performance of OPC relative to LRU under the three cache placement policies described above, depending on the ratio of fast cache memory size *per router* to the population of distinct self-identified items (chunks) in the workload, commonly referred to as the *Catalog size*. Since the number of distinct chunks was fixed in our workload, we first set the fast memory size in each caching router to correspond to 0.01%, 0.1% and 1% of the distinct items in the workload and then set the slow memory size according to the ratios presented in Sec. 4.1, i.e., 1:1 for LRU and 1:11 for OPC. For every run, we measure the number of hop-by-hop interests forwarded in the network (*Network load*), the number of interests received by the source (*Server load*) and the fraction of cache hits to cache requests (*Cache hit ratio*).

Figure 5 depicts the performance gains of OPC for each metric normalized to LRU, that is, the LRU metrics correspond to 100%. The performance superiority of OPC is clear in all cases, but is even more evident when storage resources are more limited. Specifically, when fast memory can hold 0.01% of the traffic, the gains of OPC with regard to LRU range from 260% to 400%, depending the metric and the cache placement policy. As storage resources are increased, the gains of OPC relative to LRU are reduced, since the fast memory bottleneck of LRU plays a smaller role. In addi-

tion, we observe that the improvement on edge caching is the most sensitive to cache size; for example, the gains in server load drop from 400% to 128%, with increasing cache size. This is not unreasonable, since edge caching offers less aggregated cache capacity compared to the other two policies which use all routers for caching. Finally, betweenness caching is the least affected by cache size: OPC gains on server load drop from 260% to 160%.

We then explore the impact of memory configuration on the performance of OPC. While the ratio of fast to slow memory is fixed to 1:1 for LRU by its design, regardless of actual memory sizes, OPC can adapt to different memory configurations by adapting this ratio. We thus fixed the fast cache size per router to 0.1% of the total traffic and modified the slow cache size so that the 'fast:slow memory size' ratio was 1:1, 1:2, 1:5, 1:10 and 1:20. Figure 6 illustrates the gains of OPC for each metric (again, normalized to LRU) depending on this ratio. We first notice that even with a 1:1 ratio, where both LRU and OPC exploit the same amount of slow memory, OPC performs approximately 10% better than LRU in all cases. This confirms our arguments in Sec. 3.4 that OPC better utilizes storage resources, thus providing more efficient in-network caching. We also observe that the performance gains converge at their maximum values (180% to 200%) for all metrics when the ratio reaches 1:5. This is reasonable, since in our workload the most popular traffic types are Web and Other, with the median number of chunks per object being 6 and 4, respectively.

4.3 Cache Performance assessment

We now explore the performance of OPC in terms of temporal caching costs, measuring the latency overhead of the design of Sec. 3.5 and its impact on network performance. In our analysis, we disregard processing delays, focusing on the latency overhead due to accessing the router's memory, which is considered essential for wire-speed operation. We assume that each memory access requires 0.45 ns and 55 ns for SRAM and DRAM, respectively[9]. LRU performance is charged 1 $DRAM + 1\ SRAM$ access at packet insertions and packet fetches and 1 $SRAM$ access at unsuccessful packet lookups. For OPC, we assume the design of Sec. 3.5 for managing DRAM, so we charge packet insertions and evictions with 1 $DRAM + 1\ SRAM$ access, object evictions with 1 $DRAM + n * SRAM$ accesses, where n is the number of stored object chunks, and packet hits with 1 $DRAM + m * DRAM$ accesses, where m is the number of hops followed in the linked list from the last stored chunk to the requested one. Finally, we assign a 5 ms propagation delay to all network links, and redeploy the experimental setup used in the results reported in Fig. 5.

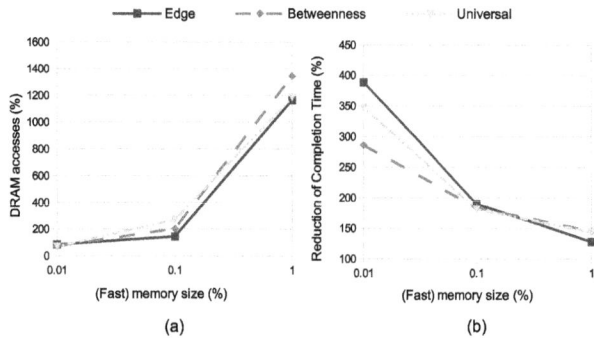

Figure 7: OPC performance normalized to LRU depending on 'fast memory size:catalog size' ratio.

Figure 7.(a) depicts the total DRAM accesses of OPC normalized to LRU for three distinct 'fast memory size:catalog size' ratios. When memory size is 0.01% of the catalog, OPC exhibits 16-32% *less* temporal overhead than LRU, despite the additional cost of maintaining the linked lists in DRAM. Since the actual hit-ratio of OPC is around 2-3% (against a roughly 1% hit-ratio for LRU), most memory accesses are due to insertions and evictions, rather than cache hits. The stricter insertion rule of OPC, which only inserts chunks in sequence, reduces the DRAM accesses for insertions/evictions by roughly 40%, leading to better memory performance. On the other hand, on cache hits OPC can require up to 1800% more reads than LRU, but as hits are only accountable for 1-2% of the total memory accesses, their cost is negligible. When memory size is increased to 0.1% of the catalog, OPC spends roughly 200% more time for DRAM accesses than LRU. This increased delay overhead is proportional to the increased hit-ratio, thus these additional memory reads are due to additional cache hits, justifying the temporal overhead. Finally, when memory size is set to 1% of the catalog, OPC's total DRAM latency reaches 1400% of LRU. OPC's larger memory can now hold bigger objects, creating longer linked-lists that amplify the DRAM accesses, as cache hits are up to 26000% more than with LRU. Nevertheless, these DRAM accesses are only triggered by cache hits, which offer network delay gains in the order of milliseconds, whereas DRAM accesses due to insertions/evictions are further reduced to 30% of LRU.

In order to understand how the increased DRAM latency of OPC impacts actual network performance, we also mea-

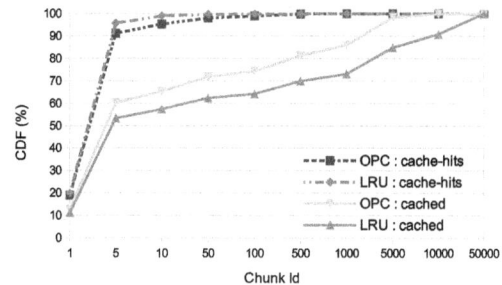

Figure 8: CDF of cache-hits and cached chunks against chunk Id.

sured the average time needed for users to complete their scheduled transmissions, also called *completion time*. As shown in Fig. 7.(b), which illustrates the reduction in completion time with OPC normalized against LRU, memory latency has a negligible impact on the performance visible to users: the plot is completely analogous to Figure 5.(b), which presents the reduction of network load with OPC normalized against LRU. This validates our claim that performance is mostly influenced by cache hits, where the temporal gains due to the increased hit-ratio of OPC dwarf its penalties in accessing DRAM.

4.4 Behavioral assessment

In order to better interpret the above results, we will also explore the state of the cache throughout the experiments. Using periodic logs, we record the stored chunks and the hits per chunk in the cache. In Figure 8 we plot these data for the betweenness centrality cache placement policy with either LRU or OPC, when the fast memory per cache is 0.1% of the catalog. Specifically, we show the cumulative distribution functions (CDFs) of cache-hits per chunk Id and of stored chunks per chunk Id, where the chunk Id is the rank/order of a chunk in its corresponding object.

We can see that 95% of the cache-hits in LRU are scored by the first five chunks of objects, whereas these same chunks account for only 53% of the cached content. In contrast, 95% of the cache-hits in OPC are provided by chunk Ids that account for 74% of the cached content, or 21% more than LRU, even though the slow memory capacity of OPC is approximately 10 times larger. Therefore, OPC "caches more" of the content that is accountable for most cache-hits, thus offering better caching accuracy. We omit plots for other policies, as they present the same tendencies.

In order to delve deeper in the results, we now focus on the 350 most frequently cached objects. We define the *caching frequency* as $\frac{\#logs\_with\_object}{\#logs}$, or the probability that an object is (partially) found inside a cache. These 350 objects, even though they represent 0.01% of the catalogue, account for 65% and 80% of OPC and LRU cache-hits. A detailed analysis of the characteristics of these objects is depicted in Figure 9, with the x-axis representing the rank of the object; note that, the 350th object has the *highest* frequency.

Figure 9.(a) presents the caching frequency of these 350 objects, showing that OPC caches store more of the most frequently cached objects than LRU caches, which is not surprising, given that OPC stores approximately 11 times more chunks in the slow memory, thus allowing for more popular objects to be cached. The significance of this design de-

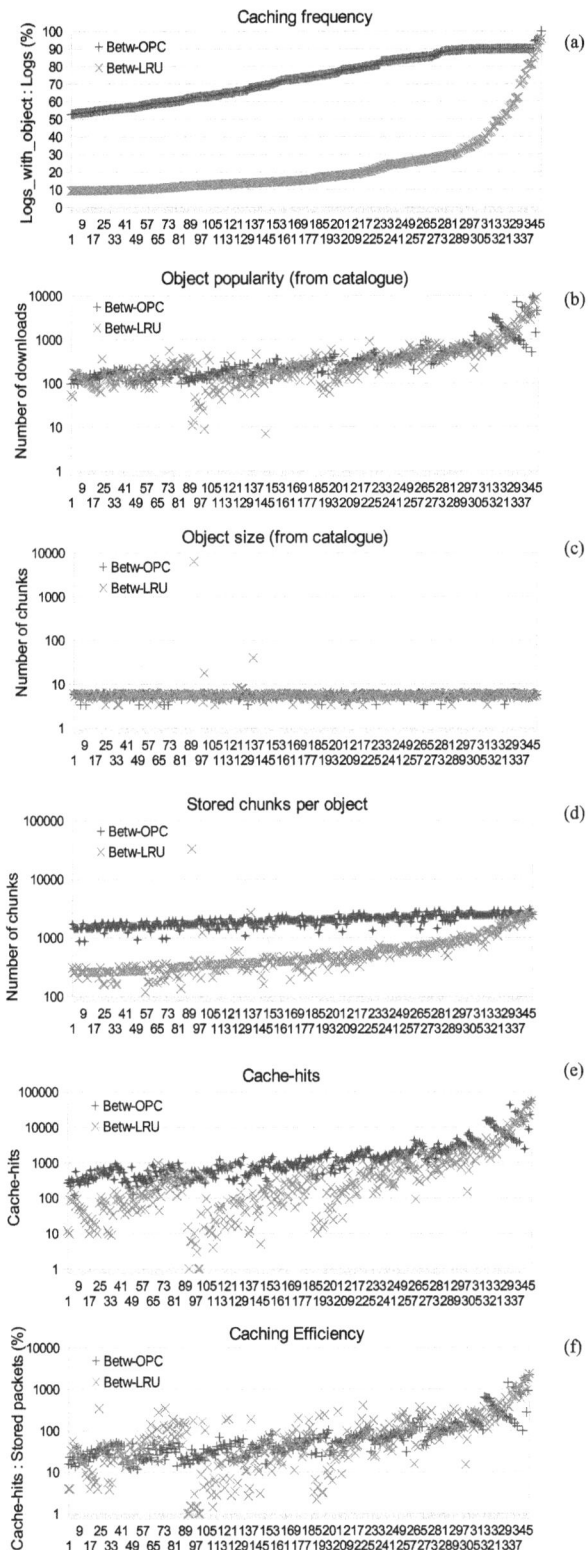

Figure 9: State analysis of OPC and LRU chunk-level caches (placement: betweenness, (fast) memory size: 0.1% of catalog).

cision is revealed by the fact that in LRU only 10 objects are found cached in more that 80% of logs, whereas 150 objects satisfy this condition in OPC. Figure 9.(b) shows that both LRU and OPC exploit popularity roughly the same, since the popularity of the most frequently cached objects is roughly the same. This is also reasonable, since OPC itself utilizes LRU replacement for the $L1$ object-level index. Nevertheless, some not so popular objects are frequently cached in LRU, implying that caching frequency is not as correlated with popularity as in OPC.

Figure 9.(c) depicts the size of the 350 most frequently cached objects, while Fig. 9.(d) shows the storage capacity occupied by each object throughout the experiment, that is, the total number of chunk occurrences for an object in all logs. These figures verify that large object cache poisoning does occur in LRU, since LRU stores some fairly large objects, some of which are also unpopular (see Fig. 9.(b)), leading to thousands of stored chunks for these objects, as shown in Fig. 9.(d). As a result, Fig. 9.(e) shows that the cache-hits per object are very low for these unpopular objects. For example, object 91 in the LRU cache has a size of 6416 chunks and a popularity of only 11 requests, yet it occupies 33,000 slots in the slow memory, while scoring zero hits. In contrast, the object at position 90 of OPC has a size of 6 chunks, a popularity of 130 requests, it occupies 1680 slots and scores 345 hits. Besides this corner case, OPC provides more cache-hits than LRU in general, even for objects with similar popularities. This is not a surprise, since the larger usable slow memory capacity of OPC allows it to store more chunks per object for a longer time.

Finally, Fig. 9.(f) depicts the per object *caching efficiency* of OPC and LRU, defined as $\frac{\#cache\_hits}{\#stored\_chunks}$. This metric exposes the gains due to inserting an object in the cache, by relating storage costs with cache hit benefits. The deviation of this metric with OPC is noticeably lower than with LRU. We interpret this stability as a positive side-effect of addressing the particular problems of packet-caches, the very same problems that directed the design of OPC and provide the aforementioned gains in almost every metric.

5. CONCLUSION

We have presented the *Object-oriented Packet Caching* (OPC) scheme for ICN architectures, a two level chunk caching scheme that fully exploits both the fast and slow memories of current routers for caching. We discussed the set of goals guiding OPC design, such as increasing chunk storage capacity and improving caching efficiency. Having identified looped replacement and large object poisoning as two critical issues for ICN packet caches, we presented a simple yet effective algorithm for chunk lookup, insertion and eviction, which achieves all of our design goals. We assessed the performance of OPC via domain-scale simulations with realistic network traffic and provided an in-depth report of the OPC gains, validating our claim that OPC provides significantly higher performance than a simple LRU cache, reducing both network and server load, in a wide range of cache placement policies and router cache sizes.

6. ACKNOWLEDGEMENT

The work presented in this paper was supported by the EU funded H2020 ICT project POINT, under contract 643990.

7. REFERENCES

[1] Cisco. (2014) Visual networking index: Forecast and methodology. [Online]. Available: http://www.cisco.com/c/en/us/solutions/service-provider/visual-networking-index-vni/index.html

[2] S. Ihm and V. S. Pai, "Towards understanding modern web traffic," in *Proc. of the ACM Internet Measurement Conference (IMC)*, 2011, pp. 295–312.

[3] G. Maier, A. Feldmann, V. Paxson, and M. Allman, "On dominant characteristics of residential broadband internet traffic," in *Proc. of the ACM Internet Measurement Conference (IMC)*, 2009, pp. 90–102.

[4] B. Ager, F. Schneider, J. Kim, and A. Feldmann, "Revisiting cacheability in times of user generated content," in *Proc. of the IEEE Global Internet Symposium*, 2010.

[5] N. T. Spring and D. Wetherall, "A protocol-independent technique for eliminating redundant network traffic," *ACM SIGCOMM Computer Communication Review*, vol. 30, no. 4, pp. 87–95, 2000.

[6] A. Anand, A. Gupta, A. Akella, S. Seshan, and S. Shenker, "Packet caches on routers: the implications of universal redundant traffic elimination," in *ACM SIGCOMM Computer Communication Review*, vol. 38, no. 4, 2008, pp. 219–230.

[7] G. Xylomenos, C. N. Ververidis, V. A. Siris, N. Fotiou, C. Tsilopoulos, X. Vasilakos, K. V. Katsaros, and G. C. Polyzos, "A survey of information-centric networking research," *IEEE Communications Surveys Tutorials*, vol. 16, no. 2, pp. 1024–1049, 2014.

[8] A. Ghodsi, S. Shenker, T. Koponen, A. Singla, B. Raghavan, and J. Wilcox, "Information-centric networking: seeing the forest for the trees," in *Proc. of the ACM Workshop on Hot Topics in Networks*, 2011.

[9] D. Perino and M. Varvello, "A reality check for content centric networking," in *Proc. of the ACM SIGCOMM ICN Workshop*, 2011, pp. 44–49.

[10] J. R. Santos and D. Wetherall, "Increasing effective link bandwidth by supressing replicated data." in *Proc. of the USENIX Annual Technical Conference*, no. 98, 1998.

[11] S. Kumar, S. Dharmapurikar, F. Yu, P. Crowley, and J. Turner, "Algorithms to accelerate multiple regular expressions matching for deep packet inspection," *Proc. of the ACM SIGCOMM*, pp. 339–350, 2006.

[12] J. C. Mogul, F. Douglis, A. Feldmann, and B. Krishnamurthy, "Potential benefits of delta encoding and data compression for HTTP," in *Proc. of the ACM SIGCOMM*, 1997, pp. 181–194.

[13] G. Carofiglio, M. Gallo, and L. Muscariello, "ICP: Design and evaluation of an interest control protocol for content-centric networking," in *Proc. of the IEEE INFOCOM NOMEN Workshop*, 2012, pp. 304–309.

[14] Y. Thomas, C. Tsilopoulos, G. Xylomenos, and G. C. Polyzos, "Accelerating file downloads in publish subscribe internetworking with multisource and multipath transfers," in *Proc. of the World Telecommunications Congress (WTC)*, 2014.

[15] Z. Ming, M. Xu, and D. Wang, "Age-based cooperative caching in information-centric networks," in *Proc. of the IEEE INFOCOM NOMEN Workshop*, 2012, pp. 268–273.

[16] S. Saha, A. Lukyanenko, and A. Yla-Jaaski, "Cooperative caching through routing control in information-centric networks," in *Proc. of the IEEE INFOCOM*, 2013, pp. 100–104.

[17] I. Psaras, W. K. Chai, and G. Pavlou, "Probabilistic in-network caching for information-centric networks," in *Proc. of the ACM SIGCOMM ICN Workshop*, 2012, pp. 55–60.

[18] S. Arianfar, P. Nikander, and J. Ott, "Packet-level caching for information-centric networking," in *Proc. of the ACM ReArch Workshop*, 2010.

[19] W. K. Chai, D. He, I. Psaras, and G. Pavlou, "Cache "less for more" in information-centric networks," in *Proc. of the IFIP Networking Conference*, 2012, pp. 27–40.

[20] S. K. Fayazbakhsh, Y. Lin, A. Tootoonchian, A. Ghodsi, T. Koponen, B. Maggs, K. Ng, V. Sekar, and S. Shenker, "Less pain, most of the gain: Incrementally deployable ICN," in *ACM SIGCOMM Computer Communication Review*, vol. 43, no. 4, 2013, pp. 147–158.

[21] G. Rossini, D. Rossi, M. Garetto, and E. Leonardi, "Multi-terabyte and multi-gbps information centric routers," in *Proc. of the IEEE INFOCOM*, 2014, pp. 181–189.

[22] Z. Li and G. Simon, "Time-shifted TV in content centric networks: The case for cooperative in-network caching," in *Communications (ICC), 2011 IEEE International Conference on*. IEEE, 2011, pp. 1–6.

[23] M. Badov, A. Seetharam, J. Kurose, V. Firoiu, and S. Nanda, "Congestion-aware caching and search in information-centric networks," in *Proc. of the ACM ICN Conference*, 2014, pp. 37–46.

[24] A. Badam, K. Park, V. S. Pai, and L. L. Peterson, "HashCache: Cache storage for the next billion." in *Proc. of the USENIX Symposium on Networked Systems Design and Implementation (NSDI)*, vol. 9, 2009, pp. 123–136.

[25] Y. Thomas and G. Xylomenos, "Towards improving the efficiency of ICN packet-caches," in *Proc. of the International Workshop on Quality, Reliability, and Security in ICN (Q-ICN)*, 2014.

[26] A.-L. Barabási and R. Albert, "Emergence of scaling in random networks," *Science*, vol. 286, no. 5439, pp. 509–512, 1999.

[27] K. V. Katsaros, G. Xylomenos, and G. C. Polyzos, "GlobeTraff: a traffic workload generator for the performance evaluation of future Internet architectures," in *Proc. of the International Conference on New Technologies, Mobility and Security (NTMS)*, 2012, pp. 1–5.

Consumer / Producer Communication with Application Level Framing in Named Data Networking

Ilya Moiseenko
UCLA
iliamo@cs.ucla.edu

Lijing Wang
Tsinghua University
wanglj11@mails.tsinghua.edu.cn

Lixia Zhang
UCLA
lixia@cs.ucla.edu

ABSTRACT

Named Data Networking (NDN) is a general purpose network layer protocol which offers a set of rich functionality: in-network storage, multi-path forwarding, multicast delivery, and data-centric security. Above the network layer, system libraries simplify application developers' tasks by providing an easy to use yet powerful API to utilize the functions enabled by NDN. This paper presents the design of a Consumer / Producer programming interface, together with several mechanisms, that supports application level framing via NDN's data retrieval protocols to make NDN application programming easier and faster.

Categories and Subject Descriptors

C.2 [**COMPUTER-COMMUNICATION NETWORKS**]: Network Architecture and Design; Network Protocols; Distributed Systems

Keywords

NDN; API; Transport; Data retrieval;

1. INTRODUCTION

Today's Internet architecture stands on IP — a universal network layer designed to create a point-to-point communication network where packets are delivered to specific destinations, enabling process-to-process communication. This was a premise for introducing the concept of the socket, which binds a running process to a communication channel, and represents a container for the current state of data transfer between two end processes [1, 2].

Over time the Internet has evolved from a network that interconnects hosts to a network that interconnects information objects broadly defined; these objects range from movie files, Facebook content, twitter messages, to sensor data and authenticated device actuation commands. This fundamental change in its usage suggests that the Internet's universal network layer would be much more organic to use a data dissemination protocol that can natively work with information objects instead of communication endpoints.

As a newly proposed architecture to meet this new usage, Named Data Networking (NDN) replaces IP's host-based addressing scheme

by names of information objects in moving packets through the network [3, 4, 5]. In an NDN network, consumers send *Interest packets* carrying application-level names to request information objects, and the network returns the requested *Data packets* reversing the path of the Interests. NDN secures data directly with a publicly verifiable signature, and with encryption as needed (Section 2).

As explained in [6], network applications work with Application Data Units (ADU) — units of data represented in a most suitable form for each given use-case. For example, a video playback application typically handles data in the unit of video frames; a multi-user game's ADUs are objects representing users' current status; and for an intelligent home application, ADUs may represent sensor readings. NDN enables applications to communicate using ADUs.

As a new way of doing networking, NDN introduces new design patterns for applications. To make the content available through the network, one needs to consider multiple design choices, which range from name structure and security model to more basic issues such as data segmentation. To fetch content, one also faces new considerations such as the presence of caching in the network and the question of data validation, in addition to conventional issues of data loss recovery and error corrections. What kind of application interface should be provided to ease the application development? And what protocols would be needed to support the interface? Clearly socket abstraction and associated protocols cannot be reused, because the model of a virtual channel between two communicating processes supported by a socket does not exist in the NDN architecture.

In this paper we present the design of a new API and its associated protocol suite that can play socket-equivalent roles in an NDN network. Our contributions can be summarized as follows:

- A Consumer / Producer programming model, which is specifically tailored for data dissemination in NDN networks.
- Associated data retrieval and content segmentation protocols.
- A number of supporting mechanisms such as a manifest and negative acknowledgement, utilized by the protocols below the API to facilitate the operation of applications.

We have implemented the Consumer / Producer API and the protocols, and validated them by using the API to develop several pilot applications. The focus of our evaluation is to have running, correctly behaving, and real-world applications, and to quantitatively measure the computational overhead experienced by a single producer publishing ADUs for multiple consumers.

The rest of the paper is organized as follows. Section II gives a brief overview of NDN architecture. Section III contains a detailed explanation of the programming model and programming abstractions. Section IV and V provide a description of important concepts and design of content fetching protocols. Section VI presents the evaluation of the design through real-world applications. Related work can be found in Section VII, and conclusion in Section VIII.

2. BACKGROUND

NDN works in a fundamentally different way than IP. To help the reader easily grasp its core concepts, in this section we first describe a toy application example, then use this example to explain the NDN basics.

2.1 A Simple-Video Application

We use a *Simple-Video* application as an example to help illustrate some basic concepts behind applications in general and possible issues that must be addressed by an application developer. Simple-Video produces two separate streams of data, video and audio, to give the consumers a choice of either watching the video with audio, listen to the audio only, or watch the video in silence. Both video and audio streams consist of a stream of data frames, and the application should allow a consumer to retrieve individual frames independently. The consumer application can, for example, stop fetching audio frames when user hits the "Mute" button, or skip some video frames after a pause in order to catch up the actual live video. In general, a video frame is likely too large to be carried in a single network packet, thus the video producer application also needs to segment one frame into multiple packets.

One of the existing technologies, MPEG-DASH [7], produces the content, with either a mixed audio/video stream or two separate streams, into a sequence of small file segments of equal time duration. File segments are later served over HTTP from the origin media server or intermediate HTTP caching servers. While there is a variety of ways applications can produce and fetch data at the level of application frames, there are repetitive and labour intensive tasks related to the segmentation of the application data frames and the retrieval of segments to reassemble an application frame. In the case of MPEG-DASH, all these low-level details are handled by the HTTP / TCP protocol machinery.

2.2 Named Data Networking

An NDN network has two types of packets: *Interest* and *Data*. Consumers send Interest packets, i.e. expressing Interests in receiving specific pieces of data. Producers produce Data packets to satisfy received Interests. Both types of packets carry a *data name*, which uniquely identifies a piece of information object carried in a *single* Data packet. A Data name in NDN is supplied by the given application and has multiple components in general. It is used to retrieve the packet across network; it also contains application specific information to facilitate packet processing. As an illustrative example, Simple-Video uses the following naming schema. The data name begins with routable components *"/com/youtube/"* which guides all Interest packets carrying this name prefix toward the data producer. The next component is the name identifier of the media resource. The component after that separates video and audio frames into separate namespaces (i.e. name subtrees). Both video and audio frames are named sequentially. Each video frame may consist of multiple segments, also named sequentially, while each audio frame is made of a single segment.

Similar to IP, an NDN network provides datagram delivery. Data consumers who desire reliable data fetching need to use reliable fetching services; they may also need to regulate data flow through pacing Interest packets transmissions.

Data production can be either on demand, or independent from data consumption. The inherent asynchrony between producers and consumers creates delicate coordination issues in between, such as the availability of data, the specifics of data, *etc.* Interest Selec-

tors is one of the available mechanisms to facilitate data fetching by *multiple* consumers, potentially from *multiple* producers. Any Interest may carry optional Selectors that specify additional conditions (besides name matching) for content retrieval. For example, when a consumer sends an Interest with a name prefix, and receives a Data packet P that is not the desired one, it can try again by resending the Interest with an Exclude selector which may contain either the exact name of P or P's digest (e.g. hash of the packet).

2.3 NDN inside a Node

The NDN Forwarding Daemon (NFD) is a multiplexer between applications and network interfaces inside a node [8]; NFD makes no distinction between applications and network interfaces, and views them all as *Faces*. NFD has a content store for opportunistic caching of passing-by Data packets. NFD may also have a face to a local repository (e.g. Repo-NG [9]), which provides managed storage of Data packets.

To make data available, the producer-process registers its name prefix with NFD to be able to receive interests for its data. The local NFD adds the prefix to its FIB (e.g. forwarding table) and also forwards the prefix to the next router. Consumer-process does not perform any registration — it simply sends Interest packets to the local NFD which then forwards the Interests toward the producer, either locally or remotely.

3. PROGRAMMING MODEL

In this section, we define *consumer context* and *producer context* abstractions, together with the rationale behind our design.

3.1 Socket is inappropriate

We aim to design a programming abstraction that would give application developers adequate freedom when handling ADUs, at the same time minimize the complexity associated with the production and retrieval of ADUs of any size.

In TCP/IP networking, similar tasks are managed by the socket API. A socket is a container for data transfer parameters holding the current state of transmission in a virtual channel between two processes running on IP hosts. Because a socket creates a duplex pipe for data to flow in both directions, server and client applications use sockets in more or less the same way with a few minor differences (e.g. *listen()* and *accept()* calls). Socket has no use without being attached to the channel (e.g. *bind()* or *connect()*). To support "time asynchrony" or delay tolerance between communicating parties, application developers often resort to higher level abstractions (e.g. ZeroMQ [10]) suitable for queuing and passing messages.

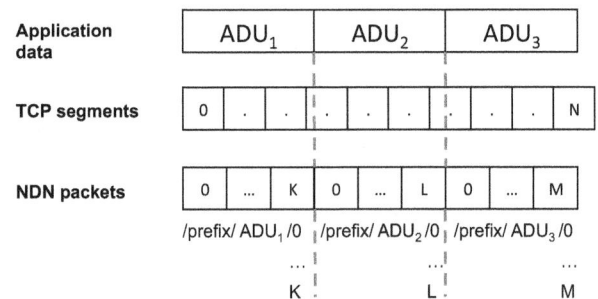

Figure 1: TCP/IP segmentation does not preserve boundaries of application frames (ADUs). NDN segmentation exposes these boundaries through naming.

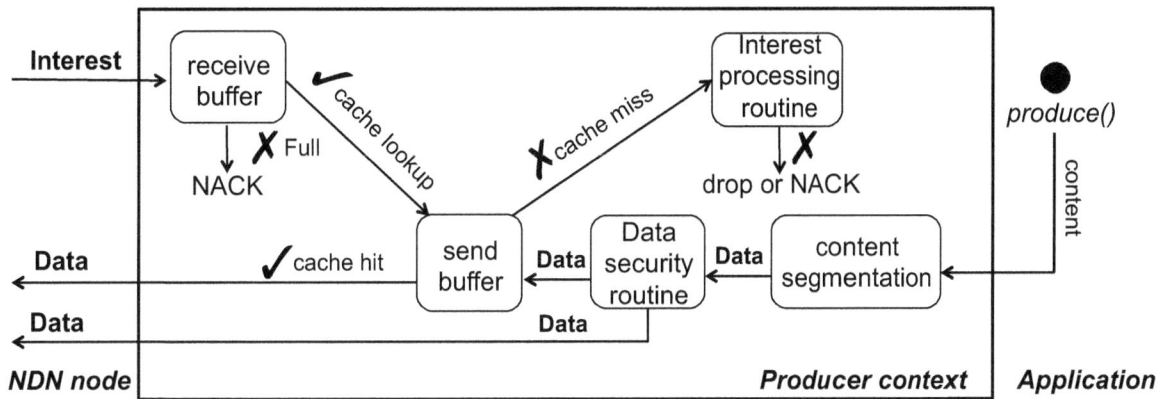

Figure 2: Producer context can publish data with or without network connectivity.

NDN is a pull-based data dissemination protocol, therefore applications that consume data behave differently from applications that produce data. Consequently these applications need different sets of data transfer parameters. Producer applications, in general, care about ADU segmentation, securing and caching/storing Data packets, and incoming Interest demultiplexing. Consumer applications, on the other hand, care about fetching all Data packets of each ADU, fetching reliability, verification of received data, as well as flow and congestion control by controlling their Interest generation rates.

These observations prompt us to design two programming abstractions: one for consumer applications, and another one for producer applications.

3.2 Design goals

To have data delivered over the Internet, large ADUs must be segmented, because the packet size is limited by network MTU. There are two major differences in how TCP/IP and NDN handle data segmentation. First, because TCP treats all application data as byte streams, TCP segmentation ignores ADU boundaries, thus ADUs can only be identified after the segment reassembly (Figure 1). NDN data packets carry the names of individual ADUs or ADU segments, therefore these packets match to application's data units directly.[1]

The second, and related, difference is the degree of insight and control that application can have during data transfer. In the simple example shown in Figure 1, if TCP/IP is used to send several ADUs back to back across the network and one of the segments is lost in transit, all the subsequent ADUs, even if they arrive at the destination, will be blocked from getting delivered to the application. This is a well known head-of-line (HOL) blocking problem. On the other hand, if NDN is used and faces the same segment loss problem, all successfully received ADUs can be immediately delivered to the applications without waiting for the recovery of the missing segment.

3.2.1 Goals for the consumer abstraction

In identifying the design goals for the consumer abstraction, we make an initial assumption that, generally speaking, individual applications would like to organize ADU fetching according to their own priorities. Therefore we describe the design goals in terms of what kinds of support that applications may desire in handling the relations between ADUs. Given we are still experimenting with this new consumer / producer API, the current sets of design goals,

as stated below, may be further revised over time as we gain deeper understanding of applications' needs. The same can be said for the goals of the producer abstraction.

At this time we believe that the new consumer abstraction model should support the following application patterns.

1. Sequential fetching of ADUs, with allowance of missing any ADU in the stream if necessary. This can be used to support real time media streaming applications.

2. Parallel fetching of ADUs to speed up content transfer. This can benefit applications like web download and torrent.

3. Fetching of individual, dynamically generated ADUs, as needed by web and IoT applications.

3.2.2 Goals for the producer abstraction

Given that NDN producers and consumers do not directly communicate, one basic question for producers is where to put the generated data. We have identified the following three application patterns to be supported at this point.

1. Realtime ADU publishing (and consumption), which can be used by a large number of applications including video conferencing, games, etc. Publishers may need to "wait for pull" and keep the ADUs in memory temporarily to handle a possible mismatch between production and consumption timing.

2. ADU publishing to stable storage, to support potentially large asynchronies between ADU publishing and consumption in terms of time, as well as in terms of data popularity ("publish once - consume multiple times"). This publication pattern can be beneficial for static content services, such as video and web-content backend applications.

3. ADU publishing to remote stable storage, to support mobile publishers and IoT publishers. This publication pattern allows smartphones and sensors to get around their resource limitations by moving the content to stable locations.

3.3 Producer context

A **producer context** is used to publish data under a common prefix (Figure 4). It is initialized by calling **producer()** primitive with a given name prefix parameter. Unlike a server side socket in TCP/IP, a producer context is ready to publish data even without being attached to the network and in the absence of any incoming Interests. Except the case of on-demand publishing, our consumer / producer model has no requirement for publishers and

---

[1]The terms "ADU segment", "data segment", and "Data packet" are used interchangeably in this paper.

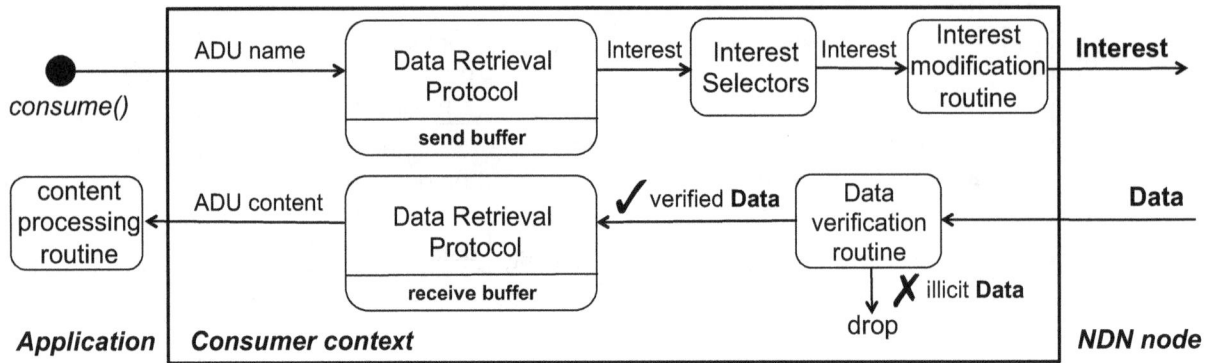

Figure 3: Event-based processing of Interest and Data packets in the consumer context.

consumers being 'connected' at the same time, therefore data publication can take place any time, including when the producer is disconnected. In our Simple-Video example, the publisher publishes data at its own pace, ahead of fetching by any consumers.

An application process calls **produce()** operation to start data publication, passing the name suffix and application frame (ADU) content. In the Simple-Video example, the name suffix is a frame number. In general cases, the name suffix parameter allows application developers to reuse the same producer context to publish data in any name subtree. In the Simple-Video application example, one context is used for publishing all video frames, and another context is used for publishing all audio frames. The locations of the producer contexts in the name tree are illustrated in Figure 4.

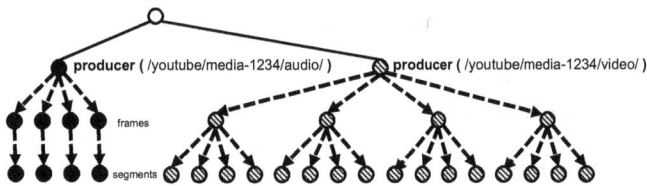

Figure 4: Producer context is initialized with a name prefix common for all information objects that it generates.

The **produce()** operation finishes when 1) the application frame (ADU) is segmented into an appropriate number of Data packets, 2) the segment number is appended to each packet name, 3) each packet is secured (e.g. signed), and 4) pushed in the send buffer and out of the context (Figure 2). By default, the segments are temporarily stored in the send buffer — in-memory storage of Data packets, while some producer applications may want to write the resulting Data packets in a permanent storage, such as NDNFS or Repo-NG [9, 11].

The context's send buffer is different from the socket's send buffer in two ways. First, the socket's send buffer is used to retransmit unacknowledged segments, whereas the producer context's send buffer is used as a temporary cache of Data packets that is being looked up by incoming Interest packet. In other words, send buffer softens the time asynchrony between data production and fetching. Second, in a socket, packets are evicted after being acknowledged, whereas in a producer context, Data packets are evicted based on memory availability, e.g. when the application calls **produce()** with an already full buffer under FIFO eviction policy.

In order to receive Interests for its data, the producer context must be attached to the local NFD by calling **attach()** operation. The arriving Interests get into a receive buffer and wait there for their turn to be matched with Data packets in the send buffer. If an

Interest matches a Data packet by the name and Interest selectors successfully, the Interests is satisfied from the send buffer. If a matching Data packet is not found, an application can be informed about the Interest.

In some conditions, the rate of incoming Interest packets may be too high for a particular producer context to process as quickly as they arrive. In other conditions, the requested data cannot be generated within the Interest's lifetime span. Instead of letting the consumers timeout blindly, application can use **nack()** operation to satisfy the Interests with a negative acknowledgement (Section 4.1), so that the consumer(s) can handle the situation in a most informed way.

3.4 Consumer context

A **consumer context** abstraction is a container that associates a name prefix with consumer-specific transfer parameters. Consumer context controls Interest transmission and processing of fetched Data packets. It is initialized by calling **consumer()** primitive with two parameters: 1) a name prefix, 2) a data retrieval protocol.

Note that, in general cases, the name prefix is not a complete name of the ADU. Since a given NDN namespace forms a name tree, an application developer can reuse a single consumer context repeatedly to fetch multiple ADUs under the same name prefix. In the Simple-Video application example, one can use one context to fetch all video frames, and another context to fetch all audio frames. The locations of the consumer contexts in the name tree are illustrated in Figure 5.

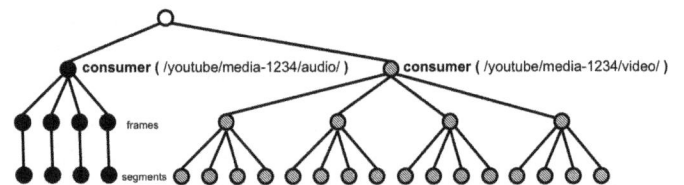

Figure 5: Consumer context is initialized with a name prefix defining the range of information objects that can be retrieved from the network.

The data retrieval starts when an application calls **consume()** operation, which takes the name suffix as an input parameter. In the case of Simple-Video application, the name suffix is a frame number. Name suffix parameter allows application developer to reuse the same context for fetching multiple ADUs (Figure 5). Inside the context, the data retrieval protocol (Section 5) generates Interests and processes incoming Data packets with other related events (Figure 3).

The data retrieval stops under one of the three conditions: 1) last Data packet of the ADU has been successfully fetched, validated and reassembled (if needed); 2) irrecoverable fetching error has occurred; or 3) **stop()** operation has been called.

4. SUPPORTING MECHANISMS

To support efficient consumer / producer communication described in the previous sections, we introduce two new mechanisms: negative acknowledgements and manifests. This section talks about these mechanisms in more detail.

4.1 Negative acknowledgement

In NDN, consumer applications pull desired Data packets from the network by expressing Interests. If an Interest does not find matching Data along the way, it arrives at the producer context, which either finds the matching Data packet from the send buffer, or otherwise informs the application to produce the requested data. The latter case happens when some specific data is being requested and produced for the first time.

Since NDN is a pull-based network protocol, it shares some common polling related challenges with HTTP [12]. An HTTP client can "short poll" the HTTP server (i.e. sending regular requests) in an attempt to receive the most up-to-date data. The HTTP server responds with empty reply in case the requested data is not ready, and the poll request will be repeated again after the client timeout. To avoid HTTP clients generating requests too frequently, which can lead to unacceptable burdens on the server and the network, HTTP long polling is commonly used. Long polling is a technique of keeping HTTP requests pending or "hanging" at the server until the requested data is ready to be sent back to the client.

Long polling works well for HTTP, because the underlying TCP connection ensures that HTTP request is reliably delivered to the server, and that the HTTP client is still waiting for the data. Since NDN network layer does not, on its own, ensure reliable transmission of an Interest all the way to the producer, and, more importantly, outstanding NDN Interests consume router resources (by occupying PIT entries), the long polling technique is not a feasible solution. In order to efficiently handle the polling of dynamically generated data in NDN, two conditions must be satisfied: 1) consumer application must be certain that its Interest packet has successfully reached the producer, and 2) producer application can regulate the polling frequency according to its current conditions.

A negative acknowledgement (NACK) can satisfy these two conditions. We define a NACK as a sub-type of NDN Data packet, which is generated when the requested data is unavailable. A NACK carries an error code, a retry timer value, and other optional application-defined fields filled by the producer application. It informs the consumer that 1) the Interest for its requested data has been received by the producer, and 2) the error code contains information to advice the consumer for best next action. Currently, two error codes are defined as follows:

1. RETRY-AFTER — prompts the data retrieval protocol to schedule Interest retransmission based on the timeout value in the negative acknowledgement. This mechanism is somewhat similar to Retry-After HTTP and SIP header field [13, 14]. NACK with Retry-After field does not change the Interest pipeline size.

2. NO-DATA — prompts the data retrieval protocol at the consumer side to terminate its operation.

Since NACK packet must be signed like all other Data packet, additional measures [15] must be taken to prevent malicious consumers from launching a Denial-of-Service attack by forcing the producer application to generate and sign excessive amounts of NACK packets.

Since NACKs are NDN Data packets, they can be cached at intermediate NDN routers, so that the same NACK packet can be used to satisfy the Interest packets from multiple consumers requesting the same piece of data. A cached NACK becomes stale when its lifetime (e.g. the FreshnessPeriod field), whose value is set by the producer context, expires. As a rule of thumb, the lifetime of a NACK packet must not be longer than the retry timeout value contained in it, otherwise the consumers attempting retry after the timeout will receive the same cached NACK again, and consequently will wait for another timeout period. One must also keep in mind that a Data packet can stay at each router hop for the FreshnessPeriod before it becomes stale, and that there can be multiple router hops between a producer and its consumers. Therefore we propose to set the FreshnessPeriod of a NACK to be within a small fraction (10%) of the application specified retry timer.

4.2 Manifest

A well-built NDN application fully utilizes "many-to-many with caching in-between" communication paradigm. To keep consumers best informed of the production progress of the data that they are interested in fetching, a producer application may package together necessary meta-information to distribute to consumers.

Manifest, proposed in [16], is one of the means to facilitate the operation of consumer applications by distributing a catalogue. The catalogue may contain either ordinary NDN names, or special names which associate the hash (e.g. digest) of a Data packet with its name. The primary benefit of using catalogues to carry data names with associated packet digests is the elimination of cryptographic signing operations for those Data packets. Instead of signing, a publisher computes a simple hash of every newly produced Data packet, populates the manifest with names carrying digests, and signs only the manifest. Consumer applications can verify Data packets by fetching the manifest and comparing their digest with the digest listed in the catalogue. As proposed in [16], manifests carrying the catalogue of names need to be fetched before data fetching, which introduces an additional round-trip latency.

We propose to embed a manifest as an ADU in the same sequence with Data packets to eliminate the undesirable latency from fetching manifest [17]. A producer context can perform this operation when an ADU is segmented by the **produce()** API primitive. The basic idea is to establish a convention of naming the manifest as the first segment of the Data packets to be published, so that consumers simply fetch the manifest together with data via Interest pipelining. In case where an ADU's size is too large so that the names of all its segments cannot fit into a single manifest packet, multiple manifest packets can be periodically interleaved with data packets as shown in Figure 6.

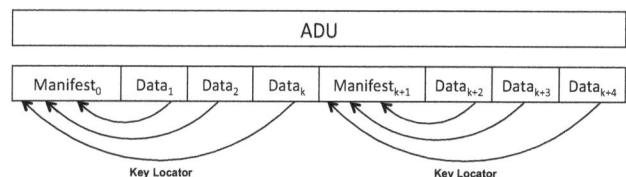

Figure 6: Manifests are embedded in the sequence of data packets when application data is being segmented.

Manifest embedding enables the consumer application an opportunity to fetch manifests together with Data packets within the same sliding Interest window.[2] By letting the KeyLocator field in each Data packet point to the corresponding embedded manifest, a consumer application is able to verify each received Data packets immediately without waiting for the rest of the Data packets.

A manifest is realized as a sub-type of NDN Data packet. In addition to the catalogue of names, manifest can also carry miscellaneous meta-information in a form of key-value pairs, such as:

- **Current data production rate.** Live streaming applications can benefit from knowing the current rate of Data packet production (packaging) and using this knowledge to pace Interest packets.

- **Other available versions.** Applications working with multi-version content can discover available versions of ADUs without iterative discovery using Interest selectors which can be time consuming.

- **First and Last ADU sibling**. In most cases, the producer of the ADU knows the total number of ADUs that constitute some larger information object (e.g. a video stream). Our Simple-Video application uses the last ADU name to understand where the video ends (e.g. frame #2500).

5. DATA RETRIEVAL PROTOCOLS

Based on our experience from developing NDN applications, we have designed an initial set of data retrieval protocols: Simple Data Retrieval (SDR), Unreliable Data Retrieval (UDR), and Reliable Data Retrieval (RDR).

5.1 Simple Data Retrieval

Any communication in an NDN network involves Interest / Data exchanges, and Simple Data Retrieval protocol (SDR) is the simplest form of fetching Data from NDN networks: send one Interest to retrieve one Data packet. SDR provides no guarantee of Interest or Data delivery. If SDR cannot verify an incoming Data packet, the packet is dropped.

SDR can be used by the applications that:

- do not know the name of the application frame (ADU) and, therefore, need to discover it using the name prefix and Interest selectors, which could be set via the **setcontextoption()** API primitive;

- know the name of ADUs and have small ADUs that fit in one Data packet;

- want to directly control Interest transmission and error corrections.

5.2 Unreliable Data Retrieval

When an Application Data Unit (ADU) is too large to fit in a single Data packet, the **produce()** API primitive automatically segments this ADU into an appropriate number of Data packets. In this case, the consumer first needs to send a sequence of Interest packets to fetch all the data packets of the same ADU, then it needs to reassemble these Data packets into the ADU, which often implies dealing with packet losses and error corrections, as well as packet ordering.

UDR is designed to meet the needs of applications that have relaxed requirements for the reliability and ordering of the Data packets, and are unwilling to pay the price in the latency of loss recovery, or in the performance overhead associated with other means of reliable delivery. UDR fetches all Data packets that belong to a single ADU in an unreliable and unordered way, with a simple flow control and best-effort Interest retransmission as explained below.

UDR makes use of the FinalBlockID, one of the optional fields carried in an NDN data packet, by having the producer set the FinalBlockID to the number of segments in an ADU. UDR fetches the ADU of a given name by starting with the segment number zero, and learns about the total number of segments to be fetched as soon as any Data packet is received. Next, the protocol enters the fast start phase and sends as many Interests as *MIN (FinalBlockID, Fast start threshold)*.[3] If the value of FinalBlockID is greater than the fast start threshold value, UDR completes fast start phase and begins to multiplicatively increase sliding Interest window size in a way similar to the TCP slow start phase. If any Interest times out during the multiplicative increase phase, the sliding windows size is reduced by half. To get the basic intuition behind this flow control scheme, consider a common use case where the ADU consists of a small number (≤ 15) of Data packets: UDR can fetch such small ADUs in two RTTs and avoid bursty transmission for much larger ADUs (e.g. hundreds of Data packets).

UDR's best-effort Internet retransmission works in the following way: at any given time, if three out-of-order Data packets arrive at the consumer, UDR immediately retransmits the Interest for the missing Data packet(s).[4] UDR can perform multiple fast retransmissions per sliding Interest window by keeping an accurate track of missing and contiguous segment numbers.

UDR does not perform any persistent error correction; it does not run retransmission timers, nor retransmits Interests upon receiving NACKs, which are passed up to the application. UDR deletes Data packets that fail data verifications. UDR delivers each received Data packets to applications as soon as possible without enforcing ordering, thus applications handle received packets directly and are responsible for the ADU reassembly. This also offers an opportunity for the applications to perform specially tailored error and loss recovery.

In summary, UDR functionality includes best effort fetching of single- and multi-segment application data frames (ADUs), and best effort fast retransmission for potentially lost segments. "Deadline-oriented" consumer applications (e.g. live streaming) can benefit from using UDR's machinery and extending it with the custom functionalities appropriate at the application level.

5.3 Reliable Data Retrieval

When an Interest packet fails to bring back the corresponding Data packet, it can be due to one of the multiple reasons:

1. the Interest is lost in transit before it reaches the data, which may reside in cache, or need to be produced;

2. the Interest reaches the producer-application but the application does not respond due to various reasons;

3. the returning Data packet is lost;

4. the returning Data packet fails the signature validation (e.g. content is poisoned, etc.).

Reliable Data Retrieval protocol (RDR) uses Interest retransmission timers to handle packet losses (cases 1 & 3 in the above), and uses application negative acknowledgements to handle case 2. The Interest is retransmitted if the expressed Interest packet is not satisfied when it times out, or if the negative acknowledgment carrying Retry-After field is retrieved instead of the actual data.

---

[2]Sliding Interest window includes already sent not-yet-satisfied Interests, as well as the Interests scheduled for transmission at the moment of time.

[3]The default fast start threshold is 16 Interest packets, which could be modified via setcontextoption() API call.

[4]The current implementation of NFD will forward a retransmitted Interest even if the original Interest has not expired, if the retransmission arrives from the same face and is at least 100ms after the original Interest.

Data verification error can be caused by packet tampering, content poisoning by a non-credible publisher, expired certificate of a credible publisher, or other cases depending on the selected trust model. Several in-network mechanisms of mitigating content poisoning attacks have been proposed by [18], and [19] describing the content ranking algorithms based on the users' feedback.

While the Data verification operation is performed separately by the security part of the library, Data retrieval protocol makes an attempt to recover from this type of error. To recover from the Data verification failure, RDR performs retransmission of the Interest packet with exclude selector set to exclude any possible Data packet having the same name and the digest (e.g. hash, checksum) of the packet that has failed verification. Because exclude selector tells NDN router to retrieve an alternative Data packet, which in general case requires an extra work to be performed by the router, large excludes (e.g. containing a lot of excluded name components or digests) can affect the performance of NDN router. RDR limits its exclude selector to five digests, which means that the protocol attempts up to five retransmissions in order to recover from the Data verification failure.

RDR provides reliable and ordered delivery of the ADU to the consumer application. Unlike TCP, RDR does not attempt to establish a connection between the consumer and producer applications. In RDR, the retrieval of every ADU begins with sending an Interest packet for segment number zero, and is finished when the last segment is successfully retrieved. Similar to UDR, the producer sets the FinalBlockID field in each Data packet to the last segment number. RDR's flow control has the same fast start and multiplicative increase phases as UDR does.

Figure 7 illustrates an example where the consumer application uses RDR to retrieve dynamically generated data and handle verification errors. The first Interest is satisfied by poisoned content from the router cache, which is returned back to the consumer context. The RDR checks the content with the user-specified verification routine, and retransmits the Interest(s) with the exclude selector carrying the digest of the poisoned content. Since the routers respect the exclude selectors, this second Interest reaches the producer context, which needs some time (e.g. several seconds) to prepare the content, and therefore replies with the Retry-After NACK. This Retry-After NACK packet has /nack in its name suffix, therefore it has no impact on the poisoned content in the cache. When the consumer RDR receives the Retry-After NACK, it schedules the Interest retransmission accordingly, which later successfully retrieves the content from the producer context. Now the router has two Data packets with identical names but different digests, they can be either stored side by side or replace one another depending on the router Content Store policies.

Producer applications can mitigate excessively high rate of Interest arrivals by responding with negative acknowledgements carrying either Retry-After or No-Data fields, depending on the data being asked. RDR's flow control utilizes these NACKs as discussed in Section 4.1. The traditional mechanism of TCP window size advertisement for flow control purpose is not applicable in NDN, given the absence of a "connection" between consumers and producers.

Congestion is controlled at the NDN forwarding plane by utilizing Interest NACK mechanism [20]. Note that Interest NACK is different from the Data NACK proposed in this paper — it is a network layer packet and its main purpose is to assist NDN routers in performing quick and informed recovery from network problems, such as prefix hijacks, link failures, and network congestion. The NFD running in the local node is expected to handle Interest NACK, perform congestion control, and enforce fairness among multiple consumer applications running on the same node. It may

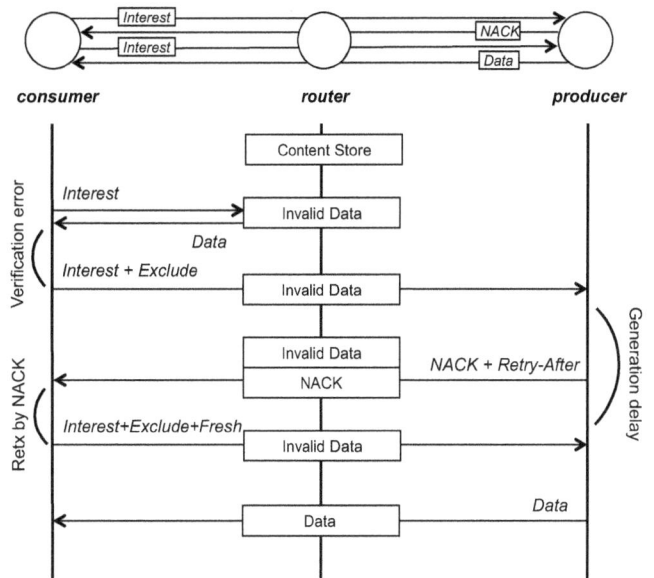

Figure 7: RDR recovers from the Data verification error and handles dynamic data generation delay.

also be beneficial to further propagate Interest NACKs up to the data retrieval protocols, an issue that we plan to investigate.

If three out-of-order Data packets arrive at the consumer, RDR performs opportunistic fast retransmission of the Interest for the missing Data packet, in the same way as UDR.

In the presence of the manifests embedded in the sequence of Data packets (Section 4.2), RDR performs verification of Data packets with help of catalogues of names in the corresponding manifest segments. If any Data packet fails its verification with the catalogue, RDR retransmits the Interest packet with the implicit digest. Since the correct digest is already known from the manifest, there is no need to use exclude selector in this case.

If a sequence of Data packets does not contain embedded manifests with catalogues of names, RDR verifies each packet's signature independently, and performs error correction using the exclude selector as described earlier.

In summary, RDR functionality includes:

- reliable fetching of a single- or multi-segment application frame (ADU) that may be either pre-generated ahead of time by the producer application and potentially cached by NDN routers, or dynamically generated upon an Interest arrival;
- low overhead consumption of dynamically generated application frame (ADU) through the use of NACK packets published by the producer application; and
- persistent recovery from the Data verification failures.

6. EVALUATION

We took an application-driven approach to guide the design and development of the Consumer / Producer API. This section reports on our experience from implementing and using the Consumer / Producer API in real environments, and some preliminary analysis of the space-computation tradeoff at the producer side.

6.1 Implementation

The Consumer / Producer API is implemented as a user-space library written in C++, which runs on Mac OS X, Linux, and BSD. The library is a branch of ndn-cxx 0.3 library [21], and is currently available at *https://github.com/iliamo/Consumer-Producer-API*.

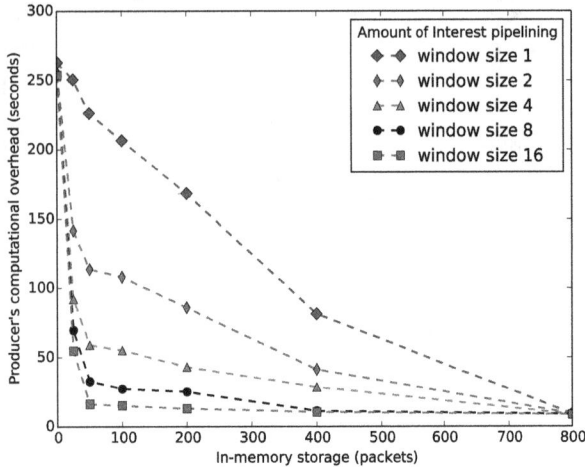

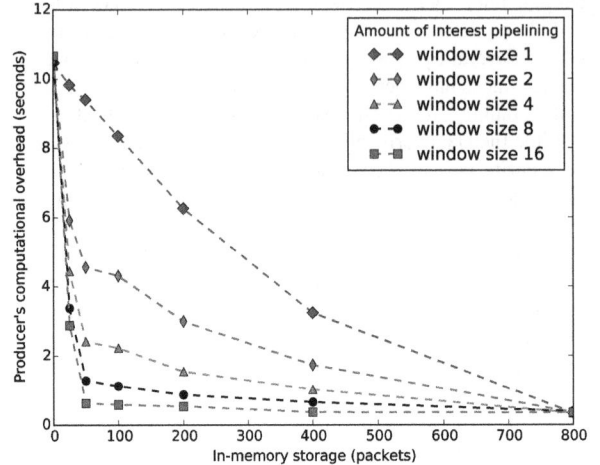

Figure 8: Benefit of having producer's send buffer for serving multi-packet ADUs to multiple consumers that pipeline Interests.

Figure 9: Benefit of embedding manifests in the multi-packet ADUs fetched by multiple consumers that pipeline Interests.

The pilot applications we developed over this new API include audio and video distributions, and sensing data collection. Our experience shows that the biggest benefit of this new API is a significant reduction in application development efforts as well as the complexity of the resulting implementation, as compared to developing applications directly on top of NDN's raw Interest / Data exchange API.

The first application we tried is NDNtube which distributes static video contents. NDNtube is an example of applications with significant time asynchrony between data publishing and consumption [22]. Video and audio frames are published once to permanent storage, and served to the consumers from storage using the RDR protocol. A similar application, NDNvideo [23], was used in a few large scale demonstrations earlier and showed that, in contrast to applications based on HTTP/TCP stack, an NDN network performs scalable content distributions without any special configuration [24].

The next application, NDNlive, is similar to NDNtube but supports live TV broadcasting instead of streaming static contents. Yet another application is NDNradio, which prototypes the iTunes radio application. It is worth mentioning that NDNradio was developed by a student without much programming experience, when she first started the project with NDN's raw Interest / Data API, she could not make much progress, and switching to the new API enabled her to successfully finished the implementation. Both NDNlive and NDNradio are examples of realtime publishing / consumption applications. Since real time data lose their value shortly after publication, these Data packets are served from short term in-memory storage — the send buffer of the producer.

Our latest application prototype developed on top of the new API is home sensor data collections. It periodically wakes up from sleep to collect new measurement samples and can also produce data on demand. If the requested data is not available yet, it uses *nack()* with *Retry-After* code to inform the consumer about the future availability of the data (e.g. in 10 seconds) and then enters the sleep mode during this time period.

6.2 Space-Computation Tradeoff Analysis

Compared to the well tuned TCP/IP implementations, we expect the performance of the Consumer / Producer API and its protocols to be largely comparable, but likely lower due to several fac-

tors: the larger NDN header overhead, the untuned implementation of the NFD and the library, as well as the cost from packet signing and verification. However in those applications where multiple users request the same data, the producer API can potentially perform significantly better than the server side socket, because every ADU (e.g. its Data packets) can serve multiple consumers. More specifically, the producer API has two mechanisms that help speed up ADU publishing: an in-memory cache of Data packets (send buffer) and an optional technique of manifest embedding in the sequence of Data packets.

Unlike a TCP socket's send buffer, which stores the segments that belong to a single connection, a producer's send buffer stores Data packets that share some common name prefix. However given the producer's send buffer has a finite size, newly produced data packet may push out the packets that were produced earlier. If those evicted packets are requested again, the producer has to generate them again. Therefore the publishing cost would be lower if the send buffer is large in size, allowing more ADUs to be kept in the memory, and would be higher if the send buffer is small, which causes more "ADU republishing events".

In a controlled experiment, we modeled the behavior of:

- multiple basic web consumers requesting 20 different personalized web resources (ADUs) in a random order. The retrieval of the random ADU can potentially cause the "ADU republishing event" depending on the contents and the size of the producer's send buffer; and
- a basic web server serving the above consumers with personalized html pages and other dynamic content. Each ADU consists of 30 Data packets.

The third factor that affects space-computation tradeoff is the Interest pipeline size at the consumer when it tries to fetch any particular ADU. Interests sent within larger Interest window, fetch more Data packets at once, leading to fewer "ADU republishing events". Figure 8 demonstrates that in the absence of the send buffer, multiple consumers that pipeline Interest packets lead to significant load (e.g. signing and segmentation) at the producer, while the larger buffer effectively amortizes publishing cost across multiple consumers.

In the experiment the send buffer size is set to [0, 25, 50, 100, 200, 400, 800] of Data packets, and the results are shown in Figure 8. It shows that without the send buffer, multiple consumers, each sending many Interests, are able to overload the producer due to the signing and segmentation overhead. A larger buffer can effectively amortize these same costs across multiple consumers.

We ran the same experiment to understand the performance implications of embedding manifests in the sequence of Data packets. This technique demonstrated up to 32 times increase of the speed of ADU publishing as illustrated by the Figure 9. Both experiments were conducted on the Mac OS X platform with trusted platform module (Mac OS X Keychain) used to produce RSA signatures with SHA256 digest.

7. RELATED WORK

Over the years multiple efforts have attempted to adapt application level framing at the transport layer (Structured Streams [25], HTTP 2.0 [26]), or above the transport layer (Publish/Subscribe [27]). However all these efforts are built over the existing TCP/IP protocol stack. A more recent effort (Named Data Socket [28]) proposed to provide some ALF support over an NDN network through a modified socket system. A few publish / subscribe systems have been proposed for NDN overlays, such as COPSS [29] and DDS-over-CDN-over-NDN [30]. In this section, we provide a brief description of the above research directions and highlight their differences with the Consumer / Producer API which is specifically designed to work over NDN.

7.1 Structured streams & HTTP 2.0

It has been well recognized that TCP's byte stream model does not match all applications' needs, while UDP's best effort datagram model leaves too much work to applications. Structured Stream Transport (SST) enhances the traditional stream abstraction with a hierarchical hereditary structure, allowing applications to create lightweight child streams from any existing stream [25]. Unlike TCP, these lightweight streams offer independent data transfer and flow control for each stream, allowing different transactions to proceed in parallel without head-of-line blocking, but sharing one congestion control context. SST supports both reliable and best-effort delivery in a way that semantically unifies datagrams with streams and solves the classic "large datagram" problem.

HTTP 2.0 proposal addresses similar issues by optimizing the mapping of HTTP's semantics to an underlying stream [26]. Its key features include: 1) multiplexing of HTTP requests over a single connection, allowing concurrent HTTP requests/responses, and 2) prioritization of the requests, providing the ability to indicate which HTTP request is more important than others, and therefore avoid head-of-line blocking.

However both SST and HTTP 2.0 are confined to IP's point-to-point packet delivery, and the application data units are invisible at the network layer. Consequently their data priority only has the effect at the end-to-end level, their scalability (for web service) must rely on other means to address, and their requirement of the direct connectivity between client and server makes them infeasible in mobile and delay tolerant scenarios.

7.2 Publish / Subscribe

Publish / subscribe communication offers multi-point non-host-based addressing: topic-based, content-based, and type-based [27]. Subscribers register their interest in events by calling a *subscribe()* operation on the event service, without knowing the effective sources of these events. This subscription information remains stored in the event service and is not forwarded to publishers. The symmetric operation *unsubscribe()* terminates a subscription. Event-based nature of this interaction leads to time decoupling between subscribers and publishers. To generate an event, a publisher typically calls a *publish()* operation. The event service propagates the event

to all relevant subscribers. Publishers also often have the ability to advertise the nature of their future events through an *advertise()* operation.

Publish / subscribe communication work with application data units, but is different from the consumer / producer communication in some important ways. First, the majority of publish / subscribe systems run on top of today's point-to-point transport layer (e.g. TCP, SCTP), which provides reliable delivery and segmentation. The rendezvous point (e.g. event service) between publishers and subscribers raise concerns about single point of failure and system scalability. Other concerns include the feasibility of supporting realtime, on-demand dynamic data production, due to the additional latency caused by the introduction of the event service.

Second, for the few publish / subscribe systems capable of running on top of Named Data Networking, their designs are not centered on the data directly. COPSS [29] introduces a push-based delivery mechanism using multicast in a content centric framework. At the content centric forwarding layer, COPSS uses a multiple-sender, multiple-receiver multicast capability with the use of Rendezvous Points (RP). DDS-over-CDN-over-NDN [30] offers a push-based delivery over simplified Content Delivery Network (sCDN). When DDS has created subscriber and publisher entities, sCDN is invoked to send a subscription message from the subscriber. This message is flooded through the network to look for an appropriate publisher. When a publisher is found, the requested content objects are forwarded to the subscriber by following the appropriate directed acyclic graph (DAG) in a hop-by-hop, reliable store-and-forward manner.

7.3 Named Networking Socket

Named Networking Socket is an implementation of the process-to-content (PCC) communication model [28]. The design extends Unix implementation of the BSD socket with a novel Named Networking domain, which implies a layered architecture with distinctive network, transport and application layers. The API does not perform conversion of application data unit (ADU) to transmission units. The assumption is that an ADU corresponds to a content segment and defines the granularity for which the application can support out-of-order packets and recovery from packet losses. Therefore, the publisher-process is in charge of defining the proper ADU size based on application constraints. NaNet socket provides a datagram ADU (single-segment) and reliable byte-stream content retrieval mechanisms.

8. CONCLUSION

The seminal paper [6], published 25 years ago, clearly articulated the value of applying the concept of application level framing to network protocol development by directly using application data unit (ADU). [31] further demonstrated that communicating by ADUs is particularly valuable in building many-to-many distributed applications. However because the work done in [31] was built upon the existing IP protocol stack where the network layer had no concept of data, the authors used IP multicast group, enhanced with various tweaks, to get packets to the interested nodes.

In today's Internet, network and transport layers are completely decoupled from application layers in namespace, because each layer has its own namespace (e.g. address and port versus application data names), and in timing, because socket simply gets a virtual channel ready, but the application decides when packets are actually sent. This insulation makes it easy to design each part on its own, however when multiple layers are put together, they often do not work most coherently. NDN's direct use of application names at network layer removed the insulation, which opens new potential for developing an overall cohesive system where applications can make the best use from the network transport.

NDN is able to support application level framing throughout the network, and Consumer / Producer API makes it easy for applications to publish and retrieve application frames from the network. Our experience with several pilot applications proved that Consumer / Producer API benefits application developers in terms of ease of development and functionality. The Consumer / Producer API is still at its early development stage, and we would like to invite others to experiment with it and help further improve its functionality.

9. REFERENCES

[1] J.M. Winett, "RFC 147 - The Definition of a Socket," Tech. Rep., 1971.

[2] W. Joy, R. Fabry, S. Leffler, M. McKusick, and M. Karels, "Berkeley Software Architecture Manual 4.3 BSD Edition," *UNIX Programmer Supplementary Documents*, vol. 1, pp. 4–3, 1986.

[3] V. Jacobson, D. K. Smetters, J. D. Thornton, M. F. Plass, N. H. Briggs, and R. L. Braynard, "Networking Named Content," in *Proc. of CoNEXT*, 2009.

[4] L. Zhang et al., "Named Data Networking (NDN) Project," Tech. Rep. NDN-0001, October 2010.

[5] L. Zhang, A. Afanasyev, J. Burke, V. Jacobson, K. Claffy, P. Crowley, C. Papadopoulos, L. Wang, and B. Zhang, "Named Data Networking," *ACM SIGCOMM Computer Communication Review*, July 2014.

[6] D. D. Clark and D. L. Tennenhouse, "Architectural Considerations for a New Generation of Protocols," *SIGCOMM Comput. Commun. Rev.*, vol. 20, no. 4, pp. 200–208, Aug. 1990.

[7] T. Stockhammer, "Dynamic adaptive streaming over HTTP: standards and design principles," in *Proceedings of the second annual ACM conference on Multimedia systems*. ACM, 2011, pp. 133–144.

[8] A. Afanasyev, J. Shi, B. Zhang, L. Zhang, I. Moiseenko, Y. Yu, W. Shang, Y. Huang, J. P. Abraham, S. DiBenedetto *et al.*, "NFD developer's guide," NDN Tech. Report NDN-0021, 2014.

[9] S. Chen, W. Shi, J. Cao, A. Afanasyev, and L. Zhang, "NDN Repo: An NDN Persistent Storage Model," 2014.

[10] M. Hurton, I. Barber, P. Hintjens, "ZeroMQ Message Transport Protocol," http://rfc.zeromq.org/spec:23.

[11] W. Shang, Z. Wen, Q. Ding, A. Afanasyev, and L. Zhang, "NDNFS: An NDN-friendly File System," 2014.

[12] I. Moiseenko, M. Stapp, and D. Oran, "Communication patterns for web interaction in named data networking," in *Proceedings of the 1st international conference on Information-centric networking*. ACM, 2014, pp. 87–96.

[13] R. Fielding, J. Gettys, J. Mogul, H. Frystyk, L. Masinter, P. Leach, and T. Berners-Lee, "Hypertext transfer protocol–HTTP/1.1," 1999.

[14] J. Rosenberg, H. Schulzrinne, G. Camarillo, A. Johnston, J. Peterson, R. Sparks, M. Handley, E. Schooler *et al.*, "SIP: session initiation protocol," RFC 3261, Internet Engineering Task Force, Tech. Rep., 2002.

[15] A. Afanasyev, P. Mahadevan, I. Moiseenko, E. Uzun, and L. Zhang, "Interest flooding attack and countermeasures in named data networking," in *IFIP Networking Conference, 2013*. IEEE, 2013, pp. 1–9.

[16] M. Baugher, B. Davie, A. Narayanan, and D. Oran, "Self-verifying names for read-only named data." in *INFOCOM Workshops*, vol. 12, 2012, pp. 274–279.

[17] I. Moiseenko, "Fetching content in Named Data Networking with embedded manifests," NDN Technical Report, Tech. Rep. NDN-0025, September 2014.

[18] M. Conti, P. Gasti, and M. Teoli, "A lightweight mechanism for detection of cache pollution attacks in named data networking," *Computer Networks*, vol. 57, no. 16, pp. 3178–3191, 2013.

[19] C. Ghali, G. Tsudik, and E. Uzun, "Needle in a haystack: Mitigating content poisoning in named-data networking," in *Proceedings of NDSS Workshop on Security of Emerging Networking Technologies (SENT)*, 2014.

[20] C. Yi, A. Afanasyev, I. Moiseenko, L. Wang, B. Zhang, and L. Zhang, "A Case for Stateful Forwarding Plane," *Comput. Commun.*, vol. 36, no. 7, pp. 779–791, Apr. 2013.

[21] http://named-data.net/doc/ndn-cxx/0.3.0/.

[22] L. Wang, I. Moiseenko, and L. Zhang, "NDNlive and NDNtube: Live and Prerecorded Video Streaming over NDN," NDN, Tech. Rep. 31, May 2015.

[23] D. Kulinski and J. Burke, "NDN Video: Live and Prerecorded Streaming over NDN," UCLA, Tech. Rep., 2012.

[24] P. Crowley, J. DeHart, and H. Yuan, "Performance in Performance in Named Data Networking," 2013 FIA PI Meeting, November 2013. [Online]. Available: http://named-data.net/wp-content/uploads/2014/05/FIA-2013-NDN-Perf-11-15-2013.pdf

[25] B. Ford, "Structured streams: a new transport abstraction," in *ACM SIGCOMM Computer Communication Review*, vol. 37, no. 4. ACM, 2007, pp. 361–372.

[26] https://tools.ietf.org/html/draft-ietf-httpbis-http2.

[27] P. T. Eugster, P. A. Felber, R. Guerraoui, and A.-M. Kermarrec, "The many faces of publish/subscribe," *ACM Computing Surveys (CSUR)*, vol. 35, no. 2, pp. 114–131, 2003.

[28] M. Gallo, L. Gu, D. Perino, and M. Varvello, "NaNET: socket API and protocol stack for process-to-content network communication," in *Proceedings of the 1st international conference on Information-centric networking*. ACM, 2014, pp. 185–186.

[29] J. Chen, M. Arumaithurai, L. Jiao, X. Fu, and K. Ramakrishnan, "Copss: An efficient content oriented publish/subscribe system," in *Architectures for Networking and Communications Systems (ANCS), 2011 Seventh ACM/IEEE Symposium on*. IEEE, 2011, pp. 99–110.

[30] C. Partridge, R. Walsh, M. Gillen, G. Lauer, J. Lowry, W. T. Strayer, D. Kong, D. Levin, J. Loyall, and M. Paulitsch, "A secure content network in space," in *Proceedings of the Seventh ACM International Workshop on Challenged Networks*, ser. CHANTS '12. New York, NY, USA: ACM, 2012, pp. 43–50.

[31] S. Floyd, V. Jacobson, C.-G. Liu, S. McCanne, and L. Zhang, "A reliable multicast framework for light-weight sessions and application level framing," *IEEE/ACM Transactions on Networking (TON)*, vol. 5, no. 6, pp. 784–803, 1997.

Efficient Content Verification in Named Data Networking

Dohyung Kim
Sungkyunkwan University
Suwon, South Korea
mr.dhkim@gmail.com

Sunwook Nam
Korea Financial
Telecommunications and
Clearing Institute
Seoul, South Korea
swnam@kftc.or.kr

Jun Bi
Tsinghua University
Beijing, China
junbi@tsinghua.edu.cn

Ikjun Yeom
Sungkyunkwan University
Suwon, South Korea
ijyeom@gmail.com

ABSTRACT

In Named Data Networking, contents are retrieved from network caches as well as the content server by their name. This aspect arises severe security concerns on content integrity. Especially, if poisoned contents lie in the network cache, called content store(CS), interests would be served by the poisoned content rather than they propagate toward the content server. Consequently, users whose interests pass through the contaminated CS cannot access the valid content. In order to resolve the problem, every content is verified before they are inserted into the CS. However, this built-in verification mechanism is not practically feasible due to its huge computational overhead. In this paper, we address problems of content integrity in NDN in details, including how to violate content integrity. We also propose a practical solution that efficiently detects poisoned contents from the CS with minimum overhead. Since the proposed scheme aligns to the basic NDN architecture, it is a practical and effective solution.

Categories and Subject Descriptors

[**C.2.1 Computer Communication Networks**]: Network Architecture and Design

Keywords

Named-Data Networking (NDN); Content integrity; Cache pollution; Verification

1. INTRODUCTION

Recently, Named Data Networking (NDN) [1] has emerged as a promising future network architecture. In NDN, content is addressed by its name, and it is stored anywhere in the network. Hence, users can access the content from

either permanent content sources or any temporal network caches, without a prior knowledge of the exact location of the content. This decoupling of content from location enables efficient content distribution by minimizing redundant transmission on the links. However, it brings about new types of security problems as well.

Several NDN specific threats have been introduced in the existing literature [2–7]. Among them, *interest flooding* and *cache poisoning* are discussed as the most representative security attacks. *Interest flooding attacks* explode the number of entries in Pending Interest Table(PIT) of routers, or they dissipate computational resource of the content server by issuing a huge number of closely-spaced interests. In [4, 7], authors present effective schemes to isolate attack sources by analyzing Pending Interest Table. By setting a limit on the number of pending interests that belong to the same namespace, routers efficiently discards malicious interests.

Cache poisoning attacks make routers fill their caches up with fabricated contents. They are classified into two categories in terms of the purpose of attack: 1)*locality attack* that ruins content locality in network caches [5,6,8] ; 2)*content poisoning attack* that excludes valid contents from the network. In *locality attack*, the cache file locality is ruined by using unpopular contents. Since every packet is stored in the limited cache space in NDN, popular content can be evicted from the cache by unpopular content. Attackers generate a large amount of unpopular contents, and minimize beneficial effects of in-network caching. In *locality attack*, checking validity of the content itself is meaningless. In [5], authors suggest to cache contents selectively according to their popularity. This scheme prevents insertion of unpopular contents into the cache, which successfully protects popular contents in the cache.

Content poisoning attack isolates valid contents from the network. This type of attack is initiated by placing poisoned content in a router's cache. If an interest whose content name is matched with that of the poisoned content passes through the router, the poisoned content would be served based on simple name matching. While the poisoned content is forwarded back to the user, it contaminates caches of intermediate routers. What is worse, though the user re-requests the content after detecting falsification of the received content, the reissued interest cannot move forward to valid content sources due to the poisoned contents in the network caches.

Theoretically, *content poisoning attack* is prevented by NDN built-in security mechanism, signature verification. However, signature verification is not mandatory at routers mainly because of its huge computational overhead [9]. The authors in [4] take advantage of hash value of the content to implement probabilistic verification. This scheme successfully reduces verification overhead, but they still have challenges such as inter-packet dependency and trust management. In [9], authors address self-certifying name and consider its limitation. And they introduce a new scheme called 'content ranking' which operates based on users exclusion information. However, user feedback has a potential risk because it can be used to exclude valid contents as well, as mentioned in [10].

In this paper, we discuss *content poisoning attacks* and their impacts in detail, and provide a simple but effective solution for them. Basically, the proposed scheme makes use of built-in signature, but its novelty is to reduce overhead by avoiding unnecessary verification. As previous work [4] points out, a large overhead is expected if every content is checked before being inserted into the cache. In the proposed scheme, verification is performed only for the contents that are actually served from the cache. This strategy gives up the cache integrity temporarily, but it successfully minimizes the effect of poisoned content on the network with the minimum overhead. Via ns-3 simulation, we observe that a large number of contents are evicted from the cache before being reused, even when the cache hit rate is reported very high. Verification for these contents is obviously a waste of resource, which is fundamentally prevented by the selective verification in the proposed scheme. But still, the impact of poisoned content is successfully minimized. In the proposed scheme, the poisoned content is detected before it influences the network, or it is simply evicted from the cache without any malicious effect.

In the implementation of the concept of "check on cache-hit", several delicate situations need to be further considered. First, massive re-requests from attackers trigger too much verification, which degrades router's performance. We solve this problem by introducing the validity mark or applying a segment LRU. If a content is successfully verified, it is stored with the validity mark in the cache. Hence, repeated re-requests for the same content are served without further verification. Besides, a segmented LRU(Least Recently Used) replacement policy is used to favor already-verified contents, which minimizes redundant verification in the cache. Second, poisoned content is distributed over the network by multiple pending interests. In this case, "check on cache-hit" cannot prevent the diffusion of poisoned content. Hence, if a response is matched with multiple pending interests, it is regarded as a cache-hit content and it is verified before being inserted into the cache.

The proposed scheme has similarity with 'check before storing(CBS) [11]' in the sense that popular contents are more likely to be verified. In CBS, content is verified and cached with a certain probability. The probability affects hit ratio as well as recency of network caches. As the probability becomes lower, verification and caching are limited to more popular contents. However, a small probability value makes caches desensitized to the change of content popularity. Hence, it is very challenging to find the optimal probability value in reality. In contrast, the proposed scheme operates upon a cache-hit event, so that it verifies popular

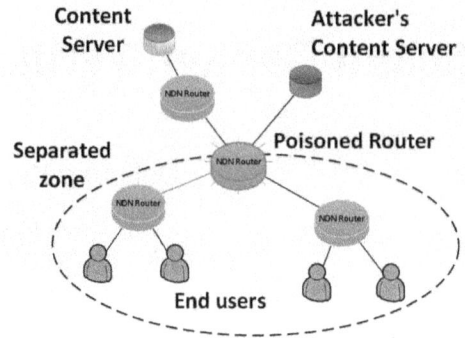

Figure 1: Global poisoning

contents regardless of the change of content popularity. In addition, the proposed scheme can work together with any type of cache replacement policies, while CBS cannot but stick to the probabilistic caching. Via ns-3 simulation, we show that the proposed scheme minimizes verification overhead up to one thirtieth maximally, when no poison content exists in the network. Since the proposed scheme aligns to the basic architecture of NDN, we believe that the proposed scheme is an effective solution for practical application.

2. CONTENT POISONING ATTACK

Content poisoning attack is initiated by placing fake content in network caches called content store(CS). It is implemented by using compromised routers or attacker-controlled end hosts. Anyhow, once the poisoned content locates in the CS of a router, future interests for the content may be served by the poisoned content in the CS based on simple name matching. While the poisoned content is delivered to the user, it also contaminates the CS of all intermediate routers. In this way, NDN efficiently distributes the poisoned content all over the network caches. It is one of the distinctive features of *content poisoning attack* that infection is accelerated by the system itself. Another feature of *content poisoning attack*, which is more serious, is to make users separated from the valid content as shown in Fig. 1. If users locate behind the contaminated CS, their requests cannot be forwarded toward the source of valid content. Unless routers check the integrity of cached contents by themselves, NDN architecture is vulnerable to this type of security threats.

Router compromise is an obvious way to contaminate the CS. Besides, *content poisoning attack* is implemented by manipulating end hosts only. Fig. 2 shows one possible scenario. An attacker puts two end hosts within the network. One of them is a client node that issues interests, and the other plays a role of a server that is responsible for injection of poisoned contents into the network. If the client node requests a content, an interest is forwarded to the valid content source by the NDN router, based on Forwarding Information Base(FIB). At this moment, the attacker's server disembogues the poisoned content into the NDN router. Since the NDN router does not check the incoming face of a response, the poisoned content is cached and forwarded back to the user by consuming the pending interest in PIT, as usual. Hence, even when the valid content arrives at the NDN router later, it is simply discarded because no pending interest exists in PIT.

NDN strategy layer brings poisoned content into the network beyond the boundary of autonomous system(AS). In terms of NDN strategy layer, different parts of the content are retrieved from multiple sources in parallel in NDN. This aspect enables fast content retrieval and load balancing. In order to find available sources, authors in [12, 13] suggest an exploration phase where interests are replicated and forwarded via randomly chosen faces in addition to the default face described in FIB. At this phase, interests may be routed to the infected AS region, and poisoned contents come into the out of AS.

Content poisoning attack could be used to implement pharming and phishing attacks, since users are exposed to poisoned content. Besides, network resources (such as link bandwidth and computing resource at routers) are exhausted by repeated transmission of the same interests, which creates a similar effect of DoS (Denial-of-Service) attack.

3. PROPOSED SOLUTION

3.1 Local poisoning

Local poisoning refers to the attack performed within an AS by using end hosts. In local poisoning, poisoned content is injected into the router via different faces from the interest-outgoing face. Hence, local poisoning is prevented by matching the incoming face of a response with the interest-outgoing face. If a response packet does not come from the interest-outgoing face, it should be discarded. Here we note that an initial version of NDN maintains the incoming face of an interest only as a bread-crumb. Fortunately, however, the recent technical report for NFD [14] specifies that the interest-outgoing face is also added to the structure of PIT for implementing various forwarding strategies(Broadcast strategy, Interest retransmission, etc.). Therefore, incoming face of a response can be checked based on PIT entry. It is worth nothing that checking incoming face of a response is necessary only at the edge router that can be directly accessed by end hosts. Therefore, we suggest that the matching functionality is provided by a configurable option.

3.2 Global poisoning

Once the poisoned content has located in the CS, it is globally spread by NDN system itself, which is called global poisoning. In order to prevent global poisoning, poisoned content should be properly eliminated from CS. Otherwise, it serves user requests and contaminates intermediate routers during its delivery. For that, NDN has a built-in security mechanism based on digital signature. However, previous research points out that signature verification incurs too much computational overhead. According to [4], only a throughput of 150Mbps is achieved by an Intel Core 2 Duo 2.53 GHz CPU, although the most convenient RSA public exponent(3) is used.

Surely, signature verification of all relay contents is a big burden to network routers. Here we question *why even the contents that are not actually served should be verified*. Here we use the term 'serving content' for the content that is served from the CS, and 'by-passing content' for the content that would be evicted from the CS without serving requests. It is obvious that verifying only the serving contents is enough to protect CS from *content poisoning attacks*. Huge computational overhead for by-passing contents is definitely a waste of resource.

We estimate the amount of serving contents in the CS by using ns-3 ndnSIM [15] simulator. In the simulation, 10^5 contents are equally distributed and served by 12 server nodes in Fig. 3. The content popularity follows the zipf-distribution function with parameters, s and $q = 0.7$ [16]. The value of s varies from 0.7 to 1.3. Each client node requests 40 contents per second with exponentially distributed inter-packet delay. The bandwidth of edge links is set to 10Mbps, while that of the core links is 100Mbps. The size of CS is proportional to the link capacity. Each CS stores the amount of contents that arrives for $5 \sim 20$ seconds. The simulation is performed for 1500 seconds.

Fig. 4 shows the hit rate and the proportion of serving contents in the CS at R2 and R7, respectively. 'r2/r7' in the legend indicates a router index. The latter part of the legend, '0.7/1.0/1.3', means the value of s in the zipf-distribution. In Fig. 4, it is observed that the proportion of serving contents is much smaller than the value of hit rate. Even though the hit rate is larger than 0.55 in the case of 'r2, 1.3', the proportion of serving contents in the CS, is less than 0.1. This is because popular contents in the CS are accessed repeatedly. The result indicates over 90% of traffic is composed of by-passing contents, regardless of hit rate. If we also consider congestion control algorithm that works for filling up the residual link bandwidth, the absolute amount of by-passing contents sustain high regardless of hit pattern.

Based on the observation, the proposed scheme implements the concept of "Check on cache-hit". In the proposed scheme, every content is stored in the CS without signature verification. Then, if a cache-hit event occurs in the CS, that

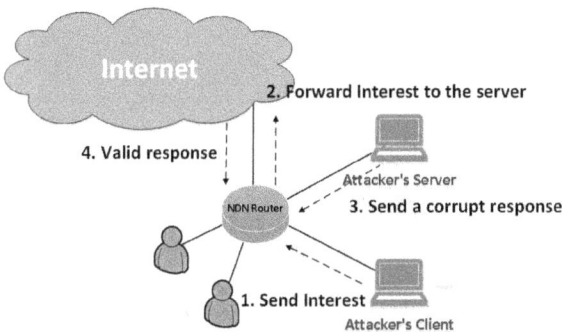

Figure 2: Local Poisoning

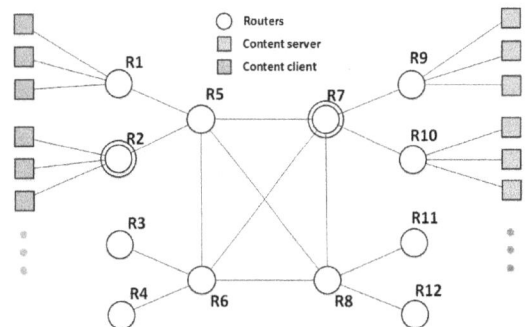

Figure 3: topology

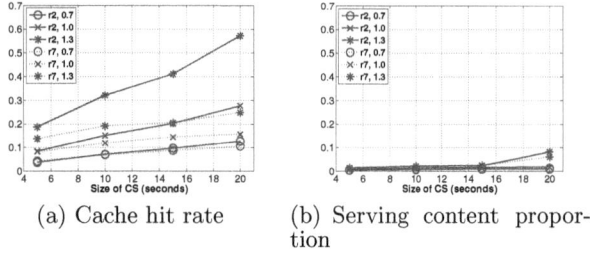

(a) Cache hit rate (b) Serving content proportion

Figure 4: Proportion of serving contents and cache hit rate

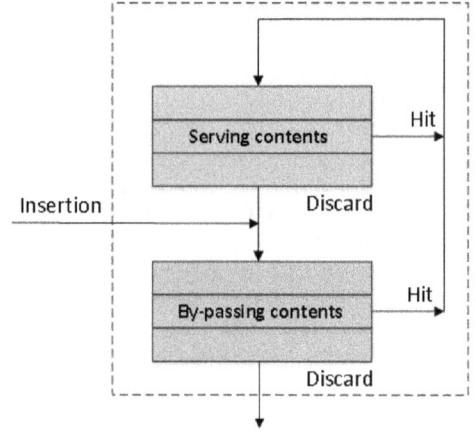

Figure 5: Application of SLRU to the content store

serving content is verified before coming into the network. The proposed scheme can save huge amount of computational resource that has been used for by-passing contents. However, with the reduced number of verification, it successfully minimizes the impact of poisoned content. Under the proposed scheme, poison content in the CS is either simply evicted without any adverse effect, or verified before influencing the network. Here, it is worth nothing that poisoned content can be diffused without the intervention of the CS by multiple pending interests. In order to handle this problem, the proposed scheme regards the content that is matched with multiple pending interests as the serving content, and checks the integrity of the content before storing it, by way of exception.

3.2.1 Enhancement of the proposed scheme

In the proposed scheme, if a serving content is successfully verified, CS sets the flag indicating that the content is flawless. The flag is used to avoid redundant verification for the already-verified content at subsequent cache-hits. The flag is valid while the content stays in the CS. It is observed that popular contents are also expelled from the CS due to the limited space, but they are soon re-inserted into the CS. Resultingly, the content is verified repeatedly at each insertion(more precisely, when a cache-hit occurs after each insertion). This inefficiency is also shown in the basic NDN security architecture. To deal with this problem, we apply Segmented Least Recently Used (SLRU) to the CS.

SLRU was originally designed in [17] for efficient disk system. SLRU divides a cache into the protected segment and the unprotected segment, and LRU policy is applied individually for each segment. If an object is hit on the unprotected segment, it is moved to the protected segment and could stay longer than the other objects in the unprotected segment. By giving preference to the frequently referenced objects, SLRU successfully improves a cache hit ratio. If SLRU is applied to our scheme, verified contents moves to the protected segment and cannot be evicted by by-passing contents. Therefore, verified contents have a higher probability of being re-accessed, which successfully lessens the overhead for repeated verification of popular contents.

3.2.2 Efficiency analysis

In this section, we analyse the efficiency of the proposed scheme in terms of the metric, κ defined by

$$\kappa = \frac{N_e}{N_v} \tag{1}$$

where N_e is the number of examined poisoned contents, and N_v is the number of overall examined contents. The values of κ in the basic scheme, κ_b, corresponds to the ratio of requests for poisoned contents to all requests, e, by definition. The value of κ in CBS, κ_c, is also equal to e because CBS simply controls the amount of N_v in the basic scheme by applying a certain probability, p.

$$\kappa_c = \frac{pN_e}{pN_v} = e \tag{2}$$

In the proposed scheme, verification is performed only for the unverified serving contents. If we let H_p the hit rate for the unverified contents in the CS, N_v for the time interval, Δt, is represented by $Re\Delta t + H_p(1-e)\Delta t$, where R is the request arriving rate. Here we note that a cache-hit occurs when a popular content is re-accessed and a poisoned content is reported by the re-request. N_e is equal to $Re\Delta t$. Hence, the value of κ in the proposed scheme, κ_p, is

$$\kappa_p = \frac{Re}{Re + RH_p(1-e)} = \frac{e}{e + H_p(1-e)} \tag{3}$$

In order to estimate H_p, we assume that the popularity of N total contents follows a "cut-off" Zipf-like distribution. All contents are ranked in the order of their popularity, and $int(i)$ is a request for the i'th most popular content. Then, the conditional probability that the arriving request is $int(i)$, $P_N(i)$, is given by

$$P_N(i) = \frac{\Omega}{i^\alpha} \tag{4}$$

where

$$\Omega = (\sum_{i=1}^{N} \frac{1}{i^\alpha})^{-1}$$

α is within the range of $0 < \alpha \leq 1$.

H_p is equal to the probability that the content i that has been inserted into the CS by cache-missed $int(i)$ generates cache-hit for the next $int(i)$. Therefore H_p is represented by

$$H_p = \sum_{\forall i} P_N(i)P_h(i)P_m(i) \tag{5}$$

where $P_h(i)$ and $P_m(i)$ are the probability of cache-hit and cache-miss for the content i, respectively,

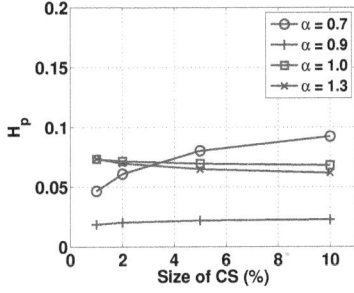

Figure 6: The value of H_p with different cache size

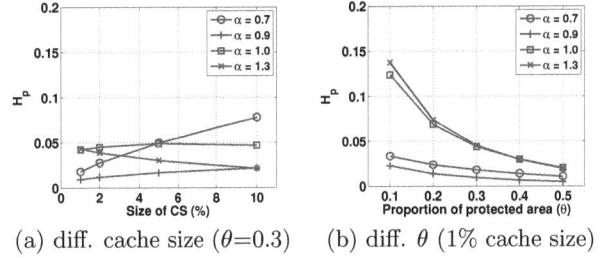

(a) diff. cache size ($\theta=0.3$)   (b) diff. θ (1% cache size)

Figure 7: H_p with SLRU

According to Che approximation [18], $P_h(i)$ is represented by

$$P_h(i) = 1 - e^{-P_N(i)t_C} \qquad (6)$$

where t_C is the solution of the following equation

$$C = \sum_{\forall i}(1 - e^{-P_N(i)t}) \qquad (7)$$

where C is the size of CS.

Based on Taylor series,

$$e^{-P_N(i)t} = 1 - P_N(i)t + \frac{(P_N(i)t)^2}{2} - \frac{(P_N(i)t)^3}{3!} + .. \qquad (8)$$

Since $P_N(i)^4 \ll 1$,

$$e^{-P_N(i)t} \approx 1 - P_N(i)t + \frac{(P_N(i)t)^2}{2} - \frac{(P_N(i)t)^3}{6} \qquad (9)$$

Hence, t_C is the solution of the following polynomial equation.

$$\frac{(\sum_{\forall i}(P_N^3(i))t^3}{6} - \frac{(\sum_{\forall i}P_N^2(i))t^2}{2} + (\sum_{\forall i}P_N(i))t - C = 0 \qquad (10)$$

Fig. 6 shows the value of H_p with different sizes of CS. Even with the CS that can contain 10% of all contents, the value of H_p is less than 0.1.

Therefore, κ_p without SLRU is

$$\kappa_p = \frac{e}{e + H_p(1-e)} \geq \frac{e}{e + 0.1(1-e)} = \frac{e}{0.1 + 0.9e} \qquad (11)$$

When SLRU is applied to the proposed scheme, H_p is equal to the conditional probability that content is moved from the unprotected area to the protected area in the CS, given that a new request arrives. That is, H_p corresponds to the hit ratio in the unprotected area. If we let θ the proportion of the protected area in the CS, contents with the rank $i(\leq \theta C)$ are served from the protected area in steady state. Hence, H_p is approximated by (6) and (7) with the normalized popularity distribution for $N - \theta C$ contents and the CS with the size of $1 - \theta C$.

Fig. 7 shows the values of H_p with different θ and C. Since the popular contents are more favored by SLRU, the value of H_p is smaller than that in Fig. 6. As the value of θ increases, smaller values of H_p are resulted because more popular contents can stay in the protected area. Here, it is shown that H_p is smaller than 0.05 with a reasonable size of

CS (less than 5%) and $\theta > 0.3$.

$$\kappa_p' = \frac{e}{e + H_p(1-e)} \geq \frac{e}{e + 0.05(1-e)} = \frac{e}{0.05 + 0.95e} \qquad (12)$$

Compared with the basic scheme and CBS, the proposed scheme achieves $\frac{1}{0.05 + 0.95e}$ times larger efficiency. Since $e \ll 1$, $\kappa_p \gg \kappa_b(\kappa_c)$. In CBS, although the value of κ is quite low, the overhead can be controlled by the value of caching probability, p. A smaller value of p lessens the verification overhead, while it helps the CS contain more popular contents. However, if a value of p is too small, it take too long that the CS is refreshed by the recent rising contents. Besides, since CBS is strongly bound together with the probabilistic caching, its application is very limited. By contrast, the proposed scheme performs verification on every cache-hit event, which does not make the CS desensitized to the change of content popularity. And it can work with any well-known caching policies without modification.

4. EVALUATION

In this section, we evaluate the performance of the proposed scheme by using ns-3 ndnSIM simulator. The simulation topology is shown in Fig. 8. 10^6 contents are served by the server node, and their popularity follows the Zipf-Mandelbrot distribution function with parameters value, s. 10 clients request contents with the rate of 40 per second, respectively. Inter-request delays at each client follow the exponential distribution with $\lambda = 0.025$. Link bandwidth is set large enough to exclude the congestion effect. CS is installed only at routers (R1 and R2) and its size is varied from 100 to 2000. Here we note that this paper focuses on how NDN routers detect poisoned contents and delete them from the CS efficiently. Hence, we simply generate poisoned contents at the server with a given error probability. It is beyond the scope of this paper to address how routers isolate malicious nodes and make alternative paths to valid content sources. When clients receive a poisoned content, they immediately re-request the content by issuing a new interest. Simulation is performed for 1000 seconds, and records for the later 500 seconds are analysed.

In the first simulation, we look at the result of verification overhead($\frac{N_v}{N_r}$), and hit rate at R1, when there is no poisoned content in the network. N_r is the number of arriving contents. Caching probability in CBS, p, is set to 0.1. In Fig. 9, the basic scheme shows much larger verification overhead than the other schemes. When $s = 0.7$, most interests are served from the content source rather than CS, which results in low hit rate. Nevertheless, routers verify

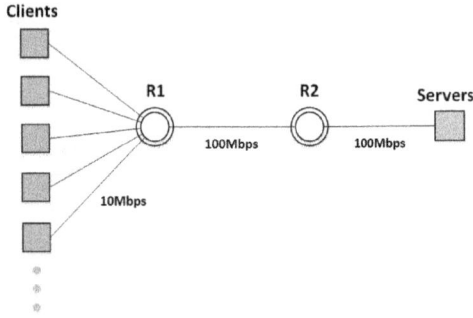

Figure 8: Simulation topology

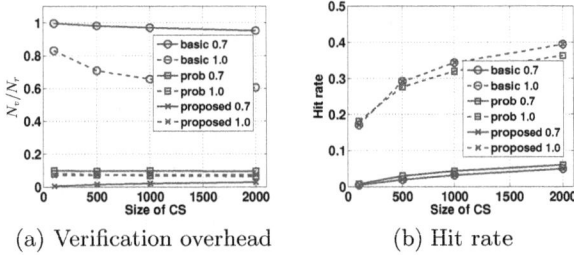

(a) Verification overhead   (b) Hit rate

Figure 9: Results without poisoned contents

(a) Verification Overhead   (b) κ

Figure 10: Results with poisoned contents

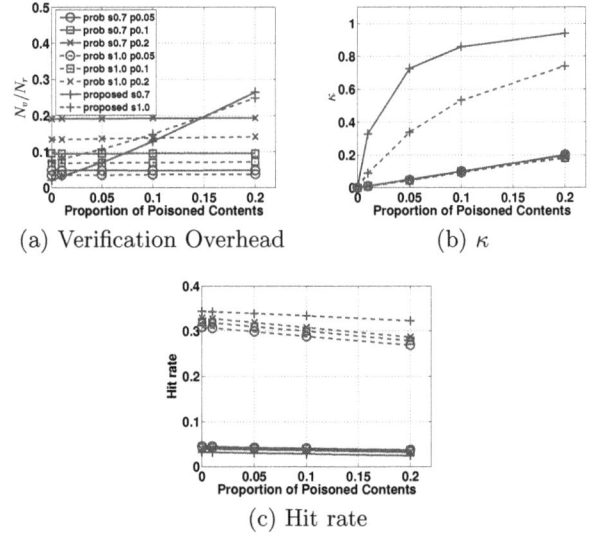

(a) Verification Overhead   (b) κ

(c) Hit rate

Figure 11: Results with dynamic content popularity

every arriving content in the basic scheme, which makes $\frac{N_v}{N_r}$ stay close to 1. In CBS, caching probability dominantly affects the value of N_v. With $p = 0.1$, N_v comes down to 0.1, and so does the verification overhead. However, caching probability affects the cache hit rate as well. When content popularity becomes less skewed ($s = 0.7$), probabilistic caching with $p = 0.1$ achieves higher hit rate than other schemes. When $s = 1.0$, on the contrary, the smallest hit rate is observed. Since content popularity in the Internet is not fixed and it is changing over time, finding out the proper value of p is not trivial. The proposed scheme achieves the minimum overhead while it does not influence the cache hit rate. Compared with the basic scheme, verification overhead is reduced up to one thirtieth. This result implies that the proposed scheme effectively minimizes verification overhead when there is no poisoned content.

The second simulation is performed with poisoned contents. With the fixed size of CS (1000), we look at the value of verification overhead and κ by varying the amount of poisoned contents in the network. Caching probability in CBS is set to 0.1. Even with different amount of poisoned contents, verification overhead does not change in the basic scheme and CBS, since verification is performed regardless of content's state(See Fig. 10). As in the previous simulation, the largest overhead is shown in the basic scheme, and the verification overhead in CBS is determined by caching probability. In the proposed scheme, however, verification overhead increases in proportion to the amount of poisoned contents. This is because more cache-hits occur in the CS by re-request messages from clients that received poison contents. Here we emphasize that in spite of an increased overhead, the proposed scheme maintains a

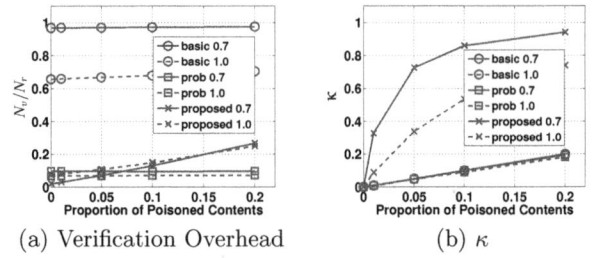

high value of κ, which indicates unnecessary verifications are effectively minimized in the proposed scheme.

In the third simulation, we compare the proposed scheme with CBS under dynamic content popularity, in terms of verification overhead, hit rate, and κ. We change ranks of content popularity on every 100 seconds. 's0.7/s1.0' in Fig. 11 indicates the value of s in Zipf-Mandelbrot distribution, and 'p0.05/p0.1/p0.2' represents the caching probability, p, in CBS. Like in previous simulations, verification overhead in CBS is managed by the value of p, while the overhead in the proposed scheme increases in proportion to the amount of poisoned contents. However, the proposed scheme obtains a much larger value of κ, which indicates that additional verifications in the proposed scheme result in the detection of poisoned contents. Here we note that caching probability p does not influence the value of κ in CBS, since probabilistic selection for caching is performed regardless of content's state. As concerns the cache hit rate, a smaller value of p results in a higher hit rate when $s = 0.7$. However, as the content popularity becomes more skewed, the benefit of probabilistic caching disappears, and CBS achieves lower hit rates than the proposed scheme.

The fourth simulation is performed to examine the effect of SLRU in the proposed scheme. We set the proportion of poisoned contents as 0.1. The overall size of CS is fixed

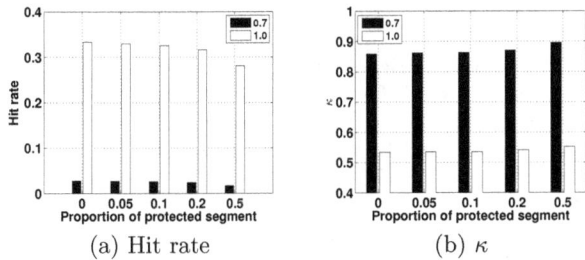

(a) Hit rate   (b) κ

Figure 12: The effect of SLRU

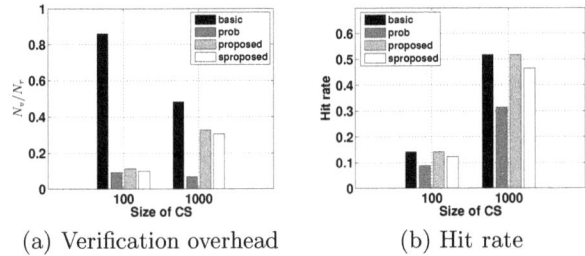

(a) Verification overhead   (b) Hit rate

Figure 13: Results in YouTube trace without poisoned contents

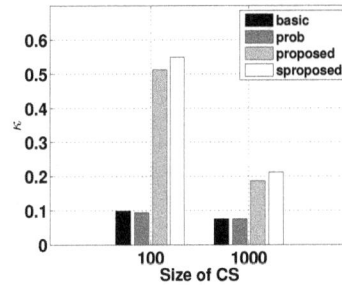

Figure 14: κ in YouTube trace with poisoned contents

as 1000, and the proportion of the protected segment in CS is varied form 0 to 0.5. Fig. 12 shows the result of hit rate and κ. As the size of the protected segment increases, the time that a content stays at the unprotected segment before eviction becomes shorter. As a result, the cache hit rate decreases. However, due to the protected segments, verification efficiency, κ, grows in proportion to the size of protected segment, which indicates that verified contents are re-used more frequently.

In the last simulation, the proposed scheme is evaluated with the youTube trace from UMASS campus during Mar. 11-17 in 2008 [19]. The overall number of contents in the trace is 158974, and we assume that all contents are of the same size as 1. In Fig. 13(a), it is confirmed that verification overhead is minimized in the proposed scheme (up to less than 25% of the overhead in the basic scheme), when the size of CS is 100. As the size of CS increases, verification overhead increases due to the high hit ratio, but it still remains less than that of the basic scheme. As concerns about the hit rate, the proposed scheme shows the similar performance with the basic scheme in Fig. 13(b). Fig. 14 shows the value of κ when the proportion of poisoned contents is set as 0.1. When the size of CS is 100, the efficiency of the proposed scheme is more than 5 times larger than that of the other comparative schemes. With a larger size of CS, more contents are served from the CS, which increases the number of verification in the proposed scheme. Hence, the value of κ decreases. However, the value of κ is still more than two times larger than that of the comparative schemes when the size of CS is 1000.

5. CONCLUSION

In this paper, we discuss NDN cache poisoning attacks, and provide simple but effective solutions for them. Especially, the proposed solution for global poisoning saves huge amount of computational resource, while it perfectly flushes poisoned contents from the CS. Both simulation and analysis study prove that the proposed scheme effectively mitigates large verification overhead without degradation of CS performance and soundness.

6. ACKNOWLEDGEMENTS

This work was supported by the National Research Foundation of Korea (NRF) grant funded by the Korea government(MSIP) (NRF-2014K1A1A2064649)

7. REFERENCES

[1] V. Jacobson, D. K. Smetters, J. D. Thornton, M. F. Plass, N. H. Briggs, and R. L. Braynard, "Networking named content," in *ACM CoNEXT*, 2009.

[2] T. Lauinger, N. Laoutaris, P. Rodriguez, T. Strufe, E. Biersack, and E. Kirda, "Privacy risks in named data networking: what is the cost of performance?" *ACM SIGCOMM Computer Communication Review*, vol. 42, pp. 54 – 57, 2012.

[3] M. Wählisch, T. C. Schmidt, and M. Vahlenkamp, "Backscatter from the data plane - threats to stability and security in information-centric networking," ArXiv abs/1205.4778, Tech. Rep., 2012.

[4] P. Gasti, G. Tsudik, E. Uzun, and L. Zhang, "Dos and ddos in named-data networking," in *IEEE ICCCN*, Aug. 2012.

[5] M. Xie, I. Widjaja, and H. Wang, "Enhancing cache robustness for content-centric networking," in *IEEE INFOCOM*, 2012.

[6] M. Conti, P. gasti, and M. Teoli, "A lightweight mechanism for detection of cache pollution attacks in named data networking," *Elsevier Computer Networks*, vol. 57, pp. 3178 – 3191, 2013.

[7] A. Afanasyev, P. Mahadevan, I. Moiseenko, E. Uzun, and L. Zhang, "Interest flooding attack and countermeasures in named data networking," in *IEEE IFIP Networking Conference*, 2013.

[8] Y. Gao, L. Deng, A. Kuzmanovic, and Y. Chen, "Internet cache pollution attacks and countermeasures." in *IEEE ICNP*, 2006.

[9] C. Ghali, G. Tsudik, and E. Uzun, "Needle in a haystack: Mitigating content poisoning in named-data networking," in *NDSS Workshop on Security of Emerging Networking Technologies*, Feb. 2014.

[10] ——, "Network-layer trust in named-data networking," *ACM Computer Communication Review*, vol. 44, pp. 12 – 19, 2014.

[11] G. Bianchi, A. Detti, A. Caponi, and N.Blefari-Melazzi, "Check before storing: What is the performance price of content integrity verification in lru caching?" *ACM SIGCOMM Computer Communication Review*, vol. 43, pp. 59 – 67, 2013.

[12] R. Chiocchetti, D. Perino, G. Carofiglio, D. Rossi, and G. Rossini, "Inform: a dynamic interest forwarding mechanism for information centric networking," in *ACM SIGCOMM workshop on Information-centric networking*, 2013.

[13] M. Lee, J. Song, K. Cho, S. Park, T. T. Kwon, J. Kangasharju, and Y. Choi, "Content discovery for information-centric networking," *Elsevier Computer Networks*, 2014.

[14] A. Afanasyev, J. Shi, B. Zhang, L. Zhang, I. Moiseenko, Y. Yu, W. Shang, Y. Huang, J. P. Abraham, S. DiBenedetto, C. Fan, C. Papadopoulos, D. Pesavento, G. Grassi, G. Pau, H. Zhang, T. Song, H. Yuan, H. B. Abraham, P. Crowley, S. O. Amin, V. Lehman, and L.Wang, "Nfd developers guide," NDN Project, Tech. Rep. NDN-0021, Tech. Rep., 2014.

[15] A. Afanasyev, I. Moiseenko, and L. Zhang, "ndnsim: Ndn simulator for ns-3," University of California, LosAngeles, Technical Report, Tech. Rep., 2012.

[16] L. Breslau, P. Cao, L. Fan, G. Phillips, and S. shenker, "Web caching and zipf-like distributions: Evidence and implications," in *IEEE INfOCOM*, 1999.

[17] R. Karedla, J. S. Love, and B. G. Wherry, "Caching strategies to improve disk system performance," *Computer*, vol. 27, pp. 38 – 46, 1994.

[18] H. Che, Y. Tung, and Z. Wang, "Hierarchical web caching systems: modeling, design and experimental results," *IEEE JSAC*, vol. 20.

[19] "Youtube traces from the campus network," 2008. [Online]. Available: http://traces.cs.umass.edu/index.php/Network

NDN-RTC: Real-Time Videoconferencing over Named Data Networking

Peter Gusev
UCLA REMAP
peter@remap.ucla.edu

Jeff Burke
UCLA REMAP
jburke@remap.ucla.edu

ABSTRACT

NDN-RTC is a videoconferencing library that employs Named Data Networking (NDN), a proposed future Internet architecture. It was designed to provide a platform for experimental research in low-latency, real-time multimedia communication over NDN. It aims to provide an end-user experience similar to Skype or Google Hangouts, while implementing a receiver-driven approach that takes advantage of NDN's name-based forwarding, data signatures, caching, and request aggregation. As implemented, NDN-RTC employs widely used open source components, including the WebRTC library, VP9 codec, and OpenFEC for forward error correction. This paper presents the design, implementation in C++, and testing of NDN-RTC on the NDN testbed using a demonstration GUI conferencing application, *ndncon*, which provides HD videoconferencing over NDN to end-users.

1. INTRODUCTION

Named Data Networking (NDN) is a proposed future Internet architecture that shifts the "thin waist" of the Internet from the current host-centric paradigm of IP to data-centric communication. In NDN, every chunk of data has a name, which is often hierarchical and human-readable, and a cryptographic signature binding name, data, and the key of the publisher. Consumers of data issue "Interest" packets for these "Data" packets by name. Signed, named Data packets matching the Interest can be returned by any node on the network, including opportunistic caches on routers. NDN's intrinsic caching can be leveraged by content distribution applications to reduce the load on data publishers in multi-consumer scenarios [8]. Duplicate Interests for the same content are also aggregated in routers, further reducing the load on those publishers and the network. NDN is described in more detail in publications on the project website[1], including [18, 19, 6].

---

[1] http://named-data.net

Efficient content distribution has long been a driver application for NDN research and the broader field of Information Centric Networking (ICN). Prior work in this area, including our own, is covered briefly in Section 4. However, low-latency applications, such as "real-time" videoconferencing, present particular design and implementation issues that have not been as widely explored in publicly available prototypes or the NDN and ICN literature. For example, obtaining the "latest data" from a network with pervasive caching, without relying on direct consumer-producer communication (which impacts scaling potential) and while trying to keep application-level latency low, appears to be a significant challenge.

The NDN project team uses application-driven research to explore NDN's affordances for modern applications and to refine the architecture itself. The NDN-RTC library was created to explore real-time communications (RTC) experimentally. Though it is based on what was learned from our NDNVideo project [8], NDN-RTC is a clean slate design with new goals. The project is ongoing; this paper presents the current design and initial evaluation. To work towards the goal of using NDN-RTC in NDN project-related videoconferences and meetings, we needed reasonable CPU and bandwidth efficiency, echo cancellation, and modern video coding performance. Therefore, NDN-RTC is built in C++ for performance and leverages the widely used WebRTC library, incorporating its existing audio pipeline and video codec.

The remainder of this paper is organized as follows: Section 2 briefly describes potential NDN benefits for real-time communication (RTC). Section 3 details our goals for NDN-RTC. Section 4 covers background and prior work. Section 5 describes the architecture of the library, designed namespace, data structures and algorithms. Section 6 discusses implementation details. Section 7 evaluates main outcomes. Finally, Section 8 provides a conclusion and explains future work.

2. WHY USE NDN FOR RTC?

Given that NDN proposes a general Internet architecture, we are motivated initially to show its viability for applications beyond the content distribution examples most often discussed in the literature. However, we can also present a few potential benefits of using NDN for RTC that are exciting for us:

- By using names rather than IP addresses for routing and forwarding, as with any other NDN application, RTC applications stand to inherit the benefits for mobility, scalability, and simplifications of network infrastructure that are currently being researched in the ICN community, a potential boon for RTCs applications. With NDN-RTC, we use a straightforward naming and communication scheme, leveraging conventions where possible, and build on the current libraries, forwarder, and testbed to increase the likelihood that these benefits can be inherited (or at least explored) in future work.

- Receiver-driven architectures requiring minimal publisher coordination can gain consumer scalability from the network, which is viable for streaming playout, as shown in past work discussed below. Early tests of NDN-RTC, described in later sections, demonstrate such network-supported scalability for RTC. This suggests that in the future, by using broadcast or group encryption schemes, NDN could efficiently support secure one-to-many or few-to-many low-latency broadcasts with very little additional application infrastructure – whether of entertainment content, presentations, closed-circuit cameras, computer vision sources, etc. – in addition to interactive conversations.

- Finally, because NDN-RTC builds directly on the thin waist of the NDN architecture, what is learned from exploring low-latency transmission of time series begins to provide broadly applicable insight into handling other high-rate and/or low-latency time series, such as sensor data feeds.

3. DESIGN OBJECTIVES

As discussed above, NDN-RTC aims to explore low-latency audio/video communication over NDN, and to support a working multi-party conferencing application that can be used by NDN project team members across the existing NDN testbed. It also aims to preserve network-supported scalability by avoiding direct consumer-producer communication (i.e., Interests that cannot be aggregated). Further, it explores if "real-time" communication can be achieved in a manner consistent with most other NDN data dissemination applications (described at a high level, as follows).

Applications using the library implement bidirectional communication by acting as a publisher of their own media streams and consumer of others. A publisher 1) acquires and transforms media data, 2) names, packetizes and signs it, and then 3) passes the packets to an internal or external component that responds to Interests received from the "black box" of the NDN network with signed, named data chunks. A consumer issues Interests with appropriate names and selectors to that "black box" of the NDN network, at the rate necessary to achieve its objectives and be a good citizen of the network[2]–as informed by the performance of the network it observes in response to its requests. It reassembles and renders them. Rate adaptation can be handled at the consumer by publishing in multiple namespaces corresponding to multiple bitrates or to layers of a scalable video stream and enabling the consumer to select them on-the-fly.

Once the namespace is defined, the publishing problem in this scenario (and in practice, at least so far) is relatively straightforward. Complexity is at the the consumer, which must determine what names to issue at what rate, to get the best quality of experience for the application. For real-time conferencing, this means low-latency access to the freshest data that the "black box" of the NDN network can deliver to a given consumer.

Conference setup and multi-party chat could be handled by applying techniques such as those developed in ChronoChat [16], which uses set reconciliation-based synchronization protocols to exchange messages in a many-to-many scenario.

Based on this high-level concept, specific design goals were developed for the NDN-RTC library:

- **Low-latency audio/video communication.** The library should be capable of maintaining low-latency (approx. 250-750ms) communication for audio and video, similar to consumer videoconferencing applications.

- **Multi-party conferencing.** Publishing and fetching several media streams simultaneously should be straightforward.

- **Passive consumer & cacheability.** There should be no explicit negotiation or coordination between publisher and consumer for the media transmission itself, to enable exploration of network-supported scaling to very high consumer to producer ratios.

- **Multiple bitrates.** The library and namespace should support multiple bitrates (from which consumers will select), enabling near future work on adaptive rate control.

- **Data verification.** The library should provide content verification using existing NDN features, as a building block for trust management and encryption-based access control.

Our design approach was further influenced by the relatively young state of NDN research:

- **Segment-level control.** At the protocol level, NDN-RTC works directly with data segments rather than video frames, group-of-pictures (GOP) blocks, or other higher-level constructs that it uses at the application level. This choice was made because most abstractions for most Interest-Data exchange explored in current research and available implementations do not handle low-latency, deadline-driven playout, assume large buffer sizes relative to network latency variations, and because frame sizes often exceed current NDN data object maximum sizes. While in the future, successful fetching and buffering patterns may be abstracted to a lower-level library, this approach enabled us to experiment with Interest expression and buffering at fine granularity. For example, NDN-RTC uses per segment metadata that can be exploited by the consumer to adjust fetching behavior.

- **Assumptions about the network.** Throughout the paper there are a number of assumptions about caching performance and other network behavior. Although future networks may have more complex behavior, the intention here is to explore the performance of basic assumptions on the NDN testbed, rather than proposing schemes to address the emergent behavior of complex ICN networks.

4. BACKGROUND AND PRIOR WORK

Most video streaming work on ICN has focused on playout without the constraints of supporting interactive conversations. For example, UCLA's NDNVideo, which supported live video and playback, was tested and deployed over NDN

---

[2]While work on congestion control and defining proper behaviour of such applications on the network is underway, it is future work with respect to this paper.

[8], scaling to approximately one thousand consumers from a single, simple publisher over plain-vanilla NDN. [4] Its data chunks were named sequentially according to NDN naming conventions [17], with a second namespace mapping sequence numbers to a timeline to enable efficient time-based random access by consumers. Though the project worked well for live and pre-recorded media streaming, it did not meet requirements for low-latency communication in its Interest pipelining approach. Also, its media architecture, based on GStreamer, was not immediately extensible for use as a conferencing solution. Subsequent work at UCLA, NDNlive and NDNtube [15] demonstrated a new API for application developers, the Consumer/Producer API [10], which works with higher-level "Application Data Units" rather than Interests/Data packets. To our knowledge, that work also does not target or achieve RTC, and like NDNVideo, is built on GStreamer, which does not easily support the audio pipeline needed for interactive conversations. Other streaming video work includes [9] and [12], which explore the advantages of using ICN networks for MPEG Dynamic Adaptive Streaming over HTTP (DASH). Although not directly related to low-latency streaming, these works also leverage ICN networks' caching ability for serving chunks of video files efficiently to multiple consumers. In contrast with the above, NDN-RTC was developed from the ground up with low latency and interactive conversations in mind.

The Voice-over-CCN project [5] was an early exploration of real-time communication over ICN, providing a similar level of quality compared to VoIP solutions with much greater scalability potential and simpler, more flexible architecture. VoCCN introduced pipelining Interests in a real-time scenario, an idea also employed in NDN-RTC. Subsequently, an audio conferencing application, ACT, was developed early in the NDN project [20]. It leveraged use of the Mumble library and successfully used NDN as a transport. Efforts for conference and user discovery were made in this work as well. However, echo cancellation quality was poor, which made it difficult to use, and only preliminary work in video was performed. This led us to build NDN-RTC on top of the WebRTC library, despite the additional, significant implementation complexity, in order to use its audio-processing capabilities and video codecs, and potentially give an opportunity for easier integration with supported web browsers.[3] Finally, the most recent related work in ICN-based real-time communication, of which we are aware, is [7]; however, as we understand, it currently handles Interest retransmission and buffering at the GOP level and does not (yet) meet our latency requirements.

5. APPLICATION ARCHITECTURE

There are two roles in the NDN-RTC library: producer and consumer. In bidirectional communication, applications use the library to play both roles, but a variety of other multi-party and one-to-many scenarios can be achieved. The library is built on a consumer-driven approach directly following NDN's Interest-Data exchange model. In contrast to the sender-driven approach of typical IP-based RTC, the producer publishes data to network-connected storage at its

own pace, while the consumer requests data as needed and manages the relationship between outgoing Interests, incoming data segments, and buffer fill.

5.1 Producer

The producer's main tasks are to acquire video and audio data from media inputs, encode them, marshal the data into packets, *name* those packets, sign them, and store them in an application-level cache[4] that will asynchronously respond to incoming Interests. Flow control responsibility is shifted to the consumer, and scaling is supported by network caches downstream rather than publishing infrastructure at the application level.

5.2 Namespace

A primary design question is how the data should be named so it can be retrieved by the consumer with the desired properties. The NDN-RTC namespace defines names for media (segmented video frames and bundled audio samples), error correction data, and metadata, as shown in Figure 1. The namespace is designed to efficiently support consumer-driven communication, as introduced in Section 5 and detailed in Section 5.4. Note that NDN-RTC handles audio and video streams independently, which enables the library to support audio-only streaming, and for applications to prioritize audio over video for increased quality of experience for interactive conversations in bursty or low-bitrate scenarios.

5.2.1 Media

NDN-RTC employs the abstraction of a *media stream*, which describes a flow of one type of media, such as video frames or audio samples, coming from a source–currently, an input device on the producer. A typical publisher will publish several media streams simultaneously–e.g., video from a camera, audio from a microphone, video from screen capture. The data from a stream may be encoded at one or more bitrates, so in the name hierarchy, each stream has children corresponding to different encoder instances called *media threads*. Media threads allow the producer to, for example, provide the same media stream in several quality levels, such as low, medium and high, so that the consumer can choose the one suitable for its requirements and current network conditions.

NDN-RTC packetizes the WebRTC video encoder output directly. Encoded media segments published under the hierarchical names described above, with video frames further separated into two namespaces per frame type, `delta` and `key`, each numbered sequentially and independently. (Section 7 elaborates more on the reasons why this separation is needed.)

The next level in the tree separates data by type, either media or parity. Parity data for forward error correction, if the producer opts to publish it, can be used by a consumer to recover frames that miss one or more segments. In the case of both parity and regular frames, the deepest level of the namespace defines individual data segments. Any media packet, except audio, consists of one or more segments.[5]

---

[3]No modifications are needed to WebRTC [2] as used in NDN-RTC, which we believe will enable us to make comparisons between IP and NDN implementations of the library in the future.

[4]Currently, this cache is provided to the application by the NDN-CCL library.

[5]For example, the average sizes of frames for 1000 kbps stream using VP8/VP9: key frames are $\approx$ 30KB, and delta frames are $\approx$ 3-7KB. Therefore, depending on the under-

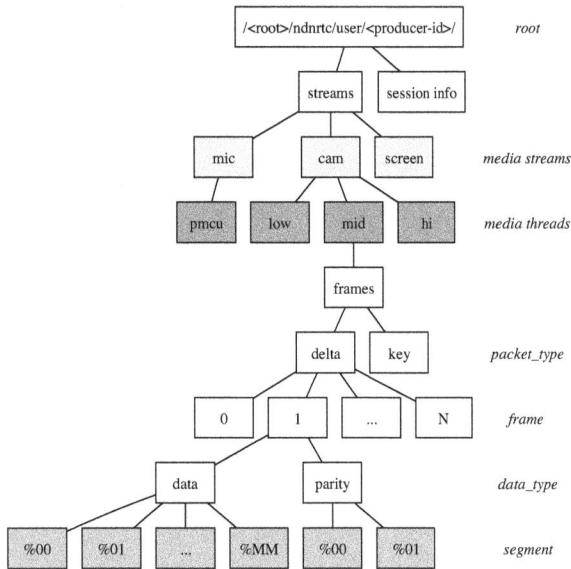

Figure 1: NDN-RTC namespace

These segments are numbered sequentially, and their names conform to NDN naming conventions [17].

Audio stream samples are much smaller than the maximum payload size, and there is no equivalent to the key/delta frame distinction in the audio codecs in use. Therefore, all audio packets are published under the `delta` namespace. Multiple audio samples are bundled into one data packet, until the size of one data segment is reached, and published only after that.

5.2.2 Metadata

NDN-RTC uses both stream-level and packet-level metadata. Consumers need to know the producer's publishing configuration and, to save them from traversing the producer's namespace, the producer publishes meta-information about current streams under `session info` and updates it whenever the configuration has changed.

Additionally, data names carry further metadata as part of each packet, which can be used by consumers regardless of which frame segment was received first. Four components are added at the end of every data segment name:

$$.../delta/frame\_no/data/seg\_no/n_{seg}/pl/pr_{seq}/par_{num}$$

n_{seg} - total number of segments for this frame;

pl - absolute playback position for current frame (this is different from the *frame*, which is a sequence number for the frame in its domain, i.e. `key` or `delta`);

pr_{seq} - sequence number of the corresponding frame from other domain (i.e., for delta frames, it is the sequence number of the corresponding key frame required for decoding);

par_{num} - number of parity segments for the frame.

lying transport's performance for delivering objects of this size, the producer may need to segment encoded frames into smaller chunks and name them in a way that makes reassembly straightforward. Based on our current observations of performance and the prevalence of UDP as a transport for the NDN testbed, NDN-RTC currently packetizes media into segments that are less than the typical 1500 byte MTU.

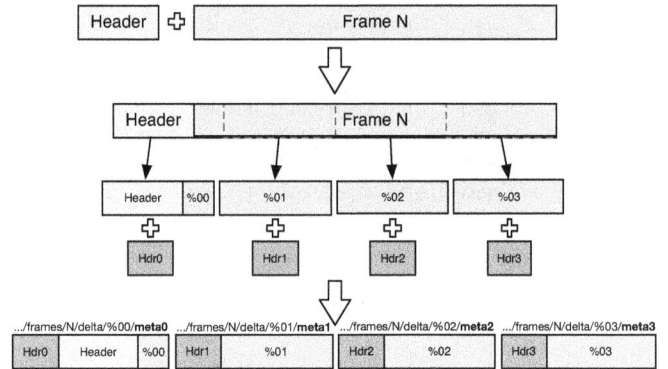

(a) Video frame segmentation.

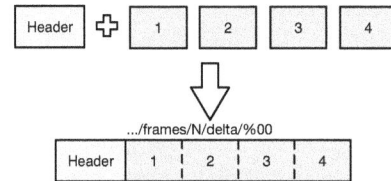

(b) Audio sample bundling.

Figure 2: Segmentation and bundling

Metadata in the name, rather than in the packet, is expected to be useful for application components or services that may not need to understand the packet payload.

5.3 Data objects

The producer generates signed data objects from input media streams and places them into an in-memory, application-level cache. These objects contain stream data and metadata.

5.3.1 Media stream

Video stream data contains raw bytes received from the WebRTC library's video encoder. For audio, NDN-RTC captures and encapsulates RTP and RTCP packets coming from the WebRTC audio processing pipeline, in order to obtain echo cancellation and gain control and other features, which are then fed into a similar pipeline on the consumer side for proper rendering and corrections.[6]

5.3.2 Metadata

Apart from metadata provided in the namespace (as was described earlier), there is also metadata supplied in the data objects themselves. Every media sample is prepended with frame-level metadata, the *frame header* (see Figures 2 and 3), which carries encoding and timing information. Another type of metadata, the *segment header*, is appended to individual segments and carries the producer's observations of Interest arrival. This information is used by consumers to adjust fetching and playback mechanisms. Segment headers make use of the Interest nonce value, and thus may not be as useful in larger multi-party calls. At this time, they are used primarily for experimental and evaluation purposes:

---

[6]This is an artifact of the current implementation to benefit from the full audio pipeline of WebRTC, which is difficult to unbundle from RTP.

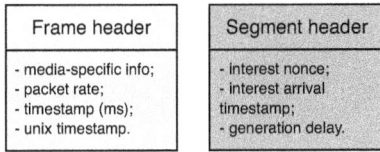

Figure 3: Frame and (experimental) segment headers.

Interest nonce: Nonce of the Interest *first* received at the publisher for a particular segment. Example interpretations include: 1) Value belongs to an Interest issued previously: Consumer received non-cached data requested by previously issued Interest; 2) Value is non-zero, but it does not belong to any of the previously issued Interests: Consumer received data requested by some other consumer; data may be cached; 3) Value is zero: Data requested after it has been produced; data is cached.

Interest arrival timestamp: Timestamp of the first Interest's arrival at the producer. Monitoring publisher arrival timestamps may give the consumer that issued the Interest information about how long it takes for Interests to reach the producer.

Generation delay: Time interval in milliseconds between Interest arrival and segment publishing. If the nonce is its own, a consumer can use this value in order to control the number of outstanding Interests.

5.4 Consumer

In NDN-RTC's receiver-driven architecture, the consumer aims to 1) choose the most appropriate media stream bandwidth from those provided by the producer, e.g., by monitoring network conditions; 2) fetch and, if necessary, reassemble media in the correct order for playback; 3) mitigate, as far as possible, the impact of network latency and packet drops on the viewer's quality of experience. The consumer implements Interest pipelining and data buffering, as shown in Figure 4(b). An asynchronous Interest pipeline issues Interests for individual segments. Independently, a frame buffer handles re-ordering of packets, and informs the pipeline of its status to prompt Interest reexpression.

5.4.1 Frame fetching

The consumer uses an estimate of the number of segments it must fetch for a given frame, issuing M initial Interests, as illustrated in Figure 5. If Interests arrive too early, they will be held in the producer's PIT and stay there until the frame is captured and packetized. The delay between Interest arrival and availability of the media data is called the **generation delay**, d_{gen}. Conceptually, this interval should be kept low, to avoid accumulating outstanding Interests with short lifetimes; however, Interests should not arrive after data is published, as this increases latency from the end-user's perspective. Once the encoded frame is segmented into N segments and published, Interests $0 - M$ are answered, and the Data returns to the requestor(s).

Upon receiving the first Data segment, the consumer knows from the metadata the exact number of segments N for the current frame, and issues $N - M$ more Interests for the missing segments, if any. These segments will be satisfied by data with no generation delay, as the frame has been published already by the producer. The time interval between receiving

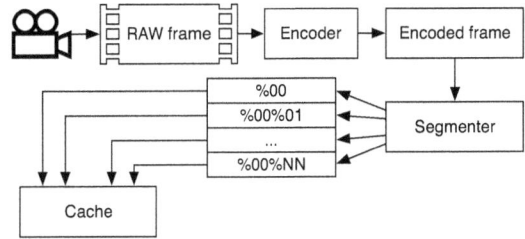

(a) Producer

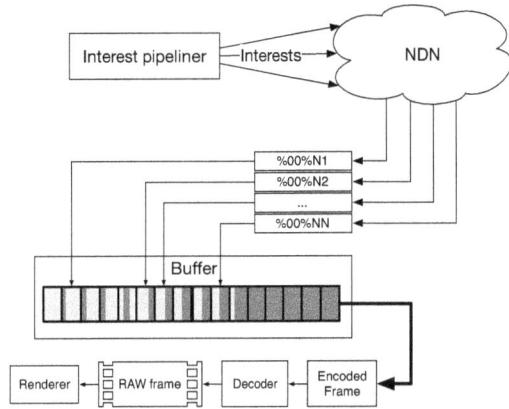

(b) Consumer

Figure 4: NDN-RTC producer and consumer operation.

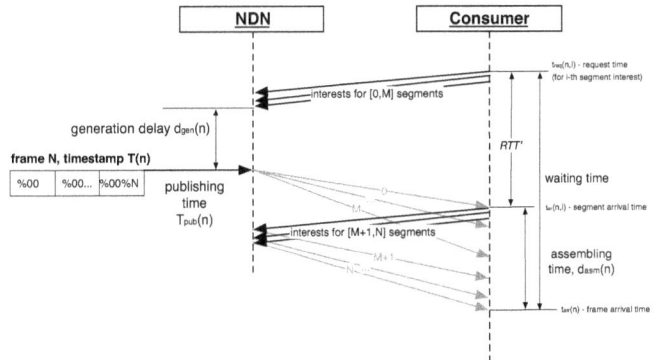

Figure 5: Data retrieval timeline.

the very first segment and when the frame is fully assembled is represented by d_{asm} and called **assembly time**. Note that for frames that have less segments than the estimate ($N < M$), some Interests may go unanswered.

More accurate estimates of the number of initial Interests per frame can help avoid additional roundtrips. The library estimates the average number of segments for each frame type for a given bitrate, and uses this evolving estimate to calculate the number of initial Interests to issue for the next frame in each namespace.

A similar process is used for fetching audio, though for now, audio bundles are carried by just one segment.

5.4.2 Buffering

The consumer uses a *jitter buffer* to manage out-of-order data arrivals and variations in network delay, and as a place

121

to assemble segments into frames. Our receiver-based paradigm requires the consumer to request data by name explicitly, and organize it by frame as well as segment. Outstanding Interests are represented in the buffer by "reserved slots" - those that have partial frame data or no data at all. The NDN-RTC jitter buffer's size is expressed in terms of two values measured in milliseconds at any given point in time. Its *playback size* is the playback duration in milliseconds of all complete ordered frames; its *estimated size* is *playback size + number of reserved slots* × $1/producer\ rate$, which reflects the estimated size of the buffer when all reserved slots have data. Each frame-level slot has an associated set of interests. The difference between estimated buffer size and playback size corresponds to the effective RTT, called RTT' (this cannot be smaller than the actual network RTT value).

Playout progress of the jitter buffer is used for retransmission control. At J milliseconds from the buffer end (see Figure 10) there is a checkpoint, after which it is estimated to be too late for another round trip. When a frame reaches the checkpoint, it is checked for completeness. If the frame is incomplete and cannot be recovered using available parity data, Interests for the missing segments are re-issued.

5.4.3   Interest expression control

A key challenge of a consumer-driven model for video-conferencing, in a caching network, is how to ensure the consumer acquires the latest data without (per our design goal) resorting to direct producer-consumer communication. To get fresh data, the consumer cannot rely on flags in the protocol, such as *AnswerOriginKind* and *RightMostChild*. The frame period for streaming video is of the same order of magnitude as network round-trip time, suggesting there is no guarantee that the data satisfying those flags will be the most recent data received by the consumer. Instead, it is necessary to use other indicators to ensure that the consumer is requesting and receiving the most up-to-date stream data possible given its (potentially evolving) network connectivity.

Our current solution is to leverage the known sample publishing rate, which is available in stream-level metadata, and note that, under normal operation, old, cached samples are likely to be retrieved more quickly than new data. [7] We define the **interarrival delay** (d_{arr}) as the time between receipt of successive samples by a given consumer.

The library currently assumes that delays in the most recent samples follow the publishers' generation pattern, but older, cached data will follow the pattern of Interest expression.[8] Therefore, by monitoring inter-arrival delays of consecutive media samples and comparing them to the timing of its own Interest expression, which is distinct from the expected generation pattern, consumers can estimate whether they are receiving fresh data or cached data (see Figure 6). The consumer's objective is to obtain fresh data at a consistent rate from the network as a black box, not for Interests to "reach" the producer directly.

------

[7]If the consumer is the *only* consumer of the stream, its Interests will go directly to the publisher, which also yields the correct behavior. A more complex challenge, for further study, is when segments are inconsistently cached in different ways along the path(s) that Interests take.

[8]Though this assumption has proved successful in tests so far, we acknowledge more work is required to address more complex network conditions.

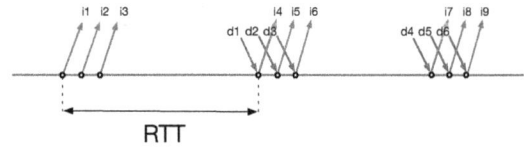

(a) Bursty arrival of cached data, which reflects Interests expression pattern and indicates that the data is not the latest.

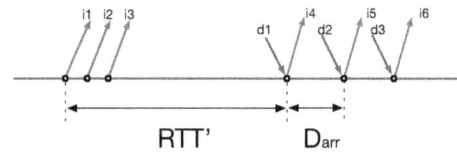

(b) Periodic arrival of fresh data, reflects publishing pattern and sample rate.

Figure 6: Getting the latest data: arrival patterns for the cached and most recent data

NDN-RTC interest expression is managed in two modes, *bootstrapping* and *playback*. During bootstrapping, the consumer "chases" the producer and aims to exhaust network cache of historical (non-real time) segments. By increasing the number of outstanding Interests, the consumer "pulls cached data" out of the network, unless the freshest data begin to arrive. In order to control Interest expression, the NDN-RTC consumer tracks a quantity called "Interest demand", λ, which can be interpreted as how many outstanding Interests should be sent at the current time (see Figure 7). The consumer expresses new Interests when $\lambda > 0$. For example, before the bootstrapping phase, the consumer initializes λ with a value which reflects the consumer's estimate of how many Interests are needed in order to exhaust network cache and reach the most recent data. In playback, every time a new Interest is expressed, λ is decremented, and when new data arrives, λ is incremented, thus enabling the consumer to issue more Interests.[9]

Bootstrapping. In the current design, there are two experimentally determined indicators that are used by the consumer to adjust λ: effective RTT (RTT') and inter-arrival delay d_{arr}. As described above, at bootstrapping (and re-acquisition), the consumer interprets d_{arr} stabilization around a relatively constant period, in order for the consumer to receive the freshest data available from the network. However, this does not necessarily ensure that the consumer issues Interests efficiently. Figure 8(a) displays that although the consumer has exhausted the cache rather quickly, RTT' is three times larger than the actual RTT for the network (100ms), which means that the majority of the issued Interests remain pending while waiting for the requested data to be produced.

The consumer makes several iterative attempts to adjust λ during bootstrapping, which can be described as follows:

1. The consumer initializes Interest demand with λ_d, and initiates Interests expression.

------

[9]While inspired by the TCP congestion window, the Interest demand, as currently employed in NDN-RTC, may play a different role in ICN networks, which we are exploring experimentally in this application.

(a) "Interest demand", λ

(b) Interest bursting ($\lambda + 3$)

(c) Interest withholding ($\lambda - 3$)

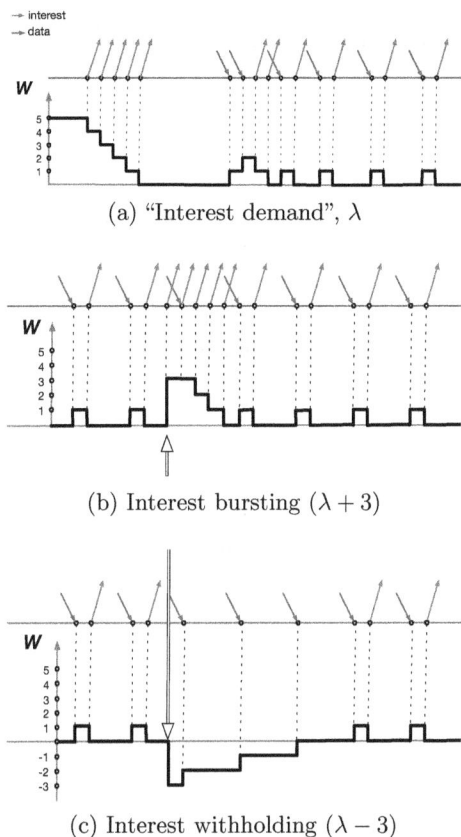

Figure 7: Managing Interest expression

(a) $\lambda = 10$: short chasing, larger RTT'

(b) $\lambda = 4$: longer chasing, smaller RTT'

(c) $\lambda = 3$: consumer can't exchaust cache, $RTT' = RTT$

Figure 8: Larger λ decreases "chasing" phase, but increases RTT' for the same network configuration ($RTT \approx 100ms$)

2. If the consumer did not receive freshest data during the allocated time[10], it increases Interest demand: $\lambda = \lambda + 0.5\lambda_d$; $\lambda_d = \lambda_d + 0.5\lambda_d$.

3. Whenever the consumer receives data determined to be fresh (cache exhausted), it decreases Interest demand: $\lambda = \lambda - 0.5\lambda_d$; $\lambda_d = \lambda_d - 0.5\lambda_d$ and waits for one of two results: a) RTT' decreases and the consumer still receives the freshest data – repeat step 3; b) d_{arr} fluctuates unexpectedly, indicating cached data – restore previous value for λ_d, increase λ accordingly and stop any further adjustments as the consumer has achieved sufficient synchronization with the producer.

Note that λ is a counter of how many Interests can be issued more whereas λ_d represents the total number of outstanding Interests allowed. The value $\lambda_d - \lambda$ shows how many outstanding Interests consumer has issued at any given point in time. The way λ and λ_d are adjusted was determined empirically and may be a good topic for further research, along with how often to re-check that the consumer is obtaining the latest data through the steps above.

Bootstrapping begins with issuing an Interest with the enabled *RightMostChild* selector, in `delta` namespace for audio and `key` namespace for video (the video decoding process can start only with a key frame). Once an initial data segment of a sample with number S_{seed} has been received, the consumer initializes λ with initial value λ_d, and asks for the next sample data $S_{seed}+1$ in the appropriate namespace.

Upon receiving the first segments of sample $S_{seed} + 1$, the consumer initiates the fetching process (described above) for all namespaces (`delta` and `key`, if available). The bootstrapping phase stops when the consumer finds the minimal value of λ, which still allows for receiving the most recent data, and the consumer switches to the playback mode.

Interest demand provides a manageable mechanism to speed up or slow down Interest expression, coupling the asynchronous Interest expression mechanism with the status of the playback buffer. An increase in λ value makes the consumer issue more Interests (Figure 7(b)), whereas any decrease in λ holds the consumer back from sending any new Interests (Figure 7(c)). Larger values of λ make the consumer reach a synchronized state with the producer more quickly. However, a larger value means a larger number of outstanding Interests and larger RTT' because of longer generation delays d_{gen} for each media sample. By adjusting the value of λ and observing inter-arrival delays d_{arr}, the consumer can find minimal RTT' value while still getting non-cached data, adapting towards a loose synchronization with the producer.

Playback. During playback, the consumer continues to observe RTT' and d_{arr}. Whenever d_{arr} indicates that no fresh data is being received, the consumer increases Interest

---

[10]In the current implementation, 1000ms.

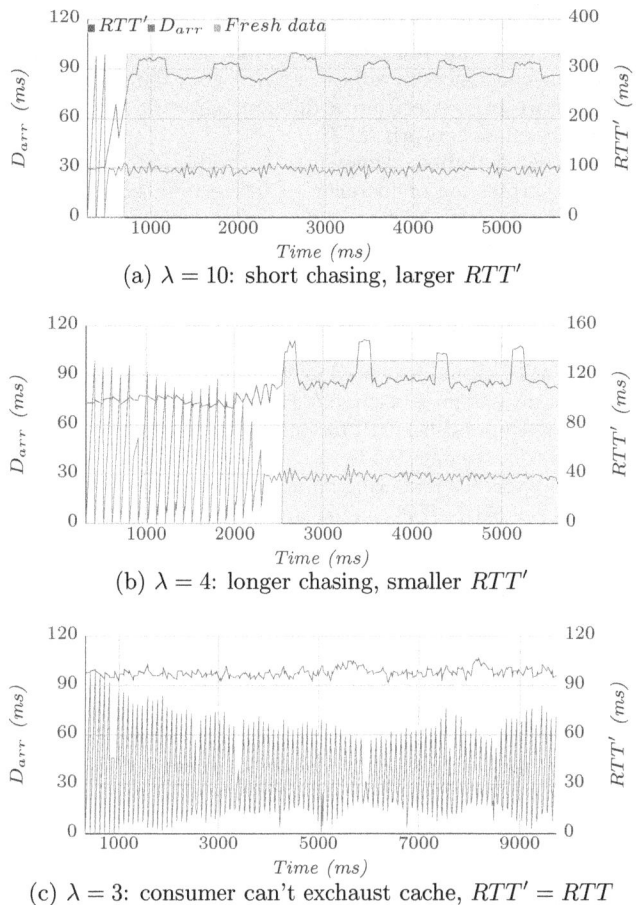

demand and starts the adjusting process over again to find minimal RTT' for the new conditions. Such an approach helps the consumers to adjust in cases when data may suddenly start to arrive from a different network hub which introduces new network RTT.

Interest batches. Practically, for video, the consumer controls expression of "batches" of Interests rather than individual Interests, because video frames are composed of several segments. λ is adjusted on a per-frame basis, rather than per-segment.

6. IMPLEMENTATION

NDN-RTC is implemented as a library written in C++, which is available at `https://github.com/remap/ndnrtc`. It provides a publisher API for publishing an arbitrary number of media streams (audio or video) and a consumer API with callbacks for rendering decoded video frames in a host application. NDN-RTC builds on functionality provided by other libraries. NDN-CPP [14] is used to access the NDN stack and to provide in-memory storage for the application. As discussed, the WebRTC framework [2] is used in two ways: 1) direct use of the video codec; 2) full incorporation of the audio pipeline, including echo cancellation. OpenFEC [1] is used for forward error correction support.

To demonstrate and evaluate the library, a desktop NDN videoconferencing application, *ndncon*, [3] was implemented on top of NDN-RTC. It provides a convenient user interface for publishing and fetching media streams, text chat, and organizing multi-party audio/video conferences. It was used, along with a command-line interface, for the evaluation below. The NDN-RTC library does not provide conference call setup functionality. This task was intentionally left out to be solved by applications that use it, and we are exploring it currently in *ndncon*. The MacOS X platform is currently supported; Linux build instructions will be added soon.

7. EVALUATION AND ITERATIVE REFINEMENT

Over the course of NDN-RTC development, numerous tests were run across the NDN testbed, as well as in isolated environments, to explore different library design patterns and implementations. These tests also helped us understand the nature of low-latency communication over NDN. We are still in the process of establishing well-defined metrics and test scenarios, but initial results generated refinements to our approach and are described below. There were several design iterations, and each introduced improvements in the overall quality of experience for the end-user, as well as in application efficiency related to bandwidth and computation. Each iteration tackled problems that were revealed during tests. These motivated namespace, application packet format and other revisions, which are reflected in the design detailed above.

7.1 Streaming performance

Separation of key and delta frame namespaces. Video streaming performance in early versions of NDN-RTC suffered from video "hiccups", even when being tested on trivial topologies. The cause of this problem turned out to be an inefficient frame fetching process. In early NDN-RTC versions, the difference in size, and thus segments, of key frames and delta frames was not reflected in the producer's

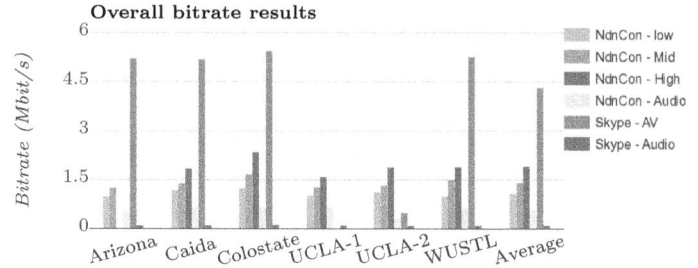

Figure 9: Two-peer conference tests compared to Skype

namespace, and consumers were forced to issue equal numbers of initial Interests (M), regardless of the frame type. This resulted in additional round trips of missing Interests and, consequently, larger assembling times (d_{asm}) for key frames that eventually led to missed playout deadlines and "hiccup" effects. Having a separate namespace for key frames enables consumers to maintain separate Interest pipelines per frame type and collect historical data on the average number of Interests required to retrieve one frame of each type in one round trip.

Audio sample bundling. Another set of tests targeting streaming performance was conducted over the existing testbed with a number of volunteers from the NDN community. Apart from monitoring application performance, we gathered user feedback and compared the experience with Skype. Each test was comprised of six runs of two-person, five-minute conference calls using *ndncon*: a) three runs of audio+video with low, medium and high video bandwidths settings (0.5, 0.7 and 1.5 Mbit/s accordingly); b) one run of audio-only conference; c) one run of Skype audio+video conference; d) one run of Skype audio-only conference. Tests were conducted between the UCLA REMAP hub and six other hubs. These tests covered both one-hop and multi-hop paths. As a main outcome of these tests, audio sample bundling was quickly introduced in NDN-RTC to reduce audio bandwidth (and the number of Interests on the consumer side), making it comparable to Skype audio bandwidths.[11] Figure 9 shows overall bitrate usage results before audio bundling was implemented. As expected, Skype adapted to use link capacity between peers, and delivered higher bitrate videos; leaving such adaptive rate control as our highest priority future work.

7.2 Consumer-Producer synchronization

Bootstrap behavior. In initial library versions based on the approach taken in NDNVideo, the consumer "chased" the producer's time-series data by exhausting cached data via issuing a large number of outstanding Interests. However, there was no mechanism to adjust Interest expression dynamically; the buffering mechanism dictated the Interests' lifetime: all Interests entering the buffer had a lifetime equal to half of the current buffer size. Thus, it was expected that data will arrive before the Interest times out. In these cases, the Interest is re-issued, even with a half-buffer length remaining to receive data before the playout dead-

---

[11]Currently, five audio samples are bundled together into one segment.

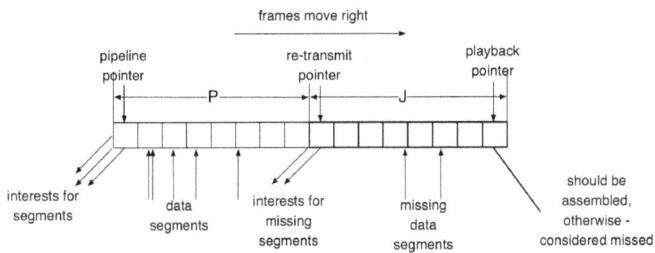

Figure 10: Frame buffer

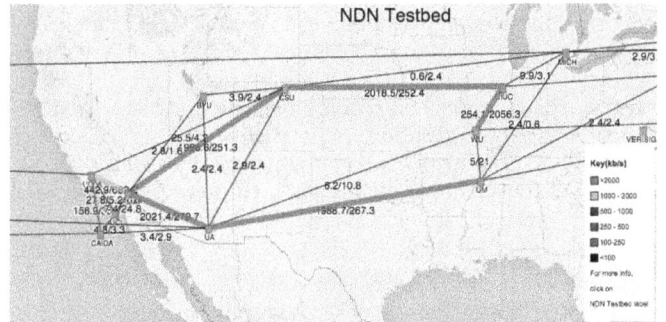

(a) NDN testbed utilization during biweekly NDN seminar using *ndncon* for simulcast.

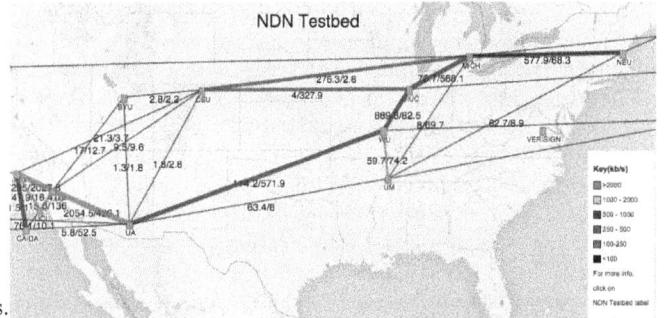

(b) NDN testbed utilization during 4-peer call between UCLA, REMAP, WUSTL and CAIDA hubs.

Figure 11: NDN testbed utilization during one-to-many and many-to-many scenarios.

Figure 12: *ndncon* screenshot.

line. This approach resulted in unavoidable Interest timeouts, in the cases when the consumer issued Interests far too early, before the actual data was produced. This was further complicated by forwarding strategies in the NDN Forwarding Daemon (NFD) that did not handle consumer-initiated retransmission over short periods. For two similar test runs (one-hop topology), the number of timed out Interests and re-transmissions varied greatly (either $\approx 1\%$ or $\approx 50\%$). This problem was addressed by increasing the Interests' lifetimes[12] and the introduction of a new NFD retransmission strategy that allowed early Interests re-transmissions. Additionally, the re-transmission checkpoint is now placed at a time estimated to be the effective RTT from the end of the buffer ($J = RTT$ on the Figure 10), which reflects a more accurate understanding of how data is received.

Moreover, the problem described above cannot occur if the consumer knows that it is issuing Interests too early. The chasing algorithm in older library versions was exhausting the network cache too aggressively; Interests were issued constantly until they filled up the buffer. With the introduction of the λ concept, the consumer exercises more precise control of the Interest expression as described previously. The number of outstanding Interests is controlled by a consumer and directly influences how fast consumer can "chase" the producer. Thus, the consumer is able to control the "agressiveness" of cache exhaustion and achieve a better synchronization state with the producer.

7.3 Multi-party use

In another experiment, *ndncon* was used to stream an NDN seminar over the existing NDN testbed. An audio/video bridge was set up using third-party tools allowing captured screen and audio feeds from existing IP-based conferencing tools to be simulcast. (Screen broadcast is now supported natively in later versions of *ndncon*.) Figure 11(a) shows an example of instantaneous NDN testbed utilization during the one-hour conference call. It is estimated that media streams were consumed by five to eight people.

Other tests of multi-party conferencing ability included four peers, each publishing three video streams and one audio stream and fetching one video and one audio stream from each of the other participants. Participants were distributed across four NDN testbed hubs - UCLA, REMAP, CAIDA and WUSTL, as shown in Figure 11(b). Even though the user experience was satisfying and multi-peer conferences

over NDN testbed have proven their viability, we plan more experimentation to explore quality of experience on a larger scale.

8. CONCLUSION AND FUTURE WORK

This paper presents the design, implementation, and initial experimental evaluation of NDN-RTC, a library intended to support experimentation in real-time communications over Named Data Networking. Our approach to this project has been experimentally driven so far, and has generated a functional low-latency streaming tool that we can now use as a platform for exploring important design challenges in real-time media over NDN. This is a rich area, and some of the future work that we have identified includes:

Scalability tests. NDN-RTC has shown that real-time communication using NDN is viable with the current open source implementation and on the current NDN testbed; we

---

[12]In fact, the dependence on Interests' lifetimes is not required anymore and every Interest is set to have 2000 ms lifetime.

are in the process of evaluating its performance in a variety of traffic scenarios and topologies. Our assumptions about the Interests and Data delivery patterns emerged from empirical observations of network behavior, and require more thorough experimentation in multi-peer scenarios, as well as simulation for much larger networks. The best schemes for 1) determining the "latest data" the network can provide at the correct rate and 2) congestion control remain open challenges that require collaboration between application developers, architecture researchers, and testbed operators.

Adaptive rate control. Multiple bitrate support is provided in the current design and implementation to lay the groundwork for adaptive rate control as a near-term effort, though for now the consuming application must manually select the best stream from bitrates offered by the producer. In ongoing co-development of an adaptive rate control solution, we are exploring if monitoring of d_{arr} and other approaches (described above) can address challenges of such adaptation over ICN, as suggested in papers such as [13].

Audio prioritization. For quality of experience in typical audio/videoconferencing applications, audio should be prioritized over video. This can be done at the application level but may also benefit from architectural support.

Scalable video coding. A more efficient way to relieve the producer from having to publish multiple copies of the same content at different bandwidths may be to use scalable video coding. By reflecting SVC layers in the namespace, the consumer will have more freedom for adapting media streams to the current network. Just as with audio, the SVC base layer may need to be prioritized; how to achieve this is an open question.

Inter-consumer synchronization. The absence of direct consumer-producer coordination shifted the complexity of "RTC-over-NDN" streaming to the consumer. A related requirement of modern videoconference not covered by this work is to ensure media playback sychronization across different consumers. This points more generally to the need for research on application-level time synchronization over NDN.

Encryption-based access control. The current NDN-RTC design supports basic content signing and verification. However, a prominent requirement of most videoconferencing is confidentiality, which can be supported in NDN through encryption-based access control. While encryption could limit the gains offered by caching, recent work exploring that application of advanced cryptographic techniques (such as attribute-based encryption to multimedia in ICN [11]) suggest new directions for meeting security requirements while leveraging key ICN features.

9. ACKNOWLEDGEMENTS

This project was partially supported by the National Science Foundation (award CNS-1345318 and others) and a grant from Cisco. The authors thank Lixia Zhang, Van Jacobson, and David Oran, as well as Eiichi Muramoto, Takahiro Yoneda, and Ryota Ohnishi, for their input and feedback. John DeHart, Josh Polterock, Jeff Thompson, Zhehao Wang and others on the NDN team provided invaluable testing of *ndncon*. The initial forward error correction approach in NDN-RTC was by Daisuke Ando.

10. REFERENCES

[1] OpenFEC Library. http://openfec.org.

[2] WebRTC Project. http://www.webrtc.org.

[3] NdnCon GiHub Repository. https://github.com/remap/ndncon, September 2014.

[4] P. Crowley. Named data networking: Presentation and demo. In *China-America Frontiers of Engineering Symposium*, Frontiers of Engineering, 2013.

[5] V. Jacobson, D. K. Smetters, N. H. Briggs, M. F. Plass, P. Stewart, J. D. Thornton, and R. L. Braynard. Voccn: voice-over content-centric networks. In *Proceedings of the 2009 workshop on Re-architecting the internet*, pages 1–6. ACM, 2009.

[6] V. Jacobson, D. K. Smetters, J. D. Thornton, M. F. Plass, N. H. Briggs, and R. L. Braynard. Networking named content. In *Proceedings of the 5th international conference on Emerging networking experiments and technologies*, pages 1–12. ACM, 2009.

[7] A. Jangam, R. Ravindran, A. Chakraborti, X. Wan, and G. Wang. Realtime multi-party video conferencing service over information centric network. In *Proceedings of Workshop on Multimedia Streaming in Information Centric Networks (MUSIC) at ICME*, 2015.

[8] D. Kulinski and J. Burke. NDNVideo: random-access live and pre-recorded streaming using ndn. Technical report, UCLA, September 2012.

[9] S. Lederer, C. Mueller, and B. Rainer. Adaptive streaming over content centric networks in mobile networks using multiple links. *âĂę (ICC)*, 2013.

[10] I. Moiseenko and L. Zhang. Consumer-producer api for named data networking. In *Proceedings of the 1st international conference on Information-centric networking*, pages 177–178. ACM, 2014.

[11] J. P. Papanis, S. I. Papapanagiotou, A. S. Mousas, G. V. Lioudakis, D. I. Kaklamani, and I. S. Venieris. On the use of attribute-based encryption for multimedia content protection over information-centric networks. *Transactions on Emerging Telecommunications Technologies*, 25(4):422–435, 2014.

[12] D. Posch, C. Kreuzberger, and B. Rainer. Client starvation: a shortcoming of client-driven adaptive streaming in named data networking. *Proceedings of the 1st âĂę*, 2014.

[13] D. Posch, C. Kreuzberger, B. Rainer, and H. Hellwagner. Client starvation: a shortcoming of client-driven adaptive streaming in named data networking. In *Proceedings of the 1st international conference on Information-centric networking*, pages 183–184. ACM, 2014.

[14] J. Thompson and J. Burke. NDN Common Client Libraries. *NDN, Technical Report NDN-0007*, September 2012.

[15] L. Wang, I. Moiseenko, and L. Zhang. Ndnlive and ndntube: Live and prerecorded video streaming over ndn. Technical report, UCLA, 2015.

[16] Y. Yu. ChronoChat. https://github.com/named-data/ChronoChat.

[17] Y. Yu, A. Afanasyev, Z. Zhu, and L. Zhang. Ndn technical memo: Naming conventions. Technical report, UCLA, July 2014.

[18] L. Zhang, A. Afanasyev, J. Burke, V. Jacobson, K. Claffy, P. Crowley, C. Papadopoulos, L. Wang, and B. Zhang. Named data networking. Technical report, 2014.

[19] L. Zhang, D. Estrin, J. Burke, V. Jacobson, J. Thorton, D. K. Smetters, B. Zhang, G. Tsudik, K. Claffy, D. Krioukov, D. Massey, C. Papadopoulos, T. Abdelzaher, L. Wang, P. Crowley, and E. Yeh. Named data networking tech report 001. Technical report, 2010.

[20] Z. Zhu, S. Wang, X. Yang, V. Jacobson, and L. Zhang. Act: audio conference tool over named data networking. pages 68–73, 2011.

MFTP: A Clean-Slate Transport Protocol for the Information Centric MobilityFirst Network

Kai Su, Francesco Bronzino, K. K. Ramakrishnan[§] and Dipankar Raychaudhuri

WINLAB, Rutgers University, North Brunswick, NJ 08902, USA

[§]University of California, Riverside, CA 92521, USA

{kais, bronzino, ray}@winlab.rutgers.edu, [§]kk@cs.ucr.edu

ABSTRACT

This paper presents the design and evaluation of clean-slate transport layer protocols for the MobilityFirst (MF) future Internet architecture based on the concept of named objects. The MF architecture is a specific realization of the emerging class of Information Centric Networks (ICN) that are designed to support new modes of communication based on names of information objects rather than their network addresses or locators. ICN architectures including MF are characterized by the following distinctive features: (a) use of names to identify sources and sinks of information; (b) storage of information at routers within the network in order to support content caching and disconnection; (c) multicasting and anycasting as integral network services; and in the MF case (d) hop-by-hop reliability protocols between routers in the network. These properties have significant implications for transport layer protocol design since the current Internet transports (TCP and UDP) were designed for the end-to-end Internet principle which uses address based routing with minimal functionality (i.e. no storage or reliability mechanisms) within the network. Several use cases including web access, large file transfer, Machine-to-machine and multicast services are considered, leading to an identification of four basic functions needed to constitute a flexible transport protocol for ICN: (i) fragmentation and end-to-end re-sequencing; (ii) lightweight end-to-end error recovery with in-network transport proxies; (iii) optional flow and congestion control mechanisms; and (iv) scalable multicast delivery mechanisms. The design of the MobilityFirst transport protocol (MFTP) framework realizing these features in a modular and flexible manner is presented and discussed. The proposed MFTP protocol is then experimentally evaluated and compared with TCP/IP for a few representative scenarios including mobile data delivery, web content retrieval and disconnected/late binding service. The results show that significant performance gains can be achieved in each case.

ICN'15, September 30–October 2, 2015, San Francisco, CA, USA.

© 2015 ACM. ISBN 978-1-4503-3855-4/15/09 ...$15.00.

DOI: http://dx.doi.org/10.1145/2810156.2810169.

Categories and Subject Descriptors

C.2.1 [**Computer-Communication Networks**]: Network Architecture and Design

Keywords

Transport protocol; future Internet architecture; Information Centric Networks; hop-by-hop transport; in-network storage; end-to-end reliability; flow control; congestion control;

1. INTRODUCTION

The TCP/IP architecture underpinning the current Internet is based on the end-to-end principle [1] of minimizing functionality in the network while handling service-specific requirements such as error and flow control at the endpoints. In addition, the current Internet architecture is based on the concept of routing between IP addresses requiring a static one-to-one association between hosts and network locators. While the Internet works well for traditional kinds of communication, increasing mobility levels, and emerging mobile content and Internet-of-Things (IoT) services have motivated consideration of clean-slate *Information Centric Network* (ICN) architectures [2, 3] which operate on names rather than addresses. Several distinct architectures for ICN have recently been proposed including MobilityFirst (MF) [4,5], Named Data Network (NDN) [6], and XIA [7]. While there are differences in detail, all the proposed ICN protocols share some common design elements that need to be considered in the design of transport protocols to be used for end-to-end services. Specific characteristics of ICN include: (a) use of names to identify sources and sinks of information; (b) storage of information at routers within the network in order to support content caching and disconnection; (c) multicasting and anycasting as integral network services; and in the MF case (d) hop-by-hop reliability protocols between routers in the network. These properties have significant implications for transport protocol design since the current protocols, TCP and UDP, were designed based on the end-to-end Internet principle, which typically assumes end-to-end connectivity during a transfer and uses address based routing with minimal functionality (i.e., no storage or reliability mechanisms) within the network.

Consider first the implications of name-based routing on transport protocol design. Communication with named objects, whether content files, devices, groups of devices or more complex context-based groups is different from conventional TCP connections in the sense that an object may have multiple end-points because the object may be multi-homed (i.e., multiple network interfaces to the same device) or multicast (to multiple devices, each with a different network interface) or multi-copy (i.e., multiple instances of the same information object can be found at different places in the network). This indicates that transport protocols need to be designed to provide appropriate service semantics for retrieving or delivering such named objects, for example, in multicast where the information object reaches all the named destinations or anycast where the object is fetched from the "nearest location". A second important property of ICN protocols is the fact that routers may store information objects such as content either for caching or for delay tolerant delivery. This implies the existence of in-network transport proxies which are in between the source and the destination, and the transport protocol should be designed to take advantage of the in-network copy to provide the desired service efficiently. For example, reliable delivery with an ICN transport would be able to utilize a copy of the information object stored at an intermediate router and avoid the need for end-to-end retransmission used in TCP. The third feature of ICN architectures is the fact that in-network storage can be associated with reliable hop-by-hop transmission of information objects between routers, thus alleviating the need for strong reliability mechanisms at the transport layer depending on the type of service desired.

In Section II, we consider the requirements for ICN transport in further detail and identify a set of core transport protocol functions needed to address an anticipated range of service requirements. These core transport protocol components are developed in further detail for a specific ICN architecture, MobilityFirst, and several examples of how these functions are integrated with the named-object network layer are given in Section III. The prototype of MFTP is discussed in Section IV. Finally, we provide a set of experimental results based on the prototype and compare its performance with conventional TCP/IP to the extent possible. The results demonstrate significant performance improvement for several example use-case scenarios.

Our contributions in designing and implementing transport protocols for an ICN architecture with explicit locators, such as MF, are twofold: (i) we examine a representative set of delivery service scenarios, and based on them, define the requirement space for transport protocols for any Information Centric architecture; (ii) with explicit locators in an ICN architecture, much richer end-to-end semantics, such as reliability delegation, and in-network retransmission, are enabled by integrating in-network transport services. We show that such features are conducive to supporting mobility, and flexibly and robustly supporting different delivery patterns. The proposed design is validated using an experimental prototype, with bulk (e.g., video) content and latency-sensitive web (text, image and video) content delivered over wireless networks to mobile clients. The general principles of our design for end-to-end transport, regardless of whether MF-like locators are used, can also be customized to work with and bring benefits to NDN as well, e.g., to apply per-hop error and congestion control to improve transmission efficiency, and employ router-proactive mechanisms to provide better and richer mobility support.

2. REQUIREMENTS FOR TRANSPORT LAYER SERVICE FOR ICN

We first consider four common service scenarios that arise in information dissemination. These are large file transfer, web content retrieval, M2M communication and multicast. Through systematic analysis of these use cases, we identify the set of transport layer features for an ICN environment to support each of these scenarios (see the summary of requirements in Table 1).

Large file retrieval. A large file retrieval is abstracted as a *get*(content_name) socket call [8] in an ICN context. Clients inject a content request, independent of the content location, with a *get*() call, and the network will route the request to the location of a copy of the content. Then a flow with a large volume which carries the content is transferred reliably from the server to the requesting client. This is often referred as *anycast*.
Key TP functions required: Because of the large amount of data to be delivered, file transfer requires: (i) fragmentation and sequencing at the source, and reassembly at the sink; (ii) efficient usage of network resources with source rate control so as not to introduce congestion. Reliable delivery, flow control, and congestion control becomes more complicated when the destination is connected to the Internet wirelessly, and especially when it is mobile. For instance, a wireless connection is susceptible to fading, may introduce random losses, and can typically provide a lower transmission rate than the nominal rate. Further, the imbalance of rates at different segments of an end-to-end path makes it difficult to perform end-to-end control at high speeds, with small amounts of buffering, and to deal with transient disruptions. This problem can be alleviated by enabling additional in-network transport features, such as temporary storage for in-transit data (we call the en-route node with transport services a *transport proxy*).

Web content retrieval. In a web-browsing application, a sequence of content requests are sent by the client to the server. Each of the requests is for retrieving a constituent named object of a webpage. Two characteristics are inherent in web content retrieval: i) these requested objects are generally small in size, i.e. of tens or hundreds of kB; ii) user experience dictates that the objects must be received in a timely manner, preferably no more than several hundred milliseconds, thus making the transfer latency-sensitive.
Key TP functions required: End-to-end error and congestion recovery need to be provided, but in a lightweight manner, because any significant setup overhead is not amortized easily. Flow control is not required due of the limited amount of data transmitted, in order to avoid unnecessary overhead contributing to increased latency.

M2M communications. In Machine-to-machine (M2M) communications, sensor data is by nature idempotent. That is, if the PDU is lost (due to bit errors or congestion) or it is delayed beyond the limits of latency for the data, the transport layer need not attempt to reliably deliver that PDU. This transfer paradigm is captured in a *send*(dst_name, content_name) API with no explicit reliability preference.
Key TP functions required: In such cases, the transport layer could simply resort to stateless communication (e.g.,

Service scenarios	Fragmentation & resequencing	Reliable delivery	Lightweight transport	Flow/congestion control	In-network proxy
Large file retrieval	✓	✓		✓	✓
Web content retrieval	✓	✓		✓	
M2M communications	✓		✓		✓
Multicast	✓	✓	✓	✓	✓

Table 1: Transport requirements for different service scenarios

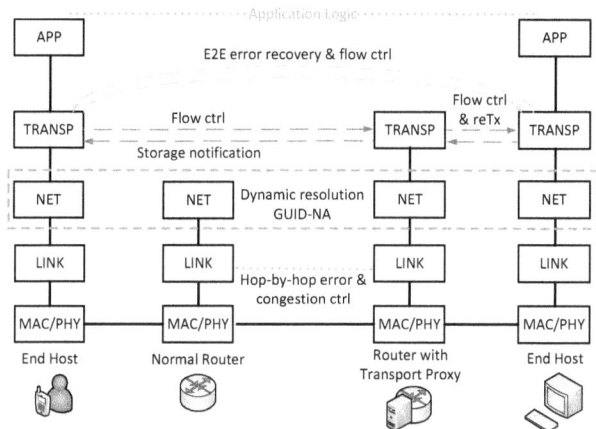

Figure 1: Protocol stack and transport layer functionalities

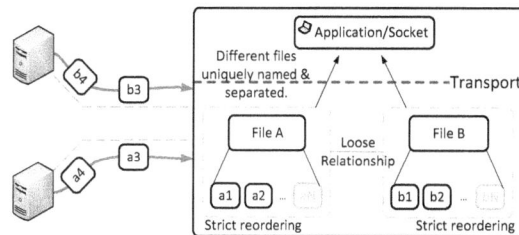

Figure 2: Illustration of named object's implication on fragmentation and sequencing. Transport layer fragments a content into large chunks. Sequential delivery is guaranteed for each content, but no strict ordering is maintained for chunks of different contents.

lightweight transport with no error recovery, and minimal flow and congestion control) to minimize overheads. Moreover, due to power constraints in devices, a sensor node may not be on all the time. End-to-end control is not always possible in this case and delegation of transport service guarantees, such as reliability, need to be made to other en-route nodes. Thus in-network proxy support is desired.

Multicast. A number of popular applications are based on multicast, such as group-based subscriptions (RSS), teleconferencing, online gaming, etc. In a name-based architecture, multicast can be realized with a *send* (dst_name, content_name) API with the dst_name referring to a group of individual endpoints names.
Key TP functions required: Guaranteeing 100% reliability in a multicast session is a well-known hard problem. To achieve reliable transport, the source relies on negative acknowledgement (NACK) from clients to initiate retransmissions. With the number of subscribers increasing, retransmission has to be implemented in an efficient manner such that the ACK-implosion (see [9]) is avoided. This may require aggregation of retransmission requests in the network, and retransmission from within the network. Thus in-network proxies are desired to handle such aggregation and storage of pieces of contents for retransmission.

3. MFTP DESIGN

MFTP is based on the four characteristics of different ICN proposals to support the analyzed requirements. Specifically, MFTP has been designed to operate on top of the MobilityFirst networking stack [10, 11], while the principles may be more broadly applicable to other ICN frameworks. As described in [5], MobilityFirst is based on a clean separation of names and network addresses with a logically cen-

tralized but physically distributed global name resolution service (GNRS). The globally unique identifier (GUID) in MF is a flat public key identifier, i.e. a name, which can be used to represent any network attached object, including devices, people, groups, content, or context. Fig. 1 shows the major layers in the MF protocol stack and the role of the MFTP transport layer above the named-object GUID based network layer which is supported by the GNRS [11, 12]. For additional details on MF, the reader is referred to [5,8,10,11].

3.1 Fragmentation and re-sequencing

Typically in ICN, a data request is abstracted by an API, *get*(content_name). In NDN, such a request, called an Interest, with an associated relative sequence number, solicits one segment of a content. In MF, the requestor only sends one request for a piece of content; the server that handles the request then segments the content and assigns the segments a relative sequence number. In any case, sequence numbers are bound to the named content, rather than the two endpoints. This has significant implication for the hop-by-hop transfer and storage capability in ICN, as we shall see later. With content-centricity, such a sequencing scheme works naturally for anycast, multicast and multipath transfers. For example, in an anycast scenario, the forwarding plane decides where the content request should be handled. The transport layer is oblivious of the server location; rather, the transport's functionality of providing ordering and reliability can be fulfilled based on the knowledge of the data being delivered, using the content names and sequence numbers.

On the sender side, the transport layer fragments the application data into large chunks[1], whose size can be negotiated by the two end-points based on a tradeoff between the

---

[1] we use "segments" and "chunks" interchangeably.

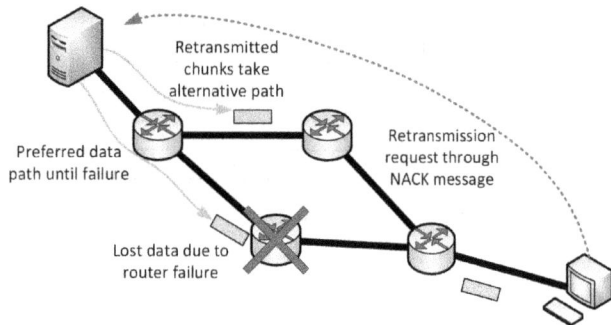

Figure 3: End-to-end signaling to recover from in-network failure

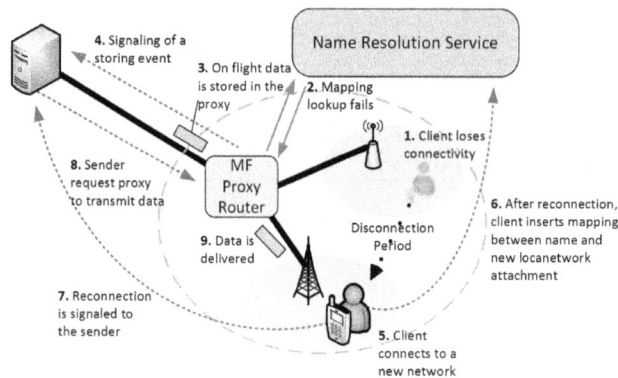

Figure 4: Procedures involved to use in-network transport proxy to handle destination disconnection and retransmission: the proxy temporarily stores chunks when the destination disconnects, and transmits to the client when connectivity is restored as indicated by the name resolution service.

overhead and the fair use of network resources across flows[2]. We allow the chunk size to go up to the order of megabytes. Note that the link layer breaks a chunk into packets to meet the link MTU requirement, but still logically maintains the semantics of a "chunk" at each hop. Figure 2 illustrates how the transport layer would support concurrent reception of multiple files. As shown in the figure, in-order delivery is strictly enforced among the chunks of a single transported file: transport will buffer out-of-order chunk arrivals. On the other hand, because each file has a unique name, retrieval of any file is fulfilled by a separate "flow". Thus there is no need for strict ordering of receiving files, say, based on the order of the requests, regardless of where the files originate.

3.2 Coordinated End-to-end error recovery and hop-by-hop reliable delivery

We use hop-by-hop reliable transfer to move each *chunk* from any node to its next hop, and use end-to-end reliability guarantees to ensure the entire *application data*, e.g. a file or content, is reliably delivered.

3.2.1 Per-hop reliability

In traditional transport protocols operating on an end-to-end basis such as TCP, loss (whether due to errors or congestion) or congestion at a link has to be detected after a feedback delay, possibly quite a few end-to-end RTTs. After the detection, recovery mechanisms, such as window reduction or retransmission, can incur an unduly large penalty to the flow. Also, due to queuing at routers, and heterogeneous transmission technologies employed along the route to destination, spurious, or premature, retransmissions are not uncommon [13]. A more efficient way to recover from congestion or error happening at a particular link is through link level mechanisms. This yields two benefits: i) congestion and errors can be detected and reacted upon more quickly; ii) reduces the possibility of spurious retransmissions. Hop-by-hop transfer maintains a per-hop reliability model: each chunk is only forwarded once it has been received reliably in its entirety from the previous node. This reliability model is suitable for ICN due in part to the fact that the segment of data being transferred is named; moreover, ICN routers can have storage capability, and can temporarily store the in-transit copy to provide delay-tolerant delivery, and also cache a copy to serve future requests. In NDN, each named data item is indeed transferred in a hop-by-hop manner: upon receiving such a data item, the router

examines whether an Interest for the data has been received earlier, and whether it needs to cache the data.

MFTP integrates per-hop error recovery and congestion control whenever the problem can be resolved locally, and only invokes end-to-end mechanisms when it is absolutely necessary, e.g., a router fails and loses all the buffered data. On each hop, after every chunk that is transmitted, a corresponding control message called *CSYN* is used to explicitly request acknowledgement from downstream, which then replies with a bitmap of reception status for every packet in that chunk. The transmission for this chunk finishes if there is no loss, otherwise the lost packets of that chunk are retransmitted locally following the same procedure until all packets are received.

3.2.2 End-to-end reliability

Taking advantage of the hop-by-hop reliability of the network, we seek to have a parsimonious end-to-end mechanism that has minimal overhead (important in mobile wireless environments) while primarily aiming to recover from node and link failures. While per-hop recovery concerns about whether all the packets constituting a chunk are delivered to the next hop, end-to-end recovery strives to guarantee all the chunks of the application data are reliably received. The end-to-end error recovery mechanism is built to be *flexible* to accommodate application and sender needs (including *don't care*, *NACK*, *ACK*). With a Negative-ACK, i.e. NACK, the transport reduces end-to-end message overhead, and the receiver provides notification only when a chunk is not delivered over a conservatively long period of time (as a result of a failure that causes the reliable hop-by-hop mechanism to lose an acknowledged chunk as shown in Figure 3). It is only for short-sessions (e.g., single PDU delivery) and for latency-sensitive interactions that the sender would enable the use of an end-to-end ACK option. With idempotent data transmissions (e.g, sensor data which the transport layer sends and forgets), the sender may choose to use the *don't care* option.

3.3 In-network transport proxy

One of the challenges for conventional transport protocols is in dealing with the content delivery to mobile devices,

---

[2]with MFTP, a "flow" is identified by a (source GUID, destination GUID) pair.

where mobility results in intermittent connectivity and the end-to-end connection experiences frequent disruptions. If the transport protocol has to re-establish the connection, then the transfer has to re-start and any data already in transit in the network will have to be discarded. ICN's architecture inherently supports mobility and resolves connection disruptions in multiple ways. For instance, in NDN, each data is solicited by an Interest packet; in case a client moves before obtaining the requested data, it can re-issue an Interest packet for the same data, which will be delivered to the new location. In the MF architecture, the network can take on a more proactive role in re-initiating data transfers when connectivity is re-established.

To this end, we postulate having routers (or at least a subset of them) which provide in-network transport service such that the original source can delegate part of the end-to-end data transfer responsibility. The router, which we call an *in-network transport proxy*, would have substantial amounts of memory, e.g., several GB, to temporarily hold in-transit chunks when the destination is unreachable. This disruption may be due to: lack of connectivity to a mobile destination node, until connectivity is subsequently re-established; alternatively, in M2M communication, when a sensor node is only powered on intermittently, it may choose to deliver information chunks to the next hop and then power down.

The mechanisms implemented by such a node are shown in Figure 4: when faced with the impossibility of forwarding chunks with the information available at the network layer (i.e. the router detects that connectivity towards the destination of a chunk is disrupted), the router pushes up to the transport proxy layer the relative data chunks. Two reasons might generate this impossibility of forwarding chunks: (i) the destination does not have an active network address (NA) binding corresponding to its GUID entry in the GNRS; (ii) the chunk reaches the destination network given by its most recent binding, but either the destination has changed its point of attachment or it has disconnected from the network before the previous NA entry expires in the GNRS server. As a consequence, the link layer is not able to deliver the chunk despite several attempts, and corresponding CSYN timeouts. In these cases, the chunk is pushed up to the proxy layer to be temporarily stored. While this is similar to Delay-Tolerant Network protocols, the innovation here is the integration of these mechanisms with the support of dynamic mobility and ICN style named object services. Note that we differentiate the *storage* operation here from *buffering* and *caching*. They all involve the action of maintaining a copy of in-transit data. However, they differ in their final purpose. Buffering usually resolves the mismatch between ingress and egress rates, and caching is to serve future data requests more efficiently. Storage, considered here, is utilized to provide delay-tolerant delivery to deal with disconnection or to provide delegation.

We limit the amount of content that can be stored for a flow. Each (source GUID, destination GUID) pair is limited to have stored content up to a size S. When a chunk for a new flow arrives, the chunk will be stored directly if sufficient space is available for the new flow; otherwise, a chunk for the oldest flow is evicted to make room for the new chunk. In other words, an LRU policy is employed for chunk eviction from the storage. Therefore, the operations for storing a chunk, and for retrieving a chunk from the storage, can be implemented with O(1) complexity. When the chunk is

stored, a timer is created to schedule future transmission. Further, a transport layer message, either *Store* or *Drop*, is transmitted back to the original source to notify it of the intermediate proxy storing or dropping the chunk. A stored chunk will be scheduled to retry a GNRS lookup to bind an updated NA to the destination GUID when its storage timer expires. The chunk will be pushed out if an NA is found, i.e., destination becomes connected again, otherwise it will be kept in storage. On the other hand, rescheduling of the chunks can also be initiated by the original source of a chunk. As is shown in Fig. 4, when the source receives a NACK message identifying a chunk as missing, if it is aware that the corresponding chunk originally destined to the requesting destination is stored in the network, based on a previously received *Store* message, it utilizes this in-network copy and initiates the retransmission from inside the network. This is done by the source sending a *Push* message to the in-network proxy to trigger retransmission.

Transport proxies also support content producer mobility by allowing the producer to delegate its end-to-end reliability guarantee to the proxy. For instance, a mobile client intending to upload a recently shot video can specify in the pushed data chunk that such a delegation is requested. Before forwarding the data chunk, the immobile access router (acting as a transport proxy) will save a copy of the chunk in order to respond to potential future NACKs.

3.4 Flow control and congestion control

With the hop-by-hop reliable delivery as a building block, MFTP uses a combination of per-hop back-pressure for congestion control and end-to-end window-based flow control.

3.4.1 Hop-by-hop congestion control

The hop-by-hop back-pressure scheme is built on top of a back-pressure buffer (of capacity B packets). As illustrated in Fig. 5, the back-pressure buffer essentially has all the chunks that are received from the network and are queued to be transmitted. In addition, between two adjacent routers on a link, the sender maintains a sending window W_{ostd}, i.e., number of outstanding packets, that is bounded by the receiver's advertised window, W_{ad}. As mentioned before, following the transmission of a chunk of data, a CSYN message is sent, which the downstream node then acknowledges with a CACK message. The receiver's advertised window is piggybacked in the CACK. The number of outstanding packets, W_{ostd}, is reduced based on the downstream node's acknowledgement. Also, whenever the router schedules to transmit on a particular outgoing interface, it attempts to transmit as many packets as W_{ad} allows. This greatly improves pipelining.

When the occupancy of back-pressure buffer reaches its capacity, the router blocks all incoming data chunks. Furthermore, it throttles the advertised window to all of its upstream nodes. This "congestion signal" eventually propagates back to the original traffic sources in a hop-by-hop manner, thus eventually limiting the traffic injected into the network.

3.4.2 End-to-end flow control

Hop-by-hop back-pressure is not sufficient to prevent the receiver's buffer from being overrun by the sender's data from an end-to-end perspective. Because MFTP does not require the receiving side to send frequent reception status

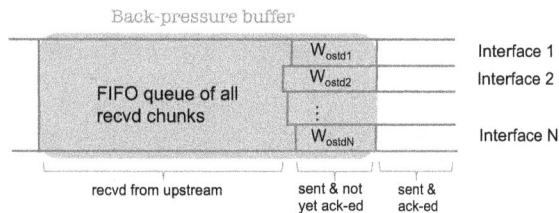

Figure 5: Back-pressure buffer and per-hop sending window.

update in the reverse path (it depends only on NACKs), the feedback from the receiver is both parsimonious and not timely for the sender to detect receiver buffer overflow. We therefore consider an explicit notification from the receiver. The sender starts at an initial end-to-end sending window W_e. For each window's worth of data chunks, the receiver then sends one window flow control message, to advise the sender to maintain, increase, or reduce the sending window to certain value based on the receiver's buffer occupancy. This message will be delivered reliably to the sender. Note that the sending window is also the atomic unit for the end-to-end NACK message, thus the NACK and flow control are fulfilled by a single message (if a NACK has to be sent, i.e., some chunks are lost). In the event that this special chunk is lost due to a node failure, a NACK timeout at the receiver would trigger the receiver to proactively notify the sender of the reception status (NACK) and receiver buffer status (flow control).

Small content transfers are not subject to such end-to-end flow control, mainly because the transfer will be complete even before the flow control notification can be generated. However, small content transfers are still regulated by per-hop congestion control.

3.4.3 Alleviating head-of-line blocking due to hop-by-hop transfer

A drawback inherent with hop-by-hop back pressure is the unfairness caused by head-of-line (HOL) blocking with FIFO queueing [14]. Consider a chunk at the head of the queue blocked from being transmitted by a back-pressure signal from the downstream node. This can prevent chunks behind it in the queue that is destined to a different destination that is not experiencing congestion. An alternative to having HOL blocking is to drop the chunk being back-pressured, but this has undesirable consequences of requiring retransmissions when a temporary buffering could overcome the short-term congestion. Theoretically, per-flow queuing solves this problem, but scheduling with per-flow queues is difficult to scale and is impractical with large numbers of flows. However, the in-network transport proxy provides some relief to this situation and alleviates the short-term unfairness. If a back-pressure signal is received for the chunk at the head of the sending queue, the transfers of chunks destined to other nodes will thus not be blocked because chunk at the head of the queue will be removed and pushed up to the transport proxy layer for temporary storage. The transport proxy will then attempt to transmit that chunk when the storage timer expires (or is dropped if the chunk is replaced in the storage buffer because of the eviction policy we described above).

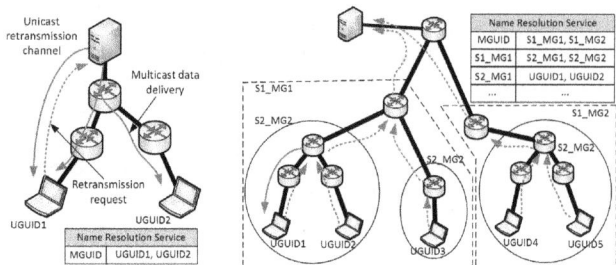

Figure 6: Multicast data delivery, small scale (left), large scale (right).

3.5 Multicast

Multicast is naturally supported by name based architectures. For instance, in NDN, data is forwarded to the requestor based on the receipt of the corresponding request: each router forwards the data on the interface(s) the request for the data was received on. Multicast is thus fulfilled by the stateful forwarding plane [6]. In MobilityFirst, a dynamically formed multicast group is explicitly identified by a globally unique identifier (GUID), which can be mapped into a set of individual clients' GUIDs or network addresses.

Depending on the scale of multicast group, multicast support varies. In the small scale case (show in the left side of Fig 6), during the transmission the source of the multicast data marks outgoing chunks with a multicast service identifier and selects as destination GUID the one identifying the multicast group. Multicast clients send NACK messages over a unicast channel and the multicast source can identify which multicast group a specific client belongs to. Further, the source aggregates retransmission requests for the transmitted chunks; it can, either employ multicast again for retransmission when the number of requestors exceeds a threshold; otherwise retransmitted data chunks can be sent using unicast destination GUIDs that identify the specific nodes that need the retransmitted data.

As the number of participants increases we can exploit in-network transport proxies to build multiple levels of *multicast group GUID to a set of GUIDs* mappings recursively. This scenario is shown on the right side of Figure 6. In order to limit potential explosion of unfulfilled requests reaching the original source, transport proxies can be instructed through proper chunk marking, to discard retransmission requests that exceed a number of traversed proxies without encountering the missing chunks. In a scenario where reliability is not demanded, the source just use the *don't care* option of the reliability preference.

4. IMPLEMENTATION

Our implementation of MFTP consists of two parts: end-system transport operations that are implemented on the MobilityFirst client stack, and an in-network transport proxy implemented as a pluggable module inside the MobilityFirst based Click router implementation [15].

Host Stack and API. The client host stack has been implemented on Linux as a user-level process built as an event-based data pipeline. Apart from the MF transport protocol, the stack contains a name-based network layer and a reliable link layer with large chunk transfer. Applications interface with the host stack through socket APIs that are available

Figure 7: Experimental Setup

as a linkable library and include the primitives *send, recv,* and *get*, and a set of meta-operations. Examples of meta-operations include those to bind or *attach* a GUID to one or more NAs. By specifying the options field in the API call, an application is able to configure transport parameters such as the i) desired chunk size; ii) end-to-end reliability preference; iii) NACK timeout; iv) willingness to use in-network proxy.

Router. The MobilityFirst software router is implemented as a set of routing and forwarding elements using Click [16]. The router implements MFTP transport proxy layer, MF network layer including intra-domain routing and dynamic binding using GNRS, and hop-by-hop reliable transfer. The transport layer (proxy) interacts with the intra-domain route look up component: if a lookup does not yield a valid next hop, the chunk is pushed up to the transport proxy. The transport proxy at the router will hold the data chunk for some time and attempt to rebind the name with one or more network addresses. When rebinding is successful, the chunk is pushed back down to the routing layer for forwarding.

Timers. There are three types of timers used in our implementation: one for triggering the transmission of an end-to-end NACK message, one for storage, and another one for link layer retransmission. For guaranteeing end-to-end reliability, timers are indispensable because a node has to learn about a remote node's failure impacting the end-end path. Previous experience with TCP end-to-end timers have taught us that timers need to be set loosely so as to reduce number of false alarms [17,18], and not have a strict dependence of the transport protocol on timers for normal operations. In MFTP's design, this goal is achievable because: (i) different end-to-end service guarantees are dissected and each timer only handles a specific job; (ii) NACK timers and per-hop timers are associated with a chunk of data, rather than a single packet; (ii) the storage timer is only concerned about disconnection, and is thus decoupled from end-to-end latency and transferred data sizes, which could otherwise complicate timer settings.

5. CASE STUDIES AND EVALUATIONS

In this section, we present how MFTP can be used in several different service scenarios, and quantitatively compare it with the performance of conventional HTTP and IP based protocols.

General experimental testbed setup. We use the OR-BIT [19] wireless testbed for our experimental evaluation. Each machine in our experiment is equipped with Intel i7 2.93GHz processor and with 8GB RAM. We use Ubuntu 12.04 with Linux kernel version 3.2. In terms of networking capability, each node has one Gigabit-Ethernet interface and one WiFi interface using Atheros' ath5k wireless drivers. Physically all the nodes are connected to a single

layer-2 switch; we use VLAN tags to create desired topology to isolate Ethernet traffic. For wireless traffic, we use 802.11g with the data rate fixed at 54Mbps. Access routers run hostapd [20] to operate as WiFi access points. We disable 802.11 authentication and use manual IP assignment (no DHCP), just to retain nearly the same amount of overhead with both MFTP and TCP for WiFi connection establishment. We considered a topology shown in Fig. 7, where a client, N_4 connects to a server N_1 through an access router N_3, which provides WiFi connectivity, and a regular router N_2.

Methodology. We evaluate three types of data delivery scenarios to compare MFTP with the current TCP/IP based architecture, in terms of the mechanisms employed, and their performance. We emulate the end-to-end RTT's of local, coast-to-coast and inter-continental communications, use the emulation tool *netem* [21] to add 10ms, 50ms, 100ms RTT between the two routers, respectively. To emulate loss in a controlled manner, we again use *netem* to introduce 1% loss. With MF, we run the MF Click router prototype (mentioned in section 4), and a local GNRS server on both N_2 and N_3. The MF client stack runs on N_1 and N_4. For specific use cases, we run corresponding applications that interface with the client stack through the MF API. In the case of TCP-based experiments, we run Click IP routers on node N_2 and N_3, rather than using Linux' default IP routing, just to eliminate processing time discrepancies of Click router compared with Linux routing (though in the experiments we found Click's overhead is negligible). TCP segmentation offloading is turned off as the basic Click IP router drops TCP packets with size larger than 1500 bytes. We enabled manual Ethernet header encapsulation on the Click IP router so no ARP message is triggered during routing. On the two end nodes, the default version of TCP on Ubuntu, TCP Cubic, is used, as it is the state-of-the-art TCP congestion control algorithm and performs better than other variants [22], e.g. TCP Westwood, including under wireless scenarios. We configured both nodes' TCP receiver buffer to be 2MB, so that it is not a bottleneck in a high delay-bandwidth path in any of the experiments.

5.1 Large content delivery over wireless

We first look into a large volume data transfer experiment. A 400MB file is requested and transferred. A simple file retrieval application in MF is running on the two end nodes. In the case of TCP, we used iperf to generate a flow of equal size with the maximum packet payload size of 1400 bytes. We repeated this experiment for a number of network conditions: RTT being 10ms, 50ms, or 100ms, and loss on WiFi link being 0 or 1%, to explore their effect on both architectures' goodput (i.e., application throughput).

Fig. 8(a) shows the average throughput comparisons for the six different network settings. Both MFTP and TCP' throughputs are consistently high when there is no loss, despite varying the end-to-end latency. MFTP is slightly higher in throughput in the lossless cases. MFTP is significantly more robust in the presence of loss, e.g., the throughput degrades by only 10% when there is 1% residual loss, with all 3 RTT profiles. On the other hand, TCP throughput drops significantly when there is loss. For instance, with 50ms RTT, TCP throughput with loss drops to only a quarter of its throughput in the lossless case. Fig. 8(b) shows a

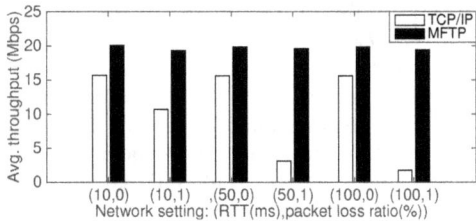

(a) Average throughput comparison for 6 different (RTT, loss rate) profiles.

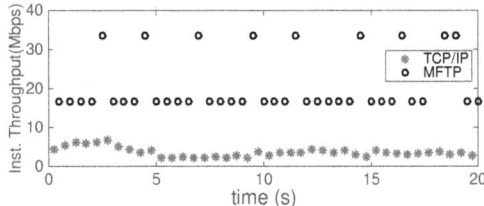

(b) Instantaneous throughput (per 500ms) for 50ms RTT and 1% loss.

Figure 8: Throughput comparison. MFTP is robust in the presence of loss.

plot of instantaneous throughput (averaged per 500ms) for 50ms latency and 1% loss. MF's PDU is a chunk of data, and in every 500ms, it receives at least one chunk (1MB), even in the presence of loss. With TCP, throughput fluctuate around 5Mbps. This is because the end-to-end congestion window is throttled whenever loss is detected. This misinterpretation of loss unrelated to congestion unnecessarily penalizes the flow. With MFTP, loss is not considered a signal for congestion, thus the sending rate is not throttled; moreover, loss happening at the last hop is recovered locally. Note in this experiment, the client suppresses the NACK messages because all the data has been successfully received.

5.2 Transport proxy for disconnection

We evaluate the benefits of using in-network transport proxies for handling client disconnections in content retrieval. In the experiments with TCP, an application client issues one HTTP GET request to retrieve one file. For experiments with MFTP, in order to keep the modifications at the application end-hosts to a minimum, we developed an MF-HTTP-MF proxy whose main job is translating HTTP request and responses into MobilityFirst content requests and messages and vice-versa. We colocate 2 instances of these proxies[3] with the HTTP components of the system, i.e., on N1 and N4. We consider the same topology as above. The end-to-end RTT is set to be 50ms, and no loss is added so that difference in performance would not be incurred by having different mechanisms for error recovery. We use *netem* to introduce 100% loss intermittently, so as to emulate client disconnections. In the experiment, WiFi connectivity is on for 10 seconds; then is turned off for d seconds; then the connection is restored. During the first 10 seconds of connection, the client requests a 10MB file at a random time. The experiment is repeated 30 times for both MF and TCP. We compare the distribution of file retrieval response times between MFTP and TCP.

---

[3]These proxies are also used for experiments in section 5.3

In Fig. 9(a), all the transfers having a response time of less than 10 seconds are completed before the disconnection. For the transfers that experience the disconnection, MFTP has at least 3 seconds lower response time (at 60th percentile). With 30 seconds disconnection, as shown in Fig. 9(b), the difference in response time is about 15 seconds at 70th percentile. It is worthwhile to understand the difference in the approaches taken by TCP and MFTP to dealing with disconnection. With TCP, the sender retransmits, based on a timer whose timeout value increases exponentially when the disconnection persists. In MFTP, the chunk in-transit is stored at the in-network proxy. A network address and next-hop lookup, rather than retransmission, is triggered when the storage timer for that chunk expires. Thus the transport proxy takes advantages of the global name resolution service in MF to learn whether there is a network address binding update for a client, and retransmits only when client is connected. This results in fewer retransmission attempts and more accuracy in the knowledge of end-to-end connectivity. Fig. 9(a) and Fig. 9(b) together suggest that MFTP's reduction in response time is nearly proportional to the length of the disconnection.

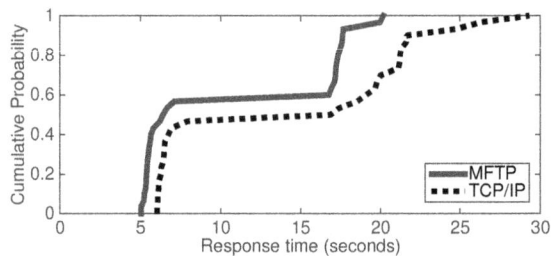

(a) With 10s disconnection

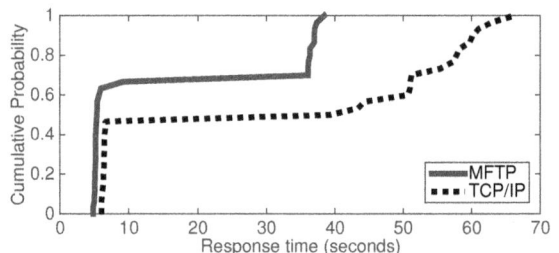

(b) With 30s disconnection

Figure 9: CDF of response times.

5.2.1 Comparison between network-proactive and receiver-driven approaches

We perform another set of experiments, with two different settings of proxy's storage and client's NACK timers. The network-proactive approach was used in the previous experiments, where the NACK timers are set conservatively, and thus client relies on the network to re-deliver the data once the network connection is restored. In the receiver-driven approach, the transport proxy does not re-initiate the delivery by itself; the client sets the NACK timer aggressively and explicitly requests retransmission, and the original server will then remotely request the retransmission from the transport proxy where the data is stored (by sending a *Push* message). As shown in Fig. 10, similar to last set of experiments,

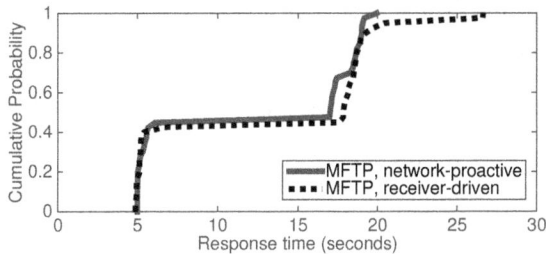

Figure 10: CDF of response times for network-proactive and receiver driven retransmissions, with 10s disconnection.

half of the transfers complete without experiencing disconnection. The long tail of the receiver-driven curve warrants a closer look: it corresponds to cases when a disconnection happens right after the client sends out the request. The content is transferred, but only a small portion gets delivered because client loses connectivity. The remaining data is temporarily stored at the proxy. The client has to wait for the NACK timeout to retrieve the data from the proxy. Thus, on the client side, whether it is an application or transport that is responsible to setting the end-to-end timer for a mobile client, a large number of characteristics, such as end-to-end path quality variations, disconnection interval, and content size, all collectively make estimating a reasonable timeout value difficult. On the other hand, retransmission from inside the network by the transport proxy only concerns itself with the connection/disconnection events. This improves performance, and more importantly, provides better manageability of end-to-end timers in mobile scenarios.

5.3 Web content retrieval

Web content retrieval is also evaluated. We use the same topology as described before to compare MFTP and TCP's performance. In addition to the routers, we run an Apache server (version 2.2.22) on node N_1, and a web browser emulator on node N_4 which requests webpages. We reuse the browser emulator, *epload*, presented in [23]. We also download the dataset introduced in [23] which consists of the real webpage objects of the 200 most accessed websites recorded by Alexa [24] in 2013. Among these we randomly select 40 pages and place them on N_1 to be hosted by the Apache server. In each run of the experiment, the browser emulator opens up 6 concurrent TCP connections (default settings in most browsers [23]) and sequentially request the 40 webpages, using HTTP 1.1 (also by default). For both MFTP and TCP, we performed 5 runs of the experiments with end-to-end RTT of 50ms, and 0 loss or 1% loss.

Fig. 11 are the plots for average page load times (PLT), i.e. the time between emitting the first HTTP request to reception of the last byte of last object, for the experiments with 50ms RTT. Page load time with MFTP is consistently lower than TCP. In the case of no loss, when there is a smaller amount of data to be transferred, e.g. page 21, 22, and 23, with TCP the PLT is about 30% higher than with MFTP. The difference in PLT can be attributed to several features of MFTP: (1) MFTP is connectionless, and thus there is no overhead due to setting up a connection; (2) TCP identifies different requested objects by differences in se-

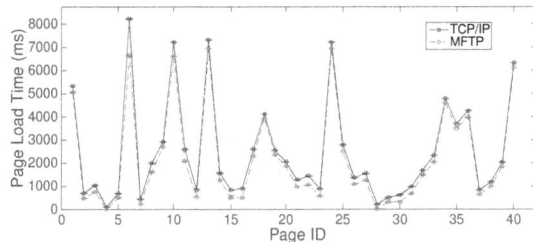

(a) 50ms RTT, no loss

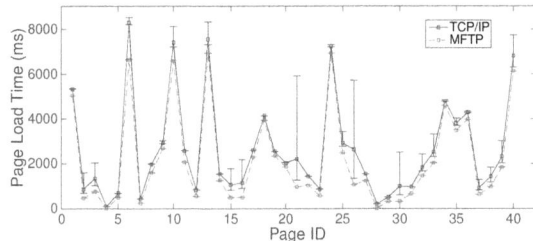

(b) 50ms RTT, 1% residual loss

Figure 11: Page Load Times (min, average, and max of 5 runs) for 40 different webpages.

quence numbers of that connection, while MFTP differentiates each requested object by a unique name, therefore HOL blocking (happens when multiple concurrent HTTP requests are fulfilled by a single TCP connection [25]) does not occur with MFTP; (3) each TCP connection "slow-starts", whereas with MFTP, short transfers, such as retrieving web objects, are not subject to flow control and are regulated only by per-hop back-pressure based congestion control, which allows sender to transmit at full rate as long as no congestion signal. As can be seen in Fig. 11(b), loss introduces a great amount of variability with TCP. For instance, for page 21, the minimum PLT is around 1500ms with TCP, but the maximum is 6000ms, which is several orders of magnitude higher than with MFTP. For all the pages, MFTP maintains minimal variability in terms of page load time.

6. RELATED WORK

Future Internet architectures (FIA): A number of clean-slate information-centric network architecture designs [4,6,7, 26] have been proposed recently to address challenges faced by today's IP network. They differ from each other in how they realize name-based service: while NDN [6] proposes a name-based routing approach in which packets are forwarded directly based on name; some other architectures (like MobilityFirst [4], XIA [7] and HIP [26]) place object names outside of the routing plane and uses a name resolution service to translate names to addresses.

Transport protocols for FIA: There have been a number of works on transport protocols for FIA, e.g. NDN [6], and XIA [7]. In NDN, a receiver asks for content by issuing a group of interest packets, i.e. requests; the corresponding data chunk is returned by the network in response to each interest. The NDN community has looked at how the transport layer can be adapted to such a interest-data interactive and multi-source/multi-path content-transfer pattern. Most of these works propose that the receiver maintains a Interest window and controls the issuing rate of interest packets (i.e., ICTP [27]), while others proposes a hop-by-hop Interest shaping scheme at each router (i.e., HR-ICP [28]). To support multi-source/multi-path transfer, CHoPCoP [29] proposes to utilize explicit congestion signaling from network to effectively notify the receiver about network conditions. In [30], a transport protocol, Tapa, for XIA architecture [7] is introduced which proposes to manage end-to-end delivery through segment-by-segment control. We share some of the techniques with these schemes here for the MFTP design. In addition, we investigate a broader set of ICN transport requirements which are derived from a collection of data delivery service scenarios. This allows MFTP to flexibly support different applications ranging from receiver-initiated retrieval, to sender-initiated publish, and from throughput-sensitive large file transfer, to latency-constrained short transfers of web objects.

7. CONCLUSIONS

This paper presents the design of a clean-slate transport layer protocol for the MobilityFirst future Internet architecture. The proposed transport layer protocol, called MFTP, is based on an understanding of the key requirements of name-based Information Centric Networks. These requirements include the use of names rather than addresses for routing, in-network storage, hop-by-hop reliability and multicasting as a basic service. Several core transport protocol components responsive to the above requirements were identified and discussed in the context of the MobilityFirst protocol stack. A proof-of-concept experimental validation has been developed and used to demonstrate feasibility and significantly improved performance relative to conventional TCP/IP for several use cases including large file transfer, web access and late binding/delay tolerant services.

8. ACKNOWLEDGMENTS

This research was supported by NSF CISE Future Internet Architecture (FIA) grants CNS-1040735 and CNS-1345295. We are grateful to Ivan Seskar for his guidance and support on the ORBIT experiments. We would also like to thank Chao Han and Feixiong Zhang for their help in the implementation and evaluation of the prototype, respectively.

9. REFERENCES

[1] J. H. Saltzer et al. End-to-end arguments in system design. *ACM TOCS*, 1984.

[2] B. Ahlgren et al. Design considerations for a network of information. In *ACM CoNEXT*, 2008.

[3] A. Ghodsi et al. Information-centric networking: Seeing the forest for the trees. In *ACM HotNets*. ACM, 2011.

[4] MobilityFirst Project. http://mobilityfirst.winlab.rutgers.edu/.

[5] D. Raychaudhuri et al. Mobilityfirst: a robust and trustworthy mobility-centric architecture for the future internet. *ACM SIGMOBILE Mobile Computing and Communications Review*, 2012.

[6] L. Zhang et al. Named data networking. *SIGCOMM Comput. Commun. Rev.*, 44(3):66–73, July 2014.

[7] D. Han et al. Xia: Efficient support for evolvable internetworking. In *USENIX NSDI*, 2012.

[8] F. Bronzino et al. Network service abstractions for a mobility-centric future internet architecture. In *MobiArch*. ACM, 2013.

[9] A. Erramilli and R. P. Singh. A reliable and efficient multicast for broadband broadcast networks. In *ACM Workshop on Frontiers in Computer Communications Technology*, 1988.

[10] S. C. Nelson et al. Gstar: Generalized storage-aware routing for mobilityfirst in the future mobile internet. In *MobiArch*. ACM, 2011.

[11] T. Vu et al. Dmap: A shared hosting scheme for dynamic identifier to locator mappings in the global internet. In *IEEE ICDCS*, June 2012.

[12] A. Sharma et al. A global name service for a highly mobile internetwork. In *ACM SIGCOMM*, 2014.

[13] S. Mukherjee et al. Evaluating opportunistic delivery of large content with tcp over wifi in i2v communication. *IEEE LANMAN*, 2014.

[14] Mario Gerla and Leonard Kleinrock. Flow control: A comparative survey. *IEEE Transactions on Communications*, 1980.

[15] F. Bronzino et al. Experiences with testbed evaluation of the mobilityfirst future internet architecture. In *EuCNC*, 2015.

[16] E. Kohler et al. The click modular router. *ACM Transactions on Computer Systems*, 2000.

[17] L. Zhang. Why tcp timers don't work well. In *ACM SIGCOMM*, 1986.

[18] I. Psaras and V. Tsaoussidis. Why tcp timers (still) don't work well. *Computer Networks*, 2007.

[19] D. Raychaudhuri et al. Overview of the orbit radio grid testbed for evaluation of next-generation wireless network protocols. In *Wireless Communications and Networking Conference*. IEEE, 2005.

[20] hostapd. http://wireless.kernel.org/en/users/Documentation/hostapd.

[21] netem: network emulation tool. http://www.linuxfoundation.org/collaborate/workgroups/networking/netem.

[22] M. Li et al. Block-switched networks: A new paradigm for wireless transport. In *USENIX NSDI*, 2009.

[23] X. Wang et al. How speedy is spdy. In *USENIX NSDI*, 2014.

[24] Alexa: the top 500 sites on the web. http://www.alexa.com/topsites.

[25] J. Erman et al. Towards a spdy'ier mobile web? In *ACM CoNEXT*, 2013.

[26] R. Moskowitz et al. Host identity protocol. *RFC 5201, April*, 2008.

[27] S. Salsano et al. Transport-layer issues in information centric networks. In *ACM ICN*, 2012.

[28] G. Carofiglio et al. Joint hop-by-hop and receiver-friven interest control protocol for content-centric networks. In *ACM ICN*, 2012.

[29] F. Zhang et al. A transport protocol for content-centric networking with explicit congestion control. In *IEEE ICCCN*, 2014.

[30] Fahad R. Dogar and Peter Steenkiste. Architecting for edge diversity: Supporting rich services over an unbundled transport. In *ACM CoNEXT*, 2012.

Beyond Network Selection: Exploiting Access Network Heterogeneity with Named Data Networking

Klaus M. Schneider
University of Bamberg, Germany
klaus.schneider@uni-bamberg.de

Udo R. Krieger
University of Bamberg, Germany
udo.krieger@ieee.org

ABSTRACT

Today, most mobile devices are equipped with multiple wireless network interfaces, but are constrained to use only one network at the same time. In this paper, we show that using multiple access networks simultaneously can improve user-perceived QoS and cost-effectiveness. We present a system architecture that exploits the adaptive forwarding plane of Named Data Networking (CCN/NDN) and implement a system prototype based on the NDN Forwarding Daemon (NFD). More specifically, we propose a set of forwarding strategies that use fine-grained application requirements together with interfaces estimation techniques for delay, bandwidth, and packet loss. Our simulation results show that our approach can improve QoS and/or reduce access costs in many wireless scenarios.

1. INTRODUCTION

Mobile and wireless terminals like smart phones and tablet pcs are becoming increasingly popular. These devices are often in the range of multiple wireless access networks like LTE, WiFi, and Bluetooth. Since each of the these access networks differs in its characteristics, like bandwidth, latency, bit error rate, security, power consumption, and network access costs, the end-user wants to select the best available network at a given time, a notion called *Always Best Connected* (ABC) [9]. The literature around ABC [12, 19, 21] contains numerous vertical handover decision strategies and network selection algorithms that aim to choose the optimal access network and to provide application transparent (seamless) handovers. However, all of these approaches assume that a terminal only uses one access network at a given time, a constraint that requires all terminal applications to agree on a single access network.

More recent solutions use multiple access networks simultaneously with the goal of improved mobility management, bandwidth aggregation, traffic offloading, or super-linear improvement of TCP performance [18]. Notable examples include SCTP, MPTCP, and IP Flow Mobility (see our previous work [17] for a review). While these approaches solve parts of the problem, they are still limited by the host-to-host communication model of IP networks. For example, IP addresses are used both as end-point *identifiers* and device *locators* for routing, which often leads to mobility problems. Moreover,

ICN'15, September 30–October 2, 2015, San Francisco, CA, USA.
© 2015 ACM. ISBN 978-1-4503-3855-4/15/09 ...$15.00.
DOI: http://dx.doi.org/10.1145/2810156.2810164.

since every device needs to maintain a globally routable IP address, vertical handovers are a rather heavy weight process. Instead of solving these issues with an IP overlay technology, we propose to adapt a rising clean-slate architecture.

The increasing share of content distribution among total Internet traffic has motivated the research field of *Information-Centric Networking* (ICN), which tries to shift from IP's communication model (*where*) to a content dissemination model (*what*). In this work, we use a prominent ICN architecture, called Content-Centric or Named Data Networking (CCN/NDN) [11], to better exploit mobile terminals with multiple wireless access networks.

This paper makes the following contributions. In Section 2, we argue that the information-centric model provides a better abstraction for exploiting multiple access networks than the host-centric model: devices no longer have to select a single access network, but can distribute smaller data units among a pool of available interfaces. We lay out our system requirements (Section 3) and architecture, which uses application profiles, interface estimation techniques, and NDN forwarding strategies (Section 4). Lastly, in Section 5, we describe our prototype implementation and simulation results of specific interface estimators and forwarding strategies.

2. THE NDN ARCHITECTURE

NDN has two packet types: 1) *interest* packets that request data, contain a hierarchical content name, and are routed towards a permanent storage location (*repository*), and 2) *data* packets that follow the path of the interests like Hansel and Gretel (intended to) follow their trail of breadcrumbs. Data packets may be cached on and retrieved from any intermediate router.

NDN routers consists of three parts: 1) The *Content Store* that acts as a temporary cache, 2) the *Pending Interest Table* (PIT) that stores a mapping of a content name to a set of requesting inbound faces, and 3) the *Forwarding Information Base* (FIB) that stores a mapping from content name prefixes to a set of outgoing interfaces (instead of exactly one in IP routers). If the FIB contains multiple alternative paths for a prefix, the NDN *strategy layer* decides where to forward incoming interest packets. In our scenario of multihomed end-devices (Figure 1) the NDN architecture shows the following differences to the IP model:

1) Content identifiers instead of host identifiers. NDN's unique forwarding layer removes all network layer host identifiers, implicitly splitting them from host locators. Since NDN hosts do not need to maintain a globally routable IP address, consumer mobility becomes automatic and seamless. Producer mobility is harder to achieve, but has been frequently discussed in the past [13, 16, 20, 24]. The NDN strategy layer is not constrained to select a single network for the whole terminal, but can decide on a set of outgoing interfaces for each incoming interest packet. This *interest distribution* is more lightweight than vertical handovers in IP, as content sources do not need to know the location (i.e., the IP address) of the requester: interest packets can be sent unmodified on any available interface; IP packets need a different source address.

2) Loop-free multipath routing. Since interest packets carry a nonce and data packets follow the exact path of the interests, neither of the two NDN packets can loop. This loop-freeness allows the NDN strategy layer to send out one incoming interest simultaneously on multiple outgoing interfaces, a feature that can be used to actively probe links and to improve the overall QoS.

3) Connectionless, yet stateful forwarding. NDN's stateful forwarding mechanism allows the forwarding strategy to store performance information about each available interface. This information can later be used to react fast and adaptively to changes in link quality. For example, NDN forwarding can detect and mitigate link failures in the order of milliseconds [23]. Moreover, stateful forwarding allows the strategy to aggregate the available bandwidth, to handle delay tolerant traffic, to improve handover performance, and to distribute data in a P2P fashion [17].

4) Support of conversational traffic. In addition to content traffic, NDN also supports conversational traffic like voice calls, video conferences, or email. Example applications include Voice-over-CCN [10], audio conferencing [25], and P2P video streaming [7].

3. SYSTEM REQUIREMENTS

Some goals of multihomed terminals, like seamless handovers, are intrinsically supported by NDN; others require additional effort. Below we list the requirements of our system that exceed current NDN functionality. These stem from a number of common observations about access network and traffic characteristics:

1) Applications differ in their requirements to the network. Some applications, like file downloads, benefit more from increased throughput, others, like voice calls, more from reduced packet loss or delay. Moreover, the function of user-perceived Quality of Experience (QoE) to network-level QoS differs for each application type (see Figure 12 in Section 5.3). For example, the voice quality of VoIP applications that use adaptive encoding will reach a threshold (in the order of 10's of kbit/s) at which coding with a higher bandwidth no longer makes any noticeable difference to the user. Such a threshold can also be seen with file transfers (a user does not care much if a file takes 0.1s or 1s to download), but there it is less clearly defined and also depends on the file size, as large files benefit more from high bandwidth. The same applies to video codecs, where the threshold depends on factors like the screen size and screen resolution.

2) Applications differ in their relative importance to the user; most users perceive the reliability of a bank transfer as more important than that of a NTP time synchronization request. Thus, they may want to prioritize these important traffic flows over others.

3) Access networks differ in their link characteristics such as bandwidth, round-trip delay, bit error rate, and availability. For example, WiFi has a higher maximal throughput and higher power consumption than Bluetooth. Moreover, the signal quality of a wireless network strongly affects the QoS: devices close to their access point typically perform better than those far away.

Figure 1: Multihomed Terminal Scenario

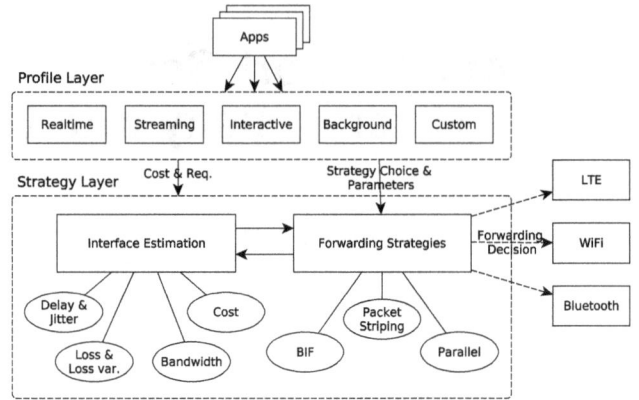

Figure 2: High-Level System Architecture

4) Access networks differ in cost factors such as monetary costs, bandwidth limits, and power consumption. Users have a different cost tolerance for each application; thus, they may want to offload low-importance traffic to less expensive networks, while keeping high-importance traffic on expensive, but high quality networks. For example, many mobile applications prefer to transfer certain high-bandwidth traffic like software updates only while connected to (inexpensive) WiFi networks. These considerations lead to the following system requirements:

1) Cost- and energy-awareness. The system should allow different notions of costs; for example, one to model energy consumption and one to model a cellular traffic limit. The system should allow to automatically offload lower-importance traffic to lower-cost interfaces.

2) Reacting to changes in link quality. The system should detect and handle both QoS deterioration and recovery. This adaptation to QoS levels should work more fine-granular than recognizing only complete link failure and recovery.

3) Exploiting multiple network interfaces. The system should use multiple network interfaces in parallel to improve overall QoS.

4) Restricting changes to the terminal. The system should not require to change devices inside the network such as access or backbone routers (other than their support of the NDN protocol stack). Limiting changes to the terminal eases deployment and allows the terminal to opportunistically exploit new access technologies.

In a related work, Detti et al. [6] proposed a cooperative video streaming application that offloads traffic from cellular networks to local peers connected by a WiFi ad-hoc network. One key difference to our approach is that they use routing to locally address content: peers add known content chunks to their FIB and the consumer application performs a longest prefix match on the chunk name, which returns only the face of the local peer. In contrast, our system relies mainly on forwarding: we assume that the FIB contains multiple interfaces per prefix (prefixes can be more coarse-grained than chunk-level) and let the forwarding strategy decide which one to use.

4. SYSTEM ARCHITECTURE & DESIGN

Our system architecture uses three components that work on and above the NDN strategy layer (Figure 2): 1) *application profiles*, 2) *estimation of interface characteristics*, and 3) *forwarding strategies*.

4.1 Application Profiles

Applications have different network requirements which we model as specific thresholds of maximal delay, maximal packet loss, maximal cost, and minimal bandwidth. These requirements are meaningful to the forwarding strategy, but not necessarily to the application developer or even end-user. To fill this gap we use a *profile layer:* application developers can select high-level profiles that contain low-level requirements and hide their complexity. We predefine four of these profiles to model common traffic classes [1]:

1) Conversational real-time services (RTS) include highly interactive applications like voice calls, video conferences, and real-time games. They are typically important to the user, require a round-trip delay below a strict threshold (less than a few 100 ms), and often tolerate packet losses up to a certain degree. Some RTS, like voice calls and certain types of games, require only moderate bandwidth; others, like video conferences, require a much higher amount.

2) Interactive services, like web browsing or email, are often delay-sensitive, that is, the RTT should not exceed a few seconds. These services often require reliable end-to-end transport and low-to-moderate bandwidth capacity.

3) Streaming services, like stored audio/video streaming and file transfers, are similar to real-time services, but with a relaxed delay requirement: they tolerate start-up delays up to a few seconds. However, they might be sensitive to delay variation (jitter). Streaming applications have a limited playout buffer (known as *jitter buffer*) and have to discard packets that arrive too late, that is, outside the buffer. These services often consume large amounts of bandwidth and, thus are a prime candidate for offloading to less expensive networks like WiFi.

4) Background applications include server-to-server email transfer and SMS-like messaging applications. These applications typically tolerate delays above 10 seconds, which allows them to perform reasonably well on lower cost network interfaces.

In addition to QoS elements, an application profile also contains one or multiple cost factors to model, for example, provider cost and energy consumption. These costs are usually a function of the bandwidth that an application consumes; thus, the cost-level can be specified relative to the number of requested packets (e.g., 5 cost units per data packet) or to the size of the consumed traffic. Another use of the cost factor is to model privacy and security requirements: insecure links can receive a higher security cost level and applications can specify a corresponding cost threshold. The semantics and usage conventions of cost attributes should be described by an API of each individual forwarding strategy.

If the application developer has deeper knowledge about network-level QoS, he can create a custom application profile. Moreover, if the application does not specify its profile, the profile layer can try to guess the traffic class by observing traffic patterns or user behavior. Lastly, a single application may define multiple traffic flows with different QoS profiles. For example, an email client may want to treat a user-triggered fetch as interactive service and treat regular polling as background traffic.

4.2 Estimation of Interface Characteristics

To forward packets intelligently, the strategy layer needs to know the characteristics of all available interfaces. In particular, our system considers the interface metrics of delay, jitter, packet loss, loss variation, bandwidth, and different types of cost (see Figure 2). These characteristics cannot be measured with perfect precision, but can often be estimated accurately enough to base forwarding decisions on them. This estimation is done by a number of interface estimator modules, which share the following design principles.

Interface estimation has to work on an appropriate abstraction level. Typically, wireless networks differ in physical characteristics like bit error rate (BER) and low-layer mechanisms like the modulation technique, FEC codes, and retransmissions. Since the presented system should work with any available access technology, these

details are abstracted away: the following estimation techniques measure network-layer performance and treat lower-layer behavior as a black box. Most of them fall into two categories: 1) passive traffic monitoring and 2) active probing.

Passive monitoring observes the "natural" traffic flow of applications to estimate interface characteristics; thereby, it avoids additional traffic overhead, but also misses some features of active probing. For example, passive probing cannot detect *link recovery*, that is, a QoS improvement of a path which is not among the current working paths; it is hard to determine the performance of an interface that does not send or receive data.

In contrast, *active probing* can probe interfaces other than the current working path to find recovered or "better" interfaces. Since active probing introduces overhead, the strategy has to adjust the probing frequency to trade-off lower traffic overhead with more precise detection of link quality.

In addition, some metrics can be retrieved from external input like hardware or network provider information. These depend on the specific metric, like bandwidth estimation, and are discussed in the next section.

Interface Estimators need to report their information to the forwarding strategy. We use a *moving average* calculation to smooth out noise and to reduce the undesirable effects of random variation. Moving averages can be computed in two ways: An *exponential moving average* (EMA) computes the average by multiplying a smoothing factor α with the current value Y_t and adding it to $(1 - \alpha)$ times the previous values:

$$EMA_t = \alpha * Y_t + (1 - \alpha) * EMA_{t-1} \tag{1}$$

This method uses all older values of Y_t, but decreases their importance exponentially. In contrast, a *simple moving average* (SMA) keeps a number of n previous values and computes the arithmetic mean over them:

$$SMA = \frac{Y_t + Y_{t-1} + \ldots + Y_{t-(n-1)}}{n} \tag{2}$$

Every time a new value is added, the oldest value drops out of the computation. A SMA can be computed over the last *n packets* or the last *m time units*, which results in a variable number of n packets, depending on how many packets were sent or received during that time period. We report specific results about the moving average calculation of the loss estimator in Section 5.

4.3 Forwarding Strategies

The main functionality of our system is implemented by NFD forwarding strategies. A forwarding strategy uses information from FIB entries, from application requirements, and from interface estimation to decide where to send on incoming interest packets. We assume that the FIB routes are correct, that is, interfaces from the FIB return content unless there is an unexpected failure. The forwarding strategies in our system are not required to probe paths outside the FIB to find off-path cache copies, but may optionally do so. Each strategy class defines an API for the profile layer which contains the strategy's set of parameters together with their semantics. Instances of these strategy classes contain specific parameter values, are bound to a name-prefix, and are looked up with a longest-prefix match. Moreover, the strategy informs the interface estimators about sent and received packets and performs active probing measurements.

Forwarding strategies can also perform interest retransmissions. These strategy layer retransmissions can be useful, because they can access more context information (e.g., about multiple paths) than higher layers. For example, retransmitted packets can be sent on a different (e.g., more costly) interface than before to increase the chance of data retrieval. A common practice is to perform strategy retransmissions if the application requests a given packet again. Another option for a router is to retransmit interests after a timeout, independently of the application. However, Abu et al. [2] argue that the latter approach is undesirable, because it increases the network load without reducing the number of PIT entries.

We categorize forwarding strategies into three classes [17]:

1) Best Interface First (BIF) strategies send out interest packets on a pre-determined "best" interface and may choose others for retransmitted interests. These strategies change their interface ranking dynamically according to variation in the QoS of the employed links (as reported by the interface estimators). BIF is the default and probably the preferred choice for most traffic classes; however, special cases may benefit from one of the other categories.

2) Packet Striping strategies can split a single application flow on different network interfaces to aggregate their bandwidth, allowing the user to run applications whose bandwidth requirement cannot be satisfied by a single link. However, since the available bandwidth per access technology varies greatly, this approach seems rarely useful on real-world terminals [18].

3) Parallel strategies send out interest packets redundantly to minimize content response time and packet loss in a trade-off against higher costs. The strategy uses the first returning data packet and discards the later arriving ones, thus reducing the overall content response time to the minimum of the response times of all involved interfaces (IF):

$$RTT_{total} = min\{RTT_i \mid i \in IF\} \qquad (3)$$

The impact on packet loss depends on the loss distribution of all involved links. In the worst case, losses are totally correlated and the overall loss rate is the minimum of the loss rates on the links (p_i):

$$p_{loss} = min\{p_i \mid i \in IF\} \qquad (4)$$

If the losses of different links are independent, the total loss rate is the product of the individual loss rates:

$$p_{loss} = \prod_{i \in IF} p_i \qquad (5)$$

Although unlikely, losses may be negatively correlated, that is, a loss on one channel makes it more likely to retrieve data on another channel. In the best case (corr = -1) the total loss rate is much lower than that of a single link:

$$p_{loss} = max\{0, 1 - \sum_{i \in IF} (1 - p_i)\} \qquad (6)$$

The question arises to which loss model most accurately approximates real-world wireless packet losses. When using technologies with different access ranges, like WWAN and WLAN, a mobile terminal may well experience independent loss characteristics. However, if technologies are similar, like a connection to two WiFi access points, correlated losses are more likely. Since parallel strategies produce a large overhead they are most useful for traffic with high importance, low total bandwidth, and strong loss and/or delay requirements, that is, for real time communication services. We provide the design and initial evaluation of one of such strategies in Section 5.3.

5. PROTOTYPE IMPLEMENTATION & PERFORMANCE EVALUATION

Below we describe a proof-of-concept implementation of our system's strategy layer. We have implemented the system based on the NFD platform, because of NFD's active development community and modular C++ code; however, with a few adjustments, one can also implement the system in CCNx [4]. We have released the source code of our implementation for experimentation at [8].

5.1 Shared Elements

Before diving into the strategy specifics, we describe a number of shared components:

Interface Probing.

The following strategies perform *active probing*, that is, they send out interest packets on paths other than the current working path to detect changes in interface performance. Since probing provides no direct performance benefit, the strategy has to trade-off the accuracy of interface estimation with the network overhead of probing packets. To control the probing effort, we follow Yi et al.'s [22] suggestion to split the probing into two functions: `bool probingDue()` and `void probeInterfaces()`.

The function probingDue() decides *if* other interfaces are probed at a given time point. We currently use two versions of probingDue: 1) one that probes interfaces (i.e., returns TRUE) every x packets, and 2) one that probes for all incoming packets during periodic time periods. Other options are to probe every y seconds, probe both every x packets and every y seconds, or use more complicated algorithms. When probingDue() returns TRUE, the strategy runs the function probeInterfaces() that decides *which* interfaces are probed. Currently, we probe all faces except the current working face (which receives the packet anyway); other options are to probe a random face and to probe faces in round robin.

Probing packets use a different nonce to avoid being dropped by the loop detection of an intermediate router. For example, in the topology of Figure 3, if an interest is sent with the same nonce both on face 256 and, for probing, on face 257, the router `Backbone` thinks that the later arriving one is looped and drops it. Consequently, one of the faces does not return a data packet, distorting its performance estimation.

Strategy parameters.

The profile layer needs a mechanism to pass parameters to the selected strategy instance. Since NFD does not natively support strategy parameters, we encode them as part of the strategy name with the syntax

$$\texttt{/strategy-name/version/}p_1{=}v_1,\ldots,p_n{=}v_n \qquad (7)$$

where p_i denote parameter names and v_i denote parameter values. Some parameters have a lower value vl_i and an upper value vu_i, which we connect with a dash: $p_i{=}vl_i{-}vu_i$

Like the strategy instance itself, the parameters are saved per name-prefix and looked up in a longest-prefix match (LPM). If the LPM does not return any entries, the strategy uses a set of pre-defined default parameters.

We currently pass the interface cost through NDN's routing cost value. If a strategy needs more than one cost attribute, this can also be done via parameters.

Measurement Information.

A forwarding strategy has to store performance measurements of the available links. For this purpose, it creates instances of the interface estimator classes described below. Some of this information, like interface cost, is the same for all applications flows and is stored per-face; other information differs for each application and must be stored per-name-prefix-per-face. For example, the round-trip delay of two flows can differ strongly if they share the same network interface, but use different paths in the backbone network.

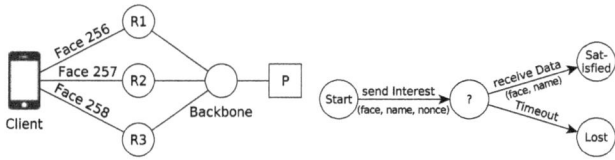

Figure 3: Topology   Figure 4: Loss State

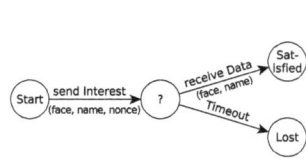

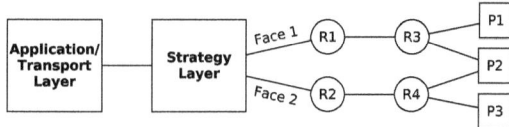

Figure 6: Packet Loss Map

Figure 5: Congestion Control Example

Our implementation currently saves this per-name-prefix information at one level upward of interest names, which by convention end with a sequence number. Thus, if an application flow requests the packets /prefix/A/seq1 to /prefix/A/seq100 they share the same measurement information; another flow that requests /prefix/B/seqXY maintains separate performance measurements. If storing measurements one level up creates too much overhead, one can aggregate measurement information further, like storing them two levels up. Measurement information is looked up in a longest-prefix match and may default to per-face information for new applications.

Performance Evaluation.

We have performed a simulation in ndnSIM 2.0 [14] to point out certain characteristics of our implementation. The simulation topology (Figure 3) models a wireless terminal with multiple access networks and is shared by all evaluation scenarios; however, the consumer applications and link characteristics differ, and are described in detail in the specific scenarios below.

Congestion Control and Caching Effects.

Congestion control in NDN is still an open research topic. Typically, NDN consumer applications use a congestion window with a TCP-like Additive Increase Multiplicative Decrease (AIMD) mechanism. The window is increased on returning data and decreased on out-of-order packets, timeouts, or delay variation [5].

Congestion control at the consumer is difficult, because of NDN's multipath strategy layer and its use of in-network caching: both are transparent to the application and create a large variation in link QoS. For example, a forwarding strategy can transparently change the outgoing face, leaving the consumer's congestion window maladapted to the new path characteristics. This adverse effect of path variability can be reduced by giving the congestion-control algorithm information about the underlying network. A first step is to use the *per-face* information of the strategy layer: all faces in the FIB (F1 and F2 in the example of Figure 5) maintain their own congestion window and measurement information, a change that improves the performance when the strategy switches between faces, but ignores path differences that lie beyond the first hop. For example, Face 1 in Figure 5 can be served by two content producers, introducing variability when the backbone router C3 changes between them. To address these path differences, one can keep *per-route* information [3], that is, one can discern between non-disjoint paths towards permanent content producers (like the 4 non-disjoint paths to the 3 content producers in Figure 5).

This per-route information allows a more fine-grained congestion control, but requires to extend NDN packets with route labels and

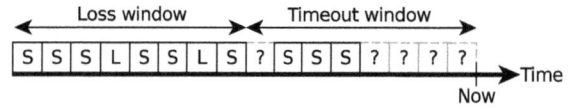

still leaves the problem of high path variability due to in-network caching. For example, a packet answered by a cache (cache hit) can have a much lower rtt than one answered by a producer (cache miss), a difference that may impair delay-based mechanisms for retransmission timeouts and congestion control. The effect of this variability is different for each of the interface estimators (delay, packet loss, and bandwidth); bandwidth estimation, for example, may be more constrained by a bottleneck link than by the cache hit ratio. One option to avoid the caching variability is to keep *per-cache* congestion windows in addition to per-producer information (8 routes to 7 caches/producers in Figure 5). However, the number of possible caches is unknown and possibly much larger than that of content providers, which could lead to an unacceptable memory overhead.

More coarse-grained solutions avoid this overhead and some argue that these are still effective in reducing congestion; examples include using congestion-control without per-path information [5] and using one shared congestion window for all routes together with per-route measurement information [3]. Another rationale for coarse-grained congestion control is that, in wireless networks, the access links often have a much higher impact on QoS than the backbone network. In this case, one can safely use per-face congestion control and ignore caching effects.

We have experimented with the *ConsumerWindow* application of ndnSIM; however, its current design is unsuitable for our scenario, since it resets the congestion window on each timeout, leading to unstable measurement results. Thus, we leave congestion control measurements for future work and, in the following experiments, use a consumer with a constant bit rate.

5.2   Interface Estimators

The current implementation estimates interface performance according to the three main QoS metrics: delay, packet loss, and bandwidth.

Delay Estimator.

The implemented delay estimator is based on the RttEstimator of the NFD prototype, which itself is based on the NS-3 simulator. On every returning data packet, it adds the new rtt value to the old ones using an exponential moving average ($\alpha = 0.1$). We use two output values of the delay estimator: 1) the mean round-trip time (rtt) and 2) the *request timeout* (rto), that is, the mean rtt plus 4 times the variance.

Loss Estimator.

Since there is no existing loss estimator in NFD, we present our own design. Unfortunately, the loss estimator cannot use an exponential moving average, because there are no discrete values like "x ms" for packet loss. Instead, an interest packet can have one of three loss states (see Figure 4):
- *Satisfied:* A data packet has returned for that interest
- *Unknown:* A data packet may return in the future
- *Lost:* No data packet has returned before the timeout

We use these states to calculate a simple moving average over the last n time units.

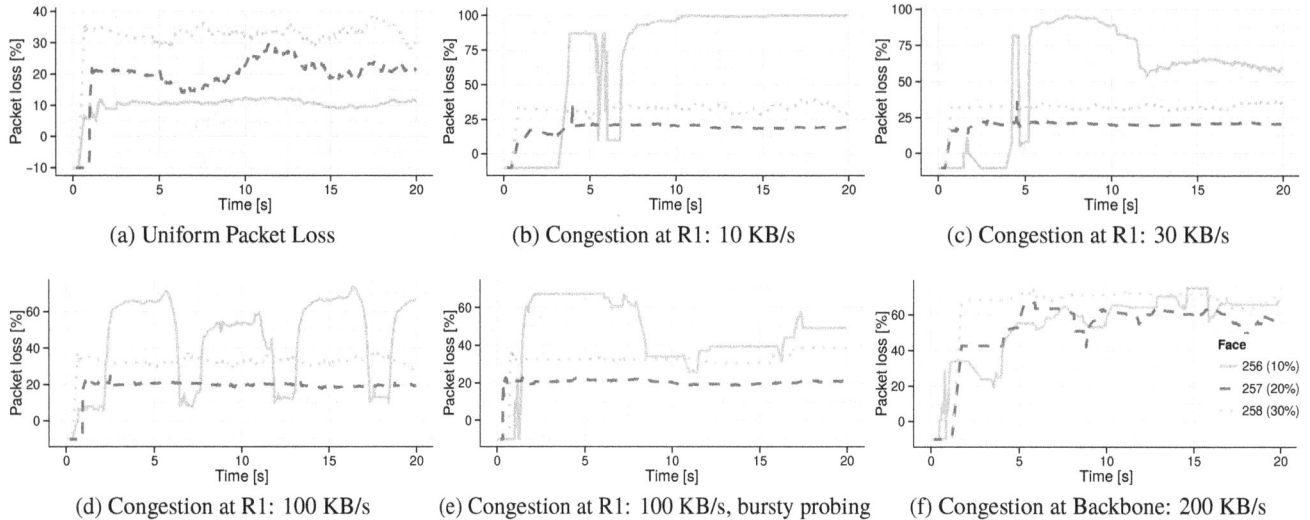

Figure 7: **Performance of the Loss Estimator**

A trivial solution is to simply count the number of sent interest and received data packets over a given time period and to calculate the loss percentage as follows:

$$p_{loss} = \frac{I_{sent} - D_{rec}}{I_{sent}} \qquad (8)$$

However, since data arrives later than interests are sent out, received data packets may count for a different interval than their corresponding interests, which causes large fluctuations in loss estimates; an interval that contains more data than interest packets even results in a negative loss estimate.

To estimate packet loss more accurately, the estimator must maintain a unique association between sent interest packets and returning data packets. Interest and data packets can be matched according to the content name and the respective interface (see Figure 4); however, the consumer application can retransmit lost packets, which results in multiple sent interests per received data packet. We assume that the strategy layer can detect these retransmissions, for example, by recognizing interests with a duplicate content name or a duplicate nonce, coming from the local application face.

Our loss estimator stores each sent interest in a key/value map `lossMap <time stamp, content name>`. For each returning data packet, it clears the content name to mark a *satisfied* packet. Entries that still have their content name are considered *unknown* before the timeout and *lost* after it (see Figure 6). The timeout is currently set based on delay estimates (the mean rtt plus 4 times the variance); another option is to use the interest lifetime (i.e., the time that an application still considers the data to be useful). When the loss estimator detects a retransmitted packet, it marks the earlier packet as *lost* and ignores all later arriving duplicates (implemented by changing the content name inside the loss map to "lost").

Finally, we calculate the loss percentage as ratio of lost to total packets during the *loss window*, a sliding window that starts after the timeout:

$$p_{loss} = \frac{N_{LOST}}{N_{LOST} + N_{SATISFIED}} \qquad (9)$$

If the current loss window is empty, the loss estimator returns a negative value (currently -10%). The forwarding strategy can decide how to handle these missing loss estimates; in the following, we treat them like a loss-free channel.

We have measured the performance of the Loss Estimator in ndnSIM with the *ConsumerCBR* application that sends 500 interest packets per second and retransmits lost ones after a delay-based timeout. The paths are modeled with a uniform loss distribution of 10%, 20%, and 30% and respective delays of 200 ms, 300 ms, and 500 ms (using the topology of Figure 3). The strategy uses a loss window of 4 seconds, sends interests on the lowest-loss face, and probes all other faces every 10th packet.

We observed that, after the individual timeout, the loss estimator is very *accurate*, that is, the mean of the reported loss value matches the actual packet loss (Figure 7a). We noticed that the loss estimation is barely affected by static differences in link delay; however, delay-based timeouts may overestimate packet loss if the delay estimation is inaccurate. This problem can be avoided by using the interest lifetime (default 2s) as timeout, but that introduces a static and high delay for the loss estimator to react to changes.

The loss estimator is more *precise* for the working path, that is, it has a low variance of reported values, as the variance depends on the traffic load on the channel, the probing frequency, and the size of the loss window. To improve the precision, one can increase the probing frequency, at a higher overhead, or increase the duration of the loss window, at a higher delay until the strategy reacts to changes in packet loss.

In addition to uniform random loss, we consider the effect of congestion-based packet losses on loss estimation and strategy behavior (Figure 7b - 7f). We have limited the bandwidth of face 256 (10% loss) below the requested data load, thereby producing additional packet drops at the queue of an intermediate router (R1 in Figure 3). If the bandwidth at R1 is limited to a degree that a large percentage of the probing packets are lost, the loss estimator reports a high loss value, allowing the strategy to avoid the congested path (Figure 7b and 7c). However, if the congested link still allows the probing traffic to go through, an oscillation pattern arises (Figure 7d): First, face 256 is selected as working face, because it has the lowest packet loss (10%). After a while, the load on the path leads to increasing packet losses (and loss estimates) at R1, so the working path changes to face 257. Path 256 now only has to transfer the lower probing load, recovers, and the pattern repeats itself. A trivial solution for this problem is to increase the amount of probing, but that also increases traffic overhead.

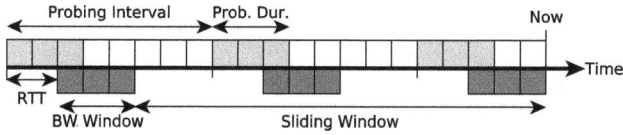

Figure 8: Bandwidth – Burst Estimation

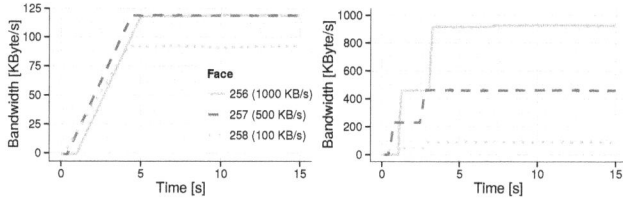

(a) Passive Estimation   (b) Burst Estimation

Figure 9: Performance of the Bandwidth Estimator

An approach that avoids additional overhead is to use *bursty packet probing:* instead of probing every 10th packet, we now probe all packets during bursts of 400 ms every 4 seconds (the probing interval must be shorter or equal to the loss window to ensure that at least one probing burst falls inside the window). In this case, a part of the probing load is lost due to congestion and the loss estimation stays at a level that discourages the use of the congested path (Figure 7e).

Another scenario is congestion at a shared router in the backbone network. In this case, the congestion-based loss often dwarfs the random loss at the local links, so that the loss estimator (with both steady and bursty probing) detects an equal congestion on each path (Figure 7f). To prevent the strategy from randomly switching between them, one can use a *hysteresis*, that is, a policy to only change the working path if another path has a loss percentage which is at least x percent lower than the current one. We discuss two specific hysteresis implementations in the next section.

Bandwidth Estimator.

A strategy could probe the bandwidth the same way as loss and delay, that is, it could send out probing packets and observe the throughput of the returning data; however, that would require to fill the capacity of all non-working paths, creating an unacceptable traffic overhead. One option to avoid that overhead is to use *passive bandwidth estimation*, that is, to observe the traffic that naturally flows over each path. However, this method only returns accurate bandwidth estimations of the current working path (or multiple working paths); for other paths, it returns the throughput of the probing traffic plus the traffic of other applications, often a much too small value.

We use another bandwidth estimator, called *burst estimator*, that uses short bursts with high traffic load (flooding) and measures the resulting throughput (see Figure 8). The burst estimator performs regular probing with a fixed interval length and probing duration, such as probing every 3 seconds for 100 ms. It measures the returning data traffic that falls inside periodic bandwidth windows which follow the probing window with a delay of one rtt, that is, the time the data of the probes is expected to return. Moreover, it calculates a simple moving average over a sliding window, which must be a multiple of the probing interval to assure that it always contains the same number of bandwidth windows. The burst estimator extrapolates the throughput during the bandwidth windows to the whole sliding window:

$$BW = \frac{\sum DataInBwWindow}{slidingWindowSize} * \frac{probingInterval}{probingDuration} \quad (10)$$

We have compared the two bandwidth estimators in the following measurement scenario: An application creates a constant data stream of 1200 KB/s, but the strategy always chooses link 258, which is limited to 100 KB/s. The other two links have a bandwidth of 500 KB/s and 200 KB/s, respectively, and are probed every 10th packet. The link delays are 1000 ms (link 256), 500 ms (link 257), and 200 ms (link 258).

The passive bandwidth estimator returns accurate values for the working path, but vastly underestimates the other two, which only receive an estimate of 120 KB/s, exactly the throughput of the probing traffic (see Figure 9a).

The burst estimator probes all paths every 2 seconds for 200 ms and uses a sliding window of 4 seconds. It estimates the bandwidth of the non-working path much more accurately (Figure 9b), without increasing the traffic overhead. Moreover, it is not influenced by static differences in link delay, as it takes the delay estimates into account; however, the estimates may be skewed by delay variability, that is, when the actual path delay differs from delay estimates.

In addition to these two estimators, there is a large literature of bandwidth estimation techniques for IP networks [15]. Future work could evaluate if and how those techniques can be adapted to NDN.

5.3 Forwarding Strategies

According to Occam's Razor, the simplest solution to a given problem should be preferred; more complex systems need to be justified by added functionality. Therefore, we describe three forwarding strategies that range from low to higher complexity, and show their merits in different evaluation scenarios.

Lowest Cost Strategy.

The Lowest Cost Strategy (LCS) takes three parameters which specify application requirements: maximal packet loss (maxloss), maximal delay (maxdelay) and minimal bandwidth (minbw). It uses an ordinal ranking of costs and sends out packets to the interface with the lowest cost that satisfies all requirements. The requirement values are considered as hard thresholds, that is, if the profile sets a maximal delay of 100 ms, the strategy considers a link with a delay of 101 ms as inappropriate and, if possible, chooses one with a lower delay. When none of the interfaces can satisfy all requirements, the strategy uses one *priority attribute* to decide where to forward packets; for example, if the priority is set to `delay` and no face satisfies all requirements, the strategy chooses the lowest-cost face that satisfies the delay requirement and, if this is not possible, the face with the lowest delay.

Even with this simple design, the Lowest Cost Strategy has a number of advantages over the currently available forwarding strategies. First, it can choose the best interface according to application requirements. Second, it can detect a QoS degradation of the current working path and switch to a better path. Third, it can detect fine-grained path recovery, like a reduction in packet loss from 5% to 2%, and switch to the recovered face if desired. We investigate how far the LCS achieves these goals in the following performance evaluation.

Figure 10 shows the functionality of the Lowest Cost Strategy in a prototypical test scenario. The client has three paths which are modeled with the following characteristics: Face 256 has a RTT of 300 ms, 5% packet loss, and the highest cost. Face 257 has 400 ms delay, also 5% packet loss, and medium cost. Face 258 has 200 ms delay, 30% packet loss, and the lowest cost. The strategy is

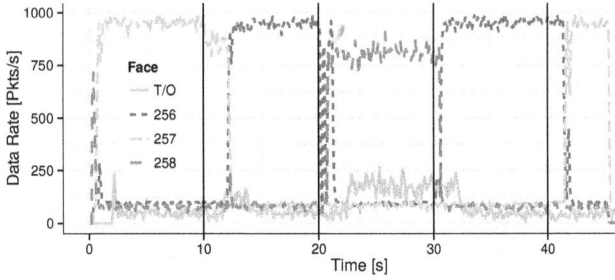

Figure 10: Behavior of the Lowest Cost Strategy in the Case of Link Deterioration and Recovery

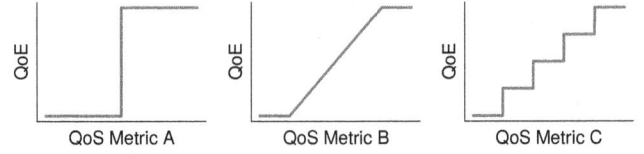

Figure 12: Generic Relationship Between Network-level QoS and User-perceived QoE

configured with the parameters maxdelay=500[ms],maxloss=10[%] and the priority attribute is set to "delay". The interest lifetime is 2 seconds and the loss estimator uses a delay-based timeout together with a loss window of 3 seconds. Moreover, we set up four events at different time points of the measurement run:

- 10 sec: Loss deterioration of path 257 to 15%.
- 20 sec: Delay deterioration of path 256 to 700 ms.
- 30 sec: Delay recovery of path 256 back to 300 ms.
- 40 sec: Loss recovery of path 257 back to 5%.

We observed the following behavior: After a short phase where no loss estimation is available yet, the strategy selects face 257 as the one with the lowest cost that satisfies all requirements. After the loss deterioration, the strategy sets the working face to 256 and after the delay deterioration to 258. Similarly, after the loss and delay recovery, the strategy selects the previous faces again.

We observe that the strategy switches paths faster after delay changes than after loss changes, caused by the differences in the two interface estimators: the EMA of the delay estimator adjusts faster to changes than the SMA of the loss estimator. The timeout face (T/O) shows the application-level timeouts (retransmissions are disabled) which follow the loss characteristic of the selected interface with a delay of the interest lifetime, that is, 2 seconds. The timeout rate increases at the start of the loss deterioration before the face changes to 256 (at 10+2 seconds) and whenever face 258 is selected. The application-level delay, which is not plotted, behaved as expected: the RTT was between 200 and 700 milliseconds, depending on the selected path.

In a second evaluation (Figure 11), we want to show how precise the selection of a path works around the parameter threshold. We set up two paths: one with low cost and a delay value of 200 ms without variance; another one with a higher cost, but lower delay (the exact value does not matter). Figure 11a shows the amount of traffic that flows on the path with 200 ms. For threshold values above 200 ms, the strategy sends all traffic except the 10% probing overhead on the expected path. However, for values below 200 ms, some traffic is sent over the path with a delay that is higher than specified. This behavior can be eliminated by using a hysteresis: all paths that are not the current working path must be at least be x (currently 20) percent better than the given requirement to become the working path; for example, if the delay requirements is 200 ms, non-working paths need to be below 180 ms. For the non-variable delay measurement, this creates a clear switching point at 200 ms (Figure 11a).

We repeated the measurement with a mean packet loss of 20% and high loss variance (loss estimation report in Figure 11c). In this case, the hysteresis no longer creates a clear switching point (Figure 11b) and moderately biases the choice towards the face with lower loss and higher cost. However, with the hysteresis, the strategy stays

much longer on the selected interface (either lower-loss or lower-cost) as seen by the number of switches of the working face (Figure 11d).

MADM Strategy.

One limitation of the Lowest Cost Strategy is its implicit and imprecise notion of costs. To allow multiple and more fine-grained cost attributes, we designed a strategy based on Multiple Attribute Decision Making (MADM). In addition to cost-awareness, the MADM strategy takes the relationship between application-level QoE and network-level QoS into account (see Figure 12 and the discussion in Section 3). Most applications show a linear (B) or step wise (C) relationship rather than a hard threshold (A). To model metric B and to approximate metric C, the MADM strategy uses two threshold values: an *upper threshold* (max_i), which achieves the maximal possible QoE for the application, and a *lower threshold* (min_i), which is the bare minimum QoS requirement, that is, anything worse is unacceptable. For example, an adaptive video streaming application could set its thresholds to $min_{bw} = 100 \, Kbit/s$ (lowest video quality) and $max_{bw} = 5 \, Mbit/s$ (highest video quality). The attributes that lie between these thresholds are then normalized to an interval between 0 and 1. The simplest option is linear normalization, as seen in metric B of Figure 12; moreover, one can use exponential, logarithmic, or sigmoidial functions [19] to model diminishing returns of higher QoS like additional bandwidth.

One must distinguish between *upward attributes* (e.g., bandwidth) where higher values denote a better QoS and *downward attributes* (e.g., delay, cost, loss) where the opposite is the case. Considering these details, we normalize each attribute i with a linear function:

$$vu_i = \begin{cases} 0 & \text{if } x_i \leq min_i \\ \frac{x_i - min_i}{max_i - min_i} & \text{if } min_i < x_i < max_i \\ 1 & \text{if } x_i \geq max_i \end{cases} \quad (11)$$

Downward attributes invert the normalized value: $vd_i = 1 - vu_i$ For example, an application profile could set the requested minimal delay to 100 ms and the tolerated maximal delay to 300 ms. In this case, $v_{del} = 1$ for any observed delay below 100 ms, $v_{del} = 0.5$ for a delay of 200 ms, and $v_{del} = 0$ for a delay above 300 ms. To model a hard threshold, like metric A in Figure 12, the application profile can specify only one attribute value. In this case, both min and max are set to this value and the same formula applies.

These normalized values are then weighted and the strategy sends the interest packet on the interface with the highest total value. Currently, we use simple additive weighting (another option is multiplicative exponential weighting) of all attribute values v_i with all weights w_i set to 1:

$$V_{SAW} = \sum_{i \in IF} w_i * v_i \quad \forall w_i.v_i \geq 0 \quad (12)$$

In addition to attribute weighting, our current implementation makes a number of fine adjustments: First, if one attribute value is 0, the total sum of the face is set to 0. This measure prevents that

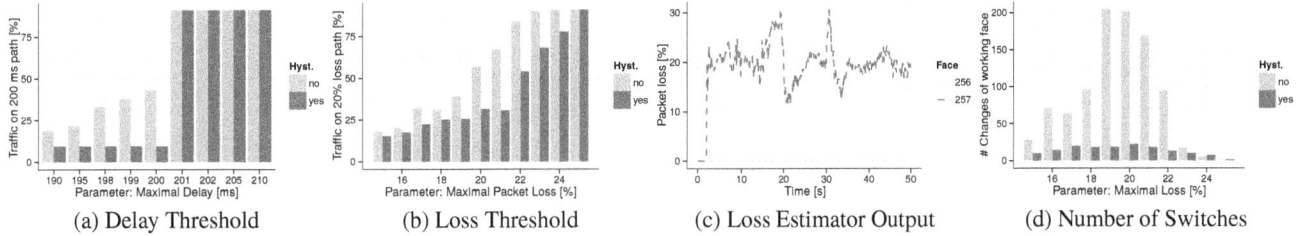

| (a) Delay Threshold | (b) Loss Threshold | (c) Loss Estimator Output | (d) Number of Switches |

Figure 11: Effect of a Hysteresis on the Precision of the Lowest Cost Strategy

a path which is insufficient in one attribute (and good in others) is chosen over one that is at least acceptable in all of them. Second, to prevent unnecessary oscillation between paths, the strategy uses a hysteresis, which is implemented by increasing the total value of the current working face by x (currently 20) percent.

The MADM strategy also introduces the concept of a *Cost Estimator*: it sees cost as a variable attribute that can change according to user requirements and traffic behavior. The strategy uses this variable cost factor to automatically react to a traffic limit on an interface (like a provider-induced limit on a cellular network): the closer the traffic gets to the limit, the costlier it becomes to use this interface. This cost adjustment allows the strategy to offload unimportant traffic to lower cost (and possibly lower quality) interfaces.

To perform this traffic offloading, the strategy needs to set a few conventions. The current implementation specifies the default cost (c_{def}) of one interface as 100 and the maximal cost (c_{max}) as 1000. If an interface has a traffic limit, a function `adjustCost()` takes the current traffic load and increases the cost as follows:

$$c = max\{c_{def}, 1000 * \frac{t_{cur}}{t_{limit}}\} \qquad (13)$$

Thus, if 90% of the traffic limit is reached, the cost will be set to 900. The application profile can use this information to define a cost limit; an application with a limit of $[600 - 800]$ discourages using interfaces that are over 60% of their limit and completely avoids those over 80%. Moreover, the strategy stops probing interfaces whose cost are above the upper limit to reduce unnecessary traffic load.

We have investigated the cost limit in a scenario with two consumer applications (Figure 13). The first application (App1) sends a constant stream of 100 packets per second (pps) and always chooses the lowest loss face; the second application (App2) sends 200 pps and uses the parameters maxloss=0[%]-40[%],maxcost=500-700, that is, it also prefers the lowest loss face, but adds a cost constraint. The topology is as follows: link 256 has 10% packet loss and a traffic limit of 10 megabyte; link 257 has 20% packet loss and no limit. This configuration roughly simulates a terminal with a high quality, but costly, cellular network and a low quality, but cheap, WiFi network.

We observed that App2 stops using the costly face after about 22 seconds when about 54% of the traffic limit is exhausted; it stops probing link 256 after about 36 seconds when *exactly* 70% of the traffic limit is reached. However, face 256 can still be probed or used by another application. Currently, every application is responsible for probing the interfaces it may want to use, which can create a large overhead when there are many concurrent applications. This probing overhead can be reduced by using a centralized probing instance. More general, interface probing leaves many questions for future work: how often to probe, which algorithms to use, and how fine-grained to aggregate probing measurements.

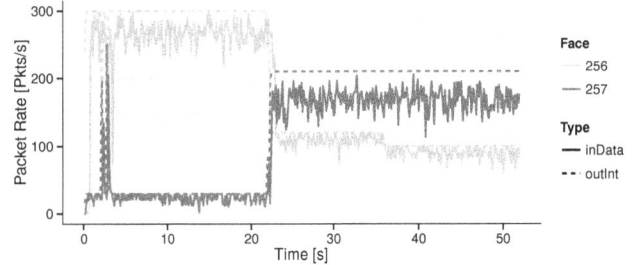

Figure 13: Behavior of the MADM Strategy in the Traffic Limit Scenario

Selective Parallel Strategy.

The Selective Parallel Strategy falls into the category of parallel strategies (Section 4.3) with the main target of real-time communication services. Like the Lowest Cost Strategy, it uses the parameters loss, delay, and bandwidth and chooses the interface with the lowest cost that satisfies all requirements. However, if one of the requirements is not met, it sends interest packets on multiple interfaces simultaneously until one face satisfies all requirements again. The number of interfaces that the strategy adds can be tuned based on the application needs. In the following evaluation, we use two alternatives: sending packets on the two best faces (*SP-Best2*) and flooding them on all available faces (*SP-Flood*).

We configure the paths of the topology from Figure 3 with delays of 200 ms, 400 ms, and 600 ms. The paths are probed every 10th packet (if the strategy uses probing) and the consumer application sends 300 pps without retransmissions. The packet loss of the paths is modeled as follows: every 2 seconds each path receives a random loss percentage between 0 and 30 %. The application profile is set to keep the total loss below 10%. We have compared a number of forwarding strategies according to their ability to do so; we compare two metrics over 30 measurement runs (see Figure 14): 1) the percentage of intervals of 3 seconds that are below 10% packet loss and 2) the amount of sent interests summed up over all faces.

We observed the following results: The best-route strategy (BestRoute) stays on one path, does not probe other paths, and thus sends exactly 300 pps. However, it has the highest packet loss of all strategies. The Lowest Cost Strategy (LCS) creates a much lower overall loss, since it changes the path as soon as a better one is available. It uses 10% more interest packets due to probing, but this amount was set manually and may be lower in practice.

To achieve an even better satisfaction of the loss requirement, one can use *redundant transmission*, that is, to send one interest packet simultaneously on multiple interfaces. The simplest of these strategies is to flood all packets among all available interfaces (Broadcast), but that method heavily increases overhead (here to 3 times the amount, since the topology uses 3 interfaces). The two versions of

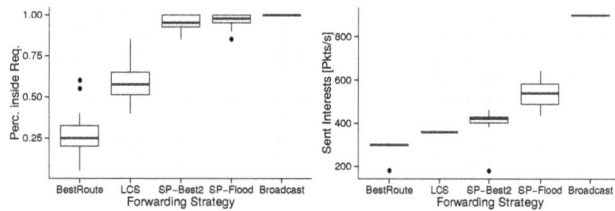

Figure 14: Performance of the Selective Parallel Strategy

the selective parallel strategy achieve nearly the same performance (as measured by the amount of intervals that satisfy the packet loss requirement), at a much lower overhead.

We use this evaluation to exemplify the possibilities of parallel forwarding. We recognize that it is a rather rough outline and future work has to expand on the details and use cases of this new adaptive forwarding method.

6. CONCLUSIONS

Today's mobile devices can transfer data by an unprecedented number of wireless technologies. To fully exploit their capabilities, one needs to move beyond the selection of single access networks towards more fine-grained control. We argue that NDN's content-oriented model is a great fit for this problem.

We have presented a system architecture that uses NDN's unique forwarding layer to improve end-user QoE and to reduce the terminals access cost and power consumption. Our prototype implementation illustrates the effects of specific mechanisms like interface probing, packet loss estimation, and the use of hysteresis thresholds. As shown in the evaluation, the system can adapt to fine-grained changes in link quality and adheres precisely to the application's cost tolerance.

Work still remains to be done in a number of areas. First, one can investigate which bandwidth estimation techniques can be adapted from IP networks. Moreover, the details of interface probing and of parallel forwarding strategies need to be worked out. A good strategy design in this area could strongly improve the QoE of real-time communication services in situations of suboptimal wireless link quality. Lastly, one should move from synthetic simulation scenarios to more realistic trace-driven scenarios and performance evaluation on real devices.

Acknowledgments

The authors want to thank Junxiao Shi and Alexander Afanasyev for helpful comments on the NFD implementation.

7. REFERENCES

[1] 3GPP. Services and service capabilities (release 12). ETSI TS 122 105 V12.1.0, Jan. 2015.

[2] A. J. Abu, B. Bensaou, and J. M. Wang. Interest packets retransmission in lossy ccn networks and its impact on network performance. In *Proceedings of ACM ICN*, 2014.

[3] G. Carofiglio, M. Gallo, L. Muscariello, and M. Papali. Multipath congestion control in content-centric networks. In *INFOCOM WKSHPS*, pages 363–368. IEEE, 2013.

[4] Project CCNx™. http://www.ccnx.org/.

[5] A. Detti, C. Pisa, and N. Blefari-Melazzi. Modeling multipath forwarding strategies in information centric networks. In *IEEE Global Internet Symposium*, 2015.

[6] A. Detti, M. Pomposini, N. Blefari-Melazzi, S. Salsano, and A. Bragagnini. Offloading cellular networks with icn: The case of video streaming. In *WoWMoM*, pages 1–3. IEEE, 2012.

[7] A. Detti, B. Ricci, and N. Blefari-Melazzi. Mobile peer-to-peer video streaming over information-centric networks. *Elsevier Computer Networks*, 81(0):272 – 288, 2015.

[8] Custom NFD strategy layer implementation. https://github.com/schneiderklaus.

[9] E. Gustafsson and A. Jonsson. Always best connected. *IEEE Wireless Communications*, 10(1):49–55, 2003.

[10] V. Jacobson, D. K. Smetters, N. H. Briggs, M. F. Plass, P. Stewart, J. D. Thornton, and R. L. Braynard. Voccn: voice-over content-centric networks. In *Proceedings of ACM ReArch*, 2009.

[11] V. Jacobson, D. K. Smetters, J. D. Thornton, M. F. Plass, N. H. Briggs, and R. L. Braynard. Networking named content. In *Proceedings of ACM CoNEXT*, 2009.

[12] M. Kassar, B. Kervella, and G. Pujolle. An overview of vertical handover decision strategies in heterogeneous wireless networks. *Elsevier Computer Communications*, 31(10):2607–2620, 2008.

[13] D.-h. Kim, J.-h. Kim, Y.-s. Kim, H.-s. Yoon, and I. Yeom. Mobility support in content centric networks. In *Proceedings of ACM SIGCOMM ICN Workshop*, 2012.

[14] S. Mastorakis, A. Afanasyev, I. Moiseenko, and L. Zhang. ndnSIM 2.0: A new version of the NDN simulator for NS-3. Technical Report NDN-0028, NDN, January 2015.

[15] R. Prasad, C. Dovrolis, M. Murray, and K. Claffy. Bandwidth estimation: metrics, measurement techniques, and tools. *Network, IEEE*, 17(6):27–35, 2003.

[16] R. Ravindran, S. Lo, X. Zhang, and G. Wang. Supporting seamless mobility in named data networking. In *IEEE ICC*, 2012.

[17] K. M. Schneider, K. Mast, and U. R. Krieger. CCN forwarding strategies for multihomed mobile terminals. In *Proceedings of NetSys*, 2015.

[18] C.-L. Tsao and R. Sivakumar. On effectively exploiting multiple wireless interfaces in mobile hosts. In *Proceedings of ACM CoNEXT*, 2009.

[19] L. Wang and G.-S. Kuo. Mathematical modeling for network selection in heterogeneous wireless networks – a tutorial. *IEEE Communications Surveys & Tutorials*, 15(1):271–292, 2013.

[20] L. Wang, O. Waltari, and J. Kangasharju. Mobiccn: Mobility support with greedy routing in content-centric networks. In *IEEE GLOBECOM*, 2013.

[21] X. Yan, Y. A. Şekercioğlu, and S. Narayanan. A survey of vertical handover decision algorithms in fourth generation heterogeneous wireless networks. *Elsevier Computer Networks*, 54(11):1848–1863, 2010.

[22] C. Yi, J. Abraham, A. Afanasyev, L. Wang, B. Zhang, and L. Zhang. On the role of routing in named data networking. In *Proceedings of ACM ICN*, 2014.

[23] C. Yi, A. Afanasyev, L. Wang, B. Zhang, and L. Zhang. Adaptive forwarding in named data networking. *SIGCOMM Comput. Commun. Rev.*, 42(3):62–67, June 2012.

[24] Z. Zhu, A. Afanasyev, and L. Zhang. A new perspective on mobility support. *Named-Data Networking Project, Tech. Rep*, 2013.

[25] Z. Zhu, S. Wang, X. Yang, V. Jacobson, and L. Zhang. Act: audio conference tool over named data networking. In *Proceedings of ACM SIGCOMM ICN Workshop*, 2011.

Interest-Based Access Control
for Content-Centric Networks

Cesar Ghali[*]   Marc A. Schlosberg   Gene Tsudik[*]   Christopher A. Wood[†]
Computer Science Department, University of California Irvine
{cghali, marc.schlosberg, gene.tsudik, woodc1}@uci.edu

ABSTRACT

Content-Centric Networking (CCN) is an emerging network architecture designed to overcome limitations of the current IP-based Internet. One of the fundamental tenets of CCN is that content is named and addressable. Consumers request content by issuing interests with the desired content name. These interests are forwarded by routers to producers, and the requested content is returned and optionally cached at each router along the path.

In-network caching makes it difficult to enforce access control policies on sensitive content since routers only use interest information for forwarding decisions. This motives our work on Interest-Based Access Control (IBAC) – a scheme for access control enforcement using only information contained in interest messages. IBAC makes sensitive content names unpredictable to unauthorized parties. It supports both hash- and encryption-based name obfuscation. Interest replay attacks are addressed by formulating a mutual trust framework between producers and consumers that enables routers to perform authorization checks before satisfying interests from local caches. We assess computational, storage, and bandwidth costs of each IBAC variant. Proposed design is flexible and allows producers to arbitrarily specify and enforce any type of content access control, without having to deal with content encryption and key distribution. This is the first comprehensive CCN access control design that only uses information contained in interest messages.

Categories and Subject Descriptors

C.2.0 [**Computer-Communication Networks**]: General—*Security and protection*; C.2.1 [**Computer-Communication Networks**]: Network Architecture and Design—*Network communications*

---

[*]Supported by the NSF grant: "CNS-1040802: FIA: Collaborative Research: Named Data Networking (NDN)".

[†]Supported by the NSF Graduate Research Fellowship DGE-1321846.

General Terms

Theory, Design, Performance

Keywords

content-centric networks; access control; name obfuscation

1. INTRODUCTION

The purpose of the original Internet in the 1970-s was to provide end-to-end communication for a few thousand users to access scarce and expensive resources via terminals. Since then, the number of Internet users has grown exponentially, exceeding 3 billion, each using a wide variety of applications: from dynamic web to content distribution. This shift of usage exposed certain limitations of the IP-based Internet design and motivated exploration of new Internet architectures.

Content-Centric Networking (CCN) is an approach to internetworking exemplified by two well-known research efforts: CCNx [19] and Named-Data Networking (NDN) [12]. CCN's main goal is to develop the next-generation Internet architecture with an emphasis on efficient content distribution, security, and privacy. Unlike current IP-based networking where data is requested by addressing the machine hosting the data, each CCN *content* is assigned a unique name. Users (called consumers) request content objects by issuing an *interest* for a given name. This interest can then be satisfied or served from any entity (i.e., producer or router) as long as the replied content's name matches that of the interest.

To facilitate efficient content distribution, a CCN router maintains a cache. This enables routers to satisfy interests, which reduces end-to-end latency and decreases bandwidth utilization when requesting popular content. Since interest messages may be satisfied by any cached version of the content, interest messages may not, and need not, reach the producer. Therefore, enforcing content access control *within the network* is a challenge. Furthermore, even if all interests are forwarded to producers, the latter might not be able to enforce access control since interest messages, by design, do not carry any form of consumer identification or authentication information.

In this paper, we propose an access control scheme based on interests – Interest-Based Access Control (IBAC). The intuition is that if consumers are not allowed access to certain content, they should not be able to generate the corresponding interests, i.e., they should not be able to learn the content's name. IBAC may also be used with or alongside content encryption to conceal both the name and the payload of the content object.[1] However, using IBAC in isolation is advantageous in scenarios where content object payloads may need to be modified by an intermediary service, e.g., a media encoding application or proxy. In this case, content encryption prevents such modifications by services or applications besides the producer. Moreover, although IBAC involves the network layer, we believe that this is necessary to allow routers (with caches) to enforce access control. To be more specific, we claim that, to support IBAC, *any entity which serves content should also be able to authorize interests for said content.*

The main contributions of this paper are:

- Architectural modifications to support IBAC without diminishing caching benefits.

- A mutual trust scheme wherein routers can verify whether consumers are authorized to access cached content.

- A security analysis of the proposed IBAC scheme.

- Evaluation of router performance overhead when serving content via IBAC compared to publicly accessible content.

The rest of this paper is organized as follows. Section 2 presents a CCN overview. Then, Section 3 provides an summarizes CCN access control techniques. Next, Section 4 presents security definitions and the adversary model, followed by Section 5 that presents the IBAC scheme. Security considerations are discussed in Section 6 and IBAC costs are assessed in Section 7. The paper concludes in Section 8.

2. CCN OVERVIEW

Content Centric Networking (CCN) is one of the main Information-Centric Networking (ICN) architectures. Related architectures, such as Named Data Networking (NDN) [25], are similar, albeit with some small protocol and packet format differences. This section overviews ICNs in the context of the CCN protocol and CCNx reference implementation. Given familiarity with either CCN or NDN, it can be skipped without loss of continuity.

In contrast to TCP/IP, which focuses on end-points of communication and their names and addresses, ICN architectures such as CCN [12, 19] focus on content by making it named, addressable, and routable within the network. A content name is a URI-like [2] name composed of one or more variable-length name components, each separated by a / character. To obtain content, a user (consumer) issues a request, called an *interest* message, with the name of the desired content. This interest will be *satisfied* by either (1) a router cache or (2) the content producer. A *content object* message is returned to the consumer upon satisfaction of the interest. Moreover, name matching in CCN is exact, e.g., an interest for `lci:/facebook/Alice/profile.html` can only be satisfied by a content object named `lci:/facebook/Alice/profile.html`.[2]

Aside from the content name, CCN interest messages may include the following fields:

- `Payload` – enables consumers to push data to producers along with the request.[3]

- `KeyID` – an optional hash digest of the public key used to verify the desired content's digital signature. If this field exists, the network guarantees that only content objects which can be verified with the specified key will be returned in response to an interest.

- `ContentObjectHash` – an optional hash value of the content being requested. If this field exists, the network guarantees the delivery of the exact content that consumer requests.

CCN content objects include several fields. In this work, we are only interested in the following three:

- `Name` – a URI-like name formatted as a sequence of /-separated name components.

- `Validation` – a composite of validation algorithm information (e.g., the signature algorithm used, its parameters, and a link to the public verification key), and validation payload (e.g., the signature). We use the term "signature" to refer to this field.

- `ExpiryTime` – an optional, producer-recommended time for the content objects to be cached.

There are three types of entities in CCN:[4]

- *Consumer* – issues an interest for content.

- *Producer* – produces and publishes content.

- *Router* – routes interest packets and forwards corresponding content packets.

Each CCN entity maintains two components:

- *Forwarding Interest Base* (FIB) – a table of name prefixes and corresponding outgoing interfaces. The FIB is used to route interests based on longest-prefix-matches of their names.

- *Pending Interest Table* (PIT) – a table of outstanding (pending) interests and a set of corresponding incoming interfaces.

An entity may also maintain an optional *Content Store* (CS) used for content caching. The timeout for cached content is specified in the `ExpiryTime` field of the content header. From here on, we use the terms *CS* and *cache* interchangeably.

Routers use the FIB to forward interests from consumers to producers, and the PIT – to forward content object messages along the reverse path to the consumer. More specifically, upon receiving an interest, a router R first checks its cache to see if it can satisfy this interest locally. Producer-originated digital signatures allow consumers to authenticate received content, regardless of the entity that actually served the content. Moreover, the Interest-Key Binding rule

---

[1]As we will discuss, IBAC does not replace access control based on content encryption. It is a complementary form of access control.

[2]Name matching is not exact in NDN [25].

[3]Currently, NDN interest messages do not provide an arbitrary-length payload and therefore cannot support the proposed IBAC scheme. However, if in the future the NDN interest format is modified to include a field similar to the CCNx payload, our IBAC scheme will become applicable.

[4]A physical entity, or host, can be both a consumer and producer of content.

(IKB) [9] enables routers to efficiently verify received content signatures before caching, in order to avoid content poisoning attacks [8]. Essentially, consumers and producers provide routers with the required trust context to enable efficient signature verification.

When a router R receives an interest for name N that is not cached and there are no pending interests for the same name in its PIT, R forwards the interest to the next hop according to its FIB. For each forwarded interest, R stores some amount of state information, including the name of the interest and the interface from which it arrived, so that content may be sent back to the consumer. If an interest for N arrives while there is already an entry for the same content name in the PIT, R only needs to update the arriving interface. When content is returned, R forwards it to all of the corresponding incoming interfaces, and the PIT entry is removed. If a router receives a content object without a matching PIT entry, the message is deemed unsolicited and subsequently discarded.

3. ACCESS CONTROL OVERVIEW

One key feature of CCN is that content is decoupled from its source; there is no notion of a secure channel between a consumer and producer. Consequently, ensuring that only authorized entities have access to content is a fundamental problem. In this section, we explore complementary approaches to access control: (1) content encryption and (2) interest name obfuscation and authorization.

3.1 Encryption-Based Access Control

The most intuitive solution to the access control problem is via encrypted content which can only be decrypted by authorized consumers possessing the appropriate decryption key(s). This enables content objects to be disseminated throughout the network since they cannot be decrypted by adversaries without the appropriate decryption key(s).

Many variations of this approach have been proposed [21, 18, 11, 23]. Kurihara et al. [17] generalized these specialized approaches in a framework called CCN-AC, an encryption-based access control framework to implement, specify, and enforce access policies. It uses CCN manifests[5] to encode access control specification information for a particular set of content objects. Consumers use information in the manifest to (1) request appropriate decryption keys and (2) use them to decrypt the content object(s) in question.

Outside of ICN, there have been many proposed access control frameworks based on encryption. Recently, access control in shared cloud storage or social network services, e.g., Google Drive, Dropbox, and Facebook, have generated much attention from the research community [26, 22, 24, 13]. For instance, Kamara et al. [14] modeled encryption-based access control framework for cloud storage. Microsoft PlayReady [1] is another popular access control framework for encrypted content dissemination over the Internet.

Despite its widespread use, encryption-based access control causes potentially prohibitive overhead for both producers and consumers. In most cases where hybrid encryption is used, it also requires keys to be distributed alongside each content object, which introduces another consumer-to-

producer message exchange. Also, encryption-based access control does not provide flexibility if content objects need to be modified by an intermediate service, e.g., a media encoding or enhancement application. Content encryption prevents such post-publication modifications without revealing the secret decryption key(s) to such services.

3.2 Interest-Based Access Control

Interest-based access control (IBAC) is an alternative technique, though not mutually exclusive with content encryption, for implementing access control in CCN. It is based on interest *name obfuscation* and *authorized disclosure*. Name obfuscation hides the *target* of an interest from eavesdroppers. As mentioned in [12], name obfuscation has no impact on the network since routers use only the binary representation of a name when indexing into PIT, CS, and FIB. As long as producers generate content objects with matching names, the network can seamlessly route interests and content objects with obfuscated names. However, interests with obfuscated names *must contain routable prefixes* so that the interests can still be forwarded from consumers to the producers. In other words, only a subset of name components (e.g., the suffix of the name) can be obfuscated.

Another goal of name obfuscation is to *prevent unauthorized users from creating interests for protected content*. In other words, if a particular consumer Cr is not permitted to access content with name N, Cr should not be able to generate $N' = f(N)$, where $f(\cdot)$ is some obfuscation function that maps N to an obfuscated name N'. For routing purposes, only the *suffix* of the name is obfuscated; there must exist a cleartext prefix that is used to route the interest with a partially obfuscated name to the intended producer. Possible obfuscation functions include keyed cryptographic hash functions and encryption algorithms. We explore both possibilities in this paper.

Authorized disclosure is the second element of IBAC. This property implies that any entity serving content must authorize any interest for said content before it is served. In this context, authorization is necessarily coupled with authentication so that the entity serving the content can determine the identity of the requesting consumer. Therefore, consumers must provide sufficient authentication information, e.g., via an interest signature. Thus, to implement authorized disclosure (in the presence of router caches), any entity serving content must (a) possess the information necessary to perform authentication and authorization checks and (b) actually verify the provided authentication information. This issue is discussed at length in Section 6.2. It is worth mentioning that disabling content caching defers authorized disclosure checks to producers. In this case, all interests will be forwarded to producers that posses the information needed to perform these checks. However, by itself, prohibiting content from being cached is *not* a form of access control and reduces the effectiveness of content retrieval.

Fotiou et. al. [5] proposed an access control mechanism similar to IBAC for non-ICN architectures, and conjectured that it should be applicable to ICNs. In [5], access control computation and overhead are delegated to a separate, non-cache entity. This entity, known as the access control provider, maintains access control policies given by a specific producer. Each content object has a pointer to a function that determines whether or not to serve the content to the requesting consumer, and the access control provider

---

[5]Manifests are special types of content that are used to provide structure and additional information to otherwise flat and simple content objects [19].

is responsible for evaluating this function. Content objects are stored at relaying parties, which are oblivious to the specific access control policy protecting the content objects. Similarly, the access control provider has no knowledge of the consumer requesting the content (for user privacy purposes), and just evaluates whether the relaying party should forward the content object. The cache, in this scenario, is not responsible for the extra computational overhead. This approach is different from our work in that we (1) maintain the association between content and authorization, and (2) provide routers with an efficient authorization verification method, thus eliminating the need for an external access control provider.

4. SECURITY MODEL

Let $\mathbb{U}(N)$ denote the set of authorized consumers for a content object with name N generated and controlled by a producer P, and let $\overline{\mathbb{U}}(N)$ be its complement, i.e., the set of all unauthorized consumers. Let $\mathsf{Path}(Cr, P)$ be the set of all routers on the path between the consumer $Cr \in \mathbb{U}(N)$ and P. We assume the existence of an adversary Adv who can deploy and compromise any router $R \notin \mathsf{Path}(Cr, P)$.[6] To keep this model realistic, we assume that the time to mount such an attack is non-negligible, i.e., longer than the average RTT for a single interest-content exchange. Table 1 summarizes the notation used in the rest of this paper.

Formally, we define Adv as a 3-tuple: $(\mathcal{P}_{\mathrm{Adv}} \setminus \{P\}, \mathcal{C}_{\mathrm{Adv}} \setminus \mathbb{U}(N), \mathcal{R}_{\mathrm{Adv}} \setminus \mathsf{Path}(Cr, P))$ where the components denote the set of compromised producers, consumers, and routers, respectively. If Adv controls a producer or a consumer then it is assumed to have complete and adaptive control over how they behave in an application session. Moreover, Adv can control all of the timing, format, and actual information of each content through compromised nodes and links.

Let Guess denote the event where Adv correctly recovers the obfuscated form of a content name. Let Bypass denote the event where Adv successfully bypasses the authorization check for a protected content object. We define the security of an IBAC scheme with respect to these two events as follows.

Definition 1. An IBAC scheme is *secure, but subject to replay attacks*, if $\Pr[\mathsf{Guess}] \leq \epsilon(\kappa)$ for any negligible function ϵ and a security parameter κ.

Definition 2. An IBAC scheme is *secure in the presence of replay attacks*, if $\Pr[\mathsf{Guess} + \mathsf{Bypass}] \leq \epsilon(\kappa)$ for any negligible function ϵ and a security parameter κ.

Replay attacks are artifacts of the environment when a CCN access control scheme is deployed. In other words, in networks where links are insecure, passive eavesdroppers can observe previously issued interests and replay them for protected content. Consequently, these attacks are considered orthogonal to the security of the underlying obfuscation scheme used for access control enforcement. The authorized disclosure element of IBAC is intended to prevent such replay attacks.

To justify our adversarial limitation to off-path routers, consider the following scenario. If Adv can compromise a router $R \in \mathsf{Path}(Cr, P)$, then Adv is able to observe *all*

---

[6]Any one of these actions can be performed adaptively, i.e., in response to status updates or based on observations.

Table 1: Relevant notation.

Notation	Description
Adv	Adversary
Cr	Consumer
P	Producer
prefix	Producer prefix
N	Content name in cleartext
N'	Obfuscated content name
$I[N]$	Interest with name N
CO	Content object
$CO[N]$	Content object with name N
$\mathsf{ID}(\cdot, \cdot)$	Key identifier function
$f(\cdot)$	Obfuscation function
$\mathsf{enc}(\cdot, \cdot), \mathsf{dec}(\cdot, \cdot)$	Symmetric-key encryption and decryption function
$\mathsf{Enc}(\cdot, \cdot), \mathsf{Dec}(\cdot, \cdot)$	Public-key encryption and decryption function
$\mathsf{H}(\cdot)$	Cryptographic hash function
$\mathbb{U}(N)$	Set of authorized consumers
$\mathbb{G}_i$	Access control group i
$k_{\mathbb{G}_i}$	Obfuscation key of group $\mathbb{G}_i$
$pk_{\mathbb{G}_i}^s, sk_{\mathbb{G}_i}^s$	Public and private signing key pair associated with group $\mathbb{G}_i$
κ	Global security parameter
$\mathbb{C}$	Set of all content objects
r, t	nonce and timestamp
$\mathbb{B}$	Nonce hash table

content that flows along this path. Therefore, we claim that on-path adversaries motivate access control schemes based on content encryption; as such, IBAC will not suffice. Moreover, we exclude adversaries capable of capturing interests and replaying them in other parts of the network – see Section 6.1 for details.

5. IBAC BY NAME OBFUSCATION

Recall that the intuition behind IBAC is that if consumers are not allowed to access certain content, they should not be able to issue a "correct" interest for it. Specifically, only a consumer $Cr \in \mathbb{U}(N)$ should be able to derive the obfuscated name N' of an interest requesting content with name N provided by producer P. In this section, we discuss two types of name obfuscation functions: (1) encryption functions and (2) hash functions.

5.1 Encryption-Based Name Obfuscation

Let $\mathsf{Enc}(k, N)$ be a *deterministic* encryption function which takes as input a key $k \in \{0,1\}^\kappa$ and an arbitrary long non-empty binary name string N, and generates an encrypted name N'. Let $\mathsf{Dec}(k, N')$ be the respective decryption function. With encryption, the goal is for authorized clients to encrypt components of a name so that the producer can perform decryption to identify and return the appropriate content object.[7] Obfuscation is based on knowledge of the encryption key and the content name under IBAC protection. In other words, even if an adversary knows the name N, it cannot generate N' since it does not possess the appropriate key.

To illustrate how encryption-based obfuscation would work, assume first that Cr uses k to generate N' as $N' = \mathsf{Enc}(k, N)$.

---

[7]Recall that a cleartext name prefix is needed to route the interest to the intended producer.

P then recovers N as $N = \mathsf{Dec}(k, N')$ to identify the content object in question and returns it with the *matching name* N' (not N). We prove the security of this obfuscation variant of IBAC (i.e., without authorized disclosure) in [7].

Supporting Multiple Access Groups: Thus far, we assumed that name encryption (obfuscation) keys are known to all authorized consumers in $\mathbb{U}(N)$. However, this might not be the case in practice. P might provide content under IBAC to several access groups each with different privileges.[8] Specifically, consumers in groups $\mathbb{G}_i(N) \subset \mathbb{U}(N)$, for $i = 1, 2, \ldots$, might be allowed access to different resources. Therefore, several obfuscation keys, one for each group, should be utilized. For notation simplicity, we refer to $\mathbb{G}_i(N)$ as $\mathbb{G}_i$. Note that in an extreme scenario, each group would only contain a single consumer, i.e., each individual consumer has a unique key used to access the content in question.

To decrypt the obfuscated name N', P must identify the obfuscation key used to generate N'. This can be achieved if such consumers specify an identifier for the key used in the interest. Such an identifier could simply be the digest of the obfuscation key $\mathsf{ID}_{\mathbb{G}_i} = \mathsf{H}(k_{\mathbb{G}_i})$, where $k_{\mathbb{G}_i}$ is $\mathbb{G}_i$'s encryption key. $\mathsf{ID}_{\mathbb{G}_i}$ can be included in the interest `Payload` field. Since matching in CCN is exact, $\mathsf{ID}_{\mathbb{G}_i}$ cannot be included in the interest name.

Recall that CCN interest messages, by design, do not carry any source information, which provides some degree of anonymity. However, including $\mathsf{ID}_{\mathbb{G}_i}$ enables interest linkability by eavesdroppers (malicious or not). In other words, $\mathsf{ID}_{\mathbb{G}_i}$ can reveal the access group identities to which consumers belong, but not the identities of the consumers themselves. If this linkability is an issue for applications, $\mathsf{H}(k_{\mathbb{G}_i})$ can be encrypted using P's public key pk^P in the form $\mathsf{ID}_{\mathbb{G}_i} = \mathsf{Enc}(pk^P, \mathsf{H}(k_{\mathbb{G}_i}))$.[9] Note that for two identifier values of the same group, i.e., with the same k, to be indistinguishable, $\mathsf{Enc}(\cdot, \cdot)$ must be secure against chosen plaintext attacks [15].

5.2 Hash-Based Name Obfuscation

Let $\mathsf{H}(k, N)$ be a keyed cryptographic hash function. The obfuscated name N' can be generated as $N' = \mathsf{H}(k, N)$ for some key $k \in \{0, 1\}^\kappa$. Since hash functions are one-way, producers must maintain a hash table that maps obfuscated names to the original content name, i.e., $\mathsf{M} : N' = \mathsf{H}(k, N) \to N$ for all deployed keys.[10] The size of this hash table is $\mathcal{O}(|\mathbb{K}| \times |\mathbb{C}|)$, where $\mathbb{K}$ is the set of all keys and $\mathbb{C}$ is set of all content objects generated or published by P under IBAC protection. This approach provides the same benefits of encryption-based name obfuscation, however, it incurs additional computation and storage overhead at the producer. Thus, while keyed hash functions are viable for

name obfuscation, deterministic encryption is a much better approach.

6. SECURITY CONSIDERATIONS

In this section we discuss the security of IBAC with respect to the adversary model described in Section 4.

6.1 Replay Attacks

Regardless of the obfuscation function used, both previously described IBAC schemes are susceptible to replay attacks. This is because both obfuscation functions are deterministic. Therefore, an eavesdropper $\mathsf{Adv} \in \bar{\mathbb{U}}(N)$ could issue an interest with a captured N' and receive the corresponding content under IBAC protection from either the producer or a router cache. In other words, the same "feature" that makes it possible for authorized consumers to fetch IBAC-protected content from router caches also makes it susceptible to replay attacks.

Such replay attacks are problematic in many access control systems. Standard countermeasures include the use of random, per-message nonces or timestamps. Nonces help ensure that each message is unique, whereas timestamps protect against interests being replayed at later points in time. Thus, to mitigate replay attacks, we use both nonces and timestamps. In particular, each consumer $Cr \in \mathbb{U}(N)$ must issue an interest with (1) name N', (2) a randomly generated nonce r, and (3) a fresh timestamp t. The reason why we use both nonces and timestamps is to allow for loosely synchronized clocks and unpredictable network latencies. Note that if (1) clocks of consumers, producers, and involved routers in IBAC can be perfectly synchronized, and (2) network latencies can be accurately predicted, only timestamps are sufficient for replay detection. Moreover, since nonces and timestamps serve a purpose which is orthogonal to content identification and message routing, they are included in the interest payload.

Consumer nonces are random κ-bit values. If a router receives a duplicate nonce, it can safely assume that the corresponding interest is replayed and should be dropped. Let w be a time window associated with authorized content.[11] To determine if a duplicate nonce was received, producers (or caches) must maintain a collection of nonces for each such content. In other words, this historical information is necessary to prevent replay attacks. Timestamps themselves are not stored, they are only used to determine if the received interest is issued within the acceptable time window w. Once this time window elapses, all of the stored nonces are erased and the content is subsequently flushed from the cache.

Although using nonces and timestamps allows detection of replayed interests, Adv capturing interests can still use their obfuscated names N' to fabricate another interest with legitimate r and t values. Therefore, we also stipulate that r and t should be authenticated via a digital signature; their signature σ is also included in the interest `Payload` field. In order to bind r and t to their corresponding interest, N' is also included in the signature computation. σ generation and verification should be performed using the public and private key pairs associated with each access group $\mathbb{G}_i$.

---

[8]We assume that each content object is only accessible by a single access group. However, this assumption will be relaxed later in the paper.

[9]Since a consumer cannot be expected to know the router from which content will be served, it is not plausible for them to encrypt these IDs with the public key of a (set of) router(s).

[10]Producers do not have to keep hash tables for all *possible* keys of size κ, only tables of keys used by producers and issued to access groups.

[11]Determining the proper value of w is outside the scope of this paper. However, a logical approach is for routers to use the lifetime of authorized content as w.

After adding nonces, timestamps, and a signature, interest `Payload` fields take the following form:

$$\texttt{Payload} = \left(\mathsf{ID}_{\mathbb{G}_i}, r, t, \sigma = \mathsf{Sign}_{sk_{\mathbb{G}_i}^s}\left(N'||\mathsf{ID}_{\mathbb{G}_i}||r||t\right)\right)$$

where $\mathsf{ID}_{\mathbb{G}_i}$ is the identity of group $\mathbb{G}_i$, and $sk_{\mathbb{G}_i}^s$ is a signing key distributed to all consumers in $\mathbb{G}_i$. To verify σ, the matching public key $pk_{\mathbb{G}_i}^s$ must be obtained. For the remainder of this paper, we use the term *authorization information* to refer to all information included in interest `Payload` fields for the purpose of supporting IBAC.

One alternative to digital signatures would be to use a keyed hash or a Message Authentication Code function such as (HMAC) [16]. In this case, consumers and routers would need to share the key used in the HMAC computation. This means that either consumers or producers need to distribute HMAC keys to all involved routers. This, however, is problematic for two main reasons: (1) compromising routers leads to HMAC keys leakage, and, more importantly, (2) if consumers provide routers with these keys, the former need to know the set of routers that their interests traverse before issuing them. Furthermore, since HMAC keys should only be shared among involved entities, i.e., Cr and all routers on $\mathsf{Path}(Cr, P)$, they must be distributed securely. Regardless of the distribution method used, this incurs extra overhead and complexity compared to simply including, in cleartext, signature verification (public) keys in content objects.

Finally, consider the following scenario where two routers R_1 and R_2 cache content object $CO[N']$ which is under IBAC protection. Assume that consumer Cr requests $CO[N']$ by sending an interest $I[N']$ with valid authorization information that includes r and t. Assume that $I[N']$ is satisfied from R_1's cache. At the same time, Adv, an eavesdropper between Cr and R_1, records $I[N']$. In this case, Adv can replay $I[N']$ to R_2 and receive $CO[N']$ from the cache since routers do not synchronize stored nonces. Therefore, there is no way for R_2 to know that r and t were already used at R_1. One way of solving this problem is to have routers share used nonces lists for each content under IBAC they serve from cache. For this method to be effective, such nonces lists need to be securely shared with every single router in the network. This might not be feasible in large networks such as the Internet. Another approach is to have more accurate synchronized clocks allowing a smaller time window for the aforementioned attack to be carried out.

6.2 Authorized Content-Key Binding Rule

Although the aforementioned method for generating authorization information mitigates replay attacks, it also raises several questions. Firstly, how does a router efficiently verify the signature in interest `Payload` fields? Secondly, and perhaps more importantly, if a router is able to *obtain* the key(s) necessary to verify this signature, how can the router be sure that such key(s) can be trusted?

To address these problems we propose a mutual trust framework for authorized disclosure. Ghali et al. [9] first studied the problem of trust in NDN, and ICNs in general, as a means of preventing content poisoning attacks [8, 6]. Even if routers can verify content signatures before replying from their cache, it does not mean that said content is actually *authentic*. Ghali et al. observed that this verification process requires insight about trust in public keys (used in verification) that is only known to applications. Consequently, this requires that all interests must either supply

---

Algorithm 1 InterestGeneration

1: **INPUT:** routable_prefix, N, $k_{\mathbb{G}_i}$, $pk_{\mathbb{G}_i}^s$, $sk_{\mathbb{G}_i}^s$, κ
2: $\mathsf{ID}_{\mathbb{G}_i} \leftarrow \mathsf{H}(k_{\mathbb{G}_i})$
3: $N' \leftarrow /\texttt{routable\_prefix}/f(k_{\mathbb{G}_i}, \mathsf{Suffix}(N, \texttt{routable\_prefix}))$
4: $r \xleftarrow{\$} \{0,1\}^\kappa$
5: $t \leftarrow \mathsf{CurrentTime}()$
6: $\sigma \leftarrow \mathsf{Sign}_{sk_{\mathbb{G}_i}^s}(N'||\mathsf{ID}_{\mathbb{G}_i}||r||t)$
7: $\texttt{Payload} := (\mathsf{ID}_{\mathbb{G}_i}, r, t, \sigma)$
8: **return** $I[N'] := (N', \texttt{Payload})$

Algorithm 2 ContentObjectGeneration

1: **INPUT:** $I[N'] := (\texttt{routable\_prefix}, N', \texttt{Payload})$
2: $(\mathsf{ID}_{\mathbb{G}_i}, r, t, \sigma) := \texttt{Payload}$
3: $pk_{\mathbb{G}_i}^s \leftarrow \mathsf{LoopupVerificationKeyForID}(\mathsf{ID}_{\mathbb{G}_i})$
4: **if** $\mathsf{Verify}_{pk_{\mathbb{G}_i}^s}(\sigma)$ **then**
5: $\quad k_{\mathbb{G}_i}^e \leftarrow \mathsf{LookupDecryptionKeyForID}(\mathsf{ID}_{\mathbb{G}_i})$
6: $\quad N \leftarrow \mathsf{Dec}(k_{\mathbb{G}_i}^e, \mathsf{Suffix}(N', \texttt{routable\_prefix}))$
7: $\quad \texttt{data} \leftarrow \mathsf{RetrieveContent}(N)$
8: $\quad$ **return** $CO[N'] := (N', \texttt{data}, pk_{\mathbb{G}_i}^s)$
9: **else**
10: $\quad$ Drop $I[N']$
11: **end if**

---

(1) the hash of the public key used to verify the signature, or (2) the hash of the requested content. In effect, the interest reflects the trust context of the issuing consumer in a form enforceable at the network layer. This framework can be viewed as one-way trust of content by routers. We extend this framework to allow producers to distribute information about authorized consumers, which can also be enforceable at the network layer. This allows routers to make trust decisions about individual interests.

Recall that in order for routers to verify which interests are authorized to access cached content protected under IBAC, the signature in `Payload` must be verified. To achieve this, producers should include the appropriate verification key with each IBAC-protected content object. To better understand this, assume the following scenario. Consumer $Cr \in \mathbb{G}_i$, for $\mathbb{G}_i \subset \mathbb{U}(N)$, requests content with name N by issuing an interest with obfuscated name N', and $\mathsf{ID}_{\mathbb{G}_i}$, r, t and σ in `Payload` as described in Section 6.1. Assume that the matching content is not cached anywhere in the network. Once this interest reaches the producer P, the latter verifies σ and replies with the content that also includes the verifying key $pk_{\mathbb{G}_i}^s$.[12] Router R will then cache $pk_{\mathbb{G}_i}^s$ along with the content itself. Once another interest for N' is received, R uses the cached $pk_{\mathbb{G}_i}^s$ to verify σ and returns the corresponding cached content object.

We formalize this in the following policy, denoted as the Authorized Content-Key Binding (ACKB) rule:

> **ACKB:** Cached content protected under IBAC must reflect the verification key associated with the authorization policy.

The protocol for IBAC-protected content retrieval relies on this rule. Algorithms 1 and 2 outline the interest and content object generation procedures. Note that the function $\mathsf{Suffix}(N, \texttt{routable\_prefix})$ returns all name components

---

[12]The content object signature must also be computed over $pk_{\mathbb{G}_i}^s$ to bind it to the message.

Algorithm 3 RouterAuthorizationCheck

```
1: INPUT: I[N′], cached CO[N′], 𝔹
2: (ID_{𝔾_i}, r, t, σ) := Payload
3: (N′, ·, pk^s_{𝔾_i}) := CO[N′]
4: if 𝔹[N′] contains r then
5:     Drop I[N′]; return Fail
6: else
7:     if Timestamp t is invalid then
8:         Drop I[N′]; return Fail
9:     else
10:        if Verify_{pk^s_{𝔾_i}}(σ) then
11:            𝔹[N′] := 𝔹[N′] ∪ r
12:            return Pass
13:        else
14:            Drop I[N′]; return Fail
15:        end if
16:    end if
17: end if
```

of N except the ones included in routable_prefix.[13] Also, the router verification procedure is outlined in Algorithm 3. If this procedure returns Pass, then the content object found in the cache is forwarded downstream to the associated interface. Note that Algorithms 1, 2, and 3 use obfuscation key $k_{𝔾_i}$ and signing key pairs $(pk^s_{𝔾_i}, sk^s_{𝔾_i})$. For completeness, a complete sequence diagram showing multiple interest-content exchanges is shown in Figure 1. Both consumers belong to the same access group, i.e., $Cr_1, Cr_2 \in 𝔾_i$.

In [7], we show that this mutual trust framework for authorized disclosure enables IBAC with stronger security guarantees in the presence of replay attacks.

6.3 Serving Content to Multiple Access Groups

One problem with encryption-based name obfuscation occurs when a content object with name N is accessible by different groups. According to Algorithms 1 and 2, the obfuscated name $N′$ contains a suffix encrypted with keys associated with each access group. Therefore, a single content object might have several names depending on the number of groups authorized to access it. Since routers employs exact matching for cache lookup[14], several copies of the same content could possibly be cached.

To solve this problem, content objects should have the exact same name regardless of access control groups permitted access. This can be achieved using the hash-based name obfuscation function described in Section 5.2. However, cached content needs to contain *every* authorization signature verification key that could be used to access said content. In other words, producers need to provide all possible public keys that can be used to access the content under IBAC protection. Consider the following scenario: a content object $CO[N]$ is accessible by two access groups $𝔾_i$ and $𝔾_j$. In this case, the producer needs to provide both $pk^s_{𝔾_i}$ and $pk^s_{𝔾_j}$ with $CO[N′]$, i.e.,

$$CO[N′] := (N′, \text{data}, pk^s_{𝔾_i}, pk^s_{𝔾_j})$$

Whenever a router R caching $CO[N′]$ receives an interest issued by a consumer in any of the authorized access groups, R uses the group identity included in the Payload field to determine $σ$'s verification key.

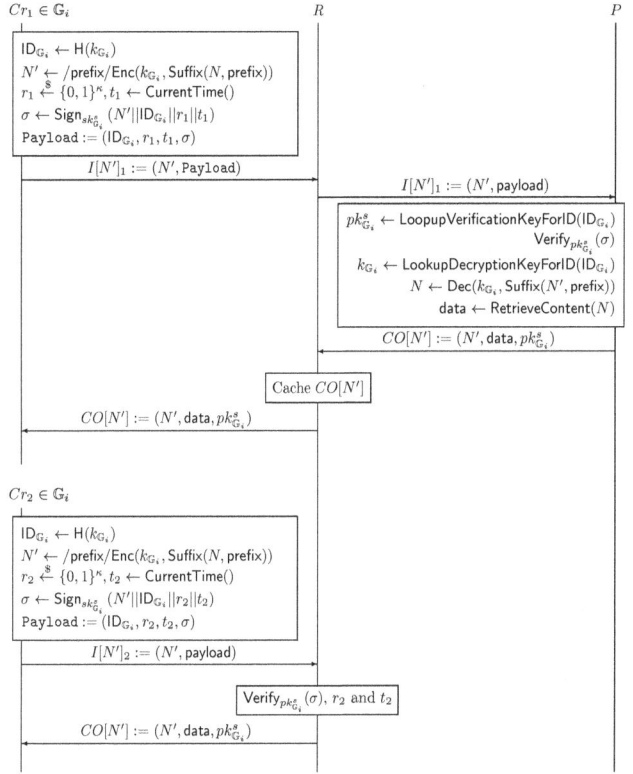

---

[13]For instance, Suffix(/edu/uci/ics/home.html, /edu/uci/) would return ics/home.html.
[14]In CCN, not in NDN.

Figure 1: Consumer and producer exchanges for IBAC-protected content.

Note that content object sizes might increase significantly depending on how many groups are allowed access. We do not discuss this issue further, since the trade-off between having multiple cached versions of the same content and having longer content objects carrying all verification keys is ultimately the application's decision.

6.4 IBAC Variations

We do not claim that any of the IBAC variations discussed above is superior to another. Each has its own strengths and weaknesses. However, to help guide the decision about which variation to use, we make the following claims based on the application needs and assumptions. Note that some claims provide privacy as well as access control.

1. If *replay attacks* are not a concern, then consumers only need to use a name obfuscation function and include their group identity in the Payload.

2. If *replay attacks* are plausible and *name privacy* is a concern, then name obfuscation must be used and authorization information, as described in Section 6.1, must be included in interest Payload fields.

3. If *replay attacks* are plausible but *name privacy* is not a concern, then only authorization information is sufficient.

Claim 3 might seem counterintuitive with the idea of IBAC. Recall, however, that router authorization checks prevent unauthorized consumers from retrieving cached content under IBAC protection. Even if content name is not obfus-

153

cated, Adv cannot forge `Payload` authorization information, and therefore cannot violate IBAC protection guarantees.

6.5 Revocation

Generally speaking, revocation is a challenge in all access control schemes involving secrets shared among group members. Recall that all consumers belonging to the same access control group in IBAC share the same obfuscation keys. If one of them leaves the group[15], the producer will have to create a new key and distribute it to all remaining authorized consumers. We will not discuss this issue further since we believe it is not part of the core access control *protocol*.

Moreover, in-network caching can cause IBAC content to be accessed by revoked consumers. Assume content $CO[N]$ is under access control and has a cached version in router R. Assume consumer Cr, connected (directly or indirectly) to R, is authorized to access $CO[N]$. However, while $CO[N]$ is cached, Cr's access is revoked. At the same time, the latter sends an interest requesting $CO[N]$. In this case, R will grant access and reply with $CO[N]$ from its cache. This is due to the fact that the cached version of $CO[N]$ is not updated with the correct authorization information (i.e., verification key(s)). However, this can be solved by setting the `ExpiryTime` field of $CO[N]$ to a value that reflects consumer revocation frequency.

Online revocation protocols, such as OCSP [20], would induce extra communication between R and P, which nearly defeats the purpose of the cache entirely. In this case, R would be better suited forwarding the interest upstream to P. Another option for the producer would be to distribute certificate revocation lists (CRLs) [4] with every fresh content. This, however, introduces further issues for routers and consumers. Firstly, routers would need to store CRLs and keep them updated frequently. Secondly, authorized consumers would need their own public and private key pair to compute σ. Finally, routers would need to perform additional verifications against the CLR. Overall, this approach suffers from increased storage, consumer management, computation, and bandwidth complexity.

7. ANALYSIS AND EVALUATION

In this section, we analyze the overhead induced by each variation of the proposed IBAC scheme.

7.1 Computational Overhead

We first focus on the computational overhead for routers and producers. This overhead is captured in terms of cryptographic and data structure operations, e.g., signature verification and hash table lookup costs.[16] Table 2 summarizes these results. To further understand the computational overhead, we compare two cases: (1) when routers perform authorization checks, and (2) when they do not. Let $\tau_{overhead} = \tau_{check} + \tau_{verify} + \tau_{update}$ be the overhead induced by the authorization check when routers receive interests, where τ_{check} is the time required to check for nonce duplication and timestamp staleness, τ_{verify} is the time to

verify the `Payload` signature, and T_{update} is the time to update the nonce data collection. Since cache lookup and interest forwarding are performed regardless of whether or not routers perform authorization checks, we omit them from this equation. Similarly, τ_{check} and τ_{update} are negligible when compared to the cost of signature verification τ_{verify}; thus, they are also excluded.

A router incurs a computational cost of $\tau_{overhead}$ for every received interest requesting content under IBAC protection. Therefore, we quantify $\tau_{overhead}$ by measuring the time it takes to perform a single signature verification. We also experiment with batch verification techniques to better amortize the cost of signature verification across series of interests. While this naturally increases content retrieval latency as signatures are accumulated in case of batch verification, it reduces router computational overhead. Whether or not to use batch verification is up to the router's discretion. Furthermore, batch verification requires that IBAC-protected content objects for which interests are being verified cannot be evicted from the cache while the batch is collected. Table 3 shows the amount of improvement using a variety of signature verification algorithms. Note that, when modeling interest arrival rates using a Poisson distribution, both individual and batch signature verification incur nearly the same overhead in certain conditions, as we will show below.

Denial of service (DoS) is an obvious concern if routers perform authorization checks (the interest rate decays to 0 in our experiments as the need for verification increases). Let λ be the rate of arrival interests for IBAC-protected content cached in router R, and let μ be the service rate for interests, i.e., the rate at which interests are processed (parsed, verified, etc.). If $\mu < \lambda$, then the router will be over encumbered with interests to process [10]. We envision that in legitimate scenarios without malicious entities generating interests with fake authorization information, only a small percentage δ of arrival interests will be requesting content under IBAC protection. To assess how susceptible routers are to DoS attacks induced by IBAC authorization checks, we empirically analyze the effect of δ on the interest service rate of a router. These service rates, which use different signature verification techniques – individual and batch – denoted μ_S and μ_B, respectively, are shown in Figure 2.

We assume that interests arrive at a base rate of $\lambda_1 = 40$ [3]; larger values for λ are provided to see at which point $\mu < \lambda$ due to authorization checks. By the exponential property of the Poisson process, μ is calculated as follows:

$$\mu = \frac{1-\delta}{\tau_{process}} + \frac{\delta}{\tau_{process} + \tau_{verify}},$$

where $\tau_{process}$ represents interest processing time not including signature verification[17], and τ_{verify} is the time required to perform individual or batch signature verification. In our experiment, we assume a constant $\tau_{process} = 0.005s$ and only vary τ_{verify}. To do so, we assume a key size of 1024b, batch size of 10, and signature size of 512KB. According to Table 3, this results in $\tau_{verify} = 0.599s$ and $\tau_{verify} = 0.322s$ for individual and batch verification, respectively. Our experiments show that the decay of μ as a function of δ is almost identical for both batch and verification techniques. This is due to the fact that only a small fraction of interests are affected by the verification step. Furthermore, our results show that

---

[15] For instance, consumers not renewing their subscription for a certain service.

[16] It is assumed that the cost of any additional checks necessary to determine if an interest requires further IBAC processing is negligible. For example, this check be done using a simple flag in the interest. Thus, this overhead is omitted from our estimates.

[17] $\tau_{process} = 1/mu$ for interests not requesting IBAC-protected content.

Table 2: Overview of per-interest IBAC-induced computational overhead for routers and producers.

IBAC Variation		IBAC-induced Computation Overhead	
		Routers	Producers
Name Obfuscation	Encryption	None	One decryption
	Hash	None	One hash table lookup
Interest Signatures	Encryption	One signature verification, one nonce and timestamp verification	One decryption, one signature verification, Two hash table lookups (decryption key and signing key resolution)
	Hash	One signature verification, one nonce and timestamp verification, one hash table lookup (signing key resolution)	One signature verification, three hash table lookups (decryption key, signing key and name resolution)

Table 3: Individual and batch ElGamal signature verification times.

Key Size	Batch Size	Sig. Size	Indiv. Time	Batch Time	Improved
1024b	10	512KB	0.599s	0.322s	46%
1024b	10	8MB	0.888s	0.615s	30%
1024b	50	512KB	2.918s	1.579s	46%
1024b	50	8MB	4.315s	2.991s	30%
2048b	10	512KB	4.065s	2.207s	46%
2048b	10	8MB	4.104s	2.269s	45%
2048b	50	512KB	20.081s	11.029s	45%
2048b	50	8MB	21.301s	12.536s	41%
3072b	10	512KB	12.406s	6.789s	45%
3072b	10	8MB	12.804s	7.122s	44%
3072b	50	512KB	60.174s	32.877s	45%
3072b	50	8MB	64.347s	35.601s	45%

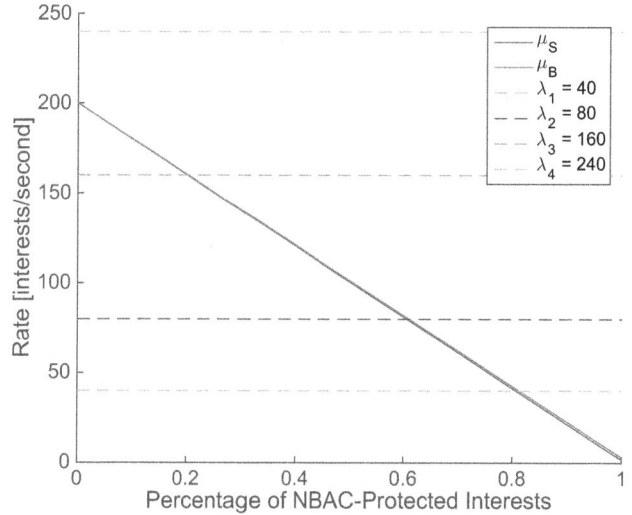

Figure 2: Interest service rates for various percentages of IBAC-protected interests.

$\mu > \lambda$ is true, i.e., the router servicing process is stable for reasonable interest arrival rates. Our experiments show that $\mu < \lambda$ when $\lambda = 160$ and $\delta \geq 0.2$. Moreover, when a Poisson process is assumed, both individual and batch signature verification perform similarly for small values of δ. However, batch signature verification prove to be advantageous in larger δ values. For instance, for $\delta = 0.2$, using batch verification provides less than 1% service rate improvement, where it provides 3% and 46% for δ values equal to 0.8 and 1, respectively.

7.2 Storage Overhead

Storage overhead varies from producer to router. If hash-based name obfuscation is used, producers incur the cost of maintaining a hash table to map obfuscated names to their original values. However, if content name contains variable name components, e.g., query string-like values in URIs, the hash table size can grow significantly since it has to contain all possible variations. Moreover, producers must bear the storage cost of IBAC access group keys if encryption-based obfuscation functions are used. Similarly, routers must bear the cost of storing variable-length tuples of key identities $\mathsf{ID}_{\mathbb{G}_i}$ and the actual verification keys $pk^s_{\mathbb{G}_i}$, along with a theoretically unbounded collection of nonces for each IBAC-protected content. Moreover, these storage costs are paid for every unique producer that generates IBAC content. Clearly, router finite storage capacities can thus be abused to mount DoS attacks.

7.3 Bandwidth Overhead

In terms of bandwidth overhead, each interest and content object is expanded to include additional authorization information, e.g., interest payloads with authorization information and content objects with authorization keys. Interests without authorization payloads will only increase (or decrease) by the expansion factor of the obfuscated name. If authorization payloads are included, then interest messages will grow by $|r| + |t| + |\sigma| + |\mathsf{ID}_{\mathbb{G}}|$, where $|r| = \kappa$. Content object $CO[N]$ grows with length $\sum_{i=1}^{L} |pk^s_{\mathbb{G}_i}|$, where L is the number of access groups allowed to access $CO[N]$ and $|pk^s_{\mathbb{G}_i}|$ is the public key size associated with group $\mathbb{G}_i$.

Note that, for interests, this increased overhead may cause them to grow beyond the MTU size, which would induce interest fragmentation. However, given that names may themselves be unbounded, this type fragmentation seems unavoidable in certain circumstances.

8. CONCLUSION

We studied the problem of access control in CCN. We proposed an Interest-Based Access Control (IBAC) scheme that supports hash- and encryption-based name obfuscation. We addressed the problem of replay attacks by formulating a mutual trust framework between producers and consumers – enforced in the network-layer – that enables routers to perform authorization checks before satisfying interests from cache. We assessed the computational, storage, and bandwidth overhead induced by each variant of the proposed IBAC scheme.

9. REFERENCES

[1] Microsoft PlayReady. http://www.microsoft.com/playready/.

[2] T. Berners-Lee, R. Fielding, and L. Masinter. RFC 3986: Uniform resource identifier (URI): Generic syntax. 2005.

[3] G. Carofiglio, M. Gallo, L. Muscariello, and D. Perino. Modeling data transfer in content-centric networking. In *ITC*, 2011.

[4] D. Cooper. RFC 3280: Internet X.509 public key infrastructure certificate and certificate revocation list (CRL) profile. 2008.

[5] N. Fotiou, G. F. Marias, and G. C. Polyzos. Access control enforcement delegation for information-centric networking architectures. In *ICN Workshop*, 2012.

[6] P. Gasti, G. Tsudik, E. Uzun, and L. Zhang. DoS DDoS in named-data networking. In *ICCCN*, 2013.

[7] C. Ghali, M. A. Schlosberg, G. Tsudik, and C. A. Wood. Interest-based access control for content centric networks (extended version). *arXiv*, 2015.

[8] C. Ghali, G. Tsudik, and E. Uzun. Needle in a haystack: Mitigating content poisoning in named-data networking. In *NDSS SENT Workshop*, 2014.

[9] C. Ghali, G. Tsudik, and E. Uzun. Network-layer trust in named-data networking. *CCR*, 2014.

[10] D. Gross. *Fundamentals of queueing theory*. John Wiley & Sons, 2008.

[11] M. Ion, J. Zhang, and E. M. Schooler. Toward content-centric privacy in ICN: Attribute-based encryption and routing. In *ICN*, 2013.

[12] V. Jacobson, D. K. Smetters, J. D. Thornton, M. F. Plass, N. H. Briggs, and R. L. Braynard. Networking named content. In *CoNext*, 2009.

[13] S. Jahid, P. Mittal, and N. Borisov. EASiER: Encryption-based access control in social networks with efficient revocation. In *ASIACCS*, 2011.

[14] S. Kamara and K. Lauter. Cryptographic cloud storage. In *FC*, 2010.

[15] J. Katz and Y. Lindell. *Introduction to modern cryptography*. CRC Press, 2014.

[16] H. Krawczyk, R. Canetti, and M. Bellare. RFC 2104: HMAC: Keyed-hashing for message authentication. 1997.

[17] J. Kurihara, C. Wood, and E. Uzuin. An encryption-based access control framework for content-centric networking. *IFIP*, 2015.

[18] S. Misra, R. Tourani, and N. E. Majd. Secure content delivery in information-centric networks: Design, implementation, and analyses. In *ICN*, 2013.

[19] M. Mosko, I. Solis, and E. Uzun. CCN 1.0 protocol architecture.

[20] M. Myers, R. Ankney, A. Malpani, S. Galperin, and C. Adams. RFC 2560: Online certificate status protocol - OCSP. 1999.

[21] D. K. Smetters, P. Golle, and J. D. Thornton. CCNx access control specifications. Technical report, PARC, July 2010.

[22] G. Wang, Q. Liu, and J. Wu. Hierarchical attribute-based encryption for fine-grained access control in cloud storage services. In *CCS*, 2010.

[23] C. A. Wood and E. Uzun. Flexible end-to-end content security in CCN. In *CCNC*, 2014.

[24] S. Yu, C. Wang, K. Ren, and W. Lou. Achieving secure, scalable, and fine-grained data access control in cloud computing. In *INFOCOM*, 2010.

[25] L. Zhang, A. Afanasyev, J. Burke, V. Jacobson, P. Crowley, C. Papadopoulos, L. Wang, B. Zhang, et al. Named data networking. *CCR*, 2014.

[26] L. Zhou, V. Varadharajan, and M. Hitchens. Achieving secure role-based access control on encrypted data in cloud storage. *Transactions on Information Forensics and Security*, 2013.

Moderator-controlled Information Sharing by Identity-based Aggregate Signatures for Information Centric Networking

Tohru Asami
The University of Tokyo
Tokyo 113-8656, Japan
asami@akg.t.u-
tokyo.ac.jp

Byambajav Namsraijav,
Yoshihiko Kawahara
The University of Tokyo
Tokyo 113-8656, Japan
{byambajav,
kawahara}@akg.t.u-
tokyo.ac.jp

Kohei Sugiyama,
Atsushi Tagami
KDDI R&D Laboratories
Saitama, 356-8502 Japan
{ko-sugiyama,
tagami}@kddilabs.jp

Tomohiko Yagyu
NEC Corporation
Kawasaki, 221-8666 Japan
yagyu@cp.jp.nec.com

Kenichi Nakamura
Panasonic Corporation
Tokyo 105-8301, Japan
nakamura.kenken@
jp.panasonic.com

Toru Hasegawa
Osaka University
Osaka, 565-0871, Japan
t-hasegawa@ist.osaka-
u.ac.jp

ABSTRACT

Information sharing services have been provided via common servers, which not only relay messages but also sometimes moderate them. A peer can become a moderator and control the distribution of messages belonging to his private message group. However, the physical transfer of a message is usually out of the peer's control. Originator-signed signatures inherent in Information Centric Networking assure the integrity and provenance of messages exchanged among peers, which makes it possible to realize moderator-controlled information sharing in which a peer can become a moderator and control the distribution of his private message group as a trustable server. However, moderated content requires multiple signatures, which increases the size of the exchanged message and is inadequate, especially for short message services. We propose the use of Identity-Based Aggregate Signatures (IBAS) to decrease this overhead, and provide a proof-of-concept IBAS implementation for Named Data Networking (NDN). We also compare the performance of the proposed IBAS implementation with existing RSA signatures. An overhead reduction of approximately 45% to 60% compared to RSA signatures is achieved for an NDN packet in the proposed configuration. Because of the properties of the identity-based signature[24], this IBAS implementation is robust and works even during a disaster or when a trustable centralized server is not online.

ICN'15, September 30–October 2, 2015, San Francisco, CA. USA.
ⓒ 2015 ACM. ISBN 978-1-4503-3855-4/15/09 ...$15.00.
DOI: http://dx.doi.org/10.1145/2810156.2810163.

Categories and Subject Descriptors

C.2.1 [**Computer-communication networks**]: Network architecture and design-distributed networks

General Terms

Performance, Design

Keywords

named data networking; identity-based aggregate signatures; moderator-controlled information sharing

1. INTRODUCTION

Information sharing through moderators has been common since the 1980's. NetNews [15] and mailing lists such as LISTSERV [16] and Majordomo [2] are typical examples. They, as well as many modern social networking services (SNSs) such as Facebook [11], have a functional division of their operations between administrators and moderators. The tasks of the administrator in these services are to change list or newsgroup settings and to add moderators and subscribers, whereas the tasks of the administrator in modern social networking services (SNSs) such as Facebook [11] are to, for example, adding/deleting peers, content storage of uploaded messages, and time-stamping received messages. The moderator's role in NetNews is to supervise posted messages to the list or the newsgroup, and the posted message will not be sent to the subscribers unless approved by the moderator, whereas each SNS peer in the SNS controls the circulation of the moderator's messages by creating friend lists or groups, which are lists of friends gathered based on intention. Once created, each circulation is usually performed without any human interventions. A server managed by an administrator is considered to be a trustable message exchange point among related peers or a kind of portal site for this SNS that is known to everybody in the serving network. In other words, the SNS administrator can observe any message sent to the public or to a specific friend group. From a privacy point of view, a future SNS service should give a peer the discretion to decide whether his messages are physically transferred only within his own closed-user group without the help of the SNS administrator's server.

Originator-signed messaging introduced by Information-Centric Networking (ICN) [28] makes it possible for each peer to become not only a moderator but also a trustable server for his friend lists by assuring the integrity and provenance of the received content. We refer to this as moderator-controlled information sharing (MIS). An MIS service is served by several moderators, and this decentralized MIS is robust in a disaster scenario, allowing safety confirmations to be exchanged among family members [26]. Such confirmations will be successful if (1) the moderator for this family exists on a network in the disaster area and (2) authentication can be performed without a trustable server online. Condition (1) will be frequently satisfied because such a friendship relation is often geographically constrained. Thus, if condition (2) is satisfied, ICN-based MIS can not only solve the privacy concerns of the current SNS but can also increase the robustness of the service as a lifeline infrastructure.

However, at least two signatures are required to convince the subscriber of the authenticities of the content publisher and the moderator. Attaching multiple signatures to a single short message increases the message size and may not be suitable for human-generated content exchanges, such as Facebook, from the point of view that the specification of short message service (SMS) by GSM/W-CDMA requires the number of message characters to be at most 140 [1]. Thus, in addition to condition (2), a method of minimizing the *Data* packet size in the above-mentioned moderator-controlled short message sharing is needed. In order to solve the above-mentioned problems, we propose the use of Identity-Based Aggregate Signatures (IBAS) [13] as yet another signature scheme for Named Data Networking (NDN), while maintaining its compatibility with the normal version of NDN. We implement this signature scheme on an existing open-source NDN implementation ndn-cxx [18] and compare its performance with the traditional Public Key Infrastructure RSA signatures. Although there have been proposals for using IBS/IBE in NDN [29], [22], to the best of our knowledge, our proposal is the first implementation of IBAS in any kind of network.

The remainder of the present paper is organized as follows: Section 2 introduces NDN, Identity-Based Aggregate Signatures, and research related to NDN security. Section 3 presents the definition of ICN-based MIS and discusses inherent problems, followed by the proposed solution in Section 4, the implementation design for NDN in Section 5, experiments in Section 6, and a discussions in Section 7. Finally, we conclude the paper in Section 8.

2. RELATED RESEARCH

This section presents a brief overview of the technologies related to our ICN-based MIS.

2.1 Named Data Networking (NDN)

Overview

Named Data Networking (NDN) [28] is a type of ICN in which communication is based on named contents, rather than host addresses, and every named content is identified, addressed, and retrieved by its name instead of its physical location (i.e., host address). In the conventional Internet, security is achieved in end-to-end connections. On the other hand, NDN routers cache contents and serve contents directly from themselves in order to achieve efficient content delivery. Therefore, in NDN, security is built into contents, rather than connections between end hosts. Consequently, content publishers must sign all of their contents, i.e., any content in NDN has a signature to prove its provenance and integrity.

Packet Structure

As specified in [20], NDN's packet encoding employs the Type-Length-Value (TLV) format [21]. An NDN packet is primarily a collection of TLVs inside a top TLV element (either *Interest* or *Data* packet), and each sub-TLV can also be further nested. *Interest* consists of five TLV elements, i.e., *Name*, *Selectors*, *Nonce*, *Scope*, and *InterestLifetime*, whereas *Data* consists of four TLV elements, i.e., *Name*, *MetaInfo*, *Content*, and *Signature*. The NDN packet does not have a fixed packet header.

Forwarding

In order to obtain content, a consumer placed the name of the desired data into an *Interest* packet and sends it out. Routers use this name to forward the *Interest* toward the intended data producer(s). The forwarding decisions at routers in this step are based on their Forwarding Information Base (FIB). While forwarding the *Interest* packet, the routers register it in their Pending Interest Table (PIT). Once the interest reaches a node that has the requested data in its Content Store (CS), the node will return a *Data* packet that has the same name as the received *Interest* and contains the requested content. This *Data* packet also contains a signature that proves that the data was indeed produced by the intended producer and has the name requested by the *Interest*. The returned *Data* packet follows in reverse the path taken by the *Interest*. On the reverse path, routers refer to their PIT to forward the returning *Data* packet to the requesting consumer. Also, the routers cache the *Data* into their CS so that they can serve it directly upon further requests.

2.2 Existing Security Proposals in NDN

In this subsection, we introduce the current key management models. Current NDN testbed key management [3] uses a simple hierarchical trust model with a root key, which signs the keys for each site. Then, the sites' keys are used to sign their users' keys, and the users' keys are used to sign their devices (Fig. 1). This trust model is essentially the same as the traditional Public Key Infrastructure (PKI) model, in which the testbed root is equivalent to a widely trusted global certification authority (CA), and the sites are equivalent to middle layer CAs. In order to verify a *Data* packet's signature signed by the ordinary RSA or Elliptic Curve Digital Signature Algorithm (ECDSA), the verifier must trace all of the parents' public keys and certificates until reaching the NDN testbed root.

There is an approach to using a Web-of-Trust in conjunction with self-certifying names for a fragmented (mobile) networks scenario [23], where connectivity to centralized en-

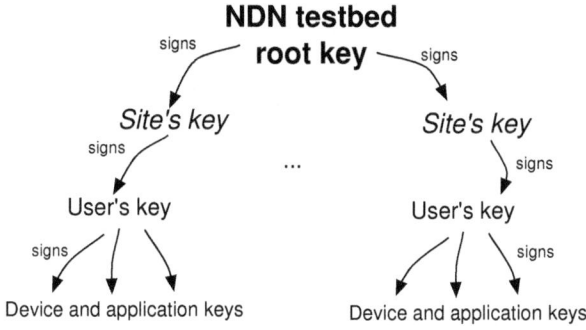

Figure 1: Key trust model on the NDN testbed [3]

tities and authentication servers are not available. However, the signature scheme itself is as described above.

2.3 Identity-based Aggregate Signatures (IBAS)

Boneh et al. proposed the concept of aggregate signatures in [4], in which it is possible to aggregate n signatures on n distinct messages from n distinct users into a single aggregated signature of constant size. This single signature (and the n original messages) will convince the verifier that the n users did indeed sign the n original messages (i.e., user i signed message m_i for $i = 1, ..., n$). The main motivation for using aggregate signatures is compactness. However, in the case of a non-identity-based aggregate signature scheme, such as that proposed in [4], verification of an aggregated signature requires the verifier to obtain the public keys of all participating signers. Furthermore, in order to verify the public keys, the verifier may need to obtain their parent certificates. Since the sizes of public keys are as large as those of signatures, the necessity for obtaining public keys and parent certificates largely negates the advantage of aggregate signatures.

Gentry et al. proposed an Identity-Based Aggregate Signatures (IBAS) scheme [13] to solve the above shortcoming of aggregate signatures. The IBAS scheme combines the Identity-Based Signature (IBS) and the aggregate signature. In the IBAS scheme, the verification information (apart from the description of who signed which message, i.e., the list of identities and their messages) consists only of a single aggregate signature and the public parameters given by the Private Key Generator (PKG). The following describes in detail the construction of the IBAS scheme (using the same notation as [13]). Compared to a normal non-aggregate IBS scheme, such as CC-IBS [7], the IBAS scheme has an extra **Aggregation** step.

Setup: The Private Key Generator (PKG)
(a) generates (elliptic curve) groups $\mathbb{G}_1$ and $\mathbb{G}_2$ of prime order q and an admissible bilinear pairing $\hat{e} : \mathbb{G}_1 \times \mathbb{G}_1 \to \mathbb{G}_2$;
(b) chooses an arbitrary generator element $P \in \mathbb{G}_1$;
(c) chooses a random $s \in \mathbb{Z}/q\mathbb{Z}$ and calculates $Q = sP$;
(d) chooses three cryptographic hash functions: $H_1, H_2 : \{0,1\}^* \to \mathbb{G}_1$ and $H_3 : \{0,1\}^* \to \mathbb{Z}/q\mathbb{Z}$.
As a result, the system parameters are $params = (\mathbb{G}_1, \mathbb{G}_2, \hat{e}, P, Q, H_1, H_2, H_3)$, and the PKG's secret key is $s \in \mathbb{Z}/q\mathbb{Z}$.

Private Key Extraction: By authenticating itself to the PKG, the client with identity ID_i receives the values of $P_{i,j} = H_1(\mathsf{ID}_i, j)$ for $j \in \{0, 1\}$.

Individual Signing: The first signer chooses a unique string (state information) w that has never been used before. In order to sign a message m_i, the signer with identity ID_i:
(a) computes $P_w = H_2(w) \in \mathbb{G}_1$;
(b) computes $c_i = H_3(m_i, \mathsf{ID}_i, w) \in \mathbb{Z}/q\mathbb{Z}$;
(c) generates a random element $r_i \in \mathbb{Z}/q\mathbb{Z}$;
(d) calculates the signature tuple (w, S_i', T_i'), where $S_i' = r_i P_w + s P_{i,0} + c_i s P_{i,1}$ and $T_i' = r_i P$.

Aggregation: Individual signatures $(w, S_i', T_i')_{1 \le i \le n}$ are aggregated into an aggregate signature
$(w, \quad S_n = \sum_{i=1}^{n} S_i', \quad T_n = \sum_{i=1}^{n} T_i')$.

Verification: The verifier checks the following equality.

$$\hat{e}(S_n, P) = \hat{e}(T_n, P_w)\hat{e}(Q, \sum_{i=1}^{n} P_{i,0} + \sum_{i=1}^{n} c_i P_{i,1}), \quad (1)$$

3. ICN-BASED MODERATOR-CONTROLLED INFORMATION SHARING SERVICE

In this section, we present an overview of our target application, moderator-controlled information sharing (MIS), and its implementation by ICN, and then discuss two problems involved in building such an application.

3.1 Overview of MIS

Our simplified model for an MIS service consists of at least three different types of participants: moderators, peers, and an administrator. Peers are content/message publishers as well as subscribers within their preferred interest groups or subscription lists. A peer can become a moderator for a specific group and can supervise posted messages to this group. In Fig. 2, the group supervised by $Moderator_1$ is indicated by solid arrows to its subscribers. The moderator can control the information released to this group. The posted message will not be sent to the subscribers unless approved by the moderator. A moderator can join a group created by another moderator as a subscriber. In Fig. 2, $Moderator_2$ has joined the group of $Moderator_1$. Another role of the moderator is to relay posted messages to related peers or subscribers if desired. In this case, moderators relay messages, like traditional SNS servers managed by administrators. Of course, a moderator can delegate this function to the administrator if desired. Thus, the administrator is a moderator who supervises a special 'public' group, indicated by the dashed arrows from the moderator to all of the peers. This group is a kind of portal site for the MIS service, and so MIS can be defined as a service that has evolved from the current centralized information sharing services.

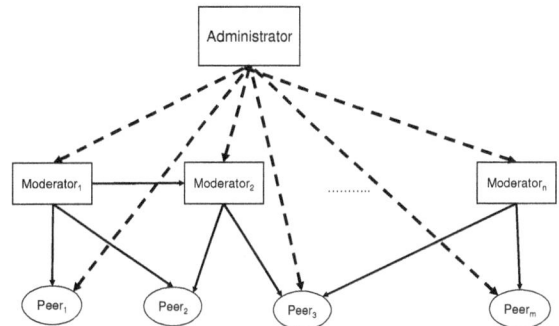

Figure 2: Structure of the MIS service

159

Messages in the MIS service can be relayed by a set of moderators including an administrator. This distributed approach has two advantages that current information sharing services in the Internet lack.

1. **Privacy:** Each moderator has the discretion to decide whether messages are physically transferred to the administrator or relayed by himself. In the latter case, the moderator can physically relay messages independent from the administrator.

2. **Fault tolerance:** All peers can communicate with each other within their preferred group when their relaying moderator is reachable by them. Even if the connection to the administrator is lost, it only prevents information sharing through the 'public' group. In such a case, Fig. 2 has three information exchange groups: $Group_1 = \{Moderator_1, Peer_1, Peer_2, Moderator_2\}$, $Group_2 = \{Moderator_2, Peer_2, Peer_3\}$ and $Group_3 = \{Moderator_n, Peer_3, Peer_m\}$. Thus, communications are possible via nodes in the intersections of these groups. For example, $Peer_m$ can communicate even with $Peer_1$ if human interventions at $Peer_3$ and $Peer_2$ exist. This advantage is very useful for safety confirmation exchanges during a disaster when the entire network is not well connected.

The requirements to achieve MIS are as follows.

1. Moderators must be trusted by their peers in any situation.
2. A peer can join a group managed by a moderator or can even become a moderator at his convenience.

These requirements must be satisfied even in a fragmented network just after a disaster.

3.2 ICN-based MIS

Information-centric networking is a promising technology for realizing the above mentioned MIS, and we refer to the result as ICN-based MIS. First, originator-signed signatures in ICN assure integrity and provenance for messages exchanged by peers. Authentications and authorizations are very easy when peers join moderators' groups. Second, any peer can be a moderator if the binding among his identifier (ID), public key, and secret key is trustable. Third, the existence of ICN network caches can reduce the load of the peer when the peer becomes a moderator. Finally, name-based routing inherent in ICN makes it possible to deliver messages from peers to their moderator even if global connections in datalink and network layers are lost. In this case, although routing is a concern for ICN, it is beyond the scope of the present paper. We herein focus on ICN-based MIS from the standpoint of message provenance, assuming routing issues are not a concern.

Information-centric networking trustability is currently supported by a real-world agent according to the traditional Public Key Infrastructure (PKI) model, consisting the hierarchy from the widely trusted global certification authority (CA) to the edge CAs. If a trustable online server is required to verify the message, fault tolerance of the service cannot be achieved. In the traditional PKI, the verification needs to obtain the public keys of both the publisher and the moderator, as well as all of the parent certificates. Fetching the required public keys and certificates results in a long delay, especially in high-latency networks, such as a fragmented network in a disaster area [26].

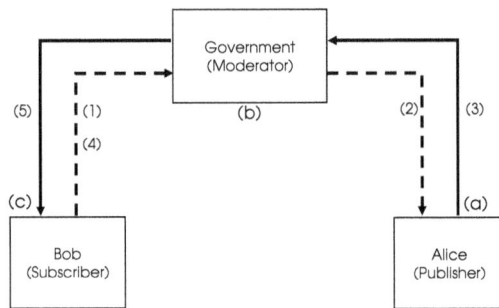

Figure 3: Information exchanges in the MIS service

Fig. 3 shows a scenario for using MIS for safety confirmation exchanges, where one peer (Alice) publishes a message and the other (Bob) receives the message or subscribes to a message service via their moderator (Government). The exchange sequence is as follows. (1) The subscriber (Bob) declares his interest through his subscription request. (2) A moderator (Government) polls the publisher. (3) If the publisher (Alice) has content to publish, she sends it to the moderator. Upon receiving the new content, the moderator first checks the content, then adds some information, such as the accepted date and the publisher's rating. (4) The subscriber requests to receive the message. (5) The moderator sends the content to corresponding subscribers or peers within his group.

In order to assure that the message is relayed via this moderator, the subscriber should have the ability to verify the authenticity of both the moderator and the publisher from the received content. Sharing a symmetric subscription key among the moderator and its peers requires additional statefull procedures among the moderator and peers, and is not suitable for use in disaster situations because connections among the moderator and peers may not be stable and it is not possible to know who will join which group beforehand. Applying a group membership to this problem has the same disadvantages.

In order to achieve this requirement using the ordinary RSA or Elliptic Curve Digital Signature Algorithm (ECDSA) signature, the moderator must attach two signatures: the signature generated by the publisher on the original content and the signature generated on the new moderated content. In the safety confirmation system [26], the content size is usually small and does not exceed 100 bytes. Most human-generated content such as that on Facebook consists of short messages, and such applications fall into a group called instant messengers. Short message transfers are also important in many sensor networks such as smart metering networks, in which the size of a message is usually small. Apart from a signature value block, the Signature element of a *Data* packet also contains a signature info block (Section 5.3), which contains a description of the signature, the signature algorithm used, and any other relevant information in order to obtain parent certificate(s) (e.g., KeyLocator ([20])). Therefore, the overhead of transmitting two signatures to deliver a single short message is huge compared to the message's size. Furthermore, if further information retrievals such as parent certificate(s) are required, received packets cannot be verified until all of the required information is received. When trustable servers are accessed in disaster situations, the connections to those servers may not be guaranteed.

The above considerations indicate that there are four requirements for message provenance in ICN-based MIS.

1. For the instantaneous reception of a message, the fetching overhead for public keys and their certificates must be reduced.
2. Verification must be achieved without any trustable servers online.
3. It is preferable to achieve a group membership using only given public key/secret key pairs.
4. It is important to reduce the signature overhead for short messages.

4. PROPOSED ICN-BASED MIS

The first and second requirements, as described for the public key retrieval delay problem in Section 3.2, can be solved using an identity-based signature scheme, such as CC-IBS [7]. As shown in Fig. 4, the proposed ICN-based MIS system adds a fourth entity, namely the Private Key Generator (PKG), to Fig. 3, which gives three other entities their secret keys corresponding to the registered identifiers (IDs) as well as the public parameters that are known to all in the network. The binding between the ID (ID_1) and the corresponding secret key ($SecretKey_1$) is assured by a physical negotiation by the signer ($Signer1$) and the PKG in our real-world activities. Once the message is known to be signed by the private key corresponding to the identifier in a received message, there is no need for the PKG to be online and instantaneous verification is achieved.

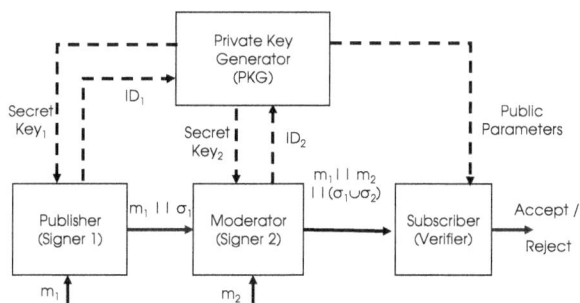

Figure 4: IBAS signing process for a message relayed by the moderator

The third and fourth requirements in Section 3.2 can be satisfied using IBAS, which is an identity-based signature. Either m_1 or m_2 in Fig. 4 indicate the signed part in the packet sent from a publisher or a moderator, which includes Name, MetaInfo, Content, and SignatureInfo. Here, σ_1 is a signature created from m_1 and $SecretKey_1$. Moreover, $\sigma_1 \cup \sigma_2$ is the aggregated signature created by σ_1, m_2, and $SecretKey_2$. In order to verify the message, a concatenation $m_1||m_2||\sigma_1 \cup \sigma_2$ must be sent to the subscriber. If m_1 can be reconstructed from m_2 in a formulated manner, sending $m_2||\sigma_1 \cup \sigma_2$ is sufficient for the verification process.

In IBS, the only information required for a verifier to check data integrity is the identity of the data producer, i.e., the publisher or the moderator, which in most cases is already known to the verifier. In NDN, in particular, the content producer's identity can be obtained from the content name. Therefore, we used IBAS, the combination of IBS and aggregate signatures, to build our MIS. In the next section, we present one implementation example for the proposed concept using NDN.

5. IMPLEMENTATION OF IBAS FOR NDN

In order to verify the *Data* packet, two different message parts signed by the publisher and the moderator are derived from the original packet. This section presents a simple example for such an implementation.

In order to measure the round trip time (RTT) in Section 6.2, the scenario of Fig. 3 is modified slightly as follows. Two peers, Bob and Alice, join the list owned by a moderator 'Government'. Through this moderator, Alice informs Bob that her new message is ready to send if requested. Bob wants to obtain a safety confirmation from Alice, and he sends an interest packet to the moderator (1). Since the safety confirmation from Alice is not yet uploaded, 'Government' sends an interest packet to Alice (2). Then, Alice replies to 'Government' by the *Data* packet with her information (3). After adding a time stamp and the moderator's name to the content part of the *Data* packet, this moderator returns the *Data* packet with the safety confirmation from Alice to Bob (4). We refer to the above scenario as the packet relay model.

Table 1 summarizes the processing performed by RSA and IBAS for the packet at each step in Fig. 3.

Table 1: Details of processing by (a) Publisher, (b) Moderator, and (c) Subscriber

	RSA	IBAS
(a)	data creation & signature generation	data creation & signature generation
(b)	signature verification & signature creation & signature concatenation	signature verification & signature generation & signature aggregation
(c)	signature verification x 2	aggregated signature verification

5.1 Naming

In NDN, naming is application-dependent, i.e., applications can design the naming system to be useful for their intended purpose. Snippet 1 contains examples of the names used in our application. Numbers (1) to (4) in Snippet 1 correspond to the numbers(1) to (3) and (5) shown in Fig. 3. (1) and (2) are the *Interest* packets sent from Bob to the moderator, 'Government', and from the moderator to Alice, and (3) and (4) are the corresponding *Data* packets generated by Alice and the moderator. In this case, '2' in (3) and '9' in (4) are the sequence numbers of the message at Alice and at the moderator, respectively. In our application, the two foremost name components of Name describe the content generator's identity, e.g., /moderators/Government and

/wonderland/Alice. The third name component is always the application name: /safetyConfirmation.

Snippet 1 Names of the packets shown in Fig. 3

```
(1) /moderators/Government/safetyConfirmation/
              wonderland/Alice
(2) /wonderland/Alice/safetyConfirmation
(3) /wonderland/Alice/safetyConfirmation/2
(4) /moderators/Government/safetyConfirmation/
              wonderland/Alice/2/9
```

Using the above naming rule, it is possible to obtain the original publisher's name from data received from a moderator, i.e., from name (4) we can derive name (3).

5.2 Message Reconstruction

Fig. 5 shows an example of the current IBAS signature for an NDN *Data* packet by the moderator, which is compared with the corresponding RSA signature. After modifying the content name, the moderator adds the dashed parts to m_1 to make m_2. In other words, two lines starting from 'From' and 'Published' are added by Alice, and two more starting from 'Moderator' and 'Accepted' are added by the moderator. In the case of RSA, the signature by the publisher is moved into the content part of the *Data* packet sent from the moderator. This is a kind of layer violation, while the IBAS *Data* packet has only one aggregated signature. Fig. 5 also shows the size of each part in an NDN *Data* packet for RSA-2048 and IBAS as discussed in Section 6.1.

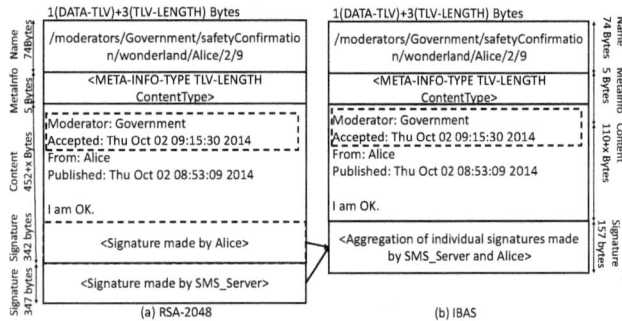

Figure 5: Structure of a *Data* packet sent from a moderator to a subscriber

5.3 Signature Structure for IBAS

The Signature element inside an NDN *Data* packet consists of two consecutive blocks as described below[20].

Snippet 2 Signature of NDN *Data* packet [20]

```
Signature ::= SignatureInfo
              SignatureBits
SignatureInfo ::= SIGNATURE-INFO-TYPE TLV-LENGTH
                  SignatureType
                  ... (SignatureType-specific TLVs)
SignatureValue ::= SIGNATURE-VALUE-TYPE TLV-LENGTH
              ... (SignatureType-specific TLVs and BYTE+)
SignatureType ::= SIGNATURE-TYPE-TYPE TLV-LENGTH
                  nonNegativeInteger
```

The size of IBAS's SignatureInfo is fixed (5 bytes) just to indicate the SignatureType in a non-negative integer,

whereas that of RSA's is variable to tell the KeyLocator information. The nonNegativeInteger value in Signature-Type represents the type of signature algorithm used in signing, as shown in Table 2. In order to implement our application, we added a new type *SignatureSha256Ibas* Signature-Type, which represents the IBAS algorithm [13] with *SHA-256* as a hash function. The size of the *Signature-Sha256Ibas* signature value is 150 bytes, 20 bytes of which is the state information w selected by the first signer, and the remaining 130 bytes consist of two equal-sized compressed elements S_i, T_i (Section 2.3).

Table 2: NDN Signature Algorithms

Value	Signature Algorithm
0	*DigestSha256*
1	*SignatureSha256WithRsa*
3	*SignatureSha256WithEcdsa*
4	*SignatureSha256Ibas*

5.4 IBAS Control Flow for Signatures

Our IBAS implementation in NDN [19] is done by extending the ndn-cxx library [18]. The ndn-cxx library uses modules called KeyChain and Validator to sign and verify *Data* packets respectively. Therefore, we added new sign(), sign-AndAggregate() and verifySignature() methods to the ndn-cxx's KeyChain and Validator modules respectively. The two modules call IbasSigner to execute any IBAS related calculation. The IbasSigner module internally uses PBC Library [17] to execute all pairing routines such as pairing and elliptic curve generation, elliptic curve addition and multiplication, and pairing computation. The implementation design is outlined in Fig.6. The library names used at each step is displayed on the left side of the figure, where "New" means *newly implemented*.

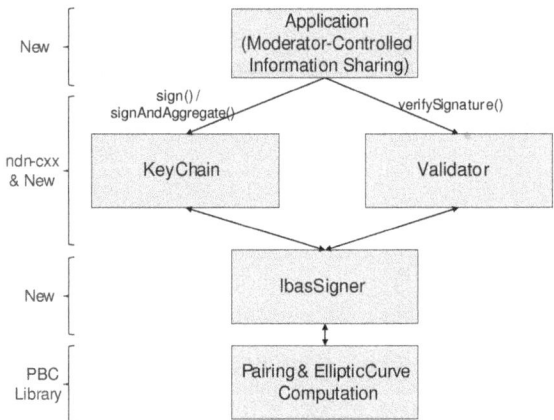

Figure 6: IBAS Implementation Design

6. EXPERIMENTS

We compare the performance of our IBAS implementation with the built-in RSA signatures in ndn-cxx. In our experiments, only the overhead of *Data* packets (not *Interest* packets) is investigated. Technically, two alternative methods are presented: using RSA and using IBAS for signatures. For RSA signatures to be used in the PKI environment, there are two cases. (1) The subscriber shall have all of the public keys and all of the required certificates in the network. In this case, there is no need to use the `Key-Locator` field. (2) Otherwise, extra handshakes are required in order to obtain the necessary certificates using the `Key-Locater` field. The throughput of the message exchanges is measured in the case of (1).

6.1 Message Size Comparison

Table 3 shows the *Data* packet size comparison in our application, where x is the size of the message published by Alice in the scenario shown in Fig. 3. The phrases N., M.I., Con., and Sig. are abbreviations of the TLV block element names `Name`, `MetaInfo`, `Content`, and `Signature`, respectively. Since each *Data* packet has DATA-TLV of one byte and TLV-LENGTH of three bytes ahead, as '1(DATA-TLV)+3(TLV-LENGTH)' shown in Fig. 5, TLV shows this size of 4 bytes. Snippet 2 shows that *Data* packet's `Sig-nature` consists of two TLV elements: `SignatureType` and `SignatureValue`. Thus, the signature sizes in Table 3 are expressed as a sum of the two numbers corresponding to `SignatureType` and `SignatureValue`. The size of `Signature-Info` for RSA is variable and in this case is 82 bytes because it contains `KeyLocator`, while that for IBAS is fixed at 5 bytes. The size of each part is also shown in Fig. 5.

Table 3: *Data* packet size comparison (in bytes)

a: Publisher to Moderator (Fig. 3(3))

	TLV	N.	M.I.	Con.	Sig.	Total
RSA-2048	4	46	5	$53+x$	$82+260$	$450+x$
RSA-1024	4	46	5	$53+x$	$82+132$	$322+x$
ECDSA-521	4	46	5	$53+x$	$82+126$	$314+x$
IBAS	4	46	5	$53+x$	$5+152$	$265+x$

b: Moderator to Subscriber (Fig. 3(4))

	TLV	N.	M.I.	Con.	Sig.	Total
RSA-2048	4	74	5	$452+x$	$87+260$	$882+x$
RSA-1024	4	74	5	$324+x$	$87+132$	$626+x$
ECDSA-521	4	74	5	$318+x$	$87+126$	$614+x$
IBAS	4	74	5	$110+x$	$5+152$	$350+x$

Table 3 shows that a message overhead reduction of 45% or 60% is achieved by IBAS from RSA-1024 or RSA-2048 in this case. If Alice sends out a 6-byte message "I'm OK" ($x = 6$), the size of the corresponding *Data* packet received by Bob is $350 + 6 = 356$ bytes in the case of IBAS, or $882 + 6 = 888$ bytes in the case of RSA-2048.

The size of the elliptic curve used by this IBAS is the default 513 bits (rbits = 160, qbits = 512) of the PBC Library [17], which is implemented in 65 bytes. Although the current ndn-cxx [18] does not implement ECDSA-521 [12], Table 3 also shows its calculated overhead because it uses the closest-sized elliptic curve to the above IBAS among three ECDSA algorithms defined in RFC4754 [12]. This shows that the overhead reduction of 43% from ECDSA-521 will be achieved by IBAS.

6.2 Computational Overhead Comparison

In a high-delay, small-throughput network, the signature verification delay can be significantly reduced by using IBAS

(Section 4) because there is no need to obtain further information such as certificates. However, if the network is healthy and all necessary public keys and certificates needed for RSA signature verification are present in the verifier's cache, the limiting bottleneck of communication throughput is the computational complexity of the signature generation and verification.

In order to make a computational comparison, we measured the average time for signature generation and verification. In this experiment, we chose the message size to be $x = 100$ bytes. The results are obtained by executing 100 operations and taking the average. The specifications of the CPU of the machine on which the benchmark was run are shown below. Although the machine has multiple cores, the benchmark was run on a single core.

```
vendor_id     : GenuineIntel
cpu family    : 6
model         : 58
model name    : Intel(R) Core(TM) i7-3520M CPU @ 2.90 GHz
cpu MHz       : 1,499.730
cache size    : 4,096 KB
cpu cores     : 2
bogomips      : 5,786.94
clflush size  : 64
address sizes : 36 bits physical, 48 bits virtual
```

Thus far, we have largely ignored the encryption strength of IBAS as compared with other signatures, and the size of the elliptic curve used by IBAS is set to the default 513 bits (rbits=160, qbits=512) in the PBC Library [17], which we hereinafter refer to as IBAS (512,160). Table 4 shows the computational costs of RSA signatures and those of ECDSA signatures. According to RFC5656 [25], RSA-1024 is comparable to the ECDSA of the key size from 160 to 223 bits, and RSA-2048 is comparable to the ECDSA of the key size from 224 to 255 bits. Another investigation on the computational costs by M. Yasuda et al[27] shows that RSA-1024 and RSA-2048 are comparable to ECDSA-133 and ECDSA-195, respectively. For the second IBAS implementation IBAS(224,112), we choose a conservative 225-bit key created by genaparam with rbits = 112 and qbits = 224 in the PBC Library [17].

Table 4: RSA vs. ECC

RSA	ECC Type 1[25] (NIST 800-57)	ECC Type 1[27] (M. Yasuda et al.)
1024	160-223	133
2048	224-255	195
2671		224
3072	256-383	
3241		247
7680	384-511	
15360	512+	

Table 5 show the computation costs of IBAS, ECDSA, and RSA for various key sizes. In RSA, signature generation is very expensive compared to verification. Therefore, the publishing and moderating time is longer than the subscription (verification) time. The difference in processing cost for ECDSA between signature generation and verification is not so large. This is why the processing time of the subscriber is equal to almost twice that of the publisher. Precisely speaking, the verification costs per signature of ECDSA-256 and ECDSA-384 are observed to be 1.21 and

1.25 times larger, respectively, than the signature generation costs. The ECDSA cost of the moderator is approximately an extra 2 ms consumed by processing other than the signing and verifying processes.

In IBAS, verifying a signature requires executing an expensive pairing function three times (Equation (1) in Section 2.3). Thus, Table 5 shows that the time required for subscription (verification) and moderating is longer than that for publishing (generation), because moderating includes verification.

Table 5: Signature processing times (ms)

	Publisher Alice	Moderator Government	Subscriber Bob
IBAS(512,160)	7.53	21.5	21.5
IBAS(224,112)	2.46	4.95	4.10
ECDSA-384	2.15	7.04	5.38
ECDSA-256	1.05	4.33	2.55
RSA-4096	10.2	10.4	0.446
RSA-2048	2.08	2.04	0.307
RSA-1024	0.738	0.841	0.246

Although the time required for verification at Bob by RSA-4096 does not increase significantly from that of RSA-1024, the generation time increases significantly and the signature processing time at the publisher and the moderator becomes more than 10 ms for RSA-4096. The processing time at Alice (publisher) and Government (moderator) by ECDSA-384 is less than that for RSA-4096. For signatures stronger than RSA-4096, we should use ECDSA instead of RSA. The encryption strength of IBAS(224, 112) may be comparable to RSA-2048 according to Table 4. Assuming that IBAS(224,112), ECDSA-224, and RSA-2048 have the same encryption strength, we can investigate the throughput comparisons. Since the processing time at the moderator is the longest and the bottleneck of these three methods, we calculated the throughput of communications via the moderator. According to Table 5, the throughputs of the moderator are is 490, 231, and 202 packets/s for RSA-2048, ECDSA-256, and IBAS(224,112), respectively. The performance of IBAS(224,112) is similar to that of ECDSA-256 but is 2.4 times slower than that of RSA-2048. In order to achieve a throughput of 1Mbps by IBAS(224,112), the message size x should be larger than 619bytes. Since the maximum data size of IEEE802.3 (802.2LLC) is 1497, IBAS(224,112) can easily provide a video streaming service at 1 Mbps.

The above results do not take into account the time required for placing *Data* packets into *Face* and processing *Interest*s. In order to obtain the average round trip time (RTT) between Bob and Alice in Fig. 3 in a delay-free network (i.e., the time for placing *Interest* and *Data* into *Face* is included, but the network has no delay), we set up the configurations to reflect the packet relay model presented in the second paragraph in Section 5. The RTT is measured 5 times by running the three different NDN clients (Alice (publisher), Government (moderator), and Bob (subscriber)) on one physical machine. The average RTT of 100-byte messages by IBAS(224,112) is 37.6ms (standard deviation: 2.8ms), whereas that of RSA-2048 is 22.7ms (standard deviation: 1.6ms). The latency of IBAS is 1.7 times larger than that of RSA-2048. In real life, the network has latency;

if we add 100ms (the average worldwide RTT to Google[14]) to both numbers, the difference may be negligible.

7. DISCUSSION AND FUTURE RESEARCH

After a disaster, even when Bob is evacuated to a shelter with no internet connectivity but with a Wi-Fi network, he can immediately confirm the safety of Alice using his smartphone via ICN-based MIS using IBAS if the corresponding moderator and Alice happen to be in the same shelter. Furthermore, Bob even knows the safety of his mother via this moderator if his brother John carries his smartphone with this information into the shelter.

IBAS can be used in other applications that require sequential signing. For example, the registration certificate of our real estate lists the current owner as well as all the previous owners with deletion marks. In this case, a modified registration certificate is signed by a new aggregated signature created from this modified registration certificate, the previous aggregated signature, and the identity of the new owner.

The following are important issues to solve in the future.

Smartphones of Different KGCs in a Shelter

Smartphones in a shelter may use different mobile carriers. In this case, the KGCs may be different, and it is difficult to set up communications among these smartphones. However, when a disaster occurs, a new Incident Command System (ICS) is launched as part of the emergency response procedure [9]. Thus, one solution is to introduce a special KGC managed by ICS, which relays other KGCs. The implementation should be investigated in detail in the future.

IBAS Key Size

The encryption strength of IBAS is beyond the scope of the present paper. The size of the elliptic curve used by IBAS(224,122) is within the range of NIST 800-57, which is equivalent to RSA-2048. However, this may not mean that the encryption strength is almost the same as that of RSA-2048. Careful investigations on the encryption strength of IBAS must be performed in the future for comparison with RSA-2048.

Hashing onto Elliptic Curves

The IBAS signature scheme [13] uses hash functions $H_1, H_2 : \{0,1\}^* \rightarrow \mathbb{G}_1$, where $\mathbb{G}_1$ is a Gap Diffie-Hellman group. Building a secure hash function with such a property is not trivial. Thus, for ease of implementation, we simply used the Crypto++ [8] library's SHA-256 hash function and converted the resulting hash value into the $\mathbb{G}_1$ field. However, note that a better hash function can be built by using the *MapToGroup* method described in [5].

Distributing Secret Parameters and Key Revocation

In our application, we save the secret key of each participant in local storage beforehand, as in the Subscriber Identity Module (SIM) card according to the GSM [10]. The `IbasSigner` module then loads the keys from storage when signing packets.

Building an efficient key revocation system is difficult in all IBC systems. In the proposed application, we do not implement any key revocation mechanism.

Other Issues

There are other issues to be solved for ICN-based MIS.

- A moderator can delegate the message relaying function to the administrator if he wishes because of the processing power of his terminal or some other temporal reasons. If the KGC is the administrator, he can be a delegate of any moderator because KGC has the secret keys of all the peers. This is another advantage of using the identity-based signature to construct ICN-based MIS.

- Currently encryption is not implemented. Since the BF-IBE scheme uses the same bilinear pairing and has similar system parameters as IBAS, we believe that the IBAS scheme can be used with BF-IBE to provide fully functional IBC.

- The significant issue in routing is that messages can be delivered from peers to their moderator even if global connections are lost.

- Although the identity names *publisher* and *subscriber* are used, the proposed application is not a pub/sub system and its communication is driven by *Interest* packets. However, this NDN's default pull-based communication model can also be extended to have push-based multicast capability (pub/sub), as demonstrated in COPSS [6].

8. CONCLUSION

We developed the ICN-based MIS, which is the first working application for Identity-Based Aggregate Signatures. The ICN-based MIS is easy to implement in the information centric networking (ICN) framework but is difficult or inefficient to implement in traditional Internet application frameworks. The current IBAS extension for ndn-cxx [18] is not optimized, and the throughput is slower than expected. Thus, the source code is openly available through GitHub [19] for use in further research on this scheme.

Moreover, we have shown that using IBAS in NDN significantly reduces the overhead of the public key and signature. Since the verification of a *Data* packet is performed without requesting additional information, it is especially appealing in our example application of a disaster, where the network delay is large, and the safety confirmation messages are small. Moreover, based on experiments using our IBAS implementation, we estimated the throughput and latency of our application in a real healthy network. Future research includes finding and implementing proper solutions for the workarounds described in Section 7. In particular, finding a proper IBAS key size is indispensable for our IBAS application to operate in the real world.

Acknowledgements

This work has been supported by the GreenICN project (GreenICN: Architecture and Applications of Green Information Centric Networking), a research project supported jointly by the European Commission under its 7th Framework Program (contract no. 608518) and the National Institute of Information and Communications Technology (NICT) in Japan (contract no. 167).

9. REFERENCES

[1] 3GPP. Alphabets and language-specific information. Technical Specification Group Terminals 23.038i version 2.0.0, June 1996.

[2] D. Barr. Majordomo. http://www.greatcircle.com/majordomo/FAQ.html. Accessed: 2015-05-04.

[3] C. Bian, Z. Zhu, E. Uzun, and L. Zhang. Deploying key management on ndn testbed. Technical Report, UCLA, Peking University and PARC, 2013.

[4] D. Boneh, C. Gentry, B. Lynn, and H. Shacham. Aggregate and verifiably encrypted signatures from bilinear maps. In *Advances in cryptology–EUROCRYPT 2003*, pages 416–432. Springer, 2003.

[5] D. Boneh, B. Lynn, and H. Shacham. Short signatures from the weil pairing. In *Advances in Cryptology –ASIACRYPT 2001*, pages 514–532. Springer, 2001.

[6] J. Chen, M. Arumaithurai, L. Jiao, X. Fu, and K. Ramakrishnan. Copss: An efficient content oriented publish/subscribe system. In *2011 Seventh ACM/IEEE Symposium on Architectures for Networking and Communications Systems (ANCS)*, pages 99–110. IEEE, 2011.

[7] J. C. Choon and J. H. Cheon. An identity-based signature from gap diffie-hellman groups. In *Public key cryptography – PKC 2003*, pages 18–30. Springer, 2002.

[8] W. Dai. Crypto++ library, version: 5.6.1. http://www.cryptopp.com/. Accessed: 2015-05-04.

[9] T. Deal, C. Mills, and M. Deal. *All Hazard Field Guide: A Responder's Handbook Using the National Incident Management System's Incident Command System*. Amazon Services International, Inc., 2011.

[10] ETSI. Subscriber identity modules, functional characteristics. Recommendation GSM 02.17 version 3.2.9 (Release 92, Phase 1), February 1992.

[11] Facebook. Controlling what you see in news feed. https://www.facebook.com/help/335291769884272/. Accessed: 2015-05-04.

[12] D. Fu and J. Solinas. Ike and ikev2 authentication using the elliptic curve digital signature algorithm (ecdsa). RFC 4754, January 2007.

[13] C. Gentry and Z. Ramzan. Identity-based aggregate signatures. In *Public Key Cryptography-PKC 2006*, pages 257–273. Springer, 2006.

[14] I. Grigorik. Latency: The new web performance bottleneck. https://www.igvita.com/2012/07/19/latency-the-new-web-performance-bottleneck/, July 2012. Accessed: 2015.02.02.

[15] M. R. Horton. Standard for interchange of usenet messages. RFC 850, June 1983.

[16] L-Soft international. Early history of listserv. http://www.lsoft.com/products/listserv-history.asp. Accessed: 2015-05-04.

[17] B. Lynn. The pairing-based cryptography library, version: 0.5.14. http://crypto.stanford.edu/pbc/. Accessed: 2015-05-04.

[18] S. Mastorakis. Ndn c++ library with experimental extensions. https://github.com/named-data/ndn-cxx. Accessed: 2014-12-22.

[19] B. Namsraijav. Ndn-cxx fork with ibas support. https://github.com/byambajav/ndn-ibas/. Accessed: 2015-05-17.

[20] NDN Project Team. Ndn specification documentation. http://named-data.net/wp-content/uploads/2013/11/packetformat.pdf. Accessed: 2015-08-05.

[21] NDN Project Team. Type-length-value (tlv) encoding. http://named-data.net/doc/ndn-tlv/tlv.html. Accessed: 2015-08-04.

[22] T. Ogawara, Y. Kawahara, and T. Asami. Disaster-tolerant authentication system for ndn using hierarchical id-based encryption. In *2013 21st IEEE International Conference on Network Protocols (ICNP)*, pages 1–2, 2013.

[23] J. Seedorf, B. Gill, D. Kutscher, B. Schiller, and D. Kohlweyer. Demo overview: Fully decentralised authentication scheme for icn in disaster scenarios (demonstration on mobile terminals). In *Proceedings of the 1st international conference on Information-centric networking*. ACM, 2014.

[24] A. Shamir. Identity-based cryptosystems and signature schemes. In *CRYPTO 84 on Advances in cryptology*, pages 47–53. LNCS Springer, August 1985.

[25] D. Stebila and J. Green. Elliptic curve algorithm integration in the secure shell transport layer. RFC 5656, December 2009.

[26] T. Yagyu and S. Maeda. Demo overview: reliable contents retrieval in fragmented icns for disaster scenario. In *Proceedings of the 1st international conference on Information-centric networking*, pages 193–194. ACM, 2014.

[27] M. Yasuda, T. Shimoyama, J. Kogure, and T. Izu. On the strength comparison of the ecdlp and the ifp. In *Proceedings of the 8th International Conference on Security and Cryptography for Networks*, pages 302–325. 2012.

[28] L. Zhang, A. Afanasyev, J. Burke, V. Jacobson, P. Crowley, C. Papadopoulos, L. Wang, B. Zhang, et al. Named data networking. *ACM SIGCOMM Computer Communication Review*, 44(3):66–73, 2014.

[29] X. Zhang, K. Chang, H. Xiong, Y. Wen, G. Shi, and G. Wang. Towards name-based trust and security for content-centric network. In *2011 19th IEEE International Conference on Network Protocols (ICNP)*, pages 1–6. IEEE, 2011.

Catch Me If You Can: A Practical Framework to Evade Censorship in Information-Centric Networks

Reza Tourani
New Mexico State University
rtourani@cs.nmsu.edu

Satyajayant Misra
New Mexico State University
misra@cs.nmsu.edu

Joerg Kliewer
New Jersey Institute of
Technology
jkliewer@njit.edu

Scott Ortegel
New Mexico State University
sortegel@nmsu.edu

Travis Mick [*]
New Mexico State University
tmick@cs.nmsu.edu

ABSTRACT

Internet traffic is increasingly becoming multimedia-centric. Its growth is driven by the fast-growing mobile user base that is more interested in the content rather than its origin. These trends have motivated proposals for a new Internet networking paradigm–*information-centric networking* (ICN). This paradigm requires unique names for packets to leverage pervasive in-network caching, name-based routing, and named-data provenance. However named-data routing makes user censorship easy. Hence an anti-censorship mechanism is imperative to help users mask their named queries to prevent censorship and identification. However, this masking mechanism should not adversely affect request rates.

In this paper, we propose such an anti-censorship framework, which is lightweight and specifically targets low compute power mobile devices. We analyze our framework's information-theoretic secrecy and present *perfect secrecy* thresholds under different scenarios. We also analyze its breakability and *computational security*. Experimental results prove the framework's effectiveness: for requests it adds between 1.3–1.8 times in latency overhead over baseline ICN; significantly lesser than the overhead of the state of the art Tor (up to 38 times over TCP).

CCS Concepts

•Networks → **Network privacy and anonymity;** *Application layer protocols;* •**Security and privacy** → **Privacy protections;**

Keywords

NDN; information-centric networking; information theory; security; privacy

[*]This work was supported in part by the US National Science Foundation grants 1241809 and 1345232 and US DoD grant 67311RTREP. The information reported here does not reflect the position or the policy of the federal government.

1. INTRODUCTION

The host-centric Internet, where a node uses domain name systems to map the canonical name (e.g., www.google.com) to the IP address, and identify the data source before getting the required data, cannot scale for the traffic trends of the future. These scalability concerns have resulted in the proposal of a move to an information-centric Internet. The corresponding *information-centric networking* paradigm is based on the concept that a node interested in a content just wants the network to provide the content, it does not really care about where the content comes from; other than perhaps the content's provenance (validate creator). Invariably, this paradigm requires a node interested in a content to know the content's name and request its chunks/packets from the network using the corresponding name—the packets are routed in the network based on their name.

Named-data based networking has received significant interest recently, resulting in the proposal of several information-centric network (ICN) architectures, such as Named Data Networking (NDN) [12], NetInf [6], Publish-Subscribe Internet Routing Paradigm (PSIRP) [1], PURSUIT [16], and Data Oriented Networking (DONA) [13]. Each architecture has it's individual nuances, however all of them share three important aspects: unique name for each data unit (packet or chunk), routing based on data name, and in-network name-based data caching. The names could be either hierarchical and human-readable or machine-readable. These inherent advantages of this paradigm make it a popular candidate for the future, more scalable, Internet.

The use of data names in ICN architectures to identify content for routing and for data searches in the network brings forth some challenges as well. One important challenge is that the explicit use of names to describe the content makes it susceptible to censorship. Let's use the popular CCN/NDN architecture to illustrate this issue. In CCN, the user sends out interest requests for the named content chunks (e.g., www.google.com/movies/Arab-Spring.mpg.1) to the network. The network's built-in intelligence retrieves the chunks, either from the content provider or an intermediate router caching them. This content retrieval requires name based routing, that is, a request's name will be processed by each forwarding network node. This enables a forwarding node to easily filter and drop requests that it wants to censor. In fact, as opposed to censorship in today's Internet: implemented by blocking data based on destination IP addresses or by time-intensive deep packet inspection at proxies; *in the ICN architecture, censorship becomes trivial, as the content name is embedded as plaintext in the interest packets.* The filtering router can simply check the content name in each packet for filtering purposes.

Monitoring and censorship of users' traffic has been widely used in the past by regimes and countries to prevent free exchange of ideas (e.g., restricted social media access by Iran/China, data monitoring by the NSA in the US). Such acts of censorship are becoming more prevalent on the Internet today, and would become easier to orchestrate on the information-centric Internet. *Mechanisms need to be proposed to prevent such censorship acts. In this paper, motivated by these observations, we propose a **novel framework** to prevent censorship based on data names.* Our framework meets the requirements of strong security needed to prevent inspection based censorship and also fast encoding to ensure that the user request rates are not adversely affected. We select the CCN architecture for illustration on account of its popularity and mature code-base. We use a 18 node CCNx [14] testbed for our implementations and experiments.

The **contributions** of this paper are: *(i)* Design of a lightweight anti-censorship framework for the users in an ICN. Our framework leverages the computation efficient prefix-free information encoding techniques (e.g., Huffman coding) and is widely applicable for mobile devices with their low-computation capabilities. *(ii)* Discussion of the protocols that utilize the framework to enable private communication between a user and a content provider in a way that the communication cannot be censored by intermediate network entities. *(iii)* Extensive evaluation of the framework's information-theoretic and computational secrecy. *(iv)* Implementation of the framework in our CCNx testbed to validate its low communication overheads compared to the state of the art anti-censorship tools, such as Tor [19].

Section 2 presents the related work. In Section 3, we present our models and assumptions. Our framework is presented in Section 4, its information-theoretic secrecy is proved in Section 5, and analysis of its breakability and computational security is performed in Section 6. Section 7 presents the implementation and experimental results in details. Finally, we draw our conclusions and present our future work in Section 8.

2. RELATED WORK

Research in both Future Internet Architecture (FIA) security and prefix-free coding are relevant to this paper. We present relevant research in both areas starting with security in FIAs. Arianfar *et al.* proposed a steganographic approach in [4] for the censorship problem. In this scheme, the content provider generates a cover file and splits both the content and the cover into smaller blocks. The provider creates chunks by mixing blocks of the content and the cover and publishes the resulting chunks into the network. The provider sends additional information to the user, such as content hash and its length in blocks, the corresponding cover blocks, and the name generation algorithm, through a secure back channel. The use of the cover, which results in a 100% overhead and the requirement of a secure back channel for each content are the drawbacks of this scheme.

ANDaNA [7] uses two proxies, one adjacent to the requester and another closer to the destination, to create a two-layer encryption of the requests. Using ANDaNA a user decouples its identity from its requests: the first-hop proxy is only aware of the user identity but not what is requested while the second proxy's knowledge is limited to the

requested content only. Despite ANDaNA's usefulness as an anti-censorship tool, it incurs significant delays (ref. results in [7]) in comparison to Tor (the Onion Routing protocol)—the popular Internet anti-censorship tool. The delays are due to the use of the CCN architecture and setting up of the secure communication channels.

Tor is one of the most widely used and effective mechanisms to ensure end-to-end data secrecy, maintain user privacy beyond the first hop, and prevent censorship by completely anonymizing the data using onion routing [19]. However, Tor also incurs significant latency and bandwidth overhead on account of the shared symmetric key operations (decryption) at each intermediate node. *The bottom line is that the state of the art approaches are expensive, requiring several specialized nodes in the network (proxies and onion routers); more importantly, they require multiple symmetric/public key encryptions, which reduces application throughput significantly.* We take a different censorship evasion approach by proposing a prefix-free Huffman encoding framework for chunk names; we prove the framework's security and demonstrate its practicality. Our framework has much lower overhead than the state of the art and has very low latency. Also the need of the secure back channel is minimal.

Encryption using Multiple Huffman Tables (MHTs) was first proposed by Wu *et al.* [20]. In this approach, n distinct Huffman tables and a vector $\mathbf{Q}$ of size m, randomly filled with integers in the range of $(0, n-1)$ are used. Each source symbol is encoded by a Huffman table, selected from the pool of n tables, based on the index of the symbol in $\mathbf{Q}$. The Huffman table selection iterates through the vector until the source message is entirely encoded. Although MHT was proved to be secure against cipher-text and the plain-text attacks, the Chosen Plain-text Attack (CPA) broke the scheme's security [21]. Updating the vector $\mathbf{Q}$ for every m look-ups, was shown to secure the MHT approach against CPAs. An alternative solution was also proposed which required the insertion of a few random bits in the encoded source sequence according to specific bit values [22].

In our scheme, we do not use MHT, instead each user has one table for encoding. The table can be changed at a user-defined rate if necessary. We prove that our framework provides higher information-theoretic security than using AES. Our approach guarantees perfect information-theoretic secrecy so long as the size of the data name is no more than a calculated threshold. We also discuss our scheme's defense against well-known cryptanalysis attacks.

3. MODELS AND CONVENTIONS

In this section, we present the system model, our assumptions, the attack model, and the convention for the generation of the key from the Huffman tree.

3.1 System Model

The network is composed of a set of users $(\mathcal{U})$, routers $(\mathcal{R})$, providers $(\mathcal{P})$, and a set of trusted proxies named *anonymizers*. A router is either a filtering router or a normal router. A filtering router (r_f) filters the incoming requests' data names and drops requests whose names appear in a blacklist of contents. The filtering process is on-line (happens on the fly), and to reduce congestion and prevent throttling of the traffic the filtering is generally performed very close to line speed (packet arrival rate). Without loss of generality, we assume that a user is directly connected to a filtering router, which is in turn connected to the rest of the network.

Assuming that the Internet Protocol is not used as the network layer, in ICN, the first hop node on the path of a request is the only one that can identify the requester (from MAC-layer header); further along the requester's identity is absent in the packet. This is the worst case scenario. If IP-based addressing is used, we assume that the requester's IP address is cloaked using some anonymization technique. With IP-cloaking the situation is the same as when IP addressing is not used. Our scheme also applies when the filtering router and the user are separated by several hops. The user requests a content by sending an *interest* packet (terminology borrowed from the CCN/NDN architecture [12]) containing the name of the content chunk. The name of an object is in a hierarchical format starting with the content provider's name, e.g., *www.youtube.com/ArabSpring.mpg.1* (the postfix number '1' is the chunk ID).

In our framework, instead of using the plaintext content name for the interest, we use an encoded name. The encoded name can only be decoded correctly by a pre-selected anonymizer which has the decoding table. No entity in the path between the anonymizer and the requester has the decoding table and hence cannot decode the name. Between the anonymizer and the data provider (source or an intermediate router) the request is transmitted as a normal request and no filtering happens. We assume that between the anonymizer and the requester the data is encrypted; otherwise the filtering entity can identify the content. Generally, a third-party entity, chosen by the user from a publicly available list, serves as the anonymizer. This is analogous to what happens today: users evade traffic censorship by choosing an anonymizing service, such as *anonymizer.com* [3], as a proxy, and bypass the censors by tunneling their traffic (e.g., Facebook, Youtube) through the anonymizer's servers. A content provider can also operate as the anonymizer.

We note that our design has a trade-off between user privacy and caching (network) efficiency. It has been shown that to guarantee strong unlinkability of users' identity with their requests in-network caching should be avoided [2, 5]. In our framework, if a user does not trust the network, it can request the content provider to be its anonymizer. This would guarantee strong unlinkability in the network, however, the corresponding cached data at intermediate routers is unusable to serve new requests. This is true with Tor and ANDaNA. The multi-layered onion-routing based encryptions render the cached private data unusable for satis-

fying repeat requests. On the other hand, if the user chooses an anonymizer in the network, the cached data is only unusable by the routers in the path between the user and the anonymizer. In-network caching can be leveraged in the rest of the path. *In this paper, we assume the content provider is the same as the anonymizer.*

3.2 Attack Model

We assume that the attacker (censoring authority) is either an active or a passive eavesdropper. The attacker's aim is to learn how to correctly decode an interest. We also assume that the attacker has bounded capabilities, i.e., it cannot do large-scale brute force attacks. A passive eavesdropper can capture all packet transmissions to perform analysis. An active eavesdropper can capture and modify in-flight requests and also masquerade as a legitimate user to send interests.

3.3 Convention for Huffman Tree Key Generation

We consider an alphabet of size N for the source messages (chunk names). The source message is denoted by M^k, where k is the message size. The encoded message is denoted by $\underline{Z}$ and is assumed to be a binary string of size n. In our framework *three sources* of randomness exist, namely the random selections of the Huffman tree structure, the conventional key, and the source alphabet order from their respective universal sets. The user and the content provider can secretly perform one or more of these three random selections, thus making it difficult to break the system. The Huffman tree is a full binary tree with source alphabet symbols placed at the leaf nodes. Hence, for an alphabet of size N there are N leaf and $N - 1$ internal nodes. However, for the same set of symbols there can be several possible trees, one of which can be chosen randomly. We will explain our convention to generate a key for a Huffman tree in detail below. The last source of randomness, is the random choice of the alphabet order, that is, the order in which the alphabet symbols are placed on the leaf nodes. Instead of the standard Huffman coding where the placement of the symbols is based on the frequency of a symbol [11], the symbol placement could follow a random distribution to further increase the framework's randomness.

In this paper, we leverage the first two methods, namely the Huffman tree structure and the conventional key. We assume that the order of the source symbols in the tree is known to everyone. Exploiting the Huffman source coding, we introduce a novel key generation mechanism from the Huffman tree. We assume that the source (user) and the destination (content provider) of a communication have secretly shared a Probability Mass Function (pmf), which represents the probability of the occurrence of the symbols of an alphabet set in a message. The pmf is selected deliberately as a part of the secrecy mechanism and does not reflect the true source distribution. We also assume that both the source and the destination have information to built the Huffman tree with the same structure. The Huffman tree is generated by assigning labels '0' and '1' to the left and the right branch respectively, at each depth of the tree.

With a little analysis one can see that for a Huffman tree with $N - 1$ internal nodes there are $2^{(N-1)}$ mutation trees, where a *mutation tree* of a Huffman tree is generated by swapping the labels of the internal nodes. Each of these mutation trees is associated with a unique string of size $2(N-1)$

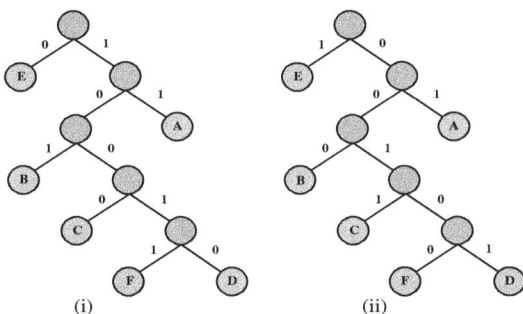

Figure 1: Key Convention: On the left, Huffman tree (i) is shown with the key 0101100110; On the right, Huffman tree (ii) is presented with 1001011001 as the key. Although the structure of both trees are the same, generated codewords are different due to different keys.

that is obtained by traversing the tree sequentially by levels and at each level picking up the labels from left to right— similar to breadth-first search. Assuming that we have an arbitrary pmf for a six symbols alphabet, Figure 1 illustrates the corresponding Huffman tree. According to our convention, the key for the tree (i) on the left hand side is "0101100110" while the tree (ii) on the right hand side, has the key "1001011001" despite having the same structure. The source and the destination can frequently switch to a new key from the pool of $2^{(N-1)}$ keys, corresponding to the $2^{(N-1)}$ mutation trees, to improve communication secrecy.

We note that this proposed convention is not restricted to the Huffman source coding. In general, every prefix-free source coding scheme with a full binary tree can use it.

4. ANTI-CENSORSHIP FRAMEWORK

Huffman coding is a promising approach to mitigate censorship in ICNs. In our framework, we encode a part of the content name, the postfix after the domain name, using the Huffman coding algorithm. The domain name is not encoded to allow for name based routing. We note that if the anonymizer is not the provider then the domain name can also be encoded. In this case, the anonymizer's domain name will be used as the prefix of the interest and used for routing. Once the interest reaches the ingress router of the domain (a CP or an anonymizer), the name in the interest is decoded into the real name. Although we use the Huffman coding technique to encode user interests other coding techniques can also be used in our framework. Our framework consists of three phases: *initialization, secure content sharing,* and *secure content response.* The initialization phase is used for sharing credentials between the user and an anonymizer to enable censorship-proof communication. For simplicity of exposition, we assume that the content provider is the anonymizer.

4.1 Initialization phase

In this phase, the user sends a membership request to the anonymizer ($\mathcal{A}$) encrypted using the anonymizer's public key and signed using the user's private key. On receiving the membership request, $\mathcal{A}$ generates a random Huffman ta-

ble, by using a random pmf for the interest, and sends the membership reply secretly to the requester; it also stores these information in its table (refer Figure 2). There are two mechanisms that need to be addressed here: a) How will the membership reply be sent secretly to user u_i? and b) How can $\mathcal{A}$ store each u_i's credentials to allow quick indexing into the table to identify the corresponding Huffman table? The anonymizer $\mathcal{A}$ generates a range of pseudonyms $(p_i^l - p_i^h)$ for u_i and creates a table entry consisting of the generated Huffman table, the pseudonyms' lower (p_i^l) and upper (p_i^h) limits, and the PKI details of u_i. It then encrypts the Huffman table and the pseudonym limits using the public key of u_i (or a shared symmetric key) and signs the message using its private key before sending the reply to u_i. At this point, the initialization phase is complete and both u_i and $\mathcal{A}$ have the required information for censorship-proof communication. Steps 1 to 3 in Figure 2 illustrate this phase. After the initialization phase, the user can request privacy-sensitive content.

4.2 Secure content request

The user needs to generate an interest packet, where the interest name has to be customized to evade censorship. Essentially, the hierarchical content name is composed of the anonymizer's domain name in plaintext (to enable prefix based routing), concatenated with the Huffman encoded postfix of the name representing the exact chunk. The Huffman encoded portion of the name may vary depending on the secrecy level required by the user. For the highest level of secrecy, the complete name postfix after the anonymizer's domain name needs to be encoded. For lower levels of secrecy, the user can encode a portion of the postfix. For instance, consider a content name for a Arab Spring video: www.google.com/movies/2012/ArabSpring/HD/TahrirSquare. The interest with highest secrecy level encodes all segments except www.google.com/ (anonymizer's domain name); while the lowest level secrecy, only encodes the last segment, TahrirSquare, the prefix is plaintext. This flexibility helps the user to adjust its desired level of secrecy.

For fast indexing at $\mathcal{A}$, u_i chooses a random pseudonym $p_i \in \{p_i^l, p_i^h\}$ and adds it as an identity field in the interest packet/chunk. Anonymizer $\mathcal{A}$ uses an ordered binary tree data structure, which has the ordered pseudonym ranges of the users as leaves, to search for u_i's ID ($u(i)$) in its table. Then, given p_i, to identify u_i $\mathcal{A}$ makes $\mathcal{O}(\log |\mathcal{U}|)$ comparisons, where $\mathcal{U}$ is the set of users. We will explore faster search using collision-resistant hashed functions in the future work. Users not interested in privacy requirements can be allocated only one identifier or can use only one pseudonym from their range. After the interest packet generation, the user sends the interest for the content chunk. Step 4 of Figure 2 illustrates this.

4.3 Secure content response

When the interest packet arrives at a filtering node, the filtering node can only infer partial information from the received interest packet. The inference is only based on $\mathcal{A}$'s domain name, but is insufficient for filtering the interest to identify the content. The filtering router can only perform longest prefix matching of the interest name with entries in its forwarding information base (FIB) and forward the interest to the appropriate next hop. At $\mathcal{A}$, a table look-up on the pseudonym (Step 5 of Figure 2) in the interest packet returns the desired Huffman tree for parsing the Huffman-

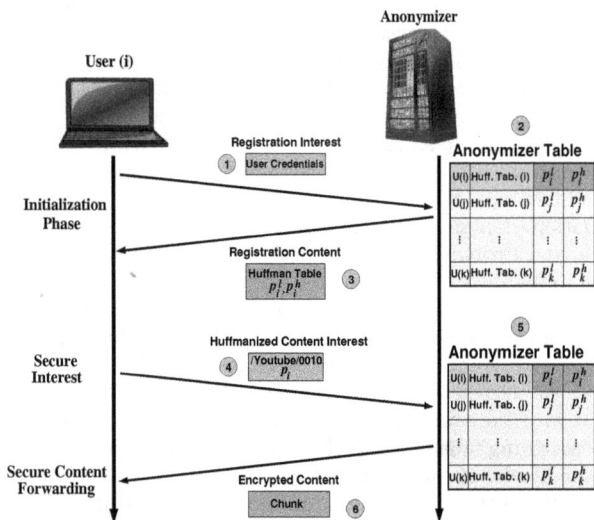

Figure 2: A schematic diagram showing our framework's three phases: initialization, secure content request, and secure content response.

encoded content name. Then $\mathcal{A}$ decodes the postfix and obtains the data from the content store(s). In the reply, $\mathcal{A}$ uses the same interest name and the same pseudonym while encrypting the content (symmetric/public key).

Our framework is also amenable to the other proposed FIA named-data architectures. Note that naming of data in all these architectures fall into one of two categories: hierarchical, human readable naming and flat machine-readable naming (hashed names). In both cases, the name in the interest can be treated as a source message and encoded using the shared Huffman table. For instance, in NetInf, the anonymizer can operate as a local or global name resolution server (outside the filtering region) and do the transformation between the encoded and the real-name of the private data. In DONA, the anonymizer can operate as a high-level resource handler beyond the filtering routers. In PSIRP, a subset of the nodes in the rendezvous system can be chosen as the anonymizer(s). These nodes do the mapping between the encoded name and the real name of the data. The anonymizers can send the forwarding identifier to the source (provider) to send the data to the requester and ask the provider to use the encoded name.

5. INFORMATION-THEORETIC SECURITY ANALYSES

In this section, we investigate the information-theoretic security of our framework and the protocols under different assumptions on the eavesdropper's knowledge of the system. As mentioned in Section 3, we use the structure of the Huffman tree and the key as the sources of randomness. We omit the third source of randomness: the ordering of the alphabet in the Huffman tree. Hence, an attacker with the knowledge of the tree structure and the shared key can reconstruct the coding table, which breaks the system. However, as these information are encrypted using PKI or symmetric keys before transmission, they are secure.

Thus there are three remaining information-theoretic attack scenarios, which we will study: (i) the eavesdropper has no parsing information, that is, tree structure and the key are unknown; (ii) the eavesdropper has key information only; and (iii) the eavesdropper has tree structure information only. Throughout this section we use the term key and the mutation tree alternatively where both refer to the key in our framework obtained using the BFS-like traversal. We also note that the source message is essentially the hierarchical data name postfix that needs to be encoded.

First, we derive basic entropy terms that we will need in the rest of the section. As mentioned before, given a tree T for alphabet size N, we have $2^{(N-1)}$ mutually independent mutation trees for T, that is, $2^{(N-1)}$ keys for T. The selection of a mutation tree (i.e., key K's selection) uniformly at random from the set of mutation trees results in K's entropy to become:

$$
H(K) = -\sum_{i=1}^{2^{N-1}} p(i) \log\big(p(i)\big) \tag{1}
$$

$$
= -\frac{1}{2^{N-1}} \sum_{i=1}^{2^{N-1}} \log\big(p(i)\big) \tag{2}
$$

$$
= \log\big(2^{N-1}\big) \tag{3}
$$

$$
= N - 1. \tag{4}
$$

Besides the selection of a mutation tree of T, the random choice of the tree structure (a uniform random distribution) is also another source of randomness. The number of mutually independent full binary trees with N leaves is given by the $(N-1)^{th}$ Catalan number (C_{N-1}) (refer Catalan Problem [8]). The Nth Catalan number (C_N) with increasing N is given by $C_N \approx \Omega(\frac{4^N}{N^{3/2}})$, thus $C_{N-1} \approx C_N$ for large N. Consequently, the entropy of using a random and secret tree structure (T_R) can be written as:

$$
H(T_R) = -\sum_{j=1}^{(\frac{4^N}{N^{3/2}})} p(j) \log\big(p(j)\big) \tag{5}
$$

$$
= -\frac{1}{\frac{4^N}{N^{3/2}}} \sum_{j=1}^{(\frac{4^N}{N^{3/2}})} \log\big(p(j)\big) \tag{6}
$$

$$
\geq \log\big(\frac{4^N}{N^{3/2}}\big) \tag{7}
$$

$$
= \log 2^{2N} - \log N^{3/2} \tag{8}
$$

$$
= 2N - 3/2 \log N. \tag{9}
$$

Also, considering the source alphabet with N symbols (e.g., $N = 512$ for Unicode or 256 for ASCII), which are uniformly randomly distributed, the source symbol entropy is given in Equation (12):

$$
H(X) = -\sum_{k=1}^{N} p(x_k) \log(p(x_k)) \tag{10}
$$

$$
= -\frac{1}{N} \sum_{k=1}^{N} \log\big(p(x_k)\big) \tag{11}
$$

$$
= \log N. \tag{12}
$$

Now we look at different eavesdropper attack scenarios.

5.1 Scenario 1: Both tree structure and the key are unknown

In this scenario, the eavesdropper has no knowledge of the tree structure or the key. Let M^k be the sequence of k symbols to be encoded and $\underline{Z}$ be the encoded binary sequence with length n symbols. The evaluation of the mutual information between the source message and the encoded sequence is provided by Equation (15) along with (4), (9), (12):

$$
I(M^k; \underline{Z}) = H(M^k) - H(M^k \mid \underline{Z}) \tag{13}
$$

$$
\leq \max\big(kH(X) - \big(H(T_R) + H(K)\big), 0\big) \tag{14}
$$

$$
= k\log(N) - 3N + 3/2\log(N) + 1. \tag{15}
$$

Equation (13) is obtained from the definition of the mutual information between the source message and its corresponding encoded sequence. The r.h.s. of Equation (14) is obtained from the fact that in this scenario the entropy of the message, given its encoded sequence, equals the entropies of the key and tree structure choices, and that the mutual information is always non-negative. The outcome of Equation (15) is the conditional entropy of the source sequence, given the encoded sequence, which is equal to the total randomness for both the structure and the key.

5.2 Scenario 2: Tree structure known, but not the key

In this scenario, the eavesdropper has complete knowledge of the tree structure and consequently can build the Huffman tree, and the key is the only secret. Hence, the mutual information between the source message and its encoded binary string is:

$$I(M^k; \underline{Z}) = H(M^k) - H(M^k \mid \underline{Z}) \qquad (16)$$

$$\leq \max\left(kH(X) - H(K), 0\right) \qquad (17)$$

$$= \max\left(k \log N - (N-1), 0\right) \qquad (18)$$

$$= k \log N - N + 1. \qquad (19)$$

Equation (19) presents the entropy of the source message assuming each symbol of this message is an i.i.d. random variable. In practice, the dependency between the letters in a word in the English alphabet reduces the entropy of the upcoming symbol (letter) given the prior symbols. We will discuss this in Subsection 5.4. Equating the r.h.s. of Equation (19) to zero, we conclude that the amount of information leakage as k becomes greater than $\left(\frac{N-1}{\log N}\right)$ is proportional to the value of k. Although the leakage increases linearly with k, it must be investigated whether the eavesdropper can leverage this leakage or not. We will investigate this in the next section.

5.3 Scenario 3: Key known, but not the tree structure

Now we investigate the opposite scenario: the eavesdropper knows the key, but does not have access to the tree structure. This can happen when the eavesdropper intercepts the key sharing communication phase between the anonymizer and the user and somehow identifies the encrypted key. Equation (23) returns the entropy of the source message under this condition:

$$I(M^k; \underline{Z}) = H(M^k) - H(M^k \mid \underline{Z}) \qquad (20)$$

$$\leq \max\left(kH(X) - H(T_R), 0\right) \qquad (21)$$

$$= \max\left(k \log N - (2N - 3/2 \log N), 0\right) \qquad (22)$$

$$= (k + 3/2) \log N - 2N. \qquad (23)$$

Equating the r.h.s. of Equation (23) to zero, we have the threshold for the information leakage to be $k = \left(\frac{2N}{\log N} - \frac{3}{2}\right)$, which has the same growth rate as the previous scenario, explained in Subsection 5.2.

Table 1 illustrates the thresholds of source message lengths (in symbols) for perfect secrecy for the three scenarios, evaluated in Equations (15), (19), (23) respectively (i.i.d. symbols in the messages). *Note that messages longer than the threshold lead to leakage; leakage is defined as the difference between the message length and the length of the threshold.*

Table 1: Maximum possible source message length k (in symbols) for perfect secrecy in i.i.d. messages.

Scenario	N=32	N=64	N=128	N=256	N=512
Scenario 1	17.5	30.3	53.2	94.3	169.1
Scenario 2	6.2	10.5	18.1	31.8	56.7
Scenario 3	11.3	19.8	35.07	62.5	112.2

5.4 Dependent source scenario's information leakage

So far, we have assumed that the source message is composed of i.i.d. random variables. Although this assumption is valid in most cases (for URL names), instances exist where there is a dependency between the source message symbols. For example, if the source message uses English words, then this changes the distribution of the source symbols and they no longer follow an i.i.d. uniform distribution. Hence, we also investigate the amount of information leakage when the symbols are dependent. Now, the probability of choosing a symbol is conditioned on the previously selected symbols in the same message, which decreases the source message's rate (i.e., the average entropy per symbol in the message).

According to Shannon [17], the $\mathcal{N}$-gram (sequence of any $|\mathcal{N}|$ adjacent symbols) entropy per symbol (F_n) is bounded as

$$\sum_{i=1}^{N} i \log i (p_i^a - p_{i+1}^a) \leq F_n \leq \sum_{i=1}^{N} p_i^a \log p_{i+1}^a, \qquad (24)$$

in a way that given the previous $a - 1$ symbols, there is a partial ordering of the symbols in the source alphabet corresponding to their probability of appearing as the next symbol. This can be discerned as a mapping between the symbols and integers such that the most probable next symbol (the ath symbol) conditioned on the $a - 1$ previous symbols, maps to $i = 1$, the second probable symbol maps to $i = 2$, and so on. Hence, p_i^a represents the probability of the ith most probable symbol (among N symbols) to be placed at the ath position in the message, conditioned on the known $a - 1$ previous symbols. Clearly, p_1^a is the most probable next symbol for the ath position in the message and p_N^a is the least probable symbol for the same position in the message. Therefore,

$$p_N^a \leq p_i^a \leq p_1^a, \qquad (25)$$

which can be inferred from [17]. The overall probability of source symbols for the $(a + 1)^{th}$ position in the source message is at least equal to the overall probability of source symbols for the ath position, that is,

$$\sum_{i=1}^{N} p_i^a \leq \sum_{i=1}^{N} p_i^{a+1}. \qquad (26)$$

In other words, the probability of guessing the correct source symbols increases with the size of the source message. For instance, for the word "the", the probability of guessing "e" after guessing "t" and "h" is higher than the probability of guessing "h" after guessing "t."

The general lower bound of the entropy of a source message with k symbols is given as [17]

$$\Gamma = \sum_{j=1}^{k} \sum_{i=1}^{N} i \log i (p_i^j - p_{i+1}^j). \qquad (27)$$

However, calculating Γ is not easy because of the dependence of a symbol on previous symbols. Consequently, for ease of calculation we try to obtain a bound that approaches Γ from below. To obtain this bound we first derive the following equation:

$$k \sum_{i=1}^{N} i \log i (p_i^k - p_{i+1}^k) \leq \Gamma \leq k \sum_{i=1}^{N} i \log i (p_i^1 - p_{i+1}^1). \qquad (28)$$

Equation (28) is obtained from the fact that Γ cannot be smaller than the entropy calculated for the source message by substituting the entropy of the last symbol (the last symbol's entropy, given the knowledge of the previous symbols is very low) in place of every source symbol; Γ also cannot be larger than the entropy calculated by substituting all symbols with the first symbol in the source.

It is easy to see that in Scenario 1 (Subsection 5.1), the lower bound entropy of the source message is at least as high as the l.h.s. of (28). This is especially true as URL addresses tend to also have symbols other than the English alphabet and sometimes contain incomplete words or meaningless strings, which would increase their randomness. Hence, we use the l.h.s. of Equation (28) to approximate the entropy of the source message, hence Equation (15) now becomes,

$$I(M^k; \underline{Z}) \leq k \sum_{i=1}^{N} i \log i (p_i^k - p_{i+1}^k)$$
$$-(N - 1 + 2N - 3/2 \log N) \quad (29)$$
$$\leq \left(kN^2 \log N \sum_{i=1}^{N} (p_i^k - p_{i+1}^k) \right)$$
$$-(3N - 3/2 \log N - 1). \quad (30)$$

Equating the r.h.s. of inequality (30) to zero, Equation (31) presents the condition for perfect secrecy,

$$k \leq \frac{3N - 3/2 \log N - 1}{N^2 \log N \sum_{i=1}^{N} (p_i^k - p_{i+1}^k)}. \quad (31)$$

Similarly, the perfect secrecy threshold for Scenario 2 is:

$$k \leq \frac{N - 1}{N^2 \log N \sum_{i=1}^{N} (p_i^k - p_{i+1}^k)} \quad (32)$$

and Scenario 3 is

$$k \leq \frac{2N - 3/2 \log N}{N^2 \log N \sum_{i=1}^{N} (p_i^k - p_{i+1}^k)}. \quad (33)$$

We note that in the dependent source case, the bound for k is dependent on the inter-symbols dependency, which is intrinsic to each message. Hence it is difficult to derive something similar to Table 1. However, in both set-ups (independent/dependent sources) an important follow-up question is, what happens when k is greater than the corresponding bounds? Then the secrecy is no longer information-theoretically perfect. Two choices exist at that point.

When k equals the bound the user and the anonymizer can use another Huffman table to continue perfectly secure communication. They can use a synchronized protocol where before k reaches the bound the anonymizer can piggyback a new encrypted Huffman table (a small overhead) with the data. Or, in the interest of speed and low overhead, the user can choose to keep using the current table and risk leaking information. In this latter case, an eavesdropper can utilize the information leakage to mount efficient brute-force or cryptanalysis attacks to break the framework. In the next section, we analyze the feasibility of such attacks.

6. COMPUTATIONAL SECRECY AND BREAKABILITY ANALYSES

In this section, we investigate and analyze the security of our framework from the perspective of well-known attacks. As per proofs in the literature [9, 10], our framework is secure against known plaintext attacks. Also, it is secure against the chosen plaintext attack as the eavesdropper cannot get

the user/anonymizer to encrypt a chosen plaintext using the corresponding Huffman table. In the chosen ciphertext attack, the attacker needs to obtain the decryption of its selected ciphertext. This is not possible in our framework as the anonymizer is the only entity with decoding capability. But, the anonymizer does not publish the decoded interest. The use of independent Huffman tables for users, selected uniformly at random, prevents the information leakage of one user from affecting others. This uniform selection of coding tables also prevents users to be able to correlate their coding tables with those of others to decode their encoded interests. Ciphertext-only attack can be mounted as the attacker has access to a set of ciphertexts, (encoded interests). If the user continues to use the same Huffman table, then the repeated interests will have the same encoded names, leaking information that the eavesdropper can use to make the cipher-text attack more potent. This leakage can be prevented by XOR-ing the postfix with a nonce and sending the nonce appended with the encoded URL.

This leaves two attacks that can be orchestrated by an attacker (active/passive): Correctly guessing the source message from the encoded sequence, i.e., ciphertext-only attack, or using brute-force to identify the correct key and the tree structure.

Correctly guessing the source message: We use *guessing entropy* [15], which is the expected number of guesses required by an attacker to ascertain the correct source message, to calculate the ease of guessing the source message. Let $G(M^k|\underline{Z})$ be the number of guesses required to identify M^k given $\underline{Z}$, in a way that $E[G(M^k|\underline{Z})]$, the expected number of successive attempts, is minimized. Equation (34) evaluates the corresponding $E[G(M^k|\underline{Z})]$:

$$E[G(M^k|\underline{Z})] = \sum_{z \in \underline{Z}} P_{\underline{Z}}(z) E[G(M^k|z)], \quad (34)$$

where $P_{\underline{Z}}(z)$ is the probability of selecting an encoded binary sequence from the pool of all possible binary sequences. Using the results in [18], the guessing entropy is lower bounded by the conditional entropy as

$$E[G(M^k|\underline{Z})] \geq 2^{H(M^k|\underline{Z})-2} + 1. \quad (35)$$

Now we evaluate the lower bound on the guessing entropy in the three scenarios. Substituting Equation (15) in Equation (35), we have the lower bound guessing entropy for Scenario 1 in Section 5 as:

$$E[G(M^k|\underline{Z})] \geq 2^{\left(3N - 3/2 \log(N) - 3\right)} + 1. \quad (36)$$

Similarly, by substituting Equations (19) and (23) in Equation (35), we have $E[G(M^k|\underline{Z})] \geq 2^{\left(2N - \frac{3}{2} \log(N)\right)-2} + 1$ and $E[G(M^k|\underline{Z})] \geq 2^{(N-1)-2} + 1$ for Scenarios 2 and 3 respectively.

Figure 3 illustrates the lower bound of the guessing entropy under the three scenarios described above, with different source alphabet size. As the conditional entropy of an unknown structure is higher than that of an unknown key, it is obvious that the attacker can extract the source message with a fewer number of guesses in Scenario 3 compared to Scenario 2.

Using a brute-force approach to identify the key and the tree structure: As mentioned in Section 3, there are $2^{(N-1)}$ mutation trees for each distribution of the Huffman code. Considering an N symbols alphabet, there exists

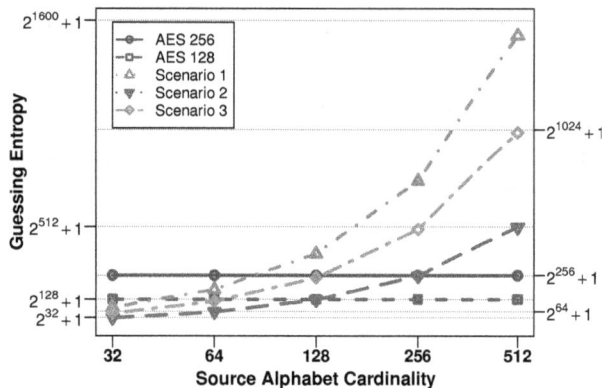

Figure 3: Guessing entropy for the three scenarios.

$C_{N'} = \frac{(2N'!)}{(N'+1)! \times (N'!)}$ different Huffman trees where $N' = N - 1$. Each of these Huffman trees has $2^{(N-1)}$ mutation trees. For brute-force attack to identify the mutation tree, an attacker needs to compute on average $\frac{2^{(N-1)}}{2} = 2^{(N-2)}$ different mutation trees–exponential in N. Given this, the attacker has to use $\frac{2(N-1)!}{N! \times (N-1)!} \times 2^{(N-2)}$ different Huffman coding tables on average to decode the encoded message when attempting the brute force attack. Even with $N = 256$ (extended ASCII) it is computationally difficult to examine this search space at a filtering router; even when it is performed offline.

So far, we have proved the information-theoretic secrecy and the computational security of our framework. In the next section, we present our experimental results, which **answer the next question**: *how efficient, applicable, and scalable is the framework for real-world mobile devices?*

7. IMPLEMENTATION AND PERFORM-ANCE ANALYSES

For our experimental evaluation, we have clients requesting content over the network to a CCN media server (content provider), which is also the anonymizer. Our testbed consists of 18 nodes, eight desktops, six laptops, and four smartphones (3 Nexus 4 and one Nexus 5). We have created a 4-tiered line topology network connected using switches and IPv4 routers. For the experiments our clients and the anonymizer are placed on either ends of the line—requests travel over five hops. The client, server, and the nodes in the network employ the CCNx-0.7 [14] code base; our framework is written in C and is integrated into CCNx. The nodes route packets using longest prefix matching.

For fair comparison, we have disabled caching, so an interest passes through all 4 tiers. We compare latency and content retrieval time over four different scenarios, namely the vanilla (Baseline) CCN implementation, CCN with our anti-censorship framework (CCN+Huffman), data retrieval using FTP, and using Tor, the state of the art Internet anti-censorship tool. We also compare the overhead of our framework and Tor over their respective baselines, Baseline CCN and FTP, respectively. For testing Tor, we setup our testbed as a Tor network where the first three network gateways (from client towards the server) are provisioned as Tor proxies—three onion layers of symmetric encryption for the client. All our results were averaged over 100 runs. The size of the contents in our experiments were chosen from the set {1 MB, 10 MB, 100 MB, 500 MB}.

One option for encoding the data name (or the postfix after the domain name) is to use a strong symmetric key algorithm, such as AES. In Table 2, we compare the time taken for encryption/decryption by two widely used AES versions and for encoding/decoding using our framework. As an alternative solution, the client can hash the content name with a salt given by the anonymizer. The anonymizer needs to pre-hash all the content names with each salt corresponding to each client. Upon receiving an interest from a particular client, the anonymizer does a look-up on the hashed content name to find the requested content. Though the storage requirement for these hashes grows infeasible with a large number of clients and/or contents, we nonetheless evaluate the performance of the Openssl SHA1 digest for the sake of comparison.

We measured the timings on a wired laptop (AMD Turion, 2.4 GHz, dual core, 2.7 GB RAM) and on two wireless Nexus 5 smartphones (Krait 2.3 GHz, quad core, 2 GB RAM). For the Huffman operations, indicated by "Huffman coding" in Table 2, the time includes reading the source symbol frequencies, building the tree, and encoding/decoding the codewords. While the "Huffman*" represents the elapsed time only for the encoding/decoding operations. The represented time for AES accounts for the encryption and the decryption operations only. The data name in our test contained 75 characters.

The optimized OpenSSL AES version is almost four times as fast as the aescrypt version; we note that this is the version we use in our Tor experiments. Encoding/decoding in our framework (Huffman*) is three orders of magnitude faster than OpenSSL (0.000034 vs. 0.010).

Table 2: Running time comparison between the AES symmetric key cryptography and Huffman encoding.

Encoding Scheme	Encoding (s)	Decoding (s)
aescrypt in unix (laptop)	0.050	0.021
AES openssl (laptop)	0.010	0.008
Huffman coding (laptop)	0.004	0.004
AES openssl (Nexus 5)	0.041	0.023
Huffman coding (Nexus 5)	0.006	0.005
Huffman* (laptop)	0.000034	0.000027
SHA1 hashing (laptop)	0.000093	

Figure 4 shows the download times on the laptop client for different content sizes and compares Baseline CCN (*denoted as C*), CCN+Huffman (*denoted as H*), FTP (*denoted as F*), and Tor (*denoted as T*); the Y-axis is in **log scale** for clarity. It is easy to understand that the download time increases for all approaches with increase in content size. CCN performs worse than FTP on account of the overheads of multiple searches on each forwarding node: searching the cache (content store) and searching the pending interests table (PIT) for the interest. This is true even if the data item is not in the cache. Having said that, *our framework on top of CCN does not add* any appreciable extra delay (less than 1.8 times). In comparison, **Tor results in significant additional overhead** in comparison to FTP, (between 2 and 38 times). Of course, the overhead for Tor is on account of the multi-layer encryption. We have not compared our approach to ANDaNA [7] as for content sizes 10 MB and greater Tor performs better than ANDaNA; most of our tests are for such larger contents. For completeness, in the future we will compare our approach with ANDaNA. We will implement the standard ANDaNA protocol on our testbed for compar-

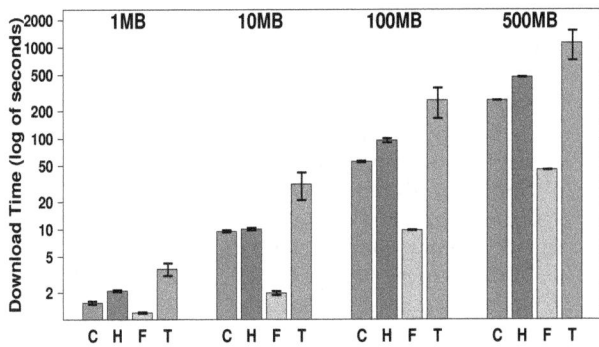

Figure 4: **Average download time comparisons between Baseline CCN (C), Huffman (H), FTP (F), and Tor (T).**

ison.

Figure 5 presents the results of a detailed comparison of the overhead ratio of our framework over the Baseline CCN with that of Tor over FTP. An interesting observation is that the error-bars for the overhead for Tor are much higher compared to those of our framework. Given that our tests were the only applications running in our testbed, it shows that the multiple levels of encryptions in Tor results in erratic behavior (Tor does not induce inter-packet delays for anonymity), which is undesirable in terms of user experience.

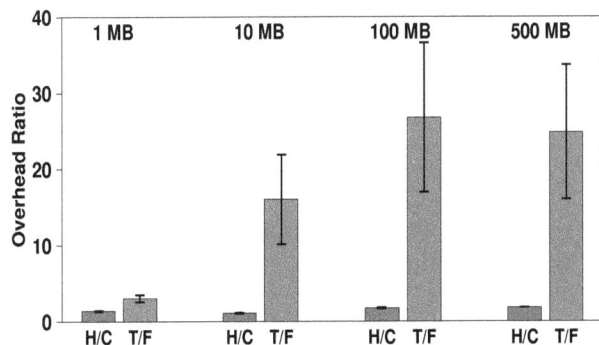

Figure 5: **Protocol overhead comparison between Huffman (H/C) and Tor (T/F).**

This fact is also highlighted by the estimated round trip time (RTT) results in Figure 6. *We have not shown the error-bars for the RTT because Tor's RTT varies a lot and undermines the graph's readability.* Baseline CCN and our approach have almost the same RTT, with very small deviations, however Tor has significant deviations. Note that the longer RTT values for the CCN and our approach in comparison to FTP are due to the extra lookups.

Figures 7, 8, and 9 present averaged results for the smartphone clients (Nexus 5) connected over WiFi. For conciseness, we only present the CCN and our CCN+Huffman results. Figure 7 presents the download times for the smartphones. Due to the wireless connections, which suffer from interference from other communications in the building, the smartphone clients require proportionally larger download times for all contents than the wired laptops.

Figure 8 presents the overhead of the Huffman framework over Baseline CCN. Again the overheads are minimal and with very low variance, which is excellent. Figure 9 presents

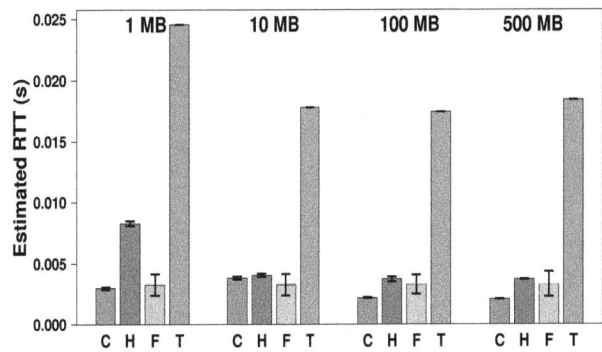

Figure 6: **Estimated average round trip time for C, H, F, and T.**

the comparison of the estimated RTTs between the Baseline CCN and our framework for the smartphone client. The RTT values are very consistent for all runs, with our framework having a very small increase in RTT in comparison to the baseline. The smartphone client results conform with those of the laptop, the variance is a bit higher because of the wireless medium and interference. The average RTT stabilizes for large contents, hence the RTT values tend to become lower. We believe that the smartphone Tor RTTs will also have commensurate trends as the laptop results.

These results show that our framework is much more efficient and scalable than Tor, the state of the art, as a mechanism to mitigate censorship of user communications.

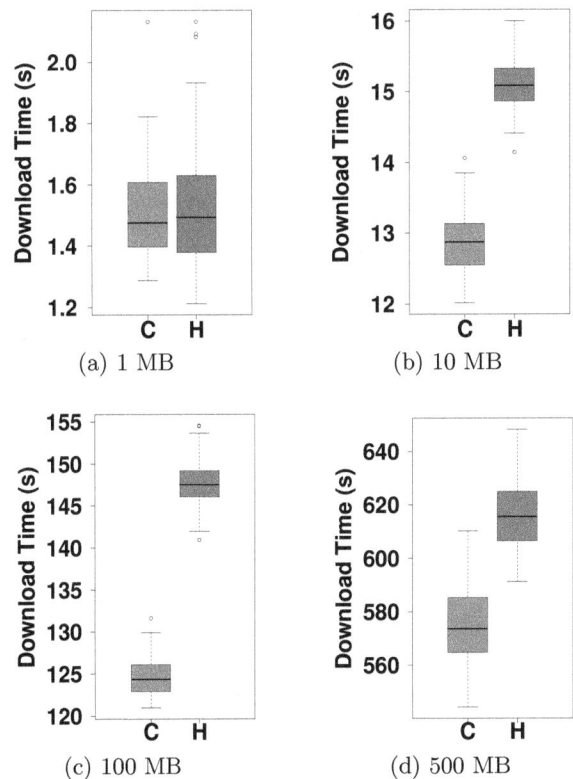

(a) 1 MB   (b) 10 MB

(c) 100 MB   (d) 500 MB

Figure 7: **Download time comparison between Baseline CCN (C) and Huffman (H) for the smartphone clients.**

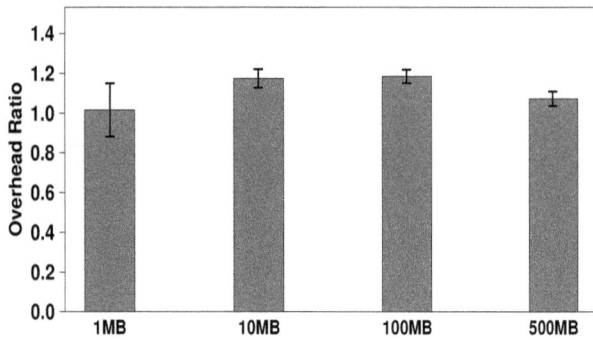

Figure 8: Protocol overhead of Huffman for the smartphone clients.

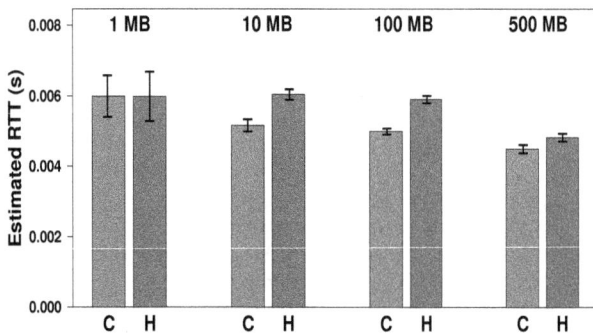

Figure 9: Estimated average RTT for baseline CCN (C) and Huffman (H) on the smartphone clients.

8. CONCLUSIONS AND FUTURE WORK

In this paper, we presented a lightweight anti-censorship framework for ICN users, specifically for mobile users. We proved conditions and thresholds for perfect secrecy as well as analyzed the computational complexity of the framework. The framework's breakability study showed the advantages of Huffman coding over AES, and the extensive experimental results demonstrated the efficiency of the framework in comparison to other frameworks, such as Tor.

In the future, we plan to implement our framework in other ICN architectures. We will analyze the trade-off between the users' privacy and caching by using an intermediate anonymizer. We will also investigate the use of hash functions based lookup at the anonymizer.

9. REFERENCES

[1] PSIRP Project, Deliverable D4.6: Final Evaluation Report on Deployment Incentives and Business Models, http://www.psirp.org/publications/.

[2] G. Acs, M. Conti, P. Gasti, C. Ghali, and G. Tsudik. Cache privacy in named-data networking. In *International Conference onDistributed Computing Systems (ICDCS)*, pages 41–51. IEEE, 2013.

[3] Anonymizer Universal. https://anonymizer.com/.

[4] S. Arianfar, T. Koponen, B. Raghavan, and S. Shenker. On preserving privacy in content-oriented networks. In *Proceedings of the ACM SIGCOMM workshop on Information-centric networking*, pages 19–24. ACM, 2011.

[5] A. Chaabane, E. De Cristofaro, M. Kaafar, and E. Uzun. Privacy in content-oriented networking: Threats and countermeasures. *ACM SIGCOMM Computer Communication Review*, 43(3):25–33, 2013.

[6] C. Dannewitz. NetInf: An information-centric design for the future Internet. In *3rd GI/ITG KuVS Workshop on The Future Internet*, 2009.

[7] S. DiBenedetto, P. Gasti, G. Tsudik, and E. Uzun. Andana: Anonymous named data networking application. *Arxiv preprint arXiv:1112.2205*, 2011.

[8] H. Dorrie. *100 Great problems of elementary mathematics*. Dover Publications, 1965.

[9] A. S. Fraenkel and S. T. Klein. Complexity aspects of guessing prefix codes. *Algorithmica*, 12(4-5):409–419, 1994.

[10] D. Gillman, M. Mohtashemi, and R. Rivest. On breaking a huffman code. *IEEE Transactions on Information Theory*, 42(3):972–976, 1996.

[11] D. Huffman et al. A method for the construction of minimum redundancy codes. *proc. IRE*, 40(9):1098–1101, 1952.

[12] V. Jacobson, D.K. Smetters, J.D. Thornton, M.F. Plass, N.H. Briggs, and R.L. Braynard. Networking named content. In *Proceedings of the 5th international conference on Emerging networking experiments and technologies*, pages 1–12. ACM, 2009.

[13] T. Koponen, M. Chawla, B.G. Chun, A. Ermolinskiy, K.H. Kim, S. Shenker, and I. Stoica. A data-oriented (and beyond) network architecture. In *ACM SIGCOMM Computer Communication Review*, volume 37, pages 181–192. ACM, 2007.

[14] Palo Alto Research Lab. Ccnx. http://www.ccnx.org/.

[15] J. L. Massey. Guessing and entropy. In *Proceedings to IEEE International Symposium on Information Theory*, page 204. IEEE, 1994.

[16] PURSUIT Project. http://www.fp7-pursuit.eu/pursuitweb.

[17] C. Shannon. Prediction and entropy of printed english. *Bell system technical journal*, 30(1):50–64, 1951.

[18] G. Smith. On the foundations of quantitative information flow. In *Foundations of Software Science and Computational Structures*, pages 288–302. Springer, 2009.

[19] Tor Project: Anonymity Online. http://www.torproject.org/.

[20] C.-P. Wu and C.-C. Kuo. Design of integrated multimedia compression and encryption systems. *IEEE Transactions on Multimedia*, 7(5):828–839, 2005.

[21] D. Xie and C.-C. Kuo. nhanced multiple huffman table (mht) encryption scheme using key hopping. In *Proceedings of the 2004 International Symposium on Circuits and Systems (ISCAS)*, volume 5, pages 568–571. IEEE, 2004.

[22] J. Zhou, Z. Liang, Y. Chen, and Oscar C. Au. Security analysis of multimedia encryption schemes based on multiple huffman table. *Signal Processing Letters, IEEE*, 14(3):201–204, 2007.

Schematizing Trust in Named Data Networking

Yingdi Yu
UCLA
yingdi@cs.ucla.edu

Alexander Afanasyev
UCLA
afanasev@cs.ucla.edu

David Clark
MIT
ddc@csail.mit.edu

kc claffy
CAIDA
kc@caida.org

Van Jacobson
UCLA
vanj@cs.ucla.edu

Lixia Zhang
UCLA
lixia@cs.ucla.edu

ABSTRACT

Securing communication in network applications involves many complex tasks that can be daunting even for security experts. The Named Data Networking (NDN) architecture builds data authentication into the network layer by requiring all applications to sign and authenticate every data packet. To make this authentication usable, the decision about which keys can sign which data and the procedure of signature verification need to be automated. This paper explores the ability of NDN to enable such automation through the use of *trust schemas*. Trust schemas can provide data consumers an automatic way to discover which keys to use to authenticate individual data packets, and provide data producers an automatic decision process about which keys to use to sign data packets and, if keys are missing, how to create keys while ensuring that they are used only within a narrowly defined scope ("the least privilege principle"). We have developed a set of trust schemas for several prototype NDN applications with different trust models of varying complexity. Our experience suggests that this approach has the potential of being generally applicable to a wide range of NDN applications.

Categories and Subject Descriptors

C.2.0 [**Computer-Communication Networks**]: General— *Security and protection*; D.4.6 [**Software**]: Security and Protection

Keywords

Security, Named Data Networking

1. INTRODUCTION

Designing secure systems and network applications involves properly authenticating multiple entities in the system and granting these entities with the minimum set of privileges necessary to perform operations. In contrast to traditional IP networks where applications usually rely on

ICN'15, September 30–October 2, 2015, San Francisco, CA, USA.
© 2015 ACM. ISBN 978-1-4503-3855-4/15/09 ...$15.00.
DOI: http://dx.doi.org/10.1145/2810156.2810170.

an additional layer (e.g., Transport Layer Security [9]) to authenticate connections, Named Data Networking (NDN) [18, 20] is a proposed data-centric Internet architecture that requires every application to name and sign the produced network-level data packets and to authenticate received packets. To utilize the data-centric security of NDN without requiring application developers and users to be security experts, system-level support is needed to automate the process of packet signing and authentication.

The power of the NDN architecture comes from naming data hierarchically with the granularity of network-level packets and sealing named data with public key signatures. Producers use key names to indicate which public key a consumer should retrieve to verify signatures of produced data packets. In addition to fetching the specified keys and performing signature verification, consumers also match data and key names to determine whether the key is authorized to sign each specific data packet.

To facilitate this matching process, we introduce the concepts of *trust rules* and *trust schemas*. A set of trust rules defines a trust schema that instantiates an overall trust model of an application, i.e., what is (are) legitimate key(s) for each data packet that the application produces or consumes. The fundamental idea is that each trust rule defines a relationship between the name of each piece of data and its signing key, e.g., both must share the same prefix, share the same suffix, and/or have specific name components at certain position of the names. Given a trust schema that correctly reflects the trust model of the application, data producers can select (and if necessary generate) the right keys to sign the produced data automatically, and consumers can properly authenticate each retrieved data packet.

In this paper we describe how NDN naming and the use of *trust schemas* enable automation of data signing and authentication in NDN applications with complex trust models. We have implemented a prototype of a trust schema in NDN application development libraries (ndn-cxx and NDN-CCL) which have been used to power the trust management of several NDN applications, including the NDN Forwarding Daemon (NFD), NDN Link State Routing Protocol (NLSR), NDN Domain Name System (NDNS), NDN Repository System (repo-ng), and ChronoChat applications [15].

We can summarize our contributions as three-fold. First, we identified a *name-based trust management* mechanism, which we hope not only can help secure NDN applications, but can also benefit other data-centric systems. Second, we invented *trust schema* as a systematic way to define application trust models and introduce the concept of *security design pattern* to facilitate application development. Third, we developed a prototype of *trust schema interpreter* that has been successfully tested to automate authentication and signing process in a set of diverse NDN applications.

We organize the rest of this paper as follows. Section 2 introduces data authentication in NDN and its threat model. We then explain the value of a trust schema (Section 3), our trust schema design (Section 4), its use in automating trust management (Section 5), and other considerations in their use (Section 6). Finally we review related work and summarize our contribution.

2. DATA AUTHENTICATION IN NDN

NDN fosters a data-centric security model at the network layer [18]: each data packet is uniquely named and this name is bound to the content using a signature. Besides being a transport unit as an IP packet, an NDN data packet is also a storage unit, so that the signature carried in a data packet secures its content whether the packet is in motion or in storage. Beside the name, content, signature, and a few other fields, a data packet also contains a `KeyLocator` field [16] to indicate the name of the public key that is used to produce the signature. In NDN, a key is simply another piece of named NDN content (Figure 1). Like any other data packet, a packet carrying a public key is also signed, making it equivalent to a certificate [19]. Because NDN names the content carried in a packet, for simplicity, we will use the term "key" to refer to an NDN data packet that carries a public key.

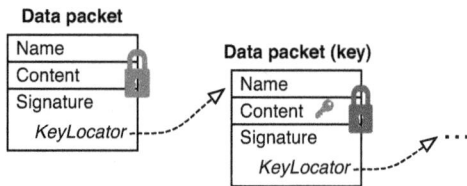

Figure 1: Authentication elements in NDN data packet

In the rest of the paper we assume that given a name, the network can directly retrieve the corresponding data packet. Other considerations, including fetching data packets whose names are not globally routed [1], may require additional steps in data retrieval but will not affect the security model described in this paper.

2.1 Example of Data Authentication

We use a simplified blog website framework as an example throughout the paper to illustrate a possible trust model and our proposed approach to schematize it. The framework includes four groups of entities (Figure 2): the website, website administrators, blog authors, and articles. The website may have a few administrators, who can authorize authors to publish articles on the website. Trust relations between these entities in NDN terms can be captured by signed data packets and chains of keys. When an administrator installs the website software, the installer generates a key[1] to act as the root of trust for the website. The installer process also creates a key for the initial administrator and signs it with the website's key. The initial administrator can further

---

[1] This key may be self-signed or later secured using some trust model, e.g., PKI or web-of-trust.

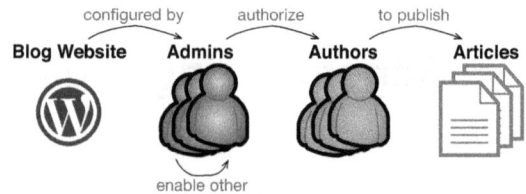

Figure 2: Entities of a simple blog website framework

delegate management privileges to other administrators by signing their keys, and any administrator can add authors into the system by signing the authors' keys. Each author can publish on the website by signing the produced articles using a valid author key.

When a reader retrieves an article, he or she can recursively follow the `KeyLocator` field in each data packet to retrieve the key of the author who wrote the article, the key of the administrator who authorized the author, and the key of the blog website where the article is published. If the reader accepts the website trust model and trusts the public key of the website (or uses PKI or web-of-trust mechanisms to verify authenticity of the key), the reader can reliably authenticate legitimate articles through a sequence of data packet signature verifications.

2.2 Threat Model

Threats to data authentication integrity in NDN include failed authentication, mis-authentication, and key compromise. Failed authentication of a legitimate key (false negative) can result in a consumer treating valid data as malicious, potentially leading to denial of service. Mis-authentication of a mis-configured or malicious key (false positive) can cause consumers to accept false data. These errors can occur when the trust schema (data-key relations) is incorrectly or unclearly defined, or when the authentication mechanism does not fully adhere to the defined schema. A set of commonly used trust schemas written by security experts not only can mitigate these threats, but also facilitate automation of both signing and authentication mechanisms.

When a legitimate key is compromised, an attacker can obtain privileges associated with this key. To mitigate this threat we enforce "the least privilege principle": each key must have a restricted non-elevating usage scope to limit the damage upon key compromise, and keys with broader privileges should be used as infrequently as possible.

3. WHY WE NEED A TRUST SCHEMA

In general, the relationship between data and key names can be complex. Depending on an application's naming structure and trust model, data authentication may involve a chain of keys (*authentication path*) across several different namespaces. We use our blog website example introduced in Section 2 to illustrate the necessity of authentication across different namespaces, and highlight the need for the trust schema to concisely express complex trust model relations.

The blog website framework defines entities in the system and also their trust relationships. Since everything is explicitly named in NDN, the framework also needs to define a naming representation of the entities. Figure 3 shows a possible representation: assuming the website owns "`/a`" namespace and allocates "`/a/blog`" to blog publishing, articles are represented as data packets under the "`/a/blog/article`" namespace, with category, publication year, and unique article identifier; each author obtains a key under the "`/a/blog/author`" namespace with an author identifier;[2] each administrator obtains a key under the "`/a/blog/admin`" namespace with an administrator identifier; and the website itself has a configuration key with the name "`/a/blog`" (e.g., created during the installation of the blog). An implementation of this blog website framework must capture the trust relationship between all these entities in terms of the relationship between NDN namespaces. However, this comprehensive naming structure leads to the fact that an authentication path following the trust model may need to traverse three namespaces: "`/a/blog/article`", "`/a/blog/author`", and "`/a/blog/admin`" as shown in Figure 3.

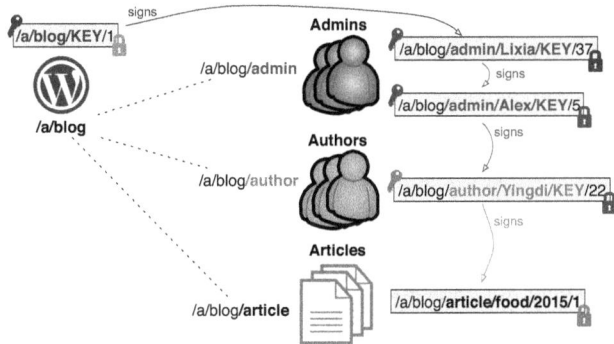

Figure 3: Example of namespaces and authentication paths in a blog website "`/a/blog`"

In theory, it is possible for application developers to hard-code all relationships in the trust model, i.e., relationships between articles and authors keys, between authors and administrators keys, between administrators keys and other administrators keys, and between administrators keys and the configuration key of the website. However in practice, even with a simple trust relationships as in our example, this process is non-trivial and error-prone. A small implementation error may compromise the security of the entire website. For example, a website implementation that accidentally associates author management with author keys rather than with administrator keys may allow authors to authorize another author without the permission from an administrator. Or, an article-publishing application that mistakenly uses an administrator key to directly sign an article violates the least privilege principle, and may also prevent browsers that comply with the trust model from authenticating articles.

In contrast, when the trust relationships are captured by a set of well-defined rules that match data and key names (*trust schema*), a system-level tool interpreting these rules can automatically execute authentication and signing procedures. This ability to automate unburdens developers from individually handling sophisticated data signing and authentication. A trust schema also makes it feasible for security experts to define a set of generalized trust models (e.g., one for blog websites, one for mail services, etc.) that other application instances of the same type can reuse. Each reuse

[2]The last two components of each key name are "`KEY`" and a key identifier. This naming convention allows authors to change keys over time.

can continue to refine and debug the schema, improving it for future applications.

4. TRUST SCHEMA

In this section, we present the trust schema as a tool to define trust models in a generalized way. A trust schema comprises a set of linked trust rules and one or more trust anchors. As we will show later in this section, the trust schema mechanism can be used to automate both authentication and signing processes. To define trust schema rules, we will use a notation similar to regular expressions to express the *name pattern*. Table 1 gives a brief summary of the syntax elements we use in name patterns that are formally defined in [17].

Table 1: Elements of name patterns used in trust schema definitions

`<name>`	Match name component `name`
`<>`	Match any single name component, i.e., wildcard
`<name><>`	Match name component `name` followed by any single name component
`<>*`	Match any sequence of name components
`(...)`	Match pattern inside the brakets and assign it as an indexed sub-pattern
`\n`	Reference to the n-th indexed sub-pattern
`[func]`	Match (for authentication) or specialize (for signing) name component according to function `func` defined pattern, i.e., wildcard specializer
`rule(arg1, ...)`	Derive a more specific name pattern from `rule`'s data name pattern with arguments `arg1`, ...

4.1 Trust Rule

A trust rule is an association of the data name with its corresponding signing key name. There are multiple ways to represent such association. For example, Figure 4(a) shows a simple direct association between an article name and its corresponding author name. This rule precisely captures that the article "`.../food/2015/1`" must be signed by author key "`.../Yingdi/KEY/22`", but says nothing about other articles or authors, even those that share the same naming patterns. If we can generalize the name relationships in trust rules, and reliably link rules to one another, we can construct concise, sophisticated, robust, and re-usable trust models.

4.1.1 Generalizing Trust Rules

A well-defined trust model usually associates the same type of data with the same type of keys, e.g., articles should always be signed by the authors. We can use the naming structure of a given application (or a set of applications that share the same naming structure) to create a set of rules to define the relationships between name patterns for data and keys in that application. This set of trust rules then captures the complete trust model for the application.

In the blog example, all articles share the same prefix "`/a/blog/article`", but each article has its own category, year, and article identifier. One way to generalize this relationship is to use name patterns as shown in Figure 4(b). In Figure 4 and later examples, we use the wildcard "`<>`" to match any name component (i.e., the schema does not impose any restrictions on the content of the name component), "`[user]`" to match alphanumerical user identifiers, and "`[id]`" to match numerical key identifiers.

179

<a/blog/article/food/2015/1 ⟿ /a/blog/author/Yingdi/KEY/22>

/a/blog/article/food/2015/1 ⟿ /a/blog/author/Yingdi/KEY/22

(a) *Explicit relationship between specific data and key name (article is valid if signed by an authenticated key with the specified name)*

/a/blog/article/**food/2015/1**	/a/blog/author/**Yingdi/KEY/22**
/a/blog/article/**drinks/2014/2**	/a/blog/author/**David/KEY/31**
<a><blog><article><>⟨⟩⟨⟩	<a><blog><author>[user]<KEY>[id]

(b) *Generalized relation between data and key names (any article is valid if it is signed by any authenticated author)*

<a><blog><article><>⟨⟩⟨⟩	<a><blog><author>[user]<KEY>[id]
<la><times><blog><article><>⟨⟩⟨⟩	<la><times><blog><author>[user]<KEY>[id]
(<>*)<blog><article>⟨⟩⟨⟩	\1<blog><author>[user]<KEY>[id]

(c) *Coupling generalized relations of data and key names (any article is valid if it is signed by any authenticated author of this blog)*

Figure 4: Trust rule generalization

	Rule	Data Name	Key Name
(a)	article	(<>*)<blog><article><>⟨⟩⟨⟩	\1<blog><author>[user]<KEY>[id]
	author	(<>*)<blog><author>[user]<KEY>[id]	\1<blog><admin>[user]<KEY>[id]
(b)	article	(<>*)<blog><article><>	author(\1)
	author	(<>*)<blog><author>[user]<KEY>[id]	\1<blog><admin>[user]<KEY>[id]

Figure 5: Generalization of trust rule linkage: (a) implicit linkage; (b) explicit linkage

In general, trust models must explicitly associate a data name with its signing key name through matching of name components. In our example, both the article name and the author name must share the same website name ("/a"). To capture this constraint, we leverage sub-patterns and repetition syntax, as highlighted in Figure 4(c). We believe this syntax is sufficiently general to capture complex trust model frameworks, allowing reuse of trust models by different application instances. In other words, the trust schema for our blog example can be used by any other blog website that shares the same trust model.

4.1.2 *Linking Trust Rules*

A trust model should also properly associate keys with their signing keys, to ensure that a data consumer can reliably construct chains of keys to authenticate data and that a data producer can correctly choose or initialize its signing keys.

Figure 5(a) defines "article" and "author" trust rules. The key name pattern in the "article" rule will always match the data name pattern of the "author" rule, therefore both rules are implicitly linked. However, in order to ensure integrity of the trust model, the schema should unambiguously describe an authentication path (or paths) for each valid data packet. Therefore, each rule has to be explicitly linked to other rule(s) in the trust schema definition.

To explicitly link rules, we assign each rule a unique identifier to be used in a function-like way as part of the key name pattern, as shown on Figure 5(b). In other words, invoking such rules is similar to invoking a function: invocation substitutes the key name pattern with the data name pattern from the invoked rule, specializing it with the supplied pat-

Rule	Data Name	Key Name
admin	(<>*)<blog><admin>[user]<KEY>[id]	root(\1)

Anchor	Key Name	Key
root	(<>*)<blog><KEY>[id]	/a/blog/KEY/1 (0x30 0x82 ...)

Figure 6: Example of linking trust rule and anchor

terns or references to the indexed sub-patterns. In our example, the "article" rule invokes the "author" rule passing to it the first indexed sub-pattern. For the "/a/blog/article /food/2015/1" article, the sub-pattern will expand to "/a" and the invocation to the "author" rule will return "<a><blog> <author>[user]<KEY>[id]" name pattern. This linkage imposes the restriction that only authorized authors of blog "/a/blog" can sign and publish articles of the blog.

4.2 Trust Anchor

To be complete, a trust schema must also include one or more trust anchors which serve as bootstrapping points for the trust model. A trust anchor is a key that is pre-authenticated using an out-of-band mechanism, e.g., manually installed or comes with software packages. In the trust schema we express trust anchors as special rules that include a key name pattern and a pre-authenticated key. Every successful authentication path must end at a trust anchor. Therefore, a trust schema must always include a way for trust rules to establish the link(s) from data or key names down to a trust anchor. Figure 6 shows an example of the trust rule "admin" linking to the trust anchor "root".

The trust anchor performs two important functions. First, it explicitly defines not only the name of the trust anchor, but also the key bits, i.e., if a packet is signed with a key that matches the name pattern in a trust anchor, this packet must be authenticated using the pre-specified key bits. Second, the anchor explicitly restricts the privilege of the pre-authenticated public key using name pattern, so that the key cannot be used to authorize anything else. For example, an administrator's key of another website "/another/blog /admin/Carl" will not be a valid administrator's key for "/a/blog": the expanded key pattern "<another><blog><KEY> [id]" will not match the blog's trust anchor "/a/blog/KEY/1". Note that the schema also prohibits another website's administrator key to be signed with the blog's trust anchor: the "admin" rule will rightfully reject such a key.

4.3 Crypto Requirements

In addition to providing a generalized formal definition of trust rules and trust anchors, a trust schema must also include cryptographic requirements on data signatures, such as the hash and signing algorithm and the minimum key size. These requirements are not directly related to naming, but can help prevent consumers from accepting data with easily compromised signatures. Therefore, a trust schema should clearly state these parameters as an essential part of a trust model.

4.4 Trust Schema Examples

We now demonstrate how the trust schema we described so far can express two different trust models. The first trust model is for our blog website framework, and the second is an example of a model that resembles the trust model of

Rule	Data Name	Key Name	Examples
article (◇*)<blog><article>◇<◇◇>		author(\1)	/a/blog/**article**/food/2015/1
author (◇*)<blog><author>[user]<KEY>[id]		admin(\1)	/a/blog/author/Yingdi/KEY/22
admin (◇*)<blog><admin>[user]<KEY>[id]		admin(\1)	/a/blog/admin/Alex/KEY/5
		I root(\1)	/a/blog/admin/Lixia/KEY/37

Anchor	Key Name	Key
root	(◇*)<blog><KEY>[id]	/a/blog/KEY/1 (0x30 0x82 ...)

Figure 7: Trust schema the blog website framework with "`/a/KEY/1`" as the trust anchor

DNSSEC and *strictly* follows the naming hierarchy to match data and key names.

4.4.1 Blog Website Framework

In the blog website example, the trust rules must capture the relationship between articles and authors, between authors and administrators, as well as between administrators and blog website configuration (the blog's trust anchor). An example of the trust schema that can achieve these goals is shown in Figure 7. Note that this schema assumes that the blog's configuration key "`/a/blog/KEY/1`" is pre-authenticated (i.e., a trust anchor). Depending on the specific usage scenario, a blog reader may further authenticate the configuration key using a hierarchical trust model similar to the example in Section 4.4.2, or using some other trust model, e.g., web-of-trust.

The first rule in the example schema, "`article`", captures the trust constraint that authors must sign their articles with their keys. Similarly, the "`author`" rule ensures that only blog administrators can sign authors' keys. The final "`admin`" rule defines two possible relations for administrators' keys in the security framework: (1) existing administrators may delegate administrator privileges to another person; and (2) authentication paths for the administrator keys must terminate at the blog website trust anchor.

Note that although every trust rule in the trust schema in Figure 7 uses the repeated wildcard "`<>*`" to match the website prefix, the prefix is always determined (specialized) at the moment when the "`article`" rule captures the original article data name. After the "`article`" rule captures "`/a/blog/article/food/2015/1`" data, prefix "`/a`" is propagated to the "`author`" rule as a reference to the first sub-pattern, then to the "`admin`" rule, and down to the "`root`" trust anchor.

4.4.2 Hierarchical Trust Model

In a linear hierarchical trust model, with DNSSEC [2] as a prominent example, a single rule can capture the relationship between all the data and key names; in plain English, this rule is "the signing key name must be a prefix of the data name." Because key names should be unique and need to include additional suffix components as shown on Figure 8, the trust schema for the hierarchical relationship in NDN needs to consider these additional components.[3] The overall trust in this model can be bootstrapped using one or more trust anchors associated with the top level namespace(s).

Figure 9 shows an example of the trust schema that defines the hierarchical trust relationships, consisting of a single rule

---

[3]For simplicity, in this example we consider only authentication of DNS keys, but the trust model and schema can be easily extended to other DNS data, as shown with the blog website example.

		signed by
Blog website key	/a/blog/**KEY**/1	
la namespace owner's key	/a/**KEY**/42	signed by
Root key	/**KEY**/2	

Figure 8: Example of naming in hierarchical trust model

Rule	Data Name	Key Name	Examples
key	(◇*)(◇)<KEY>[id]	key(\1, null) I root()	/a/**bog**/KEY/1
			/a/**KEY**/42

Anchor	Key Name	Key
root	<KEY>[id]	/KEY/2 (0x66 0x3a ...)

Figure 9: Trust schema for the hierarchical trust model with "`/KEY/2`" as the trust anchor

and a trust anchor. The rule "`key`" captures that keys at each level of the hierarchy must be signed by the keys from the parent namespace, i.e., the prefix before "`KEY`" of the signing key name must be one component shorter than the name of the key itself. The trust anchor ensures that the authentication path discovery terminates when it reaches the root namespace: when the prefix of the signing key before "`KEY`" is empty (just "`/`"), then it must be signed by the specified "`/KEY/2`" key.

The "`key`" rule is recursively linked to itself and to the trust anchor. In these cases, when matching data and key names, all specified patterns need to be considered, with anchor rules taking precedence. For a key "`/a/blog/KEY/1`", the rule "`key`" will extract the parent namespace of the key (i.e., "`/a`") and derive two name patterns: "`<a><KEY>[id]`" and "`<KEY><2>`". Given the signing key name matches the first pattern, the process recursively continues with the same rule, until there is a match with the trust anchor.

If the key's `KeyLocator` does not match any key name pattern, it implies that the key does not comply with the trust model and should be treated as an invalid key.

4.5 Schema for Authentication

For each data packet, the trust schema determines a valid authentication path(s) within the corresponding trust model. Given that the trust schema is expressed as formally defined rules, an *authentication interpreter* of the trust schema can automate the whole authentication process for any given trust model (Section 5.1).

For each received data packet, the authenticating interpreter finds the corresponding trust rule by matching the name of the packet against the specified name patterns in the rules. If the packet and its `KeyLocator` comply with constraints of the found trust rule, the interpreter can then retrieve the public key according to the data's `KeyLocator` and recursively inspect the retrieved key according to the trust schema, until reaching a trust anchor or a pre-defined limit on the number of recursive steps. In the former case, the interpreter has collected all the intermediate public keys on a valid authentication path, thus can verify signatures starting from the trust anchor up to the received data packet. When the interpreter cannot find a rule that matches the received data packet, or the constructed authentication path loops, or the path becomes overly long, the interpreter declares failure to discover the authentication path.

The received data packet is authenticated only if there is a valid authentication path according to the trust schema, and each signature on the path is verifiable and satisfies the cryptographic requirements of the schema. In other words, either failure to discover authentication path or failure to verify any signature on the authentication path implies that the received data packet cannot be authenticated with the interpreted trust model.

4.6 Schema for Signing

One can also view the trust schema as a collection of constraints on a data packet's signing key, with respect to its name, signature, key type and size, etc. Thus, the trust schema also specifies the required signing process, i.e., how to select or generate signing keys given the name of the data packet. Effectively, this allows automation of the signing process using a *signing interpreter* of the trust schema (Section 5.2).

The signing interpreter takes a data packet as an input and looks up the corresponding trust rule. Instead of checking for compliance of the data's name and `KeyLocator` to the trust rule, it infers the correct name of the key to be used to sign the data packet. If this key exists on the system, the interpreter will immediately sign and return the data packet. If the key does not exist, the interpreter will try to generate the key with the specified name and crypto requirements, and then sign this key by recursively re-interpreting the same schema again with the generated key as a new input. See further details in Section 5.2 on how the interpreter can generate key names based on rules in the trust schema.

Note that it is not always possible for the interpreter to automatically generate all necessary keys, without out-of-band verification mechanisms. For example, if a not-yet authorized author is trying to sign an article for publication, the interpreter will fail to sign it, as the author does not have a valid key to sign an article, nor a key to endorse an author on the blog, nor a key to configure a new administrator in the system. Even in this case, the interpreter can still generate useful diagnostic information, e.g., which keys are missing and how to obtain them.

5. AUTOMATING TRUST

Now that we have introduced the concept of schema-based data authentication and signing, we will describe in detail how to automate these processes, using the blog website framework as an example.

5.1 Automating Authentication

Each step of the authentication path for data (key) packets is defined by the rules of the trust schema. Rules are linked together through a function-like invocation of rule names as part of the key name pattern definition, as shown in Figure 7. The authentication process moves forward (from one step to the next) only if the data (or key) satisfies the conditions of the rule. We can model this authentication process as a Finite State Machine (FSM), with each state representing a rule and state transitions representing function-like invocations. This way, once a data packet enters the FSM, the FSM's states define the packet's authentication path, and an automatic process can walk through these states until exiting the FSM with success or failure.

Execution of the FSM processing requires a trust schema interpreter. The interpreter used for data authentication,

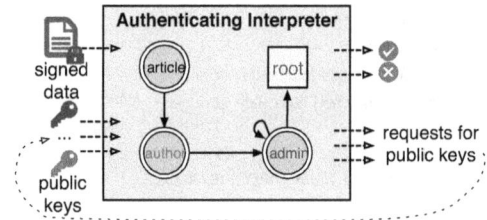

Figure 10: Finite state machine for the authentication interpreter of the blog website trust model schema

which we call *authenticating interpreter*, takes data packets as input, requests public keys when necessary, and outputs whether the received packet is authenticated or not. Given the trust schema for a trust model, an authenticating interpreter can effectively automate the process of data authentication for this trust model. Figure 10 shows the FSM of an authenticating interpreter for the blog website trust model discussed in Section 4.4.1.

5.1.1 Authentication State

Whenever a new data packet arrives at the FSM, the interpreter determines the corresponding initial state by checking the data name against the name patterns for each state. After that, the interpreter initiates the key name checking procedure, including steps to:

- extract components from the data name according to the defined sub-patterns;

- derive the key name pattern from the rule's key name functions with the extracted components;

- check if the data's `KeyLocator` matches the derived key name pattern.

If the data packet passes the key name checking, the authentication process transitions to the downstream state of the FSM: the interpreter requests the key identified by the `KeyLocator` field carried in this packet and pauses FSM processing until the key is retrieved. When the key is delivered to the interpreter, the interpreter initiates a new instance of the same checking procedure at the state on which the FSM processing previously paused. Whenever the FSM transitions to a trust anchor state, the interpreter immediately triggers verification of signatures, following the reverse path of transitions in the FSM.

5.1.2 Walking Through the State Machine

In this section we demonstrate how the authentication automation can work for the blog website trust model. We use an article data packet with name "`/a/blog/article/food /2015/1`" signed by an author key "`/a/blog/author/Yingdi /KEY/22`" as an example to show how the authentication process goes through the state machine shown in Figure 10.

Initial state.

Based on the trust schema, the article name "`/a/blog /article/food/2015/1`" will be captured by the "`article`" rule, thus the authentication process starts from the corresponding "`article`" state. When executing the key name checking procedure, the interpreter will extract "`<a>`" as the first sub-pattern and use it to derive a key name pattern through a function-like invocation of the "`author`" rule. The resulting pattern "`<a><blog><author>[user]<KEY>[id]`" will successfully match the `KeyLocator` field of the data packet and the FSM will transition to the downstream "`author`" state.

State transition.

At this point, the interpreter makes a request for "`/a/blog/author/Yingdi/KEY/22`" key and pauses processing until the key is retrieved. After retrieving the requested key, the interpreter resumes operations at the "`author`" state with the retrieved key as an input. Similarly, the interpreter extracts "`<a>`" as the first sub-pattern from the author key name and derives through the "`admin`" rule a key name pattern "`<a><blog><admin>[user]<KEY>[id]`". Assuming that the retrieved key is signed with an admin key "`/a/blog/admin/Alex/KEY/5`", the FSM will transition to the corresponding "`admin`" state.

Self-loop transition.

The "`admin`" rule in the website trust schema links to two trust rules, of which one is the "`admin`" rule itself. This self-linked rule represents a management privilege delegation from one administrator to another administrator and is represented by a self-loop transition in the FSM. This transition can capture an administrator key "`/a/blog/admin/Alex/KEY/5`" signed with another administrator key "`/a/blog/admin/Lixia/KEY/37`". In this case, the FSM transitions to the same "`admin`" state over the loopback link and the interpreter requests for the other administrator key and pauses the FSM processing again.

Note that a self-loop transition can potentially accept authentication paths that contain loops or excessively long authentication paths. To prevent these loops, the interpreter can record names of every intermediate key that each state has observed during the authentication process, and abort processing when detecting a duplicate. To prevent excessively long authentication paths, e.g., from a carefully crafted key chains in attempts to cause denial of service attacks, the interpreter should set a limit on the number of state transitions.

Transitioning towards the trust anchor state.

When the interpreter retrieves the public key "`/a/blog/admin/Lixia/KEY/37`", it can repeat the key name checking procedure on the "`admin`" again, deriving two patterns for key name matching: "`<a><blog><admin>[user]<KEY>[id]`" (from the "`admin`" rule) and "`<a><blog><KEY>[id]`" (from the trust anchor "`root`"). If "`/a/blog/admin/Lixia/KEY/37`" key was signed by "`/a/blog/KEY/1`" (the specified trust anchor), the second name pattern would match the `KeyLocator`. In this case, the process immediately transitions to the trust anchor state, triggering initiation of the signature verification procedure.

Signature verification.

Once the signature verification procedure is triggered, the interpreter will follow the reverse path of FSM back to the original data packet, terminating with failure if at any step it cannot verify the signature. In the example, the process will start with validating "`/a/blog/admin/Lixia/KEY/37`" key using the trust anchor key, following checking signature of "`/a/blog/admin/Alex/KEY/5`" using the validated admin key, similarly for the author key "`/a/blog/author/Yingdi/KEY/22`", terminating with checking signature of the received article data packet using validated author key.

5.2 Automating Signing

Another version of the trust schema interpreter, a *signing interpreter*, can use a trust schema to automate selection of signing keys and generation of keys when necessary/possible. Similar to the authenticating interpreter, the signing interpreter compiles a trust schema to an FSM (Figure 11), but processes an *unsigned* data packet as input and outputs the data packet signed with a key that conforms to the trust model (or fails). During processing, the interpreter interacts with the private key store (e.g., Trusted Platform Module, TPM) to request data signing and create signing keys when they are not yet available.[4]

The signing interpreter will fail to sign the supplied data packet if the required key is not available in the local TPM and when the key generation procedure has to cross security boundaries, e.g., a remote admin needs to sign new author's key. In such cases, additional out-of-band mechanisms are necessary to generate proper keys. For example, when a blog author is not an admin of the blog, he or she needs to call or email one of the administrators to give him or her the permission to publish articles. While it is impossible for the signing interpeter to generate keys completely automatically, it can provide assistance in creating the required keys (e.g., generate signing requests) and simplify complex cryptographic operations.

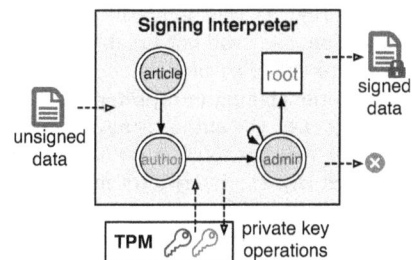

Figure 11: Signing interpreter for the blog website trust model schema

5.2.1 Key Selection

Given a data packet, the signing interpreter can derive the name pattern of a key that is allowed to sign this data according to the trust model. For this purpose, it finds the state in the FSM that corresponds to the data packet, and expands the corresponding signing key name pattern. For example, let us assume that an administrator of the blog wants to publish his article "`/a/blog/article/snacks/2015/3`". This data packet will enter the FSM from the "`article`" state, at which point the interpreter can derive the key name pattern "`<a><blog><author>[user]<KEY>[id]`", as shown in step 1 in Figure 12. With the derived name pattern and the crypto requirements from the trust schema, the interpreter will search a qualified key in the TPM (step 2 in Figure 12). In our example, the admin is publishing a blog article for the

---

[4]Ideally, a signing interpreter should be implemented as a trusted service provided by operating system.

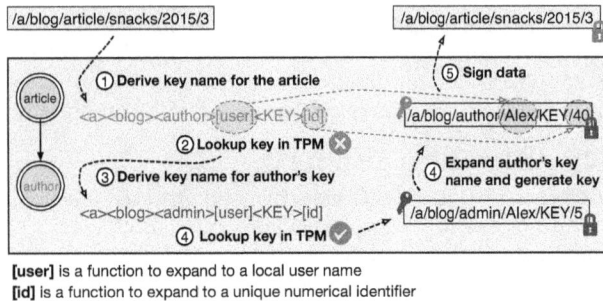

[user] is a function to expand to a local user name
[id] is a function to expand to a unique numerical identifier

Figure 12: An interpreter processing the blog website trust schema directs the procedure of signing data "/a/blog /article/snacks/2015/3"

first time, and is not yet authorized to do so, but the signing interpreter of the trust schema can automatically create such authorization, as we will show below.

5.2.2 Creating Keys

When the interpreter cannot find a signing key that corresponds to a state of the FSM (the result of step 2 in Figure 12), it transitions to a downstream state and repeats the key searching procedure. In our example, when the interpreter realizes that there are no author keys available, it will try to find out if there is any administrator key available. If not, the FSM will continue to transition downstream and repeat the search, until there are no more possible transitions available (note that self-loop transitions are skipped in the signing process when the signing key does not exist in the private key store). At this point the interpreter aborts the signing operation, as it will not be able to sign anything that will conform to the trust model.

In our example, the signing interpreter has access to the administrator's key (i.e., the author is also an administrator of the blog), and it will try to create a new author key. In order to create such key, the interpreter must derive a name for the key. In this case, the wildcard specializer [func] (Table 1) in a key name pattern can expand to specialize the key name. For example, [user] can specialize the name component for the author identifier using the local user name (e.g., "Alex"), and [id] can generate a unique identifier for the key. Therefore, at step 4 in Figure 12 (dotted blue lines), the interpreter can expand the author key pattern into "/a/blog/author/Alex/KEY/40". At this point, the interpreter is ready to generate an author key that satisfies the crypto requirements and overall trust model specified in the schema (step 4 on Figure 12), after which it will be ready to sign data packets of the article by this author (step 5 on Figure 12).

6. DISCUSSION

Having described the trust schema and its applications, in this section we discuss the lessons learned, ongoing efforts, and remaining research issues.

6.1 Design Pattern for Security

A trust schema is more than just an approach to describe the relationships between data and key names, it also represents a design pattern to implement NDN security. Similar to design patterns in software engineering [10], which provide general reusable solutions to commonly occurring

problems in software design, the trust schema provides a reusable solution of applying commonly used trust models in NDN applications. Security experts can define a set of trust schemas as the security patterns for frequently used data authentication models. An established set of trust schemas can greatly reduce the burden on NDN application developers, who can select an appropriate security pattern for their applications during the design phase, to gain all the benefit of NDN's built-in security features.

6.2 Trust Schema Retrieval

A trust schema can be represented as NDN data packet(s), i.e., it can be named and signed. In this paper, we do not define a particular naming convention for trust schema. A meaningful name of a trust schema should be related to the name of the corresponding trust anchor, so that once a consumer learns a trust anchor, the consumer can retrieve and authenticate the trust schema.

Representing trust schema as NDN data packet allows multiple trust schemas to be combined (or chained) together: one can define a meta trust schema to authenticate other trust schemas. For example, an operating system manufacturer can use this feature to limit software installation, execution, and access to private key stores on the operating system only to applications with authenticated trust schemas. This is similar to the existing application sandboxing approaches (such as Apple's App Store and Google's Google Play), but gives operating system additional flexibility in controlling applications.

6.3 Key Caching & Bundling

In our examples, data authentication processes walked through the complete authentication paths defined by the trust schema. However, these processes can be optimized by utilizing cached keys that have been authenticated, given that a single key usually signs multiple data packets (e.g., an author uses the same key to sign multiple articles, an administrator uses his key to sign keys of authors, etc.). An interpreter can cache each intermediate key of an authentication process at the state where the key is checked and verified, so that a new authentication process may find one of its intermediate keys in those states before reaching a trust anchor.

Note that even with key caching, the first authentication process may still involve several round trips of retrieving intermediate keys. This process can be further optimized by having the data producer to maintain the chain of intermediate keys and making it available in form of a key bundle. By retrieving a key bundle, an authentication interpreter obtains all the required keys in a single retrieval. In fact, it has been a common practice in existing authentication systems (such as TLS [9]) to keep a complete chain of keys at the key owner side.

6.4 Multi-Path Authentication

Trust models that define single authentication path for data (e.g., PKI [8], DNSSEC [2]) are a common concern in the security research community. Having just one way to authenticate data creates a single point of failure, e.g., failing to timely renew certificate of any of the intermediate keys will result in data authentication failure. When multiple authentication paths are available, allowing any of the paths to authenticate data improves security resiliency of applications to maintenance failures. At the same time, by imposing a requirement that a key must be authenticated through a certain number of paths, applications can mitigate the damage of key compromise.

If/when a data packet can carry multiple signatures [19], a trust model defined with a trust schema can associate the data name with key names across different namespaces. One of our ongoing directions is exploration of a variety of conditions on trust rules, such as "any valid", "all valid", etc.

6.5 Trust Bootstrapping

In describing the blog website example, we assume that data consumers have already obtained the trust anchor of the website. In general, a consumer may not always be able to obtain the trust anchor for each website it visits a priori. In today's practice, a consumer may need to bootstrap trust from a limited number of pre-configured trusted keys and eventually establish trust on a particular website's trust anchor. We believe that bootstrapping trust remains as an important and challenging open issue, which is beyond the scope of this paper but included in our ongoing efforts. Besides the use of the existing Internet style PKI in NDN networks, more exciting directions to explore this open issue include realizations of web-of-trust and evidentiality-based trust bootstrapping models.

6.6 Signature Revocation

Signature revocation is an open research problem in NDN trust management. Although this problem is beyond the scope of this paper, our ongoing efforts explore the following approaches:

- constraining validity period of issued signatures, which may require mechanisms to certify validity of the signature at the time of creation (e.g., using secure timestamp);

- using trusted services to certify current validity of the signature, similar to revocation lists and OCSP in current PKI.

6.7 Formal Trust Schema Syntax

The syntax we used to describe the trust schema is still at an experimental stage. Trust schemas share many design philosophies with logic programming languages (such as Prolog [7]). It may be helpful to unify the trust schema syntax with formal syntax used by existing languages, and we would like to encourage researchers to apply techniques of programming language to enhance the trust schema design and improve the security of NDN applications.

7. RELATED WORK

The focus of this paper is trust management automation. We are aware of similar efforts for Public Key Infrastructure (PKI), including a standardized path validation algorithm for X.509 certificate authentication [8], certificate chain discovery methods for SPKI certificate system [6, 14], and general chain discovery mechanisms [3]. However, these studies assume a specific trust model. Automation based on trust schemas is a general trust management solution for NDN applications which can have different trust models. Moreover, it not only allows automation of authentication process, but also enables (at least partial) automation of the data signing process.

The design of trust schema leverages NDN naming to enforce name-based trust policies for data packets. DNSSEC [2], a security extension of DNS, adopts a similar mechanism to authenticate DNS resource records: a key bound to a DNS domain name is globally trusted to sign only DNS resource records under this domain. DANE [11] extends the name-based mechanism of DNSSEC to authenticate a TLS public keys. At the same time, both DNSSEC and DANE assume a specific hierarchical trust model, while our trust schema can capture many different trust models that NDN applications may need.

The trust schema is basically a policy language, where rules define policies on which keys are trusted to authenticate data. Compared to previous work on policy languages for access control and authorization, such as PolicyMaker [5], SD3 [12], RT [13], and Cassandra [4], our work focuses on data authentication and integrates data authentication into the NDN network architecture.

8. CONCLUSION

Usability is a fundamental requirement for any security solution. The NDN design mandates that each network-layer data packet carries a cryptographic signature for authentication. Although this requirement on the packet format represents a significant first step toward securing networked systems, its actual effectiveness depends on the implementation. Our observations during the first few years of NDN application development suggest that it is a non-trivial task for application developers to properly define trust relationships between data and keys, to handle proper key chain creation, and to enforce authentication of data according to the defined rules. It happens too often that developers use shortcuts to get around security (e.g., using hard-coded keys, or simply turning verification off "temporarily" when it blocks development progress).

In response to the above important and urgent issue, we invented the idea of a trust schema to formally define application trust models, and to automate the signing and verification processes. We developed prototypes of two trust schema interpreters that can convert trust schemas into finite state machines and help applications to rigorously sign and authenticate data automatically. We applied our prototypes to secure a range of NDN applications, and our experience so far gives us confidence in the solution's general applicability to most, if not all, NDN applications.

We believe we have contributed a meaningful step toward a reusable approach to data authentication. We plan to apply the schematized trust management in more NDN applications and integrate the schematized trust management with operating system support. We would also like to see interested parties, especially people in security research community, to identify and define other commonly reusable trust schemas ("security design patterns") for popular network applications, to be used to secure more applications across the Internet.

9. ACKNOWLEDGEMENTS

This work was supported in part by the NSF grants CNS-1345318 and CNS-1345286.

10. REFERENCES

[1] A. Afanasyev, C. Yi, L. Wang, B. Zhang, and L. Zhang. SNAMP: Secure namespace mapping to scale NDN forwarding. In *Proc. of Global Internet Symposium*, 2015.

[2] R. Arends, R. Austein, M. Larson, D. Massey, and S. Rose. DNS security introduction and requirements. RFC 4033, 2005.

[3] L. Bauer, S. Garriss, and M. K. Reiter. Efficient proving for practical distributed access-control systems. In *ESORICS*, 2007.

[4] M. Y. Becker and P. Sewell. Cassandra: Distributed access control policies with tunable expressiveness. In *Proc. of International Workshop on Policies for Distributed Systems and Networks (POLICY)*, 2004.

[5] M. Blaze, J. Feigenbaum, and J. Lacy. Decentralized trust management. In *Proc. of IEEE Symposium on Security and Privacy*, 1996.

[6] D. Clarke, J.-E. Elien, C. Ellison, M. Fredette, A. Morcos, and R. L. Rivest. Certificate chain discovery in SPKI/SDSI. *Journal of Computer Security*, 2001.

[7] W. Clocksin and C. S. Mellish. *Programming in PROLOG*. Springer Science & Business Media, 2003.

[8] D. Cooper, S. Santesson, S. Farrell, S. Boeyen, R. Housley, and W. Polk. Internet X.509 public key infrastructure certificate and certificate revocation list (CRL) profile. RFC 5280, 2008.

[9] T. Dierks and E. Rescorla. The transport layer security (TLS) protocol version 1.2. RFC 5246, 2008.

[10] E. Gamma, R. Helm, R. Johnson, and J. Vlissides. *Design patterns: elements of reusable object-oriented software*. Pearson Education, 1994.

[11] P. Hoffman and J. Schlyter. The DNS-based authentication of named entities (DANE) transport layer security (TLS) protocol: TLSA. RFC 6698, 2012.

[12] T. Jim. SD3: A trust management system with certified evaluation. In *Proc. of IEEE Symposium on Security and Privacy*, 2001.

[13] N. Li, J. C. Mitchell, and W. H. Winsborough. Design of a role-based trust-management framework. In *Proc. of IEEE Symposium on Security and Privacy*, 2002.

[14] N. Li, W. H. Winsborough, and J. C. Mitchell. Distributed credential chain discovery in trust management. In *Proc. of Conf. on Comp. and Comm. Security (CCS-8)*, 2001.

[15] NDN Team. Libraries / NDN platform. `http://named-data.net/codebase/platform/`, 2015.

[16] NDN Team. NDN packet format specification. http://named-data.net/doc/ndn-tlv/, 2015.

[17] NDN Team. NDN regular expression. `http://named-data.net/doc/ndn-cxx/current/tutorials/utils-ndn-regex.html`, 2015.

[18] D. Smetters and V. Jacobson. Securing network content. Technical report, PARC, 2009.

[19] Y. Yu. Public key management in Named Data Networking. Tech. Rep. NDN-0029, NDN, 2015.

[20] L. Zhang, A. Afanasyev, J. Burke, V. Jacobson, kc claffy, P. Crowley, C. Papadopoulos, L. Wang, and B. Zhang. Named data networking. *ACM Computer Communication Reviews*, 2014.

VDR: A Virtual Domain-based Routing Scheme for CCN

Jie Li[†*], Jiachen Chen[*], Mayutan Arumaithurai[*], Xingwei Wang[†] and Xiaoming Fu[*]
[†]College of Information Science and Engineering, Northeastern University, China.
Email: jieli.neu.edu@gmail.com, wangxw@mail.neu.edu.cn
[*]Institute of Computer Science, University of Göttingen, Germany.
Email: {jie.li, jiachen, arumaithurai, fu}@cs.uni-goettingen.de

1. INTRODUCTION

The advent of Content-Centric Networks (CCN [1]) separates the data from its location and provides benefits like multi-source data retrieval, multicast, in-network cache, *etc.* However, the routing in CCN, especially the Forwarding Information Base (FIB) scalability becomes the Achilles' heel since the routing identities are no longer assigned by the network managers and traditional aggregation in IP cannot work efficiently.

Solutions like [2] propose ISP-based aggregation. The ISPs add (physical) domain-specific prefixes thereby renaming the data for the purpose of aggregation. *E.g.*, /alice-blog will be renamed to /att/atlanta/alice/alice-blog since Alice is a user of AT&T in Atlanta. Although the concept of aggregation can help with the FIB scalability, this particular solution faces a dilemma when the data is replicated or moved. *E.g.*, if Alice blog is replicated in Columbus, the solution should either *a*) rename the data to /att/columbus/alice/alice-blog in order to maintain the aggregation, but loses the benefits of using CCN since they are treated as two different data pieces; or *b*) maintain the same name to get the benefit of CCN thereby losing out on aggregation since the routers have to maintain 2 entries: /att/atlanta and /.../alice-blog.

In [3], the authors propose hash-based solution similar to Distributed Hash Table (DHT), wherein each router is responsible for only a subset of the global FIB. The data name is hashed to identify the router that has the necessary information (FIB entries) to reach the sources and the query is then forwarded to this router. This solution achieves FIB scalability at the cost of: *a*) longest prefix matching: since the hash is performed on the full data name; *b*) aggregation: because each data has to have an entry; *c*) single point of failure: only one router is responsible for a particular subset of names/requests; and *d*) path stretch: all the requests have to go to the responsible router in order to be routed towards the intended source(s) even if it is next to the requester.

In this work, we propose VDR, a routing scheme based on *virtual domains* – domains that are not bound to physical

ICN'15, September 30 - October 02, 2015, San Francisco, CA, USA.
ACM 978-1-4503-3855-4/15/09.
http://dx.doi.org/10.1145/2810156.2812600.

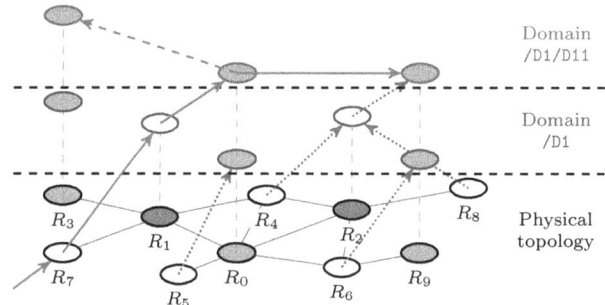

Figure 1: Example of VDR (FIB indicated with arrows).

routers – to exploit the benefits of aggregation and hashing while avoiding the issues from [2] and [3].

2. VIRTUAL DOMAIN ROUTING IN CCN

In CCN, hierarchically structured names are used to simplify the name space management and aggregation similar to IP. However, IP addresses reveal the physical domain relationships while the hierarchical names cannot. Therefore, we introduce the concept of *virtual domains* to correspond these *virtual locations* (names). *E.g.*, when a consumer is requesting a data named /facebook/simpson/gallery/..., we see it as, the consumer needs to enter the (virtual) domain facebook and then the sub-domain simpson, and so on. These domains are created with the names instead of the physical locations.

To address the unbounded name space issue caused by the variable-length names, we use hash functions similar to [3]. But we calculate hashes for *each component* of the name and use the hash values for the inter-virtual-domain routing. A virtual domain /D1/D11 represents all the names whose first component can be hashed to value D1 and second component to D11. True that calculating a hash for each component increases the computation overhead on the routers, but this overhead can be easily reduced by precalculation techniques.

VDR then embeds these virtual domains onto physical routers similar to network virtualization [4]. Each router can belong to different domains at different levels (or even no domain at all). *E.g.*, in Fig. 1, routers R_0, R_3 and R_9 belong to domain /D1/D11 (which means they also belong to domain /D1). The routers R_1 and R_2 belong to /D1 while the others do not have a domain. The FIB in the routers either store how to reach a (sub-)domain D if it does not belong to D, or store the sub-domain information of D if it belongs to D. *E.g.*, Fig. 2 shows a possible FIB layout of R_0 in Fig. 1. In the level 1 domain table (left), since R_0 does not belong to

Dom.	Next Hop		Dom.	Next Hop		Prefix	Next Hop
/D1			/D1/D11	R_1		/facebook/...	R_9
/D2	R_1		/D1/D12			/twitter/...	E_2
/D3	R_5		/D1/D13	R_2		...	...
Lv.1 Dom. Table			Lv.2 Dom. Table			Intra Dom. Table	

Figure 2: FIB implementation in VDR.

Figure 3: CDF of the states on each router.

domain /D2, the next hop for /D2 is R_1. But R_0 belongs to /D1, therefore the next hop points to a second level domain table (middle) which describes the intra-/D1 information. If the network manager decides not to separate /D1/D11 further (which means /D1/D11 is a leaf domain), the intra-domain table becomes a prefix↦next_hop table (similar to the FIB in CCN, right table in Fig. 2). The router knows how to reach the data provider(s) for each name (or prefix). A longest-prefix match can be performed accordingly. The arrows in Fig. 1 represent the FIB for /D1 and /D1/D11.

When a request is issued in the network, the routers can forward it based on the virtual domain (name), level by level till it reaches a leaf domain. *E.g.*, when R_7 in Fig. 1 receives a request for /facebook/simpson/gallery/image1.png (red arrow), it would hash the first component and know that it does not belong to the domain /D1 (we assume $hash$("/facebook") =/D1). R_7 will then forward the request to R_0, which is the nearest node that belongs to the domain /D1. R_0 does not need to do further forwarding to reach domain /D1/D11 since it already belongs to the sub-domain. Instead, it performs intra-domain routing and forwards the packet to R_9 since R_9 serves prefix /facebook/simpson/gallery. We believe that it is feasible for routers to know how to reach each other since it is not unlike the routing in IP.

In VDR, aggregation can be easily achieved. The first components are hashed and grouped into domains. Therefore, the routers that are not in these domains only need one entry for each domain rather than one entry for every name in the domain. While performing routing in the leaf domains, the routers can pick either the best source or multicast a request to several potential providers (dashed arrow in Fig. 1) just like CCN and thereby exploit the dynamicity provided by CCN design. The cache replacement rule can also be modified based on the domains, *e.g.*, data in the domain to which the router belongs can have a longer life time since the router has higher probability to serve a request for that domain and thereby increase the cache hit rate. Since the routing table of each leaf domain is maintained on multiple routers, VDR can avoid the issue of single point of failure and balance the workload on the routers.

3. PRELIMINARY EVALUATION

We simulated VDR in a RocketFuel [5] topology (AS-1239, Sprintlink) to demonstrate the scalability and efficiency of our solution. The topology contains 315 routers and we place 945 end hosts on these routers, of which 500 are chosen as providers. A name space having 20,000 4-level random names is used in our simulation. We compare VDR with hash-based routing [3] and vary the level on which the leaf domains appear.

The traditional CCN routing which maintains all the provider information on each router is similar to VDR $level=0$ (represented as VDR Lv=0 in Fig. 3). It can achieve shortest-path forwarding (with lowest network load and average la-

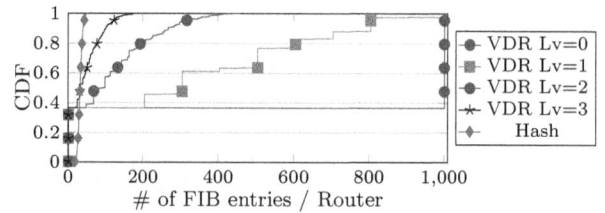

tency) but at the cost of more FIB entries maintained in the network.

With the increase of the domain levels, we can observe that the number of states stored in the network decreases. When $level=3$, the maximum number of entries per router drops to 175 and 90% of the routers store fewer than 100 entries (see VDR Lv=3 in Fig. 3). Because of the aggregation, the total number of FIB entries with VDR Lv=3 is approaching that with hash-based routing. We envision that VDR can get more benefit from aggregation when the name space is larger.

But we acknowledge that since the requests have to be forwarded based on the domains, they can be directed away from the data provider when there is no router belonging to the domain on the shortest path. The path stretch increases with the number of levels and cause (slightly) longer latency and more network traffic. This is a tradeoff between the scalability (space) and efficiency (time). We are working on finding the optimal balance in this tradeoff.

4. CONCLUSION

We propose VDR that uses the concept of virtual domains for routing in CCN. VDR addresses the FIB scalability issue in CCN by facilitating aggregation without compromising on the advantages of CCN such as ease of data replication and obtaining the data from a closer source. Preliminary evaluation shows that VDR lowers the number of FIB entries present at a router significantly without affecting much on path latency. We are currently working on a mechanism to allocate routers to different levels of the virtual domain, optimizing the solution and will perform extensive evaluations to compare the performance gain to the state of the art.

Acknowledgment

This research was partly funded from the National Science Foundation for Distinguished Young Scholars of China under Grant No.61225012 and No.71325002, the EU-JAPAN initiative by the EC Seventh Framework Programme Grant Agreement No.608518 (GreenICN), NICT under Contract No.167, the Volkswagen Foundation Project "Simulation Science Center" and the Chinese Scholarship Council.

5. REFERENCES

[1] V. Jacobson *et al.*, "Networking Named Content," in *CoNEXT*, 2009.
[2] L. Zhang *et al.*, "Named Data Networking (NDN) Project," PARC, Tech. Report NDN-0001, 2010.
[3] L. Saino *et al.*, "Hash-routing schemes for information centric networking," in *ICN*, 2013.
[4] "Network virtualization," https://en.wikipedia.org/wiki/Network_virtualization.
[5] R. Mahajan *et al.*, "Inferring Link Weights using End-to-End Measurements," in *IMW*, 2002.

Anchor-less Producer Mobility in ICN

Jordan Augé
Cisco Systems
first.last@cisco.com

Giovanna Carofiglio
Cisco Systems
gcarofig@cisco.com

Giulio Grassi
UPMC, LIP6
first.last@lip6.fr

Luca Muscariello
Orange Labs Networks
first.last@orange.com

Giovanni Pau
UPMC, LIP6; UCLA
first.last@lip6.fr

Xuan Zeng
UPMC, LIP6; IRT SystemX
first.last@irt-systemx.fr

ABSTRACT

Mobility has become a basic premise of almost any network communication, thereby requiring a native integration into next generation 5G networks. Despite the numerous efforts to propose and to standardize effective mobility management models for IP, the result is a very complex, poorly flexible set of mechanisms not suitable for the design of a radio-agnostic 5G mobile core. The natural support for mobility, security and storage offered by ICN (Information-Centric Networking) architecture, makes it a good candidate to define a radically new solution relieving limitations of traditional approaches. If consumer mobility is supported in ICN by design in virtue of its connectionless pull-based communication model, producer mobility still appears to be an open challenge.

In this work we describe an initial proposal for an anchorless approach to manage producer mobility via Interest Updates/Notifications in the data plane, even in presence of latency-sensitive applications. We detail the different operations triggered by producer movements and position our contribution in the context of existing alternatives, by discussing either user performance and network metrics.

Categories and Subject Descriptors

C.2.1 [**Computer-Communication Networks**]: Network Architecture and Design—*Network communications*

Keywords

Information-Centric Networking; Producer Mobility.

1. INTRODUCTION

With the phenomenal spread of connected user devices, mobility has become a basic premise for almost any network communication as well as a compelling feature to integrate in next generation networks (5G). The need for a mobility management model to apply within IP networks has striven a lot of efforts in research and standardization bodies (e.g. 3GPP), all resulting in a complex access-dependent

ICN'15, September 30–October 2, 2015, San Francisco, CA, USA.
ACM 978-1-4503-3855-4/15/09.
DOI: http://dx.doi.org/10.1145/2810156.2812601.

set of mechanisms implemented in a dedicated control infrastructure. The complexity and lack of flexibility of such approaches (e.g. Mobile IP) calls today for a radically new solution dismantling traditional assumptions like tunneling and anchoring all mobile communications into network core.

Native support for mobility, security and storage functionalities inside network architecture, makes ICN a promising candidate for 5G and, specifically, for relieving current limitations in mobility management by introducing a radically new model.

In ICN, mobility is managed in a very different way than in IP: the communication focuses on names rather than network addresses, hence a change in physical location does not imply a change in the data plane. Consumer mobility is naturally supported in virtue of its connectionless and pull-based transport mode, implying a simple retransmission by the consumer of Interests for not yet received Data.

Producer mobility and real-time group communication are more challenging to support, depending on the frequency of the mobility and on the content lifetime. The contribution of this work is an initial proposal for an anchorless approach to manage local producer mobility, even in presence of latency-sensitive applications.

The rationale behind is to exploit ICN features like stateful forwarding, dynamic and distributed Interest load balancing and in-network caching to define a timely forwarding update mechanism populating a Temporary FIB (TFIB) at routers relaying former and current producer location.

In the following sections we describe the design principles (Sec.2) and the operations involved by our approach (Sec.3), before concluding and commenting on future work in Sec.4.

2. DESIGN PRINCIPLES

Our mobility manager MM results from the following design principles:

Anchor-less: Mobility management approaches can be roughly divided into three classes: *rendez-vous based*, involving a resolution of identifiers into locators performed by dedicated network nodes, *anchor-based* (or indirection-based), where a fixed network node is kept aware of mobile node movements and intercepts/redirects packets to him, *anchor-less*, where the mobile node is directly responsible for notifying the network about his movements. The first class of approaches (see [1] for an ICN example) has good scalability properties and low signaling overhead, but appears unsuitable for frequent mobility and for reactive rerouting of latency-sensitive traffic. Anchor-based approaches (see [5]) show better reactivity and good path stretch properties at the cost of larger signaling overhead. Also, they suffer from single point of passage problem, preventing ICN multipath and limiting robustness to failure. Anchor-less approaches are less common and introduced to enhance reactivity with respect to anchor-based solutions (see e.g. [2], [4], [3]). Better reactivity, simplicity, insensitivity to frequency of relocations make anchor-less solutions appealing.

No name change. In order to avoid issues like triangular routing and caching degradation and to keep name semantics fully location-independent, MM does not require any change in content names.

Forwarding-based. Our approach does not rely on global routing updates (too slow and costly in presence of frequent mobility), rather it leverages hop-by-hop dynamic and distributed ICN forwarding. A temporary FIB is populated by updates/notifications originated at the new producer location and directed to its former positions.

Distributed. We design our approach to be fully distributed and limited to the edge of the network, to realize an effective traffic offload close to end-users and to eliminate dependency on in-network anchors.

Lightweight. We consider prefix granularity in updates (rather than content/chunk as in [5]) to minimize signaling overhead and temporary state kept by in-network nodes.

Reactive. We introduce network notifications and discovery mechanisms to support latency-sensitive communications even during high mobility.

3. MM OPERATIONS

In this section we describe the operations performed in MM to properly route consumer Interests to a moving producer: The sequence of operations is the following: (*I*) whenever the mobile producer moves and attaches to a new network Points of Attachment (PoA), it notifies to the new PoA the prefixes it serves. (*II*) Once it eventually relocates or regularly every T_U (e.g. 5s), he triggers a forwarding update operation. Notifications/Updates modify routers forwarding state by populating a temporary FIB (TFIB). Consumers' requests directed to the producer either follow TFIB information or, in absence, are routed to the FIB and from there towards the producer via a discovery mechanism (*III*).

3.1 Mobility and forwarding updates

Every time a mobile producer stably relocates or every T_U s, it sends a special Interest message, called Interest Update (IU) for each prefix it serves. The Interest is then forwarded based of TFIB and FIB and it eventually reaches a producer's former position (see Fig. 1(a)). While traversing subsequent routers, IU updates the TFIB replacing output interface for the given prefix with the incoming face of the IU, thus steering future consumers' Interests towards the new producer's location. To avoid conflicts among subsequent updates, every IU is tagged with a unique sequence number incremented by the producer at each mobility event. When an IU reaches a previous producer location (identified by stale face information in TFIB), the update is completed. IU acknowledgments and retransmissions are used for reliability, while a security token carried by IU packets secures forwarding update operations.

3.2 Notifications and producer discovery

Performance of latency-sensitive traffic can be further improved by introducing a fast-single hop notification mechanism: every time a producer attaches to a new PoA, it sends to the latter an *Interest Notification* (IN), a special Interest

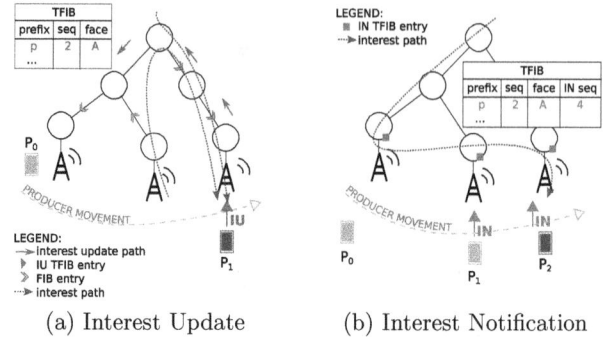

(a) Interest Update   (b) Interest Notification

Figure 1: MM Update-Notification.

message differing from an IU only because it triggers a local TFIB update without being further forwarded. When a consumer Interest reaches a previous producer location before IU completion, the Interest is broadcasted in a discovery mode to one-hop neighboring nodes (we assume that, like in LTE, neighbouring PoAs talk to each other). The presence of TFIB information about the producer (presumably left by an IN) iterates the process, thus tracking current producer location in quasi-realtime (see Fig. 1(b)).

4. CONCLUSIONS AND FUTURE WORK

To provide a quantitative assessment of MM performance and comparison with previous proposals, we are currently implementing MM in NDNSim/ns-3 and preparing a realistic simulation setting leveraging synthetic and trace-driven mobility patterns.

We leave for future work the proof of correctness of MM in terms of connectivity/convergence guarantees as well as the analytical characterization of MM with the broader objective to demonstrate the advantages of an anchorless approach over anchor-based models.

Acknowledgments

This research work has been partially funded by the Technological Research Institute SystemX, within the project on Network Architectures ARE.

5. REFERENCES

[1] F. Hermans, E. Ngai, and P. Gunningberg. Global source mobility in the content-centric networking architecture. In *Proc. of ACM NoM Workshop*, 2012.

[2] D. Kim, J. Kim, Y. Kim, H. Yoon, and I. Yeom. Mobility support in content centric networks. In *Proc. ACM SIGCOMM ICN workshop*, 2012.

[3] J. Lee, S. Cho, and D. Kim. Device mobility management in content-centric networking. *Communications Magazine, IEEE*, 50(12):28–34, December 2012.

[4] L. Wang, O. Waltari, and J. Kangasharju. Mobiccn: Mobility support with greedy routing in content-centric networks. In *Global Communications Conference (GLOBECOM), 2013 IEEE*, pages 2069–2075, Dec 2013.

[5] Y. Zhang, H. Zhang, and L. Zhang. Kite: A mobility support scheme for ndn. In *Proc. of ACM ICN*, 2014.

Analyzing Cacheable Traffic for FTTH Users Using Hadoop

Claudio Imbrenda
Orange Labs Networks
claudio.imbrenda@orange.com

Wuyang Li
Eurecom Institute
wuyang.li@eurecom.fr

Luca Muscariello
Orange Labs Networks
luca.muscariello@orange.com

ABSTRACT

We present this year (2015) statistics about cacheable traffic in the access network of Orange in Paris for about 30,000 customers served by a fiber to the home subscription. These statistics update some of the results presented in a recent work, which considered only 2 000 fiber users in 2014. The huge amount of data to be processed in the new vantage point made necessary the usage of a hadoop cluster that we have used to process the data and report new statistics in the present paper. The aggregation level at which we observe web traffic allows to draw some conclusions about the feasibility of implementing in-network caching at wire speed.

Categories and Subject Descriptors

C.2.1 [**Computer-Communication Networks**]: Network Operations—*Network monitoring*

Keywords

Network Traffic Measurements; Caching; Big Data

1. INTRODUCTION AND MOTIVATION

One of the fundamental questions about using in-network caches in the Internet is to show how much data can be really cached, if such data allows to save significant amount of traffic and if the total cacheable data requires a memory that can be implemented with a reasonable cost. The size of that memory would also determine the technology and then the access speed, which has a direct implication on the location of such memory in the communication path. Smaller memories can be very fast and installed in the forwarding engine of a router and accessed at wire speed, while very large memories are typically implemented with low rate technologies that can only be installed out of the data path and accessed at lower rate. The answer to this question depends on many factors but mostly on the nature of the traffic demand coming from the end users. It also depends on the network location where such demand is observed. In this paper we position our vantage point in the access networks of Orange in Paris to observe about 30 000 customers, served by a GPON (Gigabit Passive Optical Network)

ICN'15, September 30–October 2, 2015, San Francisco, CA, USA.
ACM 978-1-4503-3855-4/15/09
http://dx.doi.org/10.1145/2810156.2812602.

based FTTH (Fiber To The Home) access, with a per user maximum downlink rate spanning from 300Mbps to 1Gbps. In [3] all HTTP requests and replies were processed online in the probe itself, while the new scale that we face in this work required the use of a hadoop cluster to compute the relevant statistics online. The present work takes into account several ameliorations of the measurement methodology employed in [3], as it also takes into account identification of objects that are retrieved using HTTP chunked transfer encoding and range requests in order to detect partial data transfers or non overlapping pieces of a same object, that is identified by the same HTTP URI. Cacheability and traffic reduction, as introduced in [1, 3], are very important metrics, as pointed before. In order to quickly and accurately calculate these values, a log is needed containing all the requested objects, the time of the request and the real amount of traffic generated. There are already some tools that perform HTTP traffic analysis[7, 6, 2, 5], some of which are unavailable. The performance and the accuracy of the publicly available tools is in general not satisfactory for some kinds of traffic analysis, especially in relation to cacheability. Tstat[4] performs a packet-level analysis of HTTP connections, this allows it to operate quickly and with a reduced memory footprint, but on the other hand it misses many details.

Only clear-text connections can be analyzed, as obviously no dissection of SSL/TLS traffic is possible for us. Although the amount of HTTPS traffic is rising with time, especially since popular websites like Facebook or YouTube started to push in that direction, and therefore potentially rendering this approach useless in the long run, we measured in our observations that, approximately 35% of the total HTTP traffic is HTTPS.

2. STATISTICS

In addition to the usual statistics collected by other tools, like for example the client ID, the object ID, the hostname or the User-Agent string, our tool, called HACkSAw, also collects many statistics that other tools neglect, like the time between the HTTP request and the HTTP reply or the first byte of content; the indication whether cookies or ETAG headers were used, the size of the headers, the byte-range in case of range(partial) request, and the list of all present headers (without their values). The results collected by the tool allow to compute aggregate statistics as shown in [3]; those aggregate statistics are calculated with a non-trivial post-processing of the output log of the tool, which is in plain text. The relevant statistics that can be calculated easily are:

Request cacheability (*the share of HTTP requests that can potentially be cached in a given timeframe*);

Traffic reduction (*the percentage of actual traffic potentially saved assuming all cacheable items are pre-fetched during off-peak hours*);

Virtual cache size (*the minimum cache size needed to cache all*

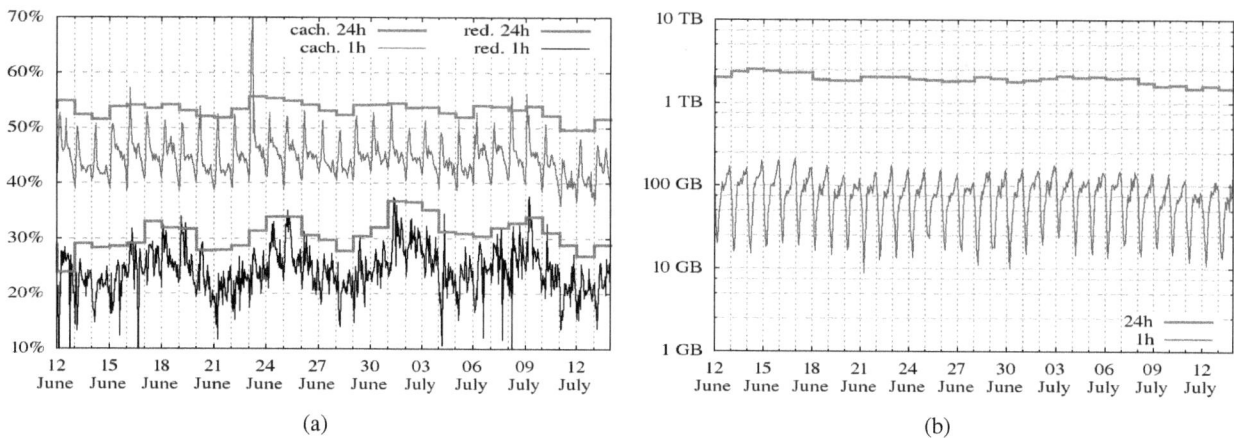

Figure 1: Cacheability, traffic reduction; (a) virtual cache size over 1h and 24h during a month from June July 2015.

cacheable content, assuming perfect "oracle" replacement);

Share of requests with cookies and/or ETAG *(ETAG headers potentially indicate different content for the same URL; the presence of cookies generally hinders cacheability)*;

Average throughput and latency of requests *(time between the first and the last byte of content, and between start of the HTTP request and the first byte of content, respectively)*;

Share of HTTPS connections *(percentage of HTTPS connections and traffic over the total of web traffic)*.

3. HADOOP FRAMEWORK

Since the amount of data generated by HACkSAw can be huge (200GB per day for an average 10Gbps of traffic), the amount of time and memory needed to compute it on any single system is prohibitive. Hence our decision to use a Hadoop cluster. In average, on a daily basis, we use 398 maps and 60 reduce tasks which read and write 93GB and 0.8GB of data respectively. The hadoop framework employs 3.5 hours of CPU time and requires 505GB of memory. The real time processing takes only 2.4 minutes which constitutes a speedup factor of 87.5 times. The current setup involves an automatic script on the probe that compresses and sends the hourly logs towards the hadoop cluster, where they are uncompressed and injected in the HDFS (Hadoop Distributed File System). At regular intervals, a script on the hadoop cluster performs all the calculations for cacheability, traffic reduction and virtual cache size; the results are then exported to a web interface.

One important process on the data is the reaggregation of chunked objects, in order to avoid miscomputing their real hit ratio and size. Due to the complexity of the task, including the chunk reaggregation, the process uses two map-reduce steps: (i) the first step takes in the raw files produced by the probe; the map phase filters out the unused columns from the rows and the reduce phase aggregates all the records by object ID and time slot, and it merges all the object slices from range requests, using the `Content-Range` data, and finally it computes intermediate statistics. (ii) the second job takes in the intermediate results obtained in the first job; little processing is done in the map stage, while the reduce phase aggregates all records by time slot and calculates the final statistics.

4. DISCUSSION

We have reported a month of on-line statistics on a hourly and daily basis in Fig.1 that allows to draw some conclusions. Today, one third of the traffic is encrypted and politics will tell if this num-

ber will increase or not. We know, however, that a significant portion of such traffic comes from Google caches which gives a rough estimation of the hit ratio in such equipment (no statistics reported here though). Two third of the traffic in non encrypted and fine grained statistics are reported here. Almost half of the requests are cacheable and about one third of the traffic could be reduced. On a daily basis 1.2TB is roughly the size of an ideal memory installed at the vantage point to cache such data. However hourly statistics reveal that no more than 200GB would suffice. The gap between these two numbers proves that time locality is a very strong component of Internet traffic. These statistics suggest that in-network storage could be implemented in router memories and serve users' requests at wire speed. An ICN architecture would help optimizing traffic engineering by also using in-network caching in the access without having to give up content encryption, if required.

Acknowledgments

This research work has been partially funded by the Technological Research Institute SystemX, within the project on Network Architectures ARE.

5. REFERENCES

[1] B. Ager, F. Schneider, J. Kim, and A. Feldmann. Revisiting cacheability in times of user generated content. In *IEEE INFOCOM*, pages 1–6, March 2010.

[2] A. Finamore, M. Mellia, M. Meo, M. Munafo, and D. Rossi. Experiences of internet traffic monitoring with tstat. *IEEE Network Magazine*, May 2011.

[3] C. Imbrenda, L. Muscariello, and D. Rossi. Analyzing Cacheable Traffic in ISP Access Networks for Micro CDN Applications via Content-centric Networking. In *Proc. ACM ICN*, 2014.

[4] M. Mellia and al. http://tstat.tlc.polito.it.

[5] V. Paxson. http://www.bro.org.

[6] B. Ramanan, L. Drabeck, M. Haner, N. Nithi, T. Klein, and C. Sawkar. Cacheability analysis of HTTP traffic in an operational LTE network. In *In Proc. of WTS*, 2013.

[7] S. Woo, E. Jeong, S. Park, J. Lee, S. Ihm, and K. Park. Comparison of caching strategies in modern cellular backhaul networks. In *Proc. of ACM MobiSys*, 2013.

Partial Adaptive Name Information in ICN: PANINI Routing Limits FIB Table Sizes

Thomas C. Schmidt
HAW Hamburg
t.schmidt@acm.org

Sebastian Wölke, Nora Berg
HAW Hamburg
{first.last}@haw-hamburg.de

Matthias Wählisch
Freie Universität Berlin
m.waehlisch@fu-berlin.de

ABSTRACT

Name-based routing as proposed in Information Centric Networking encounters the problems of (a) exploding routing tables, as the number of names largely exceeds common routing resources, and (b) limited aggregation potentials, as names are commonly independent of content locations. In this poster, we introduce PANINI, an approach to scale routing on names by adapting FIB tables simultaneously to available resources and actual traffic patterns. PANINI introduces routing hierarchies with respect to aggregation points, bimodal FIBs, and confined flooding. First evaluations show promising results in theory and experiments.

Categories and Subject Descriptors

C.2.2 [**Computer-Communication Networks**]: Network Protocols—*Routing Protocols*

Keywords

Scalable adaptive forwarding; NDN; confined flooding

1. INTRODUCTION

Information Centric Networking has introduced a new, promising communication paradigm, but continues to struggle with severe challenges [1]. NDN [2] (among others) unifies routing with names at a high level of maturity. However, the multitude and complexity of distributed content names has not been treated convincingly [3]. Even though several original approaches have been presented, the sheer number of (delocalized) names prevents a striking step forward.

Routing on identifiers can generally be achieved by aggregation or mapping to topology, the latter may be dynamically obtained from broadcasts. In the following, we will present a hybrid combination of (artificially enhanced) name aggregation at a rendezvous point, an adaptive (static) mapping by FIBs, and a dynamic on-demand flooding of Interests towards content suppliers. We sketch the PANINI routing scheme in Section 2 and give a brief evaluation in Section 3.

ICN'15, Sept.30–Oct. 2, 2015, San Francisco, CA, USA.
ACM 978-1-4503-3855-4/15/09
DOI: http://dx.doi.org/10.1145/2810156.2812603.

2. PANINI ROUTING

The PANINI approach starts from fixing an aggregation point for names in the network[1], which typically would be a larger cache repository in the fixed Internet, or a gateway in the IoT. We assume topology building mechanisms in place that generate a shortest path tree rooted at the aggregation point. This is in full analogy to the current Internet, where standard routing protocols can construct shortest paths on the inter- and intra-domain level. Given this basic topology, every node can identify up- and downward paths with respect to the aggregating root—with upward paths serving as default.

The objective of name-based routing is to link content requesters with content suppliers. In PANINI, this is achieved via the (name-specific) aggregation points that can be reached via (prefix-specific) default routes. Every node that offers content under a routable name advertises this name in a Name Advertisement Message (NAM). Per default, NAMs travel hop-by-hop towards the aggregation point, and every intermediate router can harvest the content advertisement for including in its own routing table. Filling all FIBs will generate a complete routing path from the aggregation point to the content source.

A consumer requests content by transmitting the Interest up to the aggregating root (default), and down along the previously installed paths. Data forwarding will follow the regular pending Interests of NDN on the reverse path. Routing and forwarding are thus aligned to a network hierarchy that resembles the current Internet with aggregation points located at the transit tier.[2]

Up to this point, we have required names in all FIBs, which is known to be infeasible in ICN. We now weaken this requirement as follows. Complete routing tables shall only be required at the aggregation points. This is a significant relaxation since aggregation points are designed to facilitate name aggregation and largely reduce routing table space. In addition, providers may select strong devices to serve as aggregation points. From complete, aggregated FIB tables, the (transit) root can thus always tell which branch (or lower tier ISP) holds the requested content. Without further FIB entries, flooding may lead the Interest down this branch.

Intermediate nodes are not required to carry a full FIB, but rather aim at adapting selected entries to minimize Interest flooding. In analogy to caching content, each node autonom-

---

[1]Notably, multiple aggregation points for different lexicographic ranges are possible.
[2]Extensions to multiple transits per prefix, as well as peering shortcuts are subject of future work.

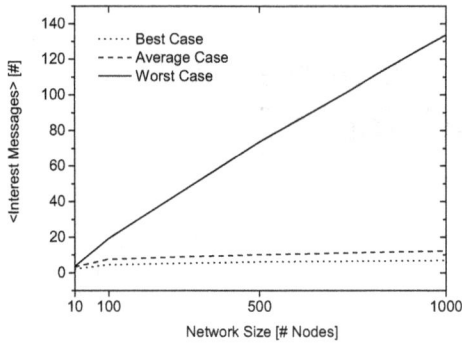

Figure 1: **Average number of interest messages for different scenarios and network sizes**

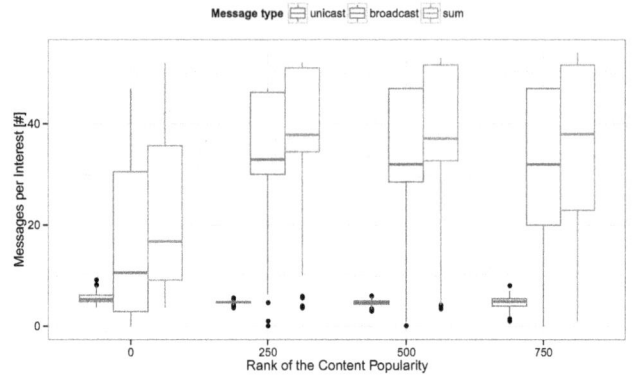

Figure 2: **Measurements of (typed) message frequencies for four selected popularity ranks**

ously decides about (a) its memory resources available for the FIB, and (b) the forwarding logic it applies within its vicinity. Traffic flows can be continuously used to adapt the FIB to relevant traffic patterns. For example, a node can hold more specific information for frequently requested names, while it may erase entries for traffic rarely seen.

To optimize Interest guidance at partial forwarding information even further, we introduce a *bimodal FIB*. This extends the FIB structure to hold two modes—include and exclude. In include mode, all Interests that match a FIB prefix will be forwarded on the associate Face, while all Interests that match a FIB exclude-prefix will be blocked on that Face. The initial state of an empty FIB reads include * which leads to a transparent forwarding (flooding) of all incoming Interests. A node that has seen no routable names from NAMs in a subtree of his may as well switch to exclude *.

3. EVALUATION AND OUTLOOK

In our brief evaluation, we concentrate on the penalty PANINI inherits from only partially filling FIBs, i.e., flooding. In the best case, PANINI ist optimal, while in the worst case, an Interest is flooded down an entire branch of the routing tree. The actual efficiency depends on (i) the available FIB sizes, (ii) the adaptation strategy of names, and (iii) the actual distribution of content within the topology.

Shortest path trees are theoretically well described by Uniform Recursive Trees (URTs) [4]. In a first evaluation step, we can use this analogy to theoretically estimate the flooding overhead inherited from the topology prior to adaptive FIB optimisations. In particular, we can derive the worst, best, and average case scenarios for flooding branches of subtrees.

A Uniform Recursive Tree of N nodes has an average depth of $\log(N)$, which is the optimal number of downtree Interest messages. In the worst case, an entire branch is flooded—on average N/H_{N-1} nodes [5], where H_N is the N-th Harmonic number. For the average scenario, we consider a random FIB on path empty and its corresponding subtree flooded. We omit the corresponding (complex) expression here and visualize the outcome in Figure 1. As can be seen from the graph, the average number of Interest messages needed for locating content follows closely the logarithmic behavior of the best case. In contrast, the worst case scenarios grow only slightly sublinearly ($\approx N/\log N$).

In a second evaluation step, we analyze the effect of popularity-based FIB adaptation. We build a (virtual) test network of 100 ICN nodes and harvest a frequency distri-

bution of name usages from Quantcast[3]. During name advertisement from randomly selected content sources, we add names to FIBs according to these popularity distributions. Content is then requested accordingly from random nodes.

Figure 2 depicts measurement results for message frequencies per type of four selected ranks of content popularity. Within this limited experimental setup, our measurements clearly reveal for routing (i) a constant unicast message effort for all conten types, and (ii) a much enhanced routing routing determinism (i.e., reduced flooding) for popular content. Given the highly skewed popularity distribution, average efforts for flooding remain close to popular content behaviour and reproduce the theoretical average scenario fairly well. In particular, we cannot encounter large deviations in single events or other indications of unexpected effects. This clearly indicates that the topological structure of routing trees (rather wide than deep) conjointly with a reasonable adaption strategy will confine Interest flooding to rather limited subtrees.

In summary, we could show that PANINI routing is a promising hybrid approach to mitigate between FIB sizes and interest flooding for locating content. Our future work will concentrate on to elaborate and evaluate the missing details of the PANINI routing scheme. It is our intend to show its feasibility even for large-scale inter-provider set-ups.

4. REFERENCES

[1] D. Kutscher, et al., "ICN Research Challenges," IETF, Internet-Draft – work in progress 01, February 2015.

[2] V. Jacobson, D. K. Smetters, J. D. Thornton, and M. F. Plass, "Networking Named Content," in *Proc. of the 5th Int. Conf. on emerging Networking EXperiments and Technologies (ACM CoNEXT'09).* New York, NY, USA: ACM, Dec. 2009, pp. 1–12.

[3] M. Wählisch, T. C. Schmidt, and M. Vahlenkamp, "Backscatter from the Data Plane – Threats to Stability and Security in Information-Centric Network Infrastructure," *Computer Networks*, vol. 57, no. 16, pp. 3192–3206, Nov. 2013.

[4] P. Van Mieghem, *Performance Analysis of Communications Networks and Systems.* Cambridge, New York, 2006.

[5] C. Su, Q. Feng, and Z. Hu, "Uniform Recursive Trees: Branching Structure and Simple Random Downward Walk," *Journal of mathematical analysis and applications*, vol. 315, no. 1, pp. 225–243, 2006.

---

[3]http://www.quantcast.com/top-sites — this distribution is even more highly skewed than the common Zipf law.

Revisiting Countermeasures Against NDN Interest Flooding

Samir Al-Sheikh
Freie Universität Berlin
samir.al-sheikh@fu-berlin.de

Matthias Wählisch
Freie Universität Berlin
m.waehlisch@fu-berlin.de

Thomas C. Schmidt
HAW Hamburg
t.schmidt@haw-hamburg.de

ABSTRACT

Interest flooding has been identified as a major threat for the NDN infrastructure. Since then several approaches have been proposed to identify and to mitigate this attack. In this paper, we (a) classify nine existing countermeasures and (b) compare them in a consistent evaluation setup. We discuss the application of pure prefix-based as well as pure interface-based mitigation strategies in different network scenarios.

Categories and Subject Descriptors

C.2.0 [**Computer-Communication Networks**]: General—*Security and protection*; C.2.2 [**Computer-Communication Networks**]: Network Protocols—*Routing Protocols*

Keywords

ICN; NDN; Interest flooding; attack; mitigation

1. COUNTERMEASURES IN A NUTSHELL

Interest flooding describes a denial-of-service attack in which a malicious node attempts to overload the distribution infrastructure by sending Interest packets [5]. The easiest implementation is the request of non-existing content as entries need to expire until they are removed. However, even the request of existing content may harm the infrastructure when the entries in the Pending Interest Table (PIT) exceed the content delivery rate (e.g., due to large network delays) [5].

Current countermeasures try to limit the number of incoming Interests, either per prefix, per interface, or per router. The main challenge is to distinguish valid from malicious Interests. As there is no clear notion of malicious Interests, several heuristics are proposed.

Considering *all* PIT entries of the (local) router, *Token Bucket* [1] and *Resource Allocation* [2] proactively try to balance the resources. The *Interest Traceback* [3] approach does not only include the size of the PIT but also the increase of entries over time. Furthermore, if a predefined threshold is exceeded, dummy data packets are sent towards all such

consumers that are responsible for stale Interests—to release states within the network and finally limit Interests at the upstreams of the supposed attackers. Note that those approaches do not explicitly try to locate the attacker at the local router.

In contrast to this, interface-based countermeasures apply thresholds and limits per interface to narrow the attack down to an interface. The *Satisfaction* [1] approaches only consider the ratio of Interest packets and data packets to identify requests for non-existing content, whereas *Poseidon* [2] additionally correlates the number of current PIT entries. Those approaches lack the option to isolate more specifically because all nodes behind the throttled interface will be affected by the limitation.

The last class of approaches that we discuss in this paper are countermeasures that analyze PIT consumption per name prefix. *Threshold-based Detecting and Mitigating (TDM)* [6] classifies valid and malicious Interests based on the number of expired Interests with respect to a specific prefix. *Prefix Pushback* [4] focuses on the overall number of Interests per prefix and alarms downstream peers.

Table 1 summarizes the countermeasures which we analyze. We argue that the concrete heuristic to identify an attack is less important. Instead, the applicability of the approaches depends significantly on the topology and the principal detection point (i.e., prefix, interface, or router).

2. PRELIMINARY RESULTS & OUTLOOK

Setup The objective of this paper is the consistent comparison of different countermeasures. Thus, we decided to extend ndnSIM, the common NDN support in NS-3. Only three [1] out of the nine approaches were supported by default. To verify the existing and our new implementations, we reproduced the measurements described in the original publications and compared the results. This extensive testing helped us to improve the quality of both code bases. Our simulation code is publicly available via http://interest-flooding.realmv6.org.

We analyzed the PIT load, caching capabilities, and the ratio of Interest request and data delivery for different topologies. In the following, we will concentrate on the Interest request ratio as this measures fairness of the mitigation strategy with respect to legitimate consumers. We deploy a one hop star topology and a scorpion topology where the producer represents the sting and (legitimate and malicious) consumers represent the feet. Attackers request non-existing content, which exhibits distinct prefix (/evil/*) compared

ICN'15, Sept.30–Oct. 2, 2015, San Francisco, CA, USA.
ACM 978-1-4503-3855-4/15/09
DOI: http://dx.doi.org/10.1145/2810156.2812604.

Approach / Acronym		Detection	Trigger	Mitigation
Token Bucket	TB [1]	per router	–	Round Robin over all interfaces
Resource Allocation	RA [2]	per router	Adaptive PIT size threshold	Drop subsequent Interests
Interest Traceback	IT [3]	per router	PIT size threshold & gain	Downstream traceback
Poseidon Local	PL [2]	per interface	Interest-data ratio	Limit PIT size per interface
Poseidon Distributed	PD [2]	per interface	Interest-data ratio	PL + alarm downstream peers
Satisfaction-based Accept	SA [1]	per interface	Interest-data ratio	Decrease probability of forwardig Interests
Satisfaction-based Pushback	SP [1]	per interface	Interest-data ratio	SA + distributed Pushback
Prefix Pushback	PP [4]	per prefix	Absolute # Interests	Drop specific ratio of Interests + alarm downstream peer
TDM	TDM [6]	per prefix	# expired PIT entries	capacity threshold

Table 1: Proposals to detect and mitigate Interest flooding attacks.

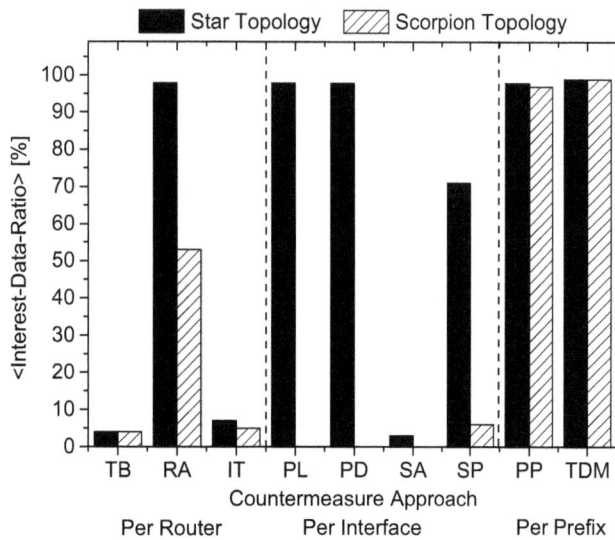

Figure 1: Fairness of different countermeasures.

to valid content (`/good/*`). Each simulation is sampled with the same parameter settings until it is converged.

Results Figure 1 shows the average Interest-data ratio over all runs and consumers, per countermeasure and topology. Higher y-values thus indicate better data delivery. We observe two key effects: (a) the results significantly depend on the underlying topology and (b) the detection point (per router, etc.). This is somewhat surprising as globally deployable countermeasures need to cope with heterogeneous networks, such as the Internet.

Prefix-based countermeasures outperform all other approaches in our scenario since these detection mechanisms can clearly identify malicious interests when the valid and the malicious data are prefix-free. Note that this changes as soon as malicious and valid Interest share a longest common prefix. This observation can be easily misused by an attacker when launching real-world attacks.

Interface-based approaches tend to exhibit similar behavior when deployed in star topologies, i.e., consumer, attacker, and producer are connected to the same router. In those scenarios, the interface complies with the maliciously requested prefix. However, in a scorpion graph the picture changes completely as the tail router cannot distinguish between

attacker and valid consumer—the complete downstream interface will be limited. Note that this single link property of the scorpion graph is very common in Internet backbone topology, in particular towards the edge networks.

Finally, we observe that most of the current per router mitigations are invariant of the specific topology but depend more on the drop Interests strategy. Strictly discarding Interests leads to worst case performance in all setups (see TB, IT). However, a more adaptive approach results in increased performance fairness. Analyzing this performance gain in more detail, will be part of our future work.

Outlook In this paper, we argue for both a comparable analysis of countermeasures against Interest flooding as well as the need for future work on this topic. In future work, we will investigate hybrid approaches, which combine different detection points (per interface and per prefix) to increase accuracy and performance while limiting PIT entries. Furthermore, we will extend our analysis, not only to cover more complex application scenarios but also to complement simulations by long-range real-world experiments.

Acknowledgments. This work was partially supported by the German BMBF within the projects SAFEST and Peeroskop.

3. REFERENCES

[1] AFANASYEV, A., MAHADEVAN, P., MOISEENKO, I., UZUN, E., AND ZHANG, L. Interest Flooding Attack and Countermeasures in Named Data Networking. In *Proc. of IFIP Networking* (Piscataway, NJ, USA, 2013), IEEE Press.

[2] COMPAGNO, A., CONTI, M., GASTI, P., AND TSUDIK, G. Poseidon: Mitigating Interest Flooding DDoS Attacks in Named Data Networking. arXiv 1303.4823, 2013.

[3] DAI, H., WANG, Y., FAN, J., AND LIU, B. Mitigate DDoS Attacks in NDN by Interest Traceback. In *Proc. of IEEE INFOCOM NOMEN Workshop*, 2013, IEEE Press.

[4] GASTI, P., TSUDIK, G., UZUN, E., AND ZHANG, L. DoS and DDoS in Named Data Networking. In *Proc. of ICCCN*, 2013.

[5] WÄHLISCH, M., SCHMIDT, T. C., AND VAHLENKAMP, M. Backscatter from the Data Plane – Threats to Stability and Security in Information-Centric Network Infrastructure. *Computer Networks 57*, 16 (Nov. 2013), 3192–3206, (original version arXiv:1205.4778, May 2012).

[6] WANG, K., ZHOU, H., LUO, H., GUAN, J., QIN, Y., AND ZHANG, H. Detecting and mitigating interest flooding attacks in content-centric network. *Security and Communication Networks 7*, 4 (April 2013), 685–699.

Secure Name Configuration and Prefix Registration

Marc Mosko, Glenn Scott, Nacho Solis, Christopher A. Wood
Palo Alto Research Center, Palo Alto, CA 94304
{mmosko, gscott, isolis, cwood}@parc.com

Categories and Subject Descriptors: C.2 [Computer-Communication Networks]: Network Protocols

Categories and Subject Descriptors: C.2.4 [Computer-Communication Networks]: Distributed Systems – *distributed applications*

Keywords: Content-centric networking; name and prefix registration

1. INTRODUCTION

Content Centric Networking (CCN) is a networking architecture that emerged from the pitfalls of today's IP-based Internet design. Contrary to host-based traffic in the modern Internet, CCN traffic is driven by explicit requests for named content. One of the main features of this name-based content retrieval strategy is that it effectively decouples content from its original producer, thereby enabling more natural content distribution. At the same time CCN enables routers to opportunistically cache content *in the network*. Cached content can then be returned in response to future interests for the same content. This avoids the need to forward every request (interest) from consumers all the way to producers, thus lowering network congestion and reducing content retrieval latency.

CCN routers are responsible for forwarding requests (called interests) for content emitted from consumers to an authoritative source (producer) capable of generating or providing the desired content (object). Generally, forwarding interest messages toward a producer is done using only their names. Routers maintain a data structure called a Forwarding Interest Base (FIB) which maps *name prefixes* to a set of interfaces to which interests should be forwarded. Like IP routing tables, FIBs are populated either manually or using a routing algorithm.

In existing routing algorithms (see [1] and references therein), producers advertise prefixes of content they are willing to serve under, and these routes are propagated throughout the network to enable routing. For example, Google might choose to serve content under the /google/ namespace pre-

fix. Routing algorithms serve to install routes to /google/ in router FIBs so that interests for any content with this name prefix are forwarded to the Google "producer." Although this arrangement is functionally correct, i.e., it will enable consumer interests to be routed to the Google producer, there is an issue of whether or not said producer is *permitted* to publish or serve content under its desired namespace. Without any form of trusted authentication and authorization, *anyone* is free to advertise content under *any* prefix. Moreover, there is the problem of registering and configuring this name prefix *in the transport stack* so that interests will be routed up towards the producer application.

We address these issues with the CCN dynamic name configuration and local prefix registration service. Together, these elements provide an application with the means to (a) securely register namespaces under which content will be served, (b) obtain the authentication token necessary to install a prefix locally so that interests can be returned to a producer application, and, (c) advertise a certain prefix to the rest of the network so that consumers may retrieve content from the target producer. Our design provides a complete end-to-end workflow that enables producers to begin serving content under a namespace they are authorized to use, thereby addressing one of the larger problem in namespace management.

2. THE CCN TRANSPORT STACK

All applications interface with the CCN transport stack using the Portal API – a lightweight interface that provides simple interest and content exchanges. The CCN transport stack is a set of components, each of which is focused on a specific task. It adheres to the chain-of-command pattern: each component processes a message and then forwards it to the next component in the chain. Each component has an outbound queue to move messages from the application toward the network, as well as an inbound queue to move messages from the network toward the application. Each transport stack requires the following two components: the API adapter and the forwarder adapter. Applications connect to the API adapter to communicate to the stack, and the stack uses the forwarder adapter to connect to the local forwarder. The forwarder is the component that contains, updates, and uses the FIB, PIT, and content store (CS) when processing inbound and outbound messages. Messages are pipelined through the transport stack components from the upper-level API to the **forwarder** by means of these adapters. Messages can be scoped to the local (i.e., endhost) machine with a special localhost prefix, thereby enabling IPC among applications running on the same endhost.

ICN'15, Sept.30–Oct. 2, 2015, San Francisco, CA, USA.
ACM 978-1-4503-3855-4/15/09.
DOI: http://dx.doi.org/10.1145/2810156.2812605 .

3. NAME CONFIGURATION AND PREFIX REGISTRATION

To address the problem of producer name registraticfxon and advertisement, we present the design of a Kerberos-like [2] name configuration and prefix registration service. Our design presupposes the existence of a Dynamic Name Configuration Service (DNCS), which is a centralized authority responsible for managing namespaces. Part of its managerial responsibilities include issuing *permission tokens* that are used by endhost transport stacks to install and advertise namespace prefixes. Each endhost has a single Dynamic Name Configuration Agent (DNCA) daemon service which is responsible for all communication with the DNCS.[1] This interaction is done on behalf of the producer to obtain the aforementioned permission tokens necessary to "use" prefixes. Specifically, when a producer application wishes to "use" a prefix N, it issues a request (in the form of a localhost-scoped interest) to the local DNCA that contains N, the producer's identity (e.g., a certificate), and a signature computed on both. The DNCA then provides this request to the DNCS in the form of an interest, which forces the DNCS to validate the request and authorize the producer to use N – returning a permission token as an acknowledgment – or deny the request and return a simple NACK. A permission token only needs to bind the namespace N to the producer's identity, e.g., it can consist of a simple DNCS-generated signature over both.

In addition to the local DNCA, endhosts also have a Prefix Registration Service (PRS) and Routing Protocol service (RP). The former is responsible for instructing the single local forwarder (FWD) to install, remove, or update FIB entries to suit the needs of a producer application. After a producer application receives a permission token from the DNCS, through the DNCA, the producer will ask the PRS for permission to perform a *specific action* with the local FIB. For example, the PRS might permit the producer to only install the namespace N in the FIB. The producer provides the DNCS permission token in the PRS request, and the PRS only authorizes the request if a valid permission token is provided. The short-term and single-use PRS token generated in response to a producer's request binds their identity to the namespace and desired forwarder action. Finally, the producer can issue this single use token to the forwarder to complete the action. Security of this procedure is rooted in the validity of each signature computed and verified, as well as the trustworthiness of the DNCS (the trust anchor). Note that installing an entry in the FIB *does not* actually advertise N to the rest of the network. To do this, the producer must request the local RP to advertise N, providing the DNCS permission token in the process. A complete overview of the end-to-end workflow is shown in Figure 1. We use the notation LT and ET to refer to the DNCS long-term permission token and PRS short-term (ephemeral) permission token, respectively.

4. ELEMENTS OF TRUST

Trust for secure prefix registration is anchored in the DNCS. The endhost PRS agent and routing process trust the DNCS (through the DNCA), and the local forwarder (FWD) trusts

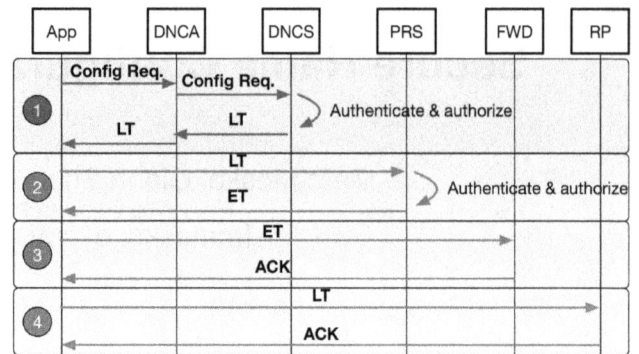

Figure 1: Kerberos-like sequence diagram showing the messages that need to be sent to install and advertise a prefix.

the PRS. Namespaces will not be advertised by the routing protocol unless given explicit permission by the DNCS (see Step 4 of Figure 1). Thus, malicious producers may only advertise namespaces under which they are not authorized to serve if they can subvert the routing process verification check or forge a long-term permission token from the DNCS.

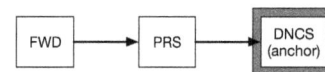

Figure 2: PRS chain of trust anchored at the DNCS.

5. FUTURE WORK

We presented the preliminary design and a complete end-to-end workflow that enables CCN producers to begin serving content under a namespace they are authorized to use. Our solution provides an application with the means to (a) securely register namespaces under which content will be served, (b) obtain the authentication token necessary to install a prefix locally, and (c) advertise a certain prefix to the rest of the network.

Future work will entail addressing issues the design of the DNCS which, as presented, is a centralized service. A more federated and hierarchical approach akin to today's DNS is needed to prevent it from becoming a single point of trust and failure. Moreover, trust delegation between parent and children DNCS instances needs to be handled securely. We will also explore issues of trust management in the routing processes and protocols, as well as ways to avoid subversion and collusion by producers.

6. REFERENCES

[1] JJ Garcia-Luna-Aceves. Name-based content routing in information centric networks using distance information. In *Proceedings of the 1st international conference on Information-centric networking*, pages 7–16. ACM, 2014.

[2] B Clifford Neuman and Theodore Ts' O. Kerberos: An authentication service for computer networks. *Communications Magazine, IEEE*, 32(9):33–38, 1994.

---

[1]Note that the DNCA is a standard CCN application that runs on top of the transport stack.

A Network-Agnostic Data Framework and API for CCN

Glenn Scott
Palo Alto Research Center, Palo Alto, CA 94304
Glenn.Scott@parc.com

Christopher A. Wood
University of California, Irvine, CA 92617
woodc1@uci.edu

ABSTRACT

We introduce the CCN Information and Data Framework (IDF). The IDF provides a Create, Read, Update, and Delete (CRUD) interface for reading and manipulating data "in the network." We show how to use the IDF API through the UNIX file I/O API, thereby placing file I/O and network communication under a single, standard interface. The IDF effectively creates a name-based layer of abstraction upon which *network-agnostic* applications can be built.

Categories and Subject Descriptors

C.2 [**Computer-Communication Networks**]: Network Protocols; C.2.4 [**Computer-Communication Networks**]: Distributed Systems—*distributed applications*

Keywords

Content-centric networking; data framework; API

1. INTRODUCTION

The suite of protocols that exist in the current TCP/IP Internet model do not adequately satisfy modern application use cases which are heavily *based on data*. All of the abstractions provided by these protocol interfaces are inherently location-dependent and provide little more than packet transmission and receipt functionality. In our increasingly content-centric world, abstractions for content are needed to build modern applications and services. Therefore, in addition to reconsidering the Internet architecture, we must also consider the interfaces by which applications make use of it.

Content-Centric Networking (CCN) is an approach to (inter-)networking designed for efficient, secure, and scalable content distribution [1, 4]. In CCN, named content, rather than named interfaces or hosts, are treated as first-class entities that are explicitly requested via interest messages. By decoupling data from its location, content can be cached within the network to optimize bandwidth use, reduce latency, and use multiple network interfaces simultaneously.

ICN'15, Sept.30–Oct. 2, 2015, San Francisco, CA, USA.
ACM 978-1-4503-3855-4/15/09.
DOI: http://dx.doi.org/10.1145/2810156.2812606 .

Apart from the aforementioned performance improvements, an important benefit of the content-centric approach to networking is that it introduces an abstraction layer in the form of requests and content responses between applications and the location where content is stored. In CCNx [1], this layer is used with the CCN Portal. The Portal API enables applications to be constructed in a *location-agnostic* way using the discrete interest and content object messages.

Many modern systems and applications rely on a file as a high-level abstraction upon which other data access mechanisms, e.g., video streams, databases, messages, and key-value stores, are implemented. While interests and content objects serve as a vehicle for transferring *raw* data, they cannot be directly used as these various abstractions without another layer of indirection. These realizations led us to the main contribution of this work: the Information and Data Framework (IDF). This component builds on top of the Portal API to provide a Create, Read, Update, Delete (CRUD) API – the Information and Data Interface (IDI) – for applications to read and manipulate network data. Internally, it interfaces with the operating system processes and remote services needed to compose content objects into these abstractions. To illustrate the efficacy of the IDF, we designed a mapping from the Unix File API to the IDI, which effectively places file I/O and network communication (for content retrieval) under a single interface.

2. THE CCN PORTAL BEDROCK

In CCN, interests and content objects are the primary elements of discourse in CCN. Consumers issue interests for data and receive content objects in response; they do not need to know the details of the transport stack to communicate. The actual contents, semantics, and representation of both interests and content objects within the network stack are entirely dependent on its internal components. Consequently, a natural abstraction for interfacing with CCN is a single interface through which discrete interest and content object messages flow. In CCN, this interface is called the **Portal**. The Portal is a minimal interface used to communicate with the **transport stack** and the network. The Portal API provides a simple interface to the transport stack allowing the application to compose, use, and maintain transport stacks and to perform discrete message operations (e.g., send interests and content objects) through the stack.

3. INFORMATION AND DATA FRAMEWORK

Unix files are an extremely powerful abstraction upon which many different applications (e.g., grep, sed, awk),

Table 1: IDI: The Information and Data Interface API.

Function Signature	Description
`(success, manifest) = IDFCreate(lciName, ACS)`	Make a file available with the given LCI encoded name and access information encoded in a CCN `AccessControlSpecification`.
`buffer = IDFRead(lciName, numbytes=0, offset=0)`	Read data (of numbytes size) from the specified name starting at the given offset.
`count = IDFUpdate(lciName, buffer, count, offset=0)`	Update the file with the given name and offset (default 0) with the specified data.
`success = IDFDelete(lciName)`	Make a file that was previously available, unavailable.

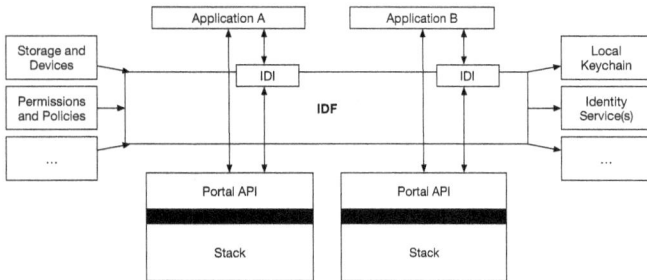

Figure 1: Component-level diagram of the IDF.

APIs, and large systems (e.g., databases) have been built. We borrow from its success to build the CCN **Information and Data Framework** (IDF), a framework that collates other services such as network communication, access control and permissions, and concurrency synchronization to provide a single, simple, file-like API. The framework is an *extension of the Portal and transport stack* that uses external services and local operating system resources to perform a variety of useful functions and provide a lightweight CRUD-like API to upper-level layers in the stack. As illustrated in Figure 1, some of these local system resources may be storage and media devices, system permissions and policies, and the local keychain. The IDF will coordinate interaction with these resources to determine whether upper-level clients can perform simple read and write behaviors, for example. The IDF may also be extended to communicate with external identity services, e.g., via LDAP [3] or OAuth [2], to obtain authentication information and other related data. These services may also provide cryptographic secrets necessary to access content protected under some form of access control, e.g., by encryption.

The goal of the IDF is to free developers from devising and implementing new protocols and mechanisms to publish and retrieve content, similar to the DOT data transfer architecture presented in [5]. The IDF API – the Information and Data Interface (IDI) – follows the CRUD (create, read, update, delete) model with ACID guarantees. Instead of file handles or network sockets, for example, each of these CRUD functions use only the name of the content in question. This name-based abstraction frees developers from the details of network communication and other content stores (i.e., filesystems). A high-level description of this API is summarized in Table 1 to illustrate its simplicity.

From the application's perspective, the IDF is meant as a more useful abstraction beyond interest and content objects. For example, applications may instantiate file instances using the framework and then read and write to them, much

like any normal file. From the system's perspective, the IDF coordinates many working services to give further meaning to the atomic interest and content object messages provided by CCN, such as: object reconstruction and access control, local operating environment access, content publication, remote authentication, and content state management.

4. NETWORK-AGNOSTIC CONTENT

The IDI enables clients to interact and treat network data as if it were *persistent* – a paradox in today's world. It enables an application to switch – on the fly – from local file based access to network based access through the same interface, much like the Juno middleware platform that enabled location and protocol agnostic content retrieval [6]. As previously mentioned, persistent data access has traditionally been access via the Unix File API. Since the IDF provides a layer of abstraction for location-agnostic persistent data, it may also be used by the very same Unix File API. To do this, we designed and specified an adapter that maps the Unix File API operations to underlying IDF functions. This adapter enables multiple benefits, including: (a) existing applications can migrate to CCN with minimal development effort, (b) richer APIs can be built upon the concept of random access files, e.g., key-value store, messaging, and data streaming APIs, and (c) security concerns such as encryption and access control are handled beneath the API.

5. REFERENCES

[1] CCNx 1.0 Protocol SpeciïñĄcations Roadmap. http://www.ietf.org/mail-archive/web/icnrg/current/pdfZyEQRE5tFS.pdf.

[2] Eran Hammer-Lahav. The oauth 1.0 protocol. 2010.

[3] Timothy A Howes, Mark C Smith, and Gordon S Good. *Understanding and deploying LDAP directory services*. Addison-Wesley Longman Publishing Co., Inc., 2003.

[4] Van Jacobson, Diana K Smetters, James D Thornton, Michael F Plass, Nicholas H Briggs, and Rebecca L Braynard. Networking named content. In *Proceedings of the 5th International Conference on Emerging Networking Experiments and Technologies*, pages 1–12. ACM, 2009.

[5] Niraj Tolia, Michael Kaminsky, David G Andersen, and Swapnil Patil. An architecture for internet data transfer. In *NSDI*, 2006.

[6] Gareth Tyson, Andreas Mauthe, Sebastian Kaune, Paul Grace, Adel Taweel, and Thomas Plagemann. Juno: A middleware platform for supporting delivery-centric applications. *ACM Transactions on Internet Technology (TOIT)*, 12(2):4, 2012.

Multipath Support for Name-based Information Dissemination in Fragmented Networks

Kohei Sugiyama
KDDI R&D Laboratories, Inc.,
Japan
ko-sugiyama@kddilabs.jp

Atsushi Tagami
KDDI R&D Laboratories, Inc.,
Japan
tagami@kddilabs.jp

Tomohiko Yagyu
NEC Corporation, Japan
yagyu@cp.jp.nec.com

Toru Hasegawa
Osaka University, Japan
t-hasegawa@ist.osaka-u.ac.jp

Mayutan Arumaithurai
University of Goettingen,
Germany
mayutan.arumaithurai@cs.uni-goettingen.de

K. K. Ramakrishnan
University of California,
Riverside, U.S.A.
kk@cs.ucr.edu

ABSTRACT

In the aftermath of natural disasters (e.g., earthquakes and hurricanes), networks are fragmented, and communication is intermittent and disruption-prone. In this paper, we propose a multipath support for publish/subscribe name-based information dissemination in such fragmented networks. Our solution helps to reduce unnecessary replication and transmission in disaster scenarios.

Categories and Subject Descriptors

C.2 [**Computer-Communication Networks**]: Network Architecture and Design, Network Protocols

Keywords

Information-Centric Networking (ICN); Content-Centric Networking (CCN); Publish/Subscribe; Safety Confirmation

1. INTRODUCTION

In the aftermath of natural disasters, existing mobile network infrastructure is damaged and isolated due to base stations and backhaul network failures. We therefore study how to improve the dissemination of information from and to these isolated networks. Hereafter, we refer to these isolated networks as *fragmented networks*.

Figure 1 shows a reference network that includes fragmented networks, a non-fragmented network, and a data mule, such as an ambulance, a fire engine, a patrol car, or a special drone. We assume a Wi-Fi access point and an ICN [1] router are installed at each fragmented network (i.e., shelter) for refugees to enable communication with others in the same fragmented network. Data mules, on the other hand, have a communication method with access points and can transfer and receive messages from/to a fragmented network and a non-fragmented network.

ICN'15, Sept.30–Oct. 2, 2015, San Francisco, CA, USA.
ACM 978-1-4503-3855-4/15/09.
DOI: http://dx.doi.org/10.1145/2810156.2812607 .

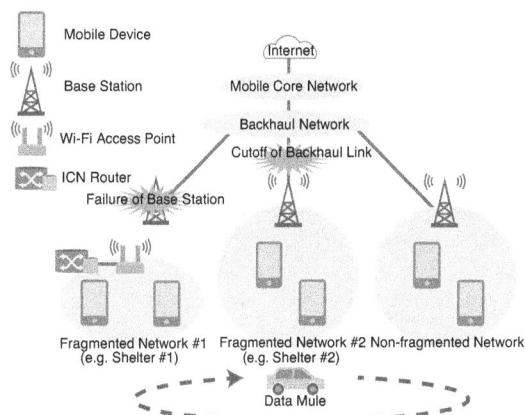

Figure 1: Hypothetical examples of fragmented networks in a disaster scenario

A rendezvous point-based publish/subscribe mechanism to support information dissemination in fragmented networks has been proposed in [6]. The basic idea is to construct a disruption tolerant logical topology over fragmented networks and build a subscription table (ST) exploiting this logical topology. The logical interfaces of a node is viewed as distinct from its physical interface. The association of a physical interface to a logical interface is established when the physical connectivity is established. The advantage is a reduction in the unnecessary transmission of messages, since messages are forwarded on the basis of a managed routing table. However, rendezvous point-based solutions could lead to a substantial increase in the length of information dissemination paths since each published message is forwarded to the subscribers via the corresponding rendezvous point. This paper proposes an extend version of our solution with multipath support in order to achieve more reduction in unnecessary message replication and transmission.

2. RELATED WORK

Delay-/Disruption-Tolerant Networking (DTN) is a promising ad-hoc communication method that provides network services continuously with a network that has no specific infrastructure. More recent studies on the interface between ICN and DTN have shown that name-based communication is superior to IP-based mobile communication [7]. Most of the work to bring information centricity on DTN, mobile ad-hoc networking, or vehicular networking is still in the early stage [8]. Recently, the authors of [5] proposed NREP, which enables named-based message dissemination based on priority. NREP is suitable for disseminating messages, such as warnings and availability of shelters and food, but not suitable for services, such as safety confirmation, since NREP does not take the specific interests of users into account.

3. DESIGN

3.1 Overview

To deal with the problem described in Sec. 1, we introduce *weighted logical topology* to support multipath forwarding in fragmented networks. Our multipath support enables the intermediate routers, i.e., ICN routers, data mules, and of course the rendezvous point, to select suitable next hops to deliver subscribe/publish messages for efficiency in the fragmented networks. The key idea is that a weight is assigned to a logical face dynamically and asymmetrically. We use two kinds of routing tables for publish/subscribe messages to construct the optimal tree with a breadcrumb model. Intermediate routers can decide which data mule is the fastest to disseminate messages to users. In that sense, multipath support helps to reduce unnecessary replication, transmission, and delay of messages in fragmented networks.

Figure 2(a) shows an example map, where there are five sites, i.e., the rendezvous point (RP) and 4 shelters. In this map, three data mules a, b, and c go around sites and have planned routes $R_a = \{$ RP, 1, 2 $\}$, $R_b = \{$ RP, 4, 3, 1 $\}$, and $R_c = \{$ RP, 3, 4 $\}$, respectively. A logical link is established based on the order of a planned route. When planned route R_a of data mule a has Shelter#1, for example data mule a and Shelter#1 are connected by a logical link. Figure 2(b) shows the weighted logical topologies, whose roots are RP and Shelter#4, respectively. The weight on a link between two nodes is the transit time between the two nodes. For example, if RP sends a message to Shelter#4, there are two routes from RP to Shelter#4, i.e., RP → b → 4 and RP → c → 4. The sums of weights over the routes are 67 (57 + 10) and 74 (42 + 32), respectively. Thus, RP chooses data mule b as the next hop because data mule b is likely to reach Shelter#4 faster compared with data mule c. Similarly, Shelter#4 selects data mule c as the next hop for a message to RP.

3.2 Two Forwarding Planes

Since the weighted logical link is asymmetric, the least-cost route is determined by the direction. This asymmetry is excellent potential for breadcrumb forwarding, like PIT and ST (defined by NDN [4]/CCN [3], and COPSS [2], respectively). Publish/subscribe communication model has multiple data packets, i.e., subscriptions and publications. The total of message delay is the sum of the delay from the publisher to the rendezvous point and the delay from the rendezvous point to the subscriber. A delay from a subscriber to the rendezvous point is not so important from the viewpoint of QoS. We, therefore, build two forwarding planes. One plane routes publish messages from a publisher to the rendezvous point, and the other plane routes subscribe messages to construct ST, which is the least-cost tree rooted by the rendezvous point.

To construct two forwarding planes on top of ICN, the rendezvous point advertises two names, i.e., /pub/rp/ and /sub/rp/. Each edge router calculates cost, i.e. transit time, according to the destination's prefix and advertises the cost to neighbor routers.

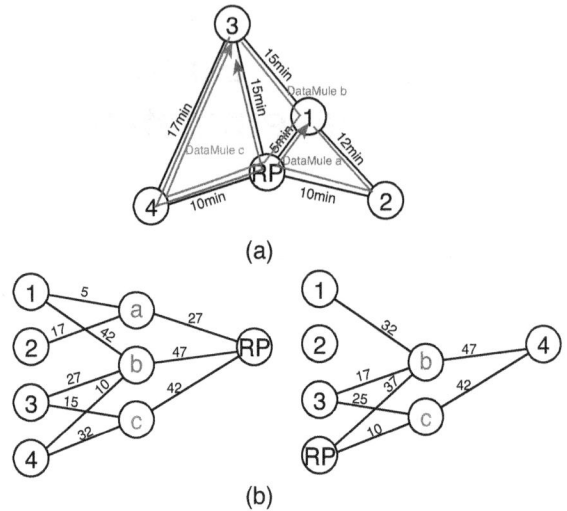

Figure 2: (a) A map with routes of data mules and transit time between sites (b) Weighted logical topologies, whose roots are RP and Shelter#4, respectively

4. CONCLUSION

In this paper, we presented a multipath support built on top of a publish/subscribe architecture, for information dissemination in fragmented networks. As future work, we need to evaluate the effectiveness of our multipath support by simulation experiments.

Acknowledgements

The research leading to these results has received funding from the EU-JAPAN initiative by the EC Seventh Framework Programme (FP7/2007-2013) Grant Agreement no. 608518 and NICT under Grant Agreement no. 167 (GreenICN project).

5. REFERENCES

[1] B. Ahlgren et al. A survey of information-centric networking. *IEEE Communications Magazine*, 50(7):26–36, July 2012.

[2] J. Chen et al. COPSS: An efficient content oriented publish/subscribe system. In *Proc. of ACM/IEEE ANCS*, pages 99–110, Oct. 2011.

[3] V. Jacobson et al. Networking named content. In *Proceedings of ACM CoNEXT*, pages 1–12, Dec. 2009.

[4] T. Koponen et al. A data-oriented (and beyond) network architecture. In *Proc. of ACM SIGCOMM*, pages 181–192, Aug. 2007.

[5] I. Psaras et al. Name-based replication priorities in disaster cases. In *Proceedings of IEEE INFOCOM NOM Workshop*, Apr. 2014.

[6] K. Sugiyama et al. Name-based information dissemination for fragmented networks in disasters. In *Proc. of IEEE/ACM COMSNETS*, Jan. 2015.

[7] G. Tyson et al. A survey of mobility in information-centric networks. *Communications of the ACM*, 56(12):90–98, Dec. 2013.

[8] G. Tyson et al. Towards an information-centric delay-tolerant network. In *Proceedings of IEEE INFOCOM NOMEN Workshop*, Apr. 2013.

Prototype of an Architecture for Object Resolution Services in Information-Centric Environment

Sripriya Srikant Adhatarao*, Jiachen Chen*, Mayutan Arumaithurai*,
Xiaoming Fu* and K.K. Ramakrishnan†
*University of Göttingen, Germany. Email:{adhatarao,jiachen,arumaithurai,fu}@cs.uni-goettingen.de
†University of California, Riverside, USA. Email: kk@cs.ucr.edu

1. INTRODUCTION

Information-Centric Networking (ICN) is a new paradigm where information is exchanged using the *Names* of the content. Recent ICN proposals like Named Data Networking (NDN [1]) and Content Oriented Publish/Subscribe System (COPSS [2]) use hierarchically structured Names and Content Descriptors (CDs) as the identity of the content. They assume the existence of some mechanisms that assist users in retrieving the "ICN-names/CDs" for the information they seek. However, these proposals lack a description of how users can obtain these "ICN-names/CDs".

In a recent work [3], we proposed an architecture for Object Resolution services in Information-Centric Environment (ORICE) that tries to mitigate this gap and thereby enhances the usability of ICN. It can be a framework for building object resolution systems in ICN. ORICE allows the object resolution systems to provide the service which may involve complex logic and large data access at the application layer that enables ICN to handle the communication in a simple and yet efficient manner. With ORICE, multiple object resolution systems can be deployed as per the need in the application layer. These systems can even communicate with each other and provide better services to users.

With the ICN as the underlying networking architecture, object resolution systems can be benefited with diversity in the recommendations along with service scalability for distribution of services and balancing the load in the network. Users can also get retrieval/dissemination efficiency thanks to the name-based routing and in-network caches along with data integrity.

In this demo, we present a prototype of ORICE, using ICN as the underlying network and demonstrate the feasibility of ORICE in fulfilling the necessity for object resolution services in ICN. We implement multiple object resolution systems using the architectural primitives proposed in ORICE and show how users can translate keywords to the names/CDs they might be interested in before retrieving the data from the underlying network.

ICN'15, September 30 - October 02, 2015, San Francisco, CA, USA
ACM 978-1-4503-3855-4/15/09.
http://dx.doi.org/10.1145/2810156.2812608.

2. PROTOTYPE OF ORICE

In this section, we describe the prototype implemented using ORICE. In particular, we demonstrate how clients can search for names/CDs in ICN (for query/response and publish/subscribe). The prototype is built on top of CCNx 0.8.0 and COPSS. We use Fig. 1 to demonstrate the working of our prototype. Here we have two object resolution services (ORS_1 and ORS_2, having 1 server each), 1 certification server (CS) and 2 users (U_1 and U_2) attached to a network consisting of 6 routers (R_1–R_6). We also implemented the broker design in COPSS (*Broker* in Fig. 1) to provide support for asynchronous data dissemination. Brokers subscribe to their responsible CDs and receive publications that can be requested by offline users. The certification server, resolution server and broker system register their respective prefixes (*i.e.*, /CertPrefix, /ORSx and /Broker) to ensure that CCNx can route the Interests to the intended server based on the prefixes. The resolution servers subscribe to the management channel (/ManageChannel) on which they receive updates in the name space from certification server. We demonstrate the system with the following scenarios.

2.1 Scenario [Post]

Data providers have the responsibility for associating appropriate names/CDs to the content they post in the network. ORICE allows them to seek names/CDs from the object resolution services.

As shown in Fig. 1a, when a user U_1 wants to publish a piece of data, he would type the title and content of the message in the graphical user interface (GUI) as shown in Fig. 1b. Instead of typing the name and CDs himself, the user can get suggestions from an object resolution service. We provide 2 basic object resolution services and the user can set the preference by setting the parameter "default search engine prefix". The application would send a request using the format /ORSx/Search/Message and the request will be routed to the corresponding object resolution service and receive the suggestions (the green arrow in Fig. 1a shows a request goes to ORS_2).

U_1 can choose any name/CD for the message before publication. If he is not satisfied with the existing identities, he can request to add a new identity by sending an Interest with name=/CertPrefix/ID and content="add". This packet will be forwarded to the certification service CS and U_1 will get the response indicating if the request is approved (flow not shown in Fig. 1a). Upon approval, CS will notify the changes to the name space via the management channel (with CD=/ManageChannel/CD) to the respective resolution servers (the red arrows in Fig. 1a).

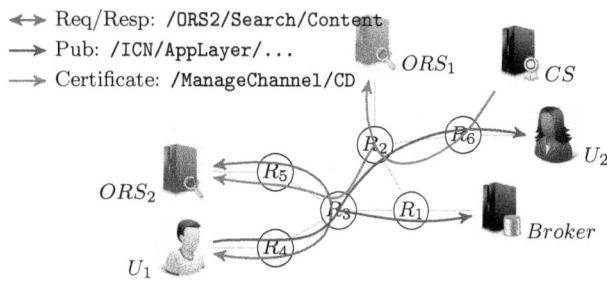

(a) Scenario: Post

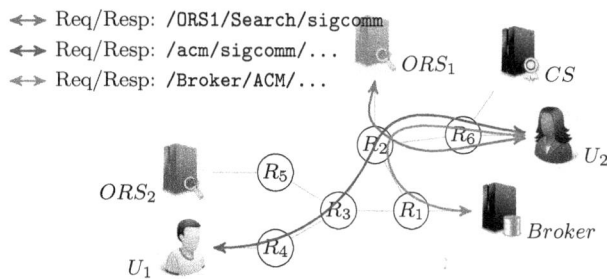

(b) Post and Messages View

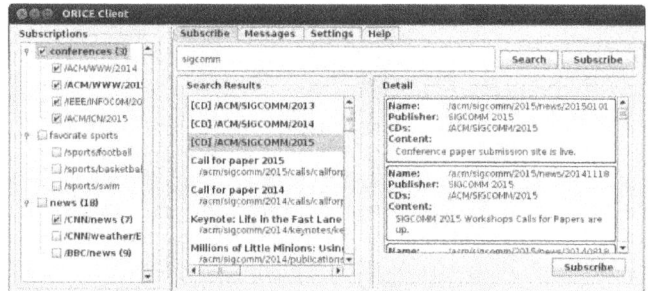

(c) Scenario: Query/Subscribe

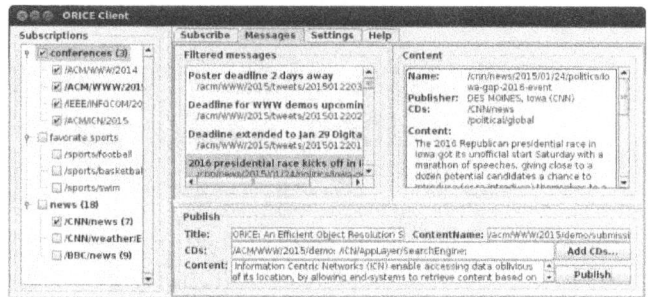

(d) Query/Subscribe View

Figure 1: Example scenario and GUI of ORICE prototype.

When U_1 clicks the "Publish" button, the application will start to serve the message and also multicast the message to the users who have subscribed to the related CDs. In the example, U_2 is subscribing to the message and her GUI will place a notification on receiving the multicast. In the demo, we use a broker (described in [2]) that listens to all the CDs as a backup server for the application. The blue arrows in Fig. 1a shows the flow of the multicast and Fig. 1b shows that the received messages are grouped into different topics based on the CDs. The user has 3 new messages in topic "conferences" and 7 new messages in CD `/CNN/news`. She can browse through the topics, CDs and also read the details of the messages in the GUI.

2.2 Scenario [Query/Subscribe]

If a user is interested in a topic, in the network (s)he can either issue a query (for past data) or perform a subscription (for future data). To simplify the procedure, we unify the two processes in our demo. The user can simply type the key words (s)he is interested in as shown in Fig. 1d.

When the "Search" button is clicked, the application sends a request using the default search engine prefix (`/ORS1/Search/sigcomm` in the example, the green arrow in Fig. 1c). ORS_1 responds with a list of candidate names and CDs and the application lists the results in the middle column in Fig. 1d.

If a user is interested in a piece of data (*e.g.*, the 4th item in the list), (s)he can click on the item and the application would send a request using the ContentName in the entry. In the example, U_2's application requests for the data `/acm/.../callforpapers.pdf` and the packet is forwarded in the network following the blue arrow. This kind of requests can fully exploit the benefits provided by ICN. *E.g.*, if R_3 has a cache or *Broker* already has the data, the request will be redirected before it goes all the way to U_1.

When a CD entry (starting with "[CD]") is clicked, the application would try to request the broker for the most recent

messages. It would send a request with name `/Broker/CD` and put "latest" as the selector (the red arrow in Fig. 1c) and the broker would reply with a list of data published recently as is shown in the GUI. These messages help the user to decide if the CD is the one that (s)he is interested in. When the user decides to subscribe to the CD, (s)he can click the "Subscribe" button in the bottom right corner and the application will subscribe to the CD (flow not shown in Fig. 1c).

When the clients come back online, the application can request the broker system using the name `/Broker/CD` and the selector to filter out all the received messages. *Broker* responds with messages accordingly.

For demonstration, we have set up the test bed as shown in Fig. 1a and Fig. 1c. With user interfaces as shown in Fig. 1b and Fig. 1d, we will show two object resolution systems implemented using ORICE framework each running on a different computer. With GUIs like Fig. 1b and Fig. 1d, we show users interacting with the object resolution systems. We will deploy the ICN platform in our lab test bed and the front-end applications will access the platform through SSH tunnels.

Acknowledgment

This research was partly funded from the EU-JAPAN FP7-NICT GreenICN project, the Volkswagen Foundation Project "Simulation Science Center" and the US National Science Funding under Grant No.CNS-1455815.

3. REFERENCES

[1] V. Jacobson *et al.*, "Networking Named Content," in *CoNEXT*, 2009.

[2] J. Chen *et al.*, "COPSS: An Efficient Content Oriented Publish/Subscribe System," in *ANCS*, 2011.

[3] S. S. Adhatarao *et al.*, "ORICE: an Architecture for Object Resolution Services in Information-Centric Environment," in *LANMAN*, 2015.

Demo:Content-based Push/Pull Message Dissemination for Disaster Message Board

Tomohiko Yagyu
NEC Corporation
Kawasaki, Japan
yagyu@cp.jp.nec.com

Kenichi Nakamura
Panasonic Corporation
Tokyo, Japan
nakamura.kenken@
jp.panasonic.com

Tohru Asami
The University of Tokyo
Tokyo, Japan
asami@akg.t.u-
tokyo.ac.jp

Kohei Sugiyama, Atsushi Tagami
KDDI R&D Laboratories
Saitama, Japan
{ko-sugiyama,
tagami}@kddilabs.jp

Toru Hasegawa
Osaka University
Osaka, Japan
t-hasegawa@ist.osaka-
u.ac.jp

Mayutan Arumaithurai
University of Goettingen
Goettingen, Germany
mayutan.arumaithurai@cs.uni-
goettingen.de

ABSTRACT

Information Centric Networking (ICN) is one of the promising technologies to support reliable communication in the post-disaster network. This demo presents the integrated framework of push and pull type content-based communication, along with proposed enhancements that make it applicable in a disaster scenario. We will demonstrate these features with the help of an example application – disaster message board.

Categories and Subject Descriptors

C.2 [**Computer-Communication Networks**]: Network Architecture and Design, Network Protocols

Keywords

Information Centric Networking, Fragmented Network, Disaster Message Board, COPSS, Logical interface, IBAS

1. INTRODUCTION

Name-based communication architecture, namely ICN (Information Centric Networking), is useful not only in ordinary cases but also in disaster cases. Aftermath of disaster, existing communication infrastructure such as the Internet and cellular networks will be severely damaged. Because of the fault of BaseStations(BS) and cable cut between BS and backhaul, the infrastructure will be fragmented into portions. We call this partitioned network a fragmented network. The fragmented network comprises of some isolated

domains. DataMules(DMs) go round and relay messages among isolated domains. Figure 1 is an example of fragmented network that we assume. In the fragmented network, it is difficult to keep connection with the server. Furthermore, securing the content itself is more feasible than establishing secure connection with the server. Therefore content-based message delivery is more desirable than host-based communication for the service reliability. This demo shows content-based disaster message board in fragmented network. Disaster message board is a bulletin board system used for communication among relatives during disaster[1]. Figure 2 shows the protocol stack of the proposed framework. This framework integrates several achievements[3][4][5][6] in GreenICN project[2] and CCN(Content Centric Networking)[8].

2. INTEGRATION OF PUSH AND PULL

In [6], we have demonstrated reliable pull-type communication in the fragmented network. Pull-type communication is useful when a user requests an existing content. However, if a user wants to obtain irregularly generated contents, push-type delivery such as pub/sub is preferable to pull. Push-type communication is also desirable for prompt dissemination of critical information to hundreds of people simultaneously. However in disaster situation, users' devices are often disconnected from the network because of saving their batteries or going outside. Therefore subscribers may fail to receive messages during their absence. When they try to retrieve missed messages, ICN is better architecture than IP network. This is because ICN allows a user to obtain a content by indicating its name without connecting the server. A user can obtain the content from cache in an intermediate node. Therefore integrated framework of push-type and pull-type communication enables reliable and efficient message dissemination in the fragmented network.

COPSS(Content Oriented Publish/Subscribe System)[3] is the name-base pub/sub protocol with Rendezvous Point (RP) node. However, COPSS can not be applied to the fragmented network because 1) intermediate nodes don't cache contents 2) subscribers can't detect missed contents. To retrieve missed messages, first of all, subscribers need to know

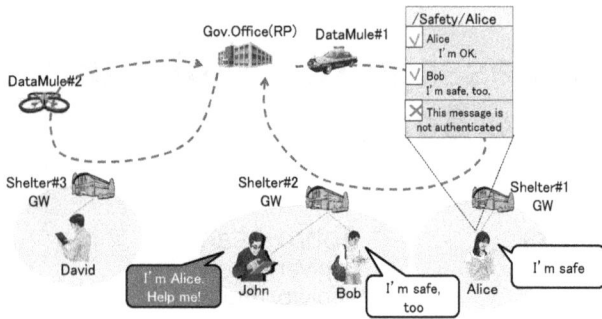

Figure 1: Demo Setup (Disaster Message Board)

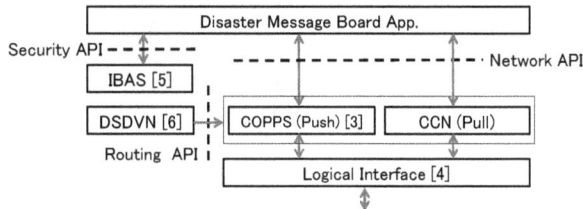

Figure 2: Protocol Stack

whether they have missed some messages or not. We extend RP of COPSS to give a sequence number to each message per topic. A subscriber can detect missed message by the sequence number. Furthermore, every intermediate node is extended to cache the messages and record the latest sequence number for the topics. A subscriber can know the latest sequence number for the topic from the nearest node. If he wants to retrieve the missed message, he pulls it by sending *Interest*. He can quickly obtain the message from the cache in an intermediate node.

3. RELIABLE MESSAGE TRANSMISSION

COPSS relies on a subscription tree rooted at an RP in order to push content from the publishers to the subscribers. In a disaster scenario, wherein there exists fragmented network, such a tree is not straightforward. Therefore, we propose that the isolated domains in fragmented network acts as nodes of the tree and the data-mules behave as logical links that interconnect these domains. Logical Interface(LIF)[4] is the technology to reliably transmit COPSS and CCN messages via intermittent links. LIF stores outgoing messages when the next hop node is disconnected. DSDVN, a routing protocol[6], informs LIF module of the link state. When a new next hop is discovered, LIF module makes a new port correspondent to it. COPSS and CCN send messages to LIF port instead of actual next hop. DSDVN populates FIB entries with LIF ports correspondent to the actual next hops.

4. SENDER AUTHENTICATION

In disaster situation, it is important to authenticate information for preventing false rumors. There are two issues: (1) Trustable servers or certificate authorities on which PKI depends may not be available due to disconnection from the global network. (2) Since bulletin board messages are usually short, the packet overhead for authentication is comparatively burden. Identity-based Aggregated Signa-

ture (IBAS)[7] is introduced to solve (1) and (2), which uses public identity such as e-mail address for authentication and reduces the signature size by aggregation. To ensure authenticity of both the message body given by publisher and the sequence number by RP, IBAS aggregates the two signatures required for publisher and RP into one.

5. DEMO SCENARIO

Figure 1 shows the setup of this demonstration. There are three shelters and one government office (Gov.Office) in the disaster stricken area. RP of COPSS is located in Gov.Office. Two DataMules are going round Gov.Office and Shelters. Alice, Bob and David are friends. They subscribe a topic of bulletin board for Alice, named as /Safety/Alice, to exchange messages with Alice. When Alice publishes a message with her signature to /Safety/Alice, it is forwarded to RP via DataMule. RP puts the sequence number to the message and aggregates signatures of Alice and RP. Then RP sends the message back to subscribers, Alice, Bob and David. Even if Bob is offline at the time, the message is pushed to Shelter GWs. He can get it from the GWs by pull-type retrieval. In addition, they can authenticate the message with IBAS, even if John sends a fake message with pretending Alice. Demonstration equipments: one laptop runs 10 VMs and wireless connection emulator. Four tablets show the application screens for four users.

6. CONCLUSIONS

We propose content-based framework for relieable, secure and efficient message dissemination in post-disaster fragmented network. In this demo, we show the disaster message board as a reliable service in disaster situation.

7. ACKNOWLEDGMENTS

The work for this paper was partly performed in the FP7/NICT EU-JAPAN GreenICN project.

8. REFERENCES

[1] Requirements for Disaster Relief System, ITU-T Focus Group on Disaster Relief System, Network Resilience and Recovery, Technical Report, May 2014.

[2] http://www.greenicn.org/

[3] J. Chen, M. Arumaithurai, X. Fu, and K. K. Ramakrishnan, "COPSS:An efficient content oriented publish/subscribe system," in Proc.ACM/IEEE ANCS, pp.99-110, Oct. 2011.

[4] K. Sugiyama, A. Tagami , T. Yagyu , T. Hasegawa, M. Arumaithurai, K. K. Ramakrishnan, "Name-based Information Dissemination for Fragmented Networks in Disasters," IEEE ACM COMSNETS 2015, Bangalore, Jan. 2015, Poster session.

[5] B.Namsraijav, Ndn-cxx fork with ibas support. https://github.com/byambajav/ndn-ibas/

[6] T. Yagyu, S. Maeda, "Reliable Contents Retrieval in Fragmented ICNs for Disaster Scenario," ACM ICN2014, pp.193-194, Paris, Sep. 2014, Demo session.

[7] C.Gentry and Z.Ramzan, "Identity-based aggregated signature," In Public Key Cryptography PKC 2006, pp.257-273, Springer, 2006

[8] CCNx implementation, http://www.ccnx.org/

Enabling Smart Grid Applications with ICN

Wei Koong Chai*, Konstantinos V. Katsaros*, Matthias Strobbe[†], Paolo Romano[‡], Chang Ge[§],
Chris Develder[†], George Pavlou* and Ning Wang[§]

*{w.chai, k.katsaros, g.pavlou}@ucl.ac.uk, [†]{matthias.strobbe, chris.develder}@intec.ugent.be, [‡]{paolo.romano}@epfl.ch, [§]{c.ge, n.wang}@surrey.ac.uk

ABSTRACT

We have harnessed the salient features of information-centric networking (ICN) and implemented a communication infrastructure, called C-DAX, for supporting smart grid applications. We will demonstrate the operations of C-DAX both in a laboratory setup and a real field trial that involves the deployment of C-DAX in a live electricity grid in the Netherlands. This demo will showcase the capabilities of C-DAX, highlighting how ICN satisfies stringent smart grid application requirements.

1. INTRODUCTION

Recent research has pointed towards a paradigm shift from the current host-centric Internet model to one which is centric to information, namely the information-centric networking (ICN) paradigm. Currently, there is a strong ongoing research effort in realizing an ICN-based public Internet, tackling important but complex open issues such as scalability. While the exact form of ICN to be realized is still evolving, there are already work pointing towards alternative domains for ICN (e.g., [1]). We harness the main salient features of ICN and implemented an ICN-based communication infrastructure, called C-DAX, for supporting smart grid (SG) applications [2][3]. We demonstrate how various ICN features can be readily exploited in a domain of smaller scale compared to the public Internet yet still with stringent and varied requirements. We demonstrate C-DAX prototype in both a laboratory setup and in a real field trial involving a live electricity grid in the Netherlands.

2. SMART GRID COMMUNICATION

Smart grids are expected to support new dynamic active components, e.g., distributed energy resources and electric vehicles (EVs). This dynamicity poses new challenges to the power system stability (e.g., voltage regulation). Monitoring and control of SG applications target these challenges, featuring several characteristics / requirements that make the ICN especially well-suited.

Flexibility – Moving the power supply of a feeder requires concurrent reconfiguration of multiple monitoring devices

ICN'15, September 30 - October 02, 2015, San Francisco, CA, USA
ACM 978-1-4503-3855-4/15/09.
http://dx.doi.org/10.1145/2810156.2812610

(e.g., phasor measurement units (PMUs) described in [4]). Maintenance operations (e.g., asset change, islanding operations etc.) require the simultaneous change of data delivery structures. Per-flow management is cumbersome and error-prone. With ICN, devices only need to express interest in specific information, regardless of the hosts.

Large-scale decentralized data exchange – The current aging Supervisory Control and Data Acquisition (SCADA) environment is centralized and supports uni-directional communications. This is inadequate for SGs involving many different stakeholders requiring access to data that originates from large number of devices (e.g., EVs [5]).

Resilience – Robust and seamless communication is critical for the operation and protection of the grid. ICN enhances resilience of information delivery (requests can be satisfied by any node/cache) against anomalies/failures.

Security – Mission-critical grid applications suffering from network intrusions often cause severe economic impact. ICN security features (e.g., location independence) are especially beneficial since host locations are not exposed.

Traffic patterns - Many SG applications involve machine-to-machine communications. The traffic patterns are more predictable than Internet traffic. This allows targeted in-network caching strategies to maximize caching gains.

3. C-DAX: ICN FOR SMART GRID

C-DAX [6] follows a topic-based publish-subscribe model, sharing some similarities with ICN projects such as PSIRP [7] and COMET [8], whereby data producers and consumers are decoupled in time and space. A topic represents a group-based communication session for data distribution and replication. C-DAX consists of control and data planes (see Figure 1).

Data Plane – Data publishers stream (real-time) data under a given topic to an entity called data broker (DB) which acts as a rendezvous point. The DB forwards received data to legitimate subscribers of the topic. This dispenses the need for explicit handling of communication. Multiplicity of DBs under a common topic is allowed for purposes such as scalability and resilience (especially for larger grids). The use of DBs enables the semantic grouping of clients in terms of management and configuration (e.g., PMUs in a certain feeder may be configured collectively). DBs may cache data for further usage and also adapt data rates toward subscribers with heterogeneous requirements.

Control plane – The topic resolver (RS) entity facilitates clients to join and leave a topic by resolving a topic join request to the relevant DB(s). Depending on the size of the grid, there may be a set of RSes forming a hierarchy for robust and efficient resolution. Once a request is resolved, the RS configures the DB(s) involved as well as the (optional) designated node (DN). DNs are introduced for scenarios where a large number of clients is expected, and their purpose is to handle/aggregate all signalling (e.g., topic join/leave requests) that originated from attached clients. Taking a proxy role, each DN is also responsible for performing local authentication of publishers / subscribers in the grid. Such operations require a dedicated security server (SecServ) in the control plane to carry out the access control and client authentication operations.

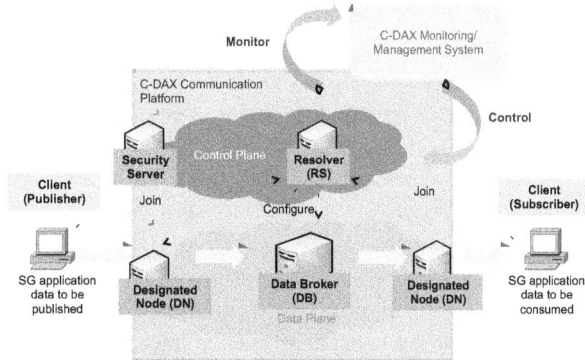

Figure 1: C-DAX architecture

4. DEMONSTRATION OUTLINE

Although C-DAX is designed to support in general all SG applications, we choose to demonstrate its functionality for near real-time PMU data delivery as it represents the most time-critical application to date (see [3] for the analysis of the requirements). Our demo consists of two parts: a lab setup where the publishers are emulated by replaying pre-recorded synchrophasor data to show the ICN-based C-DAX communication functionalities, and a live view on a field trial in a real distribution grid in the Netherlands.

Lab-based Demo. The lab-based demo will show the flexible setup, and fast and reliable transmission of data between a number of publishers (i.e., PMUs) and a few consumers (e.g., phasor data concentrators (PDCs)).

Figure 2 shows the setup of the lab demo for which will use the iMinds Virtual Wall facility[4], a testbed for emulating real communication networks. During the demo, we will show the following aspects of the C-DAX platform:

- Creation and configuration of a topic for PMU data.
- Seamless topic migration e.g., in case of maintenance.
- The resilience feature redirecting traffic to a secondary DB upon a failure, with negligible data interruption.
- Addition and configuration of new data consumers.
- The filtering feature of the DB by only forwarding a subset of the PMU data to another power application.

---

[4]doc.ilabt.iminds.be/ilabt-documentation/virtualwallfacility.html

- A management system to create, configure, start, stop, migrate, etc. different C-DAX nodes. It also provides monitoring information on resource usage and network performance statistics.

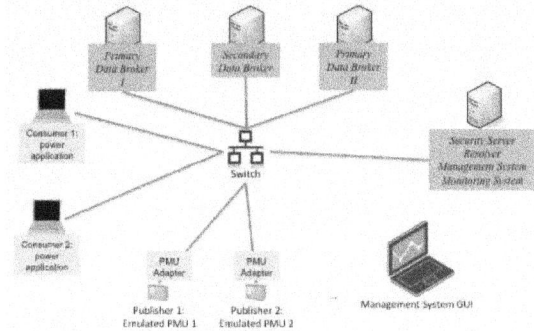

Figure 2: Lab-based Demo setup

Live Field Trial. We also demonstrate C-DAX in a live field trial, hosted in a medium-voltage (10kV) feeder that supplies electricity to the city of Huissen, the Netherlands. The feeder is equipped with 10 PMUs connected through a 4G link, to a PDC that monitors the status of the grid every 20ms and with latencies in the range of 100ms.

During the demonstration, a direct link to the server hosting the PDC will be established to show real-time measurements of the grid status with the live assessment of the latencies of the measurement chain, including C-DAX.

5. ACKNOWLEDGEMENT

The research leading to these results has received funding from the European Commission's Seventh Framework Programme FP7-ICT-2011-8 under grant agreement no. 318708 (C-DAX).

6. REFERENCES

[1] Y. J. Kim, et. al., "SeDAX: A scalable, resilient, and secure platform for smart grid communications," IEEE J. Sel. Areas Commun., vol. 30, no. 6, pp. 1119–1136, Jul. 2012.

[2] K. V. Katsaros, et. al., "Information-centric networking for machine-to-machine data delivery: A case study in smart grid applications," IEEE Netw., vol. 28, no. 3, pp. 58–64, May/Jun. 2014.

[3] W. K. Chai, et. al., "An information-centric communication infrastructure for real-time state estimation of active distribution networks," IEEE Trans. Smart Grid, vol. 6, no. 4, pp. 2134-2146, (DOI) 10.1109/TSG.2015.2398840.

[4] K. V. Katsaros, et. al., "Low latency communication infrastructure for synchrophasor applications in distribution networks," IEEE 5th Int. Conf. Smart Grid Commun., Venice, Italy, 2014, pp. 392–397.

[5] K. V. Katsaros, et. al., "Supporting smart electric vehicle charging with information-centric networking," Int. Conf. Heterogeneous Netw. Qual. Rel. Security Robustness (Q-SHINE), Greece, 2014, pp. 174–179.

[6] http://cdax.eu/

[7] http://www.psirp.org/

[8] W. K. Chai, et al., "Curling: Content-ubiquitous resolution and delivery infrastructure for next-generation services," IEEE Commun. Mag., vol. 49, no. 3, pp. 112–120, 2011.

NetInf Live Video Streaming for Events with Large Crowds

Adeel Mohammad Malik
Ericsson
adeel.mohammad.malik
@ericsson.com

Bengt Ahlgren
SICS
bengta@sics.se

Börje Ohlman
Ericsson
borje.ohlman@ericsson.com

ABSTRACT

Information Centric Networking (ICN) aims to evolve the Internet from a host-centric to a data-centric paradigm. In particular, it improves performance and resource efficiency in events with large crowds where many users in a local area want to generate and watch media content related to the event.

We present the design of a live video streaming system built on the NetInf ICN architecture and how the architecture was adapted to support live streaming of media content. To evaluate the feasibility and performance of the system, extensive field tests were carried out over several days during a major sports event. Our system streams videos successfully with low delay and communication overhead compared with existing Internet streaming services. It can scale to support several thousands of simultaneous users at a time and is well-suited for events with large crowds and flash crowd scenarios.

Keywords

ICN, NetInf, Live video streaming, Publish-Subscribe, Subscribe-Notify, Point-to-multipoint, Request aggregation, Caching, Flash crowd

1. INTRODUCTION

We demonstrate a live video streaming system built on the NetInf ICN architecture [1, 3]. The system was tested in the field at the FIS Nordic Ski World Championship in February 2015[1] in Falun, Sweden [4]. A smaller scale of this system will be demonstrated at the conference. The audience with Android smartphones will be able to participate.

The system includes many ICN architectural elements such as naming, service discovery, aggregation and caching. The system functionality is implemented on a set of fixed NetInf routers together with a mobile streaming application developed for video recording and viewing on Android phones and tablets.

The system targets the use case at sports events, or more generally, at *events with large crowds*, where people gather in a geo-

[1] http://falun2015.com/

graphically limited area for a specific time duration with a common purpose and interest. Other examples of such events are concerts, festivals and fairs. The events can take place at dedicated venues, for example, arenas, or take place ad-hoc on the streets of a city or in the countryside.

We argue that ICN technology is well suited for this use case, and especially for supporting live video streaming of the event, both user-generated and officially produced. Video streaming is otherwise very hard to cater for when a large crowd gathers. It is often the case at larger events that the communication infrastructure gets completely overloaded by current cloud-based services, since they need one unicast data stream per client. The situation is a variant of the 'flash crowd' problem that arises when there is a sudden large demand for, e.g., a video. The use case furthermore only needs a limited deployment of ICN technology – there is no dependency on a global ICN infrastructure. Another important use case for ICN technology is in DTN scenarios such as disaster scenarios as it does not depend on any remote network functionality such as cloud services or HLRs. In addition the caching makes previously downloaded material available even after the original sources get disconnected.

2. NETINF LIVE STREAMING

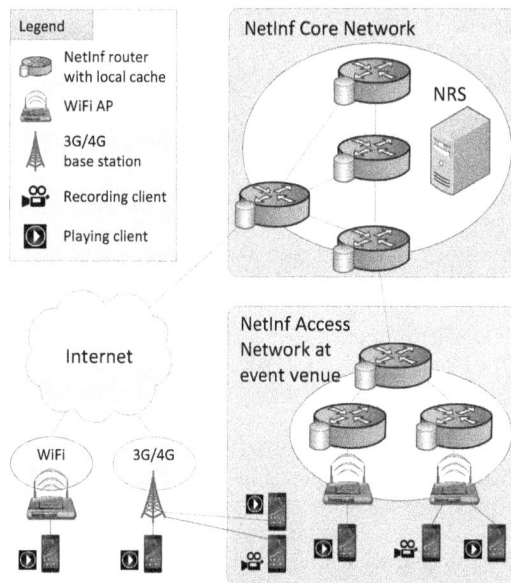

Figure 1: System architecture

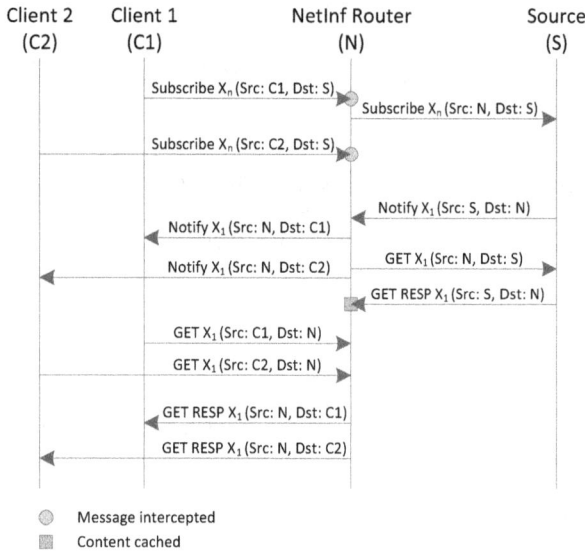

Figure 2: Subscribe-Notify protocol and Content Retrieval

Figure 1 shows the architecture of the NetInf live video streaming system. Users can record and publish video streams at a live event and at the same time other users can watch the streams live. The architecture facilitates streaming to a device anywhere on the internet so that users not present at the venue also can publish or play streams.

Recording and playing clients at the event venue can connect to the system using local WiFi or mobile internet (3G/4G). A client first has to connect to a NetInf router. Consequently this router acts as the first hop NetInf node for the client. Clients connected to the local access network at the event venue via WiFi use Multicast DNS (mDNS) to discover the NetInf router that they should connect to. Clients on the internet connect to a NetInf router in the NetInf core network using regular DNS.

The NetInf core network hosts a Name Resolution Service (NRS). This service is responsible for resolving object names into locators. It also provides search function for the registered Named Data Objects (NDOs). NetInf employs hash-based names as described in RFC6920 [2].

ICN employs ubiquitous caching. Therefore every NetInf router in the architecture is coupled with a local cache. These routers cache NDOs on-path and serve them to corresponding GET requests when there is a cache hit. This ensures that clients are served data from the local network (if the data is cached) and that the edge links (like the one between the NetInf access network and the NetInf core network as seen in Figure 1) are not choked with traffic.

The entire video stream is represented by a single Header NDO that glues together all video chunks of a stream and presents itself as a single point of reference in order to request any subset of a video. The Header NDO contains the metadata for each video, i.e., a description of the video and the geolocation of where the video is recorded. When subscribing to a live video stream, a client in fact sends a subscription request for the Header NDO.

The NetInf live video streaming system uses a hop-by-hop Subscribe-Notify protocol between the requesting client and the data source. Figure 2 illustrates a signaling sequence of the Subscribe-Notify protocol between two clients, a NetInf router and a data source.

The NetInf protocol carried in UDP/IP packets and makes use of legacy HTTP/TCP/IP to transfer large information objects between the nodes in a hierarchically scalable point-to-multipoint tree.

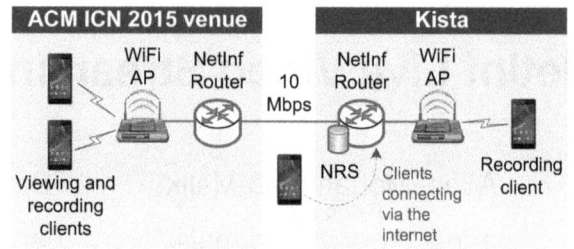

Figure 3: Demo setup

3. DEMO SETUP

Figure 3 shows the setup used for the demo in the ACM ICN 2015 conference. The setup spans across two sites, Kista in Sweden and the ACM ICN 2015 venue.

A NetInf router is installed at each site along with a WiFi access point to facilitate client connections. Clients can record streams at both the sites while several clients can view a specific stream at the ACM ICN 2015 venue. Clients can either connect to the system via the local WiFi access points or can connect via the internet. When connecting via the internet, clients connect to the NetInf router in Kista via DNS resolution of a defined service name. The NetInf router in Kista also hosts the NRS. Traffic exchanged between the two sites is aggregated over a 10 Mbps link. Aggregation is achieved using the hop-by-hop Subscribe-Notify protocol illustrated in Figure 2.

Audience at the demo have the possibility to download the Android NetInf streaming application from a web link and try recording and viewing streams. They can either connect to the local WiFi access point or use mobile internet to use the application.

4. CONCLUSIONS

We have implemented and demonstrated a live video streaming system based on NetInf supporting user-generated content. The system was deployed and field tested at the FIS Nordic Ski World Championship in February 2015. The system worked largely as expected. It proved the viability of the approach, and the relative quality and performance of the implementations.

We argue that ICN-based live streaming systems are ideal for supporting events with large crowds, especially sports events, due to limited deployment needs, and the difficulty to provide enough network capacity for cloud-based services at such events.

5. REFERENCES

[1] C. Dannewitz, D. Kutscher, B. Ohlman, S. Farrell, B. Ahlgren, and H. Karl. Network of information (NetInf)–an information-centric networking architecture. *Computer Communications*, 36(7):721–735, 2013.

[2] S. Farrell, D. Kutscher, C. Dannewitz, B. Ohlman, A. Keranen, and P. Hallam-Baker. Naming Things with Hashes. RFC 6920 (Proposed Standard), Apr. 2013.

[3] D. Kutscher, S. Farrell, and E. Davies. The NetInf Protocol. Internet-Draft draft-kutscher-icnrg-netinf-proto-01, Internet Engineering Task Force, Feb. 2013. Work in progress.

[4] A. M. Malik, B. Ahlgren, B. Ohlman, A. Lindgren, E. Ngai, L. Klingsbo, and M. Lång. Experiences from a field test using ICN for live video streaming. In *Workshop on Multimedia Streaming in Information-Centric Networks (MuSIC)*, Torino, Italy, July 3, 2015. In conjunction with ICME 2015.

CCNx Packet Processing on PARC Router Platform

Priti Goel
PARC
3333 Coyote Hill Rd., Palo Alto
+16508124821
priti.goel@parc.com

Eric Holmberg
PARC
3333 Coyote Hill Rd., Palo Alto
+16508124438
eric.holmberg@parc.com

Mark Konezny
PARC
3333 Coyote Hill Rd., Palo Alto
+16508124484
mark.konezny@parc.com

Ramesh Ayyagari
PARC
3333 Coyote Hill Rd., Palo Alto
+16508124815
ramesh.ayyagari@parc.com

Dick Sillman
PARC
3333 Coyote Hill Rd., Palo Alto
+16508124437
dsillman@parc.com

ABSTRACT
PARC's "Project 42" will demonstrate a routing platform that carries CCN over Ethernet payloads simultaneously with IP traffic. The CCN packet processing is performed on the intelligent line card data plane using embedded NPU and DPI processors. Content Objects are cached within the line cards to showcase the benefits of "in-network" caching. This routing platform enables early adoption of CCN into service provider networks.

Keywords
CCN, ICN, CCNx, Metis, Distillery, Caching, CCNoE

1. MOTIVATION
Since video is the primary component of Internet traffic, we chose to demonstrate native CCN (CCN over Ethernet) video being routed through PARC's "router platform" while running IP traffic as well. In addition, we chose simple video clients to demonstrate the low resource requirements of the CCNx transport stack.

2. OVERVIEW
Figure 1 illustrates the demo setup with following main components:

CCN and IP Video Server:

- Intel Xeon

CCN and IP Video Consumers:

- 10 "Raspberry Pi" clients
- VLC (Video LAN Client) plugin

PARC Distillery Software:

- Protocol Stack
- Metis forwarder

Data path:

- PARC's 400Gbps Routing Platform

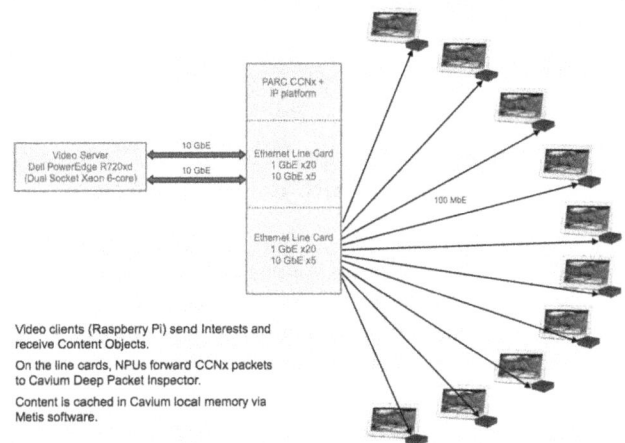

Figure 1. Demo Block Diagram

3. PARC Router platform

3.1 High level description
As shown in figure 2, the router platform is a 5-slot chassis that can house up to 4 network line cards within 6RU (Rack Units) of vertical space. Each line card slot supports 200GE of full duplex traffic. The system accepts up to two switch fabric controller cards that provide a non-blocking switch fabric between the line cards.

Following are the salient features of the platform

- CE Edge router with L2/L3/MPLS
- NSR/NSF architecture with ingress/egress QoS
- 6RU (4 line card) and 16RU (12 line card) models
- Line card family supports mix of 1/10/100GE

Figure 2. PARC Router Platform

3.2 Router Data plane

Figure 3 illustrates the data plane for the router platform.

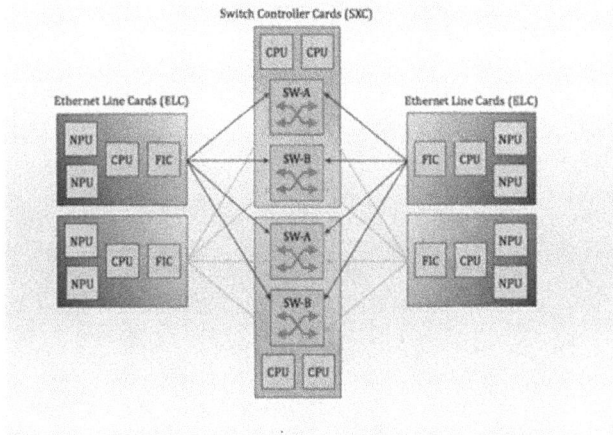

Figure 3. PARC Router Architecture

All packets come in on the line and are sent to NP4 on the line card. NP4 (in conjunction with Cavium Octeon) processes the packet appropriately and sends it to egress line card via fabric backplane.

3.3 CCN data plane

Figure 4 illustrates the CCN data plane for the platform. CCN traffic is identified by the 100GE NP4 network processor and sent to the Cavium Octeon on the line card where the Parc CCNx Metis forwarder is running. Metis forwarder sends the packet to the correct line card via NP4 and fabric backplane.

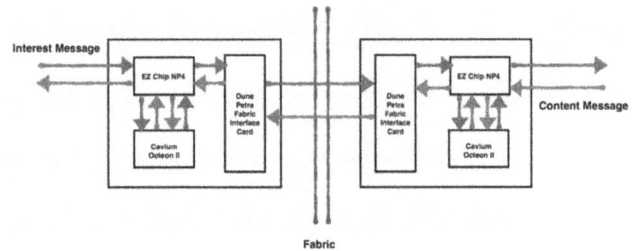

Figure 4. Router CCN Datapath

3.4 IP data plane

NP4 processes IP traffic on the line card without using Octeon and forwards the packet to egress line card through fabric backplane.

4. Demo details

The demo will show CCN video traffic getting processed by the router platform along with IP traffic. For CCN video, we are using tutorial_Server to serve the video and VLC with a CCN plugin to play the video on the RPi. In-network caching is shown and its benefits are demonstrated by removing the connection to the video server. For IP traffic, we are using VLC to stream the data from the server and VLC to play the video on the RPi.

Using CCN for Discovery of Missing Physical Items

Cedric Westphal
Huawei & UCSC
Santa Clara, CA, USA
cedric.westphal@huawei.com

Bertrand Mathieu
Orange/France Telecom
Lannion, France
bertrand2.mathieu@orange.com

Syed Obaid Amin
Huawei
Santa Clara, CA, USA
obaid.amin@huawei.com

1. INTRODUCTION

As the number of connected devices to the Internet scales up, as the amount of traffic generated by these devices explodes, it is necessary to reconsider the underlying protocols which will support the Internet of Things. As many devices in the IoT may be sensors or devices which need to provide some information but would not require complex network configuration, Information Centric Networks [1–4] and CCN/NDN [5,6] in particular, has been suggested as a potential candidate for the IoT (we just use CCN below, and in our implementation, but NDN could apply as well).

CCN offers interest-data semantics which have history in sensor networks and Directed diffusion [7] in particular. CCN issues an interest packet, which carries the name of the desired information; this packet is routed to the proper place where to find/collect/gather the information called in the name; once the information which matches the name is found, it is packaged into a data object which is returned to the original requester. In order to trace back the route of the information to the requester, the interest packet leaves a state at the router, as an entry in a Pending Interest Table (PIT), which points to the interface which received the interest, and therefore where to send back the data. This state is kept for a time-out value, which can be specified by the interest/sender and be refreshed periodically. In other words, CCN enables to place semi-persistent state in the network waiting to be fulfilled by some data.

In this demo, we propose a cyber-physical application of the abstractions natively offered by CCN to emulate an existing function called Tile [8]. Tile is a bluetooth tag combined with a cell phone application; the tag is attached to a valuable object. If the object is misplaced or stolen, a central server is contacted, which pushes the tag ID onto all the nearby devices running the application. The devices then probe for the Bluetooth signal of the tag. If they encounter the tag, they send a response to the server with the tag's position and time.

For such system to be worthwhile, it requires widespread adoption. Indeed, the distributed scanning ability required to retrieve the tag, and therefore the value of the system, hinges on the number of devices carrying out the scanning. Such a service is not valuable until it has many users to detect tags. However, since early adopters would only see little value until that critical mass is reached, they would be less likely to encourage others to adopt.

2. DEMO DESCRIPTION

We contend that having the operator provide the tag location service would break this vicious cycle; the operator would lay out a one-time deployment cost to associate the service with its infrastructure, but would then achieve coverage and be able to deliver value to the users. The operator can for instance associate the scanning with low power WiFi on top of a set of hot spots, or add a Bluetooth scanning capability to set-top boxes such as Orange's Livebox home gateway. A network operator can also ask its phone manufacturing partners to include the scanning functionality as a low-power background function on locked devices.

The point of the demo is to implement this function on top of CCN. It is of course possible to implement it over IP, but we wish to demonstrate the ease with which CCN enables us to deploy this function. Basically, CCN enables to send an interest with the tag ID that we are trying to locate, have this interest be distributed throughout the network, and to have a response to the interest (namely, a sighting of the target tag) be delivered back to the origin server. These are native semantics of CCN, and therefore come at no cost for the tag location application developer.

We have deployed such a system in an actual testbed. The testbed is described in Figure 1. For the demo, we use a Dell latitude laptop for the gateway, and some Raspberry Pi nodes running PARC's CCN code for Raspberry Pi with a CSR USB dongle attached. A script scans for bluetooth IDs at regular interval, and keeps a log of the encountered IDs at the Raspberry Pis. For the tag, we use the bluetooth interface of a cell phone, which is easy to turn on or off. On the gateway, a user interface allows to specify which tag ID to try to locate. Once a tag ID is entered on the UI of the server, it is propagated to the Pi boxes. The Pi boxes scan for bluetooth devices and keep track of the devices that they see. If they see the desired tag ID, a response to the interest is generated and propagated back to the server.

We have implemented a GUI which resides on a web server, and a gateway that translates the requests coming from the current Internet into the CCN domain.

The demo will show how to locate the tag ID of the cell phone of the demo participants (or of the demo host). When

ICN'15, Sept.30–Oct. 2, 2015, San Francisco, CA, USA.
ACM 978-1-4503-3855-4/15/09.
DOI: http://dx.doi.org/10.1145/2810156.2812613.

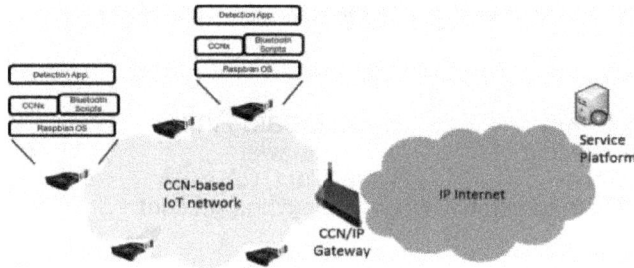

Figure 1: Testbed for tag location function.

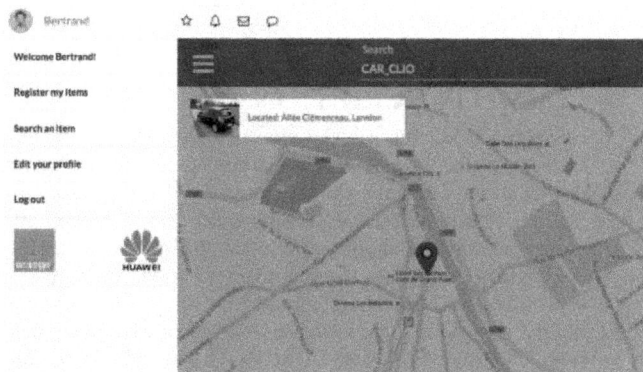

Figure 2: The user inputs the information and views the tag's location on a specific GUI

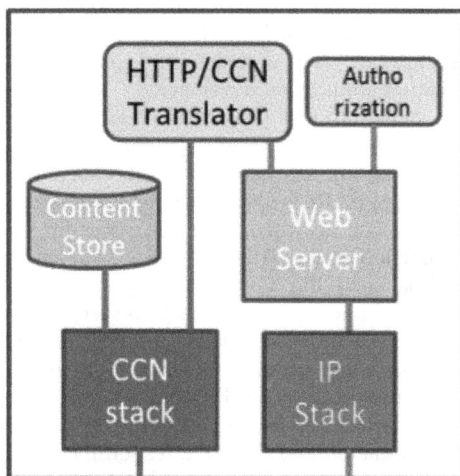

Figure 3: Gateway function to interconnect the current Internet with the CCN domain

the cell phone will be in contact with a Raspberry Pi, an alert will be send back and displayed on the screen of the gateway.

3. DISCUSSION & FUTURE WORK

The multicast features of CCN allows to forward an alert to multiple end points: the gateway of the function, but also the tag's user or the local authority to retrieve the missing tagged item. The demo uses a single interest per requested ID; therefore it would not scale to a large number of items nor to a large area to cover. Future work includes considering the scalability issues of such a set up. In particular, aggregation of the tag IDs through a Bloom Filter would allow the server to issue interest for multiple tags at the same time. Similarly, scoping the interests of specific tags to specific locations (and expanding the search radius as time goes on) would reduce the burden on the system. Building a hierarchy of servers would allow to filter out false positives of the Bloom filter without getting all the way to the

Another generalization of the demo is in the direction of logistics: can the network keep track not only of a subset of desired IDs, but of all IDs which belong to a system (say, inventory of a company on a corporate campus) and assist in the logistics. One could for instance imagine a library where miss-shelved books could be retrieved. The basic function of generating an inventory would become a function that is easily supported by the network infrastructure.

We believe that CCN easily, cleanly and natively support some cyber-physical features to locate items in the physical world and that it is a significant advantage over using IP networks in such a system. We note that such a system could be implemented over IP as well, but would require much more work, in particular to configure a new node into the system.

4. REFERENCES

[1] B. Ahlgren, C. Dannewitz, C. Imbrenda, D. Kutscher, and B. Ohlman, "A survey of information-centric networking," *Com Mag, IEEE*, vol. 50, no. 7, pp. 26–36, July 2012.

[2] A. Chanda and C. Westphal, "ContentFlow: Mapping content to flows in Software Defined Networks," in *in Proc. of IEEE Globecom*, Dec. 2013.

[3] A. Chanda, C. Westphal, and D. Raychaudhuri, "Content based traffic engineering in Software Defined Information Centric Networks," in *Proc. IEEE Infocom NOMEN workshop*, Apr. 2013.

[4] B. Azimdoost, C. Westphal, and H. R. Sadjadpour, "On the throughput capacity of Information-Centric Networks," in *Proc. International Teletraffic Congress 25*, Sep. 2013.

[5] "CCNx," http://www.ccnx.org.

[6] "NDN," http://named-data.net/.

[7] C. Intanagonwiwat, R. Govindan, D. Estrin, J. Heidemann, and F. Silva, "Directed diffusion for wireless sensor networking," *IEEE/ACM Trans. Netw.*, vol. 11, no. 1, pp. 2–16, Feb. 2003.

[8] "Tile," http://www.thetileapp.com.

An IP-based Manifest Architecture for ICN

Cedric Westphal
Huawei & UCSC
Santa Clara, CA, USA
cedric.westphal@huawei.com

Emrecan Demirors
Northeastern University
Boston, MA, USA
demirors.e@husky.neu.edu

1. INTRODUCTION

Information-Centric Networks [1–4] expose content information to the network layer. CCN, NDN and others want to replace IP as the narrow waist of the Internet. In [5], it is argued that most of the benefits of ICN can be achieved in IP through modification of DNS, and by adding a new *content record (CR)* type to the records returned by a DNS server. This CR type allows the DNS server to respond to request for Named-Data Objects (NDO) or name prefixes. The CR type is a list of IP addresses associated with the NDO.

We argue that this does not go far enough, and that the DNS could return more information about the object, namely that the DNS should return a manifest that describes the object properties. The manifest is an object (say, in xml) describing the properties of the content object that are relevant at the network layer. In particular, the manifest includes the location of the object, some security properties and some information regarding the transport of the object, including for instance its size.

Because the manifest is part of a DNS transaction, it is exposed to the network without the need of Deep Packet Inspection (DPI); because the DNS manifest is a network-layer object, it embeds only information that is exposed to the network layer, and therefore is not encrypted, or is encrypted using material that is shared with network operators.

This allows the network to observe the manifest as it is being requested, and to operate on this manifest. The typical envisioned usage is at the edge network: the client attaches at the edge network, and request a specific file to the DNS server, requesting a manifest. The DNS server (denoted DNS++) returns the manifest; the edge network is therefore informed of the content being requested by the client, and of the properties of the content.

This information can be either used and/or modified. Using the information in the manifest allows the network to accommodate certain properties of the data object. For instance, the manifest includes the size of the data, and there-

ICN'15, Sept.30–Oct. 2, 2015, San Francisco, CA, USA.
ACM 978-1-4503-3855-4/15/09.
DOI: http://dx.doi.org/10.1145/2810156.2812614.

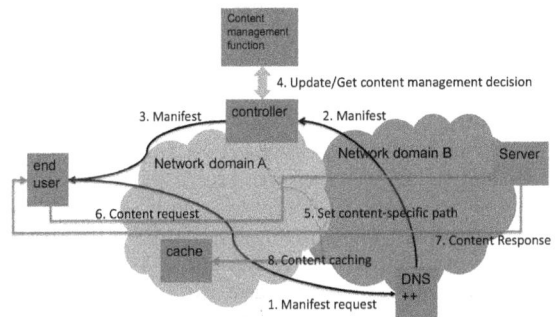

Figure 1: The Demo Architecture -all elements are implemented as VMs on two server blades

fore the edge network can make a different path selection decision depending on the content being an elephant flow or a mice flow. There is prior work on making resource allocation and traffic engineering decision based upon content properties [6–8].

Modifying the manifest allows the network to include known copies of the content that reside in a local cache for instance; this of course implies that the manifest can be updated in a trusted manner by the network. Our goal is not to describe such trust mechanism, but rather to highlight the potential benefits of a manifest.

Figure 1 presents the envisioned architecture, where an end-user (or client) will request the manifest from a DNS++ server, receive the manifest in return; the manifest is observed by the edge network on the way back before being returned to the client. The edge network can take some action based upon the manifest.

Note that manifests exist already in many contexts, including DASH MPDs [9]. The idea of notifying the network prior to a transmission is implied in many current network architecture, including SDN/OpenFlow. There, the first packet serves both as a packet within the data exchange, and a notification to the network about the incoming flow. A manifest makes this notification explicit, with the advantage of sharing object/flow properties with the underlying network (unlike an application layer manifest such as in DASH).

Manifest Request Sequence

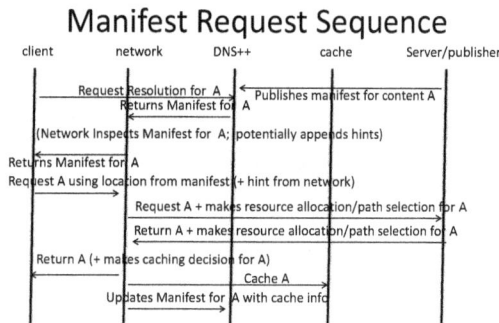

Figure 2: The messaging flow

2. DEMO SET-UP

We have implemented a DNS++ server which returns a manifest. This involves modifying the DNS++ client of the end-user and the DNS++ server. The DNS++ client needs to format the requests differently to include the whole name of the object, or the name prefix. The DNS++ request also includes the source address, as the network needs to know which client is making the request for path optimization. The DNS++ server is modified to return a manifest if it holds one for the request of a manifest record type. If it does not hold a manifest, it returns the A record corresponding to the domain name, as in a typical name resolution.

We have also implemented an edge network that listens for manifests on the DNS port 53 and is able to take a corresponding action based upon the upcoming data transfer. Figure 2 shows the data flow of the demonstration. All these elements have been implemented and will be demonstrated. The demo flow will be as follows: the client will request a file manifest from the DNS and in return, will receive the manifest. The intermediate network will observe the manifest.

- In Scenario I, it will make a routing decision based upon the size of the object mentioned in the manifest. A small object will be returned following one path, while a large object will be returned according to a different path.

- In Scenario II, the edge network will insert the address of a local copy into the manifest, so that the client can download the file from the local cache.

The demo set-up will be hosted in the Huawei data center in Santa Clara, and will be controlled remotely from the demo site. The demo equipment include a server holding virtual machines (VMs) for the server, the DNS and a virtual switch and another server with VM for the cache, the client and the network controller. Both servers will be connected over two distinct links on different ports on the physical switch connecting both servers.

3. DISCUSSION

Defining the proper manifest and what properties to include is an on-going task. There is a tension in making the manifest expressive, but at the same time, in keeping it simple. How to scale the manifest is another issue: small objects do not need a manifest, and the advantage of a native ICN

architecture is that they can be fetched directly from any intermediate cache as there is no binding of the session to a destination. There is also a concern of getting a per-object manifest, as certain content may contain many objects. For instance, a web page, or a facebook or twitter-like application, will include many pictures and referral to other objects such as advertisement embeds. While it takes only one DNS resolution step currently, per object resolution would dramatically increase the number of such steps. It could even be a new DDoS avenue to generate objects referring to many more objects.

On the other hand, the manifest of the parent web page could include information regarding the other objects. Furthermore, it could also include information on which manifests to get, and which not to (say, if all embeds are small, none of them would require a manifest resolution). This is also a topic of further study.

4. REFERENCES

[1] B. Ahlgren, C. Dannewitz, C. Imbrenda, D. Kutscher, and B. Ohlman, "A survey of information-centric networking," *Com Mag, IEEE*, vol. 50, no. 7, pp. 26–36, July 2012.

[2] V. Jacobson, D. K. Smetters, J. D. Thornton, M. F. Plass, N. H. Briggs, and R. L. Braynard, "Networking named content," in *Proceedings of the 5th International Conference on Emerging Networking Experiments and Technologies*, ser. CoNEXT '09, 2009, pp. 1–12.

[3] A. Chanda and C. Westphal, "ContentFlow: Mapping content to flows in Software Defined Networks," in *in Proc. of IEEE Globecom*, Dec. 2013.

[4] B. Azimdoost, C. Westphal, and H. R. Sadjadpour, "On the throughput capacity of Information-Centric Networks," in *Proc. International Teletraffic Congress 25*, Sep. 2013.

[5] S. Sevilla, P. Mahadevan, and J. Garcia-Luna-Aceves, "idns: Enabling information centric networking through the dns," in *Computer Communications Workshops (INFOCOM WKSHPS), 2014 IEEE Conference on*, April 2014.

[6] A. Chanda, C. Westphal, and D. Raychaudhuri, "Content based traffic engineering in Software Defined Information Centric Networks," in *Proc. IEEE Infocom NOMEN workshop*, Apr. 2013.

[7] K. Su and C. Westphal, "On the benefit of information centric networks for traffic engineering," in *IEEE ICC Conference*, Jun. 2014.

[8] J. Yichao, Y. Wen, and C. Westphal, "Towards joint resource allocation and routing to optimize video distribution over future internet," in *IEEE/IFIP Networking Conference*.

[9] R. Grandl, K. Su, and C. Westphal, "On the interaction of adaptive video streaming with content-centric networking," in *IEEE Packet Video Workshop*, Dec. 2013.

ICN based Scalable Audio-Video Conferencing on Virtualized Service Edge Router (VSER) Platform

Asit Chakraborti, Syed Obaid Amin, Bin Zhao, Aytac Azgin,
Ravishankar Ravindran and Guoqiang Wang
Huawei Research Center, Santa Clara, CA, USA.
{asit.chakraborti, obaid.amin, bin.zhao1, aytac.azgin, ravi.ravindran, gq.wang}@huawei.com

ABSTRACT

This paper proposes an audio/video conferencing architecture based on the VSER platform. The proposed solution follows a hybrid approach, where consumers are initialized to current producer's media state through a media-dependent notification framework provided by the VSER; whereas the data exchange leverages ICN features, resulting in bandwidth efficiency. The hybrid design provides better scalability and reliability when compared to the ICN based P2P conferencing systems.

1. INTRODUCTION

Real-time conferencing applications gain from the bandwidth efficiency offered by CCN/NDN architecture [1, 2]. However, challenges exist when applications with stringent real-time requirements are operated in a PULL based architecture. For example, the latency requirements for audio and video are $\leq 150ms$ and $\leq 350ms$, respectively [3]; whereas relative audio/video sync requirements are $+45ms$ to $-125ms$ [4]. Another challenge in a PULL based architecture is for the consumers to learn the names of the dynamic media particularly considering dynamic events like join/leave and transient connectivity issues in case of mobility or network degradation. To meet these requirements, this paper presents a design of an audio/video conferencing tool that uses VSER platform for notifications; whereas relies on the ICN framework for data exchange. This hybrid approach is useful in providing synchronization after a transient disconnection or a network failure and leverages ICN features, such as multicasting, for data exchange.

1.1 Virtual Service Edge Router (VSER) Platform

The audio/video conferencing solution is realized over an ICN based service platform, referred to here as the Virtual Service Edge Router (VSER), to achieve efficient service de-

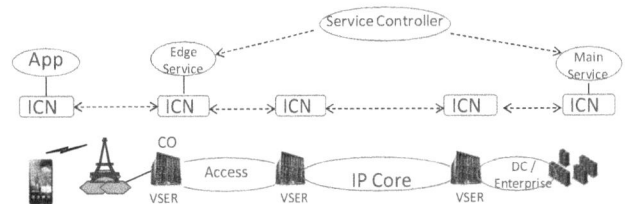

Figure 1: Deployment scenario.

livery leveraging ICN features. Considering the need for service-scaling, contextualization, agility and low latency the VSER platform is suitable for the network edge, as shown in Fig. 1. The benefits of such a platform is VSER's service hosting feature (enabling computing) along with ICN features such as unified naming, multicasting, mobility, and content-based security. Compared to NDN-RTC [5], which is a peer based conferencing system, the proposed VSER based conferencing system provides higher reliability (i.e., faster recovery from the transient network conditions) and performance with respect to media name sync among participants.

2. CONFERENCING ARCHITECTURE

Video conferencing requires synchronization of media channels (audio/video/text) among multiple participants, which is handled by the service framework of VSER. The conferencing logic within VSER is responsible for connecting UE to the closest VSER, managing participant join/leave events and mobility, syncing media status, and conference state recovery. The conferencing architecture is summarized with respect to naming schema, name sync mechanism, consumer and producer design for a participant producing and consuming audio/video/text content.

2.1 Naming Convention

The proposed naming schema comprises of three components, (i) network prefix: which represents the routeable name component; (ii) application identity: which includes the conference and user ID; and (iii) application metadata: which includes the media-type and media specific attributes. More precisely, the naming convention is: $/<vser\text{-}id>/<conf\text{-}id>/<ue\text{-}id>/<media\text{-}type>/<session\text{-}id>/<frame\text{-}id>/[<chunk\text{-}id>]$. Here the $<vser\text{-}id>$ is a routeable name prefix of the VSER attached to the producer, whereas $<conf\text{-}id>/<ue\text{-}id>$ identifies the participator context. The $<media\text{-}type>$ can be audio, video or text. The $<session\text{-}id>$ identifies a particular session and $<frame\text{-}id>$ identifies a par-

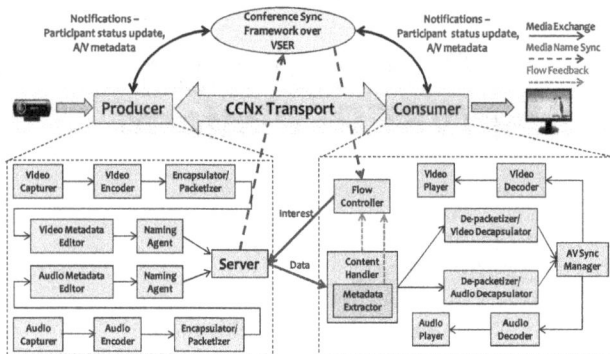

Figure 2: Audio-Video conferencing architecture.

ticular frame. The last component $<chunk\text{-}id>$ is required if the media type is video, and identifies individual chunks in a video frame.

2.2 Notification Framework

As discussed in [6], the notification framework allows name sync and recovery from network failures. Once a producer selects a media type and generates a piece of content, it notifies the VSER's service agent of the new content, which is pushed to all the participants of a conference. The consumer then pulls that content by expressing Interest for it. The frequency of the notifications depends on the media type. For text, this notification is for every chat text committed by the participant. For real-time content, the notification traffic is minimized by transmitting the notifications at a configurable periodic interval. For video, the local agent sends a notification for every Group of Pictures (GOP), equivalent to $1/second$ in our setup. There is an inverse relationship between the volume of notification traffic and processing and communication overhead incurred by the consumer to achieve producer rate. For audio we set the notification frequency to $1/second$ as well.

2.3 Producer Design

Media generation at the producer end is driven by the participant behavior, i.e. the media is generated based on what the participant chooses to enable at a given point of time. Video producer uses the open-source Xuggler Java library to encode audio and video, using the MP3 and H.263 codec respectively. Audio is sampled at $44.1KHz$ and an audio frame roughly captures $14ms$ of audio. Video uses a frame rate of $25fps$ and also a GOP size of 25. The encoded frames are then adapted to CCN transport by chunking if required and named, and synced with the consumers using the notification framework. An application level PIT is also introduced that is used to store the Interests for near-future contents, sent by the clients in pre-fetching mode (discussed in Section 2.4). This allows producer to push out the data to the network as soon as it is generated, instead of waiting for the corresponding Interest.

2.4 Consumer Design

The conference service framework allows the local agent to discover and join active chatrooms and learn about the participants. This allows consumers to select a subset of audio/video feeds. The action to view a participant is conveyed to the conference service framework, which allows the consumer to learn producers' latest video/audio name states through the notification framework. This information is enough for the consumer to start expressing Interests and sync with the real-time content generated by a participant. To keep up with the producer's data generation rate, the consumer always sends out Interests in advance for future audio/video frames (pre-fetching). The frequency of these Interests primarily depends on the data generation rate of the producer. The state and data generation rate of the producer, can be derived by the consumer from the notifications.

In Fig. 2, the *Flow Controller* manages the Interest expression rate, based on feedback from notifications and *Content Handler*. Because of variable sized video frame data, the challenge is to learn the variable number of chunks comprising a video frame. This is addressed by using a frame descriptor metadata in each video chunk, which is extracted and fed back to the *Flow Controller* by the *Metadata Extractor*. The *Flow Controller* uses the periodic notifications from the conference notification framework to sync stream information. This allows us to handle issues such as new join events and network disruptions. During network disruptions, *Flow-Controller* starts from the latest conference state clearing the outstanding Interests for stale video frames. Based on the feedback from the *Content Handler*, the *Flow Controller* can also reissue Interests for the missing frames. The audio-video sync manager (*AVSyncManager*) module uses the timestamp information from the audio/video frames to sync audio/video playback before handing the content to the respective decoders.

3. DEMO SCENARIO

We demonstrate several features of the conferencing application: 1) VSER based conference service framework, by provisioning multiple conferences dynamically that participants can choose to join at will; 2) seamless interaction among participants in a conference session using audio/video/text media; 3) content sync as participants join/leave at random intervals, dynamic participant discovery feature, usefulness of the notifications for real-time content sync towards seamless experience even after a network disruption. The CCN router in VSER is a multi-threaded TLV implementation, while the service orchestration and SDN features are enabled using OpenStack and FloodLight.

4. REFERENCES

[1] Van Jacobson, et al. Networking named content. *Commun. ACM*, 55(1):117–124, January 2012.

[2] Lixia Zhang, et al. Named data networking. *SIGCOMM Comput. Commun. Rev.*, 44(3):66–73, July 2014.

[3] Yan Chen, Toni Farley, and Nong Ye. Qos requirements of network applications on the internet. *Inf. Knowl. Syst. Manag.*, 4(1):55–76, January 2004.

[4] ITU-R BT.1359-1 1,
https://www.itu.int/dms_pubrec/itu-r/rec/bt/R-REC-BT.1359-1-199811-I!!PDF-E.pdf .

[5] Peter Gusev. Ndn real time conferencing library. In *NDN Community Meeting*, Jun 2014.

[6] R. Ravindran, et al. Towards software defined icn based edge-cloud services. In *IEEE Cloud Networking (CloudNet)*, pages 227–235, Nov 2013.

Experiments with the Emulated NDN Testbed in ONL

Ze'ev Lailari[†], Hila Ben Abraham[†], Ben Aronberg[‡], Jackie Hudepohl[§], Haowei Yuan[†],
John DeHart[†], Jyoti Parwatikar[†], Patrick Crowley[†]

[†]Washington University in St. Louis [‡]University of Miami [§]Carnegie Mellon University
{lailariz, hila, hyuan, jdd, jp, pcrowley}@wustl.edu b.aronberg@umiami.edu
jhudepohl@cmu.edu

ABSTRACT

Named Data Networking (NDN) is a recently proposed information-centric network architecture. The NDN Testbed is a global infrastructure that enables real-world NDN demonstrations. However, deploying new applications directly on the NDN Testbed requires considerable operational support and may introduce instability to shared testbed infrastructure. What's more, network performance parameters cannot be easily modified on the NDN Testbed to study application behaviors. As a result, an emulated NDN testbed, and one over which developers have full control, can benefit testing, debugging, and evaluating new NDN applications and services as a complement and precursor to testbed deployment.

In this demonstration, we present the emulated NDN testbed that runs in the Open Network Laboratory (ONL). The emulated testbed runs on real servers (there is no simulation) and uses the same NDN forwarding daemon, NFD, and the same routing software, NLSR, that are used in the NDN Testbed; this minimizes the efforts required of developers to evaluate their applications. We show how the flexibility of ONL enables the study of application behaviors in varying network environments and conditions. We also use a data collection application to demonstrate the effectiveness of using the emulated testbed to support application development.

Categories and Subject Descriptors

C.2.1 [**Network Architecture and Design**]: Network communications

Keywords

Named Data Networking; NDN Testbed; Open Network Laboratory

1. INTRODUCTION

Real-world demonstrations have been regularly performed to show the advantages of the NDN architecture and pro-

ICN'15, Sept.30–Oct. 2, 2015, San Francisco, CA, USA.
ACM 978-1-4503-3855-4/15/09.
DOI: http://dx.doi.org/10.1145/2810156.2812616.

vide feedback for NDN development. The NDN Testbed [1], a network of 26 sites around the world as of August 2015 (Figure 1), is a key building block that enables large-scale demonstrations. The NDN Testbed is remotely managed by an administrator, and each site has an operator taking care of events that require physical access, such as power cycling. To reduce the operational overhead of deploying new applications on the NDN Testbed, an emulated testbed is needed.

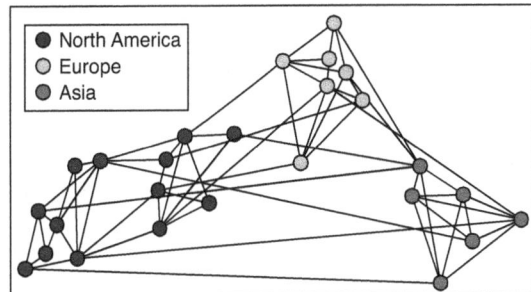

Figure 1: The NDN Testbed

In previous work, we have manually configured an NDN Testbed topology in ONL, which provides an isolated and user-controlled network environment for experiments [2], to debug and evaluate NLSR and NFD [3]. Based on our experience, we believe it would be beneficial to automate the emulated NDN testbed configuration and make it available to developers.

2. EMULATED NDN TESTBED

The emulated testbed operates as an IP overlay that requires configuring both the IP and NDN networks.

2.1 IP Topology Configuration

The underlying IP network is configured using the Remote Laboratory Interface (RLI) provided by ONL. Figure 2 shows the emulated testbed topology, where each host represents an NDN gateway router. The IP software routers (SWRs), shown as large circles, connect gateway routers. The SWRs also provide flexibility in modifying link delays, so that developers can vary network conditions to fully examine application behaviors. Our demonstration also includes NDN endhosts, which use virtual machines (VMs), shown as small circles in Figure 2. VMs require less hard-

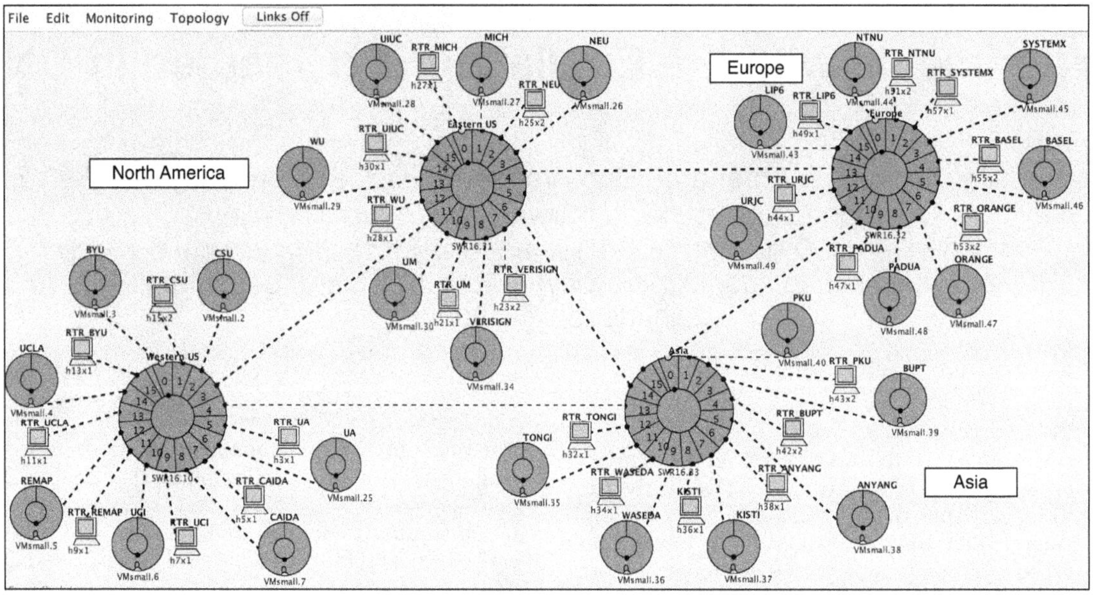

Figure 2: Emulated NDN Testbed in ONL

ware and provide developers greater flexibility, allowing for larger and more complex experiments.

2.2 NDN Topology Configuration

The NDN network requires installing forwarding entries on each node based on the NDN topology described using configuration files. NDN forwarding entries between gateway routers are configured by NLSR. The configuration files required by NLSR are generated using a flexible template program. A developer can easily set a master configuration file and automatically spawn configurations for each router. These configuration files are processed by the appropriate routers and describe the status of the network on the routing layer. The NFD links between endhosts and routers are stored as a one-to-many list. When NFD is initialized, each endhost and router creates a face and registers a next-hop for the applicable prefixes. NFD and NLSR are launched using the scripts we have developed.

3. DATA COLLECTION APPLICATION

The current data collection application collects bandwidth usage on testbed links, and it has been deployed on the NDN Testbed [1]. The application consists of a consumer (the testbed server) and multiple producers (the testbed nodes). Periodically, the consumer sends an Interest packet requesting the tx/rx counters of the producer's links. The producer replies by fetching the statistics of its faces from the NFD, and then filtering the counters of the relevant links.

We have been working on extending the application to provide a framework for users to specify the data to be collected, such as NFD process IDs and link RTTs. The ongoing development has been using the emulated testbed for testing and debugging. Eventually, the extended application will be deployed on the NDN Testbed, and we expect a smooth deployment.

4. DEMONSTRATION

This demonstration presents the emulated testbed and shows its effectiveness in supporting NDN research.

First, we show how the emulated NDN testbed is configured and launched in ONL. To demonstrate the benefits of having full control over the testbed, we show how link costs can be modified so that NLSR and NFD take action and switch to lower-cost forwarding paths.

Next, we demonstrate the flexibility of modifying network performance parameters. The extended data collection application will be deployed to monitor the link RTTs. Network performance parameters, such as link delays and packet loss rates, are modified by configuring the SWRs, and we show how the data collected by the application reflects those changes.

Lastly, an emulated testbed with link delays configured the same as the ones of the NDN Testbed is demonstrated. We collect the link delays to show the network performance is comparable to the NDN Testbed. Thus, developers could evaluate end-to-end application performance before evaluating it in the NDN Testbed.

The source code for the demo is available at https://github.com/WU-ARL/Emulated_NDN_Testbed_in_ONL.

Acknowledgment

This work has been supported by National Science Foundation grants CNS-1040643 and CNS-1345282.

5. REFERENCES

[1] NDN Testbed. http://ndnmap.arl.wustl.edu.
[2] Charlie Wiseman et al. A Remotely Accessible Network Processor-Based Router for Network Experimentation. In *Proc. of ANCS'08*, 2008.
[3] NDN Team. Named Data Networking (NDN) Project 2013 - 2014 Annual Report. Technical report, 2014.

Demonstrating a Scalable Name Resolution System for Information-Centric Networking

Jungha Hong
ETRI
Daejeon, Korea
jhong@etri.re.kr

Woojik Chun
Hankuk University of Foreign Strudies
Yongin-si, Koreae
woojikchun@gmail.com

Heeyoung Jung
ETRI
Daejeon, Korea
hyjung@etri.re.kr

ABSTRACT

In implementing Information-Centric Networking (ICN), an efficient Name Resolution System (NRS) is required since names assigned directly to the named data objects (NDOs) are location independent. On designing NRS, the most important challenge is scalability on the ever increasing number of NDO, which becomes even more critical when flat names are used in ICN. In this demonstration, we present a scalable NRS with flat names for ICN, where bloom filters are utilized to aggregate flat names. Specifically, we show the feasibility of our NRS with flat names and highlight the benefits of utilizing bloom filters.

Categories and Subject Descriptors

C.2.1 [**Computer-Communication Networks**]: Network Architecture and Design

General Terms

Design, Implementation, Experiments

Keywords

Information-Centric Networking; name resolution system; flat name; bloom filter

1. INTRODUCTION

In contrast to the host-centric networking of the current Internet, the primary communication object in information-centric networking (ICN) is named data object (NDO). In implementing ICN, an efficient Name Resolution System (NRS) is required since names assigned directly to the NDOs are location independent. This shift raises scalability issues to a new level. The current Internet is addressing on the order of 10^9 nodes, whereas the number of addressable ICN objects is expected to be several orders of magnitude higher. Thus, scalability on the ever-increasing number of NDO becomes one of the most important challenges on designing NRS.

In this demonstration, we propose a scalable NRS for ICN, where flat names are used. Flat names provide some advantages compared to hierarchical ones, such as higher

ICN'15, September 30 - October 02, 2015, San Francisco, CA, USA
ACM 978-1-4503-3855-4/15/09.
http://dx.doi.org/10.1145/2810156.2812617.

flexibility, simpler name allocation and benefits in terms of persistency and privacy [1-2]. On the other hand, scalability becomes more critical challenge on designing NRS with flat names.

In order to address the scalability issue in designing the NRS with flat name, we need to aggregate names in any form. One popular technique for flat name is Distributed Hashing Table (DHT) based approach [3-5], where multiple servers form circular linked list and the bindings are stored in the appropriate server. However, the DHT technique has some drawbacks; the binding between name and locator must be stored in a particular server other than the owner's server, which causes a serious trust problem related to the authority issue and lookup request may be propagated through the long paths.

In this demonstration, we construct NRS hierarchically and exploit bloom filters (BFs) to aggregate flat names. We will demonstrate the benefits of utilizing BFs by our prototype. We are also expecting to show how to achieve the design goals of our NRS such as scalability, locality, and low latency.

2. SYSTEM DESIGN

We construct NRS hierarchically by defining a network of NRS servers, which consists of a forest by several disjoint trees as shown in Figure 1. The network of NRS servers is defined by both parent-child and peering relationships. Each NRS server consists of a name lookup table and BFs for itself, from children, and from peers as depicted in Figure 1. A certain name can have more than one locator.

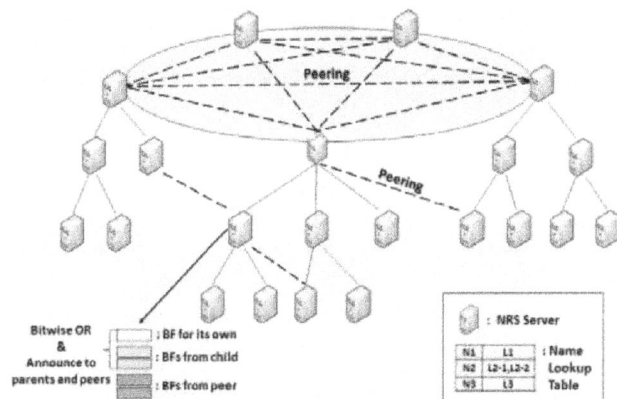

Figure 1. NRS structure.

Instead of announcing the whole list of names, each NRS server announces only one BF to parent and peer servers, which is formed as the union of BFs from all children and itself by bitwise 'OR' operation.

One of the major benefits of BF is a fixed constant time of insertion and search which is completely independent of the number of names already in a BF.

2.1 Name Registration

In this demonstration, it is allowed that a communication entity can be registered in any arbitrary NRS server since names have no structure. Because of this property, locality can be easily supported. When a communication entity is registered in a NRS server, the registration information is extracted from its name using the hash functions and inserted into its own BF first and then the NRS server updates BFs for its parents and peers, where this recursion holds until BFs at the top of trees are completely updated. When names are deleted from the lookup table, we use periodic refresh technique to reflect the deletion on BF since BF cannot handle the deletion by itself.

2.2 Locator Lookup

Requestor sends locator (LOC) lookup to its default NRS server first. On receiving LOC lookup to a NRS server, it first searches the corresponding name on its own BF. If the search fails, then it searches the name on BFs for its child and peer NRS servers. If none of the BFs return a positive answer, the LOC lookup is forwarded to its parent NRS server. On the other hand, if any BF returns a positive answer, the LOC lookup is forwarded to every NRS server that corresponds to BFs with positive answers. We note that because of the false positives of the BF, multiple BFs may return positive answers. This search is done recursively and LOC information can be eventually found. In this demonstration, LOC lookup carries the requestor's information so LOC lookup reply can be sent to the requestor directly.

2.3 Locator Update

In this demonstration, we divide LOC update into tree types: add, delete, and replace. LOC update is forwarded into the server where the name is actually stored by the name search such as processed in LOC lookup. If a name has multiple LOCs, then they are stored as a set of LOCs for the name. Because of this function, mobility and multi-homing are inherently supported.

3. DEMONSTRATION

In this demonstration, we present a scalable NRS with flat names for ICN, where BFs are utilized to aggregate the flat names. We have created prototypes for our NRS: NRS server, top server, and client. Although all NRS servers perform the same functions, we separate top server from the others for convenient implementation. We have utilized the parallel process of a graphics processor unit (GPU) to accelerate the performance of BF check at each NRS server resulting in low latency.

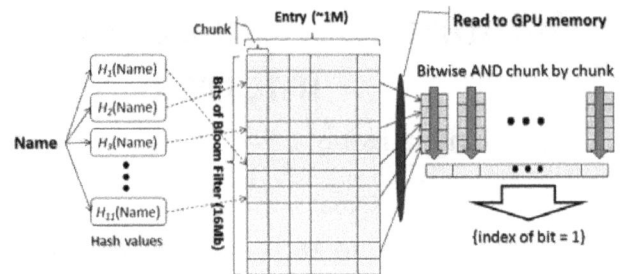

Figure 2. Overview of the algorithm for GPU usage.

Figure 2 shows the overview of the algorithm for the GPU usage. The main idea of the algorithm is to enable to extract only the corresponding bits for the given name check from all BFs at each server to GPU memory and check the extracted bits in parallel to see if any chunk gives 1 by bitwise 'AND' operation. In this demonstration, we use 16Mb BF size and 11 hash functions to keep the false positive probability less than or equal to $4.586 * 10^{-4}$ assuming that each BF can have information at a maximum of 10^6 names. We have used the static tree structure of NRS which is managed by configuration files of each server. We have also implemented the NRS without using GPUs to see the effect of the GPU usage on performance.

We demonstrate the feasibility of our NRS with flat names and highlight the benefits of utilizing BFs by our prototype. We show how scalable our NRS for ICN is even with flat names. We are also expecting to show how to achieve the design goals of our NRS such as scalability, locality, and low latency.

4. REFERENCES

[1] A. Ghodsi, T. Koponen, J. Rajahalme, P. Sarolahti, and Shenker, "Naming in Content-Oriented Architectures," In Proceedings of the SIGCOMM ICN'11, August 19, 2011, Toronto, Ontario, Canada.

[2] International Telecommunication Union (ITU), "ITU-T Recommendation Y.3031 - Identification framework in future networks," available at: http://www.itu.int/rec/T-REC-Y.3031-201205-P/en, 2012.

[3] O. Hanka, C. Spleiss, G. Kunzmann, and J. Eberspacher, "A novel DHT-based network architecture for the next generation internet," Eighth International Conference on Networks, Cancun, Mexico, March 2009.

[4] H. Luo, Y. Qin, and H. Zhang, "A DHT-Based Identifier-to-Locator Mapping Scheme for a Scalable Internet," IEEE Transactions on Parallel and Distributed Systems, October 2009.

[5] L. Mathy and L. Iannone, "LISP-DHT: Towards a DHT to map identifiers onto locators," in ReArch'08. Madrid, Spain: ACM, December 2008.

Author Index